D1176479

DIPLOMAT AMONG WARRIORS

BY

ROBERT MURPHY

DOUBLEDAY & COMPANY, INC.
GARDEN CITY, NEW YORK
1964

Library of Congress
Catalog Card Number 64–11305

Printed in the
United States of America

Acknowledgments:

To Ken McCormick, without whose genial inspiration this book would not have been undertaken; to Demaree and Dorothy Bess, on whose talent, wisdom, and skill I drew so heavily; to my cherished colleagues in the American Foreign Service, in the Armed Services, and in our Government; and to my dear wife, and our daughters, Catherine, Rosemary, and Mildred Margaret, whose patient understanding and loyal sacrifices made my public career possible.

To Four Queens—a very good hand

PUBLISHER'S FOREWORD

For more than twenty years prior to 1940, Robert Murphy pursued a conventional career in the Department of State, advancing through grades from clerk to Counselor of Embassy at Paris. His years of apprenticeship as a Foreign Service officer consisted of a mixture of routine assignments and discipline and lots of hard work. But he also had golden opportunities to observe the vast changes produced in Europe by World War I, especially the budding Nazi movement which he witnessed while living in Munich across the street from Hitler.

There was nothing sensational about this first half of Murphy's diplomatic career and it could have ended that way, as the careers of most Foreign Service officers do. But the nature of his work changed abruptly after the defeat of France, when President Roosevelt summoned him to the White House for a private conference which transformed the conventional diplomat into the President's own personal representative in French Africa.

Roosevelt's initial assignment, to assess the chances for bringing the African empire of France into the war against the Nazis, expanded into four extraordinary years, during which time Murphy made preparations for the Allied landings in Africa—the first important American combat operation of World War II. He also executed other special duties, including negotiations of the agreement which attained a certain notoriety as "the Darlan Deal"; arrangements which brought French West Africa into the war on the Allied side; and the establishment of a provisional French regime in Africa—all this accomplished without any previous professional knowledge of the Dark Continent.

When American participation in the war extended beyond the Mediterranean, Murphy was transferred to Europe where he continued to operate as Roosevelt's hand-picked agent, reporting directly to the President and carrying out his orders with little regard for military or diplomatic channels. As a result of Roosevelt's unconventional procedures, no written records were made of many significant events during the war, and the official files were long incomplete and even today suffer gaps.

Because the policies of the United States Government were of vital concern to the entire postwar world, every decision made in Washington in the 1940s was intensely scrutinized by press and public both at home and in foreign countries. Frequently those who opposed Roosevelt refrained from criticizing him personally, aiming their fire instead at the State Department or at the President's representatives. In Murphy's case, his unusual activities became part of his services as a career diplomat, duties to be performed even if he himself considered some of his government's policies doubtful or even wrong.

From the day Murphy first flew into Algiers, all his work required close association with military men, American and foreign. As General Eisenhower's political adviser in French Africa, Murphy was far too busy with immediate problems to think about the long-range effects of the cooperation he was improvising between diplomats and warriors, but a pattern emerged—the "combined operation" of military plus diplomacy—and this new type of cooperation became his chief preoccupation from 1940 onward.

Because of his ability to get along with American, British and French soldiers, sailors and airmen, his assignment in Africa led to similar duties elsewhere—first during the invasion of Italy; then in the campaign for the final conquest of Germany; afterwards in Berlin and the American zone of occupation.

Those were the years when diplomats and warriors learned that they would have to work together far more closely than they ever had done in the past. Today every American Foreign Service officer has become concerned, in one way or another, with military activities, and American generals and admirals have had to include some measure of diplomacy in their own plans. The creation of the North Atlantic Treaty Organization (NATO) and forty-odd other security arrangements and alliances became possible only through close coordination of military and diplomatic negotiators.

This form of combined operation was strikingly apparent when Murphy became the first postwar American Ambassador to Japan, and then a negotiator in the Korean armistice agreement. Later, in his work as Assistant Secretary of State for United Nations Affairs; during the landings of U. S. Marines in Lebanon in 1958; and during various other crises in which he was a participant, the value of cooperation between diplomats and military men was evident again and again.

CONTENTS

LIST OF ILLUSTRATIONS

ONE

INNOCENTS IN WARTIME SWITZERLAND (1917–19)

This book is in the form of an autobiography, but because I was for many years a professional diplomat—a career in which one's private affairs are subordinated to international affairs—this is not so much an account of my personal life as of my participation in the foreign affairs of the United States. I did not deliberately plan to enter the diplomatic service and it seems to me now, as I review the development of American foreign relations during my lifetime, that our nation's entanglement in world problems came about almost as haphazardly as my own. The government which I first began to serve in 1917 controlled an isolated country, a country whose citizens were embarking upon a World War to which they had given very little thought. The government from which I retired in 1959 was a formidable political and military complex which had accumulated responsibilities all over the globe.

My work for the Department of State began on April 23, 1917, just seventeen days after the United States entered World War I, and I was rushed to Europe and tossed into international politics before I had first-hand knowledge of any foreign country—indeed with very little knowledge of any sort. Two years later, like most Americans who had been hurried off to Europe during the war, I returned home with every intention of staying home. But the war had produced profound changes in my country. Whatever we Americans might desire as individuals, the United States never could be the same again after 1917 and, I discovered, neither could I.

There certainly was nothing in my family or educational background to suggest a diplomatic career. Before I went to Washington in 1916 as a government clerk and law student, I had lived only in Milwaukee, where I was born, October 28, 1894. This Wisconsin city had the justified reputation of being a stronghold of American isolationism, partly because so many of its residents were immigrants or descendants of men and women who had emigrated to get away from Europe's poverty, politics, and wars. My grandfather on my mother's side, Bernard Schmitz, was a blacksmith who came as a youngster to Milwaukee from Essen in the wave of emigration which followed the German revolution of 1848. Working long hours in a steel plant, he contracted tuberculosis and died before I was born, leaving a widow and four children. What I remember best about my maternal grandmother was the German language spoken in her home and in the community where she lived, some of which was transmitted to me in my childhood, a very useful legacy. My mother, Catherine Louise, was a gentle person whose natural shyness was aggravated because her face had been marred by smallpox. She was a devout Roman Catholic and had need of the comfort of her religion because life for her never was easy.

My grandfather on my father's side, Francis Patrick Murphy, left Ireland about 1850 to get enough to eat. He settled first in Brooklyn, where he acquired a small saloon, but after a few years he sought his fortune in Milwaukee, where his son and namesake was born. My father quit school in the fourth grade. Like many others of those days he thought education rather a waste of time. He tried his hand at many occupations, including operating a saloon in partnership with a friend. During long periods of unemployment, as in the depression of 1907, my father took what odds jobs he could get, and my mother helped by sewing. Nowadays when everybody is encouraged to go into debt for everything, it may seem quaint that my parents took pride in the fact that they never were in debt, although their margin of security at one time was exactly twenty-five cents.

Although my father was not financially successful, he possessed means for impressing his only son. For example, he enjoyed showing how he could crack Brazil nuts with his teeth. He never had dental care, but he still could crack nuts with his teeth at the age of sixty. He had the reputation of never losing a fight, and of having "the kick of a mule" in each fist. Like many Irishmen, my father sprinkled his speech with vivid expressions; one of his favorite epithets was "You blue-nosed Presbyterian s.o.b." That was a reminder, of course, of the ancient feud between Catholics and Presbyterians in Ireland, although my father had no religious prejudices whatever. It is curious how expressions learned in childhood stay in our memories. Long after my father was dead, when I was occupying the dignified position of Deputy Under Secretary of State, I sat one morning in a staff conference presided over by John Foster Dulles when the Secretary of State was having some skin trouble on his nose and was using a salve which gave a bluish tinge. As is well known, Dulles was an active Presbyterian layman, and I could hardly refrain from laughing aloud as my father's phrase suddenly recurred to me.

It was assumed in our family that I could scarcely expect formal education beyond grade school, and it was not easy to get even that far. I attended parish schools when we could pay tuition, and at other times I went to the public schools. When I was graduated from the Gesu Parochial School in 1909 I took an examination for a scholarship offered by Marquette University and its Preparatory Academy. A friend of mine passed with the highest mark and got an eight-year scholarship. I was a close second and was offered free tuition for four years at the Academy. That was generous, but I already had four years more schooling than my father, and I decided it was time to support myself. Several of my relatives had quit school early, and they were living useful lives. But a young Jesuit scholastic, William T. Ratigan, a teacher at the Academy, changed what might have been considered my natural destiny. Father Ratigan persuaded my parents and me that it would be unwise not to take advantage of the scholarship. I had to work nights to pay my expenses while in school, but I managed to complete the four years in three.

In the summer of 1915, when I was twenty years old, I suffered an accident which seemed at the time a major disaster. But one never knows about such things until the whole story unfolds. I was working that summer for a contracting company, and while I was in the construction elevator the cable snapped and I plunged to the bottom of the shaft, a distance of about three stories. My left foot was crushed with a triple fracture of the ankle and heel bone whose effects I still notice. I then learned the value of the newly enacted Wisconsin's Workmen's Compensation Act, very advanced for that era, which supported me through several painful months.

Being on crutches but drawing my compensation, I decided to make use of the time by studying shorthand and typing at a business college. At this school I learned about civil service examinations, which suggested the possibility of getting a job in Washington which would enable me to study law at night. The man who inspired me to become a lawyer was Senator Robert La Follette, Sr., founder of the Progressive Party in Wisconsin. "Old Bob," as he was known to everybody in his state, was as much a hero to Milwaukee's Catholic boys as he was to the Protestants. After several months in the business college and a secretarial job in a lithographing firm, I qualified under civil service as a stenographer-typist, and was offered a clerkship at one thousand dollars a year in the office of the Third Assistant Postmaster General. My father was not impressed. Said he: "That Third Assistant fellow must be pretty low down, something like the janitor." However, I discovered after starting work in Washington that the Third Assistant Postmaster General, Alexander M. Dockery, formerly governor of Missouri, was sufficiently high up so that I did not get even a glimpse of him during my first three months on that job.

Washington was still a pleasantly sleepy place when I made my acquaintance with it in 1916. It did not begin to assume anything like its present frantic appearance until after we entered World War I the next year. To me, Washington seemed completely delightful; for the first time I saw a clear road ahead to the practice of law, which by then had become my firm ambition. A Milwaukee friend, a medical student at George Washington University, recommended a boarding house on Franklin Square kept by a southern lady we called Miss Rose. For a tiny room to myself and all the food I could eat, I paid Miss Rose a munificent five dollars a week. So I was more prosperous and happy than I ever had been before. The University's night-school law course was designed then, as it still is, for students who were working days for the government. I was getting enough money from Uncle Sam to support myself, continue my law course, and send a little help to my parents. I found congenial companions at the university, I enjoyed my work, and the war—which still seemed very remote to me and to most Americans—held no threat to my ambitions. However, in a very few months the European War, as we called it then, was to change everything in my modest program and everything in the United States.

Once the American people decided to get into that war, they went in with a vengeance. The patriotic fervors of 1917 never have been repeated in such extreme fashion. Especially in Washington, young Americans were subjected to an almost hysterical wave of enthusiasm. I was dismayed by the opposition to the war led by my boyhood hero, Senator La Follette. Military service was out of the question for me because of my injured foot, but one of my law student friends, Lyle Alverson, who was supporting himself by working in the office of the Secretary of State, told me, "If you really want to go to Europe, there is great demand for young men to work overseas for the State Department as stenographer-typists. You already have passed the only civil service examinations required."

That suggestion was all I needed. When I applied as Lyle proposed, things moved more quickly than they have moved for me in Washington most times since. Within a week from the day my application went in, I was on my way to Bern, Switzerland, on the first lap of my forty-two years in the State Department.

I crossed the submarine-infested Atlantic Ocean together with several hundred American civilians who had volunteered to work with the French Army, mostly as ambulance drivers. Our ship was the French Line's SS *Chicago*, a fairly old tub, and our voyage was punctuated with frequent blackouts, boat drills, and other precautions against U-boat warfare, which was then at its peak. Even though the submarine had been the immediate cause for the declaration of war by the United States, the German General Staff, spearheaded by Admiral von Tirpitz, was deliberately gambling that the unrestricted use of the submarine could knock out Britain and France within three months. So we innocents sailed blithely into an all-out submarine attack which nearly accomplished its purpose. But Americans then, even more than now, possessed what Homer Lea called "the valor of ignorance." I cannot recall a single American on that ship who even considered the possibility that our side might lose the war.

During my few days in Paris en route to Switzerland, I gained my first appreciation of what war weariness means. Before we Americans entered World War I, the European belligerents had already endured three years of having their men slaughtered in the trenches. I never have forgotten the faces of the people whom I saw on the streets of Paris that spring—elderly soldiers, subdued workers, anxious women, solemn children. Twenty-three years later, when I watched the German army march into Paris, it was my recollection of those weary people of 1917 which helped give me compassionate understanding of the French tragedy.

The contrast in 1917 between war-saddened France and the brisk neutrality of Switzerland was startling. Ever since Napoleonic times, the Swiss have kept aloof from wars, a laudable achievement which has been accomplished partly because a neutral country in the center of Europe is useful to the belligerents. It has been remarked that if Switzerland did not already exist, it would have had to be created. The picturesque Swiss capital, Bern, high on its hill above the winding Aare River, served many of the purposes during both World Wars that the United Nations in New York does today. Bern provided a common meeting ground where representatives of hostile powers rubbed shoulders in the arcades and taverns, where they not only could spy on one another but also could arrange such humane matters as exchange of wounded prisoners through the Swiss-directed International Red Cross, and could even put out feelers for possible peace negotiations. No assignment could have been more useful to me, as introduction to the complexities of international affairs, than my two war years in Switzerland, and the respect and affection which I developed then for the Swiss people have remained with me always.

Before World War I, the American Legation at Bern was so unimportant that it had been run, almost literally, by a man and a boy. But the war brought a bureaucratic invasion, infinitesimal by today's standards, but considered overwhelming then. I arrived in the first wave and witnessed the mushroom growth of the legation staff. Those Americans were pioneers in their way, experimenting hopefully with primitive forms of intelligence, propaganda and economic warfare which now are standard features of government. Our early efforts were sometimes laughable in their innocence, occasionally sinister in their fanaticism, always extremely earnest.

The American minister, who had been given the congenial post at Bern because he was a friend of President Wilson, was a monument to the dignity of his office. He was a southern gentleman of the old school, the editor and proprietor of a newspaper in Georgia, the Savannah *Press,* and he wore striped pants, a Prince Albert coat and a pince-nez. I was reminded of him when James F. Byrnes observed in his book *Speaking Frankly:* "During my eighteen months as Secretary of State [1945–47], I met only two Foreign Service representatives wearing 'striped pants,' and both of them were political appointees." The Honorable Pleasant Alexander Stovall, Envoy Extraordinary and Minister Plenipotentiary, enjoyed wearing striped pants and, thus attired, he would meet prisoner-of-war trains from Germany and happily greet our returning doughboys. One day I overheard him introducing himself to a young Marine: "I am the American minister." To which the young man respectfully replied, "Pleased to meet you, Parson. I hope to study for the ministry myself!" Stovall did indeed resemble more than one kind of minister.

My first assignment in Switzerland was code clerk, and I thought I was doing important work because I was entrusted with putting messages into secret cipher from my superiors in Bern to their superiors in Washington. There were plenty of messages being cabled back and forth, and I felt that I was on the inside of operations right from the start. But after a few months I suffered my first disillusionment with our Foreign Service organization when I learned that some of my encoding and decoding probably had been wasted motion. The Germans rather disdainfully returned a State Department code book which had been used by the American Consulate in Leipzig, thus hinting broadly that they had keys to all our codes. The Germans were way ahead of us in cryptography; it was child's play for the German Black Chamber to break our simple book codes of that period. Moreover, most Americans had never even heard of security, and the Bern legation certainly did not practice it. Foreign employees had the run of the legation, and it would have been comparatively easy for some of them to get hold of our code books.

The indifference of the Foreign Service to security was accompanied by open aversion to Washington's hastily improvised propaganda agency, the Committee on Public Information, headed by George Creel. Our professional staff did not welcome Creel's amateur propagandists. The Committee sent to Bern an earnest and intelligent lady, Mrs. Norman de R. Whitehouse, but she had no acquaintance with any foreign language, no technical assistance or paraphernalia and only the sketchiest of instructions. Apparently she had been given this assignment largely because of her reputation as a battler for votes for women in New York. But that did not endear her to the Swiss who, nearly half a century later, still have granted votes to women in only a few localities.

I felt considerable sympathy for Mrs. Whitehouse, perhaps because she got so little from anybody else. It was only when the war was almost over that she received from Washington masses of outdated pamphlets which she valiantly undertook to distribute. The skeptical Swiss, devoted to neutrality and mistrustful of all forms of propaganda, believed that their own newspapers could supply them with all the information they needed, undoctored by foreign governments. Recalling now the cruel snubbing which this pioneer propagandist got, both from the Swiss and from her fellow countrymen, I am sorry she is not alive to be dazzled by the State Department's sponsorship of today's elaborate worldwide information services, with their network of broadcasting stations, transocean wireless and cable circuits, motion picture and television studios, traveling symphony orchestras and jazz bands, and thousands of civil servants occupying impressive buildings in Washington and around the globe.

If the State Department was slow to value security and propaganda, it was even less well organized in 1917 to appreciate intelligence work. A shocking instance which came to my attention concerned James C. McNally, the American consul general in Zurich, Switzerland's financial and industrial center. McNally's daughter was married to a German naval officer who had argued against the Berlin decision to wage unrestricted submarine warfare, because he correctly predicted that this would bring the United States into the war. McNally's German son-in-law was so embittered that he decided to help his wife's country, and through him NcNally was able to give the Allies advance notice of at least two major German offensives. For this achievement, General Pershing personally commended McNally.

But a retired American clergyman named Herbert Field, who was living in Zurich then, observed that McNally was meeting a number of Germans, and Field secretly reported to our government that the American diplomat was "consorting with the enemy." Due to the confusion of war and lack of liaison among government agencies, this ignorant accusation led to McNally's dismissal from the Foreign Service and the loss of a most valuable source of intelligence. I became convinced that McNally was loyal and had been scandalously mistreated. Thus, at the outset of my career, I realized that any official accused of disloyalty or indiscretion should be given the benefit of every doubt. There are many occasions when "consorting with the enemy" is the only means of obtaining essential information, as I myself learned during some awkward situations in World War II. More recently, in our hot and cold wars, a number of Foreign Service officers have been similarly accused. Experienced officers have endeavored to give such cases careful consideration, but in spite of what any of us in the Foreign Service could do, some Americans have been treated in recent years as unfairly as McNally was in 1917.

Incidentally, I have followed with interest the career of Herbert Field's son, Noel, who entered the Foreign Service after World War I and eventually defected to the Communists. He was last heard from in Budapest, but defectors live in danger and apparently the Communists suspected Noel Field of being a double agent. At any rate, he vanished. Perhaps some day we may learn what happened to this too-bright young man who worked secretly for the Communist side in the Spanish Civil War, using a League of Nations job as cover for his activities.

The Foreign Service normally makes about the same distinctions between its officers and clerical staff as the Army does between officers and enlisted men, but in Switzerland during World War I conditions were not normal. The customary crowds of tourists were absent, diplomatic social functions were held to a minimum, and all members of the American community were drawn together by the war. So, as a young clerk, I became more intimate with officers in the legation than would have been likely in peacetime, and in particular with the man who soon became my immediate superior, an exceptionally able consular officer named Alfred W. Donegan. As press officer, Donegan read and analyzed the German and Austrian publications which were readily available in Switzerland. Since he understood the central European scene thoroughly, he could glean inferences from his reading which might escape less informed readers. Because I knew German, he arranged to have me assigned to assist in his work.

Donegan was married to a hospitable Austrian lady, they had four children, and soon I felt almost one of their family. Early in our acquaintance, Donegan startled me by remarking that he and his wife had not visited the United States for many years, simply because they could not afford it. In those days, the starting salary of a career consular officer was $1500 a year, the maximum pay except in a few posts was $4000, and perquisites were few and far between. Congress supplied the State Department with no funds to pay traveling expenses for family vacations at home, or even to pay moving expenses when an officer was transferred from one post to another. "A promotion in the Foreign Service can be an invitation to bankruptcy," Donegan told me, "because a promotion often involves a transfer, and only men with independent incomes can afford to move family and furniture halfway around the world." Donegan said that when he was Consul at

Magdeburg, Germany, he was desperately in debt and needed $1000 urgently. His vice consul was a close friend and they agreed that the vice consul would apply to a local German bank for a loan. The banker asked the young man what security he could offer. "No security," the junior diplomat replied, "but our consul will endorse my note." The banker was impressed. "In that case, there is of course no question," he said. Donegan concluded, "What the banker did not know was that both of us were poor credit risks."

Donegan's personal story had a happy ending, without aid from the State Department. His one hobby was chess, which he played well enough to participate with moderate success in European tournaments. At one of these meets he became acquainted with a well-to-do American banker named Hallgarten, and later they became good friends and played chess together. One day Hallgarten announced, "Donegan, I drew up a new will today and named you in it." Donegan appreciated this kindly gesture, but as Hallgarten was only fifty years old and apparently in excellent health, he soon forgot about it. However, less than a year later, while Hallgarten was in the Casino at Monte Carlo, he dropped dead of a heart attack. To Donegan's amazement, he learned that his friend had bequeathed to him a quarter of a million dollars, a sum which made him the equivalent of a millionaire in today's money. This did not result in Donegan's resignation from the Foreign Service. He continued to work until his retirement several years later, his last post being Consul at Basel. Donegan was a devoted servant of the American Government. He served when he could ill afford to donate his services, and he continued to serve when he could have afforded to quit.

But my observations in Bern did not tempt me to follow Donegan's example. Much of the legation work seemed useless; there were too many instances of faithful service being unappreciated; officers were hampered by Washington politics; everyone was underpaid. As Donegan explained to me, "Congressmen know they can't win votes by appropriating big sums for the Department of State, so the Department never will be able to pay top-notch men what they are worth. That's why the Department was so poorly prepared to go into this war." A quarter of a century later, the Department was almost as poorly prepared to go into World War II.

Yet our legation in Switzerland did have some very capable men during the two years I was stationed there. The ranking career diplomat, Hugh Wilson, possessed private means and could not be intimidated by anyone. The brilliant Third Secretary was Allen Dulles, who became Director of our gigantic Central Intelligence Agency from 1953 to 1961. But in 1926, Dulles resigned from the Foreign Service in order to make money practicing law, until he felt he could afford to serve his government again.

I decided that I would go back to Washington after the war and proceed with my original plan of earning my living as a clerk until I finished my law studies, and I was impatient for the day when I could resume normal life. Yet I had to admit that in the meantime I certainly was enduring no hardship at Bern. In truth, I never had been so comfortable. I was boarding with a kindly German-Swiss family, enjoying their delicious breakfasts of hot chocolate, fresh rolls, cream cheese and cherry jam; I had several pleasant friends in addition to the congenial Donegans; and I was much attracted by a young lady, Mildred Taylor of Kansas City, Missouri, who was a secretary at the Red Cross headquarters which the Americans had established at Bern, and claimed to be a faster stenographer than I was.

One weekend I invited Mildred to go sight-seeing with me, and as we rode up the Jungfrau on a shaking rack and pinion mountain train, I said teasingly, "I bet you can't take dictation at one hundred twenty words a minute on this train!" She promptly bet ten dollars that she could—and won the bet. But I won Mildred Taylor. She promised to wait until I could qualify as a lawyer, and she has loyally shared through the years the viscissitudes as well as the satisfactions inherent in the Foreign Service.

Armistice Day 1918 came at last, and no one was more stirred by the Allied victory than Minister Stovall. He invited several hundred guests to celebrate at our legation, where he delivered a speech in the finest southern oratorical style. As a climax, he paid a flowery tribute to the courageous soldiers from his home state of Georgia who had stormed and liberated the fortress city of Metz. A British diplomat, Sir Robert L. Craigie, lost his aplomb at this point and his monocle fell to the floor—because the actual circumstances were that Metz had been evacuated by the Germans and our soldiers had strolled in without firing a shot. But we all enjoyed Minister Stovall's hospitality, and Sir Robert eventually married his charming daughter.

The improvised American bureaucracy at Bern disintegrated as soon as the war was over, largely because most of the amateurs insisted on going home quickly. However, I stayed long enough so that I was in Paris when Woodrow Wilson arrived there to attend the Peace Conference. I stood with the French crowds who gave the American messiah a tumultuous welcome as he drove in an open carriage down the Champs-Elysées. Not knowing then how many years of my life would later be spent in Paris, I lingered on a few days, visiting the war fronts, enjoying my first airplane excursion over the city, taking in as many sights as I could, from the top of the Eiffel Tower to the base of Napoleon's tomb. Then I hurried back to Milwaukee to see my mother and father and inform them of my engagement.

Two weeks later I was back in Washington, settled in a different boarding house, working days for the Treasury Department instead of the Third Assistant Postmaster General, and studying nights to finish my interrupted law course. My boarding house and my government job were not the only things changed after my return to Washington. The capital represented much more power than before the war, and this was heady wine to the men who dominated American affairs. Wealth had piled up, but politics had not improved. The way was open now for the arrival of Warren Harding and his cronies.

In less than two years, I finished law school and was admitted to the bar of the District of Columbia. I was ready at last to pursue the life I had planned, but while I was considering whether to accept an offer from a good law firm, I happened to read in the Washington *Star* that examinations were about to be held for openings in the Consular Service. To this day I cannot honestly explain why I was tempted to take those examinations. I said I was doing it merely from curiosity, to see whether I could pass, that I had nothing to lose except a little time. Yet I must have had a pretty good idea that, with the courses I had taken in international law, and with the experience I had had in government service in Washington and Bern, I would pass those tests; that then I would be eligible to become a career Consular officer; that then I might spend the rest of my life in foreign lands. Like the American nation itself, I had had a glimpse of wide horizons, a taste of life abroad, and I no longer felt satisfied just to mind my own business at home.

Anyway, my feet carried me to the examination rooms, and after I completed the written tests, an appointment was made for me to call on an examiner who would give me the oral language test. I was pleased to discover that I was acquainted with this examiner. He was Hernando de Soto, who had been our consul general in Leipzig when the United States entered the war. De Soto was married to a Russian lady who spoke German more fluently than she did English, so husband and wife had fallen into the habit of conversing with each other in German. While the couple were being repatriated from Leipzig, they were delayed for some weeks in Bern awaiting transportation to the United States, and their habit of speaking German in public excited the suspicions of some Americans there, including Minister Stovall. That ardent patriot believed that to speak the language of the enemy in preference to English was disloyal in wartime. So the De Sotos endured a very unpleasant month in Bern. Now, encountering De Soto in Washington, I made tactful reference to that episode, which inspired him to an impassioned statement of the whole affair, consuming most of the hour which had been allocated for my oral examination. Having relieved his feelings to a sympathetic listener, De Soto smiled benignly and assured me I would have no difficulty passing that part of my examination. I suppose I already was practicing diplomacy.

When I took my examinations late in 1920, the Foreign Service was a tiny fraction of its size today and held few inducements for ambitious young men, but during my lifetime it has been upgraded into a profession which can appeal to able young people. Just the other day I returned to Washington as a member of the Board of the Foreign Service Institute. I was informed that in one year recently, about ten thousand men and women had taken examinations; four thousand of these had passed the written exams; sixteen hundred got to the oral finals; and about two hundred applicants were accepted. With such keen interest, an excellent selection of junior officers is available now for our State Department.

Shortly after my examination, I was offered a choice of three posts, including vice consul at Zurich. I hastily went into conference with Mildred. I explained to her that I had no intention of following a permanent career in the Consular Service, but we liked Switzerland and we agreed it would be instructive to spend a few more years in Europe before I settled down to practice law in Washington. I took the oath of office on February 28, 1921 and we were married on March 3. I had agreed to attend a thirty-day training period for new consular officers, and the director was understandably annoyed when I immediately requested a ten-day leave of absence for my honeymoon. To placate him, I said, "I'll take along a copy of the Consular Regulations." The notion of a combined honeymoon and cram course amused him and he made no further objections.

A month later I received travel orders to go to Zurich, not as a bachelor clerk as on my previous journey to Switzerland, but as a married man, a career officer in the Consular Service of the United States Government, Vice Consul Class C, total annual emolument $2500. A fellow law student took the job which had been offered to me in a New York firm specializing in federal tax matters, and before long he was making $40,000 a year. Yet, when I learned about this, I did not envy him, for by that time I felt I had found my niche in life.

TWO

CRAM COURSE IN HITLER'S MUNICH (1921–25)

Six months after I became a consular officer, I was given by rare good fortune one of the most enlightening assignments of my diplomatic career. In November 1921 I was sent to Munich, Germany, and remained there almost four years. Only now, as I look back, can I fully appreciate how valuable those Munich years were to me. Nowhere else in Europe in the 1920s was the past, present, and future of that turbulent continent more dramatically revealed. What I learned in Munich about the behavior of victors and vanquished after the First World War enabled me to anticipate much of the behavior of victors and vanquished after the Second World War. These recollections became my greatest asset when I was appointed adviser on German affairs to General Eisenhower in September 1944 and later, during the first four postwar years, chief representative in Germany for the State Department.

When I arrived in Munich in 1921 a man whose name meant nothing to me then, Adolph Hitler, had just begun to make that city the spawning ground for his National Socialist movement. I met Hitler and other members of the Nazi high command while they were still obscure agitators. I also met Hitler's only famous collaborator of that time, the bitter and frustrated General Erich Ludendorff, who had been commander in chief on the western front when Germany surrendered in 1918. I attended several of the earliest Nazi meetings to make official reports to Washington. Like almost all foreign observers in Munich then, I found it impossible to believe that the demagogue Hitler, so unconvincing to me, would ever amount to much.

But at the same time I was learning what a dangerous situation the First World War had created in Europe. That war undermined the European system built up through many generations, before any acceptable new system had been devised to replace it. From what I saw, I developed great doubts about the wisdom of Woodrow Wilson in brashly forcing the issue of self-determination. His sweeping ideas and superficial knowledge of the practical aspects of European life helped promote European disintegration. Every other person I met in Munich seemed to be involved in some kind of intrigue, because the whole of Europe was in a state of flux. The German and Austro-Hungarian empires had been replaced by shaky republics in which most citizens had little confidence and which were viciously hated by fanatical minorities. The chaotic condition of society was such that there was genuine reason to fear that Bolshevism might take the same advantage of confusion in Germany and Austria which it had taken in Russia after the collapse of the Czarist empire. Above all, while I was in Munich I watched the wildest runaway inflation in modern history wipe out the savings of generations of Germany's and Austria's most decent, substantial people, leaving millions of them in dazed despair. That inflation, in my opinion, did more than any other single factor to make Hitlerism possible. Fortunately, the lessons it taught were skillfully utilized to prevent repetition of inflation after World War II, when a few courageous Americans resisted the shortsighted attempts of other Americans to reduce Germany again to economic chaos. Whatever stability exists in Europe today can be attributed, in my opinion, to the superior knowledge of economics and financial matters acquired between the world wars and applied in spite of understandable hatreds which might have duplicated the disastrous policies which followed World War I.

I was sent to Munich in 1921 with three other Consular Service officers to reopen our consulate general, which had been closed in 1917 by the war. An experienced officer, William Dawson, was in charge of our trio of very junior vice consuls, and he was as fine a teacher as any budding diplomat could have. Dawson had the reputation, which I can testify was thoroughly deserved, of a severe taskmaster. I offered to resign at least three times during the eight months I served under him, but he calmly ignored my offers and did not abate in the slightest his determination that his three vice consuls should not only do their work well, but also get into the habit of self-education. He prided himself upon his own linguistic ability and insisted that learning languages is largely a matter of application, not some God-given talent like being an artistic virtuoso. He was equally fluent in German, French and Spanish, and made it a rule that his vice consuls should never use English in talking with him in his office. I had to discuss everything with him in German, one of my colleagues in Spanish, the third in French. In that way, Dawson kept perfecting his own languages and obliged us to do the same.

But after only eight months in Munich, Dawson was promoted and transferred, and since I was slightly senior to the other two vice consuls, I was instructed to take charge until a successor to Dawson arrived. Probably I would have had a severe case of stage fright if I had been told that, except for a brief interval, no successor would appear for three years, during which time I would remain in Bavaria as chief representative of the United States. Fortunately for my peace of mind, I never knew from one day to another when I would be relieved. I would like to flatter myself that I was left so long in this post because of rare ability, but the evidence suggests that our Government did not think it mattered much who represented it in Munich. It was an exhilarating experience for me, as a young man, to be left so completely on my own. Before long I began to think of the diplomatic service as my permanent career rather than as a temporary adventure.

How eagerly we worked then, my fellow vice consuls and I; without their unstinted assistance I never could have held down that assignment. From the moment the consulate general reopened we were overwhelmed with work, usually spending twelve hours or more a day in the offices. The Spanish Government had looked after American interests in Germany during the war, and we found our inadequate prewar office equipment in storage. The United States Government owned no property in Munich, the city was crowded, and we had to settle for offices in a building owned by a student fraternity. Then the people poured in; it seemed to us that the whole of Bavaria wanted to emigrate to the United States. Immigration was almost unrestricted then and despite our limited facilities we soon were granting an average of four hundred visas per day. Our offices became frantically busy with such matters as approving thousands of visas for emigrants, issuing a large volume of American passports, making out consular invoices, and preparing economic reports which we had to type ourselves because the State Department could not afford to provide us with sufficient clerical help. I remember that this routine called for several hundred signatures daily. It was lucky for me that I had gone to business college, since I had to type all my own reports and correspondence.

It was a welcome relief from these chores to transform ourselves into political reporters for the benefit of the State Department, which was listed in routine regulations as one of our duties. I am rather vain about some of the political reports I made describing Hitler's earliest raucous efforts; when I looked them up recently in the National Archives in Washington, they seemed reasonably perceptive. But while we were sending in our reports so earnestly, we never knew whether or not anybody in Washington read them. They were accepted in total silence. Americans never have been more isolationist than they were in the 1920s. During my Munich years I saw nothing to indicate that the American Government or people were even mildly interested in the political developments which seemed so ominous and significant to us on the spot. The only real American interest in Germany at that time was concerned with money; a few Americans made fortunes out of the German inflation; American promoters high-pressured unrealistic loans upon German communities and corporations, loans which were defaulted later at the expense of American bondholders. Not once did our State Department ask my opinion about any political event, nor express concern over the developing Nazi movement. No comment came from Washington when I sent an eyewitness report of the Hitler group's attempt to overthrow the government of Bavaria in 1923, as a first step toward the national dictatorship which they eventually achieved. Our able ambassador to Germany, Alanson B. Houghton, periodically summoned me to Berlin for conferences of regional representatives, and listened thoughtfully to our reports of various local situations, but that was the only attention our political investigations received. Yet we were dealing with the origins of World War II.

This vast tide of emigration from Europe after World War I was a symptom of the prevailing chaos. American critics of our immigration policy complained then that we were getting the riffraff of Europe, but that certainly was not true of Munich. Moreover, I do not believe it was generally true. Unemployment was widespread and the war had been bitterly disillusioning, particularly for young people. At least 80 percent of our applicants were Bavarians, mostly young and from solid middle-class or working-class families. Many of them were craftsmen and most had some skills. They saw no future in Germany or Europe, inflation was wiping out any savings they had made or could make, and they fully intended to become permanent and serious American citizens. I am sure that the great majority of them did so. Probably it was true that our immigration laws were too lax and that some undesirable persons slipped through. Our Munich applicants were required to make out their own application forms and we did not have the facilities to check them carefully. But I am confident that, on balance, the great flood of immigrants from Europe after World War I greatly benefited the United States. Later on the 1920s, Congress swung to intensive restrictions, until today the United States has the most complicated system of immigration laws in the world.

My wife and I soon found a comfortable apartment and began immediately to enjoy life in Munich. Many Americans never have understood that Kaiser Wilhelm's Germany actually was a confederation of several more or less independent kingdoms and principalities. Munich had served for centuries as the capital of Catholic kings, the last dynasty being that of the popular and enlightened Wittelsbach family. Munich was accustomed to its own court and diplomatic corps, and its citizens had long prided themselves upon their hearty enjoyment of food and drink, music, opera, and sports. Bavaria was not occupied after World War I, as the Rhineland and Ruhr regions of Germany were, and the Bavarians tried to preserve Munich's prewar atmosphere through all postwar difficulties. The Bavarians had retained their popular monarchy and a large degree of independence under the Hohenzollern Kaisers, so they understandably were distrustful of the Weimar Republic which had dethroned their good king along with the bad Kaiser. Few Bavarians welcomed the Weimar Republic; most of them were thoroughly suspicious of it and especially of the Social Democrats (socialists) who were the republic's principal proponents. In fact, as I soon learned, Bavarians did not expect the republic to endure long; they were impatiently anticipating the restoration of some form of monarchy which would bring back their own Wittelsbach royalty. Meanwhile, they were behaving as if they were free to apply an independent foreign policy, and they treated the consular corps as if it were their prewar diplomatic corps.

After Dawson left Munich, I found myself in a peculiar position. I represented one of the richest and most powerful countries on earth in a place which European governments considered important enough to deserve high-ranking diplomats. I carried locally the impressive title of Acting Consul General, but actually I still was only a junior vice consul, drawing a vice consul's pay of $2750 a year, with almost none of the perquisites which provided my colleagues in the consular corps with ample entertainment and other allowances. If we managed to repay a few social obligations in Munich's active diplomatic society, it was thanks only to the inflation which was ruinous to Germans but temporarily helpful to those of us paid in dollars.

But we did feel seriously pinched, and when Senator Robert La Follette, Sr.—my boyhood hero from my home state of Wisconsin—came through Munich in 1922 on his way back from a visit to Russia, my fellow vice consul, Albert Halstead, and I decided to try to persuade him to plead our case in Washington. Senator La Follette was a member of two Senate committees which help to determine annually the extent of appropriations for the State Department. Halstead's wife was a Milwaukee girl, and we decided that the best way to get the senator in a proper mood would be to take him, his wife and two sons to an expensive Munich restaurant, the Walterspiel, which ordinarily was far too lush for our purses, and there ply him with food and drink before we made our pitch. Everything went off beautifully; the food was beyond reproach; the conversation was lively, the atmosphere soothing. After dinner, as the senator sat relaxed, Halstead and I, according to plan, began to describe our money troubles. The senator listened and we became more eloquent. But suddenly he looked around at the luxurious surroundings, the well-dressed and richly fed crowd, and commented: "Well, you young fellows seem to be doing not too badly for yourselves here." Too late we realized that our carefully laid plan had been psychologically unsound. We should have taken the La Follette family to the cheapest and least prepossessing restaurant in town which, in fact, we had to patronize for some time to make up for that La Follette feast.

However, we were getting experiences in Munich upon which one cannot set a price. Thanks to my official position, I had a wide and diverse acquaintance in that cultured community. Everybody in Bavaria, from highest to lowest, was accessible to the official representatives of the United States, and American visitors to Munich usually called at the consulate general. One American who slipped into town so unostentatiously that we did not know of his presence for several days was Thomas R. Marshall, former Vice President of the United States. As soon as I learned of it, I called on him. Mr. Marshall, charmingly informal, told me how he had stood in a queue to register with the police, as was required of all ordinary tourists. I knew the Munich police chief well, and immediately called on him and complained with mock indignation, "Why did you keep the former Vice President of the United States standing in line to register with the police?" The chief was horrified to learn what had happened, and exclaimed, "Why didn't he tell us who he is?" He immediately sent a written apology to Mr. Marshall, addressing him in the formal German phrase as "high-born." When I translated the apology to the Vice President, he was delighted. "I shall have that letter framed and put in the most conspicuous place in my office," he assured me. "That will silence my congressional critics who have failed to appreciate that I am 'high-born'!"

We also had a number of friends among the group of Americans who established their homes in Munich after the war. One of these was James Loeb, of the great New York banking firm of Kuhn, Loeb & Company, who after an illness retired to a country estate near Munich. He came to see me one day at the consulate, where we had a pleasant chat, and as he was leaving, he said, "If there is anything I can do to help you, don't hesitate to call on me." Not long after that, an American who was penniless came to our consulate for help. Our government provided no funds for needy citizens, and not infrequently our consular and diplomatic officers advanced their own money—which many of them could ill afford to spare—to help wandering Americans in distress. This time I remembered Loeb's offer of "help," so I telephoned to him and described the case. Loeb responded, "Of course I will give the man enough to return home," which he did. After that, Loeb made gifts and loans to a number of indigent Americans whom I referred to him, and his intelligent generosity was a great help, not only to our citizens who found themselves alone and in trouble in an alien land, but also to our consulate.

My colleagues in the Munich consular corps were exceptional men in one way or another, and all were friendly and helpful to me. They must have been astonished that the United States Government was content to leave so junior a diplomat in the Munich post, but they never treated me with anything but the kindest consideration. Today even our youngest diplomats are better equipped than I was in the 1920s, for they are given substantial preliminary training in essential matters before being sent abroad.

The titular head of the Munich consular corps was the Papal Nuncio, Monsignor Eugenio Pacelli, who later became Pope Pius XII. The Vatican always had maintained close relations with Bavaria, which remained Catholic throughout the Reformation while many other German communities were becoming Lutheran. Monsignor Pacelli, through his intimate knowledge of international politics, was one of the first to recognize that the future of Europe depended largely upon what happened in Germany. I had many enlightening conversations with him in Munich, and two decades later I was to renew my association with him after he became Pope, when I entered Rome with American troops in 1944 as President Roosevelt's personal representative. At that time someone sent me a clipping from a gossip column which detected some kind of Popish plot in the State Department, from the fact that I had been associated wih the Pope in Munich and now turned up with so much influence in Rome. But it was an Episcopalian, Franklin D. Roosevelt, who was responsible for my being in Rome, and probably nobody in the State Department remembered in 1944 that I once had served in Munich with an Italian named Eugenio Pacelli.

Another Munich colleague was William Seeds, the British consul general, an Irishman of charm and quick intelligence. He was especially helpful in showing me how to write effective political reports, something which my own government never taught me. He permitted me to read some of his reports and analyses, which combined wit with wisdom. Haniel von Haimhausen, the brilliant if cynical Minister to Bavaria from the State of Prussia, provided some of my first intimate glimpses into central European politics. Emile Dard, the French representative with the rank of minister, was a diplomat of the old school who had spent all his adult years in the Foreign Office. His one object in life at that time was to promote the French policy of "separatism." The idea was to persuade inhabitants of Bavaria and the Rhineland, Germany's main Catholic regions, to assert their independence of Berlin and to constitute independent buffer states. Many Bavarians sympathized with this general idea. Their current representative of the Wittelsbach royal family, Crown Prince Rupprecht, was an honorable and distinguished man who looked every inch a king. The French minister blew hard on every tiny flame which he hoped might re-establish an independent monarchy in Bavaria and thus make France feel more secure from German aggression.

Looking recently through my long-buried official reports from Munich, I came across one dated March 17, 1923, which described a French conspiracy I had forgotten. The purpose was to set up a southern German Catholic kingdom including Bavaria and the Rhineland and parts of neighboring Austria, with the capital at Munich. Documents had been found which indicated that French army agents had paid substantial sums to German and Austrian monarchists. So I interviewed Minister Dard and then reported to Washington that Dard had given me his "word of honor" that no money had been contributed through him to the intriguers, but he added that of course he had no knowledge of what certain military agents might be doing under instructions of Generals Degoutte and Weygand. Americans in those days did not indulge in such devious operations, but things are different today.

Dard told me frankly that the French Government had assigned him to Munich in 1920 at the same time that General Weygand had been dispatched to Poland to aid in the repulse of Bolshevism there. Dard's instructions were that if the Bolsheviks overran northern Germany, as seemed quite possible at the time, he should make every effort to separate Bavaria from the rest of Germany. But he assured me that after the Bolsheviks were defeated, his government had no further interest in a separate Bavaria. My report to my government concluded with a bit of diplomatic double-talk which I could not improve upon today: "It is believed that Minister Dard, in protesting a lack of further interest, did not strictly adhere to an entirely correct portrayal of his present mission." Which was an elaborate way of saying that my distinguished French colleague probably was lying.

One man who was more helpful to me than any of my diplomatic colleagues was a German employee of the American consulate general, Paul Drey. When we reopened our Munich office in 1921 he was working for the Spanish mission which had handled our affairs during the war, and Dawson persuaded him to come to work for us. He was in his late thirties then, a member of a distinguished Jewish family which had lived in Bavaria four hundred years. He was respected among Bavarians and could quickly arrange for me any interviews I desired. His knowledge of local politics and personalities was encyclopedic, he was in every sense a cultured gentleman, and he soon became my close friend. But Paul Drey unwittingly misled me about one man and his group: Adolph Hitler. I recall the first Hitler meeting

I attended with Paul; as we went out, he exclaimed: "How does this Austrian upstart dare to tell us Germans what to do?" Paul and I later attended many more Nazi rallies in order to report this violent political phenomenon to the State Department. But when I asked Paul, "Do you think these agitators will ever get far?" he answered firmly, "Of course not! The German people are too intelligent to be taken in by such scamps!"

The Bavarians were famous for their meticulous good manners, and one day when Paul and I went into a tailor shop to order a suit, the tailor was extremely rude. Impulsively I asked him: "Are you by chance a member of the National Socialist German Workers' Party?" He answered proudly: "Yes, I am a follower of Herr Hitler." As we left the shop, Paul said to me, "Did you notice what I did to show my contempt for that Nazi?" I said, "No, Paul, I didn't notice. What did you do?" He said triumphantly, "I did not tip my hat to him when we left!" According to Bavarian custom, men who respect each other tip hats, and by not tipping his hat Paul had subtly showed his contempt for the Nazi tailor. I hope the tailor noticed the insult, which escaped me.

Paul Drey paid dearly for his faith in the German people, among whom he firmly numbered himself until the end. In 1938, thirteen years after I left Munich, I read one morning in Paris that the Nazis had burned down a synagogue in Munich, and I immediately arranged to fly to that city to persuade my friend Paul to leave Germany, assuring him of employment with the State Department in a safer place. He thanked me, but shook his head, saying, "No, this is a temporary madness. Self-respecting Germans will not tolerate these louts much longer." Paul's faith was greater than mine, and I could not dissuade him.

I was one of the first American civilians to enter Munich after its capture in 1945, and immediately made inquiries about Paul Drey. A leading Munich banker, August Bauch, told me that he had last seen Paul in a work gang shoveling snow on a Munich street, and later heard that he had been sent to the Dachau death camp. When I visited Dachau shortly afterward and confirmed Paul's death there, I was more stricken by the fate of my friend than by the certified deaths in that horror chamber of 283,000 other victims.

Paul Drey runs all through my memories of Munich. I was with him on the memorable morning of November 9, 1923, when Hitler staged his first rebellion against the republic in the mistaken belief that Bavarian monarchists would support a break away from Berlin at that time. Paul and I arrived in the central square of Munich, the Odeonsplatz, just in time to see Hitler's storm troopers marching into the square toward a contingent of the Bavarian police. Hitler's famous collaborator, General Ludendorff, had foolishly decided to join this premature rebellion and was marching with Hitler at the head of the armed rebels. That scene has been described in many books, and the disparities in details show that reporting is not an exact science. Most reports say that when the police opened fire, Hitler lost his nerve and in order to save himself dropped to the ground with such force that he broke a shoulder, while Ludendorff marched fearlessly on. Paul and I were right there when the firing started, and we recognized Hitler and Ludendorff, whom we had seen many times. Of course it does not matter now, but for the record I can testify that both Ludendorff and Hitler behaved in an identical manner, like the battle-hardened soldiers they were. Both fell flat to escape the hail of bullets. Ludendorff's body servant, marching at his side, was killed, as were several of Hitler's cronies.

Paul and I had stayed up all the previous night reporting the rapidly moving developments. The Nazi guerrillas had seized the Bavarian Government offices, the banks, the City Hall, and of course the telephone and telegraph offices. I was refused permission to send a telegram in code to Washington, and indignantly demanded an interview with Hitler himself. After hours of argument, I finally did get in to see him at 3 A.M., only to be told rather mildly that I could not send my telegram. My protest was only a formality by that time, since I already had sent my colleague, Halstead, in a car to file the telegram from Stuttgart. And later I learned that I had demanded from Hitler rights which I did not possess.

Four months later I covered the trial of the conspirators, which I reported to the State Department under date of March 10, 1924. As is well known, Hitler was sentenced to five years in Landsberg Fortress, a sentence which was suspended after he served eight months, during which time he wrote *Mein Kampf*. Ludendorff was acquitted, and I cited as an example of the "insolent bravado" of the defendants during the trial that Ludendorff denounced his acquittal as an outrage since his comrades had been found guilty, and shouted that the decision was an insult to the uniforms worn by the judges in the court-martial. My conclusion was not too bad: "While the putsch in November 1923 was a farcical failure, the nationalist movement behind it is by no means extinguished in Bavaria. It has simply been delayed. . . . It is contemplated that upon completion of his term Hitler, who is not a citizen, will be expelled from the country. Further nationalist activity on his part, for the present at least, appears to be excluded." My disposal of Hitler was not quite so cavalier as that of the British ambassador to Germany, Lord D'Abernon. His memoirs, *An Ambassador of Peace*, did not consider Hitler worth more than a footnote, which remarked that after Hitler's release from prison he "vanished into oblivion"—which illustrates why wise diplomats think it prudent to hedge in their judgment of men and events.

I did have one interview with Hitler early in 1923 in which, according to my official report, his attitude was "cordial." I had read somewhere that the elder Henry Ford, who allegedly was financing an anti-Semitic publication in Detroit, had also contributed money to Hitler's Nazis, and I decided to ask Hitler whether the report was true. He received me amiably—the only occasion when he did so—and explained that "unfortunately Mr. Ford's organization has so far made no money contributions to our party." He added that the party's funds were coming principally from "patriotic Germans living abroad," and I believe that in those days Hitler did have more financial supporters abroad than in Germany.

Also about that time I had my first break in intelligence work, one of the principal functions of a diplomat. This experience taught me, early in my career, that it is not necessary always to become a "secret agent" in order to gather important military secrets. Our naval attaché in Berlin wrote me that it was rumored that Bavarian factories were turning out Diesel engines especially designed for Japanese submarines, in violation of the terms of the Versailles Treaty. A short time before, Paul Drey had introduced me to a young man named Diesel who said he was planning to emigrate to the United States. I remembered him well because it had not occurred to me that Diesel was the name of a family as well as an engine; this young man's father was the inventor. I was told that he was an official in the Munich-Augsburg Machine Company which made Diesel engines, and I decided to ask him frankly about the report. He said it was quite true, and that he did not like this kind of operation and would provide me with full details. Soon he brought me copies of ledgers showing the quantities and types of submarine engines being shipped to Japan labeled "agricultural machinery." So I was congratulated for my "undercover skill," and young Diesel went to the United States where he prospered.

Americans abroad call upon their consular officers to help them in many surprising ways, but Munich is the only place where I felt bound to serve as a second in a duel. One day a young American student came into my office with a problem. He said someone had stepped on someone's foot in a trolley car, and a German major who felt he had been insulted had challenged the American student to a duel. The officer had formally presented his card, saying he would have his second call upon the American's second to arrange details. The young man sought my advice and we agreed that this matter should be treated unofficially. I could remember nothing in the regulations of the State Department forbidding consuls to act as seconds in duels, but I preferred not to submit the question to higher authority. The student explained that he knew nothing about dueling, was not a good shot, and had never even handled a sword. So we studied his situation. I told him that under German dueling rules he had the choice of weapons, as the challenged party, and I asked if there was any kind of weapon he did know how to use. To my delight, he replied that he was an expert archer. Now I began to see daylight ahead and I agreed to act as his second—in a strictly unofficial capacity.

The next day, at my invitation, the major's second called on me. I informed him that we would be quite happy to have the duel occur at a time and place of their choosing, but of course my principal would assert his privilege of selecting the weapons. The major's second solemnly agreed, and asked what the weapons would be. "Bows and arrows," I replied blandly. My German visitor turned purple with indignation, protesting that nobody ever fought a duel with bows and arrows, weapons used only by savages and barbarians. I replied imperturbably that apparently he was unfamiliar with American dueling practices, since bows and arrows were standard weapons in my country, having been used by the inhabitants of the North American continent for centuries. The type of German who challenges to duels usually is deficient in a sense of humor, especially in matters regarding duels, so it required several days of discussions before I had an opportunity to meet the challenger himself. When the major finally called on me, he already had come to the conclusion that I had devised an ingenious way to save his honor and my principal's skin. I invited all concerned to the Hofbrau Haus where we engaged in a beer duel which hurt nobody, and the German officer and the American student became friends.

Possibly I have given Hitler a disproportionate amount of attention in this chapter because he became such an evil genius later. Actually, in my Munich days he and his movement were considered much less important than the one thing which affected every man, woman, and child—inflation. German money, the mark, was losing its value, gradually during my first year, then more swiftly, then in a rush which destroyed its value altogether. Americans of the Confederacy experienced similar runaway inflation after they lost the Civil War, when their money became worthless. Their inflation had some of the same psychological effects upon the people of our southern states as the 1919–24 inflation had upon the Germans, and some of the demoralizing effects still linger in both places.

Lord D'Abernon, the British ambassador to Germany from 1920–26, was a financial expert and his description of German inflation is the best I know. Day after day for years he wrote in his diary that the German Government, by permitting its printing presses to turn out paper money without limit, was heading straight for disaster. He warned Germans, he warned Frenchmen, he warned Britons and Americans, with little result. The French and Belgian governments were interested only in collecting the reparations due them, and did not care how much paper money the Germans printed. Some Germans, headed by the multimillionaire steel king, Hugo Stinnes, favored inflation as a means of avoiding payment of reparations. Other Germans discovered that they could get rich from inflation, so long as it was held within limits. But some honest German officials and bankers, according to D'Abernon, really believed they could keep the printing presses running indefinitely without destroying the value of paper money.

The prewar value of the German mark was twenty-five cents. When I first went to Munich at the end of 1921, I already could get about a hundred marks for a dollar. A year later I was getting about sixty-five hundred marks for the dollar. Then, in January 1923, French armies marched into Germany's richest industrial region, the Ruhr, and the German Government decided to finance passive resistance to such foreign military occupation. This was heartily approved by the Ruhr's mine owners and mine workers. The government undertook to pay wages to the resisting miners and subsidies to the resisting owners, and for this purpose printed enormous additional amounts of paper money. A month after the occupation of the Ruhr, I was getting more than forty thousand marks for a dollar, and the bottom of the money market began to drop out completely. By August a dollar was buying millions, in September billions, in October trillions of marks. A sad cartoon appeared in a Munich paper showing a little girl sitting beside two huge bundles of paper money, crying pitifully. A passerby was saying: "Why are you crying, little girl?" She answered: "Someone stole the leather straps off my money!" I occasionally played a dollar limit poker game for German marks. When we began that game, the limit was one hundred marks; in October 1923, one trillion marks. It was quite a thrill to raise a trillion.

Finally, that month, the German Government virtually repudiated its enormous public debt by introducing a new unit of value called the rentenmark. The State redeemed at one million-millionth of the prewar value all outstanding currency, all treasury bonds and notes, and all saving deposits and mortgages. You could figure out the value of what had been the most conservative securities in the country by knocking off twelve zeros. This meant that every German who had sacrificed and saved to provide for his old age and for his family was ruined. Our sixty-five-year-old cook, Louisa, who for years as cook for Mark Twain's daughter had thriftily accumulated German marks equivalent to twenty thousand dollars, invested in State savings bank deposits. She ended up penniless.

As Lord D'Abernon pointed out, the only gainer was the State, which was relieved of debts estimated at $50,000,000,000. Once the full circle had been completed, all classes of private creditors were wiped out. By ironic justice, the heaviest losses were suffered by individuals who had most favored inflation in earlier stages; they had piled up huge paper profits which, in the final crash, all vanished. The former British Ambassador, writing his memoirs in 1929–31, was greatly impressed by Germany's rapid recovery after the government halted its printing presses and stabilized the mark. He noted with wonder that the Germans had not lost their ingrained habits of thrift and hard work, and began at once to save and invest in government securities as they had done before. But D'Abernon was not such an expert in human psychology as he was in finance. He did not realize the immense psychological and social damage which inflation had inflicted on Germany's and Austria's most sober, useful people. He believed, at that time, that Hitler could be dismissed in a footnote; he did not understand that inflation, more than any other factor, had created a national state of mind which made Hitlerism possible.

THREE

PARIS, 1930–40: FRENCHMEN EXPECT THE WORST, AND GET IT

Not all American diplomats have an opportunity to become equally familiar with both Germany and France; those who specialize in one of these countries usually have only a casual acquaintance with the other. In this respect, I was a fortunate exception. After my years in Germany, I was privileged to serve in Paris continuously from March 26, 1930 through June 30, 1940—one of the most turbulent decades in French history. During those ten years I watched in Paris the inexorable march of events which culminated in the outbreak of World War II on September 1, 1939.

Our memories play curious tricks, and the person I recall most vividly in Paris on that first day of war is not one of the several French leaders I conferred with, but a French journalist now living quietly in France, Madame Geneviève Tabouis. Early that September morning I went to see Ambassador William C. Bullitt, who was confined to his official residence with a severe cold. The ambassador had asked Carmel Offie, his indispensable personal assistant, and me to bring him the most important of the stream of messages pouring into the embassy, so that we could dispose of these and discuss the whirl of events. We knew that British Prime Minister Neville Chamberlain would broadcast a declaration of war at eleven o'clock, and we were just tuning the radio to London when Mme. Tabouis unexpectedly was ushered into the room. We all sat silent until the somber broadcast ended. Mme. Tabouis was the first to speak. Her lively imagination served her well in her profession, and now she gave it full rein, picturing in graphic phrases her certainty that France was doomed. Finally the ambassador, who privately shared her pessimism about French preparedness, interrupted gently, "Surely things cannot be that bad!" And then he suggested that I drop Mme. Tabouis at her home on my way back to the chancery, which I did. As we stood before the door of her house on the spacious Boulevard Malesherbes, she looked mournfully at the picturesque old buildings and exclaimed dramatically: "Tomorrow all this will be gone! Our lovely Paris will exist no longer!" And she flung out her arms despairingly, as if she already stood among ruins.

I remember this little scene because it expressed the prevailing mood of the French people from the very outset of World War II. The majority of French people I met, from highest official to youngest messenger boy, exuded gloom. But there was one Frenchman whom I encountered by chance that first week of the war whose unaffected optimism set him apart from all others. This man later played an important part in American-French relations and in my own career. Simultaneously with the declaration of war the French Government ordered general mobilization, and I went one morning to a railway station, the Gare du Nord, to watch some of the mass of conscripts being shipped to the front. By coincidence I found myself standing next to a tall, very erect French officer in uniform whom I recognized as General Henri Giraud, a celebrated hero of World War I whom I had met once at an embassy dinner. Giraud said he had come to see how the mobilization was progressing and he was genuinely enthusiastic about French prospects, declaring cheerfully, "This time things will go better with us. *On les aura!*" There was little in the scene before us to justify the General's optimism. The conscripts slouched glumly through the station to their trains, without benefit of waving flags or band music or cheering crowds. Many had absorbed a good deal of alcohol which, under the circumstances, was understandable. While I knew that the French Army never had gone in for the spit-and-polish smartness of the Germans, and that some French soldiers even prided themselves on outward sloppiness, this spectacle at the Gare du Nord could seem encouraging only to a man exceptionally buoyant.

That chance encounter at the Gare du Nord undoubtedly influenced my thinking three years later, when suggestions came to me from several sources that Giraud was the right Frenchman to work with us on the American offensive in North Africa. By that time, in 1942, I was acting under President Roosevelt's personal direction, and I recalled how this French general had been almost uniquely hopeful on that morning in 1939 when the future looked so bleak to most of his countrymen. Giraud's sanguine disposition had impressed others who knew him better than I did, including Winston Churchill and General de Gaulle. In Giraud's case, unfortunately, an indomitable spirit was not accompanied by other necessary qualities, and his personal story ended more unhappily than that of his beloved France.

When World War II broke out I had been serving for three years with Ambassador Bullitt, a brilliant man with profound knowledge of

Europe and its history. He was convinced that the European conflict would directly threaten the United States, so he felt that his own role in the approaching tragedy was bound to be important. Bullitt was most helpful during our close association, and as time rushed on, some of his strong sense of destiny began to rub off a little on me, for it did seem as if my lengthy apprenticeship in the Foreign Service had been preparing me also to serve my country in this crisis. Soon after I arrived in Switzerland in 1917, I began to study French an hour every day, and I kept up this study not only during my two years in Bern but in all my later posts, until I could think as well as talk in both German and French. Those years between world wars were very valuable preparation. After leaving Munich in 1925, I spent some months in Spain as consul at Seville, and then four years in Washington, where I performed the assorted chores of a departmental officer and also managed to get an LL.M. degree by attending night law classes at George Washington University.

Those were the days of the Calvin Coolidge administration and Frank B. Kellogg and the Pact of Paris designed to outlaw war. Severe economy measures drove down our national debt to nineteen billion dollars, our defense establishment was emasculated, and our Foreign Service was threadbare. A few dedicated men, headed by Assistant Secretary of State Wilbur J. Carr, fought the battle to preserve the career Foreign Service from disintegration. It was an inspiration to work with Carr on a staggering task with pitifully inadequate means. Fortunately, the United States was the beneficiary of the protection afforded by two oceans, and of the world law and order which was maintained by the countries maligned now as "colonial." This period represented the extreme of austerity. General Herbert M. Lord, director of the budget bureau, in a talk to State Department personnel urged the workers to respect government property and mentioned, as an example of wastefulness, that he had observed one of our young ladies using a government-owned paper clip to clean her ear. The memory of those years remains in striking contrast to the dance of billions during and after World War II.

In 1930, at the beginning of the Great Depression, I was transferred to Paris. My transfer was an example of the personnel system in our Foreign Service at that time. Assignments to Washington were limited by law then to four years, and one day the Chief of Personnel, Homer M. Byington, a charming man, came by my office and said casually, "Murphy, your statutory time is about up on this assignment and you are due to return to the field. If some one should ask whether you would prefer Paris, Bremen, or Shanghai, what would you say?" Rather blankly, I replied, "Homer, what would you say?" "That's all I wanted to know," he said, and the next day I was transferred to

Paris, actually not at all certain that I did not prefer exotic Shanghai, or Bremen where I would have been in charge of my own show.

During the critical decade that I served in Paris, France endured riots, strikes, street battles between warring political factions, Cagoulards, Communists, the Popular Front, the Spanish Civil War. France was politically paralyzed as Hitler made his well-timed moves. Soon, too, the worldwide financial depression hit France, adding its strain to the Third Republic's unstable governments which changed thirty-seven times while I was in Paris. The American community there, numbering about thirty thousand residents, was seriously affected by the depression. Our embassy staff took a 15 percent cut in salaries plus cancellation of living allowances. One very lean month we were paid no salaries at all. Officers like myself, with little private income and growing families, had to do skillful juggling to keep out of debt, but we knew we were better off than millions of our countrymen hunting for jobs. In the midst of this period of penury, the Murphy family spent two summer vacations in, of all places, Monte Carlo. That Riviera resort connotes luxurious living and wild gambling, but we selected it for our holidays because it offered at that time just about the cheapest living in Europe for those who were content to enjoy its sun and sea and beauty in a modest hotel. Monte Carlo was the place where our three little daughters learned to swim.

My work in prewar Paris ran the gamut of consular activities to diplomatic responsibilities—usually a good ten- or twelve-hour day. I was executive officer of the embassy and later was designated counselor by Ambassador Bullitt, who did not have the wholehearted support of the Department of State in that action. The busy Paris embassy was in close contact with political trends in Europe as a whole. Bullitt at times was in daily touch with our ambassadors, such as Joseph Kennedy in London, Tony Biddle in Warsaw, and others in key posts. He felt he had a tacit mandate from President Roosevelt to act as his eyes and ears in Europe. Through Paris there always is a steady flow of nationalities, an assortment of international conferences, and all the various activities relating to this traditionally intellectual world center. A large and active American colony and hundreds of thousands of American visitors annually, many of whom descended on the embassy for one reason or another, provided distractions from the job of concentrating on French political, social, and economic developments, the primary reason we keep an embassy in Paris.

In the years leading to World War II, Bullitt drove his associates in the embassy to maintain close and friendly relations with French statesmen and other leaders. Thus we made invaluable contacts, ranging from the extreme left of Maurice Thorez, Jacques Duclos and Marcel Cachin, through Léon Blum, Vincent Auriol, Pierre Cot, Gaston

Bergery, Edouard Herriot, Paul Reynaud, Edouard Daladier, Camille Chautemps, Yvon Delbos, Jules Jeanneney, Georges Bonnet, Pierre Laval, Pierre-Etienne Flandin, Georges Mandel, Raymond Patenotre, Albert Sarraut—even Marcel Deat and Colonel de la Roque. Our purpose was to draw on every source and nuance of opinion to obtain the best composite of a complex and shifting political scene which affected not only the destiny of Europe but the fortunes and lives of the American people.

When the Popular Front was organized by Léon Blum with Communist collaboration, I was familiar with its leadership and recognized its weaknesses. This acquaintance helped in reporting the rush of events after the outbreak of the Spanish Civil War—that prelude to World War II. A major function of a diplomat obviously is to keep his government properly informed, and during the Spanish Civil War this involved my making some startlingly contrasted acquaintances. Sometimes I would meet General Franco's representative in Paris, and an hour later the paymaster for the Abraham Lincoln Brigade which was fighting against Franco in Spain. Franco's representative was a career diplomat, Eduardo Propper de Callejon, who was being so severely snubbed by Blum's Popular Front leaders that he felt grateful for some attention. I sympathized with him and in turn he gave me very accurate information, and he became even more helpful during World War II.

I had a more specific purpose in cultivating the Communist paymaster, a naturalized American who went by the name of Leeds. I tried to persuade him to help me recover some of the four thousand American passports of men fighting in Spain, which were being used by Communist agents. Many of these passports had been obtained fraudulently by individuals with the assistance of the American Communist Party. A favorite method was to claim birth in San Francisco, because the city birth records had been destroyed in the great earthquake and fire. The applicant would make an affidavit of birth in San Francisco, and his application would be supported by two affidavits, usually of members of the Communist Party. After his arrival in Barcelona, the owner of the new passport would turn it in to headquarters of the Abraham Lincoln Brigade so it could be used by other party members who needed a travel document for one illicit reason or another. Leeds, whose real name was Amarillo, pretended to resent this cynical misuse of American passports and agreed to help me. Through information obtained, we traced two suitcases of these passports to a small hotel in Paris. The Police Judiciare cooperated and raided the room where the suitcases were supposed to be. They had been removed an hour before. Our abortive effort gave us a clue to the extent of Communist infiltration into the French Government apparatus, including the police.

Amarillo was an intelligent Sephardic Jew of Greek origin. I rather liked him. He was remarkably frank with me, never pretending that he was not an agent of the Communist International. He told me how, when he first was assigned to the United States as a Communist organizer and later became business manager of the New York *Daily Worker,* he picked the name of Leeds. He and three other Comintern agents were in a New York café, discussing his American mission. He was using the name of Amarillo then, which in Spanish means yellow. One of his fellow Communists told him: "You can't use that name in America because yellow is a repulsive color to American workers—Yellow Legs are strikebreakers." That day the "tin-plate king," William Leeds, had just married an aristocratic Greek lady, and the newspapers lying on the table before them had his name in the headlines. One agent suggested, "Take the name of Leeds. That must be a proper American name." And so he did.

No emissary from any land ever got closer to French political life than Ambassador Bullitt, who had lived in France off and on since boyhood, spoke the language as if it were his own, and had warm friendships with men and women of all sorts. He had great influence upon French policy, judged personalities shrewdly, and used ingenuity in getting information and putting across his own ideas. Bullitt deserves great credit for bringing to his mission a dynamic imagination coupled with knowledge of internal French affairs. If he erred, it was on the side of yielding to a subjective approach, which carried him inside the French Government to an unheard-of degree. An ambassador usually is well advised to remain close enough to local politicians to enjoy their confidence but to be sufficiently aloof to ensure against their assuming control of him. But this was an extraordinary situation which called for unorthodox methods. Bullitt had the advantage of access to intimate Cabinet information which was as important at this time to President Roosevelt as it was dear to Bullitt's own instincts, derived from his early career as a newsman. When war finally was declared, he had a good general idea of what was likely to happen. He was never an emotional interventionist but he was profoundly concerned about the security of the United States in case of a French-British defeat, which he feared. Bullitt was very critical of British policy under the Baldwin and Chamberlain governments, for much the same reasons that Churchill was. But Bullitt underestimated Churchill, thinking of him as a has-been, which was the general opinion at that time in England as well as in Europe.

Ambassador Bullitt's relationship with President Roosevelt was remarkably intimate during his years in Russia and France. He often bypassed the Secretary of State and talked at length with the President by transatlantic telephone. The two men threshed out matters of policy with no correspondence to record their discussions, particularly during those first eight months of World War II which wrongly became known as the "phony war." That phrase is said to have originated with the Chairman of the United States Senate's Foreign Relations Committee. Whatever its origin, the expression proved contagious and it was eagerly adopted by the American press and public and even by many Englishmen and Frenchmen. Millions of people everywhere were eager to believe that the war was "phony," but as we know now from captured German documents, there was nothing "phony" about World War II at any time. Hitler's government never seriously considered offering peace terms tolerable to the Allied governments, nor did most British or French statesmen believe, after the failure of Munich, that a genuine peace with Hitler was possible.

For the American Embassy in Paris, those first months of the war were intensely busy. Bullitt kept in touch daily, almost hourly, with French leaders, both political and military. The Premiers of the two French Governments which were successively in power that year, and even the Commander in Chief of the French armed forces, frequently called confidentially at odd hours of the day or night upon our ambassador at his official residence on the Avenue d'Iéna, a most unusual procedure. Bullitt's well-publicized activities were deliberately intended to make the Germans believe that the United States Government was more belligerent than it actually was, in the hope of discouraging an all-out German attack. Our Ambassador was willing to face the accusations, which promptly came from many directions, that he was a "warmonger" and an American representative who was more devoted to the interests of France than those of his own country. I remained closely in touch with this rapidly evolving situation and its dramatis personae—French leaders in conflict with one another to a degree which would have done justice to the times of the Caesars.

Bullitt also was accused, both in the United States and in France, of exaggerating the help which Frenchmen could expect from the United States. Some French leaders were convinced that the repeal of the American Neutrality Act would give the Axis pause, for fear of American entry in the war. But from the very outbreak of hostilities up to the French collapse in 1940, Bullitt consistently warned French statesmen and military officers that most Americans resolutely opposed our entry. He repeatedly warned them that Congress undoubtedly would not repeal the Neutrality Act, which gave the American people a false sense of their ability to remain aloof from the conflict. I visited the United States shortly before the outbreak of the war, full of anxiety over its imminence and danger. Many of my American acquaintances chilled me with the bland assertion: "Let Europe settle its own problems. This time we will stay out of it." The seductive assumption that we had the power of choice accounted for the sense of security amazingly possessed by most Americans at that time.

More than once during that dreary, blacked-out first winter of the war, when everybody seemed waiting for an inevitable calamity, prominent French men and women asked Bullitt if he did not think France should seek a compromise peace with Germany because of the Bolshevik menace. These French "appeasers" refused to believe that the Hitler-Stalin pact could last long, and they esteemed Bullitt for one thing only: his formidable criticism of the Soviet system, based upon his experiences as the first American ambassador to the U.S.S.R. Because his hostility to Communism was so well known, the American Ambassador could argue more persuasively than anybody else in Paris that winter against suggestions that Europe could tolerate any kind of peace which would leave Hitler dominant.

However, French Communists did everything they could to weaken Bullitt's arguments. They were the most tightly knit political group in France and they faithfully followed Moscow's lead in denouncing French participation in the war. Until the Daladier Government jailed them, the fifty Communist deputies in the French Chamber openly fought every effort to speed up French military preparedness. The Premier came more than once to our embassy with definite evidence of outright Communist sabotage. Day after day Russian leaders publicly encouraged their French supporters to agitate against preparedness. But the most effective Communist contribution to Hitler came through the trade unions. Modern armies depend upon technicians, and a large proportion of French technicians were members of Communist-dominated trade unions. When these men were conscripted, they were exposed all through that melancholy winter of 1939–40 to Communist agitators denouncing war, while other agitators insidiously worked among the distraught wives of these key army personnel. Nothing did more to break down the morale of French fighting forces.

After the French collapse in 1940, a few American and French journalists who had completely misjudged the relative strengths of the French and German armies, thus misleading their readers, helped to popularize the theory that a "Fascist fifth column" had been chiefly responsible for the disastrous French defeat. I have been interested to note in General de Gaulle's war memoirs that he does not even mention the "fifth column" which these commentators so greatly exaggerated in 1940 and afterward. De Gaulle, writing after all the evidence was available to him, including that of captured German documents, concurs with what the American military attachés in Paris reported to our own government in 1940. The German blitzkrieg overpowered French and British armies because of vastly superior military preparations and generalship. However, insofar as the spirit of defeatism figured in the French catastrophe—and my own observations at the time made me feel that this spirit was a considerable factor—French and international Communists were much more responsible for defeatism than the relatively few so-called fascists. American Communists also were doing everything possible then to discourage our own military preparedness and to oppose any assistance to France and Britain. The Russian people later paid a terrible price in human suffering, due partly to Stalin's misguided and cynical policy.

In February 1940, Bullitt decided to make a hurried visit to Washington in hope of speeding up deliveries to France of the big guns and especially the fighting planes desperately needed. As De Gaulle has pointed out in his memoirs, French senior military officers even at that late date showed amazingly little concern about Nazi tanks which were so soon to destroy their forces. There was not much more that President Roosevelt could do about plane deliveries than he already had done, but Bullitt hoped to win support from some influential members of Congress. I was left in charge of the Paris embassy, and almost immediately after the Ambassador departed I received a message from Washington which greatly disturbed me, announcing that Sumner Welles, Under Secretary of State, was visiting the three belligerent countries and Italy on a peace mission. That announcement worried me because I knew that Bullitt had not been consulted about this abrupt move, and that his pride would be wounded. I knew that the Ambassador felt he had an understanding with President Roosevelt which made him the principal White House adviser on European affairs, while Welles, similarly close to the President, was the principal adviser for other areas. Secretary of State Cordell Hull had become more or less resigned to this abnormal situation, as his memoirs make clear.

When Roosevelt sent Welles to Europe without even informing Bullitt, the latter understandably concluded that Welles had violated an agreed division of functions, and a bitterness developed which, in my opinion, was a severe blow to American wartime policy-making. These two men were among the State Department's most brilliant and experienced representatives at that time, and their influence upon the President was great. Being independently wealthy, they could afford to and did participate vigorously in party politics; both had campaigned for Roosevelt in 1932 and afterward. But their misunderstanding aroused so much ill feeling that both men eventually were sidelined at a critical moment in American history. I shall always regret that efforts to resolve their private differences were unsuccessful. I am convinced that if the President had kept the ardent support of these two positive personalities during his last two years, when his health declined so disastrously, American postwar policies would have been shaped much more realistically. Bullitt in particular possessed a cool, clear awareness of Russian aims which might have proved invaluable to Roosevelt at Teheran and Yalta, and later to President Truman at the Potsdam Conference.

Welles has described his 1940 peace mission in his book *The Time for Decision,* published in 1944. Because that book appeared in wartime, while several of the French leaders he had met were in German prisons, his account of his talks with them is necessarily reticent. But I accompanied him on all his official visits in France and possess a "memo to myself" written at the time which reinforces Welles' sympathetic impressions of how lamentably inept and unrealistic were the men governing France just before the German blitzkrieg hit them. Our Paris embassy staff then included exceptionally able officers, such as H. Freeman Matthews, Maynard Barnes and Douglas MacArthur II. We did everything possible to make sure that Welles took back a clear picture of the French situation. Welles had been in Paris when World War I broke out, and he was shocked by the contrast between 1914 and 1940. As he noted, "One could almost sense in every house the feeling of sullen apathy which marked most of the faces that one passed in the nearly deserted streets. There was a sensation of general waiting: of an expectation of some dire calamity."

Having been in Paris for ten continuous years, I assured Welles that Paris had been like that, not only since World War II broke out, but for years before then. When Welles and I called upon the aging last President of the Third Republic, Albert Lebrun, the old gentleman talked at some length about the rise of Nazi Germany. I asked him only one question: "Mr. President, do you believe that the French Government could have upset Hitler's plans if it had opposed by force his illegal occupation of the Rhineland in 1936?" This distinguished Frenchman, who kept telling us that he had modeled his career upon that of Georges Clemenceau, the French "Winston Churchill" of World War I, slowly nodded in agreement, then added sadly, "But we were just too tired." As Welles and I went the rounds among government leaders, everybody seemed "just too tired," and we could discern nobody able or willing to replace these weary politicians in the terrible test they were to face in only a few more weeks. These French leaders seemed to have lost their talent for logical thought. For example, the President of the Senate, Jules Jeanneney, after pointing out how hopelessly weak he believed France to be, added solemnly that members of the Senate unanimously favored continuation of the war until Germany had been "taught a lesson such as to make it impossible for her ever again to bring about a European conflagration." But he did not suggest who could teach that lesson.

Probably Welles' most disillusioning experience in Paris was what happened after he called upon Léon Blum, who had been living quietly in retirement since the collapse of his Popular Front shortly before the outbreak of war. We visited Blum in his small apartment on the Quai de Bourbon, across from Notre Dame Cathedral. When Paris newspapers reported our visit, almost three thousand letters of protest were sent to Welles by French men and women. Most of them were written in insulting terms, condemning President Roosevelt's personal representative for thus honoring a Jew. Welles commented that this incident made him realize "how widely the poison engendered by the Nazis had already seeped into western Europe." I mention this episode because the Vichy Government subsequently was accused of foisting anti-Semitism upon a reluctant French people. Unfortunately, as Welles' experience demonstrated, anti-Semitism was prevalent in France before the Vichy epoch. On the other hand, some members of the Vichy Government consistently resisted efforts of the German Nazis and their French sympathizers to impose anti-Jewish decrees in France. As for the sentiment against Léon Blum, it was due also partly to the fact that his government had neglected rearmament, which embittered many military officers and their supporters.

Recently, in looking over the list of French leaders whom Welles and I interviewed in March 1940, I was struck by how the war variously affected these men. For one reason or another almost all these Frenchmen in the government at that historical moment were destined to be passive during the war. Some were imprisoned, first by their own countrymen and then by the Germans. The vigorous and courageous Minister of the Interior, Georges Mandel, was murdered by Frenchmen in the Forest of Fontainebleau in July 1944. A majority of the Third Republic's political leaders and members of the legislature did endorse the authoritarian state set up at Vichy a few weeks after the armistice, but most of them soon decided to hold aloof both from the Vichy Government and from De Gaulle's unofficial organization in London. The Third Republic and the men governing it during its downfall never did recover from defeat; they were equally unsuccessful with the Fourth Republic after the war.

In my 1940 notes I find a copy of a petition which was brought to me during Welles' visit to Paris, summarizing the views of several former French premiers and foreign ministers. This petition urged that Ambassador Bullitt should not return to Paris unless he could persuade President Roosevelt to side openly with the Allies and grant immediately important credits to France to carry on the war. Otherwise, the petitioners argued, the Welles' visit would appear to repudiate the

Ambassador. If, as the visit seemed to indicate, Roosevelt was taking the initiative toward encouraging a compromise peace—which could only be regarded as defeat for the Allies—then American policy would be the reverse of that advocated by Bullitt. But the truth was that Roosevelt, like many other Presidents before and since, probably was using foreign policy for domestic political purposes on this occasion. With a campaign for re-election coming up, he could see the advantage of making American voters believe that he was not overlooking any possibility of preventing all-out war.

My notes also remind me that Joseph Kennedy, then American ambassador to Great Britain, arrived in Paris from Switzerland on the same train with Welles. I jotted down without comment: "I enjoyed a half hour with Ambassador Kennedy who told me of his bad health, his discontent over returning to London, his belief that everything he could do there could just as well be done by a $50-a-month clerk, that he wanted to quit but didn't see how he gracefully could before the elections. He said the United States would be crazy to go into the war, and that he didn't mind telling the British that they were kidding themselves if they believed otherwise."

Just as the first soft blandishments of spring were beginning to beguile Parisians, Bullitt returned from Washington to witness the "phony war" swiftly transform itself into the blitzkrieg. The war in Finland and the German occupation of Denmark and Norway had revived hopes of some French and British leaders that it still was possible to avoid making France a battleground. This form of wishful thinking prevailed right up to the blitzkrieg itself. On the actual eve of the Battle of France, on May 9, Bullitt gave a dinner party in honor of the current French Premier, Paul Reynaud. Among his guests were Raoul Dautry, Minister of Armament; Pierre Fournier, Governor of the Bank of France; British Air Vice-Marshal Barratt, commander of the tiny British air force in France; Vincent Sheean, the author; and Dorothy Thompson, the American journalist. Although the German attack on the Lowlands would begin in a few hours, none of us knew that, and a lively argument developed at the dinner table about whether the Germans would attack some time in 1940 or defer such action until 1941. Dautry stated his positive conviction that there would be no attempt to invade France that year; he told us that the entire French armament program was based on the assumption that the attack would not come for another year. The Germans, he asserted, were in need of time more than the French and British. Fournier, the banker, listened to Dautry's exposition with growing impatience. "If that is your theory," he interrupted, "then we are in greater danger than I suspected. The German attack could happen at any minute now and might well come in a matter of days." Our group listened in amazement to this sharp disagreement between influential members of the government. When the dinner ended at the customary diplomatic hour of eleven, a few of us, including Air Vice-Marshal Harris, accepted an invitation from Miss Thompson to continue the discussion in her apartment in the Hotel Meurice, where we talked until long past midnight. The British airman got back to his headquarters at Compiègne near Paris barely in time to be informed that the German attack had started.

Details of the days which followed are rather blurred in my memory, partly because all of us got so little sleep. Never before or since, I am sure, has one battle so stunned the entire world. The invasion of the Netherlands began at three o'clock on the morning of May 10 and only five days later Premier Reynaud cried into Winston Churchill's bedside telephone in England: "We are defeated!"

On May 14 the French Foreign Office notified us that it had begun to burn its records and advised the American and other embassies to do the same. Burning records is a tedious job. We had a modern chancery and a good furnace, which made our task easier, but the British Embassy, purchased by the Duke of Wellington in 1815, still retained its primitive heating equipment. The British also had a tremendous accumulation of confidential documents. My colleague in the British Embassy, Harold Mack, told me a little story about Winston Churchill at that time. The Prime Minister had responded to Reynaud's frantic appeal by flying to Paris on May 16, sleeping that night at his embassy. The circumstances must be remembered: Holland had fallen, Belgium was about to fall, British and French armies were virtually ripped to shreds, so Churchill had many overwhelming things to think about. But the next morning he summoned Mack to his bedroom and pointed out of his window to the superb embassy lawn which had been lovingly cultivated for generations. Now it had great scorched spots where the archives had been burned. "What is going on here?" the Prime Minister demanded, and Mack reluctantly informed him of the loss of many precious documents, realizing as he spoke that Churchill, as an historian, would be shocked. But the Prime Minister, saying nothing about the documents, grumbled: "Was it necessary also to mutilate this magnificent lawn?"

I had to call at the Foreign Office shortly after its staff received an order to evacuate. The courtyard at the Quai d'Orsay presented a scene of wildest confusion. A large number of old Renault buses had been requisitioned, and bundles of files were being flung from office windows on the upper floors to the courtyard for loading. Others were being burned. For months afterward, whenever I took up various matters with the Foreign Office and later in Vichy, officials seemed helpless. Nobody could find anything in the files, and how can a government department function without files?

Our own embassy's primary concern was with American citizens, and Americans flooded in on us from the conquered countries to the north, then from many parts of France. One morning at four o'clock, Bill Crampton, manager for France of the Standard Oil Company of New Jersey, telephoned to inform me that he had just received an irrevocable order from the French General Staff to destroy the enormous stocks of petroleum in the Paris area. He said he wanted to touch base with the embassy before blowing up the oil accumulated at great expense over many months. I told him to go ahead, since everybody agreed that Paris was about to be occupied. For days thereafter the city was covered with heavy black smoke, which provided a kind of Dante's Inferno background for the pitiful refugees from several countries who flowed in and through and out of Paris, most of them not knowing where they were going. Fourteen million French men, women, and children fled on foot and in anything with wheels from the north to southern France. We in the embassy felt more sympathy for these victims than we did for a considerable number of Americans who became panic-stricken at the last minute and behaved as if they were particular targets of the Nazis. They had much less reason than any Frenchman to become alarmed, since we were not at war. Although none of us in Paris could know it then, the United States would continue to stay officially out of the war for another year and a half.

Now the time had come when Ambassador Bullitt must decide what he himself should do. The French Government was leaving Paris, first to pause briefly in Tours, then moving to Bordeaux. Other ambassadors decided to follow the fleeing government, but Bullitt, after much soul-searching, decided to remain in Paris. He felt that he had an American tradition to uphold, since American ambassadors had stayed in the capital in 1870 and in 1916 when emissaries of other nations had followed the fugitive French government. He sent an advance embassy group to accompany the government, headed by Interim Ambassador Anthony Drexel Biddle and H. Freeman Matthews, and kept me and several secretaries, together with his military and naval attachés, with him in Paris.

Personally, I agreed with the Ambassador's decision, but Secretary of State Hull and General de Gaulle, among others, have severely criticized Bullitt for remaining in Paris. Hull wrote in his memoirs: "This decision, in my opinion, was unfortunate. It deprived Bullitt of all contact with the French Government during the crucial week between June 10, when it left Paris, and June 17, when it asked for an armistice. Had Bullitt, with his unequaled contacts with the leaders of the French Government, been able to represent us during those historic days, it is possible, if not probable, that that Government would have taken the fleet, gone to North Africa, and continued the fight from there." De Gaulle makes much the same comment in his own memoirs.

This raises one of the most interesting hypothetical questions about World War II: What would have happened if the remnants of the French Government had retreated to North Africa in June 1940, and then continued to fight from there? How would the Germans have responded to such a move? The question still fascinates me because my own wartime experiences were so intimately concerned with French North Africa, the place where Americans first fought in the European Theater and where General Eisenhower first made his reputation.

Nowadays, whenever I return to Paris, I reflect with satisfaction upon one contribution which Bullitt and his staff were able to make in 1940 by remaining in the city. That Paris survives in all its glory today seems a miracle when I recall how we in the embassy assumed that the capital would be ground to rubble when the German armies were approaching, and Reynaud proclaimed that the French would fight from street to street and house to house. Churchill and De Gaulle both record in their memoirs that they urged such suicidal resistance. It was only at the very last moment that Reynaud asked the American Embassy's intervention in making Paris an open city. Bullitt was in constant touch with the French Premier and doubtless had some influence in his decision. By prompt and vigorous negotiations, conducted in association with the Swiss Minister in Paris and the American Legation in Switzerland, an agreement was concluded with the Germans that Paris would be undefended, and thus would not become a battleground.

Most military experts now agree that a destructive battle in the streets of Paris would have been merely a delaying action of a few days which could not have affected appreciably the course of the war. Churchill has stated frankly that his major objective in 1940 and 1941 was to involve the United States in the war, since he did not see how a British victory could be possible otherwise. I suspect that he felt, consciously or subconsciously, that the brutal destruction of Paris, the city so many Americans love, with inevitable bombings, conflagrations, and disappearance of celebrated monuments, might so outrage the American people that we would be precipitated into the conflict, or at least moved closer toward declaring war against Nazi Germany. However, Churchill admits in his memoirs that he underestimated how widespread, in 1940, was American resistance to entering the war. Bullitt and his staff never had any illusions about that, and we could see no good reason why Paris should be uselessly sacrificed.

There never has been anything like the eerie atmosphere in Paris during the two days between the departure of the French Government and the arrival of the German troops. One day the vast metropolis was more active than ever, as its agitated population and refugees churned around not knowing what to do. Then they were gone, many of them to their death on congested highways. The Paris from which they fled was left almost empty. On June 13, the day before German troops reached the center of the city, I went at noon from our embassy into the adjoining Place de la Concorde and looked up the broad expanse of the Champs-Elysées toward the Arc de Triomphe. As every visitor to Paris knows, this is one of the world's greatest traffic hazards. But now the only living creatures in sight were three abandoned dogs cavorting beneath the large French flags which still hung at each corner of the great concourse.

That midnight, six hours before the first troops arrived at the Place de la Concorde, I decided to take a walk with Commander (later Vice Admiral) Roscoe Hillenkoetter, our naval attaché. It had been a long, hectic, hot day, and our embassy staff was sleeping that night in the chancery. As we came out of the guarded embassy door, we were confronted by the Grand Rabbin of Paris, his wife and two friends, all French nationals. The Grand Rabbin was the greatly respected leader of the Jewish community of Paris, and he had courageously decided to remain there, regardless of what might happen to him. But after the departure of the French Government, the Grand Rabbin changed his mind at the last moment—for very understandable reasons. He asked us if we could not provide seats for him and his little group in our embassy automobiles which were going to Bordeaux. I had to inform him that Paris already was surrounded by German armored divisions and that most of our staff had departed for Bordeaux long before. But in order to convince him that I was not misinformed, I summoned one of the few remaining automobiles and instructed the chauffeur to drive his party to the outskirts of Paris, where the Germans turned them back, as I was almost certain they would do. I never saw the Grand Rabbin again but learned afterwards that he died in Paris. As Hillenkoetter and I walked along the ghostly boulevards that sultry night, not a café was open, no lights showed anywhere, we met no one. The few people who remained in the city were buttoned up in their shuttered homes. From the direction of Melun came occasional flashes of artillery fire.

The first German troops appeared at dawn on June 14, undisturbed by a single untoward incident. They were disciplined men, carefully selected to carry out the predetermined German policy of "correctness." About ten o'clock that morning little detachments of German soldiers were assigned to escort men of the fire department—just about the only Frenchmen who had remained to protect Paris—on a tour of the boulevards, hauling down the Tricolor and raising the Swastika. An especially large Nazi flag was hoisted at the Arc de Triomphe, where the everlasting flame continued to flicker over the Tomb of the Unknown Soldier.

We had been informed that the German Provisional military governor, General von Studnitz, intended to make his headquarters at the Crillon Hotel, directly opposite the American Embassy. Ambassador Bullitt instructed me and our military and naval attachés to pay a formal call upon the general as soon as he appeared to be settled, so when the Swastika rose above the Crillon, we decided the moment had arrived for us to make our call. We were to obtain as much information as we could, ascertain the German attitude vis-à-vis the French Government and population, and in accordance with our promise to Prime Minister Reynaud, see whether we could be helpful. The three of us left the embassy together, and as we stood on the sidewalk waiting for a military convoy to pass so we could cross the street, one car detached itself from the procession and drew up beside us. A uniformed German lieutenant stepped out and said to us in English, "You are Americans, aren't you?" We nodded. He explained that he had lived several years in the United States, and then went on, "Can you tell us where we might find a suitable hotel here?" The question was so unexpected and so incongruous that we all laughed. Then one of us said, "The whole city seems to be in your possession. It has hundreds of empty hotels. Take your pick."

The lieutenant hesitated a moment, saluted, and returned to his automobile. We continued, with some misgivings, and entered the Crillon lobby. There, pacing up and down, obviously agitated, was a French police commissioner whom I knew. I asked him how things were going. He exclaimed, "Oh, you can't imagine what happened!" I noticed that he was perspiring freely. When "they" arrived, he told me, the German colonel had summoned him, handed him a Swastika flag, and said: "Open that hotel. It will be our headquarters. Take down the French flag from the roof, and replace it with this German flag." But the hotel was locked and empty, the steel shutters on the windows were closed. "We tried to get in and then we tried to get a locksmith," the police commissioner continued. "Precious time went by. Then the colonel summoned me again and said: 'If that hotel is not open in fifteen minutes and the French flag is not down, we will shoot it down and shoot you, too!' " Fortunately, a locksmith was found in the nick of time, but sweating it out was hard on the police commissaire. "*Comme j'ai transpiré!*" he said dejectedly.

We then made our way to the Prince of Wales suite of the hotel, where we were informed the General could be found. Standing at the door of the suite was a German colonel who exclaimed: "Murphy! What are you doing here?" I looked at him in astonishment; his face was vaguely familiar. "I am Colonel Weber," he announced, and then I remembered that he was a Bavarian army officer whom I had known fifteen years before when I was vice consul at Munich. He was the General's aide, and now he welcomed us as if we all were old friends, ushering us immediately into the drawing room where the general was talking with a dozen staff officers. We had expected to spend only a few formal minutes with the general, but he had previously ordered champagne from the Crillon's excellent cellars and was in a mood to answer all the questions of our military and naval attachés. The only information we had about the progress of the war was what we had heard from western and Berlin radio broadcasts, which necessarily were confusing. General von Studnitz, who had served as German military attaché in Poland, said he appreciated it was the duty of attachés to gather intelligence for their governments and he was quite willing to inform us fully and frankly.

After listening to the General's clear and concise summary of the military campaign to date, I asked him what would happen next. With complete confidence, he replied that mopping up operations in France would not require more than another ten days, after which preparations would begin for crossing the channel to England. He confirmed our information that the British, after evacuating France, did not have a single division intact and that they had been forced to abandon most of their heavy equipment. Therefore, he concluded, further resistance was impossible. Our naval attaché inquired how the Germans were going to get across the English Channel, but von Studnitz brushed aside this question with the comment that plans were all made and he repeated that, since the British had nothing left, the war would be over by the end of July, six weeks hence.

As we walked back across the street to our Embassy, reviewing that conversation, we agreed that the General was expressing his honest convictions, and none of us was at all sure that he might not be right. Bullitt had said that he would have no contacts with the occupying forces, but after we told him that von Studnitz had offered to call upon him to repay our courtesy call, and that he seemed disposed to talk freely about Nazi plans, the Ambassador agreed to receive him the next day. The Germans were so confident in June 1940 that the war was almost over, that their military headquarters and embassy in Paris assisted us to obtain exit permits, not only for Americans who wanted to leave the occupied zone, but even for hundreds of French people and a few English ones.

Our chancery in Paris is enclosed by a very high metal grille, which we kept locked during those days. Included in a particularly loyal and capable staff, both French and American, we had at that time a picturesque colored doorman, George Washington Mitchell of North Carolina, who remained faithfully on the job guarding our building. He had come to Europe originally with a Buffalo Bill show which had gone broke. He had played the part of an Indian and he may have had a little Cherokee blood; he was an excellent horseman. Our consul general in Marseilles, Robert P. Skinner, had provided him with a job as messenger in our consulate many years before, and later he had followed Skinner to a number of posts, ending in Paris. Although George was practically illiterate, he had learned in the course of his travels to speak German; in fact, he had been married, so he said, to a German girl in Hamburg. On the day the Germans arrived in Paris, I gave George strict instructions not to admit any uniformed Germans to our premises, but as I looked out my office window that first morning, I saw to my dismay that George was assisting two German soldiers to climb over the embassy grille. They were running a telephone wire across our courtyard to the Crillon Hotel. When George came inside our building again, I was waiting to scold him, but I had scarcely begun to ask why he disobeyed my order, when he explained earnestly, "Why, Mr. Murphy, they's from Hamburg! They know people I know in Hamburg. They's very nice fellas!" It was no use trying to explain to George that we regarded these "very nice fellas" as unwelcome. Several years later, in 1949, I was in Paris on diplomatic business with Secretary of State Dean Acheson and was told that George Washington Mitchell was dying. Secretary Acheson and I visited him in the hospital to bid farewell to this faithful servant of the American Government.

Ambassador Bullitt prolonged his stay in German-occupied Paris a little beyond what he had originally planned because the Germans were so unexpectedly communicative about their accomplishments and intentions. We also knew that the French Government, en route from Bordeaux to Vichy, was in a state of utter confusion. It seemed advisable to give it time to assemble itself. The Germans were not only willing but eager to talk, and our military and naval attachés easily arranged meetings with high-ranking German officers, some of whom they had known as attachés in Paris before the war. The information thus obtained was transmitted to Washington immediately after we left Paris and thence relayed to London. Paris proved to be one of the best, if not the best, of intelligence centers of Europe at that moment.

My own chief contact during those three weeks was Ernst Achenbach, who was in charge of the reopened German Embassy pending the arrival of the new ambassador, Otto Abetz. Herr Achenbach's wife was American, a native of California. He was a protégé of

Abetz who, as we know from captured German documents, really believed and sold Hitler the idea that France, if treated considerately, might quickly accept a subordinate place in Hitler's "new order." It was the same idea which French Premier Pierre Laval wholeheartedly shared—so wholeheartedly, in fact, that Laval eventually was executed as a traitor. In the crazy upside-down state of affairs prevailing during those weeks, it did not seem very odd that Hitler's principal diplomatic representative in Paris should be a professed Francophile, married to an equally Francophile American. Achenbach was useful to the American Embassy in many ways and helped us to settle our affairs properly and to depart from the occupied zone when the time came.

I was amazed in those first occupation days to discover how thoroughly the Germans had prepared for every phase of military government. It became apparent that they had drafted comprehensive blueprints long in advance to suit whatever conditions they might encounter in conquered countries. Years later, after the war, I glanced through those plans in captured documents, and noted that they were even more comprehensive than we had realized. I reflected ruefully that the United States Government might have practiced to advantage some of that German foresight. In our own early ventures in military government, Washington's neglect of this phase of waging war created unnecessary difficulties for General Eisenhower, and especially for me as his political adviser.

Before leaving for Vichy we received an inquiry relayed from Washington via Berlin that New York banks which had branches in Paris were anxiously requesting advice regarding the future of their Paris establishments. Accordingly I went to the Bank of France building to call upon the former president of the Bank of Danzig, who was installed now as the Commissioner of Finance in France. He received me politely and listened to my inquiry. He was well informed concerning the financial picture in Paris, and after a few comments he smiled quizzically and said: "You know, when we Germans arrived here the other day we found 137 [I am not certain that I remember the number accurately] banks in the city of Paris. We think that is too many." He paused, and then said mildly: "Does that answer your question?"

Although Hitler's war machine usually operated with inhuman impersonality, individual sentiments sometimes intervened. Just before Paris was occupied, the American Embassy was notified that a large consignment of food and cigarettes for our staff had arrived from the United States and was in the central customs house. In the rush of events we were too busy to collect our shipment, so that it was still there when the Germans took over. When the new administrators inquired about this shipment, the French customs inspector explained that it was American diplomatic property, belonging to the embassy. The inspector told us later what happened then. A German colonel, noting that the cases were addressed to Ambassador Bullitt, in conformity with regulations, exclaimed: "So these are Bullitt's cigarettes! Well, he won't get them. I used to live in Philadelphia and I never did like Bullitt. Take them away." And that was one shipment which our Embassy did not receive.

One of the last services I was able to render the French administration of Paris was to rescue the French police official who was in charge of individual political records, the equivalent of our F.B.I. records, which the Paris police kept in as complete detail then as we do now. When the French government evacuated Paris, only two skeleton staffs were left behind, one from the Prefecture of Police and the other from the Prefecture of the Seine. The first dealt with policing and public security; the second with public utilities and food supply. Both performed marvels, and it was understood that our Embassy would act with them in matters concerning the open city agreement which we had helped to negotiate.

One of the first moves made by the German High Command was to send a detachment to commandeer these elaborate police records. Entering the office of M. Jacques-Simon, Director of Police Intelligence, the Germans demanded access to his files, which would have provided them with detailed information about all their potential enemies in France. Actually the French, working day and night, had removed these confidential archives from Paris, taking them on a river barge as far south as Roanne, where the barge was sunk deliberately when the German Army threatened to overtake it. The French refloated it later, before the sodden papers dissolved. The less important files had been burned and the Germans found in the Prefecture's furnaces smoldering evidence of this technical violation of the open city agreement which provided that everything would be preserved intact. Jacques-Simon was arrested and an angry German officer declared that he would be executed promptly. The Prefect of Police, M. Langeron, telephoned to beg me to intercede on behalf of his chief subordinate, and I wasted no time in taking up the matter with the amiable Herr Achenbach. He really went to a great deal of trouble to find out where Jacques-Simon was and finally traced him to St. Cloud, awaiting summary trial. Jacques-Simon has written that I saved his life, and perhaps he is right. He was technically guilty and his German captors, without failing to be "correct," could have shot him.

During those last three weeks of June 1940, government policymakers all over the world were just beginning to realize what profound changes had been wrought by the blitzkrieg. Never before had the balance of power in Europe been shifted so completely in so short a time. Except in England, where Churchill's government had direct and immediate threats to face, international policy-making during those three weeks was virtually suspended. Bullitt, upon whose advice Roosevelt had depended for years, devoted hours of intense thought every day trying to figure out how the American Government should proceed next. Bullitt was inclined to believe that he could be useful no longer in a Europe dominated by Hitler's Germany, since he had made his personal detestation of Hitler and everything he represented unmistakably clear. So he tentatively decided that after leaving Paris he would propose to President Roosevelt and Secretary of State Hull that he should return to Washington after presenting himself briefly to whatever French administration survived to govern the fraction of France which the Germans had agreed not to occupy. I cannot recall that it ever occurred to any of us that our government had any alternative other than to maintain relations with whatever French Government was established in France.

When we were notified that French leaders had chosen for their temporary capital the resort city of Vichy, we wondered whether this was a bit of Gallic humor. It seemed wryly appropriate that the government of defeated France should choose a place hitherto celebrated only for its rather disagreeable medicinal waters used to treat unpleasant but not necessarily fatal diseases. Actually, Vichy had been selected because it had so much room in its hotels, casinos, and villas. On the morning of June 30, Ambassador Bullitt left Paris by motor caravan for Vichy, accompanied by Carmel Offie, his military and naval attachés, and me. It was understood that in a few days I probably would be left in temporary charge of our embassy, accredited to the government which soon became known as Vichy France. The weather was fine on June 30, 1940 and we traveled at a moderate speed, although the journey could have been made in six hours over the almost empty roads. Once across the line of demarcation between the Occupied and Unoccupied zones, we stopped for a picnic lunch in a shaded grove near the highway, in a setting which could not have been more peaceful. None of us could know then that France was destined to serve as a battleground for almost five more years.

FOUR

CHARGE D'AFFAIRES IN WARTIME VICHY

Not long ago I had occasion to drive again through the once-famous health resort of Vichy which figured so spectacularly in French-American relations during World War II. Vichy, my friends inform me, has never regained since the war its previous popularity, either with Frenchmen or Americans. Bernard Baruch once told me that he had been an ardent booster of Vichy between the world wars and had helped set the fashion for Americans to take the "cure" there. No doubt the medicinal repute of Vichy water is as esteemed as ever, but Vichy's popularity seems to have been affected by the unhappy political notoriety which this spa acquired during the years of Nazi domination of Europe, when Vichy was headlined in the blazing controversies of world politics. To many Americans, Vichy still carries the connotation of Fascist, pro-Nazi, collaboration, anti-Semitism, totalitarian, treachery. But to me, who watched the dazed French Government trying to pull itself together during that anguished summer of 1940, Vichy suggests mostly an assortment of bewildered Frenchmen staggering under catastrophic military defeat. In the beginning, at any rate, most of the French politicians were groping their way toward possible solutions of their immediate problems, wondering how they could ever manage to live with the Nazi war machine which so suddenly had blasted its path through the entire continent.

Before Ambassador Bullitt and his little group of aides started out for Vichy that sunny June 30, 1940, the Paris police informed him that German agents had proposed to French gangsters that they assassinate him during his unprotected journey. The idea was that German propagandists could then proclaim that indignant Frenchmen had revenged themselves upon a man who had lured their government into a disastrous war. But Bullitt laughed off this alleged plot, saying, "Can't you see that the Germans believe the war is over? Why would they bother now to get rid of a mere ambassador?" However, Bullitt himself lent a little spice of danger to our departure from Occupied

France by including in our group a British couple who were subject to internment, Mr. and Mrs. Francis Gilroy. Philadelphia-born Mrs. Gilroy was a hometown friend of the Ambassador, and he said that with so many irregular things happening, he saw no harm in adding one more irregularity. So he smuggled out his British friends by having American passports issued to them, and Gilroy did his best to behave like an American when we came to the line dividing Occupied and Unoccupied France. All of us were relieved when the German inspector handed back the Gilroys' fresh American passports without comment.

During those momentous three weeks in Paris we had been completely cut off from communication with Washington, except for an occasional rare message via Berlin. We had burned our codes and the Germans notified us that, because of military exigencies, our open cablegrams would have to be routed through Berlin and be subject to indefinite delay. They did not exaggerate. We left Paris knowing only what we had picked up from radio broadcasts, plus what the Germans themselves had told us about the last tumultous days of the Battle of France. In order to inform himself fully before making his presence known at Vichy, Bullitt had reserved rooms in a small hotel in the nearby hamlet of La Bourboule for his own party and for the members of his staff, headed by Ambassador Biddle and "Doc" Matthews, who had been assigned to stay with the itinerant French Government after it left Paris.

We sat up most of that first night in La Bourboule while Biddle and his associates gave us a thorough briefing. They had managed with great difficulty to keep in constant touch with the distraught French Government as it paused briefly in Tours and then went on to Bordeaux where the armistice was arranged. The confusion, they told us, had been wild beyond description, with cabinet ministers, bureaucrats, soldiers, and hundreds of thousands of terrified refugees of many nationalities jamming the highways southward. The harassed French Premier, Paul Reynaud, often out of touch with Army Headquarters, only belatedly received news of one military disaster after another. Our own diplomats, like everybody else in and around the government, had gotten very little sleep because meetings of the war council were held any time of the day or night. These chaotic conditions made it impossible for the French Government to give calm consideration to decisions of the most vital importance. Our colleagues told us how Churchill and his aides flew over from London in an effort to persuade the disintegrating Reynaud Government to seek refuge in French Africa, or any place beyond German reach, and continue the war.

As Bullitt listened to this melancholy report of his staff, he was more than ever convinced that he had been right to remain in Paris, where he was at least able to help save that city from destruction. In fact, it was only Bullitt's strong sense of duty which brought him back to France at all after his February trip to Washington before the blitzkrieg. He had discovered then that the same American politicians who blustered and postured about the evils of Hitlerism hastily backed away when specific military measures were proposed. The Ambassador told us, after he returned to Paris, that he had come back only because he would be accused of letting France down if he did not, and thus would embarrass the Roosevelt administration. He knew all too well that in any critical situation, French leaders would inevitably demand more help from the United States than they could possibly get. Nobody had been more emphatic than Bullitt in warning Reynaud and other French ministers that there was not the slightest chance that the United States would declare war in 1940, unless attacked. He had constantly explained that only Congress could declare war, and that American sentiment in and out of Congress was overwhelmingly opposed then to entering the war. The situation which had developed in Tours and Bordeaux was very much what Bullitt had feared, and he now expressed thankfulness that he had been spared the ordeal of explaining for the last time to distracted French ministers the facts of American political life. He congratulated Biddle for handling the nightmare situation at Bordeaux as well as anybody could have done.

Ambassador Biddle went on to tell us that Washington, judging by the torrent of instructions he had received, was worried chiefly about the French fleet, a real cause for worry. Biddle said he had been authorized to promise almost anything—short of involving the United States directly in the war—which would take the French fleet beyond any possible German control. But the best our diplomats had been able to achieve was to exact from responsible members of the incoming Pétain Government the promise that they never would permit the Germans to seize their fleet. And history records that despite anxious years and many vicissitudes, that promise was kept.

In La Bourboule that evening we also heard the details of a personal scandal which had attracted wide attention even in the midst of universal catastrophe. I mention it here only because, as I was to discover later in Vichy, it had more political significance than historians usually have attached to it. Premier Reynaud, upon whom the fate of France chiefly rested during the final months of the Third Republic, had lived for years with Mme. Helene des Portes, a former friend of his wife. The Premier and Mme. des Portes often were seen gaily cycling together in the Bois de Boulogne, and when M. and Mme. Paul Reynaud were invited to dine at the American Embassy, there always was a question which lady would attend. At one dinner both arrived, providing a neat protocol problem. Mme. des Portes was an exceptionally determined Frenchwoman, and her frenzied political activity and her doubts about the war were the gossip of Paris. Even after war broke out, she persistently urged Reynaud and his ministers to negotiate peace with Hitler's Germany.

When Reynaud finally decided to resign rather than accept an armistice, he relinquished the government to his vice premier, Marshal Henri Philippe Pétain, hero of World War I. At the same time, the Pétain Government approved Reynaud's request to appoint him ambassador to Washington. This was believed to be Mme. des Portes' objective, and she certainly planned to accompany Reynaud. But Destiny intervened. As Reynaud and Mme. des Portes were riding together near the Spanish frontier in an automobile loaded with baggage, their car stopped too abruptly and the luggage toppled over on the occupants. Mme. des Portes, who was driving, lost control of the car which left the road and hit a tree, killing her and injuring Reynaud so badly that he was unable to travel. The Premier, who had been among the most effective of the Third Republic's statesmen, was thus immobilized, and a few months later he, Léon Blum, and other prewar Premiers were imprisoned by the Germans for the duration of the war.

What appeared to be irregular personal behavior, occurring in the midst of national tragedy, affected the reputation of Reynaud and indirectly involved General de Gaulle, because Reynaud had been virtually the only influential political supporter of the then obscure colonel. De Gaulle's emphasis upon the importance of mechanical warfare, in his book *L'Armée de Métier,* had greatly impressed Reynaud, and perhaps it is for this reason that no mention of the Reynaud scandal appears in the De Gaulle memoirs. But the incident had a profound effect in 1940 upon those Frenchmen, like Marshal Pétain, who had contended for years that the Third Republic's politicians were not merely weak but were morally rotten. When Pétain was French ambassador in Madrid in 1939, some of his friends visited him in an effort to persuade him to return to Paris for the purpose of arresting the deterioration of the Daladier Government. The Marshal was reported to have said, "What would I do in Paris? I have no mistress!" It was notorious that some of the ladies who were intimate with members of the French Government were ambitious to play political roles, and their *salons* were active in the tradition of Mme. de Staël. Both Nazi and Soviet espionage found this source of seepage of secret information most useful and, for that matter, so did our own Embassy. Pétain was one of many patriotic Frenchmen who had come to believe that only an authoritarian regime could cleanse the corruption in French public and private life. Such ideas fitted nicely, of course, into Hitler's proclaimed "new order" for Europe, and into the plans of those Frenchmen who were ready to concede that Germany had won the war in 1940, and that France could obtain a favored position in the "new order" only if Frenchmen promptly seized the opportunity to get in on the ground floor. Those were the ideas which American diplomats, among others in Vichy, had to combat.

After learning from Biddle and his associates how matters had stood in Bordeaux, Ambassador Bullitt concluded that it would be better not to present himself in Vichy officially at all. Instead, he decided to remain at La Bourboule for a few days to have informal talks with the Government's principal members, and then proceed to Washington, leaving me in charge of our Embassy. With America's national holiday so near at hand, Bullitt said that if he refrained from moving personally into the Villa Ica, the property of Mrs. Jay Gould which was assigned to us in Vichy, we could avoid holding our traditional Fourth of July reception under distressing circumstances. But, before departing for Washington, Bullitt took pains to reassure himself concerning the French fleet. He had a long talk with Admiral Darlan, Minister of Marine, and the following day he conferred with Marshal Pétain and others. His report of these conversations, dated July 1, is described by William L. Langer, Coolidge Professor of History at Harvard, as "one of the most remarkable and revealing documents in the entire annals of this great war."

Thus it came about that I was officially in charge of our embassy on July 3, 1940—one of the most unfortunate dates in the long history of Anglo-French relations. On that July day the Churchill Government, desperately anxious about possible German capture of the French fleet, decided that it must at any cost get control of all units of the French fleet within British reach. The British Navy therefore boarded and took over French warships in British ports and in Egypt, with only token resistance. But at Mers el-Kebir, the port of Oran in western Algeria, the French commanding admiral, Marcel-Bruno Gensoul, refused after several hours' parley to accept the British ultimatum to proceed to some British or neutral port, safe from the Germans. Acting under irrevocable orders from Churchill's war cabinet, the British Mediterranean Fleet thereupon destroyed or crippled many French warships, killing or wounding about two thousand French sailors.

I learned of this British attack only a few hours after it happened, when French Foreign Minister Paul Baudouin called me to the Foreign Office in Vichy to inform me that his government was breaking off diplomatic relations with the British Government. This meant that all British consular officers would be obliged to depart from French Africa, and Baudouin knew that this in turn would be followed by a naval blockade imposed by Britain against France and French overseas possessions. Baudouin was so angry and humiliated that he even hinted the French Navy might cooperate with the Germans. But as I listened carefully to his outburst, I decided I would be justified in reporting to Washington that the Pétain Government probably would not declare war against its recent ally and would keep its pledge to us about the fleet.

In his memoirs, Churchill makes out the best possible case for the British action at Mers el-Kebir, showing that he was more determined than anybody else to use force against what he considered an imminent menace. But it is my own feeling, based upon the reaction which I witnessed in Vichy then, that General de Gaulle, in his memoirs, more accurately estimated what he calls this "lamentable event." After examining the evidence presented in the Churchill account, together with all the postwar revelations in France, De Gaulle concludes, as I did at the time, that the British attack was unnecessary and cost much more than it gained. Perhaps this was the most serious British mistake of the war, because it simultaneously undermined the influence of the pro-British moderates in Vichy and of De Gaulle in London.

Indeed, one of the chief victims of the British naval attack was De Gaulle, whose campaign to organize French resistance from London was thus abruptly checked before it had fairly started. Representative French politicians and officers who were preparing to go to England to join him were so outraged that they gave up the attempt. History, of course, has proved that De Gaulle was the most forceful French personality of his generation, but in that chaotic spring and summer of 1940, the General presented an obscure and somewhat dubious aspect to many of his most earnest anti-Nazi countrymen, as well as to nearly all the foreign diplomats who came to Vichy. Many of De Gaulle's compatriots wrongly regarded him as a British vassal.

We who were in the American Embassy in German-occupied Paris on June 18, had listened there to the French General's stirring appeal for continued resistance, and had been moved by it. But we asked each other: "How has this man suddenly become so important?" Until that hour, I cannot remember ever having heard De Gaulle's name. It was not until we arrived at Vichy that I learned the details of how he had been brought into the government by his sponsor, Premier Reynaud, only after the blitzkrieg started, and only then was promoted from colonel to brigadier-general. It was understandable why many politicians distrusted him. In the same book in which he had courageously jeopardized his army career by criticizing the High Command's neglect of tanks, he also had recorded his grave doubts about parliamentary democracy. In the parlance of those days, he had been denounced as a Fascist.

But, as I recall it, there was no widespread hostility in Vichy toward De Gaulle until that British naval attack on July 3. Five days later, the General made a speech, broadcast by the London radio, which was misinterpreted by angry Frenchmen as an attempt to justify the British. A careful reading of that speech shows that De Gaulle made no apology for the action of the British Government, which he deplored as unnecessary. He merely urged that the ghastly blunder should not be allowed to interfere with the war against Germany. The self-exiled officer was presenting in London precisely the same arguments I was using in my talks with Marshal Pétain and other Frenchmen in Vichy. But it was not easy during those weeks immediately following Mers el-Kebir to induce Frenchmen to discuss the affair calmly. French naval officers bitterly told me that the British always had been jealous of the French Navy, always were looking for a chance at international conferences to weaken it, and now had seized the moment when France was knocked out by Hitler's Germany to destroy a large part of the helpless French fleet. The effect on French naval officers in North Africa was catastrophic and caused us endless difficulties there later. When copies of London newspapers belatedly reached Vichy, French indignation turned into fury. English papers, no doubt to bolster morale at home, featured the seizure and widespread destruction of the French fleet as if it had been a great British naval victory.

During those days there was real danger that outraged French politicians might commit themselves completely to an alliance with Berlin. In this precarious situation my personal inclinations were wholly in accord with the instructions I received from Washington, and I like to believe that American policy at that moment helped considerably to save the French Government from a disastrous move. I could say to French officials with complete truth that the American Government had no prior knowledge of the British naval attack, and deplored it. But I also was authorized to say that our interests and sympathies in the war were entirely on the side of Britain. Our relations with France would depend therefore upon whether any further concessions were made to the Nazi Government.

At that crucial moment German victories seemed so complete that millions of Europeans thought that Germany already had won the war, and many Americans agreed. Allied propaganda and our own wishful thinking had led us to believe that France and Britain were more than a match for Germany, so the Allied collapse found Americans as unprepared psychologically as we were militarily. Hitler's triumphs posed a fundamental question for Washington's top policy-makers: Should the United States remain passive in the wake of the Allied debacle, or should we oppose the peace overtures which Berlin was offering to the distracted peoples of western Europe? The Nazi conquests had shattered the balance of power in Europe and were compelling us to choose between a Nazi victory and American intervention.

This question was decided in Washington behind closed doors, and the secrecy which cloaked the discussions still obscures the events of that period. Only a few months earlier, Congress had passed the Neutrality Act, designed to prevent American participation in Europe's war, and that legislation was so effectively drafted that it blocked any military intervention regardless of the alteration which had since occurred in the European balance of power. Instructions to our embassy in Vichy were classified as top secret, not only to conceal Washington's plans from the Germans but also from the American public. There was no doubt that most Americans sympathized with England and France and hated and feared the Nazis, but there was a great deal of doubt about American willingness to risk war against Hitler. That year of 1940 was a presidential election year and Roosevelt, as an astute politician, could never forget that any move which the voters might consider too warlike would jeopardize his chances for re-election, already uncertain because he was breaking precedent by seeking a third term.

The secret directives which we in Vichy received from Washington expressed the opinion that France offered the most promising opportunities for anti-Nazi activities by Americans, and we were informed that our government intended to make vigorous attempts to prevent Europeans from concluding peace settlements with Hitler, since any peace settlement would consolidate the Nazi triumphs. It thus became the chief mission of our embassy staff to persuade French statesmen that Germany had not yet won the war, and that France would profit by refusing to make any concessions to Germany beyond what already had been made in the armistice agreement. Our Embassy was authorized to offer American support to French leaders by every means permissible under the Neutrality Act, so long as the French Government avoided making a peace settlement with Germany. The Allied collapse had been so complete that the Germans did not press for a final agreement. They expected London would surrender very soon, and meanwhile they were satisfied with the armistice which they had concluded with France.

In those first weeks at Vichy, I think most of us felt as if we had been knocked on the head and were slowly recovering our senses. History has rarely, if ever, moved with such dizzy speed as in that summer, and it seemed almost impossible to readjust our thoughts to a Europe dominated by one man, as in the Napoleonic era more than a century before. In this new Alice-in-Wonderland atmosphere, Vichy seemed an appropriate capital for that portion of France, one-third of the country, which the German armistice permitted Frenchmen still to govern. Offices were located in gambling casinos, music halls, and tourist hotels designed to lighten the hours of health-seekers. The Hotel du Parc, long popular with fashionable invalids, became the seat of government. All of us felt absurdly isolated in this inbred community, making our diplomatic rounds in this artificial, gaudy, improvised political center which nobody expected to serve this purpose for long.

Normally, Vichy had about thirty thousand permanent residents, and during its peak tourist season it could accommodate one hundred thousand. Now it was called upon to house in one way or another some 130,000 persons, including an excessive proportion who regarded themselves as V.I.P.s. It amazed me, as we moved into Vichy, to observe how smoothly, in the midst of national chaos, the protocol officer of the French Foreign Office, kindly M. Loze, arranged accommodations for the bedraggled members of the diplomatic corps straggling in from Bordeaux. I was impressed, as I had been in Paris after the government's departure, by the indestructibility of the French civil service, whose organization dates from Napoleon's reign. We in the American Embassy had sometimes been irritated by the arrogance of French functionaries, cigarette butt in mouth, but in this crisis they behaved superbly. These civil servants actually had administered France during the increasingly frequent periods when the politicians were indulging in their game of political musical chairs and now, while whole European nations, including France, were being bowled over like tenpins, French government employees stayed on their jobs as a matter of course. Some of these faithful officeholders in Vichy paid dearly for performing what they conceived to be their duty. They discovered, too late, that France was involved in a curious kind of civil war from which even the bureaucracy could not remain aloof.

Very few observers in Europe that summer could feel any confidence that Britain would be able to hold out against Germany, and Britain was the only remaining obstacle to German conquest of Europe—or so it seemed then. However, we in the American Embassy had scant leisure to indulge in theoretical worries about the future of Europe; our greatly reduced staff was working far into the night and was not standing on ceremony. I found myself performing some of the same clerical work I had done at the outset of my career, and so did other members of the fine staff which Ambassador Bullitt had assembled. Having met and survived the greatest crisis, the British naval attack, in our first days at Vichy, we began to breathe easier. Now all of us undertook to "sell" the American Government's line to French ministers of assorted beliefs. I personally concentrated upon Marshal Pétain who now had the new title of Chief of State, and his Vice Premier, Pierre Laval. These two men bore the responsibility for arranging the armistice. The old soldier and the suave lawyer-politician had almost nothing in common except their conviction that Germany had won the war and that Frenchmen must somehow adapt themselves to this fact.

In my first conversation with Pétain at Vichy, I expressed confidence in eventual Allied victory. The Marshal was then eighty-four years old and in his eyes I was only a young diplomat substituting for an ambassador, so he smiled at me indulgently. Then, in his cool, clear, rather formal French, he said that continuance of the war would have been insanity, and that France would have been completely destroyed, since neither France nor Britain should have gone into a war for which they were wholly unprepared. With some emotion he declared that France could not afford again to have a million of its sons killed. In later conversations he brought up the subject of De Gaulle who, he said, he had favored as a junior officer on his staff, adding bitterly, "He was a viper I clutched to my bosom!" The old Marshal seemed more irritated, in those early Vichy days, by memories of De Gaulle's temerity in questioning the Marshal's military competence than he was by De Gaulle's denunciation of the armistice. Each time that I talked with Pétain he expressed in some way his friendly feeling for the United States, implying that it was only his affection for our country that made him tolerate my rather unwelcome arguments.

Pierre Laval, who was destined to be executed as a traitor after a summary trial by a special French postwar commission, was by all odds the shrewdest, most forceful personality in Vichy, and I studied him earnestly in the several talks I had with him. We in the Embassy believed that he, more than any other man, would determine how far French-German collaboration would extend. Of course I had met Laval before in Paris, since he had been prominent in French politics during all of my decade in the capital, but he never had occasion to pay attention to me, as he did in Vichy. This ruthlessly ambitious politician possessed a plan for action from the very beginning in Vichy, as most other members of the government did not, and he cultivated me—as the ranking American representative—because the United States figured in his plan.

Vichy was an ideal setting for Laval because this was his native region. In nearby Chateldon, his hometown, Laval had a luxurious château which he had bought with some of the fortune he had made as a lawyer and politician. The château was the pride of the village, and one aspect of this many-sided self-made man was revealed when he invited me there for lunch. Explaining how he had taken pains to restore the château to its original form, Laval took me out on his private hill overlooking a beautiful valley, and told me I was seeing the place where a battle had been fought in the days when Jeanne d'Arc was saving France from the rapacious British. Then he led me into the great drawing room, one wall of which was covered with an enormous oil painting, showing British soldiers storming this very hill and being repulsed by French defenders. Laval described that French victory of four centuries ago as though it had happened yesterday. Obviously, he had staged for my benefit this little lesson in Anglo-French historical conflicts and then, it seemed to me, had let his emotions run away with him. I asked why he personally was so bitter about the British who, after all, had been allies of France throughout history as many times as they had been rivals. Talking very rapidly, he recounted a litany of incidents—financial, political, military—in which the British during his own career had thwarted France and him as Premier and Foreign Minister. During World War I, he declared, the British had let France bear the brunt of the bloodletting, so that France had lost 1,500,000 killed, from which loss the nation never had recovered. This time the British had tried the same trick again, he cried, but this time the British and not the French would pay for the war. Throughout his several conversations with me, there ran a curious thread of chauvinism, a fierce, earthy sort of patriotism.

I discovered early in my talks with Laval that he was astonishingly ignorant about Germany and the Germans. He expressed a naïve contempt for them which the circumstances hardly seemed to justify. I never saw any evidence that he really sympathized with the Nazis, despite his collaboration with them. What he did show was supreme confidence in his own ability to outsmart the Germans. The future, as he pictured it that summer of 1940, was perfectly clear. Within a few weeks, or months at the latest, the British would have to sue for peace. Meanwhile, the foolishly stubborn British were providing him, Laval, a crystal opportunity to negotiate for France that no. 2 role in the New Europe. If I had any influence at all upon Laval, it was to make him feel that perhaps he underestimated Nazi ruthlessness and the extent of Hitlerian ambitions.

But I certainly failed to impress Laval with my intimations that the United States might eventually intervene again in Europe. He replied, with a shrug and a smile, that the future of Europe would be settled long before Americans could even make up their minds what to do. Whatever may be said about Laval's political judgment on this point, he certainly was not unfriendly to the United States. Laval was devoted to his family and this devotion seemed to be fully reciprocated by his wife and his intelligent daughter, José. The latter and her husband, René de Chambrun, who enjoys American citizenship under the laws of the State of Maryland as a direct descendant of the Marquis de Lafayette, played an active part in Laval's political career. Immediately after Dunkirk, René de Chambrun traveled to Washington to make a personal report on the French disaster to President Roosevelt, later incorporating his thoughts and experiences in a book *I Saw France Fall; Will She Rise Again?* It seemed to me in Vichy that Laval relied considerably on De Chambrun's knowledge of the United States, hoping that some form of negotiations would involve the American Government in an eventual European settlement.

Meanwhile, on the other side of the earth, in the Far East, the Japanese began to take advantage of the weakness of France by starting tentative moves in French Indochina. These Japanese maneuvers naturally alarmed Washington, and I was instructed to make one "representation" after another to the French Government in Vichy about Japanese demands. The foreign minister, Paul Baudouin, had been general manager of the Bank of Indochina, and was married to an Indochinese lady. He understood fully the significance of events there, but he also understood that his government was in a position to do little if anything to check the Japanese. He referred me to the Premier, and I went to see Laval, who was not an Asian specialist but who was equally noncommittal about Indochina. Laval even suggested, with a sly smile, that the Japanese had not menaced Indochina until the British fleet had put the French fleet temporarily out of commission.

On one of these occasions while we were conversing, Laval's chef de cabinet, Fernand de Brinon (who also was executed after the war), interrupted to say that the German ambassador in Paris was on the telephone asking to speak with the Premier. I rose to leave, but Laval motioned me to an extension telephone near his desk, saying, "Listen to our conversation." I expected to hear the voice of Ambassador Otto Abetz, but instead it was his second in command, my acquaintance Achenbach. It developed that Laval had sent the German Embassy in Paris a list of about ten concessions he hoped the Germans would make to fortify his own position. His requests included general release of French prisoners of war, who then numbered some 1,850,000; evacuation of enough occupied territory to permit the French Government to return to Paris; and provision for feeding the French people better.

Speaking in French, Achenbach was very businesslike. He took up Laval's requests one by one, in order, reading the Premier's own words, and then replying either "No" or "Yes." Every major request was followed by "No." Only two minor concessions were granted. But after Achenbach hung up, Laval turned to me with a satisfied air and said, "I just wanted you to see how well things are going between us and the Germans." I thought at first that he must be speaking sarcastically, but he was quite in earnest. During the two and a half months I remained in Vichy, before I was recalled to Washington for my assignment to

Africa, I talked several other times with Laval about the Germans, but he did not show any reduction of self-confidence. Adroit lawyer that he was, he apparently had sold himself on his case and was determined to prosecute it to the limit—which he certainly did. The limit for him was ignominious death.

Into our improvised embassy during the first week in July came many members of the French Senate and Chamber of Deputies, politicians of all parties except the Communists, seeking encouragement about the immediate intentions of the United States. I felt a great deal of sympathy for the appalling predicament in which these French legislators found themselves. They were being convened to sit jointly as a Constituent Assembly for the purpose of abolishing the Third Republic, established in 1875, and replacing it with an authoritarian regime headed by Marshal Pétain as Chief of State. Pierre Laval was running this show. He produced a Constitutional Law, very brief and broad, which assigned to the Chief of State powers equivalent to those of an absolute monarch. The legislators were told that if they did not make this change promptly, the Germans probably would occupy the rest of France and could not be expected to evacuate Paris or release the prisoners of war. Moreover, if Britain fell, or sought a negotiated peace as many Europeans expected, then France would miss the opportunity to assure for herself a high place in Germany's "new order." That was an effective argument among men who were miserably aware of their own defeat and of the formidable task confronting them to restore some kind of order in chaotic France.

Some of the legislators with whom I talked were virtually in a state of shock. Their humiliation and despair were so deep that they suffered paralysis of will. Yet there also was courageous opposition and sharp debate concerning Laval's Constitutional Law, about which we were informed promptly even when the Assembly sessions were secret. Although open opposition was personally dangerous, as was soon proven by the arrest and trial of leading opponents, eighty senators and deputies voted against the Constitutional Law, and an even larger number abstained from voting at all. But 569 legislators, more than the required two-thirds of the 850, did approve the Constitutional Law as presented, and thereby formally legitimized the new regime. These men had been freely elected as representatives of the French people before the German defeat. But in July 1940, they no longer were acting in freedom. Hitler's war machine held France in an iron grip.

I remember one very human incident on the day, July 10, when the Constituent Assembly was taking its decisive vote. I was lunching with the former Minister of Aviation, Guy La Chambre, and his wife, and at a nearby table sat M. and Mme. Paul Reynaud, he swathed in bandages after his close call with death on the highway, but grimly determined to participate in the historic parliamentary session which would make Pétain the Chief of the French State. Everyone was somber and dispirited—except Mme. Reynaud, who came over to our table and recounted to Mme. La Chambre the pungent details of the highway accident which took the life of her husband's mistress. As she rose to rejoin M. Reynaud, she exclaimed with some emotion, "And now, *cherie,* for my revenge!"

Indicative of how precarious was the position of French politicians then, Guy La Chambre was one of those arrested soon afterward and put on trial for treason. He and his wife were among our embassy's close French friends, and after she visited him in prison she came to my office one day and threw a sealed envelope upon my desk, crying: "Open it and see what it contains!" When I did so, a mass of dead bedbugs poured out. "I caught those in my husband's cell," she told me. "That is how they are treating him!" In such cases, I was authorized to do nothing more than ask informal questions, but I was greatly pleased when Guy La Chambre was one of the ministers soon released.

During that summer in Vichy I saw very little of the two Frenchmen who later were to make me a controversial public figure for the first time in my life. These two were Admiral Jean Darlan, then Minister of Marine, and General Maxime Weygand, then Minister of National Defense. Our naval and military attachés undertook to keep in contact with these two officers, and I left that business to them. Thus I had met Darlan only casually once or twice and had no formal conferences with him until he confronted me in Algiers, more than two years later, with the most difficult decision I ever have been compelled to make.

Darlan was a political admiral who had struggled for decades to pry money out of French parliaments and had succeeded in making the French fleet more powerful than at any time in its history. His influence with naval officers was so great that he could have taken the fleet abroad if he had chosen to repudiate the armistice, as General de Gaulle did. But he believed that Britain was defeated and that France must negotiate with triumphant Germany. However, he did solemnly promise both his British allies and the American Government that he never would permit the fleet to come under German control. So when the British Navy attacked French warships at Mers el-Kebir, Darlan was more outraged than anybody else, and his resentment surpassed all reasonable bounds. As he saw it, the British not only had partially wrecked the fleet he had done so much to create, but also had flaunted his honor by doubting his pledges. At that moment he would have thrown in his lot with Hitler if he had not been even more anti-Nazi than he was anti-British. Our attachés used every persuasion on Darlan to prevent his anger from running away with him, and soon he agreed to renew his pledge to the American Government to keep out of German control what was left of the French fleet.

General Weygand, World War I hero revered almost as much as Marshal Pétain, had been recalled from retirement in 1939 at the age of seventy-two to command the French forces in the Levant, and then dramatically in May 1940, to become supreme commander of the French and British armies in the Battle of France, after it already was apparent the battle was lost. He recommended to the French Command in June 1940 that an armistice was mandatory, and later agreed to serve briefly as Minister of National Defense in the Pétain Government. But, unlike Pétain and Darlan, Weygand had no political ambitions, and soon he asked to be relieved of his cabinet post and to be sent to North Africa in command of French forces there. It was the General's shift to Africa which inspired President Roosevelt to entrust me with my African mission.

The State Department did not explain why it was recalling me to Washington in September 1940, and I hoped this was a good omen for the project which most interested me then: how to prevent starvation among the French people during the approaching winter. Richard F. Allen, European director of the American Red Cross, had been gathering information for us, and the report we sent to the Department in September painted a graphic picture. Into the one-third of France for which the Vichy Government was responsible, twenty million people had been crammed, six million of them refugees. The French fugitives from the north were mostly old people and women and children whose husbands and fathers were still prisoners of war. They had fled in frantic multitudes, mingling with victims from the Benelux countries who had brought little or nothing with them. They had scrambled into a region already thickly populated with earlier escapees—anti-Franco Spaniards, anti-Nazis and Jews from Germany, Austria, Poland and Czechoslovakia. France, even then, was the safest sanctuary for displaced persons. Most of these unfortunates had endured the anguish of separation from home and family and were living in congested, unsanitary quarters, facing a winter without fuel, warm clothing, proper food or jobs. Military operations had reduced the 1940 harvest to a third of normal and the Germans still held as prisoners hundreds of thousands of farmers. Railroads had stopped running for lack of fuel, as had truck and bus transportation.

One obstacle stood in the way of Americans rushing food and clothing to famished France: the British blockade. Churchill's government, believing a blockade of Europe to be Britain's only offensive weapon in 1940, was determined to enforce it relentlessly. This blockade had even cut off much of the normal large food shipments from France's overseas empire. While I expressed sympathy with Britain's objections to unrestricted importation of food and clothing to the continent dominated by Hitler, I earnestly recommended some relaxations in the blockade. I proposed that Allen head a control commission similar to the commission I had observed operating from Switzerland during World War I. There was no question of charity; the French Government had sent gold and other assets to the United States ample to pay for its urgent needs of food and fuel. Our Red Cross survey showed that a mere sixty thousand tons of automotive gasoline would start traffic moving again, and Allen had persuaded the German Armistice Commission to exert no claim on relief stocks purchased abroad.

My report pointed out that "abandonment of the French population by their ally Britain and their oldest friend the United States would compel the French to consider making new friends. If the winter is severe [it turned out to be the coldest in ninety years], and the situation desperate, they will turn to Germany or anywhere. . . . Whoever wins the war, the United States will be blamed if callous indifference to French needs persists." My report concluded: "I am convinced that relaxation of the present British blockade to permit minimum food imports has no bearing of any importance in the present military situation."

But when I arrived in Washington I had to work hard to arouse any interest in French relief. By that time the terrible Nazi air raids on London had begun and the Battle of Britain overshadowed every other foreign interest. And, of course, even the Battle of Britain had to take second place in Washington's interest in the Roosevelt-Willkie election campaign. I confess that I was not proud of a few of my countrymen in Washington in 1940. Many of our politicians were even more insistent upon a total blockade of Europe than was the beleaguered British Government. And in that presidential election year, although not one important public official advocated military participation in the war by the United States, many Americans were brutally critical of defeated France. Roosevelt's Secretary of the Interior, Harold Ickes, noted in his diary at that time: "It is ghastly to think of the suffering that is ahead of Europe. Literally millions will die of starvation. . . . But we ought not to send a pound of flour to any country that is controlled by Germany." It was a bad time for those of us who knew France and could not contemplate the starvation of our friends with such detachment. British statesmen, despite their own precarious situation, soon took measures on their own initiative to relax the food blockade.

That summer of 1940 created what eventually came to be known as our "Vichy policy." During the next two years our relations with the

French Government aroused as many controversies among Americans as any of our wartime tactics. Secretary Hull, in particular, was subjected by some American commentators to much unfair criticism and this made him very unhappy. So he decided, even before the war ended, to commission Professor Langer to prepare an independent account of American relations with the Vichy Government from June 1940, to the time when our troops landed in French North Africa in November 1942. Langer was given access to secret files in the Department of State and in the Pentagon, and he produced an admirable volume. Unfortunately, however, the Harvard professor did not have access to the White House papers essential to complete the story. President Roosevelt's deep personal interest in French Africa induced him to bypass both the State Department and our military establishment, as Secretary of War Henry L. Stimson has disclosed in his memoirs.

When Langer's book appeared in 1947 it bore the title *Our Vichy Gamble,* which helped perpetuate an impression that American policy involved a choice among alternatives. Our embassy was not conscious then of having any choice, which also was true of the Canadians, Russians, Chinese, and all other governments represented at Vichy. We found ourselves there in the summer of 1940 because our diplomats had automatically followed the French Government to Vichy just as they had followed it at first to Tours and then to Bordeaux. Nobody, including Churchill, questioned the legality of the French Government which finally settled in Vichy, and negotiations between this government and London were broken off only after the British naval attack provoked the Vichy administration into severing diplomatic relations. Although the British Ambassador decided not to go to Vichy, after the armistice at Bordeaux, the Canadian Minister, Pierre Dupuy, continued the trek as a matter of course. The Canadian Government, a member of the British Commonwealth at war against Germany, looked after its own and Great Britain's interests at Vichy right up to the landings in North Africa. Our relations with Vichy, with which I was intimately associated from beginning to end, never were a "gamble." At all times we had much to win and we never risked a substantial loss. It was not until 1943 that General de Gaulle presented a clear-cut alternative to the Vichy Government.

FIVE

ROOSEVELT SENDS ME TO AFRICA (1940–41)

For almost four years, beginning in September 1940, the French empire in Africa was the be-all and end-all of my existence. Those years provided me with more adventurous assignments than many diplomats achieve in a lifetime, but there were occasions when I would gladly have traded my adventures for a nice placid job in Sweden or Switzerland. The American invasion of Africa created grave controversies among all the governments concerned, and not infrequently I found myself caught in the middle of those controversies. Nowadays Africa is so much in the news that it is difficult to remember how utterly unknown that vast continent was only twenty years ago. Today every quarter of Africa—north, south, east and west—receives our serious attention; the United Nations struggles for months on end with African problems; swarms of reporters roam the continent to record the transformation of former European colonies into infant nations. But during my ten years in Paris before the outbreak of World War II, my colleagues in the American Embassy and I paid almost no attention to France's huge African empire, and our French friends seemed almost equally indifferent to their lands across the Mediterranean.

It never occurred to me to visit French Africa and I heard little discussion of international developments there until, soon after the defeat of France, Commander Hillenkoetter, naval attaché of the U. S. Embassy, returned to Vichy following a quick trip to Morocco and Algeria. Hillenkoetter was agreeably surprised and encouraged by what he observed during his brief excursion. Contrary to rumors which were being broadcast from London, he found that the Nazis had left French Africa almost completely to its own devices. He said only a few German consuls and Italian members of the Armistice Commission were in evidence, while Frenchmen were administering the territories practically the same as before the war. Furthermore, said our naval attaché, the military establishment was far stronger than he had expected, with about 125,000 combat-trained men on active service and about 200,000 more in reserve. Hillenkoetter added that these experienced army, navy and air force officers and men had not lost their traditional French fighting spirit. They had accepted the German armistice and had sworn allegiance to the Pétain Government, but they were confident they could protect and control their African empire despite the collapse of the mother country. "The atmosphere over there is not comparable to the confusion in Vichy," Hillenkoetter told us. "If France is going to fight again anywhere in this war, I believe North Africa will be the place." He impressed us all with his hopefulness, which was reflected in the reports our Vichy Embassy sent to Washington. However, these reports elicited no comment from the Department of State, and we did not know whether they were arousing any interest.

Then, suddenly, I received a cablegram ordering me to proceed to Washington at once. That was a chaotic period in Europe, transatlantic communications were erratic, and when I received this summons to return home, without any explanation why, I assumed that the Department wanted from me a firsthand account of conditions at Vichy. But when I called on Under Secretary of State Sumner Welles, he told me that our reports on French Africa had been brought to the attention of President Roosevelt, that he had read them carefully, and that I had been summoned at the President's request. Welles arranged for me to go to the White House almost immediately.

There is no official record, so far as I know, of that hour-long conversation which opened very informally. The first time I ever had met Roosevelt was at Hyde Park in 1920 when as a guest of James A. Farley, who later became Postmaster General, I stood with a group on the lawn and listened to Roosevelt deliver his front porch speech accepting the nomination for the vice presidency. That was before Roosevelt was stricken with polio, and I was impressed that day with his magnificent physical form. He was, as the Irish would say, a fine figure of a man. Now, twenty years later, when Welles presented me to the President, I remarked that I already had been introduced on the occasion of the Hyde Park speech. Roosevelt commented genially that I must have been in short pants then, and after a few other casual words the President disclosed why he had summoned me.

When the French-German armistice had been signed the preceding June, Hitler had agreed that about one-third of continental France and all of its African empire would be granted a semi-independent status and would not be occupied by German troops. This situation intrigued Roosevelt, who believed that North Africa was the most likely place where French troops might be brought back into the war against Nazi Germany. Spread out on his desk was a large map showing all of French North and West Africa, and the President told me that he had given much thought about how to help French officers who were operating in the relatively independent conditions prevailing in Africa. The President then said that he wanted me to return to Vichy and work unostentatiously to get permission to make a thorough inspection tour of French Africa and to report my findings to him. The French African policy of the United States Government thus became the President's personal policy. He initiated it, he kept it going, and he resisted pressures against it, until in the autumn of 1942 French North Africa became the first major battleground where Americans fought Germans.

One reason why the President hoped for anti-Nazi action in French Africa was because General Maxime Weygand had recently been appointed Delegate General there, a position newly created by the Vichy Government to give Weygand supreme authority in Africa. Roosevelt could not believe that this honorable old soldier would tolerate indefinitely French subservience to Germany, even though Weygand had conceded the defeat of France and had helped to negotiate the armistice. Weygand had been Chief of Staff to Marshal Foch in World War I, and Roosevelt was impressed with the fact that Foch then had been the Supreme Allied Commander. Weygand thus had worked with British and American as well as French troops and was accustomed to thinking in terms of coalitions.

It was obvious that the President had been briefed not only about conditions in French Africa but also about my previous work in the State Department. He knew I had served several years in Germany and a decade in France, so that I was familiar with the languages, politics, and personalities of both these countries. Roosevelt also knew I was a Roman Catholic, and he said frankly that was one of the reasons he had chosen me to investigate French Africa and to help maintain our relations with the French Government in Vichy. During the American election campaign in 1960, there was lively public discussion about whether our President might be politically influenced by his religion, but I cannot imagine any Roman Catholic President ever being as fascinated as was Roosevelt with the thought of the Church in world politics. Roosevelt had established informal diplomatic relations with the Vatican in 1939, for the first time in American history, and had appointed a prominent Protestant industrialist, Myron C. Taylor, as his envoy. The President seemed to have exaggerated ideas of the bond existing between Catholics because of their religion. In urging me to become as intimate as possible with General Weygand, who like many other Frenchmen is a Roman Catholic, Roosevelt said with a wink, "You might even go to church with Weygand!" That suggestion conjured a more amusing picture to me than it apparently did to the President.

From his lifelong interest in naval affairs, Roosevelt was particularly concerned about the fate of the French fleet, and he discussed with me various means by which it might be kept out of German control. The President was in the midst of his campaign for a precedent-breaking third term, and had no illusions about the widespread determination of the American people to keep out of the war in Europe. He remarked that naval rearmament was the only form of preparedness politically possible. "American mothers don't want their boys to be soldiers," he said, "so nothing really big can be done at present about expanding the Army. But the Navy is another matter; American mothers don't seem to mind their boys becoming sailors."

Roosevelt expressed much interest when I related a conversation I had had in Vichy with the Spanish ambassador there, Señor Don José Felix Lequerica, who later became ambassador to Washington and Spanish delegate to the United Nations in New York. After the German armies swept across France in June 1940, they found themselves poised with ten powerful divisions on the Spanish frontier. Many observers assumed they would immediately push on through Spain to capture Gibraltar, and perhaps spill over into North Africa which, nine miles away, is visible on a clear day. Nothing seemed to stand in the way of such an operation, for Gibraltar at that time was practically an empty shell. The Spanish chief of state, Generalissimo Francisco Franco, was indebted to Hitler for military support during the Spanish Civil War and was widely though inaccurately regarded as an outright ally of Hitler.

But when the French armistice went into effect on June 25, the German divisions gradually were pulled back from the Spanish frontier and from all of unoccupied France. Lequerica said that he had acted as an intermediary in the French-German armistice, and that Franco had dissuaded Hitler from moving through Spain to overrun Gibraltar, which I believe some members of the German General Staff were urging. Hitler had a blind spot concerning the Mediterranean. I reported to Roosevelt that Lequerica told me: "If the Germans had been aggressive, Spain would not have resisted them. We had nothing with which to resist ten German divisions, but we kept them out by diplomacy." My report of that conversation may have had some influence on Roosevelt's subsequent wartime policy toward Spain.

Although the President discussed every pertinent topic with me during our unhurried conversation, and even touched upon several incidental matters, he barely mentioned Charles de Gaulle. Only a few months had elapsed since the General had broadcast from London his historic denunciation of the French-German armistice, but

Roosevelt apparently had already decided that he need not consider him a major factor in French affairs. The President's only reference to him was to say that the ill-fated attempt to capture Dakar confirmed his poor opinion of De Gaulle's judgment.

As Roosevelt concluded his suggestions for my African assignment, he said casually, "If you learn anything in Africa of special interest, send it to me. Don't bother going through State Department channels." Later I asked Welles if the President really meant for me to communicate directly with the White House. "That is the way he often operates," Welles assured me. Thus I became one of President Roosevelt's "personal representatives," assigned to carry out secret missions under his orders during World War II. Roosevelt delighted in ignoring departmental procedures in this way, preferring to work informally through men chosen by him and responsible directly to him. This sometimes compelled me to bypass my superiors in the Department of State, contrary to twenty years of disciplined training. Embarrassing as that was, it was a situation which had to be accepted as one of the occupational hazards of Roosevelt's special assignments. And there always was the consolation that the President, though he might let one down in a public utterance, gave very stanch support in private.

Before leaving Washington on my exploratory expedition, I tried to find out what I could about Africa by reading the secret files of our government departments, but I unearthed very little useful information from official archives. Up to that moment in 1940, the American Government had not rated Africa high on its list of vital interests, and our military and naval attachés had given it only casual attention. Our country had not participated during the nineteenth and early twentieth centuries in Europe's rough and dangerous scramble for African colonies, and the United States had shown virtually no concern after the First World War in the redistribution of the African colonies previously held by Germany. My preliminary information, therefore, came mostly from documents assembled in France, Britain, Italy, and Germany, many of which had not been translated into English.

Late in November I returned to Vichy for the purpose of obtaining the permits necessary for my African tour. I had intended to remain in Vichy only a few days, but I was delayed there almost a month by a major crisis which developed within the Pétain Government. The associates of the old Marshal split among themselves on the issue whether or not to make further concessions to their German conquerors. The group led by Pierre Laval was gambling everything upon a German victory, so they became unabashed collaborators. But most of Pétain's other ministers disagreed with Laval, although it was difficult for them to see just how Britain singlehandedly could overcome German domination of the continent. However, as months went by after the French-German armistice, the anti-Laval faction began to suspect that maybe Britain would not be compelled to sue for peace, and that it would be expedient to cooperate with the Germans as little as possible. In any case, many of Pétain's associates detested Laval's personality as much as his policy. One of the most effective of these opponents of Laval was Marcel Peyrouton, Minister of the Interior, who helped to organize the *coup d'état* in December 1940 which temporarily overthrew Laval.

I first became acquainted with Peyrouton during that critical December in Vichy. I was interested in meeting him just then because I thought that, as a former Resident General of Tunisia, he could fill in some of the immense gaps in my knowledge of that French colony which I was about to visit. But when he invited me to dine alone with him one evening, he was less concerned with the problems of Tunisia than with the presence of Laval right there in Vichy. He related in confidence that he was planning to use the Brigade Mobile—the crack central police then under his control—in a maneuver to oust Laval from power. There was a rumor that the Germans had wind of this plot, would try to prevent it, and that there might be fighting in Vichy. As I listened to Peyrouton's recital of his conspiracy, it seemed to me that he was a courageous man trying to foil the Nazis and that he therefore was serving American as well as French purposes. Two years later, after our troop landings in Algeria, my knowledge of Peyrouton, based on this observation of him in Vichy in 1940, caused me to concur in his appointment as Governor General of Algeria, an appointment which promptly aroused worldwide controversy. Some imaginative but not well-informed Allied journalists depicted me as an American Machiavelli who had conspired with Peyrouton during those Vichy days and who had worked with him behind the scenes ever since. But such reports gave me and the State Department altogether too much credit for guile. The fact is that no Americans participated in French factional intrigues at Vichy. We played no concealed part in Laval's overthrow there in 1940, although we did emphasize in all our talks with Pétain's ministers, including Laval himself, that the American Government was convinced that its interests demanded the defeat of Nazi Germany. But that was merely repeating what Roosevelt was stating publicly time and again.

Five days after Laval's overthrow, permission was granted for me to tour French Africa. The man most helpful at this point was Charles Rochat, Secretary General of the Foreign Office, a career civil servant like myself. He not only obtained my permits, which had been held up by the Laval group, but he accomplished this so as not to arouse

German or Italian opposition, which was quite a trick. Charles Rochat did not figure again in my African adventures, but I should like here to give him credit for his services to the Allied cause. He was one of many French patriots who chose to remain in France through the war rather than seek refuge abroad. They believed it their duty to stay at their posts in France, even though this involved contact with the Germans. But sentiment ran against such men after the liberation. Charles Rochat, who declined opportunities to live abroad during the dangerous years, was compelled to go into exile after hostilities ended, until wartime animosities faded.

A few hours after leaving Vichy on December 18, my Air France seaplane touched down in the harbor of Algiers, which later became familiar to hundreds of thousands of Americans in uniform. The State Department had estimated that my exploratory trip would require three months but I completed it in three weeks. I had not realized that the President wanted me to go slowly so I could make more detailed observations of possible military significance. The French air line did an amazingly good job with the few outmoded trimotor Dewoitine transport planes it still possessed, enabling me to execute this itinerary:

December 18—Arrived at Algiers.
19—Departed for Dakar in West Africa, two days en route. (No flying at night.)
20—Arrived at Dakar. Remained for several days for talks with Frenchmen who were governing the Africa empire.
25—Arrived at Gao in French Sudan.
26—Returned to Algiers.
27—Arrived at Tunis for consultation with Resident General of Tunisia.
29—Returned to Algiers, en route to Morocco.
30–31—Casablanca, Rabat, Tangiers, Spanish Morocco.
January 1—Returned to Algiers, pausing en route at Mers el-Kebir.
5—Departed for Lisbon.

It would have been impossible, of course, to fulfill this schedule if my appointments with French administrators had not been carefully arranged in advance, and if these military and civilian officials had not agreed before my arrival to trust the United States Government implicitly and to give me a great deal of confidential information without delay. Many of these details had been attended to by an old friend of mine, Felix Cole, the American consul general at Algiers, a specialist in Russian and eastern European matters and now well informed on Algerian affairs. The State Department had notified Cole that I was coming on behalf of President Roosevelt, and he made preliminary approaches to Delegate General Weygand in such a tactful manner that my mission got off to an excellent start. François de Rose, a young French diplomat on Weygand's staff, made the arrangements possible. Without French cooperation throughout the following two years, it would have been utterly unrealistic for any foreign representative to function successfully in that abnormal situation, under the watchful eyes of the Axis armistice commission.

As has been mentioned in a previous chapter, General Weygand, then seventy-two years old and weighed down with the responsibilities and honors of his five stars, had been pulled out of well-earned retirement when the French and British were on the verge of total defeat. After the armistice, he had reluctantly agreed to serve temporarily as Minister of National Defense while Marshal Pétain's government was being set up in Vichy, but he soon persuaded the Marshal to create a new post for him as Delegate General of French Africa, which enabled him to get away from Vichy's political intrigues. Weygand's new appointment was announced on September 9 and immediately aroused the interest of Roosevelt. As the President explained to me when I saw him in Washington, he wanted to know the extent of Weygand's real authority in Africa, what did the old soldier have in mind for the future, and what could the United States do to encourage him?

When I arrived in Algiers, Weygand was in Dakar on an inspection trip, and I decided to begin my African tour by going first to Dakar to pay my respects to the General. My talks with him there initiated the French-American economic agreement which became known as the Murphy-Weygand Accord. This was based on the assumption that French Africa could retain its relatively independent status if it received moderate economic support from the United States. Weygand and his associates admitted that their position was very precarious, because they feared that the Germans would attempt to occupy these possessions in the spring of 1941, but the French forces in Africa were determined to resist such an attack and they believed they could do so successfully. The General had more than one hundred thousand trained soldiers, airmen, and sailors under his command, with a potential reserve of two hundred thousand more, but they could not even plan an offensive for lack of equipment. Weygand had infused new life and hope into the military group, reorganized it, made new plans, and carefully hoarded the meager supplies of ammunition and equipment. Many French officers were confident that they could defend at least some of the area indefinitely if the United States would supply them with the necessary equipment, petroleum, and other supplies, plus enough consumer goods to satisfy the restive native populations. These of course vastly outnumbered the European residents.

Weygand and his chief subordinates differed greatly in experience and in temperament. I had extended talks with all the highest officials, sometimes in Weygand's presence, sometimes alone. Of the top men in the French administration, two were five-star generals, several were admirals, and others were high-ranking civilian governors and administrators. Many of these administrators encouraged me to talk separately with their own subordinates in Algeria, Morocco, West Africa and Tunisia. Little information was withheld from me. For example, there was much interest in what had happened to the important shipments of gold which had been sent to Africa from the Bank of France just before the Germans entered Paris. I had worked in Paris on this gold transfer with Jacques Rueff, Vice Governor of the bank, and a cruiser had been provided by the United States to ship part of the gold from Bordeaux to Dakar. I was told exactly where it was: in a fortress at Kayes in the French Sudan, almost four hundred miles east of Dakar. There were about fifteen hundred tons of French gold, two hundred tons of Belgian gold and fifty-four tons of Polish gold. I was told frankly that, at German insistence, some of the Belgian and Polish gold was being flown back to Paris, as the armistice terms apparently stipulated. I greatly admired the skill with which Maurice Couve de Murville and Paul Leroy Beaulieu conducted for Vichy the negotiations with the Germans at Wiesbaden on French-German financial questions. There naturally was some doubt about the eventual fate of the French gold, but we were given the same assurances about this as we were about the French fleet—that the Germans never would get control of it. And they never did.

General Weygand and his associates were straightforward, giving me not only the material facts of their situation, but also confiding their sentiments and intentions. It was not their fault that misunderstandings developed later. My talks with these Frenchmen convinced me that there was no disagreement among them on basic policies. All of them noted with approval my emphatic assertions that the American Government intended to support the British by all means "short of war," and that we therefore supported in principle the British blockade, which then was one of London's few effective weapons. But Weygand himself intimated that it was high time for the United States to produce its own independent and definite American policy, since we were not at war and Britain was. He continually said he hoped and was ready to believe that Hitler would be defeated, but he asked: Where are the divisions coming from? Will the United States provide them? In 1940, nobody could say.

The old French soldier, accustomed to taking the long view, pointed out that the British Empire could never be the same again, regardless of the outcome of the war, and that the world power it had held would pass to the United States. As evidence of Britain's declining power, he cited our trade of old destroyers for British air and naval bases in the Western Hemisphere. I was somewhat disconcerted when the General congratulated Washington for driving such a sharp bargain, declaring that in Britain's more glorious days, she never would have given so much for so little. I had not thought of this transaction in that light.

Although the ostensible reason for beginning my African inspection at Dakar was to pay my respects to Weygand, who was there at that moment, there was another important reason for my visiting Dakar immediately. Dakar was the largest French naval base on the west coast of Africa, and it was feared that the Germans would try to establish themselves and a submarine base there. Several times it had been erroneously reported that they already had done so. If they were to capture that base, German submarines would menace American and Allied shipping. The American Government had closed our consulate at Dakar before the war in order to save money, but Roosevelt had instructed the State Department to reopen it, and an American consul, Thomas Wasson, later killed in Jerusalem by a stray bullet, arrived there on September 15, 1940, just one week before the Battle of Dakar occurred. Thus the President and the State Department received an excellent eyewitness account from our own representative.

To the surprise of the outside world, the attack on Dakar was made not by Germans but by French and British forces led by Charles de Gaulle. The leader who had denounced the armistice had not yet been able to inspire more than a small scattering of Frenchmen, in and out of France, to join him, but De Gaulle thought he detected in the heart of Africa an opportunity to demonstrate that many Frenchmen wanted to follow his leadership. The Negro Premier of the Chad, an obscure French colony in Equatorial Africa, announced allegiance to De Gaulle, thus providing encouragement at a moment when the General badly needed it. Unfortunately, however, this unexpected recruit caused De Gaulle to overestimate his personal following in other sections of the African empire. The exiled leader in his patriotic fervor conceived the idea that with the help of the British Navy and a handful of French followers, he could rally all the French possessions below the Sahara Desert including the naval base at Dakar. He prevailed on Prime Minister Churchill to support a British-De Gaulle expeditionary force which was organized in the hope that it would be able to occupy Dakar by a combination of persuasion and force. The idea was that after a face-saving show of defending the port, the Frenchmen at Dakar would gladly join the De Gaulle movement.

The result was a bitter disappointment. After a few days of confused fighting, the expedition withdrew ignominiously, and the manner of the defeat was more serious than the defeat itself. From the reports which Roosevelt received from our consul inside the naval base, and from Churchill who reported what happened outside, Roosevelt—who never had liked the Dakar operation—concluded that De Gaulle had started what amounted to a French civil war, putting his own ambitions above French and Allied interests. Roosevelt never lost the distrust of De Gaulle's judgment and discretion which he formed then, and this distrust was a major factor in French-American relations right up to the President's death in 1945. As for security, he regarded the De Gaulle headquarters in London as a leaky sieve, not to be trusted with secret military information.

When I arrived at Dakar three months after the battle, I was astonished at the attitude of Pierre Boisson, High Commissioner at Dakar, who told me that he was pro-British despite the recent British battering of the French naval base. Boisson who had lost a leg while fighting against the Germans in World War I, said he hoped and prayed for British victory now, and he thought that the British would realize before long that Frenchmen in Africa wanted them to win and could be of great assistance to them. He went on to relate that there was a moment after the attacks on Dakar and Mers el-Kebir—to say nothing of the Dunkirk disaster—when French officers, "goaded to desperation by the distress and humiliation of it all," were on the point of war against the British. Boisson added that he was sure the American Government, ". . . on reflection, will see in the self-control exercised by the French a basic sympathy with the British cause."

Boisson blamed only De Gaulle for what had happened at Dakar, and he described indignantly how De Gaulle, completely misjudging the situation, had sent a staff officer, De Bois Lambert, ashore to induce Boisson's junior officers to revolt. He said this clumsy and amateur effort at subversion between Frenchmen was contemptible, and he regretted that the De Gaulle emissary had not been shot. Boisson never forgave De Gaulle for his attack on Frenchmen and his reckless attempt to seize the naval base by force and guile. Boisson was convinced that if De Gaulle had succeeded, the German High Command would have been obliged to occupy ports in French North Africa and perhaps Gibraltar. I never really understood why they did not. But in December 1940, when I stood on the dock in the harbor of Dakar, gazing past a huge mountain of peanuts (Senegal was a prime source of edible oil for Europe) at the beautiful French warship *Richelieu*, badly damaged by the British, I could better understand Boisson's partiotic sense of outrage. De Gaulle, for his part, cherished everlasting enmity against Boisson for so easily repulsing his attack on Dakar. Boisson became the daily target of a vitriolic barrage of personal invective leveled at him by the De Gaulle radio out of Brazzaville. De Gaulle eventually revenged himself and Boisson paid dearly for defying him.

After the Battle of Dakar, Churchill publicly assumed personal responsibility for the fiasco and reasserted his support of the De Gaulle movement, but I learned during my travels that the British Prime Minister apparently lost confidence in De Gaulle after Dakar and tried to inveigle Weygand to replace him as a leader of the French resistance forces. When I arrived at Algiers in December, Weygand's political adviser, Count de Rose, lost no time in informing me that the General had just received a personal letter from Churchill, urging him to break away from the Vichy Government and to put himself at the head of a dissident government in Africa, with guarantees of British support. Churchill declared that the French fleet and the entire African empire would follow Weygand in such a move, which then would bring about the early collapse of Italy, shatter the Axis, and demoralize Germany. Count de Rose went on to tell me that Weygand forwarded the Prime Minister's extraordinary message to Pétain at Vichy, who replied that he also had recently received a letter from Churchill, but that Pétain's letter contained no intimation of the proposal made to Weygand. Weygand told De Rose that he considered such furtive maneuvers behind Pétain's back as a reflection on both Churchill's intelligence and honor, and he added: "This confirms my distrust of Churchill's judgment. During the Battle of France, he flew over from London and told us he was waiting for a miracle to save the situation. I am a good Catholic, but in military matters I prefer not to depend upon miracles."

The Frenchmen with whom I conferred in Africa believed that Churchill and De Gaulle had been inexcusably rash in their attempt to capture Daker. Boisson suggested that I talk separately with his staff section chiefs, and everyone showed sympathy with the British cause, coupled with admiration for British courage, but much as these men wished to see Britain win the war, they felt that French Africa was their sole remaining trump and that it must be played only on a well-timed, carefully planned basis. A premature move could easily lead to German blockade of the western Mediterranean. They were recovering from the fury and grief engendered by the attack on their naval base, but they were making every preparation to defend Dakar against any future assault, although they said they believed the British would not try again. Nevertheless, their slogan for the moment was resistance to aggression by any foreign power, including Britain.

The chief anxiety at Weygand's headquarters, while I was there, were repeated radio announcements from London that Weygand was planning independent action in Africa. Both the British and American press were depicting the old Frenchman as a David preparing to slay the German Goliath. The General and his staff were determined that their territory should not be made a battleground prematurely, and they found it difficult to believe that this was not a deliberate attempt to sabotage their efforts to strengthen North African defenses. Some even speculated that this might be a subtle De Gaulle scheme to undermine Weygand's position and force his departure under Axis pressure, which later did occur. As Weygand's associates explained to me, the foundations must be carefully laid, the native population groomed, and an intelligent program arranged before they could fight. First of all, they felt an economic basis must be established which would make the Arabs and Berbers more disposed than they then were to engage in hostilities. Weygand said to me: "There are so many ways in which we could help the British if, for once, they could learn something of subtlety and did not feel that everything must be shouted from the rooftops." I reported to the State Department: "German suspicion is at a high peak, and this ill-advised publicity is a terrible headache for Weygand. He never knows at what moment the Germans may force him out."

When I arrived in Casablanca early in January, I was dismayed an hour after arrival to receive a telephone call from a German career diplomat, Theodore Auer, whom I had known before the war when he was counselor of the German Embassy in Paris. He wanted to see me urgently, but I did not reciprocate this desire. I had rather liked Auer in Paris, but I did not want him poking into my affairs. However, the French authorities said it might be useful to meet Auer because, since his recent appointment as consul general in Casablanca, it was rumored that he was forerunner of a German group which was to replace the Italians who had been allowed to staff the Armistice Commission in Morocco, to see that the armistice terms were being observed. When we did get together for a drink at my hotel, I regretted that I had not seen Auer sooner and oftener because he proved as eager to talk as General von Studnitz had been during his first day in Paris.

Auer came to the point at once: What was I doing in Africa? I explained fulsomely that our consular establishments had not been inspected for a long time and that, as he knew, we were a nation of businessmen. We thought that French Africa might offer openings under present circumstances for the sale of American goods. He listened to this rigamarole patiently, but I could see that he did not believe a word of it. When I finished, I asked him in turn what he was doing in Casablanca. He said: "Murphy, I will be more honest with you than you were with me. I came here for one purpose only, to convince that prize ass in Berlin, our Fuehrer, of the importance of the Mediterranean and of Morocco in particular. Herr Hitler does not seem aware that this area exists. He always looks in every direction except south." He then told me that he had persuaded the Nazi Foreign Office to replace the Italians on the Armistice Commission and soon would have enough Germans here to do that job properly. But he said he could not seem to stir up much real interest in Berlin. Notwithstanding Auer's geniality and the highballs, my spirits sank. The last thing we wanted was active Berlin interest in the western Mediterranean.

Auer's remarks were of importance to me because Weygand and his associates were anticipating a German attack in the spring of 1941, and all of their proposals for American cooperation were based on that assumption. Since the Germans were such faithful record-keepers all through the war, the history of their conduct of the war is an open book now. Their records disclose that some of Hitler's leading generals, notably Goering and Guderian, supported men like Auer who tried, but failed, to persuade Hitler to push on through Spain into Gibraltar and thence across the nine-mile channel into Africa immediately after the collapse of France, while Frenchmen still were in a state of shock. But Hitler—unlike Roosevelt, Churchill, De Gaulle and Weygand—was not Africa-minded. And already, in December 1940, while I was talking with Auer, Hitler had given orders to prepare for an attack on Russia the following spring. That Russian project naturally took precedence over all lesser plans, including those for the Mediterranean. But neither Auer nor I had been informed of Hitler's grand scheme for an invasion of Russia, and Auer blithely went ahead building up his German staff in Morocco, which had more than a hundred members when the Allied troops landed two years later. Auer himself barely escaped a trap we had set to capture him, and it might have fared better for him if he had not. He and his group failed to give Berlin any warning of the Allied troop landings in November 1942, and such gross incompetence was not lightly forgiven by the Auswaertiges Amt. He was cashiered by Ribbentrop and captured by the Russians in Berlin. I respected him as an intelligent diplomat.

All my life I had heard so much about the British Intelligence Service that I kept an eye out during this tour for British agents who might help me. But if there were any such agents, they kept themselves well concealed. I did encounter in Rabat, French headquarters for Morocco, one Frenchman who might be described as a British agent, but there was nothing secret about his activities. He was Emmanuel Monick,

Secretary General to the Resident General, and he was an undisguised Anglophile who was negotiating with the British Board of Economic Warfare in an endeavor to get shipments into Morocco through the British blockade. He was particularly eager to buy such things as sugar, tea, and cotton textiles for the dissatisfied Arabs and Berbers. But when I met him, he was beginning to despair of persuading his British friends to adopt a consistent African policy. Some British officials, he said, apparently aimed at the decomposition of French Africa, thus playing directly into Axis hands, while others wanted to help build up a French Africa which, in a decisive moment, might be of vital importance in the outcome of the European war. The British never did resolve this conflict between the objectives of different governmental agencies, and our official agencies in Washington tried to outdo the British in fighting against each other. In this sense these bureaucratic quarrels created more troubles for me later than the Germans did.

On Christmas Day, when I was homesick for my family in Washington, I found myself in Gao, deep in the Sudan, where I had flown to get a glimpse of conditions in French West Africa. The Resident General, in lieu of a Christmas dinner, invited me to his annual feast for about twenty sheiks, Negro Moslems all at least six feet tall. I sat next to one giant, decked out in a brilliant green silk jelaba, who spoke reasonably good French, and I told him I had been reading a French translation of the Koran on my plane trips to get some idea of Islam and Moslem thought. To make conversation, I said jestingly that we Americans were impressed by Mohammed's encouragement of multiple wives, because we found that even one wife could present many problems. The chief could not believe that I would joke about such a serious subject. He explained solemnly that he never had the slightest difficulty with his four wives, since he kept them in separate villages about fifty kilometers apart. It seemed to me that the French administrators here, and everywhere else I traveled, retained surprisingly firm control of their African colonies, despite defeat and chaos in France. Without such control, the Allied landings would have been impossible.

Those three weeks in French Africa made a tremendous impression upon me. I was fascinated by the immensity of the French possessions, their vast potentialities in war or peace, and their complicated problems apparently so well handled by the French military and bureaucracies. Above all, I was delighted to meet Frenchmen who were strongly anti-Nazi, who were much more pro-British than I had anticipated, and who acted as if they really would fight for their independence in their African empire. It seemed to me that the least we Americans could do was to give these Frenchmen the modest economic support they required. If the United States later entered the war, the French military establishment in Africa and the area's strategic importance could be of immense value. General Weygand had agreed to accept American supervision of everything we might supply, to make sure that nothing fell into German hands.

On January 17, 1941, less than a month from the day I departed from Vichy, I cabled from Lisbon, Portugal, the official report of my preliminary survey of French Africa. I had brought with me from Algiers my first draft of the economic agreement which Weygand had approved, and I wholeheartedly recommended its acceptance. I was more enthusiastic about this project than any other with which I had been associated since the beginning of the war. My original report, now in the files of the State Department, bears this notation: "I have read this with great interest," signed FDR. Later I was told that President Roosevelt used this survey as the basis for his African policy.

SIX

STRUGGLE TO SAVE FRENCH AFRICA

During the twenty months prior to September 4, 1942—when President Roosevelt personally informed me of his decision to invade the Dark Continent—the African agreement which I negotiated with General Weygand passed through a bewildering variety of hopes and frustrations. The project was tentatively accepted; then it encountered objections; it was approved; it was thwarted; it was on; it was off—until I felt like a jack-in-the-box popping up and down in Africa at the whim of every pencil-pusher in Washington. As sometimes happens in the Foreign Service, these experiences produced in our little group in French Africa an acute case of "localitis," meaning that the local situation seemed to us the most important in the world, and we could not understand why so few outsiders failed to recognize its earth-shaking importance.

Although we knew in a general way about the tremendous events which were occurring all over the globe during those twenty months, we were isolated in Africa so much of the time that we could not adequately appreciate how the policy-makers in Washington were obliged to dovetail the African project with dramatic developments elsewhere. The Battle of Britain was fought to a finish in the skies over England. On Sunday, June 22, 1941, German armored divisions fatefully lumbered into Russia. On another Sunday six months later, Japanese bombers propelled Americans into global warfare. All of these events affected Africa, in ways not always apparent at our distance, so that Washington's behavior toward us was not as capricious as it sometimes seemed.

The essence of the Murphy-Weygand Accord was that French officials should be permitted to use French funds, then frozen in banks in the United States, to buy a limited amount of non-strategic American goods acutely needed in French North Africa; and be permitted to ship such cargo through the British naval blockade which was enforced after the rupture of Anglo-French diplomatic relations in July 1940.

The Weygand group beseeched me to try to obtain supplies immediately because they believed the Germans were planning to occupy French North Africa early in the summer of 1941, and consumer goods were urgently required as an incentive to Arab cooperation in defense of this area. But the American Government, itself not yet at war, lacked a wartime sense of urgency, and the State Department noncommittally instructed me to wait in Lisbon for a decision about French Africa. Three weeks later I received a coded cablegram signed Hull. This directive from the Secretary of State read: "You are instructed to return for a final visit to North Africa before proceeding to Vichy to report, previous to your return to the United States. You may state to Weygand that the United States Government is prepared in principle to proceed with the matter of extending economic cooperation to the North African territories."

During the following four years, when North Africa served as my headquarters and I flew in and out again and again, I often had occasion to remember wryly those instructions "to return for a *final* visit." But on that February day in 1941 when I received this message in Lisbon, I thought only that our African project was starting off now with American approval, and I hastened to carry the glad tidings to Weygand. But when I arrived in Algiers, my friends there greeted me with disquieting news: radio broadcasts from London and New York were reporting that hundreds of Germans were swarming into Morocco, many of them disguised as tourists, and the presumption was that they were about to take over the French administration.

This was the first of an elaborate series of similar false reports which disturbed and delayed our African supply plans during the next five months. On February 19 the British Ambassador in Washington, Lord Halifax, called upon Under Secretary of State Sumner Welles to urge that negotiations with Weygand be suspended indefinitely. The Ambassador accepted as a fact a wildly incorrect report from the British Consul General in Tangier that a German delegation, including specialists in preparing airfields and submarine bases, had taken over the French Air Force in Morocco.

On March 14, even my experienced friend Felix Cole, American Consul General in Algiers, became the victim of rumormongers, and cabled to Washington: "All reports here indicate massive German infiltration Morocco, maximum six thousand, with eight hundred officers and men at Casablanca." He followed this up on March 21 with reports that the Germans had been given submarine bases in Casablanca and Tangier, plus three major air bases. Then, in mid-May, the British Embassy in Lisbon reported "from a reliable source" that some sixty thousand German troops were massed in Spain, poised for an imminent attack on Gibraltar and Morocco.

These false rumors and reports were received with peculiar eagerness by officials of both the American and British Boards of Economic Warfare. The group in Washington seemed ready to believe almost any story about Axis influence and control in French Africa. At the same time they viewed my reports, and reports from American consular officers who were on the spot, with the gravest suspicion. At times they seemed to believe we were Nazi agents and that their own knowledge, far removed from the scene, was somehow more dependable. Each time "authentic information" of German infiltration, German attacks, and German conquests reached Washington, it became my immediate business to drop everything else and investigate these rumors. Thus, although I had flown from Lisbon for the purpose of continuing negotiations with Weygand at Algiers, I had to postpone calling on the General while I went to Morocco to hunt for the Germans allegedly disguised as tourists.

Arriving at Rabat, French headquarters in Morocco, I was received immediately by the Resident General, five-starred Auguste Nogues, who told me that one lone German had appeared in Morocco with a tourist visa, which had been issued at Paris. Nogues had promptly shipped the visitor back and had ordered that similar visas should be rejected. The General assured me that the only newly arrived Germans in the region were fifty-three additions to the Armistice Commission, and that most of these were clerks and noncommissioned soldiers. To show how good French Intelligence was, Nogues presented me with a complete list of these recent German arrivals, with remarkably detailed descriptions of the background, habits, and characteristics of each individual. Nogues said that the German Consul General in Casablanca, Theodore Auer, had not attempted any real interference with French control of Morocco, and this was confirmed by American Consul General Gould in Casablanca.

Every time a new German rumor blew through the Mediterranean, investigation disclosed it to be as exaggerated as the tourist tale. Regarding the British report from Tangier, a trustworthy informant in the French Foreign Office told us that the Germans had not even requested French African bases and certainly had not been granted any. When I flew to Madrid in May to check the report that sixty thousand German soldiers were massed in Spain, the British Ambassador there, Sir Samuel Hoare, explained that his compatriots in Lisbon had fallen for baseless rumors and that there were practically no German troops in Spain, which proved correct. These and similar fabrications which chewed up my time and plagued my work all through the first half of 1941, ceased abruptly on June 22 when a startled world learned that the Nazis were invading, not Morocco, but Soviet Russia.

Nazi agents had planted those cover stories about German plots and German troops to distract attention from Germany's approaching attack on Russia, and their psychological warriors certainly did a good job in getting Washington agitated about Axis penetration of North Africa.

As I listened on the radio, that pleasant Sunday morning in Algiers, to Hitler's strident voice announcing from Berlin the attack on the Soviet Union, there came to me a vivid recollection of that same voice which Paul Drey and I had heard twenty years before at so many political rallies in Munich. "Never again," Hitler had shouted, "will Germany fight a war on two fronts!"

When General Weygand was informed that the Nazis were on their way to Moscow, he telephoned me urgently to come to his residence. I found him minus his usual composure and in a state of exhilaration. He said without further ado: "When we discussed the war and you expressed your belief that Britain would win in the end, I asked you where the divisions would come from. Now I know where they will come from—Russia. Germany has lost the war!" But Weygand's opinion was not shared by other French military men in North Africa, especially some high-ranking naval officers. One admiral offered me a bet which I accepted that Germany would defeat the Soviet Union in two months. This reflected a widely held French belief that since Germany had been able to defeat France in thirty days of combat, the Nazis certainly could quickly crush a backward country like Russia.

Perhaps Weygand's attitude, which of course I reported to Washington immediately, influenced a move made a month later by Roosevelt. On July 17 I received in cipher a top secret personal message from the President to be transmitted orally to the French General. Roosevelt tentatively suggested military assistance for French Africa at some future date, from a pool of fighter planes then being flown to British colonies in west Africa. I was instructed not to make written notes of any kind in conveying this message. This was almost five months before Pearl Harbor, and the President naturally did not want any specific warlike propositions made public. When I carried this oral message to Weygand, he expressed keen interest and requested me to repeat it so he could fix it correctly in his mind. Then he asked if this meant the United States would become a belligerent. I replied that, in a sense, we already were that. Weygand reflected for a moment and then said he had hoped the United States might remain aloof in order to exercise its enormous power as arbiter. But now he could see that matters were developing in a different direction. My report to Roosevelt concluded: "That fact did not appear to distress him."

But while the President was hinting at American fighter planes for

Weygand and his associates, the French in Africa actually were receiving no military aid at all and only a few driblets of economic aid. The Murphy-Weygand Accord had been approved in principle early in February and had been formally ratified at Vichy on March 10, yet in late June the agreement still was dormant. One cause for delays and postponements was the false threats of a German invasion of Morocco, but the trouble which emanated from Berlin was insignificant compared to the trouble our plan encountered in London.

To begin with, Churchill had no confidence in the French leaders who had accepted an armistice with Germany. In a wartime speech to the Canadian Parliament, Churchill said: "It was their duty [in 1940] to go to North Africa, where they would have been at the head of the French Empire. In Africa, with our aid, they would have had overwhelming sea power. They would have had the recognition of the United States, and the use of all the gold they had lodged beyond the seas. . . . But their generals misled them."

Most British officials shared the Prime Minister's distrust of French generals, and the British Board of Economic Warfare was particularly opposed to sending any American consumer goods to North Africa. The British felt that Africa was the place where the French Government should still be defying the Nazis, as Churchill and his people were doing in the British Isles. But this comparison never made sense to me. The idea that the demoralized French in 1940 could make any sort of substantial stand in Africa was surely an illusion. Had the French Government tried to establish itself there, the Germans unquestionably would have moved through Spain and seized Gibraltar. The Nazis then could have sealed off the Mediterranean at its western end, thus making the British position extremely precarious. The failure of the Germans to do so when they had the power in June 1940 will go down in military history as one of the great errors of the war.

In addition to the attitude of their Prime Minister, there were two more reasons why influential Britons objected to cooperating in 1941 with the administration in North Africa. One group in Churchill's cabinet contended that the French regime in Africa was pro-German, else the Nazis surely would not allow these Frenchmen to maintain their virtually independent administration. North Africa was in the enemy camp, this group argued, and it should be sabotaged rather than aided. Another group in London conceded that the French in Africa might be anti-Nazi, but declared that if such were the case it was the duty of these allies to stage an immediate offensive against the Germans. The British Isles were in desperate danger and British troops fighting in the Libyan Desert urgently needed a diversion in their area. If the French forces in Africa were ever to be useful in this war, the time for them to fight was now, not in the sweet by and by.

I gave very serious consideration to these British objections before I recommended to Washington that the United States should cooperate with the French leaders in Africa. While I sympathized with the British views, I was convinced that Weygand's plan would be best for Britain as well as for the United States and France. From what I had seen and heard in Africa, I was persuaded that the great strategic area of the western Mediterranean might easily be lost if the Allies opened a premature offensive. Weygand's military experts had demonstrated to my satisfaction that the British could no more provide adequate military support for the French African empire in 1941 than they had been able to provide for the French homeland in 1940. It was essential that the French military establishment be reinforced with some supplies, and that the loyalty of the Arab population be strengthened with some desperately needed civilian goods, before active warfare would be a good risk.

The three weeks I spent marking time in Lisbon at the beginning of 1941, waiting for a decision on my preliminary report, was consumed by Washington-London conversations concerning these British objections. And the cablegram which Secretary of State Hull dispatched, instructing me to go to North Africa for a final visit, added that the British had agreed to permit American supplies to be shipped through the British blockade only under certain conditions. The first of these conditions was that American observers must inspect French African ports and railways to make sure that none of the imports from the United States went to the Germans. On this point all of us—French, American and British—were in complete agreement. But the British also stipulated that British observers should work alongside our American observers in Morocco. This secondary condition was wholly unrealistic. It took no account of the fundamental fact that Britain was formally at war against Germany while the United States then was not. I felt sure that neither Weygand's group nor the Germans would tolerate this condition. The French assumed that an agreement could be negotiated without overt German opposition only because the United States was technically neutral. So this British inspection stipulation was omitted from the Murphy-Weygand Accord.

After signing this Accord, I departed for Washington where I learned immediately upon my arrival that the British Ambassador had already called upon the State Department to repeat that His Majesty's Government could not approve an agreement to ship supplies to French Africa which were to be inspected there only by Americans. Furthermore, London's consent to clear such shipments through the blockade would depend now on two additional demands. First, British consuls must be permitted to return to French Africa and reopen their offices there. Second, the portions of the French fleet which still remained anchored in France must be removed to ports beyond German control. In my conversations with Lord Halifax, he manifested the greatest doubts about the possibility of cooperation with the French in North Africa, and he gave me no encouragement or support.

Fortunately, however, our side gained an invaluable British ally, David Eccles, who deserves more credit for his war efforts than he has received. Eccles, who went into Parliament after the war and has been a minister in a number of Conservative cabinets, is a remarkable economist who understood how to make effective use of economic concessions, which was the most formidable weapon that Britain had in 1940-41. He arrived in Washington about the same time I did, and soon he succeeded in reversing the attitude of the British Embassy and swung its support to our African venture.

On April 24, Under Secretary Welles summoned several of us who were involved in the Accord and announced that it was definitely decided to go ahead now with the much-delayed agreement. I was assigned to Algiers as a sort of High Commissioner for French Africa, although I still was listed simply as Counselor of Embassy to France. It would be my job to maintain contacts, especially with Weygand; to supervise our inspectors and our consular officers; and to report developments to the State Department. This was an executive assignment I had neither sought nor expected. Welles then called in David Eccles, who was waiting in an adjoining room, told him of the American decision, and asked for comments. Eccles explained that sentiment in London had changed and that the British Government probably would agree now to include even Dakar in our cooperation sphere, an idea which would have been hooted down a few weeks earlier.

Everything seemed clear at long last. I made various preparations in Washington and then flew back to Africa—only to learn there that our hard-won Accord had been suspended before it went into operation. The hitch this time was a message from Secretary Hull dated May 16 which declared: "Pending clarification of the situation, all activities in behalf of France and French North Africa are at a standstill." The Secretary's sudden order was the result of that false report from the British Embassy in Lisbon that sixty thousand German soldiers were massed in Spain. My French friends implied that this latest breakdown in our aid program was another British device for preventing American supplies from reaching Africa. Even Emmanuel Monick, Secretary to the Resident General at Rabat, who was so pro-British that I nicknamed him The Anglophile, greeted me with the sarcastic question: "Are you Americans ever going to have an African policy of your own, or do you intend to keep on letting London make your policy?" Since my previous visit to Rabat, the British had suffered serious defeats in Yugoslavia, Greece, Crete and Libya, and

Monick went on to say: "When you were here in January, the British had prestige. Now they have none. The question before Frenchmen today is: What is the United States going to do? If the United States does intend to act, what is the timetable?"

I could not give Monick any specific encouragement under the circumstances, but I notified the Department of State that my latest investigations on the spot reaffirmed the soundness of the arrangement we had previously agreed upon. I cabled: "It is my opinion that we should go forward boldly with the plan of economic cooperation, establishing our control organization and using it to the best advantage." During the next few disturbing weeks, the Accord was restored, then halted again, and then restored once more.

Several of the hindrances to sending American equipment to Africa originated in Washington. For example, on one occasion after we had laboriously compiled a list of supplies desperately needed to keep the African administration afloat, and had won grudging approval from both the American and British economic warfare agencies, Secretary of the Treasury Henry Morgenthau abruptly canceled the release of seven million dollars in French funds earmarked to pay for these purchases. This cancellation occurred without warning or explanation, and interferences of this sort were not infrequent. They were one of the hazards of working in the too loosely administered Roosevelt regime.

Another stumbling block was the problem of rounding up suitable Americans to inspect ship cargoes. It was by no means sheer perversity which caused the British to demand that their nationals should work side by side with American inspectors. The British had a good many men who had made careers in Africa, who could speak Arabic, who understood the customs of native populations, and who were experienced in shipping. Such Britons could be relied upon to supervise cargo arrivals and to make certain that they would not slip by devious routes into German hands. The United States, on the contrary, had few citizens who had even visited Africa, and we found it very difficult to recruit men for the peculiar work we were arranging.

Because, although the only job stipulated in the Accord for these men was to supervise the shipments, it was understood by everybody concerned—from Pétain and Weygand down—that these Americans really would be intelligence agents. A few farsighted men in Washington had become aware of how little we knew about what was going on in Africa. They saw the need for dependable American observers, instead of having to rely entirely upon our French colleagues. We had American consulates in five French African cities, staffed by about a dozen officers altogether, but these State Department officials had been trained only for the duties normally associated with their work. It was decided, therefore, that we now must appoint a dozen observers, whom we would call vice consuls, and that this special group would work under my personal direction.

To demonstrate his confidence in the United States Government, General Weygand made an unprecedented concession: our consular staffs, including the twelve new "vice consuls," would be permitted to use secret codes and to employ couriers carrying locked pouches, a privilege usually restricted to diplomatic missions and not extended in wartime to consular offices in French North Africa. This secret understanding, noted on the margin of the agreement which Weygand and I initialed, became the basis of one of the most effective intelligence operations of the war, for it provided that Americans not only could watch what transpired in French Africa, but also could get out uncensored confidential reports to our Government.

But how to find competent American observers? Assistant Secretary of State Adolf Berle was put in charge of selecting this staff, and he admitted at once that our limited number of regular Foreign Service vice consuls could not provide the specialized personnel called for by this project, involving as it did a certain amount of irregular activity and danger. It occurred to him that what was needed were experienced Army and Navy officers, brave, patriotic, disciplined men who could appreciate objects and events of military significance. So he consulted with the chiefs of Army and Navy Intelligence to persuade them to assign resourceful specialists for work in Africa. This was my first experience in dealing with the heads of our military Intelligence in Washington. With all due respect to these dedicated officers, and with the benefit of subsequent experience which all of us have enjoyed since then, it must be confessed that our Intelligence organization in 1940 was primitive and inadequate. It was timid, parochial, and operating strictly in the tradition of the Spanish-American War. To the chiefs of the Army and Navy Intelligence groups, North Africa seemed something new, almost another planet. We had traditionally depended on handouts from the British and French services for information about the Mediterranean and North Africa area. We had absolutely no personnel qualified in Arabic. The only commodity our military Intelligence organization seemed to have in abundance was time. Months of delay and inaction was the rule.

Our military services were reluctant to associate themselves with a State Department enterprise, but after considerable discussion, the chiefs of Intelligence at length agreed to assign to Africa several reserve officers, commissioned as vice consuls, and to pay their salaries—providing the State Department would pay their other expenses. The men thus selected all had some experience in France and knowledge of the French language—businessmen, engineers, lawyers who held reserve commissions in the Army or Navy. Then somebody pointed out that commissioned officers, if they performed civilian functions while on active duty, could be shot as spies if war broke out. So some of the officers who had been selected were discharged. So now they were civilians—and who would pay them? The services were operating on a financial shoestring. It finally was decided to pay them from the President's emergency funds.

After my decades in government service, I should have known that matters cannot be rushed when several agencies are confronted with an unprecedented situation, but I did plead that at least two of these "vice consuls" should be transported to Africa by air, in order to get things started as quickly as possible. However, they all crossed the Atlantic by ship to save a few dollars, and the first batch did not arrive in Algiers until June 10. The Germans stationed in French Africa soon became aware, of course, of the presence of our new "vice consuls," and a confidential report concerning them was dispatched to Berlin. The French police in Morocco gave me a copy of this report which said in part: "The vice consuls whom Murphy directs represent a perfect picture of the mixture of races and characteristics in that wild conglomeration called the United States of America. We can only congratulate ourselves on the selection of this group of enemy agents who will give us no trouble. In view of the fact that they are totally lacking in method, organization and discipline, the danger presented by their arrival in North Africa may be considered as nil. It would be merely a waste of paper to describe their personal idiosyncrasies and characteristics."

This unkind report was a gross exaggeration, but it was true that the Departments of State, War and Navy had failed to produce a single American familiar with the Arabic language or with conditions in Moslem communities. With one exception, Ted Colbert, a graduate of the Naval Academy who had represented Pratt & Whitney in Europe before the war, our little group had no expert knowledge of shipping, so important to our project. As I reported to Washington: "One or two of us, with luck, might be able to distinguish a battleship from a submarine on a particularly clear day."

However, very soon after our "vice consuls" settled down to work, we were aided by the attention of General William J. ("Wild Bill") Donovan, Medal of Honor hero of Rainbow Division World War I fame. Donovan had induced President Roosevelt to turn him loose in French Africa, among other places, with plenty of money to create the kind of spy-subversive secret service long employed by European powers but previously scorned by Americans. The American Army and Navy had consistently down-graded their Intelligence sections, and Donovan proposed now to fill the gaps. We surely were glad to welcome his representatives, being ourselves rank amateurs in the Intelligence field.

But even my limited experience in Africa won me the reputation in Washington of an Intelligence specialist.

The Donovan organization made important contributions to our enterprise, but one of its ventures almost pushed a bull into our china shop. For generations, the French in Africa had jealously guarded their empire from any outsiders who might be disposed to meddle with the native populations. Knowing this, I had repeatedly assured the Weygand group that the only interest of the American Government in Africa was strategic, and that we considered relations between France and the African peoples in French Africa to be purely an affair between them. However, during our delicate waiting period, Arabs made overtures to us a number of times. On one occasion they approached an American consular officer in Tunisia with an offer to replace—for a reasonable price—the pro-German Bey with a pro-Allied one. The well-meaning but misguided American official passed on this proposition to Donovan, who promptly set aside fifty thousand dollars to bring off this coup.

Fortunately, the General placed the matter in the hands of his chief representative in Africa, Colonel William A. Eddy, who had grown up in the Middle East and was fluent in Arabic. This Marine officer, partly disabled by World War I wounds, was stationed in Tangier as the American naval attaché, and he was invaluable throughout the various stages of the African operation. Eddy was always meticulous in coordinating his activities with mine, and no American knew more about Arabs or about power politics in Africa. He was one of a kind, unique; we could have used a hundred like him. When he informed me about the proposal to "purchase" a pro-Allied native ruler, I was as much shocked by mention of the amount of money as I was by the project itself. Nothing would have enraged our French colleagues more than this kind of monkey business, or been more ruinous to our chances of obtaining the support of French military forces. As for fifty thousand dollars! Our whole operation in Africa had not cost that much over a period of many months.

Another American who performed invaluable services during the long preparatory period before the landing of Allied troops in Africa was our new ambassador to France, Admiral William D. Leahy, who succeeded Bullitt in this post. I first met Leahy when I went to Vichy for the ratification there of the Murphy-Weygand Accord. I did not know it then, but that was my last visit to wartime Vichy, although I continued to be listed as Counselor of Embassy there. The main reason it never became necessary for me to return to Vichy was because Leahy and I worked harmoniously together from the day we met. The Ambassador entrusted to me the African end of our project, while he handled the multiple complications at Vichy. I was to enjoy similar friendly cooperation with Leahy through all the war years, since he later became Roosevelt's personal chief of staff, where he was largely instrumental in directing Roosevelt's very personal conduct of the war.

The President named Leahy as Ambassador to Vichy in the hope that this retired officer, who had held the highest positions in our Navy and was then serving as Governor of Puerto Rico, might be able to get closer to Marshal Pétain than any civilian diplomat could. Roosevelt's hopes were justified, and the Admiral exercised great influence at Vichy for eighteen months. He told everybody there that he was no diplomat and that he knew very little about European politics, but that he did know something about military matters and that these were of major concern in wartime. He was keenly interested from the outset in the African project, and during our first meeting he put me through a detailed and critical examination. After that, he supported my efforts at every stage. For instance, during the late summer of 1941, the American and British press waged an intensive campaign against the relations of the United States with France. Reports were published that French Africa was being staffed with "100% collaborators," that Dakar was being heavily reinforced "under German initiative," and that American supplies sent to Africa were getting into German hands. On September 18 Secretary Hull cabled to Leahy and me asking for our opinions of these press reports. The Ambassador fully supported my own detailed refutations of these false reports, and recommended continuance of our relations with both Vichy and Africa.

The most important anxiety which Leahy and I shared for a year was the fate of General Weygand, whom the Nazis were determined to force out of Africa because they were well aware that he was no friend of theirs. The Nazis continually brought pressure on eighty-five-year-old Marshal Pétain to recall Weygand—and they could exert enormous pressure because two-thirds of France was under their control and 1,500,000 Frenchmen were their prisoners of war. At length, on November 18, 1941, Pétain informed Leahy in Vichy that the Nazis had threatened to occupy all of France and to let the French population starve while the German Army lived off the land, unless the Marshal removed Weygand from Africa. On the same November day, Weygand at Algiers gave me the same information. The General also gave me a copy of a memorandum which he had written and which he said he intended to read personally to Pétain and his associates. This turned out to be his political testament, and is therefore of particular interest:

"I moved to Africa when Britain had proved ability to survive air attacks. This immensely increased the potential importance of French Africa. France possessed a trump essential in the general diplomatic situation. At the beginning of the present year [1941] the United States offered us an economic accord which has not given all results hoped for, because of British and German opposition. But from the political standpoint, this accord offered an important advantage. France, thanks to its empire, remained the only European power retaining its economic relations with the United States. . . . Thus, in addition to the duty as I understood it, of protecting the empire against the conqueror, there was added a further possibility, that of maintaining cordial economic and political contact with a power which, in any event, will be one of the arbiters of the situation at the end of the war. The evolution of the situation in 1941 only confirms the growing importance of French Africa. . . . Opening Africa to Germany means in the last analysis giving to Germany a unique opportunity to continue the war for ten years, and to impose her will upon France without the possibility of any reaction."

As he handed me this declaration of faith in Africa's importance, the old soldier urged me to impress upon the American Government that American-French collaboration in Africa did not depend upon one man, but upon the vast organization which had been fortified since 1940, and would remain.

That was General Weygand's last public act; he had always held himself aloof from politics, and now he disassociated himself permanently from military affairs. He retired to a small estate in the south of France, where he was visited after Pearl Harbor by a representative of President Roosevelt, Douglas MacArthur II, who offered him complete American support if he would head a separatist movement in Africa. The general politely said "No," and gave the same answer to renewed approaches after the Allied landings. He refused to flee when the Germans occupied all of France, and so finally became a prisoner of war, since the Germans did not trust him. He worked on his memoirs in a German prison, and after the war continued in Paris a lifetime of dedication to his country.

Ambassador Leahy was even more upset than I was by Weygand's recall, and his first reaction was that the American string in Vichy had played out. He cabled Washington recommending that the Government should recall both him and me "for consultation," suspend the African Accord, and give maximum publicity to these moves and the reasons for them. But I could not concede defeat so readily, and my own cablegram to Washington recommended: "All here urge it would be folly for the United States to abandon the field at a moment when its influence is demonstrated and can become indispensable. If we make Weygand an issue, it will support the German argument that Weygand was negotiating over Vichy's head. My contacts say the setup is virtually unchanged except for Weygand personally. Men with whom I have worked for a year still are on the job, and say Weygand's removal will calm Nazi apprehensions regarding French Africa and give us a breathing spell. I urge that we intensify rather than abandon the supply program. May I recommend that before a final decision on policy is taken that a brief period be allowed in which to gather all essential facts."

However, two hours before my cablegram was received by the State Department, it was publicly announced that the United States Government had suspended its program in French Africa. For several nights I did not get much sleep, turning over in my mind new arguments for resuming the Accord. One such argument came to me secretly in a handwritten message from General Weygand himself. This read: "Continue I beg of you to favor the supply program. As the Marshal told Admiral Leahy, nothing is changed in French policy by my departure. My messenger will tell you how much I count on the maintenance between our two countries of the union necessary for the near future of the world." Forwarding this message to the State Department, I also pointed out that if we gave up the Accord we were unnecessarily depriving ourselves of the great advantage of diplomatic courier service, use of cipher messages, and the presence of our own trained observers in this strategic area. In still another cablegram to the Department, I said: "By retaining our present position intact we risk nothing, making the Germans take the initiative in breaking the Accord. In any case, during nine months of the Accord, little came of it in goods. Only 7 percent of authorized quotas were delivered. If more had been done, stronger public reaction might be expected now." Leahy, after his first moments of discouragement at Vichy, reconsidered his early recommendation and now reinforced my arguments with his own.

During my year in Africa, I had become intimate not only with Weygand himself but with his principal associates in the Algiers headquarters. And I had come to understand that, much as I admired the general personally, the African hierarchy was not just one man upon whom we should pin our hopes. I had grown to trust some of Weygand's associates as much as I did him and, with Leahy's support, I eventually was able to persuade Washington that we could deal with many Frenchmen remaining in Africa on the same basis as we had dealt with the General himself. But the main thing which saved the Accord from extinction, after the downfall of Weygand, was not so much our reasoned arguments as the Japanese attack three weeks later on Pearl Harbor.

I was dining in Algiers at the home of my French friend Count de Rose when the radio announced the Japanese bombings in Hawaii. Everyone turned to me as the only American present. I certainly underestimated both the power of the Japanese and their willingness to take risks, for I told the dinner guests that I could hardly believe the Japanese would be so reckless. But, I added, if the news should prove to be true, it would solve the principal problem which weighed on President Roosevelt: How would the United States enter the war? The next day, as I listened on the radio to Hitler's speech before high Nazi party members in Berlin, with his heavy sarcasm and contemptuous jibes at the poor benighted American Government, I could feel only relief that the chips were down at last, and Americans no longer need pretend to be neutral.

On December 22, Prime Minister Churchill arrived in Washington to discuss war strategy with President Roosevelt. Although Japan had made the Pacific a major battleground now, and America's entry into the war against Hitler had opened up innumerable possibilities, that pre-Christmas conference in the White House was devoted almost exclusively to French North Africa. Churchill and Roosevelt wanted to send their first expeditionary force to this area, and they wanted to make this move at the earliest possible moment. Only Japan's spectacular victories in the Pacific and further German conquests in Russia and in the eastern Mediterranean area compelled postponement of the African expedition.

Secretary Hull and Under-Secretary Welles attended that White House conference, and on the following day they sent me some cautious encouragement. They cabled that our on-again, off-again Accord was being revived. Two small French ships, then waiting in New York Harbor, were being permitted to sail with a selected cargo, provided that two similar ships at Casablanca would simultaneously return to the United States. This had been our agreed arrangement from the beginning. But even though we now were openly at war, I was informed that "no movements of tankers or petroleum products are contemplated at this time." Those of us waiting in North Africa persisted in our belief that this region would become extremely important in the war, but it looked as though we still had an uphill struggle against the doubters. And so it proved to be, right up to the arrival of the Allied Expeditionary Force nearly a year later.

The last threat to our African project occurred in April 1942 when Pierre Laval, with the help of a German ultimatum, maneuvered his way back into power at Vichy. Once more Laval became Vice Chief of State, and this time Foreign Minister and Interior Minister in control of the police, as well. There was no doubt whatever about Laval's stubborn determination and his belief that he could outwit the Germans, even with both the United States and Russia now fighting the Nazis. So it was only to be expected that Washington would again suspend the African Accord, as it did. We had to dig out all the well-worn arguments that French Africa and Vichy were two separate entities, only loosely associated, and this time Ambassador Leahy was firmly on our side. So was "Wild Bill" Donovan, because our amateur spies had learned enough by now to become really effective. The British Intelligence Service also praised our efforts, and the American Joint Intelligence Committee in Washington warned that if our group were withdrawn from Africa "there would be virtually a blackout of an entire and crucial region." So the Accord was resumed once more, although every small shipment involved inter-agency arguments, reductions and delays until the Allied Expeditionary Force actually landed.

One of the useful results of the months I lived in Africa, traveling constantly and talking with Frenchmen who had lived there for decades, was my growing awareness of what complicated human problems this French African empire had mastered. Inside this far-flung domain there were almost as many administrative and ethnic divisions as in Europe. Morocco and Tunisia were French protectorates, whose Arab rulers had considerable independence; one of my duties was to maintain friendly personal contacts with these influential Arabs, without offending the French. Algeria's miscellaneous Moslem tribes and mixed urban population had been illogically incorporated in European France. The Arab, Berber and Negro inhabitants of French Africa outnumbered Europeans ten to twenty times and included hundreds of tribes, many famous for their fighting qualities. The one bond which held most of them together was Islam, a religion foreign to the French administrators.

Moreover, the Europeans who dwelt in wartime French Africa were an incredible medley. Living conditions along the southern shores of the Mediterranean were attractive compared with the hardships in war-torn Europe, and every ship crossing from the Continent brought refugees seeking escape from cold, semi-starvation, German military rule, and Nazi persecution. It was estimated that at least two hundred thousand Europeans had come to French North Africa since the outbreak of war, some of them very rich, many very poor. Bankers and businessmen were clandestinely transferring their money and investments to Africa to avoid inflation or confiscation; paupers found shelter in rude, makeshift camps. Scattered among these fugitives were hundreds, perhaps thousands, of restless and even dangerous men and women, most of them anti-Nazi, but also anti many other things. In Africa's camps or living underground in its cities were Communists, Spanish Loyalists, refugee European Jews, also twenty-five hundred Poles who had fled from their homeland in 1939, first to France itself and then to Africa.

The more I learned, the more I realized what a potentially explosive area this was, and the more I was impressed by the skill with which French administrators had retained control over these diverse and often hostile communities, even during years of French defeat and occupation. What would these mixed-up people do if French Africa should become a battleground? The answer, it seemed to me, was that only French administrators already familiar with the complexities of these variegated local situations could possibly maintain the order in French Africa which an Allied Expeditionary Force would require. This was a point which I particularly stressed when the time came for me to discuss the African expedition with its planners in Washington and London.

SEVEN

SECRET AGENT FOR EISENHOWER (1942)

When I returned to Washington on August 31, 1942, I discovered a remarkable change in the American capital's attitude toward French Africa. During the many months I had been immured in Algeria, Morocco and Tunisia, those French territories seemed to rank near the bottom of Washington's priority list. Now they suddenly had risen to the top. I did not learn just why until President Roosevelt asked me to come to Hyde Park a few days after my return, so that he could "brief" me himself. Meanwhile I had my first round of talks with war strategists in the State and War Departments, including Secretary of State Cordell Hull; Under Secretary of State Sumner Welles; Secretary of War Henry L. Stimson; General George C. Marshall, Chief of Staff of the Army; Admiral Ernest J. King, Chief of Naval Operations; and Admiral Leahy, who by then was the President's personal Chief of Staff.

One of the first who asked me to come to see him was Stimson, who told me the War Department had been closely following developments in Africa, but that he deplored the loose talk in Washington regarding our possible plans there. A columnist had just published in a Washington newspaper bits and pieces about the expedition project. All planners believed that if the North African operation was to succeed, and especially if heavy casualties were to be avoided, surprise was imperative. I heartily agreed, and added that I even felt uncomfortable about coming to his office because of undesirable publicity if the press became aware of it. The Secretary said he had overlooked this possibility when he asked me to call, and he immediately instructed a staff officer to eliminate any record of my visit. A little later when General Marshall joined our conversation, Stimson requested him to arrange my exit by a side door.

Stimson and Marshall did not conceal their misgivings about the African venture which was being planned, or their disappointment that their own project for an early cross-channel invasion of Europe had been indefinitely postponed. The strategy they favored was to attack the Germans directly on the continent, and at first the British had reluctantly accepted this American proposal. But early in July, Churchill—acting on the unanimous advice of his military commanders—flatly refused to participate in a cross-channel attack in 1942. The Allied raid, code name Operation Jubilee, in August 1942, across the English Channel on Dieppe, was made as a test, a so-called "dry run," principally by 5000 men of the Canadian 2d Division. It was a disaster costing about 3500 casualties. It convinced the British and many Americans that the Nazi coastal defenses were too powerful at that time for Allied strength. While the cost in brave men was high, perhaps as Lord Louis Mountbatten has said, the experience saved many lives on D-Day two years later. Since an invasion of this nature could be launched only from the British Isles, Churchill's refusal brought to a halt for the time being all such schemes.

Roosevelt thereupon revived his own plan for Allied landings in Africa, which he and Churchill had approved immediately after Pearl Harbor. The President had promised Stalin that Americans would be fighting Germans before the end of 1942, and French Africa now seemed the only practical place to open the "second front" which the Russians were demanding. So an African expeditionary force was hastily organized, although the American high command was far from enthusiastic about it. The decision to go to Africa was made on July 22, and Commander Harry C. Butcher, General Eisenhower's personal aide and wartime confidant, noted in his diary: "Ike thought that July 22, 1942, could well go down as the 'blackest day in history,' particularly if Russia is defeated in the big Boche drive now so alarmingly under way."

In the course of my talk with Stimson, I mentioned that French officers who wanted to fight again were thinking of battles in France itself rather than in the French empire, and talked of being ready to cooperate with American forces in Europe by the spring of 1943. That remark seemed to interest the Secretary more than anything I said about Africa. He commented that a direct assault on Europe in 1943 seemed much wiser than some kind of second front to meet popular clamor. In his memoirs written after the war, Stimson indicated that even then he still believed the African expedition had been an unnecessary diversion from proper strategy.

General Marshall's lack of enthusiasm for the African project was also apparent during our first talk. He heavily discounted the idea I had been working on so earnestly for nearly two years—getting important help from French collaborators. In a memorandum I prepared at the time for Welles, I wrote: "Marshall seemed to favor a straight-out American attack on French Africa in sufficient force to ensure its success." The general repeated several times his concern about the danger of confiding our plans to Frenchmen. His attitude in this matter never did change and it influenced our relations with French associates before and during the landings. There were a considerable number of French military and civil administrators whom I trusted by that time, but my instructions discouraged me from confiding our plans to any of them until the last moment, which led to serious misunderstandings.

When I met Admiral Leahy for the first time since we had worked together in France, he greeted me with the words, "Well, maybe you and I didn't waste our time cultivating those people in Vichy!" He said he would take me to see the President in the White House soon, but two days later, on September 4, word came that an Air Force plane was waiting to take me quietly and unescorted to Hyde Park. The President received me in the library, accompanied by Harry Hopkins, both men tieless and in their shirt sleeves. Hopkins spoke very little during the hours we spent together that hot afternoon; Roosevelt did most of the talking.

The President obviously was delighted that the African enterprise finally was under way. Although I do not underestimate Churchill's persistent influence, Roosevelt had been more responsible for the adoption of the African venture than anyone else, and despite his innumerable preoccupations elsewhere, he had found time to read our reports about Africa. The North African expedition appealed to his sense of adventure, especially as it involved a major naval operation. The President was keenly aware of the delicate situation which would be created by sending American troops into the territory of a professedly neutral government with which we had amicable relations. In view of our declared principles, it would be difficult to establish a case for landings in French Africa without the formal consent of the Vichy Government. And, lacking such approval from Marshal Pétain's administration, we must anticipate that a military invasion would be forcibly resisted by some French commanders who had sworn allegiance to the marshal. There were only two possible ways to conquer this inevitable French resistance—by transporting overseas Allied troops and equipment vastly superior to the French fighting forces already stationed in Africa; or by diplomatic maneuvers to persuade the French commanders that victory over Germany would result from cooperating with the American expedition, and that allegiance to France was more important than allegiance to Pétain.

During our conversation, the President repeated what he had told me in the White House nearly two years before, when he assigned me to an inspection tour of French Africa. He declared that his wartime policy vis-à-vis the French was to refrain from the recognition of any one person or group as the Government of France, until a liberated French population could freely choose their own government. To me he said, very solemnly and firmly, "You will restrict your dealings to French officials on the local level, prefects, and the military. I will not help anyone impose a Government on the French people." This remained his credo and it governed my relations with the French before and after the Allied landings.

Of course, this was in direct conflict with General de Gaulle's philosophy—or, I should say, his passionate conviction. Some influential American commentators, led by Walter Lippmann, had for two years put pressure upon the President and the State Department to recognize the De Gaulle movement as representing the people of France. Our relations with the French Government at Vichy had been under continuous fire by these journalists. But Roosevelt and Churchill agreed that De Gaulle should not even be informed in advance about the expedition to Africa. There had been grave breaches of security in De Gaulle's headquarters in London on other matters—for example, the Anglo-De Gaulle attack on Dakar—and Roosevelt and Churchill believed the men around De Gaulle could not be trusted to keep secrets. Moreover, Roosevelt and Churchill believed that if De Gaulle participated in the African venture, the presence of his men would produce fighting between Frenchmen, as had occurred not only when De Gaulle forces attempted to capture Dakar, but also during a small similar expedition to Syria. Opposition to De Gaulle was particularly virulent at this time among French naval and air officers in French Africa.

After describing our new invasion plans, which had taken final shape only that week, the President said, "Don't tell anybody in the State Department about this. That place is a sieve!" When I mentioned that this might put me in an awkward position with Secretary Hull, Roosevelt replied, "Don't worry about Cordell. I will take care of him; I'll tell him our plans a day or so before the landings." This impressed me because I always had believed, and I think not too inaccurately, that more leaks emanated in those days from the White House than from the State Department.

Having been thus instructed by the Commander in Chief himself, I resumed my rounds of conferences and met all the expedition's major planners. Marshall decided I should make a secret visit to Eisenhower's headquarters in London, despite the danger of being recognized there. The General said, "We'll disguise you in a lieutenant colonel's uniform. Nobody ever pays any attention to a lieutenant colonel." So I was given accreditation as "Lieutenant Colonel MacGowan." To make the disguise complete, it was decided that a passport in this assumed name would be desirable, and Secretary Hull and Assistant Secretary Howland Shaw ordered that this be issued. But my dear friend Mrs. Ruth Shipley, chief of the Passport Division of the State Department, who was vigorously independent, refused to disregard regulations even at the Secretary's behest. "It's never been done and never will be while I am here," she declared. So the Secretary and Assistant Secretary meekly backed down, and I made the round trip to London by special military arrangements with no passport at all.

I traveled to London on September 15–16 on one of the warplanes being delivered by Ferry Command, and during our stop at Prestwick, Scotland, I was startled to hear a familiar voice shouting, "Why, Bob! What are you doing here?" It was our "Vice Consul" Don Coster, from Africa. The bewildered man suddenly found himself being rushed off under arrest, and he was kept incommunicado until after the landings. My old colleague Julius Holmes, formerly in the Foreign Service and then a colonel on Eisenhower's staff, ordered the arrest. Coster's innocent error was that he almost betrayed my presence in England, which was supposed to be top secret. Fortunately, there were thousands of Bobs in the Army, some of them doubtless lieutenant colonels, so no harm was done. Escorted by Holmes to a military airport near London, I was driven by car to Eisenhower's hideout in the country, Telegraph Cottage, where I spent a day and a night in almost continuous conferences with the General and his planners.

I was pleased to learn that the General's political advisers in London included experienced diplomats who knew France well. But even these capable men had no first-hand knowledge of Africa. I was the only person at that London conference with prolonged experience in Africa itself, and from questions asked I could see that Eisenhower and some of his officers had mental pictures of primitive country, collections of mud huts set deep in jungles. I assured them that French North Africa was more like California than a tropical wilderness, and I described briefly the creature comforts of Algiers and Casablanca. Eisenhower then prudently inquired whether winter underwear would be necessary, and I told him it was, especially on the high plateau in eastern Algeria. Thousands of American soldiers appreciated that the following winter.

During those hurried hours in London and hurried days in the Pentagon, I became aware of my own appalling ignorance of military matters. Here I was participating as a key figure in the initial important American offensive of World War II, and I did not know the first principles of military science. My interests always had been political and my professional training was in diplomacy. But I took comfort in the knowledge that the expedition to French Africa would require political as well as military strategy. I was relieved to find that although Eisenhower had been as displeased as Marshall about the shift in operational plans, he did not share Marshall's indifference to help from Frenchmen in Africa. In an astute analysis made at the time, Eisenhower wrote that the African expedition was too risky to justify on purely military grounds. Its success would depend, he observed, upon such political factors as correct estimates of French and Spanish reactions to our landings. Butcher wrote in his diary: "Ike feels we are sailing a dangerous political sea, and this particular sea is one in which military skill and ability can do little in charting a safe course."

Eisenhower and many of his brother officials had the benefit of previous instruction in political problems, such as the excellent course given at the Army War College and other military schools, but I had had no equivalent training in military matters. Nowadays we try to teach our professional diplomats a great deal about military affairs, and we try also to teach our professional soldiers more about world politics and diplomacy. In 1942, American soldiers and diplomats alike had to contend with large areas of ignorance. That African venture probably was more unpalatable to Eisenhower than any other assignment in his distinguished career. The General disliked almost everything about the expedition: its diversion from the central campaign in Europe; its obvious military risks in a vast, untried territory; its dependence upon local forces who were doubtful at best and perhaps treacherous; its bewildering complexities involving deadly quarrels among French factions, and Spanish, Italian, Arab, Berber, German and Russian politics. Eisenhower listened with a kind of horrified intentness to my description of the possible complications. Perhaps some of the things I said were as incomprehensible to him as military mapping and logistics would have been to me. The General seemed to sense that this first campaign would present him with problems running the entire geopolitical gamut—as it certainly did. And in those days Eisenhower, in accordance with American military tradition, still preferred to regard himself as a soldier who paid attention to politics only when military operations were affected.

During our marathon conversation, most of the time with a dozen other American and British military and civilian planners, we covered all the points about Africa which had been bothering me. I explained how seriously French officers cherished their oath of fidelity to Marshal Pétain, and how they feared that Americans would underestimate the strength needed to establish themselves in Africa. I explained that these factors indicated we might encounter French resistance in several places. Eisenhower shared Marshall's doubts about entrusting our plans to Frenchmen, so it was agreed that I should withhold the date of the Allied landings, November 8, 1942, from even our closest colleagues, and that I should wait until the last possible moment before disclosing the actual date of arrival of the forces, giving a maximum of four days' notice. I did emphasize that our French colleagues were at least as eager as we were to save North Africa from the Axis. But American and British war planners were unanimous in their insistence that surprise was of the essence. With the miserable communications existing in the two thousand-odd miles of territory from Tunis to Casablanca, four days' notice was fantastically inadequate for any coordination with our French friends. In fact we lost the friendship of some of them who were indignant over the method used.

Back again in Washington after my London trip, I endured several frustrating weeks. Knowing how desperately short of consumer and incentive goods the population of French North Africa was by that time, we wanted to send substantial supplies to Casablanca in four cargo vessels in advance of the landings. Shipments of almost everything would be useful for the approaching campaign. For example, native stevedores could hardly be induced to work overtime unloading our ships, except by an array of simple but tempting goods they wanted for themselves and their families. But only a few Americans shared the tight secret of our assault plans, which were not revealed to the staff of the Board of Economic Warfare. So I had to argue with a group of dedicated but hostile economic warriors in Washington who had no sense of urgency and viewed my frantic appeals with increasing suspicion. I recall in particular one cock-sure young lawyer who practically accused me of being a Nazi sympathizer and grilled me for two precious hours. "How can you prove, Mr. Murphy, that these cotton textiles you say are for the Arabs will not be seized to make uniforms for Rommel's troops in Libya?" inquired this representative of the Board of Economic Warfare. In desperation I appealed several times for help to Admiral Leahy, who personally tackled the obstructors with all the prestige of the White House behind him, but without success. Finally I went to Roosevelt himself and he gave me an order in his own handwriting authorizing the immediate dispatch of two French freighters whose sailings had been delayed by picayune objections to some items in their cargoes. One example was tobacco, which was challenged on the ground that it might give "aid and comfort" to Nazis if it fell into their hands. But even the President's handwritten order was ignored by the Board of Economic Warfare. The ships were not released in time to arrive before our Armed Forces did, and the urgently needed supplies did not get there for many weeks.

Meanwhile, at my own request, the President's office prepared a directive for my protection, placing on record my secret temporary separation from the State Department and my assignment to the President. This unusual document instructed me to work in close cooperation with Eisenhower, first as "personal representative of the President" prior to the arrival of military forces in French North Africa; and thereafter as "the Operating Executive Head of the Civil Affairs Section and Adviser for Civil Affairs under General Eisenhower." Thus to my surprise I became the first civilian in American history to serve on the inner staff of a military commander's headquarters in a war theater, with access to all military information. Marshall and Eisenhower were disturbed by this irregular situation and they made a mild effort to get me into uniform, inside the regular "chain of command." But I had acquired enough experience at French military headquarters in Africa to observe the advantages of preserving civilian status, and I managed to retain civilian status in all the military headquarters to which I was attached during and after the war. Harold Macmillan, who became my opposite number as British Political Adviser, ascribed equal importance to his civilian status.

The presidential directive relieved me of responsibility to the State Department for the time being, and instructed me to establish communications directly with the President and with Eisenhower "through channels as General Eisenhower and you may arrange." As a result, the Department of State failed to see some important communications during several months of 1942 and 1943, and even today some of my reports are not in the department's files. This was manifestly wrong and an indication of a certain weakness in the civilian side of the government. The British Foreign Office had ready access to Macmillan's messages. The presidential directive spelled out the rationale under which American troops would move into Africa, giving the exact words used by me to explain our conduct to our French colleagues:

"Information having been received from a reliable source that the Germans and Italians are planning an intervention in French North Africa, the United States contemplates sending at an early date a sufficient number of American troops to land in that area with the purpose of preventing occupation by the Axis, and of preserving the French sovereignty in Algeria, and the French administrations in Morocco and Tunisia. No change in the existing French civil administrations is contemplated by the United States. Any resistance to the American landing will of course be put down by force of arms. The American forces will hope for and will welcome French assistance.

"The American forces will provide equipment as rapidly as possible for those French troops who join in denying access to French North Africa to our common enemies. . . . The American Government will guarantee salaries and allowances, death benefits and pensions of those French and other military, naval and civilian officials who join with the American expeditionary forces. The proposed expedition will be American, under American command, and it will not include any of the forces of General de Gaulle."

Clearly this directive involved a certain amount of deception of our French colleagues. It gave the impression that the expedition would be wholly American, whereas the planners were well aware that they must depend to a large extent upon British armed forces. At that stage of the war, our troops generally were without combat experience, green and untried. American commitments in the Pacific war made it impossible for the United States to mount the African expedition single-handedly. But my directive did not permit me to explain that situation to Frenchmen. My instructions were precise on this point. I was to describe the expedition as American, not Anglo-American, and to take only partly into my confidence "those French nationals whom you consider reliable." The directive imposed heavy responsibilities upon my judgment, but it also restricted me to specific limits. It concluded: "After the necessary preparation is made by French patriots in French North Africa, which should be accomplished with the utmost expedition, at least twenty-four hours' notice will be given to our friends of the time of the landings, and in your discretion of the approximate places." The directive was dated September 22, 1942, almost seven weeks before the landings.

With time running out, I naturally was eager to return to Africa, but was unable to get away from Washington until the first week in October. During a final session with Marshall he asked if I needed anything immediately. Much on my mind was the problem of how to assure dependable clandestine communications with Eisenhower, so I suggested that I might take back with me some small, lightweight radio transmitters like one which the Polish underground in Algiers had obtained somehow, and which our group in Africa had tested successfully. Upon inquiry, Marshall was informed that the only transmitters and receivers available to the Army Signal Corps were much too heavy for me to transport by air to Africa. Fortunately I happened to be having lunch that day with General "Wild Bill" Donovan, and mentioned the Polish transmitter. The general said, "You may be in luck. Only this morning we received some lightweight radio equipment. Let's go have a look at it." The sets were just what I needed, and when I flew back I carried five of these "top secret" transmitters and receivers in ten sealed diplomatic pouches. But I forgot to obtain from the State Department a certificate appointing me an official courier, so when I arrived in Lisbon in the middle of the night, Portuguese customs officials insisted that they must examine the contents of my pouches. In this emergency an old friend in the American Legation at Lisbon, Consul General Samuel "Pat" Wiley, came to the rescue. He spoke Portuguese well and was regarded as a friend of Portugal, so he was able to persuade the conscientious customs inspector to pass my bags at 5 A.M. in time for me to catch a seven o'clock plane for Tangier. Those transmitters were immensely useful to us. One of them was installed in the attic of the Casablanca consulate general, and this disturbed one of our senior consular officers who thought it might be contrary to regulations. He said to me rather dejectedly, "Murphy, I hope you know what you are doing. But I should like to make clear that I disapprove of espionage."

EIGHT

FIFTH COLUMN ACTIVITIES IN AFRICA

Getting back to Algiers in mid-October 1942, three weeks before the Allied military operation, I had to present a nonchalant appearance, going daily to my office and about my routine affairs as if nothing were happening, while urgently looking for French assistance in every direction. By that time we had secret sympathizers in every military headquarters, in various governmental and police establishments, the youth organization, and a tight little group of ardent civilians. But most of the civilians in French Africa were complacently neutral. Far from wanting to be liberated, they just wanted to be left alone. Many believed it was too late and that French Africa should stay out of the war. Some were making more money than ever before, and this was particularly true of certain European landowners, the wealthiest and most influential group. The demand for agricultural products was enormous, and governments at war were bidding extravagantly against each other for foodstuffs. To a lesser degree, city merchants also were enjoying an abnormal prosperity through black market dealings of various sorts. This was true of Arabs and Berbers as well as European residents. Pearl Harbor revived the hopes of aggressive French patriots, but they were a small minority.

My own description of the evolution of the French "fifth column" in Africa is recorded in a series of confidential letters which I addressed to Under Secretary Welles, who was the State Department's liaison man with President Roosevelt in this matter. Two of my earliest reports to Welles are dated on Pearl Harbor day, December 7, 1941. Almost every day for the next eleven months fresh offers of help were presented for our consideration. Some were sensible, others wildly impractical. My reports emphasized how extraordinarily mixed were the motives of these Frenchmen. A few of them were royalists who hoped to restore the Count of Paris as king. Many supported different versions of a reformed republic, as did General de Gaulle. A considerable number frankly advocated the type of authoritarian regime established by the Pétain-Laval Government. The one common bond among these Frenchmen was their desire to defeat Germany and Italy and to liberate France, and this desire also was their only common bond with the United States.

Our French friends plotted with us for almost a year, patiently enduring Washington's in-again, out-again hesitations. In Algiers, some five hundred French conspirators were loosely organized around a nucleus which called itself the Group of Five. This was the point of contact of the Algiers resistance underground to which I gave support. Similar underground fighters were recruited secretly in Morocco and Tunisia and throughout Algeria. There also was a small undercover De Gaulle group in Algiers, headed by René Capitant, editor of the clandestine newspaper *Combat*. Some of the Frenchmen in the Group of Five did not trust the De Gaullists because of their urge to propagandize under Capitant's direction. They also felt that the De Gaullists talked too much and that their security was bad. So while there was no open hostility between the two groups, there was lack of confidence. General de Gaulle told me a few months later that I had failed to appreciate the extent of his popular support in North Africa. But in 1942 we Americans were interested not so much in the question of eventual popular support as we were in the control then of the French military establishment of 125,000 trained and experienced Army, Navy and Air Force personnel, plus about 200,000 reservists, many of whom were Arabs who did not care a rap about De Gaulle. The French Navy and Air Force officers were predominantly hostile to De Gaulle then, and so were a good many Army officers.

All through 1942, the activities of the Group of Five became increasingly conspiratorial, as we resorted perforce to methods of the underground. The game we played became ever more dangerous, as a small minority of pro-Nazi Frenchmen became increasingly alarmed about their own future. French informers and Axis representatives were ubiquitous. Some of our helpers, detected before the invasion, were summarily shot. Never before had Americans been confronted with a situation like this, and we had to play it by ear. Because of the great distances and limited communications, coordination among our scattered groups was woefully inadequate. Naturally we tried to enlist the most powerful Frenchmen we could, in the hope that when our troops arrived these key figures might sabotage the Vichy extremists. When we were thwarted by highly placed officials who wanted to keep Africa aloof from the war, subordinates often were ready to plot against their commanding officers. For instance, suggestions were made to junior army officers to countermand orders of their superiors, and many of them did.

It was not always easy for Americans to work with disparate French personalities, whose volatile temperaments were enhanced by their feelings of defeat, humiliation, pride, and exile, but we could have done nothing without their generous assistance. The French helpers whom I remember most appreciatively were the unassuming patriots who sought no political or personal advantage. An example was Roger de Sinety, who lived with his family in a beautiful suburban estate, the Bordj el-Ahmin, outside Algiers. Isolated, it was a remarkable vantage point. Two days before the landings I went to these good friends and said I could not tell them why, but we wanted to take over their property for reasons they could perhaps divine. They asked no questions and moved the next day with their several small children. In Bordj el-Ahmin we installed our Algiers clandestine radio equipment and staff with perfect security. After the landings, the property became the headquarters of our OSS in Algiers, and it was not until long months later that the De Sinety family was able to recover its home, in very badly used condition. I regret that I cannot give detailed credit here to all the other French and American patriots who made possible the success of the Anglo-American expedition, but an account of their magnificent services in the African underground would require a book in itself. It was an inspiration to work with these men.

After General Weygand was recalled in November 1941 at German insistence, French Africa had no over-all commander because the position which had been specially created for Weygand was abolished when he departed. Admiral Raymond Fenard was given the title of Delegate General, and he took over part of Weygand's functions and occupied the same quarters, but he had no military command authority. We Americans were compelled, therefore, to investigate the capabilities and sound out the sentiments of numerous French Army and Navy officers to try to ascertain which ones probably would oppose our invasion, which might assist us, and which could go either way. When I came back from Washington in October 1942, one of the most important men whom I hoped against hope to bring to our side was the five-star Resident General of Morocco, Auguste Nogues, and I decided to make a final attempt to enlist him in our enterprise. Hitherto he had been warily friendly but always had refused to budge from the proclaimed policy that French Africa would be defended from attacks from any source whatever, Nazi or Allied. When this capable and intelligent officer and administrator decided to support the French-German armistice, after three days of struggle with his conscience in June 1940, the die was cast so far as he was concerned. I knew that this shrewd soldier, with several decades of experience in Morocco, familiar with all the intricate problems of the region, would be of incalculable assistance if only he would change his mind.

Nogues received me in his Rabat headquarters politely as usual, invited me to dinner, and after dinner gave me an opportunity to speak with him privately. I described as graphically as I could what an enormous war capacity the United States was developing, sufficient to supply all our global fronts. Then I delicately asked if, by any chance, the United States should reach a position where it could send half a million men to North Africa, fully equipped with planes, tanks, guns, warships, and all the rest, the General might not be interested. His reaction was explosive. "Do not try that!" he cried. "If you do, I will meet you with all the firepower I possess. It is too late for France to participate in this war now. We will do better to stay out. If Morocco becomes a battleground, it will be lost to France!" I reluctantly concluded we must eliminate Nogues from our schemes, and I reported his attitude to Washington and London and to our French associates in Algiers.

The over-all French command along the entire coast of North Africa was in the hands of the Navy, and Admiral Michelier—who later was responsible for much of our trouble—was violently opposed to American intervention. Unable to enlist the cooperation of Nogues or Michelier, we turned to General Emile-Marie Bethouart as the best alternative, and induced him to join our cause. Bethouart was only the divisional commander at Casablanca, but he bravely undertook to immobilize Nogues, his superior officer, on the night of the Allied landings. Bethouart, an honorable officer in the best French tradition, unfortunately did not prove adept in the unfamiliar role of a conspirator, and when the crucial hour struck—with inadequate notice—he let Nogues evade him and organize resistance, as Nogues had warned us he would do. I always have regretted and blamed myself for my failure to persuade Nogues to support the Allied invasion. Perhaps if I had been authorized to give him a more detailed description of our plans, he might have been more amenable. But I doubt it. In fact, if he had known more about it, Nogues might have considered our project irresponsibly reckless, as many American officers did, and might have communicated the whole plan to Vichy. And events since the war have demonstrated that his anxiety about French colonial relations was well founded, because the fighting in French Africa did indeed stimulate the movement for independence, not only in Morocco but in Tunisia and Algeria.

Nogues presented a serious problem, because he was powerful—and he was against our intervention. But a much more perilous problem was presented by Admiral Darlan, because Darlan had greater power than Nogues—and we did not know how he would fit into our plans.

Jean Charles François Darlan, a five-star admiral, had clung to his post of Commander in Chief not only of the Navy but of all French forces—naval, army and air. Darlan had been an Anglophobe through most of his naval career and was a bitter enemy of Britain's protégé, General de Gaulle. Darlan told me that his distrust of perfidious Albion dated from the Naval Conference of 1922 and its famous 5-5-3 ratio of naval power. Britain, he said, always feared and opposed a powerful French Navy. Darlan had resigned himself in 1940 to a Nazi victory and acted accordingly. British and American newspapers and propaganda agencies had vilified him for almost two years as the blackest of opportunists. And now this Admiral Darlan was secretly sending word to me that he was willing to participate in joint French-American military operations.

Darlan's proposal did not come as any bolt from the blue; he had been making discreet overtures to us for thirteen months. I had known this controversial naval officer for several years, but our early meetings had been casual. It used to be said in Paris and Vichy that Darlan's strategy was more clever in the realm of politics than on the high seas, but the Admiral certainly held the respect and admiration of most French Navy men. It was Darlan who had wangled appropriations to modernize and expand the French fleets, and it was Darlan who had induced the Nazis to release sixty thousand French sailors who were prisoners of war. It was inevitable that Marshal Pétain should appoint Darlan as Minister of Marine at the time of the armistice.

But when I returned briefly to Vichy in March 1941, I found myself conferring with the Admiral not as a Navy man but as "heir apparent" to the old Marshal himself. Darlan had succeeded in ousting his political rival, Pierre Laval, and had become Vice President of the State Council. Admiral Leahy was the American Ambassador at Vichy then, and Leahy has recorded in his memoirs: "As one sailor to another, we talked shop easily." Notwithstanding his professional bond, Ambassador Leahy told me that he regarded the Frenchman as ambitious and dangerous. "It was impossible for me to put any confidence in him," Leahy wrote in his book *I Was There*. "Darlan was a complete opportunist. He endeavored to walk a tightrope between the warring powers. . . . But he once told me that if the Allies appeared with sufficient force in North Africa to be successful against the Nazis, he would not oppose us."

On April 14, 1942, when Laval returned to power, Leahy decided that his own usefulness in Vichy had come to an end. The Ambassador would have returned to Washington immediately, but his wife was fatally ill and could not be moved. She died on April 21 and Leahy left for home on May 1. As he has recorded: "My final call was on Darlan in his Hotel du Parc office. He endeavored to put a good face on his changed status, emphasizing that he had full command of the national defense directly under Marshal Pétain. Once again he pledged that the French fleet would not be used against the U.S. Darlan also said that he personally wished to maintain the existing friendly relations with America and, with equal emphasis, that he did not wish to have any friendly relations with Great Britain."

After Leahy's departure, Darlan transferred his overtures to me through his agent in Algiers, Admiral Fenard. Darlan was not without a sense of humor. In speaking of Fenard, he once said that Fenard was the kind of naval officer who was not popular because he would give an order to have something done on the hour, and then five minutes before the hour inquire why the order was not executed. Fenard's first direct approach to me came on May 6, after he returned from consultations at Vichy with the deposed Darlan. Fenard pointed out the unpublicized fact that Darlan still retained top authority over the entire African military establishment. He went on to propose that henceforth the United States should regard French Africa as a separate unit which could and would resume hostilities against the Axis at the proper time—"but only when the Americans are able to provide the material which will make such action effective." Darlan was wary lest the Americans blunder into Africa before we had sufficient strength to outmatch the Germans there. The hit-and-run Anglo-De Gaulle fiasco at Dakar had not been forgotten, and it was feared that any similar abortive raid would provoke German occupation of North Africa, France's last high trump.

Throughout the next six months, up to the very last week before the Allied forces landed in Africa, Fenard kept in close touch with me, as did also Alain Darlan, the Admiral's young naval officer son, who seemed ardently pro-Allies. I reported to Washington that these two men begged us to believe that despite the necessity of keeping up deceptive appearances at Vichy, Darlan was convinced now of ultimate Allied victory and therefore was determined to defend both the fleet and French Africa against Nazi seizure. In this connection, Darlan proposed that French ships and soldiers should be assigned some place in the Allied military plans for Africa and for France itself. Fenard and Alain urged that Americans should be more understanding about Vichy's minor concessions to the Germans, so long as major demands were resisted. When I suggested that Americans would have more faith in Darlan's intentions if he had taken Ambassador Leahy into his confidence before "minor concessions" had been made, Alain explained that his father did not believe Americans could keep secrets. If Darlan talked to Germans, Alain said, he could be sure that nothing would leak out later in Berlin. The reverse was true in Washington,

Alain declared. While I let his remark pass without comment, I had to admit to myself that there was some truth in it. I had been embarrassed when some of my own confidential reports got into newspapers and broadcasts. When we sent secret telegrams to Washington, it was a standard joke to ask: "How soon will this one be broadcast by the BBC out of London?"

No response whatever came from Washington to my reports of Darlan's overtures in the spring and summer of 1942. It was only when planning started in earnest for the African expedition that the "Darlan problem" began to be seriously considered in London and Washington. So far as I know, it was first discussed by Eisenhower's Anglo-American staff during my visit to London in September. The expedition's planners were acutely conscious that their undertaking was extremely precarious and needed all the help it could get. And both Churchill and Roosevelt always kept their eyes fixed upon French warships, which were under Darlan's control.

During the nineteen months preceding the invasion, I had no personal meeting or correspondence of any kind with Darlan. Although the French Admiral and I were in Algiers at the same time on a few occasions, Darlan deliberately avoided meeting me personally. His son explained that any such meeting would be imprudent because German spies noted everybody who approached me. So on the night of November 7–8, while Allied troops were disembarking on the beaches of North Africa, the participation of Darlan in this campaign was still in doubt. There were two main reasons why no understanding with him had been reached up to the twelfth hour. For one thing, none of the Allies really trusted Darlan, especially in view of his intense dislike of the British. The second reason was that a firm agreement had been made two weeks before the landings to include General Henri Giraud in the Allied strategy, and it was thought impossible on such short notice to induce the two Frenchmen to accept joint operations.

The American purpose in working first with Weygand and then, after he was cashiered by Vichy, hitting almost in desperation on Giraud, was that we needed a well-known military leader who would be satisfied to fight the war and postpone political decisions for post-war France. The suggestion that Giraud might be the heroic General to inspire French support in Africa had been broached to us from several directions. This extraordinary old soldier had a brilliant service record as a young officer in North Africa. He knew the country well and he knew Arabs well and was generally respected by them. Giraud was somewhat of a specialist in escape. In World War I, as a wounded captain, he escaped from a German military hospital. In 1940, during the Battle of France, he again became a prisoner of war, but in the spring of 1942 escaped from the German fortress of Königstein on the

Elbe in Saxony. The Nazis had agreed under the armistice terms to respect Unoccupied France as a sanctuary, and the indomitable warrior went straight to Vichy to report to Marshal Pétain. Churchill and De Gaulle both spoke on the British radio to praise Giraud's feat, describing him as a splendid French patriot. As for myself, I recalled Giraud's optimism the first week of the war when I encountered him at the dismal railway station in Paris. I felt that he possessed at least the right temperament to lead Frenchmen from the Slough of Despond.

Giraud's position was unique in other respects. Having escaped by his own efforts, skillfully aided by French Army Intelligence, he was under no obligation whatever to the Nazis. Some French military leaders holding African commands had been released by their captors on the proviso that they would not take up arms against the Germans during the period of the Armistice. This stipulation was a part of the Franco-German Armistice, and the paroled French officers had no doubt had representations made on their behalf through the Armistice Commission at Wiesbaden. Giraud had made no promise, nor had he sworn allegiance to Marshal Pétain. So he was free to set about organizing French resistance against the Germans, preparing for the day he confidently anticipated when American forces would arrive.

We had no problem getting into confidential communication with Giraud because one of our boldest French colleagues, Jacques Lemaigre-Dubreuil, was available to sound out the hero of the hour, who was then living under cover in the south of France. Lemaigre-Dubreuil was a wealthy, aggressive industrial promoter. Through his wife's family, he had acquired a great deal of the peanut oil industry both in France and in French Africa—of prime economic importance during Europe's shortage of fats—and his business interests gave him an excuse for maintaining immensely useful high-level contacts. He had ready access to top people like Laval in Vichy and German and French authorities in Paris. Freedom of movement, which required French and German permits for everything, constituted a serious practical problem in our underground operations. Communications were exceedingly tight and difficult. Lemaigre-Dubreuil exploited his advantages with hardy courage.

My acquaintance with Lemaigre-Dubreuil dated from my early days in Algiers in 1940, when in our first private talk he assured me he would do anything he could to bring about the defeat of Germany. He told me that he had arranged a carefully concocted police record of himself which indicated that he had been a pro-Nazi collaborator long before the war, and that he had placed this false record in files available to the Germans. By this means, he explained, he had obtained permits to travel wherever he had business interests, in Occupied France, Vichy France, and both West and North Africa. After such trips he would give me an account of his conversations, which provided invaluable information. He warned me that some French big businessmen believed that their interest would best be served by a German victory, because they thought that a British victory would result in the bolshevization of Europe. He said he opposed such ideas but that he had to pretend to agree with them. Lemaigre-Dubreuil's melodramatic tale was pretty hard to believe but I passed it on to Washington, sprinkling my report liberally with salt.

As time passed and the magnate continued to bring me information about relations between French industrialists and the Germans which proved correct, my confidence in him grew. We tested him out in various ways and became convinced of his trustworthiness. Certainly nobody else could have provided the kind of support he gave to our African project for two years; nobody else combined his important contacts with his inspired daring. For our purposes he was a perfect intermediary as he continuously traveled the lengthy route from Dakar, where he owned one huge peanut oil plant, to Dunkirk, in Occupied France opposite the coast of England, where he owned another. He was falsely accused by Pertinax, the celebrated French journalist, of being a Nazi collaborator who was profiting by his perfidy, amassing a huge fortune as a "king of petroleum." Actually, he was in the peanut oil business, and after the war he successfully sued Pertinax for libel on account of the false charges. Lemaigre-Dubreuil, his charming wife and two fine children, all anti-Nazi and eager for the French to resume combat, were a source of inspiration and comfort to me.

Lemaigre-Dubreuil soon reported to us that he had talked alone with Giraud and learned that the General was planning for the day when American troops would land in France. It required several other clandestine meetings with Giraud before the General would agree to participate in a campaign in Africa. He assented only on condition that the expedition would be an American operation only, that the Americans would land simultaneously somewhere in France, and that he or another French officer would be placed in over-all command of American as well as French troops who fought anywhere on French soil. During my September visit to Eisenhower's headquarters in London, I explained that Giraud was not likely to come out of France unless promised that the command in North Africa would be French. This was not personal ambition, which Giraud never had, but a matter of guaranteeing French sovereignty and of demonstrating to the Arabs and Berbers American acceptance of it. Eisenhower replied that the question of command must wait; it could not be settled at that time. The matter was still unsettled when I finally informed Giraud of the approximate date of the invasion, only a few days before the Anglo-American troops actually arrived.

Soon after we began negotiations with him, Giraud named General Charles Emmanuel Mast to represent him in Algiers. Mast was deputy commander of the XIX Army Corps stationed in Algeria, and he was the first French general officer to commit himself decisively to the support of our expedition. Mast had been a military attaché in Tokyo and he possessed an unusually broad grasp of world politics. Thus, on my return to Algiers from Washington on October 16, I was confronted on the one hand by General Mast, representing Giraud; and on the other hand by Admiral Fenard, representing Darlan. Both officers sensed that some kind of decision must have been made about a campaign in Africa, and both made new and encouraging overtures to me. By that time I was reporting on such matters only to the White House and to Eisenhower, as instructed by Roosevelt. On October 17, I sent several messages about these new overtures, and on the same day Admiral Leahy, acting for the President, sent me a cablegram authorizing me to initiate any arrangement with Darlan which, in my judgment, might assist the military operations.

Upon receiving my messages, Eisenhower devised a formula which he hoped might induce Giraud and Darlan to work as a team, dividing the top French command between them. This formula was discussed by military and political planners in both London and Washington and was unofficially approved. Churchill was particularly enthusiastic about the possibility of Darlan's participation. As Eisenhower notes in his book *Crusade in Europe:* "Just before I left England, Churchill had earnestly remarked, 'If I could meet Darlan, much as I hate him, I would cheerfully crawl on my hands and knees for a mile if by doing so I could get him to bring that fleet of his into the circle of Allied Forces.'" There was no thought in the minds of American war planners that a "Darlan deal" would not be acceptable in Washington, although none was attempted before the landings.

While I was not permitted to inform General Mast how soon military operations were to commence, I was authorized to give him positive assurances of American support, and he urged that the time had come now for staff talks between French and American officers. This was a possibility I had discussed with Eisenhower in London, and after an interchange of messages, the general asked me to arrange a secret meeting somewhere along the Mediterranean coast to which the Americans could come in a submarine. The intensive Vichy and Axis policing of the area made this the only feasible means of access. The place chosen was an isolated farmhouse owned by Henri Tessier, one of our French associates, near the town of Cherchell, about seventy-five miles west of Algiers. There a French group headed by Mast met an American group headed by Eisenhower's deputy commander, General Mark Clark. The American group included two officers who afterward gained military renown: General Lyman Lemnitzer, who became Chairman of the Joint Chiefs of Staff; and Captain (later

Admiral) Jerauld Wright, recently retired as chief naval commander of NATO and of U.S. forces in the Atlantic.

That meeting at Cherchell was one of the oddest conferences of the war, because the French participants in those staff talks were ignorant of the essential details of the Allied plans. Both Clark and I were under instructions to avoid giving the French conferees specific information about the timing of the expedition or the exact locations selected for troop landings. So these discussions inevitably misled our French associates, who assumed they had months in which to prepare for African D-Day, whereas we Americans knew they had only sixteen days. In fact, the first slow convoys of the expedition already were starting from the United States as we talked. Because of the secrecy imposed upon the American negotiators, the Cherchell meeting failed to clarify the status of French commanders either in military or political affairs. For example, Giraud's representatives requested from Clark positive assurances that Giraud would have over-all command of the Allied forces, American as well as French. Clark explained that this was impractical during the preliminary operations, but he agreed that Giraud would be given over-all command "as soon as possible"—a purposely vague phrase. The question of Darlan's participation also was discussed at Cherchell. Clark outlined the Giraud-Darlan formula devised by Eisenhower, but Mast objected vigorously to the inclusion of Darlan. He declared that the Admiral was belatedly trying to climb on the Allied bandwagon, and that the Allies did not need him because Giraud could swing the support of the African Army and Air Force, and the Navy would soon fall in line. So the conference at Cherchell left Darlan's status unresolved.

A few days after the invasion, Clark gave a picturesque account of the Cherchell meeting to war correspondents attached to Eisenhower's temporary headquarters in Gibraltar. Since wartime security made it advisable to conceal the serious complications which had arisen at Cherchell, Clark diverted attention from the political aspects by describing some comical aspects of the venture. At one point the local police had burst in upon us, forcing the American visitors to hide in a wine cellar, while I posed as a somewhat inebriated member of a raucous social gathering. Fortunately the police were not looking for military conspirators but for smugglers. They had been tipped off by our host's Arab servants, who suspected that smugglers were involved in the unusual activities around the remote farmhouse, and hoped to collect the generous rewards for information leading to seizure of smuggled goods. This incident made lively newspaper copy, a welcome diversion from the war's somber happenings, and Clark further embellished his tale by relating how he lost his pants while getting back into the submarine. But the amusing manner in which Clark described the dangerous French-American meetings added unintentionally to the British-American public's downgrading of the importance—actually the vital necessity—of French assistance to our precarious expedition. Few Britons or Americans appreciated at the time of the invasion, or in the months which followed, how serious prolonged French resistance would have been to the Allied operations. Support from the French military and political administrations in Africa was even more essential to the campaign's success during the months following the invasion than it was on African D-Day.

The Cherchell talks ended on October 23, leaving me just two weeks to complete my share of preparations for arrival of the troops. Lemaigre-Dubreuil flew off immediately to the south of France to report latest developments to Giraud, and on October 27 he brought back a disturbing letter from the General, who wanted an agreement in writing that he would be placed in charge of the "Interallied Command" forty-eight hours after the expedition's arrival. Giraud also wanted assurance of Allied intervention in France itself very soon after the African operations began. He proved quite innocent of the shortage of Allied maritime shipping, that terrible bottleneck affecting most American military efforts. Obviously Giraud's conception of the imminent campaign differed sharply from the American-British plans, as did the conception of many French officers, and the question was how to reconcile these differences promptly, while still observing security regulations. It seemed to me that we would have to give the Giraud group more specific information about our plans, and on October 28—my forty-eighth birthday—I requested and received permission from Eisenhower to inform Mast that the expedition would arrive "early in November." Mast's reception of this news was far more agitated than I had expected; for a time there seemed some danger that in his excitement he might give away the whole show. He was distressed by American lack of confidence in their French allies, and by what he described as a form of political blackmail so far as he and his fellow conspirators were concerned. However, he regained control of his emotions, and we arranged to send word to Giraud.

On November 1 an alarming letter came from the general, declaring it was absolutely impossible for him to leave France before November 20. He seemed so positive about this that, after a prolonged unhappy discussion with Mast, I sent a message to President Roosevelt late that day recommending that the expedition be delayed for two weeks. My message concluded: "I am convinced that the invasion of North Africa without favorable French High Command will be a catastrophe. The delay of two weeks, unpleasant as it may be, involving technical considerations of which I am ignorant, is insignificant compared with the result involving serious opposition of the French Army to our landing."

In the years since I sent that message I have learned enough about military operations to realize how ridiculous it must have seemed then to Marshall and Eisenhower. The intricate movement of vast fleets from the United States as well as England was already under way, and a delay of even one day would upset the meticulous plans which had been meshed into one master plan by hundreds of staff officers of all branches of the armed forces of both Allied powers. Eisenhower cabled to Marshall: "It is inconceivable that Murphy can recommend such a delay with his intimate knowledge of the operation and the present location of troops and convoys afloat." What Eisenhower did not know was that I never had had any military training, that I lacked even the elementary instruction in strategy and tactics which is required today of all Foreign Service officers, and that I had no "intimate knowledge" whatever of the North African expedition. Everybody assumed that somebody else had "briefed" me thoroughly, but nobody had. Eisenhower's message added: "It is likewise inconceivable to me that our mere failure to concede such demands as have been made would result in having the French North African Army meet us with serious opposition. Recommend the President advise Murphy immediately that his suggested action is utterly impossible in view of present advanced state of operation and that we will proceed to execute this operation with more determination than ever."

The reply to my desperate recommendation came to me not from Eisenhower but from Leahy in Washington, who cabled on November 2: "The decision of the President is that the operation will be carried out as now planned and that you will do your utmost to secure the understanding and cooperation of the French officials with whom you are now in contact." This presidential directive clearly left it up to me to deal with our French allies in whatever ways I thought best. So late that same day Lemaigre-Dubreuil flew again to the south of France, carrying my assurances couched in ambiguous phrases that everything could be arranged to Giraud's satisfaction. In that final frenzied week I was the only American in contact with Giraud, and it was my responsibility to decide how much to tell him. While I completely trusted this French patriot's good faith, I had been warned so frequently against possible leaks that I felt I could not tell him everything without endangering our expedition.

My final letter to Giraud emphasized two points. First: "The Government of the United States considers the French nation as an ally, and will treat it as such." Second: "So far as the command is concerned, the Government of the United States has no thought or desire but to put the military command of the region in the hands of the French as soon as possible. However, during those phases of the operation that involve the landing, establishing the security of French North Africa and providing the necessary bases, it is considered essential that the American command organization which has been set up with so much effort and difficulty for this special operation should remain unchanged." This was the most direct reply I dared to make to Giraud's insistence that he become commander of American as well as French forces forty-eight hours after the invasion started. I said nothing about the British troops in the expedition or of the decision not to make simultaneous landings in France. These omissions misled the General and his group, but under the circumstances I felt that I could not be more explicit.

Our irreplaceable intermediary, Lemaigre-Dubreuil, returned quickly, reporting that Giraud had greeted him with an "avalanche of reproaches" because of the short notice. The General declared that the underground network in France was so far advanced that it needed his constant attention now. However, he finally consented to come to Algiers a day or two before the invasion so he would be on the spot when the Americans began to land.

During the final pre-invasion fortnight I followed my orders to communicate directly with the White House and with Eisenhower through military channels. The British had better communications than we did in the Mediterranean, and the British Navy picked up and forwarded to London many of my radio messages. The State Department, which I still formally represented, did not receive my most significant reports until some time afterward. For instance, the State Department asked me on March 10, 1943—four months after the invasion—to forward my last-minute correspondence with Giraud, which Secretary of State Hull and his Washington staff had not seen even at that late date. Roosevelt's decision to draft me for work under his personal direction, and his determination not to confide in Secretary Hull so far as Africa was concerned, had one unfortunate consequence. At the first news of the invasion, on November 8, before Hull really knew what was happening, the Secretary called a press conference and claimed a large measure of credit for the State Department. Hull's impulsive action was understandable. For years he had been unfairly criticized for his "Vichy policy," which in fact was Roosevelt's personal policy, and which the President often shaped without consulting his Secretary of State. Now, when our relations with the Vichy Government seemed to be paying off, Hull was disposed to exult at the discomfiture of his journalistic and other critics. If he had been informed of the actual circumstances in Algiers on the day he held his press conference, the Secretary would have been more prudent in his remarks, for his critics soon would acquire an abundance of new ammunition to use against him.

When the fateful day of November 7 arrived, I endeavored to maintain my pose of outward calm, remaining in my Algiers office until early evening. We had set up assembly points in nearby apartments to avoid any abnormal activity around the American consulate general, and our American staff checked and rechecked in secret stations the pre-invasion assignments of our own men and their French associates in Algeria, Morocco, and Tunisia. As usual, I received a number of uninvited and unexpected callers at my office. Among my visitors that day was Ferhat Abbas, already then the most ardent Algerian Arab nationalist. He had approached me before once or twice to discuss Algerian independence, and now he had learned that I had recently returned from Washington and he wanted to inquire what was the American Government's latest attitude toward an autonomous Algeria? I repeated what I had told him before, that Americans were generally sympathetic to all desires for independence but that our present purposes in Africa, as everywhere else, were concentrated upon defeating the Nazis. We earnestly hoped, I added, that all our friends would join us in winning the war. Abbas gave me the impression then of being a moderate and reasonable man, and his organization made no difficulties for our military operations later when he might have hampered us seriously. I was disappointed after the war when Abbas, as head of the exiled Algerian Provisional Government, became involved in one of the longest and most unhappy wars in French history.

Another visitor late that afternoon, when the arrival of our forces was only a few hours distant, was an old acquaintance of mine from Paris and Vichy, former Premier and Foreign Minister Pierre-Etienne Flandin. He was very excited about unfounded rumors of a threatened Axis invasion of Tunisia, and dropped in to warn me. "If you Americans do not come here in full force within a month," he cried, "it will be too late!" It was with some difficulty that I restrained myself from giving any hint to the veteran statesman of the imminent Allied arrival.

Among last callers that afternoon were three charming and friendly French ladies, volunteer members of an Army ambulance unit which had come to Algiers from France soon after the armistice in 1940 and had done excellent work for more than two years. But now, they informed me, things were so quiet here that they were becoming bored and were thinking of returning to France where they might find more useful work to do. They asked my advice about this, and I pretended to consider their problem thoughtfully. Finally I suggested, "Perhaps it would be a good idea for you ladies to come back again in a few days. I'll think the matter over in the meantime."

NINE

A FRANTIC NIGHT, NOVEMBER 7–8, 1942

African D-Day, November 8, 1942, arrived at last. From England and from the United States great convoys of eight hundred ships, carrying 110,000 Americans and Britons, were converging upon a score of landing beaches strung along twelve hundred miles of Atlantic and Mediterranean coasts. The time had come to test our two years of hopeful soundings and schemings. From a military standpoint, Operation Torch was a partial bluff. Allied war planners had estimated that at least half a million men were needed for this operation, and the United States and Britain could spare less than a fourth that number for Africa because of other commitments all over the globe.

No campaign of World War II depended upon so many intangible factors. If Franco should decide to intervene, because of Spanish interests in Morocco and alleged sympathy with Hitler and Mussolini, Spanish troops might easily overwhelm the less than invincible Rock of Gibraltar which Eisenhower had boldly chosen as his temporary headquarters. I was convinced that Franco had no intention of intervening in French Africa, but there was grave suspicion and doubt in the Pentagon. Nor was it certain how the Germans might react, whether their own invasions of Libya and Russia had left them with reserves sufficient to defeat us in French Africa. But the most dangerous intangible was what the French themselves might do. Time and again Marshal Pétain and French military officers had proclaimed that they would resist any invasion attempt from any source whatever. If French armed forces should resist us strongly, our risky operations would be jeopardized, and the Spaniards and Germans and Italians might be encouraged to leap into the battle while it hung in balance. Thus the French had it in their power to be of immense help or hindrance to our expedition. It is my belief that our French sympathizers could have eliminated nearly all resistance to the invasion if we had given them sufficient advance notice to prepare for our landings. But we were allowed a maximum of four days! The Combined Chiefs of Staff and the Anglo-American planners believed it more important to safeguard the element of surprise than to inform our French associates.

Eisenhower's skeleton staff had flown into Gibraltar just thirty-six hours before D-Day. From his command post in caves dug deep inside the great rock, Eisenhower would receive reports of the far-flung operations and shape his strategy accordingly. I was to keep in communication with Gibraltar by clandestine radio. Our local plans, as finally fixed, provided that Giraud would arrive in Algiers the day before the landings, and that British submarines would deliver twenty tons of modern small arms, walkie-talkies, and similar equipment for French underground fighters whom we had recruited. Colonel Van Hecke, the leader of thirty thousand trained members of the youth organization, *Chantiers de la Jeunesse,* was one of the very few Frenchmen to whom I gave the maximum four days' notice. Like General Mast and the others, he complained that four days was totally inadequate to provide really effective French assistance, but my instructions on this point were strict.

Millions of Americans who have served in our armed forces are more familiar now with military operations than I was then. These millions know that it was too much to expect that such a tremendous and complicated enterprise as the African military expedition would go strictly according to plan. Even so, an excessive number of major mishaps disrupted our military and political schemes during the critical twenty-four hours before the expedition was established in Algiers, the controlling center for the whole of French Africa.

For instance, Roosevelt himself had informed me that the expedition would seek to land about five thousand men in Tunisia in the first wave, and our resistance leaders were alerted on that basis. But there was a last-minute cancellation without notice to me. Postwar reports show that the Allied Chiefs of Staff found that the necessary shipping for this risky operation was not available. Since we in Algiers were given no warning of the change in plans, our friends in Tunisia naturally believed they had been deliberately deceived by us.

Then General Giraud, whom we had selected to be the top-ranking Frenchman on the spot, did not arrive when expected. I sent repeated radio queries asking: "Where is Giraud?" I received the surprising reply that he was at Gibraltar and would arrive "shortly." I could not understand why Giraud had not come directly to Algiers, as planned. Later I learned that he had gone to Gibraltar at the suggestion of two wise and experienced diplomats, H. Freeman Matthews, my successor in the American Embassy at Vichy, and Harold Mack of the British Foreign Office, who were accompanying Eisenhower as political advisers on the French African venture. They knew from copies of my correspondence with Giraud that the Frenchman expected to assume command of Americans as well as French troops almost immediately after the landings, and that he held other misconceptions about Anglo-American plans. The political advisers felt that these matters should be clarified before Giraud moved into Africa, so they proposed to Eisenhower that he talk with Giraud before the landings. Although there were excellent reasons for this decision to set the record straight with Giraud, the last-minute stopover at Gibraltar seriously upset our local plans at Algiers, which were predicated upon Giraud's presence before the start of the invasion.

Giraud was accorded so little advance notice that he could be evacuated from his hideaway in southern France only by submarine. The French general insisted that it must be an American submarine. There was none in the Mediterranean. So Captain Jerauld Wright was placed in technical command of a small British submarine to make it "American." This is said to be the first time an American naval officer commanded a British naval vessel in wartime. When Giraud arrived at Gibraltar and Eisenhower informed him just what his status would be, Giraud promptly announced that he would withdraw from participation. He argued—correctly, as matters turned out—that his position would be gravely compromised with other French generals if he agreed to subordinate French troops to Americans in a campaign on French territory. He would have been even more balky if he had been told that the expedition included as many British as American soldiers, a fact withheld from all our French associates before the invasion. Giraud yielded only after two days of round-the-clock persuasion at Gibraltar, and by the time he arrived in Algiers thirty-six hours after the landings, the political situation had drastically changed. His absence on that night of November 7–8 compelled hasty improvisations in our local operations which affected the whole of French North Africa and of France itself.

Not only was Giraud absent on that critical night, but our underground fighters never did receive the weapons which had been promised through OSS channels. Colonel Eddy, our brilliant naval attaché in Tangier, had assurances from the OSS and the British SOE that deliveries would be made on isolated beaches at night in plenty of time. So it was maddening to us all when night after night, despite messages that deliveries would be made at specific points, the Frenchmen dispatched to receive the precious equipment were disappointed. Both Eddy and I were later convinced that the British SOE let us down because they had no confidence in our judgment or our French underground. As a result, most of our French supporters in Algiers and at other military centers along the coasts had to depend on a weird collection of inadequate weapons, and their military capabilities were largely symbolic.

But the Allied expedition was inexorably approaching the African shores and would not wait for us to repair our disrupted plans. During the last daylight hours of November 7, many in Algiers learned of a huge Allied convoy steaming majestically through the Mediterranean, said to be bound for Malta, which was in dire need of supplies. Only a few possessing our secret even suspected that these ships would soon turn sharply toward Algiers and unload their military cargo.

Shortly before midnight our clandestine radio received the agreed code message from London that the Torch landings were beginning. The BBC broadcast was in French: "*Allo, Robert. Franklin arrivé.*" So, two hours before armed American forces were supposed to enter Algiers, I signaled full speed ahead for our local operation. Our resistance groups began to seize key points in Algiers, taking over quietly and with little opposition. They soon controlled the city's police and power stations, military headquarters, communication and transport centers. They placed patrols inconspicuously around military points, to be seized as the Americans appeared. The hope was to capture Algiers without firing a shot. Being assured that plans were going smoothly thus far, I proceeded to call upon General Alphonse Juin, the ranking Army officer at the moment in the whole of French Africa. His title under the Vichy Government was Commander in Chief of Ground Forces, and he lived in the suburb of el-Biar at the official residence formerly occupied by Weygand. I had intended to have Giraud accompany me on this call, and was worried about that general's failure to arrive.

In Churchill's war memoirs, he states that the Allies had a prior understanding with Juin and that he directed the underground in Algiers. That is an error. We had no prior understanding of any kind with this important commander, although he never concealed from us his hatred of Nazis and Fascists. Juin had been considered as a possible no. 1 Frenchman in the African campaign but he had been ruled out because he had given his word of honor, when released from a Nazi prison, not to fight against Germans again in World War II. Although I believed he would consider this pledge invalid because made under duress, it would have been too dangerous to count upon that. Juin might have felt obliged to inform Vichy of anything we told him.

When I reached Juin's residence, the Villa des Oliviers, he was sound asleep and the place was guarded by tall Senegalese soldiers. After some difficulty I was admitted and persuaded a servant to wake the general. He came to the drawing room in pink-striped pajamas, tousled and sleepy, but my news snapped him wide awake. I told him, as calmly as I could, that an American expeditionary force of half a million men was about to land all along the coasts of French North Africa. According to my instructions, I multiplied the size of the expedition and made no mention of its British components. I explained: "I wish to tell you about this in advance, because our talks over the years have convinced me that you desire above all else to see the liberation of France, which can come about only through cooperation with the United States."

Juin was startled and shocked. He ejaculated, "What! You mean that the convoys yesterday in the Mediterranean are not going to Malta but will land here?" When I nodded, he said, "But you told me only a week ago that the United States would not attack us!" I replied that the American expeditionary force was not coming to attack the French, but was coming at French invitation to cooperate in the liberation of France. Juin asked, "Who gave this invitation?" When I said, "General Giraud," he asked whether Giraud was in Algiers. I said we expected him momentarily. Juin began to walk agitatedly up and down, stopping now and then to express vehement regrets that he had not been consulted sooner. But he did not question my explanation that Giraud's freedom from pledges to the Germans and to Vichy had predisposed Americans in his favor. I added earnestly that, having heard Juin express his sentiments so often, we had been confident of his support when the time came. After a few more minutes of floor-pacing and thinking out loud, Juin said, "If the matter were entirely in my hands, I would be with you. But, as you know, Darlan is in Algiers. He outranks me and no matter what decision I might make, Darlan could immediately overrule it." Without any hesitation I replied, "Very well, let us talk with Darlan."

The melodramatic role played in the African campaign by Admiral Darlan provoked one of the bitterest controversies of the war. For more than two years Darlan had been broadcasting anti-British and anti-De Gaulle statements from Vichy, and apparently collaborating closely with the Nazis. British and De Gaulle propagandists naturally did everything possible to discredit him. So when an arrangement was made with Darlan in Algiers, protests in the United States and Great Britain became so intense that they distracted attention from the brilliant military achievements of the campaign, and threatened to affect seriously the reputations of those responsible for making the agreement with Darlan, including Eisenhower. If Eisenhower had not displayed the same aptitude for handling political emergencies as he did for meeting military emergencies, his African campaign might have failed disastrously. In that case, Dwight D. Eisenhower's place in history would be very different, because somebody else would have become Supreme Commander in Europe.

But that night at Juin's residence, I entertained no doubts whatever about bringing Darlan into our enterprise, because my authorization in this matter had come from Roosevelt himself in the cablegram sent October 17 by Leahy, directing me to initiate any arrangement with Darlan which in my judgment might assist the military operations. So at the very hour when our invasion forces were beginning to disembark, I asked Juin to telephone the Admiral. Among the several dramatic features of the "Darlan deal," not the least was the circumstance that the Admiral happened to be in Algiers that night. He had arrived unexpectedly because his son, Alain, who had talked with me on behalf of his father, had been stricken with infantile paralysis. Darlan was staying at the home of his representative in Algiers, Admiral Fenard, and Juin immediately got him on the telephone. Juin informed Darlan that I had just arrived with a most urgent message for him, and Juin offered to go with me to Darlan. But the latter said he would come to Juin's residence, and arrived with Fenard in less than twenty minutes.

Meeting Darlan again for the first time in nineteen months, I told him the news in the fewest possible words. His first reaction was to turn purple, exclaiming, "I have known for a long time that the British are stupid, but I always believed Americans were more intelligent. Apparently you have the same genius as the British for making massive blunders!" He went on to say that if the Americans had waited even a few weeks, we could have received effective French cooperation in a program of simultaneous military operations in France itself as well as in Africa. Now that the Americans had made a premature unilateral attack, he asked angrily, what would happen to France?

For at least fifteen minutes Darlan paced the floor of the long room, puffing vigorously on his pipe, and I paced right along beside him, adjusting my stride to fit the steps of this exceptionally short naval officer. I employed every argument I could conceive to persuade Darlan of his unique opportunity to strike an effective blow now for the liberation of France. His behavior left no doubt in my mind that our action had come as a complete and disagreeable surprise to him, and that he was wondering how much of my story to believe. Among other arguments advanced, I reminded Darlan how in July 1941 he had told Ambassador Leahy that if ever the United States would be prepared to send a half million equipped American soldiers and several thousand tanks and planes to Marseilles, to notify him and he would be ready to cooperate. "That moment has now arrived!" I exclaimed with as much eloquence as I could, and with considerable stretching of the facts. "It is your responsibility to arrange that no

French blood will be shed by senseless resistance to the American landings already in progress."

At the end of a half hour during which I did most of the talking while Darlan seemed to be following his own thoughts rather than my words, he still was undecided, murmuring, "I have given my oath to Pétain and preserved allegiance to the Marshal for two years. I cannot revoke that now. This premature action is not at all what we have been hoping for." I asked then whether he would cooperate if Pétain authorized him to do so. Darlan considered my question for a few moments, and finally said that of course he would cooperate if the marshal approved. He called in Admiral Battet, his secretary, and drafted a message while Juin and Fenard and I looked on, outlining the situation and asking for a free hand in dealing with it.

The message written, we came next to the matter of dispatching it, and this confronted us with a most embarrassing situation. Unknown to me but intended for my protection, a group of forty volunteer underground men commanded by a courageous youth in the uniform of a French *aspirant* (there is no equivalent rank in our Army; an *aspirant* is one who is hoping to become a lieutenant) had surrounded Juin's house and taken the regular guards into custody. So when Juin, Darlan, Fenard, and Battet walked out the front door to the graveled patio, expecting to send a naval message to admiralty headquarters on the waterfront, we were stopped by the young soldier and his colleagues, all elaborately armed with a miscellaneous assortment of weapons. Surprised, Juin demanded of the *aspirant*, "Who are you?" Calmly the youth replied, "I have no information to give you except to say that no one will be permitted to pass except the representative from the American Consulate General." Everyone turned to me and Juin asked, "Does this mean we are prisoners?" I truthfully replied that it looked that way, but that I was as much surprised as they.

I then offered to have Vice Consul Pendar, who was waiting in an automobile in the street, deliver the message to the admiralty. This offer was reluctantly accepted and we returned to the house. My hosts obviously still doubted that I had been unaware that Juin's residence was surrounded, and they were disagreeably affected. There began a miserably awkward period of waiting and pacing up and down. Not much conversation. Later I learned that when Pendar delivered the message to the French naval officer in charge of the port, the latter became suspicious, checked with Darlan on the telephone, and then took Pendar into custody for several hours. The message never was acknowledged. The word which did go out to Vichy was that Darlan and Juin were prisoners of Americans.

Meanwhile the hour of 2:30 A.M., when American troops were due to reach Algiers, had long passed. I had prolonged the talks with Darlan and Juin as much as I could, expecting every minute that the arrival of armed Americans would lend force to my elocution, but the hours dragged on to six o'clock and still no word came from the expedition. For many days I had gotten very little sleep, and I hazily began to wonder if I had made the terrible mistake of starting things a day early. Certainly something had gone wrong. While I was becoming more tense, Darlan became more relaxed, and we sat down and had a dispassionate discussion of the possibilities before us now. When I told him the entire story of how we had arranged matters with Giraud, he shook his head, saying positively, "Giraud is not your man. Politically he is a child. He is just a good divisional commander, nothing more." Unfortunately, that analysis proved correct.

At 6:30 A.M., four hours after American troops were due, we heard excited voices outside and discovered that our underground helpers had been overpowered by a group of state police, Gardes Mobiles. Our friends had done more than had been asked of them, controlling the city for hours beyond the time appointed for their relief. But when daylight came, regular French Army headquarters discovered the strange situation, and Juin's residence was one of the first places they investigated. I went out into the garden just as fifty Gardes Mobiles equipped with submachine guns rushed the place. I was brusquely taken into custody, with a tommy gun poked in my back, and unceremoniously hustled together with Pendar into a small pavilion which served as a guardhouse. It was guarded by Senegalese soldiers and one of them, not doubting that we were to be shot, offered me a Gitane cigarette. Admiral Fenard got me released some minutes later. The Gardes Mobiles explained later that in the confusion they had understood we were Germans.

General Juin's aide, Major d'Orange, came in swinging his heavy-caliber Army pistol, swearing he would kill that *cochon,* Jean Rigault, for his stupidity in plotting the seizure of Algiers. D'Orange and I had been good friends, but he was understandably aggrieved to be caught unawares by the Allied landings and he told me sternly that I was under arrest. Darlan said he would accept responsibility for me. He asked Fenard to stay with me in Juin's house while he and Juin drove off to Fort L'Empereur, the military headquarters in Algiers. They said they had grave doubts about my story, for which I did not blame them. By that time I also was experiencing grave doubts, owing to the non-appearance of American soldiers or any word from the "vice consuls" posted on the assigned beaches to receive our troops and guide them into the city. However, it was not long before Juin's headquarters informed Fenard by telephone that Americans were indeed landing all along the Algerian and Moroccan coasts, and that our expedition undoubtedly was a large one. I kept up a running argument with Fenard to let me loose to find out what had gone wrong, but I was not permitted to leave Juin's heavily guarded house until mid-afternoon.

Darlan returned about three o'clock and requested me to establish contact with Major General Charles W. Ryder, the Eastern Task Force commanding general, who was said to be on a beach about ten miles west of Algiers. Darlan provided a chauffeur-driven automobile bearing both a French and a white flag for the drive through the advancing American forces. By that time there was a volume of brisk small arms fire in front of the house. Before getting into the car I made a quick reconnaissance down the street and saw a platoon of American soldiers hugging the wall and firing as they advanced in our direction. With the white flag prominently displayed on the front fender of our car, we moved cautiously in their direction. They stopped firing and waited. I came up to them, introduced myself, maintained a respectful distance as ordered by the young lieutenant in command, and shouted an explanation of the circumstances. The lieutenant asked me to repeat the story slowly. Then, apparently convinced it was not a ruse, he allowed me to walk up to him. I asked his name and he replied, "Lieutenant Gieser." I could not help a smile and the remark, "You are the best looking Gieser I have seen in a long time!" That seemed to convince him I was a bona fide American. He detailed one of his men to accompany me and we drove down to the landing beach without further incident.

The first person I met on the beach was Randolph Churchill in a Ranger uniform. He seemed to know about me and said something to the effect that the British diplomatic service could use a few like me. I considered that quite a compliment. He took me to General Ryder, whom I had never met. I explained quickly the situation at Algiers, the decision of Darlan to ask for a local cease-fire, and said I was ready to drive Ryder at once to French headquarters where the entire staff awaited him. The General was short of vehicles and readily accepted my offer of a lift. Then he paused and said, "But I must send a message to Gibraltar and get into a fresh uniform." I expressed the hope that he would hurry. He sat down on a rock to dictate the message to an aide. It took him forever to dictate a paragraph. He seemed dazed. He referred vaguely again to his need for a fresh uniform. Sensing my impatience he said, "You will have to forgive me. I haven't slept for a week." I knew then exactly how he felt because I also had not slept much for several days. I took him by the arm gently but firmly and we were in the car and on our way to Fort L'Empereur. Ryder was a delightful man and a fine soldier. He told me that political matters were not his specialty, and that he hoped General Mark Clark would "buzz over fast from Gib" to take charge of that work.

When we arrived at the fort we found about fifty French officers standing rather formally in a large room with Darlan and Juin at the head of a table covered with green baize. Just as we entered the room, one of our American planes came over and dropped a stick of bombs at what seemed a distance of perhaps a hundred yards. An ecstatic smile spread over Ryder's face, and he stood still and exclaimed, "How wonderful! This is the first time since World War I that I have been under fire." His pleasure was not shared by the French officers, and a moment of icy silence followed. I presented General Juin and talked fast. After a short discussion, both parties signed a preliminary cease-fire which enabled orders to be issued immediately to stop the shooting in the Algiers area.

As darkness fell on Algiers on November 8, the city's heterogeneous population was remarkably placid. The day's events had given the outward impression of brilliant planning, executed with precision. Only a few hours after the first American and British troops hit beaches near Algiers, two of the highest-ranking French officers in Africa had personally arranged a local cease-fire, and this had been imposed almost without incident. They also had tentatively promised to arrange similar cease-fires throughout French Africa. To my embarrassment, several French acquaintances whom I encountered that night offered their hearty congratulations. They did not suspect how deceptive was this outward appearance of spectacular success, how badly some of our plans had misfired, how close Algiers had come to a disastrous bombardment, and how unsettled the relationships were between disputing French factions.

One of the unscheduled events which occurred during the Algiers landings was that a British destroyer carrying American soldiers attempted to force its way into port—setting off explosions in gasoline tanks, damaging other installations, causing unnecessary casualties—and was then compelled to withdraw without unloading its troops. Even more grave was the error in the landing operations of the Eastern Task Force. Instead of disembarking at prearranged points where American "vice consuls" and French underground members were waiting to provide guides and assistance, Ryder's troops landed on a beach four miles distant. It was this inaccuracy which caused the agonizing thirteen-hour delay in the arrival of our troops in the city. The British Navy, which was responsible for landing the entire expeditionary force, explained that an error in navigation occurred in the darkness. But the British Navy was so familiar with this Algerian shore that many persons believed the landings were made on an undisclosed beach on purpose, to guard against possible treachery in the French underground.

I was only too well aware, that night of November 8, of how potentially explosive the situation still remained between Frenchmen and Anglo-Americans throughout Africa. A dozen important matters awaited decisions, and each urgent problem should get Eisenhower's prior approval, if possible. But I discovered that the overburdened radio facilities at Gibraltar had fallen hours behind in handling reports and queries. Urgent dispatches were pouring into Eisenhower's command post from London and Washington, from landing parties all along the African shores, and from warships still at sea or engaged in duels with French warships. This was my first experience with military communications in combat, and I began to understand better how errors could occur which would be inconceivable in a normal situation. So I got no sleep that night, badly as I needed it. Having been compelled by circumstances to assume exclusive responsibility for initiating the "Darlan deal," I now was compelled by this communications delay to continue making independent decisions throughout the night and up to five o'clock on the afternoon of November 9, when Eisenhower's deputy commander, Mark Clark, finally flew into Algiers.

TEN

ASSASSINATION IN ALGIERS: THE DARLAN ENIGMA

Mark Clark, it would seem, is one of those romantic generals destined to move always in an atmosphere of high drama. There was nothing especially picturesque about the arrival in Algiers of any of the other Torch commanders, so far as I know, but Clark arrived in the midst of a German bombing raid with a Messerschmitt flaming down dangerously close to his Flying Fortress. The General landed at Maison Blanche, the airport which later became so familiar to hundreds of thousands of Americans, and we drove into Algiers to the orchestration of the city's first air raid. About twenty-five German and Italian planes came over just at dusk and the British warships in the bay let loose with all the antiaircraft guns they had, a spectacular show which threw the Arab residents into a frenzy of excitement. The people of Algiers learned afterwards to stay off the streets during raids, but this attack caused a number of casualties, mostly from antiaircraft splinters.

I had arranged with Pierre Giauchain, owner of the St. George Hotel, to reserve that beautiful establishment for Allied Force Headquarters, and as soon as Clark and I reached the privacy of his suite there, I told him about my negotiations with Juin and Darlan. How ironical it was, I remarked, that while Clark was arguing with Giraud at Gibraltar, events in Algiers were already rendering obsolete his Giraud agreement. Clark astonished me by the sharpness of his reaction. "This really messes things up!" he exclaimed, and then informed me what had happened at Gibraltar that very morning. He and Eisenhower, after their prolonged discussions with Giraud, had been so pleased when the Frenchman finally agreed to serve with an American over-all command, that Eisenhower had broadcast an extremely optimistic statement about the important position which Giraud would hold. Eisenhower's statement had gone to great lengths in committing the American Government to support Giraud. Now if the Frenchman did not get a position near the top of the administration, both Eisenhower and the American Government would look ridiculous. Clark appreciated that his own reputation also was at stake, since he personally had conducted most of the conversations with Giraud at Gibraltar. "We've got to put Giraud back into this business right away," Clark declared.

It had been planned at Gibraltar that Giraud and Clark would depart for Algiers simultaneously in separate planes on that morning of November 9. But after Giraud's plane left the Rock, weather closed in, delaying Clark's departure for five hours, so the French General landed at the Blida airfield, forty miles from Algiers, unannounced and unaccompanied by any Americans. When I was notified that Giraud had at last arrived, I went to see him with some misgiving, anticipating that he might reproach me for the misleading correspondence I had exchanged with him while he was in France. But he listened quietly to my explanation that the safety of our expedition was the only motive behind my ambiguity. Nor did he show undue agitation when I told him that, while he was arguing at Gibraltar concerning the exact status of his command, it had become necessary to bring Darlan into the picture at Algiers. Giraud did not doubt Darlan's claim that he, too, had been secretly preparing for joint French-American action against the Germans, and Giraud evinced no surprise when I told him that Darlan and Juin blamed him for "jumping the gun."

Giraud had no desire to engage in any political controversy. His only interest was to preserve French sovereignty and to make sure that French commanders had an appropriately important share in military operations conducted on French soil. On this subject all French officers were in complete agreement, but when I tried to explain this to Clark, he was in no mood to listen during his first tense hours in Algiers. Clark had little acquaintance with French politics and could not understand the intricate play of French personalities and the psychology arising out of France's defeat in 1940. Clark wanted to concentrate at that moment on military operations, yet his immediate responsibility was the negotiation of an agreement with the French authorities which was more political than military. What Clark wanted was a prompt unconditional agreement to give our forces all the support which the French could provide. He felt that we were entitled to at least that much because, after all, without us the French had no salvation. He noted in his diary that night: "What a mess! Why do soldiers have to get mixed up in things like this when there is a war to be fought? It's awful!"

After talking with me, Clark decided to put off until the following morning his meeting with Darlan. Clark wanted first to explain the situation to Eisenhower by radio, and he announced that he was going to get a good night's sleep in the meantime, and advised me to do the same. Clark kept with him throughout the war a devoted sergeant who stood guard while the General slept and could be depended upon to make sure his sleep would be interrupted only in case of dire necessity.

Having no such guardian or sensible rule of life, I stayed up that night of November 9, my fourth successive night with little sleep. I conferred endlessly with our assorted French helpers, who were excited and worried about the unexpected turn of events. I had to soothe them, while trying to piece together from radio reports a coherent account of what was happening. Darlan also stayed up the whole of that night, in conferences and studying radio reports. These dispatches which we picked out of the air were confusing and contradictory, often garbled and frequently mixed with Nazi and other propaganda. Darlan was hoping for some word from Marshal Pétain before his meeting with Clark, but no word came. I kept in touch with Darlan throughout the night and became increasingly convinced that he really would play ball with us if he could be sure that French sovereignty in Africa was clearly defined.

I knew that Darlan was confronted that night with difficult and disagreeable decisions, and when I saw him again at the St. George Hotel the following morning, he showed the strain and lack of sleep. Describing that first meeting, in his book *Calculated Risk*, Mark Clark observed that Darlan, "a little man with watery blue eyes and petulant lips . . . seemed nervous and uncertain, obviously ill at ease. . . . He shifted in his chair and his hands fumbled with the papers on the table in front of him." Like me, and unlike Clark, Darlan had failed to fortify himself with sleep.

After conferring with Darlan, I met the leaders of our underground group who were instrumental in bringing Giraud to Algiers, and late that evening of November 10 Clark and I met with Giraud alone in an automobile where we could talk without being overheard. During the previous thirty-odd hours, Giraud had been exposed to all the complexities of the situation. He was a guest in the home of Lemaigre-Dubreuil in an Arab quarter in Algiers, and there he talked with many high-ranking French officials and learned, to his amazement, that most of them considered him a dissident and refused to recognize that he had any authority over them. Giraud sympathized with the importance which most French military officers attached to "legality," and told Clark and me that he was appalled by the complexities of civil authority and wanted to be free to devote himself to combat. To our surprise, and admittedly to our relief, he went on to say that Darlan obviously was essential to the success of our enterprise, and that he would be content to serve under him. Giraud hoped that Darlan would agree to an arrangement by which the Admiral would be a sort of High Commissioner while he, Giraud, would become Commander in Chief of the French forces. Thus, without a word of persuasion from Clark or me, Giraud provided what proved to be an effective working formula for the early weeks of Operation Torch.

Developments in Algiers during the next few days demonstrated that mere specialized knowledge can be a handicap under certain conditions. Clark did not pretend to understand French politics, so he found it easy to hold unwaveringly to an oversimplified view of French-American relations, and to ride roughshod over all delaying tactics. In Clark's reports to Eisenhower during his first days in Algiers, he made frequent use of his private code word "YBSOB." This stood for "yellow-bellied son-of-bitch" and was applied at one time or another to most of the French officers with whom Clark conferred. In his opinion, any Frenchman who would not immediately and unconditionally support the Anglo-American expedition deserved this appellation. In like manner, Clark punctuated his French negotiations with frequent table-thumpings and colorful epithets in English, a language which most of the French officers understood to some extent. The general believed that those tactics served him well, and perhaps he was right. For instance, he might not have been able to threaten so convincingly that unless French commanders composed their differences straightaway, he would put them in jail and impose an American military government over French North Africa. That threat scared me more than it did any Frenchman, because I was afraid that Clark really might do it. I tried to imagine what would happen if Americans undertook to fight Germans in North Africa and simultaneously to govern twenty million assorted civilians in a vast territory, without knowing any Arab dialects or even, in the case of most Americans, the French language.

After one such session, I escorted Darlan to his car. Pausing at the door, he said to me, "Could I ask a favor? Would you mind suggesting to Major General Clark that I am a five-star admiral? He should stop talking to me like a lieutenant junior grade." I repeated this to Clark, who took it in good spirit. Fortunately, most French officers already were reconciled to fighting with Americans against the Nazis, so Clark's bulldozer methods were suited to an occasion when hesitation could have been fatal. The last obstacle to an agreement with French officials was overcome when Nazi troops began to pour into Unoccupied France, in violation of the 1940 armistice.

When Darlan consented on November 8 to give his personal approval to the local cease-fire, he and I both understood that we were initiating what soon became known as the "Darlan deal." The stakes were very high: a cease-fire at once, not only in Algiers but throughout

French Africa, and the beginning of a firm working agreement there between Frenchmen and Anglo-Americans which would consolidate our military position and assure availability of several hundred thousand French-trained troops as soon as they could be equipped. Nobody else in Africa possessed Darlan's authority with the French military and civil administrators, whose good will might make or break the Allied campaign. For example, General Nogues in Morocco had outmaneuvered our secret ally in his headquarters, General Bethouart, and was directing resistance to the invasion, as he had warned me he would do. Darlan was the only man in Africa who could persuade Nogues to stop the fighting and so make Morocco safe for our troops and their operations. Then, too, there was the tempting thought that Darlan might have the power to remove the French fleet from Toulon beyond reach of the Germans.

On November 12 Nogues flew to Algiers and he and members of the Darlan and Giraud groups agreed to a formula for the French command which was almost identical with the plan Eisenhower had proposed in London three weeks before the landings. The Supreme Command pledged itself not to disturb the French administrative control of North Africa, nor Darlan's status as its highest-ranking officer, and Giraud was accepted as over-all French military commander. Apparently nobody in high Allied authority anticipated the intensity of opposition to this "Darlan deal" in certain circles in the United States and the United Kingdom. Clark, understandably proud of the progress of his negotiations, held a press conference at the St. George Hotel where he related a lively account of the proceedings. Eisenhower was the first to feel the brunt of public reaction in a spate of messages sent to him at Gibraltar, headed by inquiries from Roosevelt and Churchill and continuing with reports from military chiefs describing public criticism, complaints, and cries of dismay. Right or wrong, it was President Roosevelt's belief that French domestic politics should be subordinated to winning the war, and this was the policy under which we operated in 1941 and 1942. The Good Lord knows we needed a military success in 1942. We could not discuss this publicly at the time, and the storm of charges that the United States was foisting Darlan on postwar France had to go unanswered then. I regretted these charges because they cast a temporary shadow on the first major American success in World War II. Eisenhower had every reason to believe that he was authorized to negotiate with Darlan or any other French leader who might be useful to the expedition. Nevertheless, a less courageous man might have become alarmed by the outcry. But Eisenhower unhesitatingly accepted responsibility for the negotiations, approved the agreement, and decided to make a hasty trip to Algiers on November 13 to confirm the "Darlan deal" on the spot. Meanwhile, he advised Clark to hold no more press conferences.

Arriving at Algiers by plane, Eisenhower listened carefully to my detailed account of how various mishaps had combined to produce unforeseen but fortunate results, at least from the military viewpoint; how the "Darlan deal" had been arranged; and how it had begun to operate even before Clark's arrival. After meeting the group and shaking hands with Darlan and Nogues and all the other officers, Eisenhower asked me to fly back with him to Gibraltar to help prepare dispatches to the Allied governments to explain just what had happened, no simple matter. When the Eisenhower plane reached Gibraltar after dark on November 13, I was so groggy from lack of sleep that I was dozing as we tried to land and so missed an unpleasant thrill. The incident is best described in Eisenhower's own words: "We flew around the Rock in complete blackness, making futile passes at the field. I saw no way out of a bad predicament and still think the young lieutenant pilot must have depended more upon a rabbit's foot than upon his controls to accomplish the skillful landing that finally brought us safely down."

There was a staff dinner that night in the official residence of the Governor of Gibraltar, General Sir F. N. Mason-MacFarlane, where I spoke my piece again, more or less by rote by this time. Then several of us combined our information and experience to produce the first drafts of the explanatory dispatch for Eisenhower, so important to his personal career and to the fortunes of our enterprise. But, as he usually did, Eisenhower rewrote the explanation in his individual style. In this dispatch, the General committed himself irrevocably to the "Darlan deal," knowing that he would stand or fall upon its acceptance or rejection by the Allied governments, and upon whether or not it worked out as anticipated. He declared: "It is of the utmost importance that no precipitate action be taken which will upset such equilibrium as we have been able to establish." He expressed his confidence that Darlan was trying to induce the French fleet to leave Toulon, and added: "Even if he fails, it should be realized that he is not empty-handed, so far as affairs in North Africa are concerned. Murphy, who has done a grand job, will, as head of my Civil Affairs section, be very close to Darlan."

I was indeed close to the enigmatic little French admiral during the next six weeks, until he was assassinated in Algiers on Christmas Eve. Probably I got to know him better than any other American ever did and, strangely, I grew to like him. I was particularly impressed by how cleverly Darlan safeguarded French national interests. Although he was leading from weakness, knowing the hostility toward him in Britain and the United States, no negotiator could have obtained more Allied concessions for the benefit of France. While discussions in Algiers were still in a critical stage, Roosevelt was induced to make a statement describing arrangements with Darlan as a "temporary expedient," justified solely by the stress of battle. The Roosevelt statement was interpreted by some French commanders as a partial repudiation of assurances already given, and Darlan had to move fast to hold his subordinates in line. The agreement signed on November 23 provided guarantees of French sovereignty in the African empire, and left unimpaired French imperial controls over African populations. Moreover, Darlan exacted from Americans even more lavish pledges to reconstruct French armed forces than Clark had offered to Mast at Cherchell.

Out of the military clauses in the Clark-Darlan agreement emerged the massive American military aid program for France while World War II was in progress. Under that program the United States fully equipped and trained eight French divisions in North Africa, partially outfitted and trained three more in France, supplied equipment for nineteen air squadrons, and also extensively re-equipped the French Navy. Under this wartime program the United States supplied the French with fourteen hundred aircraft, thirty thousand machine guns, three thousand artillery guns, five thousand tanks and self-propelled weapons, and fifty-one million rounds of ammunition. Whatever Darlan's apparent failings during his Vichy period, he proved during his last weeks that he was a French patriot.

While thus protecting the interests of France, Darlan also contributed more to the Allied cause than most people knew at the time. He invited me to listen on extension telephones to several of his conversations with French commanders during the first critical days of the invasion, and to read some of his messages before he sent them. No one but Darlan, I am sure, could at that time have induced Nogues to end resistance in Morocco so quickly, or have persuaded General Pierre Boisson, Governor General of French West Africa, to deliver that great territory and the port of Dakar without the firing of a shot. This was the port which had been of more concern to Roosevelt than any other in Africa; he considered it the greatest potential threat to the Americas. On long-distance telephone I listened to Darlan urge Admiral Jean Esteva, then Governor General of Tunisia, to resist the imminent invasion of German airborne troops. Darlan asked: "Esteva, are you willing to become an American?" Esteva replied: "Yes, but when are they coming?" He was referring to our pre-landing assurances that American troops would disembark in Tunisia the first day of the invasion, as had been originally planned. The change in Allied plans, and Vichy's acquiescence to German demands, permitted the Germans to occupy Tunisian airports and prolonged the fighting in Tunisia and eastern Algeria for many frigid winter weeks.

Darlan tried his utmost to persuade Admiral de la Borde to move the French fleet out of Toulon to Algiers. Relations between Darlan and De la Borde had been strained for some time. De la Borde's service had been extended; perhaps if he had retired earlier, another admiral might have been more intelligent and more cooperative. In reply to urgent pleas sent by Darlan, there came only the laconic and contemptuous one-word reply from De la Borde—"Merde"—which, politely translated, conveys some of the meaning of General McAuliffe's "Nuts" at the Battle of the Bulge. Darlan never even contemplated revoking his standing order to the French fleet to scuttle rather than capitulate to Nazi control. At the time of the 1940 armistice, and frequently during the twenty-eight months thereafter, Darlan promised that the fleet never would fall into Nazi hands. When the fleet at Toulon was scuttled, the little admiral at least had the satisfaction of knowing that his pledge had been honored.

Several times Darlan said to me, "Please tell your President that any time he decides I am more of a liability than an asset to him, I will gladly step down." He even offered to leave with us a signed resignation, undated, which could be put into effect whenever we desired. "All I ask," he said, "is the privilege of visas and transportation to the United States for myself and my wife."

The reason Darlan wanted to go with his wife to the United States was because their son Alain was at Warm Springs, Georgia, undergoing treatment at the infantile paralysis clinic made famous by Roosevelt. Infantile paralysis, in fact, figured rather importantly in the "Darlan deal." It was responsible for Darlan's presence in Algiers at the time of the invasion, and it influenced the emotions of both the French Admiral and the American President. When I informed Leahy by cablegram two days before the landings that Darlan had arrived in Algiers because of his son's paralysis, Leahy promptly informed Roosevelt. Describing this incident in his memoirs, Leahy wrote: "The first thing that impressed Roosevelt was the nature of the boy's illness. Roosevelt remembered his own illness and proposed that we send a letter to Darlan. I replied I thought it would be a very nice thing to do. Later Roosevelt sent Darlan's son to Warm Springs and kept him there for a considerable time. Darlan was most grateful, and it is my belief that this thoughtfulness on the part of the President helped us in the critical situation that was developing." After Darlan's assassination, his widow visited her son as a guest of the American Government.

Twenty-four hours before Darlan was shot, I lunched with him and a group of Allied naval officers headed by Admiral Sir Andrew Browne Cunningham, Allied Naval Commander in Chief. During the luncheon, Darlan proposed a toast to a British victory. Then, as we were leaving,

Darlan asked me to come with him to his study, saying he wanted to discuss a number of problems. But after we were alone, he pushed aside the business communications on his desk and told me he had been thinking of the current situation. "You know," he began, "there are four plots in existence to assassinate me." He went on in a detached manner, "Suppose one of these plots is successful. What will you Americans do then?" Pulling a slip of paper from his pocket, he said he had listed several names, speculating who might succeed him. The list included De Gaulle. Darlan commented that if De Gaulle came then, we would have trouble. It would be premature, he explained. Perhaps in the spring of 1943, De Gaulle would be possible. As for Giraud, Darlan repeated his opinion that Giraud was only a good divisional commander, nothing more. There followed the names of some civilians—Flandin, Herriot, Reynaud, and others whom I do not recall now. For one reason or another, none of these men was available. Darlan seemed sincerely disturbed over the prospect, but as though he were talking about the death of someone else, not himself. Then he shrugged, drew back the pile of business papers before him, and took them up item by item.

The motive for the assassination of Darlan still remains a mystery. The man who shot him, Bonnier de la Chapelle, was of a good Algiers family and was a member of an insignificant group of youths who wanted to restore the monarchy. Whoever influenced young De la Chapelle to commit the murder, supplying him with the pistol and apparently assuring him that he would be a national hero and would be fully protected from harm, never has been identified. Darlan's personal assistant, Air Force General Jean-Marie-Joseph Bergeret, who was completely loyal and devoted to Darlan, was responsible for the security of Darlan's offices where the assassination took place, and the ease with which De la Chapelle entered the premises was a reflection on Bergeret's management. Bergeret summarily ordered the assassin's execution the following day, thus extinguishing the best source of information and opportunity to ascertain the facts.

Mark Clark and I reached the French military hospital a few minutes after Darlan died on the operating table. Many commentators in the United States and England wrote that Darlan's death was a fortunate break for the Anglo-Americans, relieving us of the intolerable burdens of the "Darlan deal." That never was my feeling. President Roosevelt knew he could have Darlan's resignation instantly if he requested it. Clark and I, talking over matters in the hospital, agreed that Darlan had contributed as much as any Frenchman to the success of a highly speculative military and diplomatic venture.

ELEVEN

EVERYBODY GETS INTO EISENHOWER'S ACT

During my first meeting in England with Eisenhower, two months before the African expedition, I asked him how large his staff in Algiers would be and how long he expected to stay there. I was thinking of the housing and office space he would require. The general told me he wanted to keep his staff as compact as possible and would try to hold it to about two hundred members. He added that a city like Algiers was not suitable for military headquarters, and that if the landing was successful and "if we can hang on after arrival," he would like to move eastward in about six weeks. As events turned out, Allied Force Headquarters in Algiers mushroomed to over six thousand persons, who remained in Algiers for twenty months, and Eisenhower himself stayed in that city for more than a year. This startling discrepancy between estimates and results reflects no discredit upon the General. He was calculating on an African campaign based on the plans of the Combined (American and British) Chiefs of Staff, but that strategy did not prevail for long.

As for myself, I naturally thought about my own staff in even more modest terms than Eisenhower did about his. When President Roosevelt authorized me to organize a civil affairs section within Allied Force Headquarters, I was given only a few weeks' notice and no additional expense money for this purpose. So I made no arrangements to expand my group beyond the twelve "vice consuls" and the regular American consular personnel who already were assigned to French Africa. I thought that after the arrival of our expeditionary force, I still would be concerned chiefly with Frenchmen as I had been throughout the previous two years. Realizing how few Americans had any firsthand knowledge of North Africa, it seemed obvious that we must depend almost entirely upon French military and civil officials, and that the work of the civil affairs section would be mostly to maintain liaison with these professional administrators. I could not have been more wrong. From the day when General Mark Clark flew into

Algiers, bringing as an assistant, not a professional soldier but the motion picture producer Darryl Zanuck, my chief preoccupations in Africa concerned Americans. Being on duty in Algiers after November 8, 1942, seemed like the old days in Paris before the war, when both visiting and resident Americans expected our embassy to give them top priority over all other responsibilities.

I had supposed that the Americans we would have to worry about in Africa would be mostly soldiers; it never occurred to me that we would be called upon in Algiers to deal with a continuous parade of Very Important Persons—or those who thought they were. But I soon became aware that almost every organization in the United States wanted to participate in this first major American campaign of World War II, and had drafted plans accordingly. Many of the newcomers assumed that Americans, not Frenchmen, were entitled to decide how French Africa should be administered while our soldiers were there. That assumption was entirely contrary to arrangements we had made with French officials before and during the landings, and it was contrary to promises which had been given with the full approval of Roosevelt and Eisenhower. Nevertheless, hundreds of Americans, including the President himself, yielded to impulses to interfere with the formal agreements we had concluded with the French authorities. Roosevelt never could quite make up his mind whether we had "occupied" or "liberated" French Africa. In a letter written to us on January 2, 1943, he declared:

"I feel very strongly that, in view of the fact that in North Africa we have a military occupation, our C.G. has complete control of all affairs, both civil and military. Our French friends must not be permitted to forget this for a moment. In the same way they must not be led to believe that we are going to recognize any one group or committee as representing the French Empire or the French Government. The French people will be able to settle their own affairs when the war ends with victory for us. Until that time, wherever our armies are in occupation in former French territory, we will deal on a local basis with local Frenchmen, and if these local officials will not cooperate, they will have to be replaced."

Secretary of War Stimson likewise was inclined to regard French Africa as subject to temporary American rule. He had been Governor General of the Philippines in the 1920s, when those Pacific islands still were administered by the War Department, and he had become familiar there with the type of military government necessary in conquered or dependent countries. When the United States became a belligerent in World War II, Stimson was one of the first American officials who appreciated the importance of special training for officers who were to administer conquered enemy territories, and he was influential in creating a useful training center at Charlottesville, Virginia. But suddenly, with no advance notice, seventeen officers ranked as colonels and lieutenant colonels reported to me in Algiers. They announced that they had been instructed at Charlottesville how to administer French North Africa, which apparently they had divided into seventeen regions. They were an admirable group of men, but totally misinformed as to the requirements of this situation. One or two spoke French; none spoke Arabic. Eventually they were reassigned, understandably disappointed that Eisenhower was unwilling to permit seventeen inexperienced Americans to try their skills at governing Morocco, Algeria, and Tunisia in the midst of a critical campaign against German armored divisions.

Among the Americans who received considerable attention from me during the early weeks in Algiers were the newspaper and radio correspondents. During my career in Europe I had maintained cordial relations with American foreign correspondents, and a few of my old acquaintances accompanied our troops to Algiers. But most of the press corps were novice war correspondents, unfamiliar with international politics. Communication facilities were inadequate for several months, and there was a feeling of frustration among these correspondents which sometimes was reflected in their dispatches. Like all reporters, they also feuded with the cautious military censors. In mid-December, two correspondents whom I had known in Paris called upon me and said they had come to say goodbye. They were returning to England, they informed me, because now that a political censorship had been imposed in Algiers, working conditions had become impossible for them. "Political censorship?" I asked. "What political censorship? You must be misinformed." The correspondents thought I was joking. Since I was the political adviser at Allied Force Headquarters, they could not believe that a political censorship had been imposed without my concurrence, or even my knowledge.

Not until after their departure did I learn what had happened. Eisenhower's Chief of Staff, General Walter Bedell Smith, told me that the political censorship, restricting all local newspapers as well as war correspondents, was a "command decision" by Eisenhower. I said that in my opinion this was a mistake, but the political censorship continued in effect for several more weeks, adding to the already numerous complaints about alleged reactionary policies of Allied Force Headquarters. The State Department in general, and I in particular, were blamed for this censorship about which we had not even been consulted. In his memoirs, Eisenhower admits that the imposition of the political censorship was an error, "even though from a good motive." I still do not know who inspired this error.

Another group which dumfounded me was a delegation representing Jewish-American soldiers, who called upon me one week after our expedition landed. Their spokesman declared: "We are informed that you have been in Algiers for more than a year, yet you have done nothing about the Jews here! Don't you think you have outlived your usefulness in Africa and should get out fast?" These Americans never had seen anything like the segregated Jewish quarters of Algiers and Morocco, and they were so appalled by the wretched conditions that they were in no mood to hear that this was French territory, where I had had no authority whatever before the landings. My agitated visitors did not know that the Jews of North Africa have lived in separate quarters for centuries—as they still do today—and that their standard of living is not appreciably higher than that of their Arab neighbors. These American coreligionists were under the impression that the misery they now were glimpsing had resulted from Nazi decrees which I should have nullified. I told them that I had visited several synagogues prior to the arrival of the Allied expedition, in order to express the sympathy of the American Government for the Jews, and that one rabbi had shown his appreciation by presenting me with a copy of the Torah.

I also tried to explain why it was essential to move very cautiously in revoking Nazi decrees while the outcome of military operations in Africa was still indecisive. German propagandists were agitating the Arabs by broadcasting that the United States was controlled by Jews, and if Americans won the war they would elevate Jews to supreme power in North Africa. Great care was necessary if we were to prevent racial uprisings which would be detrimental to the Allied military campaign.

Nobody understood this precarious situation better than Major Paul P. Warburg, a member of a distinguished Jewish banking family whom Eisenhower detailed to my staff for some months to advise me on Jewish affairs. When Secretary of the Treasury Henry Morgenthau, Jr., visited Algiers, Warburg—who was of invaluable assistance to me—did his best to guide Morgenthau, and prudently recommended that he avoid public meetings with the resident Jewish community, lest such association appear to confirm Nazi propaganda. But when Morgenthau asked my opinion on this matter, I told him that I felt it would be more useful than harmful for him to confer with the Jewish leaders in Algiers. "That's just what I wanted to hear," said Morgenthau. "Will you arrange a meeting?" So I invited thirty prominent Jewish residents, fifteen North Africans and fifteen French Metropolitans, some of whom I knew personally. They met in the large reception room of my residence, and it could be seen immediately that the Europeans were not acquainted with the local inhabitants. The two groups moved to opposite sides of the room and were thus separated when Morgenthau entered. To break the ice, Morgenthau proposed that each guest describe his own personal experiences.

As one after another related tales of exile, petty discriminations, and mounting fear because Nazi-like decrees were belatedly coming to light in North Africa, Morgenthau became perplexed. For instance, one of the leading North African Jews told how he had been forced to sell half his interest in a profitable chain of motion picture theaters. The Secretary inquired sympathetically, "And I suppose you never received payment for this half?" The movie magnate replied, "Oh, yes. I received seventy million francs, much less than the property was worth. I have the money. Would you like to see it?" It was obvious that Morgenthau had expected to hear lurid accounts of physical torture and wanton destruction of Jewish property, such as had taken place in Germany and some other countries under Nazi domination. Finally a French Jewish banker and a distinguished professor at the University of Algiers explained that their difficulty lay in anxiety and the general humiliation suffered, and pointed out that the most extreme anti-Semitic decrees had not been enforced in North Africa where the French administration had been relatively independent of Nazi pressure. Morgenthau returned to Washington with an accurate conception of the situation, and he helped to correct misunderstandings there.

In another matter, however, Morgenthau seriously disturbed the French civil administration. The U. S. Treasury Department was concerned with several French-American financial questions, and two Treasury agents arrived in advance of the Secretary to initiate investigations in North Africa. During Morgenthau's first talk with me, when he dined at my residence, he brought up the name of Maurice Couve de Murville, a brilliant French civil servant. Couve de Murville was doing excellent work on financial matters, actually a de facto Minister of Finance attached to the French High Commissioner. Morgenthau startled me by saying, "About this man Couve de Murville. I think we should get rid of him."

"I'm sorry to hear that, Mr. Secretary," I replied, "because Couve de Murville is a good friend of mine and, I believe, of the United States."

Morgenthau shook his head. "No, he will have to go."

Hoping to change his mind, I described how, just before the German occupation of Paris in 1940, I had worked with Couve de Murville, then an official in the Ministry of Finance, of transport to a safe place the French gold reserves. An American cruiser had carried to French West Africa several hundred tons of the precious metal, which later was stored in a central African fortress. I explained how Couve de Murville had been largely responsible for keeping this gold out of Nazi hands, preserving it for the people of France. When Morgenthau still seemed doubtful, I suggested that he should at least have a talk with Couve de Murville, who spoke excellent English, and he agreed. I arranged a meeting in my office with Morgenthau, who was accompanied by Harry Dexter White, then Assistant to the Secretary of the Treasury, and Couve de Murville. Morgenthau did most of the questioning and White said practically nothing. Much of the interrogation concerned Couve de Murville's record as Vichy negotiator at Wiesbaden, where his skill prevented the Germans from obtaining many of the financial concessions they sought. The conversation in my office lasted almost two hours and I was confident at the end that our visitors were as favorably impressed by Couve de Murville's superior qualities as I was.

But that evening, at a dinner given by Eisenhower for the V.I.P.s then in Algiers, the Secretary took me aside and declared: "I haven't changed my mind about Couve de Murville. He must go." It proved impossible to get this decision reversed in Washington, so we were compelled to inform French headquarters that the man who probably was their most effective civilian administrator in Algiers was unacceptable to the American Government, and he was sidetracked. This excursion by Morgenthau into the field of foreign policy was based upon the assumption, very common among Americans in 1943, that any Frenchman who had remained in France and served the Vichy Government was thereby suspect. This notion was encouraged by General de Gaulle for his own propaganda purposes, but in practice he did not hesitate to employ the services of distinguished "Vichyites." Shortly after Couve de Murville was dismissed as Secretary General of the High Commissioner's headquarters, De Gaulle appointed him as the French member of the Mediterranean Advisory Council, although Couve de Murville never had pretended to be an ardent De Gaullist. The British member of this Council was Harold Macmillan, who later became Prime Minister, and I represented the United States. Years later, in 1960, when De Gaulle paid a triumphal visit to America as the President of France, he was accompanied by his Foreign Minister—Maurice Couve de Murville.

Another Very Important Person who came to Algiers was Milton S. Eisenhower, brother of the General, who arrived on December 11, 1942. Milton Eisenhower at that time was Associate Director of the Office of War Information, our wartime propaganda agency, and when we learned that he was coming to Africa, Allied Force Headquarters had an uneasy feeling that the purpose of his visit might be to bring pressure on us to obtain the release of prisoners in French internment camps, which the OWI then was urging. A statement written by the

OWI for the President, which Roosevelt had released under his own name eight days after our landings, had included this sentence: "I have requested the liberation of all persons in North Africa who have been imprisoned because they opposed the efforts of the Nazis to dominate the world." That "request," which in the circumstances amounted to an order, sounded harmless enough, and our first inclination was to exert our influence to persuade the French authorities to release everyone and to close the camps.

But French officials pointed out that the camps held nine thousand persons, most of whom were destitute and had no place to go because the Allied armies were making such heavy demands upon living space in North Africa. Moreover, these nine thousand internees were a very mixed lot, including dangerous fanatics and a good many common criminals. They also included twenty-seven Communist deputies, the equivalent of American congressmen, who had been arrested by the French Government in 1939 because they denounced the war as an "imperialist struggle" for which England was largely responsible. These legislators had agitated and voted against every war measure, and thus had played the Nazis game while the German-Russian alliance was in effect.

In recommending that Roosevelt should arrange for the release of Communist prisoners in French Africa, the OWI policy-makers were influenced by one of their own chief functions at that time, which was to emphasize that Soviet Russia was now "on our side." Of course the battles then raging in Russia were of great military importance to the Allies, but the President's "request" arrived at a moment when we had to do everything possible to maintain stability behind our expedition's own combat front. So Allied Force Headquarters agreed that the French authorities should proceed with caution in releasing prisoners. So far as the Communists were concerned, they had not been imprisoned because they "opposed the efforts of the Nazis to dominate the world," but for precisely opposite reasons. But one poorly chosen OWI representative in Algiers seemed to consider it his personal mission to force the release of all Communists immediately.

I was preparing to explain this complicated situation to Milton Eisenhower when he called upon me, but my visitor soon made it clear that he had come to Algiers mainly because he was concerned about his brother's reputation. General Eisenhower not only had assumed responsibility for the hotly criticized "Darlan deal," but now he was tolerating still more Frenchmen who had been prominent in the Vichy Government. Milton Eisenhower told me that some newspaper and radio commentators were even calling his brother a "Fascist," and that unless drastic action were taken immediately, the General's career might be irreparably damaged. "Heads must roll,

Murphy!" he exclaimed. "Heads must roll!" He wanted to know what French leaders we were planning to get rid of, and when I asked whom he considered objectionable, he mentioned the only name he could remember at the moment, General Nogues, whose resistance to the landings in Morocco had cost the lives of several hundred Americans.

Milton Eisenhower was right in protesting the authority being flaunted by Nogues, but he was mistaken if he thought that I, or even General Eisenhower himself, could take drastic action in Morocco immediately. The expeditionary forces in that area, almost exclusively American, were under the command of Major General George S. Patton, Jr., and relations between that flamboyant warrior and Nogues had become embarrassingly cordial. News reports had been published in the United States about the extraordinary cooperation between these generals who so recently had been fighting against each other, and these dispatches aggravated sentiment against the way French Africa was being administered. This was the first time, but by no means the last, when Patton created a problem in public relations for General Eisenhower. The Patton-Nogues story, as we finally pieced it together, was as follows:

After three days of fighting in Morocco, with hundreds of casualties on both sides, the Americans and French arranged a cease-fire just in time to prevent the bombardment of Casablanca. Patton then invited Nogues and members of his staff to the Anfa Hotel, Patton's headquarters, to attend a formal truce signing. Two American staff officers who were present told me later what happened there. Patton slowly read aloud to the assembled group a document labeled "Treaty C," which had been given to him by the War Department before he left Washington, with instructions to apply it if the French opposed our landings. This treaty, which I had not been consulted about, ignored the special conditions prevailing in Morocco under the French protectorate. If its surrender terms had been enforced, the treaty would have virtually abolished the protectorate, thus infuriating all patriotic Frenchmen and creating chaotic administrative conditions. Patton was well aware how shocking this document would sound to the French officers, so he read with deliberation and emphasis and then paused for the anticipated effect. Then, looking at the mortified and angry French officers, he dramatically tore "Treaty C" into small pieces, declaring: "You and I fought side by side in the First World War! I am confident that we can work together now on a basis of mutual trust."

In this fashion Patton, partly because of his supreme self-confidence and partly by force of circumstances, took upon himself to become an independent policy-maker in Morocco as well as the field commander. His action certainly was irregular and probably illegal, but it won the full military cooperation of Nogues, who thereupon worked so smoothly with Patton that the rapidly expanding American bases in Morocco were secure, requiring merely token protection. Patton thus was left free to reorganize his own troops for combat, for which they soon would be badly needed.

As Patton viewed matters, Nogues behaved "correctly" at all times. He gave the Americans fair warning in advance that he would resist an invasion from any source; he patriotically defended his territory with all the forces he had; and now, having struck a bargain with the Allies, he was cooperating with us completely. Nogues delivered everything Patton requested for military purposes. He maintained public order. He supplied ample native labor for handling the massive supplies pouring into Moroccan ports, and safeguarded the transport of these shipments to the front over hundreds of miles of Moroccan narrow-gauge railways and rough roads. Above all, Nogues relieved Patton's headquarters of the complications which American officers lumped under the heading of "French politics," matters which they had neither time nor inclination to investigate.

This state of affairs was so agreeable to the American commander that he was not disposed to interfere in any manner with the French administration. He was not even in a hurry to arrange the release of General Bethouart and other pre-invasion American supporters, whom Nogues had arrested as rebels. When news reached Washington and London of Patton's indifference to the fate of Frenchmen who had helped the Allies, and his amiability toward French officers who were responsible for the death of American "liberators," public opinion was outraged. But it required some weeks and considerable tact on the part of Eisenhower to reduce the authority of Nogues.

One example of Patton's amiable attitude toward Nogues was not publicly known at the time, but it created something of a problem for me. The White House cabled that Roosevelt had not received any answer to the message he had dispatched for delivery on D-Day to the Sultan of Morocco, expressing hope for the Sultan's friendly support of our expedition. Although the American Government did not oppose the French protectorate in Morocco, it maintained unusually close relations with the Sultan's government. Morocco was the only place in the world where, by agreement with the Sultan, the United States still retained extraterritorial privileges. So the Sultan's failure to reply to the President's letter was strange indeed, and I sent "Vice Consul" Pendar to Casablanca and Rabat to investigate. After some difficulty, he discovered that Roosevelt's message had been pigeonholed because Nogues did not like its tone. Nogues feared that under the circumstances it might encourage the Sultan to feel more independent in his relations with the French.

When Pendar explained to Patton what had happened, and showed him the President's letter, the general read the message carefully and commented: "I don't like it, either. Not enough mention of the French in it." Patton began to insert additions of his own, ignoring Pendar's protest that nobody should change a President's message without the President's consent. Patton replied impatiently that he would take full responsibility in this matter. Pendar described the situation to me by long-distance telephone. Only after some additional delay and some prodding from Allied Force Headquarters did the American and French generals, who were equally reluctant to do so, belatedly deliver President Roosevelt's letter in its original wording to the Sultan.

Another American officer on Eisenhower's staff created a different kind of situation for me to handle. This officer telephoned me that the general sorely needed a day's rest, which he wanted to arrange the coming Sunday. A pleasant place to get away from it all would be a hunting lodge in the mountains near Algiers which Eisenhower had visited once or twice before. This lodge had been taken over by a five-star French general, Georges Catroux, the former Governor General of Indochina who had been an early supporter of De Gaulle and had come to Algiers as De Gaulle's representative. Eisenhower's assistant inquired if I would mind asking Mme. Catroux if the Supreme Commander could use the lodge on Sunday. I called Mme. Catroux, a member of an aristocratic French family who was active as supervisor of volunteer nurses, and she told me that her husband was tired, too, and had planned to rest in the mountain lodge that Sunday, but of course they would cancel their own plans and feel honored to turn over the lodge to General Eisenhower.

Monday morning, having occasion to call upon Eisenhower on other business, I remarked that I hoped he had enjoyed a good rest Sunday. He looked at me as if I had made a joke in poor taste and said, "I was at my desk here all day—if you call that a good rest!" My suspicions aroused, I said nothing about the hunting lodge. A little later Mme. Catroux phoned to inquire rather indignantly what had happened to General Eisenhower? Her servants had informed her that only an American officer and a young lady had come to the lodge. I recognized that this was a situation which required diplomacy of sorts, so I made profuse apologies on behalf of Eisenhower. He had intended to come, I explained, and had sent one of his officers and a WAC secretary in advance, but unexpected circumstances had arisen suddenly which made it impossible for him to leave headquarters. He greatly appreciated Mme. Catroux's gracious hospitality and deeply regretted that he had inconvenienced her. Mme.

Catroux was mollified. I decided to say nothing to the general. He had too many important things on his mind to be bothered about this petty affair. As for the staff officer, I never said anything to him, either. But the next time that Catroux's name came up during a conference with Eisenhower, I gave the offender a good hard look. He had not been especially cooperative with me before, but thereafter he became exceedingly so.

Another indignant lady—American this time—also required some attention from me in an awkard complication which involved La Saadia, a modernized Moorish palace in the Moroccan city of Marrakesh. A New York banker had spent a fortune on this exotic estate years before, but his widow had no intention of coming to Africa in wartime so "Vice Consul" Pendar, who was acquainted with her, arranged for the State Department to rent La Saadia for a nominal price. Marrakesh, because of its ideal flying weather, became a stopping point for most of our transatlantic planes after the invasion, and we knew that the hotels there were bound to be overcrowded.

Besides providing accommodations for our Air Force, we also used La Saadia for confidential meetings with both French and Arabs. I am not sure how confidential these meetings actually were, because our Secret Service people subsequently discovered a number of microphones hidden in several rooms, some of the equipment French, some German. The head servant of La Saadia, Louis, was a Eurasian who spoke French, English, German and Arabic, and under his supervision the fabulous estate extended hospitality to hundreds of American airmen and V.I.P.s. Louis later accompanied me to Europe, but after he ran my house in Berlin a few months, I regretfully had to part company with him because he became the proprietor of a restaurant in Paris.

When Roosevelt came to the Casablanca Conference in January 1943, Churchill persuaded him to spend a day in Marrakesh on his way home. The two men and their entourage drove the 158 miles from Casablanca between lines of American troops who had been ordered out by Generals Patton and Clark, as much to impress the Moroccans as to safeguard the distinguished visitors. Meanwhile, Pendar had been instructed to prepare La Saadia, which had six master bedrooms each with its own sunken marble bath. The only stipulation which had been made by the owner was that her own bedroom, ornately furnished and containing her personal effects, should not be used under any circumstances. However, when Mike Reilly, the President's Secret Service chief, examined the four-acre estate enclosed within high pink plaster walls, he decided that the only bedroom with security which he considered adequate for the

President was this ground-floor bedroom of the owner, with its private courtyard. So Roosevelt was installed there.

When news of the visit to Marrakesh was released after the President's safe return home, the mistress of La Saadia deduced from newspaper accounts just what had occurred, and her annoyance was aggravated because she was one of those "economic royalists" who never would speak Roosevelt's name; to her, he was "That Man in the White House." She wrote one furious letter after another to the State Department, which sent copies of the correspondence to me for comment. During my diplomatic career I sometimes have had to negotiate concerning broken international treaties, but never have I endured more protracted maneuvers than those which resulted from the alleged breach of contract concerning the lady's bedroom. At one period she threatened to sue for heavy damages. The affair still was unsettled when I finally departed from Africa, and I had to leave it to the State Department to convince her that no jury would award damages to a lady merely because the President of the United States had slept in her bed.

What with one thing and another, maybe I did earn the Distinguished Service Medal which General Eisenhower personally pinned on my jacket on December 16. This decoration is rarely awarded to a civilian and I always have felt deeply grateful for this tribute from the Army. The citation which accompanied my award stated: "To Robert D. Murphy, a Foreign Service Officer of the United States and of the Department of State, while serving in a position of great responsibility with the Army of the United States. He displayed exceptionally outstanding qualities of leadership, courage, and sound judgment, often under extremely hazardous circumstances. Additionally he rendered outstanding and effective service by assisting in the negotiations with French authorities in North Africa, by which hostilities were ended. By command of General Eisenhower."

This generous approval of my efforts was by no means unanimous at Allied Force Headquarters in Algiers, where several of the staff officers were disturbed by my novel status as a civilian assigned to highest military headquarters. My Arab chauffer also was distressed by this, because my car did not display the stars denoting high rank. Since it was my policy to emphasize that I was not a soldier, I did not place upon my Army automobile the stars of my assimilated rank, which matched those of the commanding general. So my chauffeur could not share the pleasures of military drivers who delighted to speed through red lights and otherwise demonstrate their immunity from civilian restrictions. What bothered the American officers, however, was not the matter of stars on my automobile but my access to their military papers. I shared this privilege with a colleague from the British Foreign Office, whom British staff officers accepted unquestioningly because foreign office participation at military headquarters is a long-established British practice. As political advisers, we were permitted separate channels of communication, and we had our own cryptographic sections and separate codes. One day an American major general asked me: "Will you please tell me what in hell the State Department has to do in an active theater of war?" He was asking for information, so this, in effect, is what I told him:

"War is a projection of policy when other means fail. The State Department is responsible to the President for foreign policy. Our prewar policy, under the personal direction of the President, was to support the western Allies against the Nazi drive. The North African theater played an active role in the period prior to the U.S. entry into the war; its political trends were important to our policy-makers. The State Department had direct responsibility in the preparatory stage leading to the invasion. It was directly concerned in the political decisions inevitably to be made during the military operations, and it will have to deal with the postwar political effects of this campaign. Furthermore, General Eisenhower needs someone to deal with French officals and leaders on the civilian level. And that is why I am here."

As I have indicated in this chapter, my duty to keep in touch with French officials and their problems was interrupted by many American distractions after the arrival of the Allied expedition. Perhaps it was my own fault that I permitted myself to get bogged down by these miscellaneous matters, but the fact remains that I could not devote as much time and thought to "French politics" as I should have done. In particular, I still am haunted by two episodes where more attention on my part might have prevented serious difficulties. The first case involved an injustice to one of our faithful French friends, Yves Chatel, whom I should have supported and did not. The other case involved his successor, Marcel Peyrouton, whom I did support—without adequate investigation.

My association with Yves Chatel began the day I arrived in Algiers in December 1940. He was then Weygand's right-hand man in Africa and he stayed on as Governor General after Weygand's recall. In the secret message which Weygand sent me after his return to France, he said that he was urging two key administrators to remain on the job—Yves Chatel in Algiers and Pierre Boisson in Dakar. Chatel told me that he remained only because the general urged him to. For almost two years this distinguished French patriot vigorously supported French-American cooperation, despite numerous setbacks which the preliminary negotiations suffered during that period. He and I often played golf together on the little nine-hole course near Algiers, a perfect place for security-proof discussions. Chatel never misled me, either regarding material facts or mental attitudes. Nobody knew more about the involved personal relationships both in Vichy and French Africa, and no Frenchman wanted more earnestly to beat the Nazis. I felt sure that Chatel would welcome a successful Allied expedition, though he said on more than one occasion that he never would do anything without the approval of Marshal Pétain.

I was dismayed, therefore, when about a week before the invasion, Chatel casually remarked that he was leaving on a routine trip to Vichy. He knew so much about our plans that I could not suggest that he postpone his trip or hurry back, because any such hint would have disclosed to him that the invasion was imminent, and I was under strict instructions to give no more than four days' advance notice to any Frenchman. So Chatel happened to be in Vichy when news of the landings broke, and I can imagine how embarrassed and humiliated he must have felt. He was known in Vichy as my friend; it was hard for anyone there not to believe that he was in on the secret of the invasion. Yet he was not. He thus came under the suspicion of Americans and Vichy Frenchmen simultaneously.

Chatel managed to fly back to Africa immediately, landing at Constantine, two hundred miles east of Algiers, where he made an emotional statement denouncing the Americans and reaffirming his devotion to Pétain. Unfortunately, he delivered his tirade before he had opportunity to hear Giraud's radio broadcast which appealed to all patriots to support the expedition against the Germans. It was Chatel's bad luck and mine that he let righteous indignation get the better of him at the worst possible moment, while resistance to the landings was still in a critical stage. He thus handicapped himself at the outset, but nevertheless he returned to Algiers on November 10, after Clark issued a sweeping statement that "all [French] civil and military authorities will be maintained in their present functions." That statement automatically confirmed Chatel's position as Governor General of Algeria, probably the most difficult of all French African posts at that time. Every move by the Governor General was scrutinized by high officials, French and Allied, who also had headquarters in Algiers. Every move by the Governor General was publicized by the large corps of British and American war correspondents in that area.

It soon became apparent that it would be impossible for Governor General Chatel and High Commissioner Darlan to work together, because neither man could forget their differences since 1940. Chatel had repeatedly criticized Darlan's concessions to the Nazis when the admiral was the real power in the Pétain government. Chatel was a Weygand man, and Darlan and Weygand always had been in opposing political camps. So Darlan made the most of Chatel's outburst at

Constantine, and persuaded Eisenhower that Chatel should be replaced as Governor General of Algeria. I feel that Eisenhower was unjust to Chatel under a misapprehension of some sort. It is unlikely that he ever met him personally, because Eisenhower's contacts with French civilian officials were almost always made through my office, and even I never saw Chatel again after his unlucky departure for Vichy a week before the invasion. Certainly Darlan was solely responsible for Chatel's removal. Eisenhower was understandably disposed to grant most of Darlan's requests after the Admiral did so much to hold together the various complex administrations in Africa. I still reproach myself for not having done more to defend Chatel at Allied Force Headquarters. If I had argued his case more effectively, it might have saved all of us the trouble which resulted from the appointment of his successor.

The selection of Marcel Peyrouton to succeed Chatel was made by Darlan, who told me that Peyrouton was better qualified for the job than anybody else available. Darlan's proposal raised no storm warnings in my mind. I already have related how my only previous acquaintance with Peyrouton was at Vichy in December 1940, when he played a major part in overthrowing Pierre Laval, who wagered the future of France on a German victory. Peyrouton's coup against Laval succeeded so well that he had to flee from France to escape Nazi vengeance. Darlan, who became Laval's successor, then arranged for Peyrouton to be named as Vichy's ambassador to Argentina, where he served inconspicuously for sixteen months until Laval got back into power again, when Peyrouton immediately resigned. From the American point of view, Peyrouton's record seemed better than that of many other Vichy officials. So when Darlan asked whether the American Government would facilitate Peyrouton's transportation from Argentina to Algiers, since travel in wartime was under government control, I passed Darlan's request on to Eisenhower, adding that I saw no objections. It never occurred to me that the appointment of Peyrouton would provoke almost as much indignation and controversy in England and the United States, weeks after Darlan was dead, as had been aroused by the "Darlan deal" itself.

There were two reasons why the appointment of Peyrouton blew a hurricane of public protests into Allied Force Headquarters. For one thing, he had been Minister of the Interior at Vichy, in charge of the police, and the Vichy police had become a symbol of persecution to their fellow Frenchmen. Even more calamitous was the circumstance that during the two months in 1940 while Peyrouton was Minister of the Interior, the Vichy Government promulgated its first decrees against the Jews in France. As I have previously described, anti-Semitism already was widespread in France during the period of the "phony war," aggravated by the fact that some prominent Communists were Jews, and that a Jewish Premier, Léon Blum, was blamed by the French Armed Forces for their own military unpreparedness. But Peyrouton's association with Vichy's earliest decrees against the Jews was interpreted in the United States as evidence that Allied Force Headquarters approved the appointment of an anti-Semitic Governor General in Algeria.

Actually, the career of Peyrouton under Allied auspices was in no way so adroitly planned as some of our critics assumed. When Darlan's recommendation was relayed to Washington, the first thing which happened there was that Under Secretary Welles strongly advised against the appointment, which he believed would create more controversy than it was worth. Welles was shrewdly aware of public sentiment and the power of propaganda, and his advice was sound. However, a strained situation existed between Under Secretary Welles and Secretary of State Hull. The latter was the superior officer, but Hull knew that Roosevelt often dealt directly with Welles without even informing the Secretary of State what was happening. Understandably, Hull was inclined to belittle recommendations from Welles, and in this case he ruled that since both Eisenhower and I had cabled asking for travel facilities for Peyrouton, this request from Allied Force Headquarters should certainly be granted. But, as I have explained, this request really originated with Darlan, not with Eisenhower or me.

No public announcement of the appointment of Peyrouton was made until his arrival in Algiers, and in the meantime Darlan was assassinated. Efficient administrator that he was, one of Darlan's first acts as High Commissioner of Algeria had been to devise a six-man Imperial Council with power to elect a new High Commissioner if that post became vacant. After the death of Darlan, Eisenhower felt that he should use his influence to see that Giraud finally acquired the status he had been promised at Gibraltar, and the result was that Giraud was unanimously elected to succeed the little Admiral.

One of the first problems of Giraud's new administration was that he was blamed, along with the State Department and me, for the appointment of Peyrouton, whose belated arrival did not occur until after Giraud became High Commissioner. As a matter of fact, I doubt that Giraud was ever even consulted by Darlan concerning the new Governor General whom Giraud inherited. Peyrouton's appointment was announced on January 19, 1943, while Roosevelt and Churchill were attending the Casablanca Conference. The uproar was immediate, especially in England, where this selection of a former high Vichy official incensed the supporters of General de Gaulle, who were demanding a top spot in Algiers for the De Gaulle group. Fortunately, Eisenhower and I could take the matter up at once with Roosevelt personally at Casablanca, and he gave his approval to the new administration in Algiers.

The other grave objection to Peyrouton, his alleged anti-Semitism, was also inherited by Giraud, who attempted to ease the situation by issuing a decree on March 14 which abolished the Nazi-inspired laws in all districts under his jurisdiction. Giraud's decree restored sequestered properties, restored civil rights, and removed various lesser discriminations. Major Warburg, on Eisenhower's staff, acted as the liaison officer in this matter, and the Grand Rabbi of Algiers, Maurice Eisenbeth, endorsed every phase of Giraud's program. Far from soothing public opinion in the United States, however, this decree was seized upon as additional evidence of the anti-Semitism of Giraud and Peyrouton. A full-page advertisement in the New York *Times* of March 18, signed by Edouard de Rothschild as President of the Central Consistory of French and Algerian Jews, proclaimed: "French Jews born in Africa are now forced into economic and social status below Arabs or Negroes of any part of the Empire. A monstrous heresy! I protest with great grief and indignant energy." The baron also cabled me from New York expressing his indignation at this turn of events.

The explanation for the dissatisfaction in the United States with Giraud's efforts to make amends to the Jews in Algeria was that Giraud's new decree failed to restore the Crémieux law of 1870, which Vichy had abolished. This Crémieux law gave Algerian Jews a special privilege not granted to Moslems, the right to automatic French citizenship at birth. Moslem natives of Algeria could acquire such citizenship only by formally applying for it and by renouncing their religion. Since the Jews of Algeria had been entitled automatically to French citizenship for seventy years, until Vichy rescinded this right, it was difficult for most American Jews to comprehend why the Crémieux law had not been restored by Giraud at the same time that he nullified other Vichy decrees. Henry Torres, chairman of the French Jewish Committee in New York, published a pamphlet in English which declared: "Abrogation of the Crémieux decree is actually the most unjust racial discrimination ever inflicted upon the French citizens of Jewish faith who are natives of Algeria."

What the Jewish people in the United States did not understand, and Major Warburg and the Grand Rabbi understood very well indeed, was that to restore the Crémieux law required extremely delicate handling, in view of the passions which had smoldered for generations among Algerian Christians as well as Moslems. The population of Algeria was then divided approximately as follows: Jews, 140,000; Christians, 850,000; Moslems, six million. To infuriate nearly seven million inhabitants in order to favor some 140,000 inhabitants was simply more than Allied Force Headquarters felt capable of tackling while the war against the Nazis was being waged. General de Gaulle, when he took over administration of Algeria, also thought there was more political turmoil than he could control without adding religious riots, and, until Algerian independence, the Crémieux decree of 1870 remained in abeyance.

After my retirement from the State Department, I served in New York as the Roman Catholic co-chairman of the National Council of Christians and Jews, an honor which I took seriously. I believe that it is high time to eliminate ancient prejudices among all the religious communities in the United States, and I am doing everything in my power to further this objective. But in 1943, like the Grand Rabbi of Algiers and High Commissioner Giraud and Governor General Peyrouton, I realized that the conditions in Africa were very different from conditions in America.

TWELVE

CELEBRITY CONFERENCE AT CASABLANCA

When President Eisenhower vacated the White House in January 1961, Harold Macmillan was Prime Minister of Great Britain and Charles de Gaulle was President of France. I shall now relate what occurred eighteen years earlier, in January 1943, when the destinies of these three great men became entwined and when I worked in close association with all of them. What happened then explains why Eisenhower spent almost as many months in Algiers as he had intended to spend days, and why his staff rose to thousands of persons instead of the few hundreds anticipated.

When the United States Government agreed to send an expedition to Africa, the American plan was to conduct merely a brief campaign to expel the Germans and Italians from that continent. American military chiefs were under the impression that their British colleagues agreed that after the African campaign, they would without delay invade Europe from bases in the British Isles. But the British General Staff never did favor this American strategy. From the moment in the summer of 1942 when Roosevelt consented to dispatch Americans to North Africa, British strategists began planning a whole series of Mediterranean campaigns. The British were determined to invade Hitler's Europe first from the south, and some of them even believed that with luck they might conquer Germany from Mediterranean bases, thus avoiding altogether the dreaded cross-channel operations. However, the British did not reveal their real intentions during that summer of 1942. In order to assure Anglo-American harmony while planning the African expedition, they awaited a propitious moment to resubmit their case. That moment arrived at a meeting of the Combined Chiefs of Staff, together with President Roosevelt and Prime Minister Churchill, at Casablanca, Morocco, in January 1943.

This meeting had been conceived originally as the first of the Big Three conferences with the Russians. Immediately after the African landings, Roosevelt and Churchill began to talk about sitting down somewhere with Stalin. Both were enthusiastic about the idea and sent invitations to the Kremlin. But Stalin was busy directing battles in Russia—and he also was suspicious. Declining the President's invitation in courteous language, the Soviet generalissimo nevertheless added a tart reminder: "Allow me to express my confidence that the promises about the opening of the second front in Europe given by you, Mr. President, and by Mr. Churchill in regard to 1942, and in any case in regard to the spring of 1943, will be fulfilled." This was not a propaganda maneuver; Stalin's reminder was not made public at the time. Obviously Stalin did not consider the African expedition a substitute for the promised "second front."

Roosevelt and Churchill realized that Stalin's attitude demanded an immediate Anglo-American conference to decide the next war moves, and as the problems seemed entirely military, Roosevelt suggested North Africa for the meeting place since Eisenhower and his staff were there. He wrote Churchill that he would bring "no State Department people," only his military chiefs plus his personal adviser, Harry Hopkins, and his Special Representative, W. Averell Harriman. When Churchill suggested that Foreign Secretary Anthony Eden be included, Roosevelt objected: "In view of Stalin's absence, I think you and I need no foreign affairs people with us, for our work will be essentially military." Churchill concurred, and that is how it came about that neither the State Department nor the British Foreign Office was represented at Casablanca.

However, after all arrangements for the conference had been completed, the assassination of Darlan suddenly made the French political situation an explosive issue. Churchill felt that under the circumstances he, like Roosevelt, should have a personal representative at Allied Force Headquarters. Up to that time, the expedition had been functioning under American agreements with Frenchmen, while British connections with the French were restricted to the De Gaulle group in London. Now the Prime Minister asked Roosevelt for permission to appoint a personal representative in Algiers, and permission was granted. The man selected for this pioneering post was Harold Macmillan, whose relationship with Churchill thus became similar to my own with Roosevelt. It was no sinecure to serve as the personal agents of these brilliant but unpredictable statesmen, whose national and individual objectives sometimes were at cross-purposes, and Macmillan and I became involved in one controversial matter after another. But we got along famously together, not only during our Mediterranean years but also in such postwar crises as the Suez fiasco of 1956 when we again worked together in a matter concerning Great Britain, the United States, and some difficult Frenchmen.

Macmillan's official title in Algiers was Minister Resident, so President Roosevelt elevated me to ministerial rank to match his status. Macmillan was not a career diplomat, nor did he bring to Algiers any exceptional knowledge of French or African affairs. What he did bring was exceptional common sense and knowledge of British politics. Churchill wrote Roosevelt that one reason he chose Macmillan was because, like Churchill himself, he had an American mother. But no American would suspect that ancestry. Macmillan—in dignity, voice, manners, dress, and personality—was and still is almost the American popular image of an English gentleman. He had been a member of Parliament since 1924. This is a part-time job, unlike being a member of Congress, and Macmillan had devoted much of his time before the war to his family's prosperous publishing business. When assigned to Algiers, Macmillan was Parliamentary Under-Secretary of State for Colonies and he often had been invited to sit with the War Cabinet, the highest policy-making group in Britain. His political weight in London was vastly greater than mine in Washington, but I cannot recall a single instance when he invoked this to swing the balance of opinion at Allied Force Headquarters.

Macmillan's assignment in Algiers required more delicate diplomacy than mine did. He had to avoid the appearance of untoward influence, not only upon military leaders, but upon Americans of every kind. Churchill also was careful not to draw attention to his personal representative. Even after the war was long over, Churchill listed Macmillan in the index of his war memoirs as "assistant to the American political representative North Africa"—that is, me. According to one story which circulated in Algiers during the war, Macmillan told his British staff: "These Americans represent the new Roman Empire and we Britons, like the Greeks of old, must teach them how to make it go." Whether or not he ever spoke such words during his service in Algiers, he did indeed exercise greater influence upon Anglo-American affairs in the Mediterranean than was generally recognized.

For one thing, Macmillan's government kept him better informed than my government did me. More than once I learned first from Macmillan and other British colleagues of decisions taken in Washington of vital importance to our joint enterprises. This was not a personal matter but a defect in Washington's coordination. The British Foreign Office cabled duplicates of relevant reports to all its representatives concerned. When I complained that I had to depend upon the British to keep up to date with what was happening in Washington, the reply came that the State Department could not afford the expensive British procedure. That explanation sounded ironic, coming at a time when the British Government was frankly bankrupt and was getting billions in Lend-Lease from the United States. But the finances of the

State Department were subject to the discretion of congressional committees.

The Casablanca Conference was one of the most significant meetings of World War II, and a number of fundamental decisions were made there which have affected American relations with Europe to this day. But because of security regulations, the conference never was adequately reported. The press did not even know it was being held until the final two days, when correspondents were flown in. Then the superficial features of the meeting were exaggerated, while some of the basic decisions were ignored or misinterpreted. The setting of the conference was too theatrical, too fantastic, to be regarded entirely seriously. Roosevelt had insisted upon coming to this active war theater despite the objections of the American Secret Service and Army, which were responsible for safeguarding the formidable assembly of high officials. The conference began only two months after the arrival of American troops, when Morocco was known to be swarming with German agents, and when Casablanca still was attacked occasionally by German bombers. The Berlin radio delighted in reporting unpublicized events in Morocco an hour or so after they happened.

Since no place in Casablanca was really safe, the security agents decided the visitors might as well be comfortable. The modern Anfa Hotel, which had been used by the German Armistice Commission, was made ready for the new guests, together with a group of nearby elegant private villas conspicuously set in tropical gardens. A kind of miniature country club suburb was thus created, but guarded more tightly than any prison. The whole area was triply fenced in and protected day and night by an almost solid line of military police, who issued new kinds of passes every few hours for those of us who had to move in and out of the enclosure. For security reasons, almost all the Moroccan servants were replaced by American and British soldiers. Aside from these soldiers and the security agents, almost everybody inside that luxurious prison was of the highest rank or influence in his respective field.

The tone of the conference was set by President Roosevelt, who repeatedly expressed his delight over this brief escape from Washington's around-the-clock politics. His mood was that of a schoolboy on vacation, which accounted for his almost frivolous approach to some of the difficult problems with which he dealt. Inside Casablanca's toy Suburbia, with its languid climate and exotic atmosphere, two world problems were discussed simultaneously. In one large banquet room of the Anfa Hotel, American and British military chiefs debated global war strategy. In Roosevelt's sumptuous villa, he and the British Prime Minister debated French politics with Giraud, and later, in a deliberately dramatized manner, with De Gaulle.

When Roosevelt agreed to the appointment of Macmillan as Churchill's personal representative, he made certain that Eisenhower should have the last word about everything in Africa. The President completely supported General Marshall's dictum that anything bearing upon military operations must be controlled by the top commander in a theater of war. So the British Prime Minister put in writing that his agent would be as much subject to Eisenhower's orders as I was, and that all French political questions must be referred to the General. This arrangement was well intentioned, but it involved Eisenhower more deeply than he liked in French politics. To advance their own intrigues, French factions tried by every ruse and blandishment to exploit Allied Headquarters, and both Roosevelt and Churchill were constantly demanding that Eisenhower should give his personal attention to these relatively unimportant maneuvers. I heard Eisenhower lament more than once that French, Italian, and other European politics were consuming more of his time and thought than waging the war.

When the Casablanca Conference assembled, the military campaign in North Africa was reaching a crucial stage, and Eisenhower decided he could not possibly spare more than a few hours with the Combined Chiefs of Staff plus Roosevelt and Churchill, and he flew back to Algiers from Casablanca the day following his arrival. I remember the Supreme Commander coming into Roosevelt's bedroom where Macmillan and I were having an early morning meeting with the President while he was still in bed. Eisenhower gave a very smart salute before leaving, and Macmillan whispered in my ear, "Isn't he just like a Roman centurion!" As for the French political details at the conference, the General simply loaded that diplomatic donkey work on Macmillan and me. We took our orders every day, sometimes several times a day, directly from our famous chiefs, Churchill and Roosevelt, both of whom immensely enjoyed the political game at Casablanca.

Of course I did not participate in any of the military discussions at the conference, whose issues I was incompetent to judge, but the outcome of the war strategy decisions had direct bearing upon my political work. From my very first talks with Macmillan, he was remarkably frank with me about British problems in the Mediterranean. That great inland sea and the countries bordering upon it had loomed importantly for centuries in the history of the British Empire. Macmillan told me that Churchill's disaster at Gallipoli in World War I added a personal factor to the Prime Minister's strategic planning now—he deeply desired to justify in this war the Gallipoli campaign which had failed under his previous sponsorship.

Ever since the outbreak of World War II, British forces had never ceased fighting in the eastern Mediterranean. They had managed to cling precariously to Egypt and the Suez Canal, to Malta and Gibraltar, taking enormous losses at sea while pushing convoys through to beleaguered garrisons, even while the British people themselves were enduring food shortages. To the British, the Mediterranean was an essential link in their imperial system, and they were gravely concerned about what would happen in this area after the war, as well as during the war. So when they moved into French North Africa with the Americans in November 1942, they arrived with an outlook altogether different from ours. To nearly all American strategists, the Mediterranean was a temporary battleground and little more. To our Navy, the Japanese war in the Pacific was all-absorbing; our Army was intent upon an invasion of Europe from British bases. Our military chiefs had almost unanimously opposed the African expedition in the first place. Now they wanted to pull out as quickly as possible, return to England, and proceed there with preparations for a massive cross-channel attack. To them, the French African campaign was an unwelcome distraction from "getting on with the war."

These divergent British and American war policies were blended at the Casablanca Conference by a "compromise." Macmillan told me something about how the new joint strategy was agreed upon; I myself observed some of the maneuvering; I guessed some of the other details. But it was not until the publication in 1957 of *Turn of the Tide*, based on the diaries of Field Marshal Lord Alanbrooke, that my information about what occurred at the conference was officially confirmed. A diary of the Chief of the British Imperial General Staff reveals that the British planned their debating campaign at Casablanca as skillfully as they planned their combat campaigns against the Axis. Alanbrooke's diary records that Churchill, in a kickoff talk to the British military chiefs just before the opening of the conference, instructed them not to hurry the Americans or try to force agreement, but to take plenty of time, the "dropping of water on stone." The Prime Minister said he would do the same with President Roosevelt. These tactics worked perfectly.

According to Alanbrooke, the British anticipated that Marshall would continue to argue at Casablanca that Mediterranean hostilities were "diversions" from the main show, and that the American Chief of Staff would be strongly supported by Harry Hopkins. So the British devised what they called a compromise. They proposed that, after Africa was cleared, Sicily should be occupied by an Anglo-American force in order to assure a relatively safe shipping route through the Mediterranean Sea. The Americans had not come prepared to debate this proposition, but the British brought to Casablanca a six-thousand-ton ship, converted into a reference library. It was crammed with all the essential files from the War Office and had a complete staff of file clerks. The outcome of such thoughtful preparation was inevitable. The "compromise" was adopted. It had been adroitly designed to persuade reluctant Americans to accept the strategy which kept them fighting for more than two years in this traditional sphere of British influence. Instead of the quick campaign which Eisenhower had expected to fight in Africa, he had to plan and direct several additional campaigns on Mediterranean islands and in southern Europe. More than a year passed before he could even get back to England to prepare at last for the kind of invasion of Europe which he and other Americans had wanted in the first place. But the American High Command never changed its Mediterranean outlook. For the two years we fought there, we were a reluctant tail to the British kite, and thus failed to exploit several opportunities.

When the Combined Chiefs of Staff, supported by Churchill and Roosevelt, thus substituted British Mediterranean strategy for the previous American plans, they automatically rendered obsolete the ideas which had governed American war relations with Frenchmen up to that time. The British, assuming that the Mediterranean campaign would extend into Europe, tried to establish a strong central French authority which could deal with matters affecting French long-range interests. Americans were slow to recognize this need, partly because our military strategists never ceased trying to detach themselves from the Mediterranean, and partly because of Roosevelt's ideas about the future of France.

Casablanca afforded my first opportunity to report in person to the President since I initiated the "Darlan deal," and he commented favorably upon our French negotiation. Then he added, looking mildly reproachful, "But you overdid things a bit in one of the letters you wrote to Giraud before the landings, pledging the United States Government to guarantee the return to France of every part of her empire. Your letter may make trouble for me after the war." That was the first indication to me that Roosevelt was planning to encourage extensive reductions in the French empire, but it was apparent at Casablanca that this project was much on his mind. He discussed with several people, including Eisenhower and me, the transfer of control of Dakar, Indochina, and other French possessions, and he did not seem fully aware how abhorrent his attitude would be to all imperialist-minded Frenchmen including De Gaulle and also those with whom I had negotiated agreements.

No problem has been more disturbing to France than her overseas empire. This has been an explosive issue for generations—as it still is today—and patriotic Frenchmen have argued about every aspect of this sensitive question. Roosevelt was in agreement with the opinion of the greatest French statesman of World War I, Georges Clemenceau, who wrote: "I have always been opposed to colonial ventures for France, and always will be. We can never be good colonists, and should not try. It was Bismarck who treacherously encouraged France to embark on schemes for colonial expansion, knowing that they would weaken her. He it was who incited France to go into Tunisia. And it was Napoleon, that evil genius of France, who plunged France into adventures overseas and was responsible for the comparative weakness of his country."

Roosevelt's intense personal interest in French affairs was not always helpful, as events at the Casablanca Conference demonstrated. Having a thousand and one things on his mind, he simply did not have time to follow through some of his personal decisions. He forgot that he ever made some detailed agreements and usually there was no record of them in any regular government department. Often Harry Hopkins was the only witness to presidential decisions, even on such technical matters as the exchange rate between dollars and French African francs. The President discussed replacement of French officials and changes in French laws in Africa as if these were matters for Americans to decide. But when I asked whether American policy had changed, and if we now regarded our presence in French Africa as a military occupation, Roosevelt replied there had been no change in policy. The President's inconsistency on this point remained an awkward problem all through the Mediterranean campaigns.

It may not be altogether an oversimplification to say that Roosevelt at Casablanca approached French politics in terms of two French generals: Henri Giraud and Charles de Gaulle. The President listened attentively to my résumé of what happened after the death of Darlan—how De Gaulle cabled Giraud on the very day of the murder, proposing that the two of them meet on French soil to discuss a merger, and how Giraud put off the requested meeting. One reason Giraud did not want to talk then with De Gaulle was because he believed that members of De Gaulle's London staff had connived with the assassins. Another reason for postponing the get-together was Giraud's preoccupation with rearming French troops and sending them into battle. When we introduced Giraud to Roosevelt, the French general completely confirmed what we had reported about his lack of interest in politics. Giraud's attention wandered whenever Roosevelt raised political questions, and he turned back the conversation as quickly as possible to pleas for more American equipment for French troops. Clearly, this fighting general was willing to accept any political arrangement which respected French sovereignty over its empire and left Giraud in command of the French forces.

At one of the informal meetings which were held in the President's bedroom first thing in the morning, Roosevelt referred to Giraud as a rather simple-minded soldier and commented jocularly on my judgment—or lack of judgment—in having picked him as the provisional leader in French North Africa. I reminded the President of his expressed desire to treat with French authorities during the remainder of the war on a local level only. That is, no individual was to be recognized as representing the Government of France. Although Giraud was totally disinterested in politics, he had an unblemished name and an excellent reputation as a fighting general in Morocco who knew that area. He also was part of the French underground in metropolitan France. On his record, Giraud was an ideal selection to fill Roosevelt's own prescription.

As for De Gaulle, it was apparent that Roosevelt had not altered in the slightest the opinion which he expounded to me at Hyde Park the previous September. The President still deplored what he called De Gaulle's readiness, almost eagerness, to start civil wars, and he told me that it was important as ever to prevent any disputes between Frenchmen which might interfere with military operations. He could see for himself in Morocco how valuable it was to retain the support of the local French administrators, even though some of them still proclaimed loyalty to the Pétain regime. He could see that the success of the military campaign depended upon how well these Frenchmen maintained order in the vast territories through which our supplies moved to the fighting fronts. Roosevelt was more convinced than ever that he had been right in dealing with Vichy from 1940 through 1942, and that he should continue to refuse to recognize De Gaulle or anybody else as the sole governing authority for France until the French people were free to make their own choice. Roosevelt never abandoned that attitude, although it became increasingly difficult to maintain.

British relations with De Gaulle were quite different, however. As Macmillan explained to me in one of our private talks, the British Government had invested a great deal of prestige and money—he mentioned the sum of seventy million pounds—since it had backed this French dark horse in the gloomiest days of 1940. Admitting that De Gaulle was a "difficult person," Macmillan pointed out that the indomitable Frenchman nevertheless had shared British determination to continue the fight against Nazi Germany when the odds against British victory seemed tremendous. Macmillan declared that British self-interest and prestige and honor all demanded that the British Government should support De Gaulle's political aspirations. The French leader was determined to push his own London Committee into the African administration, and Macmillan said that the British

Government felt bound to support that objective insofar as it could be satisfied without endangering military operations.

In December 1942, Eisenhower still hoped that the Germans in Tunisia might be routed in short order, and that Giraud's French-trained professional soldiers, most of them Moslems, might prove a decisive factor. Darlan's assassination occurred at a critical moment in the campaign, but De Gaulle's well-developed political instincts made him feel that this was the moment to strike, and to strike with all his force. He protested publicly as well as privately against the delay in permitting him to go to North Africa, and this stimulated another press uproar by his British and American supporters. These tactics particularly annoyed Roosevelt, but public reaction showed him that De Gaulle's aspirations could not be ignored. The urgent diplomatic problem was how to include De Gaulle in the Algiers administration without creating civil disorders which would disrupt the military campaign. Macmillan and I accordingly were instructed to make a satisfactory arrangement with the French Imperial Council in Algiers before the opening of the Casablanca Conference.

The formula which we devised, and which was approved by Eisenhower, was to offer De Gaulle joint political leadership with Giraud immediately, and to combine those members of the Imperial Council who had assisted the Anglo-American expedition with members of De Gaulle's London Committee, in an enlarged Algiers organization. When we escorted Giraud to Casablanca to be presented to Roosevelt, it was understood that De Gaulle would be invited to meet Giraud there and that a French merger would be concluded with some pomp. The prospects for such a settlement seemed hopeful because De Gaulle on several occasions had spoken respectfully of Giraud; De Gaulle had proposed that they meet on French soil; and De Gaulle had taken the initiative in suggesting a merger. Giraud deserved the respect of De Gaulle; he greatly outranked him, having earned his fifth star before the war while De Gaulle was only a colonel. In fact, rank was the only point on which Giraud insisted during our preliminary discussions. He would not serve as a subordinate in military matters to a two-star junior. If De Gaulle had been a civilian official, this question of rank never would have arisen.

During Roosevelt's first three days at Casablanca, Churchill persuaded him to agree to the settlement which the French Imperial Council and Eisenhower had approved. The Prime Minister and the President proposed to confound critics of both British and American policies by appearing at the conference as the benevolent sponsors of a "shotgun marriage"—as Roosevelt put it—between two French factions separated, according to their interpretation, only by the whims of two temperamental French generals. The proposed new arrangement was much more favorable to De Gaulle than his previous status, and Churchill naturally was very pleased. For one thing, the merger promised to remove De Gaulle and his associates from the British payroll, which had supported them for two and a half years since the fall of France. The French exiles in London had no access to French funds because part of the French gold reserve was frozen in the United States and a larger part was held by Frenchmen in Africa who opposed De Gaulle. The General himself was entirely dependent upon the British for the airplanes in which he made his wartime trips and even for his personal expenses.

So Churchill happily sent word to De Gaulle in London that he had arranged an immediate meeting with Giraud at Casablanca to conclude a merger. For security reasons, this first Churchill invitation did not mention Roosevelt's presence in Africa. Experience had shown that few if any secrets were safe in De Gaulle's London headquarters. But then, to Churchill's intense mortification, De Gaulle rejected his invitation, declaring that he and Giraud did not require a British intermediary to bring them together to discuss purely French affairs. At first Roosevelt was more amused than disturbed by this development. All through the informal meetings and social gatherings at Casablanca there was a great deal of joking about bringing together the French "bride" and "groom," and the President rather enjoyed Churchill's discomfiture. Roosevelt was confident that the Prime Minister could get De Gaulle to Casablanca whenever he chose to exert enough pressure.

That proved to be true, but the proud Frenchman kept the conferees waiting several days, and before he finally arrived on January 22 there was some real doubt about whether he would appear at all. So he focused everybody's attention upon himself and he did not overlook this opportunity to make the most of the fact that Roosevelt and Churchill needed his cooperation at that moment as much as he needed theirs. For thirty-one months the British wartime propaganda machine had built up De Gaulle as the symbol of French resistance, and the Nazi-Vichy propagandists had done almost as much for his reputation by denunciations of him. De Gaulle, despite his lack of material resources, was well aware now of his symbolic value to Roosevelt and Churchill, as well as to his own French cause.

The evening of the day De Gaulle arrived at Casablanca, just before he and Roosevelt were to meet each other for the first time, the President gave a dinner in honor of the Sultan of Morocco. This affair was entirely Roosevelt's own idea. He had not forgotten the reluctance of General Nogues to deliver his letter to the Sultan at the time of the landings, and one of the first things the President asked me to do was to arrange an intimate little dinner at his villa.

The Sultan was accompanied by his eldest son, and the other guests were Nogues—who was invited as the Sultan's Foreign Minister under the French Protectorate—Churchill, Macmillan, Marshall, Patton, Hopkins, Elliott Roosevelt, and me. In deference to the Sultan's Moslem code of behavior, no alcoholic beverages of any kind were served before, during, or after the dinner. Perhaps it was this rare abstinence which caused the British Prime Minister to be unnaturally glum throughout the evening; or perhaps he remained silent because he regarded the whole occasion as deliberately provocative.

The President began the serious conversation by expressing sympathy with colonial aspirations for independence, and soon he was proposing to the Sultan that arrangements should be made after the war for American-Moroccan economic cooperation. Nogues, who had devoted his career to fortifying the French position in Morocco, could not conceal his outraged feelings. Hopkins noticed his restlessness but misunderstood why the Frenchman was perturbed. In an aside to me after dinner, Hopkins observed that Nogues seemed to be uneasy "because he knows we may throw him out any minute." I suggested to Hopkins, "Perhaps the President's approaches to the Sultan also aggravate Nogues' fears about American designs on the French empire. From the point of view of any imperialist—including De Gaulle and Churchill—the President's conversation with the Sultan could seem subversive." With an impatient shrug, Hopkins changed the subject.

Of course, De Gaulle's informants told him about the President's overtures to the Sultan, and this increased the General's distrust of Roosevelt. Although it was De Gaulle, and not the Americans, who eventually threw Nogues out of his position in Morocco, De Gaulle saw eye to eye with Nogues on what De Gaulle has described as Roosevelt's "insinuations" to the Sultan. De Gaulle recorded in his memoirs that the Sultan remained loyal to France in spite of Roosevelt's interference, and added: "It must be admitted that the influence of Nogues, in this regard, had been happily exercised on the sovereign's mind." When De Gaulle wrote this, he did not foresee that a postwar French Government would imprison and exile the Sultan, and that this sovereign later would lead Morocco to the independence which Roosevelt "insinuated" in 1943.

De Gaulle consented to appear at the Casablanca Conference only because Churchill finally issued a flat ultimatum that if he did not come, he would forfeit his position as Britain's chosen instrument. The general flew to French Africa from London by grace of the British Royal Air Force. No French guards welcomed him upon his arrival at the airport, or en route to the enclosure, or within it. But American soldiers were everywhere. Four villas had been assigned to the "wedding party"—the two best for Roosevelt and Churchill, and two slightly smaller houses for Giraud and De Gaulle. The latter two villas were almost identical, to suggest equality between the French generals.

Roosevelt had commissioned me to introduce De Gaulle to his pleasant villa and then accompany him across the street to meet the President. I greeted the general politely and said, "It must be good to be back again among your own people." De Gaulle replied haughtily, "I never would have consented to stay in this house, surrounded by American barbed wire and bayonets, if I had not been informed that it is owned by a Dane, not by a Frenchman!" After this inauspicious beginning, the general asked me to sit down and we had half an hour's talk before going to the President.

I had given a good deal of thought to what I could say to De Gaulle which might induce him to come to Algiers with a friendlier attitude toward the United States. Now he seemed to be listening carefully as I went on, "We all are happy that you are here. While I would not presume to advise you about French and North African politics, I feel I should say that it would be very helpful to everybody concerned if you could come without making legalistic conditions. I am certain that if you do, you will have complete control of the French political situation within three months, because General Giraud is interested solely in his military command and has no political ambitions." De Gaulle smiled thinly and replied, "Political ambitions can develop rapidly. For example, look at me!"

This unexpected expression of wry humor encouraged me, and I went on to explain the policy of Roosevelt in regard to France. I said that the President was determined to deal with Frenchmen only on a local basis until the people of France could choose their own form of government and their own leaders. I described how our relations with the Vichy Government had arisen, how the President's one idea from the beginning was to help the French people and keep alive French hopes of resistance and eventual victory. De Gaulle listened in silence. I did not know what impression I was making. When it came time to go, he said abruptly, "I have come down here a prisoner of my London Committee. I am not empowered to make any binding decisions while in Casablanca." That was fair warning. He never budged from that position despite every argument or device which Churchill, Roosevelt, Macmillan, and the rest of us could contrive.

Churchill and Roosevelt had devoted much careful attention to preparing the ceremonies at Casablanca which they hoped would solve their French difficulties, at least for the time being. But De Gaulle, having deliberately delayed his arrival until the last moment, made a grand entrance and stole the show. This professional soldier, who never had participated even in national politics before the war, now put on such a sparkling performance in international power politics that he took the star role away from the two greatest English-speaking politicians. On one occasion at a meeting in Roosevelt's villa, with several of us present, Churchill, in a white fury over De Gaulle's stubbornness, shook his finger in the General's face. In his inimitable French, with his dentures clicking, Churchill exclaimed: *"Mon Général, il ne faut pas obstacler* [sic] *la guerre!"* (General, you just cannot place obstacles in the way of winning the war!) De Gaulle, disregarding the Prime Minister's outburst of temper, vehemently asserted that he enjoyed the popular support of the citizens of French North Africa and should not have been excluded from the Allied landings. De Gaulle scorned the hostility against him of the French Armed Forces in Africa, especially the Navy, whose top officers openly characterized him as a British stooge because of the British attack on the French Navy at Mers el-Kebir in July 1940—when fourteen hundred French sailors were killed—and the British-De Gaulle attack on Dakar two months later. The United States had believed it could not afford to ignore that hostility at the critical moment of the Allied landings.

From the point of view of De Gaulle, the entire Casablanca setup was all wrong for a settlement between Frenchmen. He was offered a formula which he considered the handiwork of Roosevelt, Churchill and their agents. To accept it was to acknowledge before the world that France no longer was a great power—which De Gaulle never for one moment has admitted at any time in his life. Our plans were designed to appeal to his desire to speed along the common victory, but our elaborate preparations were wasted upon him. He came to the conference firmly resolved to make no agreement, and throughout his two days there he maintained the pose of a Frenchman righteously indignant at the arrogant behavior of Anglo-American interlopers on French soil, who had come there without his permission.

So the French merger which was supposed to provide the highlight of the Casablanca communiqué was not consummated. However, De Gaulle did agree to make a conciliatory gesture for the benefit of the British and American correspondents and photographers who had been flown in. (The French press was not invited.) De Gaulle composed an innocuous statement declaring that he and Giraud had met and exchanged views, and the two Generals solemnly shook hands while Roosevelt and Churchill smilingly looked on. Then they obligingly repeated this performance for the photographers. Oddly enough, this staging of an artificial reconciliation misled Roosevelt and Churchill almost as much as it misled the press representatives. When pictures of the French handshake were released a few days later, public agitation in England and the United States subsided temporarily, and Roosevelt expressed confidence that the conference had made a giant step toward solving "the French problem." The President persuaded himself that he had "managed" De Gaulle—Roosevelt's own word—and could continue to manage him. This illusion that a French solution had been found was one of the most unfortunate consequences of the conference. The President held to this mistaken view for several months.

As the conference was closing, Harry Hopkins remarked to me, "It seems a pretty feeble effort for two great countries in 1943." Hopkins was still lamenting the postponement of his favored knockout blow from Britain. But Casablanca was no feeble effort for the British, who won American approval for their Mediterranean program, both military and political. De Gaulle also got at least as much as he expected at Casablanca. He persuaded Giraud to receive his representatives immediately at Algiers, and that was the beginning of the end for Giraud. Within less than five months, the political ascendancy of De Gaulle in French Africa was absolute, although Roosevelt never did formally recognize it.

Meanwhile the Allies were completing their military campaign in Tunisia. For me, that campaign to eliminate the Nazis from North Africa was the culmination of years of effort. It marked a turning point in the war—the first major Allied victory—the destruction of the myth of Nazi invincibility. During the last days of the fighting, I toured the Tunisian front in a jeep in the happy company of Colonels Julius Holmes and Harvey Gerry. Along the way, we encountered long convoys of Allied trucks laden with disarmed and subdued prisoners of war going to the prison cages at Mateur, usually with only one brisk Allied sergeant in charge. In the final week alone of that Tunisian drive, the Allies captured 240,000 prisoners, of whom 125,000 were Germans, including all the survivors of Rommel's famed Africa Korps. Tunisia had been the testing ground of the American troops, most of them green and untried, and of their ability to work in harness with the British. The exhilarating results which I witnessed compensated for all the tribulations since 1940 in the buildup of the African venture.

Later I interviewed some of the German officers in the prison cages to ascertain their political reactions. The refrain which ran through most of their remarks was that we Americans would regret our military intervention because the Nazis were the last bulwark against Bolshevism, and that we would see Bolshevism spread over all of Europe and eventually America. Indoctrination of those Nazi officers had been thorough; even in defeat they entertained not the slightest doubt that their cause was right.

On May 20, 1943, a Victory Parade and review of troops was held in Tunis, and Macmillan and I were invited to participate in the celebration. There we learned that the Bey of Tunis intended to bestow medals on the top Allied personnel—Eisenhower, Montgomery, Alexander and many others, including Macmillan and me. Although we appreciated the Bey's courtesy, neither Macmillan nor I could accept his awards because the American and British governments do not permit diplomats to receive such honors from a "foreign potentate." To avoid an awkward situation, Macmillan and I decided not to attend the reception but to go directly to the airport after the parade. We were on board our plane, ready to take off, when the Bey's protocol officer rushed up and tossed two parcels through the plane door, one for Macmillan and one for me. Each parcel contained the collar and insignia of the Tunisian Order of Nicham Iftikar ("Medal to be Proud Of"), First Class. Wearing these rather gaudy decorations, we played bridge on the plane returning to Algiers. Perhaps it was because I lost at bridge on that occasion that I never wore the medal again.

The unproclaimed victory which De Gaulle won at the Casablanca Conference was a great step forward in his plan to assure France the largest possible share in Allied conquests, including full restoration of the French Empire. The miscalculation which all of us at Casablanca made about De Gaulle was our belief that winning the war had top priority with him, as it did with us. But De Gaulle's memoirs which he wrote after the war, during his long years of seclusion at his country estate in France, show that his thoughts were two jumps ahead of everybody else's. By 1943, with Russia fighting strongly against the Nazis and with the United States moving into all-out global hostilities, De Gaulle correctly calculated that Allied victory was certain, and that France would share in that victory regardless of what French soldiers accomplished or failed to do. This politically minded General decided that it was his function to concentrate upon restoring France as a great power, which he considered its rightful position. He sensed that he could exact greater concessions for France in the midst of total war than later, even though France then possessed less military and economic power than in centuries.

When De Gaulle's three volumes of memoirs were published in France during 1954–56, I was astonished to see how much space he devoted to me. This eminent Frenchman apparently believed that I had more influence with Roosevelt than I actually did, and therefore more effect upon French-American relations. Until I read De Gaulle's memoirs, I did not realize that his conception of my character and my importance was based largely upon the wartime fabrications of the Nazi-subsidized newspapers in France. The Germans feared Roosevelt's Vichy policy and were more eager than even De Gaulle to discredit it. Nazi propagandists worked diligently to blacken the reputations of all members of the American Embassy at Vichy, from Ambassador Leahy down. It was the Nazi press in Paris which first depicted me as a conspirator who had associated with the wrong kind of Frenchmen throughout my long residence in France, with decadent aristocrats and rich schemers. The French exile press picked up some details of this Nazi fiction, as did some English and even American periodicals. Somewhere along the line, De Gaulle absorbed this erroneous impression of my activities, and his memoirs show that his mistrust of Roosevelt, and of me as Roosevelt's agent, never abated.

Churchill and Roosevelt left Casablanca confident that they had fitted De Gaulle into a subordinate place, whereas De Gaulle actually set in motion there a series of events which soon would confound and humiliate his French enemies in Africa, would give him absolute control of French African administrations, and would cause persistent worries for Eisenhower as long as he remained in the Mediterranean —in fact, would have disturbing after-effects which Eisenhower would have to consider right up to his retirement in 1961 as President of the United States.

But De Gaulle never could have moved so far so fast without the help of another Frenchman, Jean Monnet, who in many respects is more remarkable than De Gaulle himself. It can be plausibly argued that Monnet has been the most influential man in France of his generation, and he also has exerted a major influence upon the affairs of the United States, Great Britain, and other countries. He is the kind of international figure who avoids publicity, preferring to remain in the background no matter how much power he is wielding. It is characteristic of Monnet that he never has claimed credit for his part in De Gaulle's elevation to power in Algiers in June 1943.

It was Roosevelt who first suggested to me at Casablanca that Monnet might be useful in Algiers. I had known Monnet in Paris. He is a member of an old Cognac family, a wealthy private banker who earned a formidable reputation helping to finance France during World War I, then served between the wars as First Deputy Secretary-General of the League of Nations. In 1940 he was in London directing the financing of France in World War II, when his country's Army suddenly collapsed. But Monnet did not join the De Gaulle movement, or publicly endorse De Gaulle's defiance of the armistice. Instead, Monnet went to Washington as a member of the British Supply Council, by personal appointment of Churchill. Thus Monnet had no formal ties in 1943 with any French faction, and he had won the confidence of many influential Americans, including Harry Hopkins.

It was Hopkins who proposed to Roosevelt at Casablanca that Monnet should be appointed political adviser to Giraud. Time and again the President had completely ignored the State Department in more important African matters than this seemed to be, but now he cabled Secretary Hull asking for advice about appointing Monnet. Hull replied that Monnet seemed to be more closely linked with De Gaulle than appeared on the surface, and Roosevelt let the matter drop. But after returning to Washington, Hopkins again urged the appointment, and in February Monnet appeared in Algiers with letters from Hopkins to Eisenhower and to me, saying that the President wanted him to have every help we could give him. I received no word from Hull about this development, and Jean Monnet is not even mentioned in Hull's voluminous memoirs. For that matter, Monnet also is not mentioned in Eisenhower's African recollections, nor in the detailed diary of Eisenhower's personal aide, Harry Butcher. This is a tribute to Monnet's genius for self-effacement.

In Monnet's first talk with me, he frankly stated that he had come to Algiers not so much to serve Giraud as to seek a solution which would create unity among all French factions. This was what all of us were eager to accomplish, but months passed before we learned that Monnet's idea of French unity challenged Roosevelt's conception. Monnet found a quiet villa for himself on the outskirts of Algiers and spent long weekends there in private negotiations or, as he told us, just thinking. I assigned my deputy, Samuel Reber, to give him whatever assistance he required, and Eisenhower asked his Chief of Staff, General Smith, to do the same. Smith assigned to Monnet a French-speaking American sergeant who was even more impressed with the Frenchman than were the rest of us. Unfortunately for the sergeant, he misinterpreted Smith's orders and showed Monnet top-secret military files. The day when the irascible Chief of Staff discovered this, he could be heard all through the St. George Hotel headquarters shouting: "Take this blankety-blank fool out and shoot him right now!" But French-speaking men were scarce in our Army, so the well-meaning soldier was retained on the job, though he became a corporal.

All through that spring of 1943, as Americans, Britons, Frenchmen, and Arabs fought and died in the concluding battles against Germans in Africa, a political civil war was being waged simultaneously around Algiers. Thousands of De Gaulle supporters drifted in from several directions, some arriving from other French African colonies, some coming from England and France, some from Montgomery's British Eighth Army in Egypt. After operating on a shoestring for so long, De Gaulle somehow had acquired ample funds which now enabled him to offer handsome pay increases to induce French officers and civil servants to throw in their lot with him. These offers were tempting to the underpaid Frenchmen in Africa. Such recruiting dangerously weakened French fighting morale, but De Gaulle was playing for higher stakes than a subordinate role in Allied military campaigns. His purpose, as he repeatedly stated, was to organize around himself a central French authority, recognized as such, qualified to bargain on even terms with Great Britain and the United States.

Soon after the arrival of Monnet, high-level negotiations started between representatives of De Gaulle and Giraud. As Giraud's adviser, Monnet always attended these sessions and he summarized their results for Macmillan and me. Since he was entitled to participate in these French negotiations, and we were not, this arrangement seemed excellent. We assumed that we were being informed of all important developments. Monnet did not conceal from us his impatience with Giraud's political ineptitude. He exclaimed: "When the general looks at you with those eyes of a porcelain cat, he comprehends nothing!" But Monnet worked skillfully to win Giraud's confidence and soon succeeded.

As the battles in Africa drew to a close in May, it became apparent that De Gaulle and Giraud were near agreement. Being advised of this, Prime Minister Churchill and Foreign Secretary Eden arrived in Algiers to celebrate the "marriage" which had been a major British objective, so long delayed. On June 3 it was announced that De Gaulle had accepted a formula which seemed almost identical with the one we had proposed at Casablanca five months earlier. Giraud and De Gaulle were to become joint chairmen of a seven-man French Committee of National Liberation which would replace the Imperial Council. Monnet was to be a member of this committee, as Giraud's chief political representative. The next day, June 4, the British group entertained the French committee members at a "victory lunch" to which no Americans were invited. It seemed fitting that the British should celebrate the smooth interposition of their protégé into the Algiers administration, and Macmillan told me that everything went off well at the luncheon except that De Gaulle was even more reserved than usual.

Three days later the skies fell. Navy Commander Viret, the genial aide of Giraud, telephoned me about six o'clock in the morning and asked urgently if I would please come right away to French Headquarters. I was not unaccustomed to early morning calls because Giraud normally began his day at 4:30 A.M. His favorite quip was that the difference between generals and diplomats was that the former arose very early to do nothing, nothing, all day; while the latter arose very late for the same purpose. So I went to Giraud's office immediately, where the conscientious Viret showed me several decrees which Giraud, after weeks of negotiations with Monnet, had signed during the night in his capacity as Chairman of the French Imperial Council, the de facto governing body in French Africa. Glancing hastily through the pile of documents, I saw that Giraud had practically signed away all his powers to De Gaulle. I asked the Commander: "Does General Giraud know what he has done?" Viret shrugged wearily.

I went in to see Giraud and explained the effect of the decrees. Giraud cried in obvious astonishment: "But I never was told that!" He read the decrees carefully, as though for the first time. Then after a moment's reflection he too shrugged his shoulders, saying that he had been informed that these matters were purely internal French affairs which required no prior consultation with Americans or Britons. This did not seem to displease Giraud, a fighting soldier, who was under the impression that he would retain control of French military forces in any event, an authority which he cherished much more than political strength. In taking leave of Giraud that morning, I told him as sympathetically as I could that he had signed himself out of power. Soon after De Gaulle took over, Giraud was relieved of his command.

Returning to my office, I telephoned Macmillan and described what had happened. We then asked Monnet to join us, and related to him the circumstances as we saw them, pointing out that the three of us had worked rather closely for several months during which we had given him our confidence. Monnet was non-commital and in effect told us that he really had no information to impart regarding French internal affairs. He referred to the fact that Rene Massigli, a career diplomat, was handling Foreign Affairs in the French Imperial Council. Monnet thus politely declared French independence.

Events in Algiers moved swiftly after Giraud signed away his authority, and De Gaulle's mastery of French internal politics became virtually absolute. He quickly formed what was still called a Committee but actually was a de facto French Government with a cabinet of De Gaulle's choosing, including Massigli as Foreign Minister. This skillful maneuver was not made public, and Roosevelt with many burdens pressing upon him perhaps did not fully comprehend the important role of Monnet in the transition in Algiers from Giraud to De Gaulle. I never discussed the matter with the President. It was a delicate subject since Roosevelt himself, through Harry Hopkins, had provided letters which gave Monnet almost the status of a personal envoy of the President in French Africa. It was this authority which led to the establishment of De Gaulle as a challenge to Roosevelt's own attitude toward the French Empire. Understandably, this political triumph increased immeasurably Roosevelt's distrust of De Gaulle's organization, and it helps to explain the President's subsequent refusal to recognize De Gaulle's Committee as the Government of France long after it was firmly established. Contrary to the then vehement

Gaullist opposition to relinquishing an inch of territory anywhere, Roosevelt never doubted during those war days that the French Empire was visibly withering on the vine.

Monnet never impressed me as Gaullist in the usual sense. At times he was almost as critical of De Gaulle as of Giraud. I believe that France has always come first with Monnet, above personalities. His adroitness in international politics has been at the service of his country for half a century, but never more impressively than at Algiers. Having accomplished what Roosevelt did not want to see accomplished, Monnet returned to Washington later that same year with apparently undiminished influence on the Roosevelt administration. When Lend-Lease ended, it was Monnet who negotiated a loan to take up the slack in France—a $650,000,000 loan which greeted General de Gaulle when he made a state visit to President Truman after the end of the war. Since then Monnet has done much to ensure that American funds were available to stimulate the French and European economy. Having observed him operate at close quarters in Algiers, I have followed with profound appreciation his subsequent maneuvers in the development of his design for Europe.

In Algiers, too, I formed an opinion of De Gaulle as an ardent French patriot, but I never regarded him as a close friend of my country. I did not find that he then was a great admirer of American military or political sagacity. He knew little of the United States or of Americans, and it seemed to me that he was cynical in his appraisal of how the United States could be "played" vis-a-vis the Soviet Union and Europe for the benefit of France. In his references to Britons and Americans, De Gaulle termed them "the Anglo-Saxons" which, curiously enough, was Hitler's terminology.

One of the first actions taken by De Gaulle's reorganized committee was to accept the resignation of Marcel Peyrouton and to dismiss from office Pierre Boisson, the Governors General of Algeria and French West Africa, respectively. Later De Gaulle ordered that they be brought to trial for alleged collaboration with the Nazis. Both of these Frenchmen had been given assurances of Allied protection, by Churchill in person and by Roosevelt in writing. When their arrest was announced on June 11, 1943, Roosevelt cabled: "Please inform the French Committee as follows: 'In view of the assistance given to the Allied armies during the campaign in Africa, you are directed to take no action against Peyrouton and Boisson at the present time.'" Eisenhower asked me to convey this message orally to De Gaulle, which I did the same evening—in more diplomatic language.

I found De Gaulle in an unexpectedly amiable state of mind. He talked for half an hour on the need for better understanding with the United States. He declared that he had been fully aware, from the day in June 1940 when he denounced the armistice with Germany, that the outcome of the war and the future of France would depend upon what America did. He said that Americans should be better able to understand the aspirations of the "new France" than Britons. When I assured him that American and British policies toward France were now almost identical, he looked skeptical. He referred repeatedly to Boisson, whose case particularly troubled Roosevelt because, as I explained to De Gaulle, this Governor General of French West Africa had peacefully transferred to the Allies the great port of Dakar, which had been a grave source of worry to the President lest it fall into German hands.

But De Gaulle had his own reasons for also considering Boisson a special case. As Governor of Dakar in 1940, Boisson had humiliated De Gaulle in the eyes of the world by the embarrassing ease with which he drove off De Gaulle's abortive attempt to capture Dakar. De Gaulle told me that if he retained Boisson in office, or failed to punish him, his own authority would be undermined before his Committee of National Liberation was soundly established. When I pointed out that the committee, and not De Gaulle personally, would presumably decide such matters, De Gaulle agreed. But he added that he could not remain a member of any committee which would brook interference by a foreign power in any purely French matter. I tried to convince him that, because of the war, French, American and British affairs were now inextricably mixed in French Africa, and therefore could not be treated simply as national affairs, but he remained obdurate.

During that summer and autumn of 1943, while the collapse of Italy diverted Anglo-American attention from French to Italian affairs, I had to endure many frustrating experiences. The bases in Africa became more valuable than ever when Sicily was conquered in thirty-eight days and the chaos of southern Europe opened many tempting prospects to Allied Force Headquarters. Macmillan and I were involved in Italian affairs from the moment Mussolini was overthrown, but French affairs also continued to occupy us until October. A few French generals were more interested in combat than in politics, and prepared troops to fight in Italy, but De Gaulle's interest remained almost exclusively political.

It was painful for me, during those months, to watch Frenchmen who had helped my early efforts and the Anglo-American expedition being pushed inexorably out of all key posts. Some of the most prominent among our friends were imprisoned and maltreated. Mme. Boisson called one day, just after a tiring trip by bicycle, her only means of transport to visit her husband in his cramped prison cell. She told me that he had been refused even a comfortable chair, despite the fact that one of his legs had been amputated due to battle injuries in World War I. She came to me only to ask for a replacement for his hearing aid, which I obtained for her. But she asked me not to intercede again on her husband's behalf, because she said that would only make his imprisonment more unpleasant.

After Roosevelt's cabled request for protection of Peyrouton and Boisson was spurned by De Gaulle, the President and Eisenhower had little or no success in helping Frenchmen who had incurred De Gaulle's displeasure. Soon they quit trying. The war was making too many other urgent demands on the attention of Americans. Besides, Washington officials were "sick and tired of French politics." But Churchill refused to keep quiet about Boisson and Peyrouton, with whom he had lunched and to whom he had given personal assurances of protection. He persisted in sending messages to his erstwhile protégé, De Gaulle, but the only thing Churchill was able to accomplish was to arrange for these two Frenchmen to be transferred to a more agreeable prison until the war ended.

To me, the most unfortunate case was that of courageous old General Giraud, who in careless innocence had handed over all his high cards. He was deprived of one honor and position after another until, on the great D-Day in Europe—to which he had looked forward with such patriotic earnestness—he was isolated in a country house in Algeria, permitted no place whatever in the Armed Forces of France. Adding injury to insult, an Algerian soldier hiding in a hedge fired a rifle at Giraud one evening when he was strolling in the garden with his daughter. The bullet perforated Giraud's jaw but did not kill him. An investigation by the Gaullist authorities failed to disclose who was responsible for the attempted assassination. When Darlan was murdered, Giraud suspected that extremists in the De Gaulle movement had plotted to get rid of him, and now Giraud believed that these same fanatics had instigated the assault against himself.

By July of 1943, De Gaulle's committee had every appurtenance of a full-fledged government, and all of us in Algiers accepted the inevitable. De Gaulle's campaign had been adroitly planned and it had achieved all of its objectives except one—formal Anglo-American recognition as the Government of France. In the middle of the month, Macmillan recommended to Eisenhower that he deal with the French committee as such, rather than with individuals, thus making discussions impersonal. I saw no objection, but when Roosevelt received word of this recommendation, he cabled Eisenhower in vigorous language, forbidding even such implied recognition. Churchill nevertheless decided to recognize for all practical purposes the French Committee of National Liberation as the Government of France, and he attempted at the Quebec Conference in August to persuade Roosevelt to do likewise. The President finally yielded somewhat on this point and agreed to assign an American representative, with the rank of ambassador, to work with the committee.

I felt that my mission had been accomplished, that the time had come to terminate my four-year preoccupation with French affairs in Africa, and I requested the President to relieve me. He agreed, but asked me to serve next as his personal representative in Italian affairs. When I told Macmillan what had happened, he said that he had made the same request to Churchill and had been given an Italian assignment similar to mine. So I had the pleasure of working with Macmillan for several additional months at Allied Force Headquarters on the Advisory Council for Italian and Balkan Affairs.

I am indebted to John Lardner, war correspondent for *Newsweek* at Eisenhower's headquarters in Algiers, for a concise summary of the work which Macmillan and I did in French Africa on behalf of our governments. Lardner wrote: "There are career diplomats all over the world. They begin as neat, tactful, well-spoken young men and usually nothing exceptional happens to them. Bob Murphy and Harold Macmillan, however, were asked to make history and, as part of their official duties, they did so."

THIRTEEN

FRESH FACTS ABOUT ITALY'S SURRENDER (1943)

The Allied conquest of Sicily, Operation Husky, began July 9, 1943, and was completed in thirty-eight days. But midway through the campaign, "politics" demanded the attention of General Eisenhower and his staff once again. On Sunday evening, July 25, the Rome radio announced that the Fascist dictator, Benito Mussolini, had been divested of power and that King Victor Emmanuel III had resumed control of his realm, including command of all Armed Forces. Eisenhower was disposed to take immediate advantage of this internal dissension in Rome and summoned his staff to discuss the situation. The General said that the new regime in Italy probably was anti-Nazi and that its policies might affect not only the Sicilian campaign but even the war in the rest of Europe. He proposed, therefore, that a message be broadcast at once to encourage the King's Government. But Macmillan and I pointed out that Allied Force Headquarters lacked authority to initiate a political maneuver. If the General wanted to broadcast such a message, the matter should be referred first to Washington and London. The Supreme Commander replied rather wearily that in the old days, before rapid communications, generals were free to do whatever they thought best; nowadays an opportunity could be lost while officers argued back and forth.

None of us at that staff meeting cared to mention, even among ourselves, that Italy had no monopoly on internal dissension. The Anglo-American alliance also suffered from internal dissension and this dispute now prevented exploitation of the upheaval in Italy. As the Casablanca Conference had demonstrated, the United States and Britain supported two different military strategies. The British wanted to throw nearly all available resources into Mediterranean operations, while Americans were determined to fight only a limited war in that area, conserving most resources for the scheduled invasion of northern France. This dispute resulted from an honest difference of opinion, but the arguments had persisted so long that Americans had become distrustful of British strategic intentions. The disagreement among the Allies was concealed, of course, since knowledge of it would have been invaluable to the Germans, and the American and British public never were aware of it. But the tragic effect of this American lack of confidence in British proposals was that the Allies were unable, at the critical moment of Mussolini's downfall, to make the quick decisive moves which might have achieved spectacular success and reduced to a minimum the cruel warfare in Italy.

As we at Allied Force Headquarters well knew from previous discussions, the British were hoping that a quick success in Sicily, followed by a Fascist collapse, would induce the Americans to assign men and supplies for an accelerated drive into Italy and the Balkans. Churchill's interest in this strategy was much deeper than a mere desire to compensate for his responsibility in the Gallipoli fiasco of World War I, and although I knew nothing about the military aspects of the British proposal, I did recommend the political advantages which might result if our forces could gain northern Italy and conceivably Budapest. The collapse of the Fascist government had now occurred exactly as British strategists had predicted.

On the very day while we were discussing what could be done to take advantage of the new circumstances in Rome, Secretary of War Stimson arrived in Algiers. His brief tour had been arranged earlier and the Secretary had spent a week in London, while en route from Washington, as the guest of Churchill. The Prime Minister had assembled a group of high strategy planners to try to persuade the influential American visitor that the Allies could not afford to ignore the opportunities in the Mediterranean area. Far from being impressed by this British sales talk, Stimson had become alarmed. Discussing this with Eisenhower and his staff, Stimson stressed that Americans had yielded to the British in 1942 by agreeing to the African expedition; again at the Casablanca Conference by accepting the plan for an attack on Sicily; and a third time by consenting to follow up the conquest of Sicily with a limited invasion of southern Italy to make use of airfields there. Now, he said, the British were pressing for still further assaults in Italy. The news about the downfall of Mussolini did not alter Stimson's convictions in the slightest. The time had come, he insisted, to stand firm against any more British schemes in the Mediterranean. The Secretary informed Eisenhower that, while in London, he had talked by transatlantic telephone with General Marshall, who agreed with him.

While Stimson was in Algiers, the Combined Chiefs of Staff were in Quebec, Canada, for another of their periodic meetings to discuss global warfare. Roosevelt and Churchill joined them there later. It was from Quebec on August 12, a few days after Stimson's departure for home, that Marshall cabled that Eisenhower's orders remained unchanged despite the events in Rome. Roosevelt had decided to hold the British to their agreement not to divert to the Mediterranean any resources earmarked for the invasion of northern France. Accordingly, Eisenhower never did have the formidable expeditionary force which was generally supposed available for use in Italy. That is why the capture of Rome, hopefully expected in the autumn of 1943, was delayed until June 1944.

The Italians made tentative peace overtures by first approaching British diplomats at Lisbon on August 3 and then at Tangiers on August 9. These unofficial spokesmen for the new government at Rome confirmed reports that King Victor Emmanuel had taken the initiative in arranging the arrest of Mussolini, and that the King had induced Marshal Pietro Badoglio to become Prime Minister. Badoglio was Italy's ranking soldier at the beginning of the war, and now his political prestige was even higher because he had been rudely dismissed by Mussolini as Chief of General Staff at the end of 1940.

The British diplomats in Lisbon and Tangiers had no authority to do anything except report to their Foreign Office the first Italian peace feelers, which mentioned no precise proposals. But on August 15 a fully accredited Italian envoy reached Madrid and informed the British ambassador there, Sir Samuel Hoare, that he had come by order of King Victor Emmanuel to make a specific and impressive proposal. This envoy, General Giuseppe Castellano was, like Badoglio, a high-ranking professional soldier who had served in the Italian Army long before the Fascist regime. When Castellano's overtures were relayed to Quebec, Eisenhower was instructed to send one American and one British staff officer to talk with the Italian general. The meeting was confined strictly to military channels, lest Roosevelt and Churchill be charged with "making a deal with Fascists." General Walter Bedell Smith, Eisenhower's Chief of Staff, and Brigadier K. W. D. Strong, the British Chief of Intelligence at Allied Headquarters in North Africa, flew to Lisbon under fictitious names and in civilian clothes.

The proposition which Castellano offered was far more sweeping than the Allies had anticipated. The Italian envoy offered a complete about-face from the Italian-German Axis, replacing this with an Italian alliance with the Anglo-American forces against Germany. General Smith and Brigadier General Strong were not empowered to negotiate on such broad terms, which went far beyond "unconditional surrender." They could only fly back to Algiers for further instructions, while Castellano returned to Rome at great personal risk to report to the King and Badoglio.

Shortly after Smith and Strong returned from Lisbon, the King's Government sent to Algiers another Italian staff general, Giacomo Zanussi, accompanied by his aide, Lancia de Trabia, with another startling proposal. General Smith was in charge of the negotiations and invited Macmillan and me, as political advisers to Allied Force Headquarters and in our capacities as personal representatives of Churchill and Roosevelt, to participate in the conversations. This was my first direct participation in Italian affairs. When the attack on Sicily was originally planned, I had been rather brusquely informed by the State Department that my services would not be required in connection with the occupation of that island, because the Departments of State and War had coordinated their own plans for military government of conquered Italian territories. But the officers at Eisenhower's headquarters had gradually become accustomed to the presence of Macmillan and me at their conferences. These campaign planners tolerated us partly because we tried to prevent European politics from interfering with their military operations. "If you can restrain the politicians," they said, "we soldiers can win the war." So when the meeting was set up to negotiate an Italian cease-fire, Macmillan and I went along.

What Zanussi proposed was that the Allies should land airborne troops on three airfields near Rome. The Italian general told us there were only about one and one-half German divisions in the vicinity, and they were about two hours' distance from the city. If the Allies would land at least one division of paratroops on the Rome airfields, the Italians would support the operation with six well-equipped divisions. These seven divisions, Zanussi asserted, could easily stand off the German forces in the area and also render untenable the position of three German divisions in the Naples area. If the Allies moved boldly and quickly, they could capture Rome and also rally to the Allied side a substantial part of the Italian Armed Forces.

Zanussi was the first Italian envoy whom I met and he was an eloquent advocate. Macmillan and I were enthusiastic about his scheme for military cooperation. At that stage of the war, and in light of the severely limited Allied resources, it seemed to offer advantages not only of a military nature but also for the future political evolution of Italy and the Balkans. Many of Eisenhower's staff planners, especially the British, believed the venture was feasible if the Italians were serious. There followed numerous interchanges of messages between London, Washington and Quebec, and it was agreed that a meeting to discuss Italian surrender terms should be held immediately in Sicily with Badoglio's emissaries.

Formal surrender negotiations were begun on August 31, 1943, in an Army camp hidden in an olive grove not far from Palermo, near the headquarters of General Sir Harold Alexander, the British Commander in Chief in Sicily. In the opinion of many of his American associates, Alexander then was the ablest of British generals in the Mediterranean theater of war. I am still of that opinion. At a small private dinner at his headquarters, he explained to General Smith, Macmillan, and me the problems involved in the approaching campaign which he had planned and would direct against the Nazi forces entrenched in Italy. His description was brilliant—and hair-raising. The operation, he told us, was a dangerous gamble because such inadequate Allied forces had been allocated to it. The Germans already had some nineteen divisions in Italy, built up during the month since Mussolini's overthrow. The Italians had sixteen divisions, who might jump either way. But Alexander said he would have only from three to five Anglo-American divisions for our initial landings, to a maximum buildup of eight divisions over the following two weeks. So Italian cooperation must somehow be obtained immediately. Without aggressive assistance from the Italian Government and Armed Forces, the operations were almost certain to fail or, at best, prove excessively costly for minimal gains. Alexander declared he would be willing to risk his reputation and, if necessary, retire from the Army, should his government disapprove his insistence on immediate signature by the Italians of the armistice terms, and Allied acceptance of Italian military cooperation. Alexander and Macmillan both were profoundly disturbed by the possible consequences upon Great Britain of an Allied repulse in Italy. They dwelt upon the fatigue of the British people and British soldiers, many of whom had been separated from their families for more than three years. Some Englishmen, they said, were beginning to believe the Allies should seek a compromise peace.

Just before we left Algiers for Sicily, Eisenhower had received from Churchill and Roosevelt two sets of surrender terms, one called the "short term," the second the "long term." The text of the former dealt exclusively with military affairs, providing for "unconditional surrender" by the Italians. The "long term" documents contained detailed political, economic, and financial provisions, putting complete control of every aspect of Italian affairs into Allied hands indefinitely. It imposed the harshest kind of peace upon Italy. According to instructions from the British and American Governments, Eisenhower's negotiators were not to show the "long term" text to the Italian envoys until the latter signed the "short term" unconditional surrender. Apparently it was feared that if the Italians knew what they were letting themselves in for, they might refuse to go through with the deal. Allied instructions also forbade making the "long term" documents public under any circumstances. Eisenhower was not happy about this. He grumbled that it was a "crooked deal," and said that these secret documents would not be published even ten years after the end of the war. He underestimated the durability of this particular secret; the "long term" Italian surrender documents never have been published to this day.

As a matter of fact, some of the most onerous clauses became obsolete almost immediately. They were based upon the assumption that the Italians could retain control of their own country, whereas even before the Anglo-American negotiators met the Italian envoys in the Sicilian olive grove, the Germans already controlled most of Italy, for all effective purposes. Hitler had wasted no time after the overthrow of Mussolini. Captured German documents show that he comprehended immediately the full significance of the Rome coup, and secretly assigned one of his most skillful soldiers, Field Marshal Erwin Rommel, to take charge of Italian affairs. Rommel promptly seized control of the Alpine passes which, if they had been blown up with the explosives which the Italians had in readiness, would have prevented German reinforcements from reaching their forces in Italy, and would have cut off the Germans' main supply source. Instead, as Alexander learned, the Germans had sent to Italy enough German divisions to hold it indefinitely, and were imposing a tight grip on the entire peninsula.

The Italians who met with the Allied representatives in Sicily were all professional Army officers and diplomats. Zanussi accompanied our Allied group which flew in from Algiers; Castellano and his associates arrived by plane directly from Rome. It soon became evident that the Italians were less concerned about our surrender terms than they were about the German threat to their country. "Are you strong enough to protect us from the Germans?" they kept asking. As I wrote to President Roosevelt: "It is a nice balance in their minds whether we or the Germans will work the most damage in Italy. They are between the hammer and the anvil." The Italians insisted at first that they would not sign any agreement unless the Allies would guarantee to land some troops north of Rome. If we restricted our landings to south Italy, they declared, the Germans surely would occupy Rome and everything north of there, with slaughter, pillage, and destruction too terrible to contemplate.

No Italians suspected that the Americans and British had already decided to reduce their Mediterranean operations to a minor sideshow while they concentrated on preparations for invading France across the English Channel. Of course the Allies had no intention of confiding that we lacked sufficient forces to invade northern Italy. However, Smith did mention favorably Zanussi's proposal that we should land airborne troops on airfields around Rome. The Italians responded eagerly, saying that they could guarantee to overcome any German or

Fascist opposition to such landings in the Rome area. The fate of the Italian fleet also was a major Allied interest; most of it was later delivered safely into Allied control. In this maneuver the Italians were more determined and skillful than the French had been, but this did them little good in the end. Among other things, the Russians demanded and got a substantial part of the Italian fleet.

After the war there was a general impression that the Soviet Union had acquired one-third of the Italian fleet, but this report was the result of an incorrect announcement which Roosevelt gave to the press on March 3, 1944. He said on that occasion that Italian warships were ready to be sent to the Russian Navy and that discussions were under way to transfer about one-third of Italy's ships to Russia. Churchill, learning of this, sent Roosevelt a rocket pointing out that the Russians had not even asked for that much. What the Russians had requested was:

1 battleship (out of 5)
1 cruiser (out of 6)
8 destroyers (out of 10)
4 submarines (out of 22)
40,000 tons of merchant shipping

The British had agreed to this, as had we; Roosevelt had modified it in the grand manner.

After the military discussions, Macmillan and I conversed briefly with the leaders of the Italian delegation. We impressed upon them that this was their last chance, valuable only if seized quickly. We pointed out that if no surrender agreement eventuated here and now, three results were indicated: King Victor Emmanuel would lose all consideration; the Allies would be obliged, as a war measure, to incite anarchy throughout Italy; we also would be obliged to bomb all Italian cities, including Rome. The Italian envoys had seen in the rubble of Sicilian towns what all-out bombing could do. At five o'clock on that afternoon of August 31, the Italian group flew back to Rome with our ultimatum that if the King's Government did not accept the Allied terms by midnight the following day, Rome would be bombed.

As soon as the Italians departed, Allied staff officers flew to Eisenhower's Tunisian headquarters to urge that an Allied airborne division be dropped in the Rome area on September 8, at the same time that Allied troops were to land at Salerno, near Naples. The next morning, Eisenhower approved this recommendation, and word of this was sent by radio to the Italian envoys, who were back in Rome now. This message sounded like a firm Allied commitment, and a reply came promptly that the envoys would return to Sicily the next day, September 2.

But when the Italians arrived at the rendezvous in the olive grove, they incensed all of us by confessing that the King's Government had not empowered them to sign any surrender terms, short or long, prior to the Allied landings, which they understood were imminent. This seemed like procrastination and bargaining, and Smith, Macmillan, and I went into conference with Alexander. We agreed that the British General should pay a formal call on the Italians, whom he never had met, and he decided to make the occasion impressive. Donning his full-dress uniform, with decorations and shiny boots, Alexander assembled his aides. At this point, an incongruous circumstance threatened to mar the formality of the hastily improvised ceremony. A large tent for the Italian delegation had been reserved in the center of the extensive encampment, and the General's own tent was pitched at the rear, just inside the volcanic rock wall which surrounded the camp and the olive trees. It was discovered that the Allied officers could drive into the main gateway of the enclosure only by first climbing out over the wall and then getting into their jeep. Otherwise, Alexander and his staff would have to make an unimpressive approach from the rear. The General and his beribboned staff climbed over the wall, brushed the dust from their uniforms, and drove through the front entrance with great éclat.

Presentations were made and Alexander greeted the Italians cordially but with a certain reserve. He said he was happy to understand that they had returned from Rome prepared to sign the armistice. With voluble protestations they regretted they could not. Thereupon the General staged a magnificent bit of histrionics, declaring that our patience was at an end and that we doubted their good faith. With every appearance of cold fury, Alexander announced that if the Italians failed to sign within twenty-four hours, the Allies would be obliged to bomb Rome. His motive was to convince the delegation that the Allies could and would do more damage to Italy than the Germans. Alexander's performance was impressive because it was by no means just an act. He told us that he was prepared to employ any ruse or subterfuge which might be required to compel the Italians to sign immediately, because he believed that the outcome of the war itself was at issue. And he instructed us that the envoys should under no circumstances be permitted to depart until they signed. We decided that the best means of impressing the Italians with our displeasure was to leave them pretty much to themselves for the rest of the day.

That same afternoon we were greatly relieved to receive word that Roosevelt and Churchill agreed that the Italian negotiations should be guided by military considerations only. In other words, our hands were not to be tied by arbitrary formulas which might prevent us from dealing with Italians who had been members of the Fascist party.

After twenty-one years of Fascist dictatorship, every Italian of consequence who had remained in Italy was tarred in some way or other with the Fascist brush. Any restrictions in negotiating with these men would have blocked obtaining effective Italian assistance in the military campaign against the Nazis. Allied Force Headquarters was confronted in Italy with the same kind of dilemma we already had encountered in French Africa; Anglo-American critics who had cried out against dealing with "Vichyites" in Africa now objected even more sharply to negotiating with Fascists in Italy.

Radio communications with Rome were erratic, and it was not until the afternoon of September 3 that the Italian envoys waiting in Sicily received the necessary instructions from their government to sign the surrender. Authenticity was verified by a wireless message from the British Minister accredited to the Vatican, and it was agreed that Allied Force Headquarters and the Rome Government would simultaneously broadcast their acceptance of the armistice a few hours before the time fixed for the Allied invasion at Salerno. Late in the afternoon, Eisenhower flew in from Tunis for the signing of the "short term" papers. He still was unhappy about this procedure and stayed only a few minutes, entrusting to his Chief of Staff the unpleasant task of handing the Italians the merciless "long term" documents. A covering letter made it clear that these stern provisions had come into effect automatically with the signing of the "unconditional surrender." When Castellano glanced through the lengthy secret conditions, he did not conceal his shocked surprise. He decided on his own responsibility to withhold the contents of the document from the King and Badoglio until they publicly committed themselves to the armistice.

The Italians were not informed where the Allied invasions would take place, but they flew back with a definite impression that the Allies would use airborne troops in a cooperative effort with the Italian Army to seize and hold Rome. However, when the Allied negotiators returned to Eisenhower's headquarters near Tunis, we discovered that the commanders of the American 82nd Airborne Division, General Matthew B. Ridgway and his deputy, General Maxwell D. Taylor, were skeptical about this venture. Ridgway was understandably averse to a gamble which might result in the loss of the entire division. But Macmillan and I argued that failure to go through with the operation would destroy whatever chance there was of organized Italian military cooperation and especially of the six divisions they had promised. It also would look like bad faith on our part. Ridgway finally growled that he would agree only if the two double-damned political advisers went to the Rome landings in the first place. Macmillan and I had not thought about this but suddenly the suggestion seemed exactly right. "It's a deal," we told Ridgway.

When the Rome airborne landings were discussed a little later at a staff meeting in Tunis headquarters, Eisenhower approved the venture, which was supported by a majority of his staff. To prepare the way, Taylor had been given the dangerous assignment of going to Rome with portable sending and receiving radio equipment. The trip was made by an Italian frigate which picked up the General on the Island of Ischia and took him to the port of Gaeta, where he was put into an Italian Red Cross ambulance and sent to the home of an Italian admiral. As soon as the project was definitely approved, Macmillan and I informed Eisenhower that, by agreement with Ridgway, political advisers would be in the lead plane. The General replied, "That's good. Send some of your men who really know their way around." Macmillan explained that we were not planning to send anybody; we intended to go ourselves. Eisenhower looked at us for a moment, and then said dryly, "Well, all right. There's nothing in the regulations which says diplomats are not expendable."

Macmillan and I made eager preparations to embark upon this assignment which we believed offered incalculable political advantages. But at the very last moment, when we were all set to go, Taylor sent a radio message from Rome that the Italians had withdrawn their support. His information was that additional German armored units had moved into the Rome area, making it impossible for the Italians to control the airfields. Of course Taylor thought his information was correct, but later the Italian Army chiefs who had conferred with us in Sicily denied they had withdrawn support. It always has been my feeling that our airborne commanders had set their minds against this expedition from the start for standard military reasons and because nobody trusted Italians. Moreover, the 82nd Airborne Division was an important feature of the Salerno assault plans and the commander of that invasion, Mark Clark, counted upon using those paratroops.

Ridgway and Taylor are, I believe and hope, good friends of mine. These two great soldiers later achieved two of the finest records in American military annals. Each served, among other things, as the Army's Chief of Staff. But I still feel that on this occasion their judgment should not have prevailed and that the Rome landings should have taken place. Alexander when he talked so earnestly with us concerning his need for help from the Italians, calculated that he might capture Rome at the latest by mid-October. Actually, the Allies did not reach Rome until June 4 of the following year, and the intervening eight months were immeasurably costly to Allied soldiers in Italy as well as to the Italians. But who am I to question the judgment of two of our greatest soldiers? I dare to do so only because I remember how often some of my soldier friends have expounded their opinions about political and diplomatic questions.

Nowadays nobody commemorates the date of September 8, 1943, but this was an eventful day in the history of World War II and in the history of Italy. Four outstanding events occurred on that day: Allied troops made their first assault on the Italian mainland, at Salerno. The armistice between Italy and the Allies was publicly announced. Germans seized control in Rome. And Victor Emmanuel was forced to flee from The Eternal City, never again to return as King.

It is said that the most dangerous situation a soldier ever encounters is when he attempts to surrender, because at such times he is menaced by his own side as well as by the enemy. On September 8, 1943, the entire Italian nation was faced with this perilous predicament. The last-minute decision of the Allies not to land near Rome threw the Italian forces there into complete confusion. The Italian negotiators had assumed and hoped the Allies would employ at least fifteen divisions in that invasion, and would land north of Rome, perhaps at Genoa, instead of farther south, near Naples. Field Marshal Rommel, Hitler's great general, reached the same conclusion. He noted in his diary that he was surprised and relieved when the Allies displayed what seemed to him inexcusable caution. Of course he did not know the limitations imposed upon Eisenhower.

But the Italians had agreed to broadcast an announcement of the armistice with or without landings in Rome, and although the King's associates pleaded for postponement, Eisenhower held them to their pledged word. At the agreed time, 6:30 P.M., two hours before the start of the invasion of Salerno, Algiers broadcast the armistice terms. The Italian negotiators kept their promise but showed their confusion by hesitating almost two hours after Allied Force Headquarters had broken the news. The King and Badoglio were thus put in danger of capture and had to flee out of German reach, risking travel through German lines by automobile from Rome to Pescara on the Adriatic, where they embarked on an Italian cruiser for Brindisi. They were accompanied by only a small group of generals and courtiers. The King told me later that to avoid suspicion on departure, he took no baggage whatever; he had nothing but the uniform he wore. Most members of the King's Government remained in Rome, either by their own choice or through ignorance of what was happening. Immediately after the Algiers radio announced the Italian surrender, German armored cars moved into key positions in Rome, and German units disarmed the Italian divisions stationed in and around the city. The Italians as a matter of policy put up virtually no resistance, and the Germans took over Rome without serious opposition. The next day the Germans began to bring into Italy several more divisions, moving some far to the south of the capital.

As soon as Allied Force Headquarters learned that the King and

Badoglio had escaped and reached Brindisi, Eisenhower decided to send an exploratory diplomatic mission there. All communications with Rome were cut off now, and none of us knew what the Germans were doing or whether Italy possessed a coherent government capable of enforcing the surrender terms. The Governor of Gibraltar, Major-General P. A. Mason Macfarlane, was named head of the mission and Macmillan and I were instructed to accompany him, remaining discreetly in the background, available to the British General for advice on political questions which might arise. When Macfarlane flew in from Gibraltar, he was just recovering from an attack of jaundice, which reduced further his conspicuous lack of enthusiasm for this assignment. His contempt for Italians was even more bitter than that of most other British officers at that time. Mussolini's disastrous policies had deprived the Italian people of almost everybody's sympathy. Our French and British associates hated the Nazis, but they despised Italians. Macfarlane expressed disbelief that Italians could contribute anything to the Allied war effort, and he said Badoglio was a "has-been" who never had been an effective soldier even in his prime. Macmillan and I tried to modify his misgivings by telling him that Alexander said he must have Italian cooperation in order to prevent an Anglo-American catastrophe, but Macfarlane remained skeptical. Macfarlane, for whom we had great affection, was one of Britain's best intelligence officers, with a broad knowledge of European affairs, but his attitude toward Italians in 1943 was jaundiced in more senses than one.

On our way to Brindisi our plane touched down at a badly battered airfield near Taranto, the great Italian naval base which had just been captured by British forces. We were surrounded immediately by a swarm of genial Italian soldiers, sailors, and aviators, who did not know whether they were still at war or whose side they were on. "Is the war over for Italy?" they asked excitedly. "Will the Germans recognize the armistice?" The word "armistice," broadcast from Algiers and Rome, meant to them the end of fighting. We were not at all sure then just what it did mean. We were kept busy for three hours answering their questions, while we waited for the Italians to locate a small automobile for us. Obviously these men wanted to be on the Allied side, or at least out of the German alliance. Macfarlane muttered, "The bloody bastards tried for years to do us in, and now look at them!"

Early the next morning, September 12, we set off for Brindisi, an ancient city which has served as a naval port for Romans since the third century B.C. We found the new government located in gloomy Admiralty headquarters near the waterfront, while the King occupied another Admiralty building close by. In the adjacent harbor the six-thousand-ton cruiser which had brought the party to Brindisi was kept under full steam in case German raiders got wind of the King's whereabouts. The King-Badoglio Government, consisting of a grab-bag assortment of military officers, diplomats, and members of the King's palace staff, was far from impressive. But Victor Emmanuel provided a nucleus for a legal government, which no other Italian did just then, and Macmillan and I thought that this little retinue gathered loyally around their monarch might be the only kind of Italian Government which could serve Anglo-American military purposes at this moment. We were disappointed to observe that Macfarlane almost ignored the King. The general explained to us afterward that the seventy-three-year-old ruler looked "gaga" to him. But it seemed to us that the King had taken considerable initiative in forcing Mussolini out, and later in escaping from Rome when Allied protection failed to arrive. Victor Emmanuel had shown a great deal more enterprise and anti-Nazi spirit than most of the ministers in his post-Mussolini administration.

Later in the day Macmillan and I talked privately with Badoglio. We strongly emphasized that his new government was starting with enormous handicaps. The Anglo-American press was describing the King as a Fascist-minded opportunist who abandoned Fascism only when it was beaten, and whose sole interest now was in clinging to his shaky throne. We also informed Badoglio that the Allied press was rehashing old reports of Italian atrocities in the Ethiopian campaign. The seventy-one-year-old Badoglio reminded me of General Giraud in his complete indifference to political issues. Solemnly he told us that he had agreed to organize a non-Fascist government for one reason only—his King commanded it and he always obeyed his King.

Before leaving Brindisi, Macmillan and I arranged to have a talk with Victor Emmanuel without the discouraging presence of Macfarlane. The King, describing how hastily he had been compelled to escape from Rome, mentioned that he and the Queen had rushed off without any of their personal possessions. I inquired politely if I could be of any assistance. After a hesitant pause, he said: "The Queen has been unable to get any fresh eggs. Is it possible that we could somehow get a dozen eggs?" That was all he asked of us, so with a dozen eggs we sealed our concord with the thousand-year-old House of Savoy.

Our exploratory mission to Brindisi was followed on September 29 by a formal meeting of Eisenhower with Badoglio on board the British battleship *Nelson* in Valetta Harbor on the island of Malta, amidst the ruins left by Italian bombs. The main purpose of this Malta Conference was the formal signing of the "long term" surrender document. The entire Italian delegation, including most of the ranking men with whom we had dealt up to that point, flew into Malta in the same big plane. The pilot made a clumsy landing and the plane bounced an amazing distance above the ground. "There go all our signatories!" one American officer shouted in horror—but the plane descended, miraculously in one piece, and no one was hurt.

As soon as the discussions started, it became apparent that Italian plans were based upon the assumption that the Allies would capture Rome in the very near future. The Italians believed that available Allied forces were much greater than they actually were, and they recommended several likely places for additional invasions. Nobody corrected their illusions. On the other hand, almost every proposal made by Eisenhower was countered by Badoglio with the suggestion that it be postponed until Rome was reached. He said the King's decisions could be announced more impressively from Rome, where power had been established for so many centuries. Eisenhower probably would have pressed more urgently for Badoglio to broaden the base of his government and declare war on Germany immediately, if the Supreme Commander likewise had not believed that the capture of Rome was imminent. Almost everybody in Algiers thought that the Germans, for military reasons, would withdraw to a line north of Rome, which would permit the new Italian Government and the Allies to establish themselves in the old capital. As Rommel's diary reveals, he himself advised such withdrawal of German troops. But Hitler sensed the political importance of Rome and he ordered his soldiers to hold the city, which they did for eight more long months.

It was at the Malta Conference that Count Carlo Sforza's name was first brought into the Italian negotiations. Sforza was regarded as the most distinguished politician among the anti-Fascist Italians. He had been Minister for Foreign Affairs and Ambassador to France in the years just before Mussolini seized power. When the Fascists marched on Rome, Sforza immediately resigned his post in Paris and began his fight against Fascism which was to continue unceasingly for more than a score of years. During much of that time, the Count lived in the United States, where he made many influential friends, including Secretary Hull. He also made a formidable enemy, Prime Minister Churchill.

It is doubtful that Eisenhower had any personal knowledge of Sforza's background when, according to instructions, he informed Badoglio at Malta that the American Government wanted the Count to visit Brindisi in the near future to meet members of the new Italian Government. Badoglio replied that he remembered Sforza well, having attended international conferences with him after World War I. He added, however, that the King could scarcely be expected to receive Sforza, since the Count only recently had publicly demanded Victor Emmanuel's abdication. Eisenhower listened somewhat impatiently, and then declared that the American Government's interest in Sforza's return to Italy had been expressed so emphatically that the King's attitude to the celebrated anti-Fascist might be decisive in such matters as whether Italy should be regarded as a beaten enemy or as a cobelligerent against Germany. Badoglio repeated that only the King could decide such questions, but he said he would advise the King to receive Sforza, since the American Government wished it.

As the conference concluded, Eisenhower told Badoglio that he would instruct his own staff to say nothing to the press about Sforza or the signing of any documents, and that he hoped Badoglio would adopt a similar policy. Badoglio replied that he had just as much affection for the press as he had for Fascists. We all laughed, and Eisenhower commented that Badoglio's opinion seemed to be shared by everyone in the room. As a matter of fact, Eisenhower usually got along amicably with the press, but he already had discovered that his negotiations with an Italian Government headed by King Victor Emmanuel and including many former Fascists was being denounced by American and British commentators as vehemently as the "Darlan deal" had been.

A few days after the Malta Conference, Sforza arrived in Algiers en route to his homeland, which he had not seen for twenty-one years. The voluble Italian was sponsoring a compromise plan which would retain the historic House of Savoy but demanded the abdication of Victor Emmanuel III and his son, Prince Humbert. Sforza believed that the King and the Crown Prince had been inexcusably chummy with Mussolini and other leading Fascists, and he proposed a regency on behalf of the King's ten-year-old grandson, who was then in school in Switzerland. Sforza recommended that the regency be headed by Badoglio. This plan was supported by Secretary Hull, but was opposed by Churchill who even attempted to prevent Sforza's return to Italy. Knowing what a precarious military campaign was in prospect there, the British Prime Minister believed that politics in Italy should be postponed indefinitely. Sforza's argument was that even the Allied military cause would be served by dumping the discredited King immediately and giving Italians a taste of party politics, almost forgotten.

When Churchill was informed that Washington had granted Sforza facilities to return to Italy, the Prime Minister invited the Count to stop in London on his way to Algiers to have lunch with him. But this meeting only exacerbated the antagonism between these two statesmen who differed profoundly on policies and also irritated each other personally. After conferring with Sforza, Churchill sent a memo to Allied Force Headquarters which said in part: "I have made plain to him that he is now going into Ike's zone, and that anything he said which was not helpful might result in his being sent out of it. He struck me as a foolish and played-out old man, incapable of facing, let alone riding, the storm." When this memo was passed around for comment, I wrote: "The P. M.'s description of Sforza as 'a foolish and played-out old man' is harsh. The difficulty is that both of them wish to do all the talking." Thanks largely to Churchill's support, Victor Emmanuel managed to stay on his throne for several months more, despite all the maneuvers which Sforza could contrive. The monarch produced one excuse after another for delay, usually by insisting that Rome was the place to decide the future of Italy. Victor Emmanuel was a far more clever political operator than most people gave him credit for, and he overlooked no device to defer his fate.

On October 12, the King's Government reluctantly declared war against Germany, thus acquiring for Italy the status of cobelligerent with the Allies. However, the Americans and British reserved the right to retain military government wherever they considered such administration necessary. This resulted in great confusion, infinitely more than in French North Africa where local administrations functioned much better than military government did in Italy. But this was not entirely a matter of government organization. The fighting in Italy was more devastating than it had been in North Africa; air raids and German demolitions were much worse. During that winter of 1943–44 the Italian people witnessed the destruction of their beautiful country in one of the cruelest military campaigns that age-long battleground has ever suffered. The Germans and the Allies jockeyed for position with small regard for the civilian population. The military stakes were too high for either side to afford much human kindness.

During October, Allied Force Headquarters established its Italian base at Caserta, near Naples, and Macmillan and I—together with Couve de Murville and Alexander Bogomolov, the French and Russian members of the Advisory Council for Italian and Balkan Affairs —began to spend much of our time there. Until Rome was occupied, Caserta and Naples were the center for Italian politics as well as Allied activities. After the Italian Government was moved from Brindisi early in 1944, we persuaded Victor Emmanuel and the Queen to reside in the Villa Sangro near Ravello. But the monarch and his wife enjoyed salt-water fishing, and they kept pressing for permission to occupy their villa on the Bay of Naples. This royal abode adjoined the historic mansion once occupied by Lady Hamilton, mistress of England's most famous sailor, Lord Nelson, which was being used by the British Navy as a guest house for visitors who required special protection. When King George VI came to Naples that winter, the waters surrounding the Hamilton mansion were cleared of all traffic. But one morning a British naval lieutenant on patrol in a speedboat observed a shabbily dressed elderly couple fishing placidly directly under the windows of King George's suite. The young officer pulled up alongside and motioned for them to leave, but the old lady stood up in the boat and declared imperiously in English: "This is the King and I am the Queen!" She opened her handbag, took out a calling card, and held it toward him. No one had been informed that Victor Emmanuel had come to Naples, and the British lieutenant decided to obey his own orders. "It doesn't matter who you are," he shouted. "Nobody can fish here now. Go away!" A few hours later Allied Force Headquarters received from the Imperial Household a formal protest against discourtesies shown to their majesties.

So long as Victor Emmanuel clung to his regal status, he was an inevitable target for Italian political parties and also for all the critics of Allied policies. A day rarely passed without fresh demands for his abdication, and by the spring of 1944 the King of Italy had become a lively issue even in American politics. Roosevelt was up for re-election that year and the status of Victor Emmanuel was troubling American voters of Italian descent. The President summoned me to Washington for consultation early in April and told me that he had consented to the King's retention longer than he believed wise, because Churchill felt so strongly about this matter, but now an abdication must somehow be arranged. He left it up to me to figure out how this could be accomplished, if possible without angering Churchill.

I flew back to Naples where I found Sforza waiting to talk with me. The Count had achieved his objective of reviving party politics in his homeland, but the game was not being played at all as he had anticipated. Italian Communists were making tremendous progress, he informed me, and were being openly supported by Soviet Russia. Sforza blamed Churchill as much as the Russians for Communist gains in Italy. He declared that the Prime Minister's "blind and stubborn adherence" to the notion of supporting the King and his weak Badoglio Government was playing directly into Russian hands. Sforza went on to say that his countrymen had an instinct for smelling out success, and too many of them were concluding now that the Communists were to be the winners in Italy. He described long queues which he had seen of applicants for membership in the Communist Party, which he said included a growing proportion of business executives and professional men.

I lost no time in telling Macmillan about my instructions from Roosevelt to force the abdication of the King, and I also told him that Sforza believed retention of the King was aiding the Communist Party in Italy. Macmillan saw the point, saying, "It is a matter of domestic politics for you Americans, as well as international politics." He and I decided to deliver the President's personal message to the King without any fresh correspondence with London, and Macmillan agreed to accompany me to add dignity to the occasion. The tiny King, who had been advised in advance of the purpose of our call, received us while standing before a very large wall map of Italy. I explained the President's position as tactfully as I could, but the King's emotions suddenly overcame him. He continued to stand very erect and dignified, but his chin quivered and tears came into his pale blue eyes as he spoke with pride of the thousand-year history of the House of Savoy. He said mournfully: "A republican form of government is not suited to the Italian people. They are not prepared for it either temperamentally or historically. In a republic every Italian would insist upon being President, and the result would be chaos. The only people who would profit would be the Communists."

We listened respectfully, but I did not modify the virtual ultimatum I brought from the President. The King finally agreed—or so Macmillan and I thought—that his councilors would work with members of our staffs to produce a proclamation of his immediate abdication in favor of his son. But we reckoned without Victor Emmanuel's tenacity. After twenty-four hours of around-the-clock conversations, a text finally emerged beyond which the King refused to budge. Instead of announcing his immediate abdication, his proclamation concluded: "I have decided to withdraw from public affairs by appointing my son, the Prince of Piedmont, Lieutenant General of the Realm. This appointment will become effective by the formal transfer of powers on the day on which the Allied troops enter Rome. This decision, which I firmly believe furthers national unity, is final and irrevocable."

Well, that was not exactly what President Roosevelt had stipulated. The King had concocted a formula intended to postpone his abdication for several more weeks, and Macmillan and I felt we would have to accept this formula. For one thing, Macmillan had supported me further than he really should have done in view of the attitude of his Prime Minister. Moreover, the King's position had suddenly been strengthened by unexpected support from an astonishing source. The Soviet Government, without consulting or even notifying its Big Three "partners"—the United States, Britain, and France—had formally recognized the King-Badoglio Government and offered to exchange ambassadors. This was a sample of Soviet tactics which later were to become all too familiar. Victor Emmanuel thus engineered one more little triumph, but it was his final one.

The King retained his power during April and May, as the Allies slowly battered their way through Italy along the route which Churchill had hopefully called the "soft underbelly of Europe." Allied hesitations and Hitler's swift intervention had combined to thwart Alexander's plans. As the general had foreseen, his undermanned Allied expedition bogged down for lack of effective help from Italians. Most Italian troops were cut off and disarmed in their own country by their former Axis partners. All through Albania, Yugoslavia, Greece, and Mediterranean islands, Italian soldiers interpreted the armistice as an end of fighting for them. So instead of taking Rome in mid-October, as Alexander had believed feasible, Allied troops under Mark Clark did not reach the capital until June 4, 1944—just thirty-six hours before D-Day in Normandy.

When the moment finally came to enter Rome in triumph, Victor Emmanuel to his intense disappointment was not among those present. The political pot was boiling fiercely in Rome, where anti-Fascists who had been fighting underground for years now expressed their political sentiments with violence. Allied security agents declared they could not assure Victor Emmanuel's safety if he entered Rome before the situation calmed. The Allied Command decided it had troubles enough in Italy without risking a royal assassination, so the old ruler was not permitted to return to the capital to formalize his abdication, which had been proclaimed a few weeks before. The exuberant Roman crowds did not seem to notice his absence.

Members of the Allied Advisory Council flew into Rome on June 6, and one of my first assignments was to carry a personal message of good will from President Roosevelt to Pope Pius XII. It was a delight to meet again this great and good man who had been so helpful to me two decades earlier, when he was Papal Nuncio in Munich and I was a vice consul. The war had severely tested the diplomatic ability of the Pope, who had to steer a tortuous course among many possible pitfalls for the Vatican state and for the Roman Catholic Church. His Holiness had met the test, and was grateful that Vatican City and Rome had been preserved from destruction. He told me that he was trying to express his gratitude by meeting and talking with as many American and British soldiers as possible, regardless of their religion. But he said he was puzzled by the behavior of the soldiers he received. When he appeared before them and spoke to them in English, they remained completely silent. This seemed strange to the Pope because Italians and other Europeans always greeted him with enthusiasm, often clapping hands boisterously. He asked me whether he was failing for some unknown reason to communicate with these English-speaking soldiers. I explained that our men, by their silence, were showing their respect, even awe. His Holiness seemed much relieved, and he repeated several times at our subsequent meetings that one of his greatest joys had been seeing these thousands of young Americans and Britons.

During my reunion with the Pope, His Holiness took a few minutes to reminisce about the events in Germany when Hitler failed to seize power during the so-called beer hall *putsch*. All the foreign representatives at Munich, including Nuncio Pacelli, were convinced that Hitler's political career had ended ignominiously in 1924. When I ventured to remind His Holiness of this bit of history, he laughed and said, "I know what you mean—Papal infallibility. Don't forget I was only a monsignor then!"

The capture of Rome did not conclude the Italian campaign. Almost eleven months of bitter fighting went on before the German armies finally surrendered on April 29, 1945. But during those miserable eleven months, the attention of the world shifted to more dramatic battles which were taking place simultaneously in northern Europe and the Pacific. The generals and the G.I.s in Italy were equally discouraged. They had to make do with whatever resources could be spared from other theaters of war. Some of their experienced divisions were taken away from this secondary front. Italian civilians were even more wretched. Other peoples' armies, using their country as a battleground, were not gentle with them. During my stay in Italy it gradually became apparent that the Communist Party, outlawed by Mussolini, was coming back stronger than ever. The political operations of the Soviet Government in Italy during 1943–44 were more important in the long run than either the German or the Allied military operations, and an account of these Soviet maneuvers follows in the next chapter.

FOURTEEN

ENTER THE RUSSIANS

Soon after De Gaulle entrenched himself in North Africa in the spring of 1943, Alexander Bogomolov, former Soviet Ambassador to France, turned up in Algiers. His status there was roughly equivalent to Macmillan's and mine, loosely attached to Eisenhower's headquarters. But Bogomolov retained his diplomatic rank as ambassador, he was accompanied by his own staff, and he behaved in Algiers as though he were still running an embassy in France. Bogomolov was not given access to secret military files at Allied Force Headquarters, as Macmillan and I were, but Eisenhower and the rest of us had instructions to provide him with every other facility. Those were the days when Stalin's demand for a "second front" was clamorous, and the American and British Governments were glad to have Soviet observers see for themselves that the Anglo-American forces really were fighting Germans in the Mediterranean area. Our military officers also were friendly to the Russians because they appreciated that the Red Army was fighting much better than had been expected.

Prior to the Nazi attack on Russia in June 1941, the Soviet Government practiced the same policy toward France which the United States did. The Russians followed the fleeing French Government out of Paris and settled down in Vichy after the French-German armistice. When the German Army invaded Russia, it was the Vichy Government —not Moscow—which broke off diplomatic relations, a cheap gesture to placate the Nazis. Bogomolov then went to London where he devoted particular attention to French affairs, shrewdly cultivating De Gaulle at a time when he was being rebuffed by American and some British officials. The Soviet diplomat became virtual ambassador to the French Committee of National Liberation in London, where he established himself on excellent terms with De Gaulle and his associates.

In Algiers, Bogomolov was not required—as Macmillan and I were—to oppose De Gaulle's immediate program. Stalin was openly

1. U. S. leaders in Africa during first negotiations with Admiral Darlan; 1942. *Left to right:* General Eisenhower, Admiral Darlan, General Clark, Robert Murphy. (U. S. ARMY SIGNAL CORPS)

2. Marshal Henri Philippe Pétain, Chief of the French State at Vichy.

3. General Maxime Weygand, Delegate General in French Africa; 1942.

4. Shotgun wedding at the Casablanca Conference; 1943. General Henri Giraud and General Charles de Gaulle shake hands, while standing in front of President Roosevelt and Prime Minister Churchill. (U. S. ARMY SIGNAL CORPS)

5. General Eisenhower in Algiers conferring the Distinguished Service Medal on Robert Murphy; 1943.
(U. S. ARMY SIGNAL CORPS)

6. Robert Murphy in Tunisia pins Distinguished Service Medal on General Eisenhower; 1943.

7. Mr. Churchill holds a press conference in Algiers; 1943. *Left to right:* Robert Murphy, Anthony Eden, Prime Minister Churchill, Harold Macmillan. (U. S. ARMY SIGNAL CORPS)

8. Harold Macmillan and Robert Murphy confer on Italian armistice in wartime Sicily; 1944. (U. S. ARMY SIGNAL CORPS)

9. Members of the Allied Control Council in Berlin; 1945. In the front row on Robert Murphy's left are Field Marshal Montgomery, General Zhukov, General Eisenhower, French General Koenig and Russian Political Ambassador Semenov. (U. S. ARMY SIGNAL CORPS)

10. John Foster Dulles, then U. S. Delegate to the United Nations, confers with General Lucius D. Clay and Robert Murphy; Frankfurt, 1948. (U. S. ARMY SIGNAL CORPS)

11. Dinner at the Elysée Palace in Paris; 1949. *Left to right:* General Sir Brian H. Robertson, British Military Governor, Germany; Charles E. Bohlen; General Vassily I. Chuikov, Russian Military Governor, Germany; Robert Murphy. (AGENCE PHOTOGRAPHIQUE FRANÇAISE)

12. Meeting with Mr. Eugène Jungers, the Belgian Governor General of the Congo in Leopoldville; 1950. (CONGOPRESSE)

expressing his contempt for Frenchmen as "quitters" in the war, but Bogomolov was not required to transmit these sentiments. Instead, he lavished upon De Gaulle the formalities customarily accorded to a Chief of State. These courtesies cost nothing and paid off handsomely. Bogomolov's French acquaintances kept him informed about the controversies in which De Gaulle was incessantly involved with Churchill and with Roosevelt, and the Russian envoy sometimes amused himself by telling us about French maneuvers which he learned before we did. Bogomolov deserves a major share of credit for De Gaulle's tolerance toward—sometimes practically an alliance with—French Communists in Algiers and later in France in 1944–45.

The Soviet Government could not have chosen for its purposes in Algiers a better man than Bogomolov. He was a career diplomat, more like a nineteenth-century ambassador than what might be expected of the representative of a Communist state. His background and education were much less "proletarian" than my own. He had been schooled before the Russian Revolution and his learning was wide and elegant. It interested me to see that Bogomolov was supervising solid diplomatic training for the young Russians working under him, the same attention I had the good fortune to receive from some of my superiors in the Foreign Service.

Bogomolov missed no tricks for the Soviet Government which he faithfully served, but he also was well liked by his colleagues in Algiers, and he was so approachable that soon everybody around Allied Force Headquarters was calling him "Bogo." He was hard working, well informed, had a sense of humor, and suffered from ulcers—the occupational disease of professional diplomats. On several occasions "Bogo" insisted to me that he was NOT a member of the Communist Party. I don't know why he thought this would impress me; it really did not matter. Hervé Alphand, who later became French Ambassador at Washington, was one of De Gaulle's associates in North Africa, and sometimes Alphand would good-naturedly amuse us by enacting the scene of the Soviet diplomat's arrival in Algiers. Bogomolov's ulcer was hurting him; nobody met him at the Maison Blanche airport; the only room he could get in the Hotel Aletti had a window broken by bombing; the weather was cold and the food was terrible for the ulcer. Alphand, mimicking a Russian accent, would imitate Bogomolov's indignation at the treatment he received, threatening every minute to telegraph to Moscow. The episode had a happy conclusion—"Bogo" ended up by getting one of the most pretentious villas in Algiers as his official residence.

Bogomolov's conversation was sprinkled with quotations from his favorite philosopher, Friedrich Wilhelm Nietzsche. He would declaim, "Listen to a wise German's estimate of his countrymen. Nietzsche wrote: The Germans are like women. You can scarcely ever fathom their depths—they haven't any!" Bogomolov would pause for the appreciative laugh, and then continue, "Or listen to Nietzsche again: I believe only in French culture and regard everything else in Europe which calls itself culture as a misunderstanding. Wherever Germany extends her sway, she ruins culture." We could well imagine how such quotations might assuage De Gaulle's ruffled feelings. The Soviet Ambassador also used Nietzsche-isms to tease his wife, a self-proclaimed "new Soviet woman," who proudly informed acquaintances that she was a graduate engineer. Her husband would infuriate her by quoting Nietzsche: "God created woman, and from that moment boredom ceased. But many other things ceased as well. Woman was God's second mistake." Somebody gave Mrs. Bogomolov a nickname which stuck; we all knew her as "Operative Number Forty-six."

Bogomolov originally was assigned to Allied Force Headquarters to represent his country in relations with the French. But, as with Macmillan and me, his duties were extended to Italy after he became a member of the Allied Advisory Council on Italian and Balkan Affairs. This council was created in Moscow in October 1943 when the Foreign Ministers of the Big Three—the United States, the Soviet Union, and Great Britain—conferred there. The American representative at this meeting was Secretary of State Hull, who insisted on making this arduous wartime journey in person although he was then seventy-two years old, in very poor health, and had never before flown in an airplane. Upon his doctor's advice, Hull traveled the transatlantic portion of his voyage on a cruiser, and I met the warship at Casablanca and rode with the Secretary on his plane to Algiers.

I was astonished to discover how emotional Hull was about the conference he was about to attend. He expressed confidence that it would be an epochal event. I had not thought about it in that light, considering it merely a preparatory discussion, but Hull was almost mystical in his approach. The veteran Tennessee politician had become fascinated with the possibilities of establishing close, friendly relations with Soviet Russia. During Hull's eleven years as Secretary of State, his attitude on many matters was misjudged by the Washington press corps, especially his attitude toward Russia. Hull often was depicted as the most anti-Soviet member of the Roosevelt cabinet, whereas he was virtually co-creator with the President of the "Grand Design" for the postwar world, a plan which assumed that the United States and Soviet Russia could become partners in peace because circumstances had made them partners in war.

Cordell Hull's personal enthusiasm for this idea enhanced the exaggerated outburst of public optimism which greeted the results of the

1943 Moscow Conference. The aged Secretary, almost at the end of his career, was given a tumultuous ovation when he returned to Washington, and he became the first Secretary of State in history to be invited to address a joint session of Congress. The utopian tone of his speech is indicated in one sentence: "There will no longer be need for spheres of influence, for alliances, for balance of power, or any other of the special arrangements through which, in the unhappy past, the nations strove to safeguard their security or to promote their interests." It was a noble dream, but this extravagant confidence in a lasting Soviet-American partnership, this climate of opinion, did not make it easy for us who had to pioneer the Allied Advisory Council in Italy.

The significance of that organization—the first attempt at a co-operative venture of the Big Three—was not appreciated for many months. The council was intended to provide "guidance" for whatever Italian Government would succeed Fascism; as matters turned out, the council opened the Italian door to Communism. When the American and British Governments welcomed Bogomolov in Algiers, they tacitly acknowledged the Soviet Government's joint interest in Mediterranean affairs. When Bogomolov accompanied Macmillan and me into Italy, the English-speaking governments in effect shared with the Soviet Government sponsorship of the revived Italian Communist Party. On Bogomolov's arrival in Italy, Mark Clark even had a little ceremony to bestow a decoration on the Russian envoy.

The purpose of the Moscow meeting of Foreign Ministers, in addition to preparing for the administration of conquered countries after the war, was to make preliminary arrangements for an immediate conference in Tehran, Iran, between Roosevelt, Churchill, and Stalin. Churchill already had journeyed to Moscow on two occasions to confer with Stalin, but this was to be the first meeting of Roosevelt with the Soviet dictator. The day after Hull's triumphant return to Washington, Roosevelt departed for Tehran, stopping en route at Eisenhower's headquarters near Tunis, where I met him. Roosevelt showed the same delight at getting away from Washington that he had displayed at the Casablanca Conference nine months before, but now he was even more buoyant at the prospect of talking with Stalin personally, a meeting he had been trying to arrange ever since Pearl Harbor. Roosevelt gave me the impression that Soviet-American partnership had become as much an article of faith to him, in his own more sophisticated fashion, as it was to Secretary Hull. The latter's exuberant reports of Stalin's responsiveness naturally raised the President's own hopes.

During my discussion of French and Italian affairs with Roosevelt, it soon became apparent that he had not been told, or had forgotten, that the French Committee of National Liberation had been invited to participate in the Italian Advisory Council. The President did not welcome this news, commenting tartly that De Gaulle would be sure to find some means of complicating the already too complex Italian political picture. I explained that the Foreign Ministers had agreed at their meeting in Moscow that France should be a full member of the council, and I added that Bogomolov had been the first to inform De Gaulle of this decision, doubtless receiving credit thereby for initiating the idea. When I went on to say that the Russians now were treating the French Committee as the Government of France, Roosevelt was plainly irritated and abruptly changed the subject.

It had been arranged that before proceeding to Tehran, Roosevelt would stop for a few days at Cairo where he would meet Generalissimo Chiang Kai-shek of China to discuss the war in the Pacific against Japan. The President asked me to accompany him to Cairo because the Russians were sending an unofficial observer there, Andrei Vishinsky, Vice Minister of Foreign Affairs, who later would be coming to Algiers and Italy. Roosevelt and Hull were largely responsible for the presence of Vishinsky at Cairo. They had urged the Soviet Government to participate in this conference, but Russia had not yet declared war against Japan and believed it would be impolitic to join in strategy talks which included Chiang Kai-shek. For this reason Vishinsky did not attend any formal sessions of the conference, and even his presence in Cairo was kept secret.

However, Roosevelt told me that he wanted Vishinsky to be kept fully informed about what transpired. The President's plan for dealing with the Soviet Government was first demonstrated to me at Cairo. It was to make the Russians feel that Americans trusted them implicitly and valued Soviet-American cooperation in war and peace above any other prospective alliance. The President was very pleased that Stalin had sent Vishinsky to Cairo, because he knew that Vishinsky was one of Stalin's most intimate "personal representatives," whose reports would assuredly go straight to the Soviet dictator.

At this preliminary conference in Cairo, Churchill tried for the last time to persuade Roosevelt to expand the fighting in Mediterranean areas. Several American strategists, including Eisenhower, were more favorably disposed to this British plan now than they had been at the Casablanca Conference nine months earlier. The British once more made elaborate preparations to present their case effectively, and Churchill was hopeful that an Anglo-American program could be fully agreed upon before meeting Stalin at Tehran. But Roosevelt thwarted Churchill's scheme by keeping the Cairo discussions almost entirely on Far Eastern matters. The President obviously had made up his mind to go to his first meeting with Stalin unhampered by any additional commitments in the Mediterranean, and without releasing the British from their own commitments to invade northern France. Thus when Roosevelt, Churchill, and Stalin assembled at Tehran they were confronted with an amazing situation. Because American and British leaders disagreed upon strategy, they left it to the Soviet dictator, in effect, to decide how the English-speaking nations should fight the remaining eighteen months of the war in Europe. When Stalin cast his vote for all-out invasion of France, American strategists gained their objective and Churchill's Mediterranean aspirations faded. From that time on, fighting in the Mediterranean area stayed far down on priority lists, and the Italian campaign in particular became a slow, sad, frustrating affair.

Few Americans understood that the issues at stake at the Tehran Conference were not only military but were geopolitical. Stalin's ascendancy at Tehran was due less to Bolshevik cleverness than to two Washington policies. The first of these American policies was established soon after Pearl Harbor, when Roosevelt agreed with General Marshall that international political considerations should defer to military requirements so long as the war lasted. The second policy, emerging in 1943, was that everything possible must be done to win the confidence of Stalin and his associates. These two policies tipped the ideological balance toward Soviet Russia.

When Roosevelt and Churchill departed for Tehran, I was left in Cairo with instructions to escort the Russian envoy, Vishinsky, and his party of ten on a tour of Allied-held portions of Italy. I was somewhat dubious when the President first informed me of this assignment, because Vishinsky was notorious as the State Prosecutor who had sent to death many pioneer Bolsheviks whom Stalin accused of treason. Vishinsky's reputation led me to expect a steely eyed, ice-cold individual, but he proved as approachable in private relations as Bogomolov. His public career seemed to have nothing to do with Vishinsky personally. His manner was a Bolshevik device, put on and off like robes of office. Americans later were to become familiar with Vishinsky's public personality during his television appearances while he was Soviet Foreign Minister and chief of the Soviet delegation to the United Nations. In those UN debates, I suspect that Vishinsky derived sardonic pleasure by playing the villain for American audiences. Actually, his strong point was not international conferences, which are mostly talk, but undercover maneuvers. In Italy, during a period of five months in 1943–44, I watched with fascination his manipulations which laid the foundation for Soviet policy in western Europe. During that same period, Vishinsky simultaneously organized several satellite governments in eastern Europe so effectively that they remained intact through years of postwar strains.

Vishinsky and his group flew from Cairo to Algiers, the first stop on our tour, in a much-worn American Douglas plane, a C-47, obtained under Lend-Lease. They insisted on using this plane, and I understood why when, at Eisenhower's suggestion, I offered to facilitate their communications with Moscow. Vishinsky declined politely, explaining that his plane carried complete radio sending and receiving apparatus. The plane made them self-sufficent in other respects, too, producing an inexhaustible supply of caviar and vodka. While in Algiers, Vishinsky stayed in Bogomolov's villa. He paid all the proper formal calls, showing particular deference to De Gaulle and the French Committee, whose influence in Italian affairs he encouraged from the outset.

En route to Italy, Vishinsky and I stopped in Sicily for supper at an American Army mess. The Russian was in an affable mood and asked many questions about our operations, including remarks about the G.I. rations we were eating. To make conversation, I asked whether the Russians were using similar canned food rations for their troops on the eastern front. Vishinsky flushed and replied rather angrily that the Red Army supplied no canned foods. Surprised, I asked: "How, then, are the soldiers fed?" Vishinsky answered curtly that Russian soldiers were given flour and potatoes; for the rest they lived on the country. Although it had been far from my intention to draw unfavorable comparisons, it was evident that Vishinsky was embarrassed. The fact that the Russians were fighting so well on such meager resources seemed to give him no satisfaction. In the years since then, I have had similar experiences with other Soviet officials; they are supersensitive to any suggestion of lack of material things. They never took pride, as the British did, in austerity endured for patriotic reasons.

Vishinsky's party included five Red Army officers, two of them generals, and these military men were flown promptly to General Clark's headquarters in Italy. From this point they were taken on a front-line tour which enabled them to observe the type of warfare—desperate struggles for lofty mountain peaks—which had delayed the advance on Rome and would continue to do so for another seven months. Meanwhile I showed Vishinsky where we intended to establish the Allied Advisory Council, in a section of the huge air training school which the Fascists had built at Caserta, which was being converted into Allied Force Headquarters to supplement Algiers. The Germans controlled Rome and points north, the most prosperous two-thirds of Italy. The Allies held Naples and the impoverished southern third of the country, where food had to be imported to feed the people. And the Italian Government had to be content with Brindisi, where it was completely out of touch with Allied headquarters and also with the population it was presumably governing.

When I took Vishinsky to Brindisi to meet Badoglio, he saw for himself that this was a government in name only. The Russian was wryly amused by the wary manner in which he was greeted by Badoglio and his staff. For more than two decades the public statements of these Italians had automatically included denunciations of Soviet Communism and all its works. Now the Soviet Government, although it was sending no combat troops into Italy, had arrived officially as one of Italy's conquerors, sponsored by the Government of the United States. When I asked Vishinsky whether he cared to call upon King Victor Emmanuel, he went into a huddle with his associates and after an hour told me that he would let me know the following day. He evidently felt that he should consult Moscow before deciding this point. Our staff at Allied headquarters had thought the Russians would be without communications equipment when they arrived in Italy, but they had immediately unloaded the wireless apparatus from their plane and installed it in the fine residence which was requistioned for Bogomolov outside Naples. So the day after I asked Vishinsky whether he wanted to meet the King of Italy, he had his reply ready. "In our country we do not have much use for kings," he said smilingly. "Is it not the same with Americans?" But Vishinsky later proved willing to make expedient use of Victor Emmanuel.

As the days passed, my relations with Vishinsky became so relaxed and he seemed so willing to discuss any subject, that I brashly asked him how so many veteran Bolsheviks had been induced to confess conspiracy against Stalin during the famous "purge" trials of the 1930s, in which Vishinsky had been the Chief Prosecutor. He smiled broadly at the question, quite unembarrassed, and replied, "Oh, I know what you have in mind. You are thinking of those wonder drugs dreamed up by sensational bourgeois journalists. There was no need for anything like that. It was simply a matter of careful collection of the evidence, like weaving a fine tapestry. It took patience and tenacity—only that." The answer did not satisfy me, but since we were on a diplomatic mission it seemed advisable not to continue this line of inquiry.

While touring with Vishinsky, I tried to look at Italy through his eyes. Italians were suffering severely from the war, but not so severely as the Russians. His lack of pity was understandable. What interested him most was how the King and his associates had almost succeeded in getting out of the war cheaply. The King's group believed they had timed their offer to change sides in July so as to obtain maximum benefits for their country—and for themselves. They were bitterly disappointed when they discovered that they had been tricked, in some respects, into a costly surrender. Vishinsky's survey of Italy evidently convinced him that this former Fascist stronghold offered promising possibilities to Moscow. Once more, Anglo-American disagreements favored Soviet objectives. Each of the English-speaking governments was inclined to impose its own image upon the country which had created Fascism. The British, especially Churchill, wanted Italy to revert to a British-type monarchy, retaining the royal House of Savoy. Americans favored an American-style federal republic. And the Russians? They also were thinking of imposing their own image—Communism—but this was a ticklish matter and Vishinsky handled it with cautious astuteness.

During his first tour, Vishinsky's only mention of Italian Communists was that they seemed to be waging effective guerrilla warfare in the north behind the German lines—which was true. Later Vishinsky and Bogomolov diplomatically avoided becoming involved in some basic decisions which affected Russian interests. For example, Eisenhower decided for military reasons to forbid freedom of speech and press and activity by Italian political parties. But when this decision was criticized in England and America, Macmillan and I were belatedly consulted and we recommended that, in contrast to Fascist practice, political parties and the press be permitted reasonable liberties. Eisenhower then reversed his original decision, but it is debatable whether this reversal was prudent. Because the political party which benefited most from the liberal ruling was the Communist. Perhaps we should have given more weight to the fact that the Communist Party had come very close to power in Italy after World War I, and might repeat that performance after World War II if given a good head start—which turned out to be the case. But it would have been difficult, if not impossible, to suppress the 1943 Communist revival in Italy because of the war's incongruous alliances, and the eagerness in Washington to support Soviet-American cooperation.

As the attack on Rome stalled during the winter of 1943–44, Anglo-American Intelligence agents repeatedly confirmed that the best-organized and most active and daring guerrilla fighters were Communists and their sympathizers. Allied Force Headquarters naturally wanted to encourage Italian resistance in the German-occupied portions of Italy, so more equipment and money were allocated to Communist guerrillas than to any other resistance group. It was only after this arrangement had gone into effect that Bogomolov one day casually suggested the return to Italy of the world-famous Italian Communist, Palmiro Togliatti, who had made his base in Russia for seventeen years. Togliatti was the Italian member of the executive committee of the Communist International, and Mussolini had put a huge price on his head. Bogomolov told us that Togliatti had some interesting ideas about extending underground support for the Allied armies.

Eisenhower by this time had departed for England to prepare for the long-awaited invasion of France, and he was succeeded in the Mediterranean area by British General Sir Henry Maitland Wilson, who approved the return of Togliatti to Italy in January 1944 to encourage Communist underground fighters. The American Government welcomed this decision because it fitted in with the Roosevelt-Hull idea that Italy, the first enemy country to surrender, provided the first real testing ground of Big Three cooperation. My instructions from Washington were to give Togliatti the same courtesy and attention accorded to other Italian party leaders. Togliatti was not at all the popular image of a Communist chieftain. He had the manners and vocabulary of a professor of philosophy, and was such a gifted orator that he could hold any Italian audience spellbound. He behaved with such circumspection during his first months in Italy that he won the respect—almost the trust—even of anti-Communists like Badoglio. That naïve old Field Marshal told me wonderingly, after he had dickered for weeks with assorted politicians about forming a coalition government, that Togliatti had been the most helpful of the lot. The Communist from Moscow had resolved several arguments by repeating "The war always comes first!"

For a short time the Soviet and American Governments jointly made this slogan their guiding principle in Italy. It served Soviet purposes as well as our own to support a common Italian policy temporarily, but some Americans mistakenly assumed that this Soviet accommodation would be extended into permanent cooperation. Neither the Russians nor Togliatti can fairly be charged with misleading us on this point. Americans were entirely willing to deceive themselves. During his years in exile, Togliatti had been one of the most forthright advocates of international Communism. He had proclaimed in exhaustive detail his plans for promoting Communism in his own country. So far as I know, nobody ever asked Togliatti to renounce or even moderate his well-known opinions before the Allied Supreme Commander in the Mediterranean gave him permission to return to Italy.

As a matter of fact, Togliatti did have some practical ideas about guerrilla warfare, having studied the subject in Russia, and he soon was communicating with the Communist resistance behind the German lines. This made him useful at Allied Force Headquarters where he worked with American and British staff officers. He also was an agreeable dinner guest, so he sometimes was invited to lend a piquant touch to gatherings in honor of touring V.I.P.s who found Italy even more attractive than Algiers. At one luncheon given by American Ambassador Alexander C. Kirk, I casually asked Togliatti whether he was glad to be back in his own country after his long absence in Moscow. His reply was fervent: "More than happy! A lifetime will not be long enough to get Russia's intense cold out of my Italian bones. And I shall never forget the smell of cabbage!" Allied support of the Communist guerrillas, and our small courtesies to Togliatti, helped to make Communism respectable again in Italy, where it had been outlawed for more than two decades.

Another factor which aided the Communist cause in Italy was Churchill's intense dislike for Count Sforza, who also had lived in exile during Mussolini's regime but for quite different reasons than Togliatti. The personal antagonism of the British Prime Minister was responsible for preventing Sforza from becoming Premier in the first six-party Italian coalition at Naples, and later from becoming Foreign Minister at Rome. Twice after the Italian Government's return to Rome, the coalition parties offered the Foreign Ministry to Sforza, and twice the British Government used its veto powers to block the appointment. This widely publicized antagonism between Churchill and Sforza was exploited by Russian and Italian Communists who must have been delighted by this personal feud between two of Communism's implacable foes.

Togliatti had been in Italy more than three months before he had occasion to come to my office in April 1944. Prior to that visit, my meetings with him had been casual and had not gone beyond a polite exchange of greetings. He said he was calling upon me to ask my opinion about how Italians could be more helpful to the Allied campaign in their country. He said many Italians were eager to fight the Nazis but lacked the means to do so. In this roundabout manner, Togliatti finally got to the purpose of his call, which was to urge the United States to rearm ten Italian divisions. Vishinsky already had made this proposal to me several weeks earlier, and I knew that the Russian was telling Italians that he hoped to get American support for this scheme. Now Togliatti was taking up the campaign. I lightly pointed out that his Russian friends surely had explained to him that Americans could not spare arms and equipment for ten Italian divisions because we were preparing the "second front" which the Soviet Government was insisting upon. I could not know whether Togliatti was just making a demagogic gesture for Italian consumption, or whether he really hoped the United States might modernize enough Italian divisions to serve as the power nucleus of a Communist state after the war.

According to press regulations drawn up by the Allies, Italian commentators were not permitted to criticize any of the Allied powers, including Soviet Russia. But one day, while we were preparing at Caserta for our long-deferred entry into Rome, Bogomolov complained to me that a pamphlet had been published by a Roman

Catholic archbishop in southern Italy which violated this rule. Upon reading the pamphlet, I noted that it exposed the tactics of the Italian Communist Party but did not mention the Soviet Government. I reminded Bogomolov that the Catholic hierarchy was directed by the Vatican, not by the Italian Government, and I inquired whether Moscow had made any effort to approach the Vatican which, as he well knew, was a separate and neutral state with its own diplomatic representatives. Bogomolov did not pursue the subject but I sensed that he was mulling it over.

On June 6, two days after Allied troops entered Rome, Bogomolov and I arrived in the city at the same time and both of us were quartered in the Grand Hotel. Learning that I was to have an audience with Pope Pius XII, Bogomolov said to me confidentially, "You know, I am not satisfied with the state of relations between the Soviet Union and the Vatican. How do you think they could be improved?" To this artful question, I replied, "Well, how about negotiating a concordat? That is one of the standard procedures." Establishing a concordat is the Vatican's method of maintaining relations with many countries, and Bogomolov said, "Oh, that might be a good idea! I also would like very much to visit the Vatican. Do you suppose that could be arranged?" During my audience with the Pope, I mentioned this conversation with the Soviet envoy. His Holiness commented thoughtfully, "That can wait. I want deeds, not words. Where are the churches, where are the priests in the Soviet Union?"

Ever since Pearl Harbor, Roosevelt had tried to persuade Stalin to give some indication, for wartime propaganda purposes, that the Soviet Government was becoming less hostile to organized religions. But His Holiness told me that the Vatican's own intelligence reports showed that the Soviet official attitude to all religious organizations was basically unchanged. Probably Bogomolov's purpose in discussing the matter with me was that he hoped to be received in audience by the Pope, merely for the effect such a meeting would have upon Italian public opinion. For it had become clear by that time that the most formidable factors in the Italian political struggle were the Communists and the party which had been organized by Roman Catholics, the Christian Democrats.

The entrance of the Soviet Government into Italian politics, with the open approval of the American and British Governments, had repercussions beyond Italy's borders. When the time came to conclude postwar settlements in Europe, political maneuvers of the Italian Communists distracted attention on several critical occasions from Russian activities in the Balkans, eastern Europe, and Germany. The Soviet Government, by helping to establish a vigorous Communist

Party in Italy during the war, often was able to put the Allies on the defensive in postwar negotiations elsewhere. Vishinsky and his fellow operators achieved maximum results at minimum cost. The Communist base in Italy, unlike those in eastern Europe, never required any Red Army garrison to hold it and keep it in line.

FIFTEEN

MEETINGS WITH TITO (1944)

As every Foreign Service officer knows, there are times when our government seems to lose interest in certain portions of the globe. The blank spot, after the capture of Rome, was Italy and the Balkans. I felt that many happenings in this area merited attention by the American Government, but Washington policy-makers did not share my view. The American Joint Chiefs of Staff had decided to make the Italian front a mere holding operation and, after the abdication of King Victor Emmanuel, Roosevelt showed little further concern about Italian politics. The President's attention was diverted by military campaigns in Europe, war in the Pacific, postwar plans for Germany, and his own vision of a United Nations based upon Soviet-American cooperation. Day after day I cabled reports and suggestions to the State Department which often did not even elicit comment. This apparent indifference in Washington was in striking contrast to the attitude of Churchill and Vishinsky, who continued to take active personal interest in the fate of Italy. Vishinsky maintained close touch with the Italian Communists, and Churchill flew to Italy several times despite manifold other matters demanding his attention. Inasmuch as the British had definite plans for Italy—political, economic, financial—and Americans seemed willing to trail along, the British practically took over the administration of the country, challenged only by the Communists.

Left largely to my own devices without guidance from Washington, I utilized my opportunity to observe the activities of Italy's eastern neighbor Yugoslavia, which showed indications of becoming a very important postwar country. If Yugoslavia should swing into the Soviet sphere of influence, the impact would be immense upon all of eastern and southern Europe. The rugged people of this mountain country had dared to defy Hitler at the height of his conquests in the spring of 1941, thereby delaying the Nazi attack upon Russia for a few decisive weeks. The Germans destroyed the Yugoslav Army in a few days, but defiant remnants retreated into the mountains and organized effective resistance there. British and American propagandists made a hero of one guerrilla leader, General Draja Mihailovič, a professional Army officer and monarchist.

But in July 1943, Churchill ordered a small British mission to be parachuted into the mobile headquarters of another guerrilla leader who also was fighting the Nazis, and who seemed simultaneously to be engaged in a civil war against Mihailovič. The name of this warrior was Josip Broz, but he called himself Tito. One American air force officer, Major "Slim" Farish, was attached to the British parachute mission, and his optimistic reports soon began to reach Eisenhower's headquarters. When the Italian King proclaimed an armistice, Tito strengthened himself by disarming six Italian divisions stationed in his territory, using their equipment for his own guerrillas. He also recruited enough Italians to form about two new divisions for himself. The only disturbing report we received about Tito was that he was a Communist who had been trained in Russia.

When I accompanied Roosevelt to the Cairo Conference, I attempted to explain to the President the situation existing between Tito and Mihailovič, in the hope of getting some definite policy directive. But Roosevelt was not interested. "We should build a wall around those two fellows and let them fight it out," he said, not altogether in jest. "Then we could do business with the winner." Neither then nor later did Roosevelt ever have any consistent policy toward Yugoslavia.

One reason why I was dubious about recommending that the United States should assist Tito was because it was so obvious that Vishinsky considered Tito to be Moscow's man. In view of Washington's conciliatory attitude toward the Soviet Union at that time, Vishinsky could hardly be blamed for making the most outrageous suggestions. With a disingenuous air of camaraderie, Vishinsky asked me one day whether the Americans could not send a few cargo ships to the Russian port of Odessa to transport some supplies to Tito. This would have involved trans-shipment of Lend-Lease goods which the American Government already had sent free of charge to Russia, and the only purpose in moving such goods again would be to give Moscow credit for helping Tito. I tried to treat Vishinsky's request as a joke, saying that the longest way 'round is not the shortest way home, but when he persisted, I referred his request to Washington with the recommendation that it be disapproved. I was by no means sure what the reply might be, but Washington upheld my objections.

After Allied headquarters were transferred from Algiers to Caserta, General "Wild Bill" Donovan, head of the American Office of Strategic

Services (OSS), spent much time in Italy. He occupied an imposing villa owned by Mrs. Harrison Williams, on the island of Capri in the Bay of Naples, where he received reports from OSS agents in Yugoslavia. Some of these reports were forwarded directly to the President, but Donovan was no more successful than I in stirring up any interest in Yugoslavian operations.

However, one report which Donovan received caused me to reconsider my own appraisal of Tito. The OSS agent who wrote this dispassionate report was Major Richard Weil, Jr., a New York lawyer in civilian life. Weil had been parachuted into Yugoslavia and had spent a month there making a detailed survey of Tito's organization. Tito made him welcome in the hope of getting American supplies, and on April 4, 1944, Weil wrote: "In spite of his known affiliation with Russian Communism, most of the population seem to regard him first as a patriot and the liberator of his country and secondarily as a Communist. . . . For whatever it may be worth, my own guess is that if he is convinced that there is a clearcut choice between the two, on any issue, his country will come first." That was a remarkably shrewd guess. Four years later, in 1948, Stalin confronted Tito with just that choice, and the Yugoslav Communist demonstrated that his country did rank first with him.

In the summer of 1944, Tito was forced to leave his mountain territory because the Germans almost captured him and his chief associates. The Yugoslav Partisans then set up new headquarters on the Adriatic island of Vis. Meanwhile, Churchill became increasingly enthusiastic about Tito and urged General Wilson, who had succeeded Eisenhower as Supreme Commander in the Mediterranean, to arrange staff talks with Tito "as one Commander in Chief to another." After considerable correspondence, Tito agreed to meet Wilson in Caserta on July 12, but on July 11 word was received from Vis that he had decided not to come. We suspected that a Russian military mission, which flew into Tito's headquarters some months after the British parachutists, persuaded Tito that he should not entrust himself in British-controlled territory. However, in a few weeks he changed his mind and did fly to Caserta early in August. Wilson put him up at a guest house near the Supreme Commander's official villa, and I was invited on the day of his arrival to a small luncheon party in his honor.

Although it was a scorchingly hot day, Tito wore a woolen uniform of his own design with a dazzling display of red facing and gold braid, with a tight collar reaching to his chin. His retinue was magnificent. Tito had requested permission to bring with him sixteen personal bodyguards but he actually brought only twelve, and now three of these formidable Partisans followed Tito closely into Wilson's reception room and stationed themselves in corners with submachine guns trained upon the British host. The party also included a statuesque girl dressed in Partisan uniform. This was the celebrated Olga Ninchich, daughter of an ultraconservative minister in the prewar Royal Yugoslavian Government. She had been educated in an English finishing school and had returned home to join the Communists whom her father hated. She had served Tito for two years as a secretary and interpreter, enduring all the perils and hardships of guerrilla warfare. Finally, among his close companions, Tito was accompanied by Tigger, an unusually large Belgian sheepdog who had been trained for war duty and captured from the Germans.

Another picturesque addition to Tito's party was his British adviser, Brigadier Fitzroy Maclean, a lanky Scotsman wearing rather dirty kilts, who had done much to promote the cause of the Partisans. When the war broke out, Maclean was a career diplomat attached to the British Embassy in Moscow. The Foreign Office refused to release him for military service but he conceived the original idea of escaping from diplomacy by getting himself elected to Parliament. Thus freed from obligation to serve the Foreign Office, Maclean joined the Army immediately and participated in a number of daring irregular military operations in the Middle East and Africa before being dropped into Tito's territory.

The room where we lunched was rather small and stuffy, but two of the bodyguards pushed in and took corner stations with tommy guns ready for action. Tigger also clung close to Tito, lying at his feet under the table. General Wilson's waiters were Italians, uneasily aware that the Yugoslavs had excellent reason to hate Italians since Mussolini invaded their country. The atmosphere proved too nerve-wracking for one waiter, who dropped a plate of beans with a loud crash. The bodyguards leaped to attention, the war dog bounded out from under the table—and Wilson and Tito roared with laughter. The luncheon ended in an atmosphere of cordiality.

Tito spoke almost no English, but I guessed correctly that he was fluent in German. He had learned German while serving in the Austro-Hungarian army during World War I. We got along well together and he accepted an invitation to dine with me that same evening. I was occupying a requisitioned house called the Villa Lauro, a magnificent medieval structure on the Bay of Naples. The property stood in the midst of a private park which contained a curious plaything built to resemble a small chapel, the creation of a Greek former owner who liked practical jokes. The structure had four steps leading to its entrance, and when pressure was applied to the top step the double doors flew open and a life-sized dummy of a Dominican monk swung within inches of the visitor's nose. I called this tricky apparatus my icebreaker, and it amused Tito as much as it had other guests.

The evening was almost as hot as the afternoon had been, but Tito again wore his heavy uniform. He brought along two of his bodyguards, the charming Olga, and the watchful sheep dog. Tito said he had spent a pleasant afternoon touring Naples and calling at the villa occupied by Donovan on Capri. Tito's confidence obviously was expanding. I told him that our dinner was unofficial and that it was our custom on such informal occasions to make ourselves comfortable by removing our coats, because of the heat, and I asked his permission to do so. "*Ist das erlaubt?*" (Is that permitted?) he asked, and he unhooked his high collar and took off his coat. When dinner was announced, I told him that his bodyguards could be served in a small room opening into our dining room, where they could relax and eat in peace, if he had no objections. He agreed and began talking much more freely than at luncheon, laconically describing some of his hairbreadth escapes from the Nazis. As he was taking his departure, Tito unexpectedly invited me to visit his headquarters on Vis, and I promptly accepted.

Before Tito left Caserta to return to Vis, Churchill decided that he must meet this enigmatic figure. The Prime Minister was anxious to merge the Royal Yugoslavian Government-in-Exile, set up in London in 1941, with the Provisional Government which Tito had organized. So Churchill flew from London to Naples for a tête-à-tête with the famous guerrilla fighter, and Macmillan told me that the two men thoroughly enjoyed each other. But Tito took no chances even with the British Prime Minister; he was again accompanied by his bodyguards and the dog Tigger.

My visit to Vis provided a lively conclusion to my five years' wartime service in the Mediterranean. On August 14 the State Department informed me that I was being transferred to Supreme Allied Headquarters in France as Eisenhower's political adviser on German affairs. I was glad to be released from the frustrating duty of marking time in Italy, but I asked and was granted permission to accept Tito's invitation before departing. The American Government did not want to give even the appearance of official relations with Tito and his Provisional Government, so I was instructed to make this a personal visit and to go unaccompanied by anyone on my staff; but a B-26 plane was assigned for my trip. The plane developed engine trouble immediately and returned to Ciampino airport, where I climbed into another B-26. But the engine of this second plane faltered over Foggia airport and we were lucky to get down. I had to telephone to Naples for a third plane, and I feared that my flight was jinxed when the officer in charge at Foggia told me that the exchange number there was "Oil Can Thirteen." However, the third B-26 delivered me to Vis—two hours late. Vis is a rocky island with a double row of parallel low hills, and the valley in between provided the site for a small airstrip. The island was well defended by a brigade of Partisans and some British Commandos, and was given air and naval support by Allied Force Headquarters.

Tito had politely delayed his luncheon party and was waiting at a pleasant terrace restaurant in the lovely harbor of Komisa, a fishing village at the end of the island. This was my first meeting with Tito's close associates, some of whom still are in his government today. The Russian inspiration of the Partisans was evident. Several of the men were Communists who, like Tito himself, had been trained in Russia. Uniforms were Russian-style, and about half the guests were members of the Red Army mission. Their manner was cordial, but our conversation did not get beyond the usual toasts and small talk. After lunch we reviewed the Partisan brigade, with its women soldiers. The record of this brigade proved that both sexes were capable of sharp fighting, and they looked it. Tito then invited me for a ride on a small yacht anchored near his house. I was told that Tito had lived in caves for so long that he preferred them to houses, and that he had a cave on Vis where he often slept. But he did not invite me to inspect his cave.

Aboard the yacht, Tito explained that he never discussed political matters except in the presence of one or more members of his National Committee, but that he had arranged a little meeting for me without the presence of any Russians. Tito was quite frank with me, and I believe with everybody, about his belief in Communism and his devotion to Soviet Russia. But I got the impression, as Major Weil had, that Tito was more a national patriot than an international Communist. In talks with him and his staff that day, he appraised his Russian allies objectively. When I explained how enormous America's war production had become, but that it had to be divided many ways, Tito said he knew most of his outside support could come only from America, not from hard-pressed Russia. He dryly mentioned that the Russian pilot who had "rescued" him, when Tito left his mountain headquarters to go to Vis, was flying an American plane from an American-controlled airfield in Italy according to arrangements set up by British officers. This encouraged me to tell him how Vishinsky had requested the loan of American cargo ships to sail under the Soviet flag to bring American Lend-Lease supplies from Russia. Tito and several of his associates smiled broadly. I did not discuss any definite political matters with Tito because the American Government still had no Yugoslav policy and I had been instructed, in effect, not to talk with him concerning his future intentions. After pleasant farewells I took my departure before dark, doubting that I ever would see Tito again. He had many hazards before him.

But as matters worked out between his country and mine, my association with Tito did not end that summer day. Years later, in September 1954 and again in September 1955, I returned to Yugoslavia to discuss controversial territorial, military, and economic matters, and on both occasions Tito warmly welcomed the first American who had accepted his hospitality on the island of Vis, and our negotiations were concluded in friendly fashion.

SIXTEEN

PLANNING THE GERMAN OCCUPATION

When I flew into Washington from Italy on September 4, 1944, to be briefed on my new assignment as Eisenhower's political adviser on German affairs, I was quite out of touch with Allied preparations for dealing with postwar Germany. That problem had not been among our responsibilities in the Mediterranean area. But I was aware that an Anglo-American-Russian agency, called the European Advisory Commission, had been at work in London all through 1944 trying to decide how to administer Germany, and I assumed that at this late date a detailed occupation plan must be in readiness. Paris had been liberated on August 25, Allied armies were advancing from the west, Russian armies were closing in from the east, and the surrender of Germany appeared imminent.

To my astonishment, I learned in Washington that no American plan was ready yet because President Roosevelt had not made known his own views, and three departments of the government were wrangling among themselves about postwar Germany. The State Department had drawn up its plans under the expert direction of two of my best friends in the Foreign Service, H. Freeman Matthews and James W. Riddleberger. The War Department had developed other plans under the skilled supervision of Secretary Stimson and Assistant Secretary John J. McCloy. And the Treasury Department had produced a third program which became known as the Morgenthau Plan, named for the Secretary of the Treasury who sponsored it. Although the occupation policies of the State and War Departments disagreed in details, they were essentially similar, and Secretaries Stimson and Hull were willing to merge them. But the Morgenthau Plan was based on a drastically different conception—the proposition that Germany should be transformed from an industrial to an agricultural economy. It was the contention of the Treasury Department that the world could protect itself against a revival of militarism in Germany only by depriving that country of its heavy industry and by shutting down its coal and iron mines.

These policy disputes encompassed much more than the fate of Germany alone; the future of the entire continent of Europe was involved. Hull and Stimson and Morgenthau were in agreement that the Germans must be made to pay for Nazi crimes, and no one in Washington was recommending any "soft" occupation. But opponents of the Morgenthau Plan believed that the postwar reconstruction of all Europe depended on utilizing Germany's resources and skilled workmen, and they were aghast when the President became so impressed with the Treasury Department's proposal that he wrote on a preliminary draft of it: "O. K. FDR." Stimson soon persuaded Roosevelt to withdraw his unqualified approval of the Morgenthau Plan, and a Joint Committee representing the White House and the three departments tried to reach a compromise which would satisfy the President.

During the two weeks I spent in Washington preparing for my new post, I was given so many different versions of Roosevelt's ideas on Germany that I became very anxious to hear what the President himself had to say on this subject. I was more than usually pleased, therefore, when I received a message from the White House that Roosevelt wanted to see me. But in our conversation, the President did not even mention any disagreements on occupation policy, and since he did not bring up the subject, I did not feel free to question him.

In any case, Roosevelt monopolized the conversation, as he usually did when some matter particulary interested him. His topic that day was the future of Soviet-American relations. He declared we must arrange the German occupation in a manner which would convince the Russians that Americans really desired to cooperate with them. The President told me that he expected to talk soon with Stalin and Churchill in a second Big Three conference, and that he was confident that a permanent Soviet-American understanding could be reached. He urged me to bear in mind that our primary postwar objective was Soviet-American cooperation—without which world peace would be impossible—and that Germany would be the proving ground for such cooperation. That was my parting word from the President before I returned to Europe, and I considered it the equivalent of an oral directive.

Not until several weeks later did the President explain to Secretary Hull why he was determined not to be stampeded into a decision about postwar Germany. In a memorandum to Hull dated October 20, Roosevelt wrote:

"It is all very well for us to make all kinds of preparations for the treatment of Germany, but there are some matters in regard to such treatment that lead me to believe that speed on these matters is not an essential at the present moment. It may be in a week, or it may be in a month, or it may be several months hence. I dislike making detailed plans for a country which we do not yet occupy." The President added this comment about the European Advisory Commission which was then working in London: "We must emphasize the fact that the European Advisory Commission is 'advisory,' and that you and I are not bound by this advice. This is something which is sometimes overlooked, and if they do not remember that word 'advisory' they may go ahead and execute some of the advice which, when the time comes, we may not like at all." His memo to Hull concluded: "In view of the fact that we have not occupied Germany, I cannot agree at this moment as to what kind of a Germany we want in every detail."

When I reported to Eisenhower at his Versailles headquarters near Paris, meeting him for the first time in nine months, I learned that the Supreme Allied Commander was not paying much attention to what would happen in postwar Germany. He rightly believed that this was not his responsibility. The General was burdened with the stupendous task of directing the military campaign which was swiftly moving toward its end, and he could spare little thought for non-military problems. However, he did tell me that he had made one suggestion which both Washington and London turned down. He had proposed retaining the administrative machinery of SHAEF (Supreme Headquarters, Allied Expeditionary Force) for some time after the surrender. Eisenhower was justifiably proud of the way Britons and Americans had learned to work together in his various headquarters, and he thought that if the Anglo-American staffs could be used in joint administration of the American and British occupation zones, the Russians might be induced to come into a unified organization. But Moscow's reaction to this suggestion was emphatically negative. The Russians apparently suspected a scheme to perpetuate an Anglo-American combination against them. Since the help of Moscow was then being sought in the war against Japan, the Anglo-American military chiefs did not want to antagonize the Russians, and Eisenhower's sensible idea was shelved.

The General told me, during our first talk in France, that he was entirely in favor of the decision which had been tentatively made in Washington that a civilian High Commissioner should head our military government in Germany. Eisenhower said that civilian supremacy was the American tradition, respected by all professional soldiers, and he cited some of his experiences in the Philippines as evidence that the American Armed Forces were not an appropriate instrument for administering conquered territories. He believed the Army should serve merely as a garrison, not a government, and he suggested that garrisons of all the occupying powers might even be housed in a special military district. Eisenhower assured me he would do everything possible to urge civilian responsibility for the American share of the occupation, and remarked that he would seek to arrange matters so the Army could transfer authority at the top within a matter of weeks after Germany's surrender. Speaking of the occupation, he exclaimed, "Thank the Lord that will not be my job!" And he added with a grin, "They'll probably wish a good part of it off on you!"

Despite Eisenhower's conviction that military commanders should not usurp civilian functions, he and his staff were required during the final months of the war to make a number of political decisions which have had lasting international consequences. These decisions were imposed upon the Supreme Commander because the civilians responsible for American foreign policy—the President and the Secretary of State—did not choose to assert their authority. The most important example was the decision not to try to capture Berlin, a decision of such international significance that no Army chief should have been required to make it. When the time came to decide about Berlin, the entire responsibility was placed upon General Marshall, as Chief of Staff, and General Eisenhower, as Theater Commander. Both of these Army officers accepted this responsibility without complaint, then or afterward, but it was inevitable that they would regard Berlin from the military point of view.

As a matter of war strategy, the Eisenhower-Marshall decision was irreproachable, being based on careful consideration for saving the lives of American soldiers. According to SHAEF estimates, it would have cost from ten thousand to a hundred thousand American casualties to capture the German capital and the area surrounding it. These estimates proved wildly wrong, but that is beside the point. Eisenhower reasoned that, since Berlin lay deep inside the agreed Russian occupation zone, SHAEF forces would be obligated to evacuate the metropolitan district almost as soon as they could capture it, turning it over to Russian control. So the Anglo-American troops were directed toward Leipzig and the Red Army was left to seize Berlin—with results which none of us foresaw.

A number of other decisions of great political importance were left entirely to the judgment of Supreme Allied Headquarters during those final months of the war. In order to concentrate upon military operations, Eisenhower depended upon his Chief of Staff, General Smith, to see that he was not distracted by what seemed unnecessary interruptions. In later years Smith served with distinction as Ambassador to the U.S.S.R., Director of the Central Intelligence Agency, and as Under Secretary of State. But in 1944–45 Smith would have been the first to admit that he then lacked detailed knowledge of European affairs, and that political aspects of many events were downgraded or disregarded at SHAEF. In retrospect, I feel that I might have done more to correct that situation. As the President's personal representative, I could request direct access to the Supreme Commander whenever I desired, but I used the privilege sparingly because I knew that both Eisenhower and Smith preferred it that way, and I considered myself a civilian guest in their military headquarters.

Having learned in Washington that American plans for Germany were still indefinite, and having learned from Eisenhower that the Army hoped to be relieved of top responsibility soon after the surrender, I flew to London to find out what progress the European Advisory Commission was making with its occupation plans. The State Department had instructed John G. Winant, our Ambassador to Great Britain who was serving also as the American member of the EAC, to cooperate with me as Eisenhower's political adviser, and the Ambassador provided me with an office in the embassy where I could study the EAC secret files and consult with our men who were working on this project. They were an exceptionally competent group of Foreign Service officers and academic experts, but they were a harassed group because their discussions had been difficult and frustrating.

Just before I arrived in London, the EAC on September 12, 1944, had finally concluded a draft for an occupation program. This draft was the culmination of nine months of laborious negotiations, during which the EAC negotiators sometimes had despaired of ever reaching agreement. The Russian member, Ambassador F. T. Gusev, had to refer even minor questions back to his government, and sometimes Moscow did not reply for weeks or months. Stalin was directing the military campaigns of the Red Army, as well as supervising political settlements in the portions of eastern Europe already overrun, and he was in no hurry to make binding agreements concerning Germany's future.

Roosevelt and Churchill proved even more difficult. After the commission members agreed that each of the Big Three nations would occupy a separate zone in Germany (France was not included), and after the boundaries of the Russian zone had been accepted by all three governments, the President and the Prime Minister still could not agree which areas the Americans and Britons would occupy. Both statesmen wanted the port of Hamburg and control of the Ruhr, Germany's richest industrial region. So the draft agreement of September 12 delimited two western zones but postponed decision about which western government would occupy which zone. It was not until late in the autumn that Roosevelt yielded on this point, giving Churchill the northwestern area he desired.

The draft agreement also stipulated that Berlin would become the administrative center for the three occupying powers—for the United States and Great Britain as well as Russia. But when I examined the approved occupation map, I observed that Berlin was more than a hundred miles inside the Russian zone and no provision had been made for the Anglo-American powers to reach the city. James Riddleberger, while studying this map, had also taken cognizance of this omission and he proposed that the occupation zones should converge upon Berlin like slices of pie, thus providing each zone with its own frontage in the capital city. Nothing ever came of this ingenious suggestion, however, and some time later I asked Riddleberger what had happened. He explained that he had been adamantly opposed to putting the American sector one hundred miles behind the Soviet lines in Berlin, but that Winant had been equally vigorous in defending the plan. They "had a head-on clash," but of course the Ambassador was in a much more influential position than the career officer. Riddleberger told me: "Winant accused me of not having any faith in Soviet intentions and I replied that on this he was exactly right. In an effort to find some way out, I then suggested that the three zones should converge upon Berlin as the center of a pie, but this idea got nowhere because Winant was very much opposed to it."

Although I was not responsible for any decision of the EAC, this lack of a precise agreement about entrance to Berlin disturbed me. The geography of access corridors had been defined, but not the right to use them. Our right to be in Berlin was based, of course, on the right of conquest—the unconditional surrender of Nazi Germany—and not on any agreement or lack of agreement with the Soviet Government, but I felt that our access through the Russian zone should not be taken for granted merely as a derivative right. It seemed to me that this important point should be spelled out in the EAC agreement. I mentioned my concern to some of Winant's assistants on the commission, but they replied, "Yes, that worried us, too. But the ambassador does not wish to press the matter now."

This subject was very much on my mind when the ranking American naval officer in London, Admiral Harold R. Stark, invited me to luncheon with Winant in the Admiral's apartment in Grosvenor Square. There were only the three of us, and Winant talked for two hours about his difficulties with the EAC. Finally I ventured to say that I thought a serious effort should be made to define the right of access from the American and British zones to Berlin. I told Winant that judging by my experiences with the Russians in Italy, they were sharp bargainers who expected other people to be the same. To my surprise, Winant exclaimed vehemently, "You have no right to come along at this late date and make such a proposal just after we have agreed upon a draft!" Winant went on to say that the September 12 agreement had become possible only because he had established close personal relationship with Ambassador Gusev, after months of patient effort, and had gained the Soviet envoy's confidence. In Winant's opinion, if we now belatedly raised the access question, this might upset the hard-won draft agreement and make further settlements impossible. Winant argued that our right of free access to Berlin was implicit in our right to be there. The Russians, he declared, were inclined to suspect our motives anyway, and if we insisted on this technicality, we would intensify their distrust. He would not do it.

Ambassador Winant's deputy on the EAC was Professor Philip E. Mosely of Columbia University, a distinguished specialist on Russian affairs. Several years after the war and after Winant's death, Mosely and I met in New York and compared our information about Winant's grave responsibility for the personal diplomacy which he exercised in the Advisory Commission negotiations. Winant, a highly sensitive man of many tensions, joined the Roosevelt administration in 1935, after three terms as Republican Governor of New Hampshire. By 1941, when he was appointed Ambassador to the United Kingdom, Winant was so intimate with Roosevelt that he had authority in London to use the U.S. naval code to communicate directly with the White House. The Ambassador thus was in a position to bypass the State Department to which he was officially attached, and to develop policies of his own which were likewise independent of the War Department, which also had vital interest in his negotiations. Mosely told me that Winant never consulted the State Department on the subject of access to Berlin. A thorough check of the 1944 files has shown that Winant never communicated in writing with either the State or War Departments on this problem, but Mosely recalled that the ambassador did mention once that he had talked with somebody in the War Department who assured Winant that there was no military necessity for an access stipulation in the EAC agreement, that the Berlin question could be settled later.

When Winant so sharply objected to reopening the access question, I felt it would serve no useful purpose to appeal to higher authority in Washington. The President himself, in his recent talk with me, had emphasized that he thought the most important thing was to persuade the Russians to trust us, a sentiment which apparently motivated Winant's negotiations. As for Eisenhower, I knew that the Supreme Commander would prefer not to become involved in a controversy more likely to hinder than speed the conduct of the war. I did mention to the General and his principal staff officers my concern about the undefined arrangements for Berlin, but their minds were on more immediate problems. During those final months of the war, Eisenhower consistently differentiated between decisions which had to be made before the surrender—which he regarded as military matters which directly concerned him—and decisions which were to go into effect after the surrender—primarily political and diplomatic business.

So the matter of a defined right of access to Berlin was left hanging—and it is still hanging today. In retrospect the danger appears obvious, and it would seem that all of us who were in a position to do something, and who failed to act, were culpable. Unlike the situation in Poland, for example, where all-out war might have exploded if Americans had attempted to enforce the Yalta agreement, the United States possessed adequate military power in Germany, during the early postwar days, to compel an understanding with the Russians.

There can be no doubt that the deliberate decision not to seek a specific understanding on the Berlin access question had a disastrous aftermath. But at the time, many wise men did not so view the problem. Winant's idealistic notions about Soviet-American relations were matched by Roosevelt's confidence, frequently expressed in his phrase, "I can handle Stalin." After the war other occasions arose, as the months and years passed, when the Berlin issue might have been settled under conditions more favorable to the United States than were ever to occur again. Two such opportunities came at the beginning and at the end of the Berlin Blockade in 1948–49. But the fateful decision about Berlin, made in London in September 1944, was a personal decision based upon the all-too-prevalent American theory that individual friendships can determine national policy. Soviet policymakers and diplomats never operate on that theory.

SEVENTEEN

SURRENDER OF THE NAZIS

After the liberation of Paris on August 25, 1944, some of Eisenhower's staff went with the General to France, while others remained in England. My work required close contact with officers in both places, and during that long hard winter of 1944–45 I made frequent trips back and forth. SHAEF was installed at Versailles amidst summer palaces of former French kings and ancient mansions of court nobility. Versailles, twelve miles from Paris, was where the conquering German Army established its headquarters in 1870–71 and where the peace treaty of World War I was signed in 1919. Now this historic suburb was providing offices and billets for Eisenhower and his staff. Supreme Headquarters were in the former Grand Trianon Palace, and Eisenhower lived in a pleasant modern villa not far from the Petit Trianon, the exquisite make-believe cottage of Marie Antoinette. My residence was a requisitioned house nearby on the Avenue de Paris. The Hotel Raphaël in Paris was also requisitioned for the Supreme Commander's staff, and a suite there was assigned to me for use in the city.

Because of De Gaulle's attitude toward me as Roosevelt's agent, I had stipulated that I should not serve as Eisenhower's adviser on French affairs, but of course I was still deeply interested in the country where I had lived so long. Many of my French acquaintances had never left France during the difficult and dangerous years of the Nazi occupation, and they were extravagantly exuberant during the first weeks of the Paris victory celebrations. But as the war continued to drag on, they experienced an inevitable letdown. Almost every family had members who still were in German prison camps or enduring forced labor in German factories. Food in Paris was scarce, fuel almost nonexistent, and fear of the Nazis was succeeded by fear of vengeful Frenchmen. Members of the resistance movements had kept their own political differences in abeyance while they were working underground against the Nazis, but after the departure of the Germans some of the groups began to fight each other. These former guerrillas ranged politically from extreme left to extreme right, and the war years had provided them with many grievances, many suspicions of treachery, many accusations of collaboration with the Nazis. It was not surprising that some groups, particularly the Communists, took advantage of the unsettled times to eliminate their enemies and rivals. France was swarming that winter with millions of Allied soldiers wearing the uniforms of a dozen countries, so disguise was easy. Summary justice was dispensed in thousands of cases, some never made public.

Several French friends appealed to me for protection. Among these friends was Gaston Henry-Haye, former French Ambassador to Washington, who came to the Hotel Raphaël one midnight in fear of his life. I first met Henry-Haye before the war when he was Mayor of Versailles. While the German Army was entering Paris and many neighboring French mayors were fleeing in panic, Henry-Haye persuaded the people of Versailles not to join the headlong exodus, and thus saved many of them from accidents and death on the jammed highways. His calm courage at that time made a favorable impression upon Ambassador Bullitt and other members of the American Embassy in Paris, and we were pleased when the Vichy Government appointed Henry-Haye as Ambassador to the United States. In Washington, I found the new Ambassador helpful in my efforts to obtain American food and medicines for the people of Unoccupied France, especially the children.

Later he also was of assistance in our efforts to get civilian supplies to North Africa, until the Vichy Government severed diplomatic relations with the United States when our troops landed in Africa. The following day, according to protocol, Henry-Haye was presented with passports for himself and his staff. When the Ambassador said he preferred to remain in the United States until France was free, he was astonished and chagrined to have the American Government intern him as an "enemy alien." The Ambassador had a hot temper which he did not always control perfectly, and he was not popular with everyone in Washington. After the liberation of Paris, Henry-Haye returned to France, assuming rather naïvely that he could resume his status as a government official, as many other Vichy officials had done in the De Gaulle administration. Instead, Henry-Haye became a fugitive in his own country, under sentence of death by two resistance groups. He told me that for weeks he had not dared to sleep two consecutive nights in the same room, and he asked me to help him go abroad until conditions became normal in France. But I convinced him that to leave then would imply admittance of guilt. He accepted my advice and continued his hideaway existence through that turbulent winter.

The French Provisional Government which De Gaulle had formed at Algiers in 1943 was not officially recognized by any of the Big Three until it established itself in Paris in October 1944. President Roosevelt persisted in his conviction that the French people should be given an opportunity to elect an administration of their own choosing, but when the Germans continued to hold out and it became apparent that elections would have to be postponed indefinitely, Roosevelt reluctantly agreed to join London and Moscow in granting diplomatic recognition to the "united front" government which De Gaulle had created. In forming his coalition, De Gaulle included members of the Communist Party as ministers in his cabinet. The French Communists were better organized than any of the prewar political parties, and De Gaulle felt bound to make concessions to them in order to avoid a showdown which he might not have won just then.

In December I was asked to arrange a dinner conference in Versailles between French and American financial experts, including De Gaulle's Minister of Finance, René Pleven, the French economist Charles Rist, and the Americans John J. McCloy and Lewis W. Douglas. The disordered French financial situation troubled a number of Washington agencies which were trying to help the French Government, and the American visitors were impressed when Pleven described to them his proposals for currency reforms. One of Pleven's schemes was an ingenious device similar to drastic measures already enforced in Belgium and the Netherlands. The Minister of Finance explained that French collaborators and black marketeers were hoarding their money largely in five-thousand-franc notes, and he proposed withdrawing these notes from circulation with no advance notice. New franc notes would be printed but in order to exchange canceled notes for the new issue, holders of the old money would be required to explain how they had acquired it. Pleven said immense sums of illegal profits could thus be wiped out and French currency stabilized. But months went by and the Pleven scheme was not put into effect.

When I discreetly made inquiries among my friends in the French Government, they admitted that Communist ministers had sidetracked the project. During the chaotic weeks just before and after the liberation, the French Communist Party had seized and stockpiled huge quantities of currency, especially five-thousand-franc notes, which they had removed from French banks and other institutions. By delaying the Pleven plan for more than a year, the Party was able to exchange its hidden hoards for other assets, thereby accumulating funds to support Communist activities for years to come. The delay was equally helpful, of course, to black marketeers and collaborators.

De Gaulle's prestige among his own people rose throughout that winter. Some Frenchmen who had regarded the General as a British puppet, and who had not been thrilled by his celebrated repudiation of the armistice with Germany, now became enthusiastic about him. Their allegiance was won by De Gaulle's determination to restore France as a Great Power and to relinquish nothing of the French overseas empire. At the moment when French strength was at its lowest point in modern history, I could see that the men of France—and the women even more—were grateful to De Gaulle for bolstering their sense of national pride. Most of my acquaintances in Paris completely disagreed with Roosevelt's theory that France would be better off if the Republic did not try to hang on to its far-flung colonies in Africa and Asia. It is ironic that, in later years, De Gaulle initiated an empire-reducing program which resembled Roosevelt's recommendations for France more than De Gaulle's wartime visions.

When I first reported to Eisenhower in September 1944, no provision had been made for France in any plans for the German occupation. France was not even represented on the European Advisory Commission, although it had been a member of the Italian Advisory Commission from its beginning. France was admitted to the EAC later that autumn, but no occupation zone in Germany was assigned to France until February 1945 when Stalin, Roosevelt, and Churchill came together at Yalta in the Soviet Crimea for their second personal conference. At that meeting Stalin was at first opposed to giving France any part in the occupation of Germany. He argued that Frenchmen had not fought long enough to earn that privilege, and that Yugoslavia or Poland deserved such recognition more than France. Stalin asserted that many woes of the Soviet Union occurred because France surrendered so quickly to the Germans. He added that when De Gaulle had visited him in Moscow the previous December, the French General had shown a wholly unrealistic attitude in equating vanquished France with the Big Three victors.

Roosevelt supported Stalin's contention, but the British "fought like tigers for France," as Harry Hopkins expressed it in his notes. The British did not attempt to change Stalin's mind but concentrated upon Roosevelt, and after the Yalta Conference was more than half finished, the President agreed that France should become a partner in both the German and Austrian occupations. Roosevelt then arranged to have a private meeting with Stalin to explain the reasons for his change of heart. The President told Stalin that he had become convinced that no settlement in Germany could be lasting unless France were given a share in the occupation. Stalin replied that his own views about France remained unaltered, but that he no longer would oppose French participation if Roosevelt considered it necessary. Thus it came about that the final communiqué of the Yalta Conference announced that the Big Three statesmen had agreed to accept France as a full partner in the occupations.

Neither SHAEF in France nor the EAC in London had been given any advance notice of this dramatic decision. Eisenhower was not consulted about a French zone in Germany until he suddenly was notified that France had one. The Supreme Commander had not paid much attention to what was transpiring at Yalta; his mind was on the war, not on postwar settlements. The decision at Yalta necessitated eleventh-hour rearrangements for independent French zones. Since the Russians were not even asked to contribute any territory from their allotted zones, the French areas had to be carved out of the American and British zones—and most of them came from the American. Our officers at SHAEF were inclined to yield to the French as much territory for occupation as they reasonably could. "For God's sake, let's not have another row with De Gaulle" expressed the attitude. The division of areas was made mostly by the military authorities, who paid scant attention to Germany's previous administrative organization. The states of Baden and Württemberg were each neatly sliced in half. Knowing how difficult it always had been to reach agreement with De Gaulle's Government about anything, I was appalled at the prospect of trying to rush plans for these complicated territorial transfers involving millions of people. In fact, it did prove impossible to complete the transfers in time. Many details were still unsettled when Germany surrendered in May.

The Yalta Conference also granted full membership to France in the Allied Control Councils to be located in Berlin and Vienna. This decision was made also against the position orginally taken by Stalin. The Soviet dictator told Roosevelt that De Gaulle should be content with the grant of French occupation zones and should not be given authority in the Allied Control Councils equal to the Big Three. Stalin commented that Frenchmen, smarting from the humiliation of defeat, would be tempted to abuse their power merely to reassert their pride. As our experience later showed, that was a percipient forecast.

The discussions at Yalta specified what would be done when the war ended, but those discussions could not end the war. When Allied troops had triumphantly entered Paris the previous August, everyone thought that the fighting was practically over. Even Eisenhower made a small bet that Germany would surrender before the end of the year. But he lost the bet. The Germans fought desperately for eight and a half months longer, including a frightening counterattack in the Battle of the Bulge during Christmas week. About this time it was discovered that the Germans were conducting an operation to assassinate members of the top Allied command in France, including Eisenhower, Bedell Smith, and others. The daring venture was being directed by Lieutenant Colonel Otto Skorzeny, the Nazi special operations chief whom Hitler had sent to Italy months before to rescue Mussolini; about two hundred Germans dressed in American uniforms and speaking French and English had been parachuted back of our lines. When Allied Intelligence reported this, there was considerable commotion around headquarters. Guards were doubled on all lodgings and there was a lot of trigger-happy shooting with some unnecessary casualties, including four unfortunate French officers in a jeep who did not stop at sentry's orders and were killed. I spent the night at Bedell Smith's quarters which were surrounded by a large, wall-enclosed garden. Nine guards were on duty. In the middle of the night we were awakened by a fusillade. With Smith leading in pajamas and equipped with a carbine, we deployed into the garden and began shooting right and left. The next morning a stray cat was found in the garden riddled with bullets. However, most of the Skorzeny operatives were captured shortly thereafter, and many eventually were executed.

As the blackouts and troop movements and bombardments continued, and Germany still would not surrender, everybody stopped making bets about when the war would end and went to the opposite extreme of overestimating Nazi defenses. The favored rumor was that diehard Nazi battalions were preparing enormous mountain redoubts in central and southern Germany from which they could wage guerrilla warfare for years. The principal redoubt area was supposed to be in Bavaria. Anything seemed plausible that spring. The Germans already had held out months longer than most experts believed possible, and last-ditch fighting was encouraged by the American Government's insistence upon unconditional surrender. At a SHAEF meeting which I attended in Versailles, a British staff officer claimed to have information that Roosevelt had weakened in his stand on unconditional surrender, and some American officers there were nearly persuaded in spite of my vigorous denials. Afterwards I got confirmation from Washington that there had been no change in the President's attitude.

On this subject of unconditional surrender, my personal views were in complete agreement with the President. I was at the Casablanca Conference when Roosevelt first announced his policy in a talk with war correspondents there. The President declared that the Allies would demand the "unconditional surrender" of Germany, Italy and Japan. Roosevelt used the phrase casually but it became astonishingly popular. However, British officials never did like the idea. The phrase had not been defined, and Macmillan, among others, thought it would be a stumbling block in peace negotiations. Eisenhower was dubious but did not really oppose it. The point, as I saw it, was that if conditions were to be negotiated, with whom were we to negotiate? American public opinion was highly inflamed, and if we attempted to make a deal with Nazi representatives, the reaction in the United States can be imagined.

However, Nazi propagandists used the chilling phrase "unconditional surrender" to great effect after details of the Morgenthau Plan leaked out. The Nazi radio shouted day and night that Germans would become starving peasants if they surrendered. Both the Soviet and British Governments decided that the slogan was needlessly prolonging the war, and Eisenhower agreed with them. Several of us on his staff, Americans and Britons, drafted a number of declarations suggesting various forms of "conditional unconditional surrender," similar to arrangements made for the Italians. But none of the proposals proved acceptable in Washington. The mighty war machine commanded by Eisenhower rolled on inexorably to meet the millions of soldiers of the Red Army, and the Germans battled until the Nazi regime literally fell apart. The German surrender was the only genuinely unconditional surrender of World War II.

After Hitler's death was announced on May 1, everybody knew that the end was a matter of days. Throughout Europe frantic German commanders tried to negotiate mass surrenders to western armies in order to escape avenging Russians, Poles, Yugoslavs, and Czechs. German soldiers knew how brutally all Slav people had been treated, and they had no reason to expect less harsh treatment if they fell into Slav hands. If Eisenhower had desired, he might have accepted the surrender of millions of Germans who had fought on the Russian front, but he refused. He acted in harmony with Roosevelt's wishes, and was determined to do nothing which might increase Russian distrust.

During the last weeks of the war Eisenhower moved his headquarters to the ancient cathedral city of Reims, with its enormous champagne cellars which provided protection against air raids. And it was in a little school house in this French town that the Germans surrendered at 2:41 A.M. on May 7, 1945. The surrender ceremony was something Eisenhower found distasteful and he decided not to participate in the procedure, delegating the signing of the documents to his Chief of Staff, General Smith. It was a very personal decision.

The precise text of Germany's unconditional surrender had been discussed for months by experts in Washington, London, and Moscow. The European Advisory Commission had written a number of drafts and finally produced a set of terms which all the Big Three governments formally approved. These documents were sent to me late in March and I turned them over to Smith, informing him that they were to be signed simultaneously by the Big Three and Germany and then released to the press. The surrender ceremony at Reims was strictly military, but as soon as the formalities ended, I had access to the texts. It was then I discovered that a strange document—that is, strange to me—had been used. General Smith, exhausted, had gone to bed, but I telephoned him and asked what had happened to the EAC-approved text. At first he could not recall having received any surrender papers from me. "But don't you remember that big blue folder which I told you were the terms approved by everybody?" I asked. The Chief of Staff, now thoroughly awakened, jumped into his uniform and raced back to headquarters. We found the big blue folder exactly where he had filed it in his personal top-secret cabinet. Moments later an urgent cablegram arrived from Washington saying that Moscow was protesting that the surrender terms which had just been signed were not the EAC agreement which had been endorsed by the Russians.

What had happened was that Smith, harassed by a thousand complex matters of highest importance, had suffered a rare lapse of memory and had been under the impression that the EAC never had approved a surrender agreement. Accordingly, when the first message came from General Montgomery's headquarters that the Germans might be ready to surrender, Smith used his own discretion and secretly ordered three officers to assemble surrender documents based on miscellaneous reference material. The Russians had sent a liaison officer to Eisenhower's headquarters, General Ivan Susloparov, and when Smith asked him to certify the improvised documents, the obliging Russian did so. Susloparov told us later that his government never had informed him of any other terms, which doubtless was true, but he was abruptly recalled to Moscow when he admitted that he had certified the terms which Smith had hastily adapted.

The bungled affair was covered up immediately by an announcement by SHAEF early in the morning that the documents which had been signed in the middle of the night merely "formalized the surrender" and that "the official surrender" would be signed in Berlin on May 9. SHAEF's announcement offered no adequate explanation for this complicated arrangement, and the curiosity of many witnesses then and of several historians since remained unsatisfied on this point. One scholar, after a meticulous examination of all the official documents and personal records he could find, evolved an impressively elaborate explanation, but he missed the key fact—Smith's lapse of memory—which never was put in writing. As at Reims, Eisenhower also declined to participate in the Berlin surrender ceremony, and he delegated his British deputy commander, Air Chief Marshal Sir Arthur W. Tedder, to represent Supreme Allied Headquarters.

It required almost two months to complete the extremely complicated surrender of the huge German armies and their auxiliaries. The utmost care was necessary to prevent accidental conflicts between Anglo-American and Soviet armies rushing toward each other across Europe with enemy troops in between. Meanwhile, one major question for Eisenhower's political advisers was whether or not any German Government still existed. The surrender at Reims had been arranged through Grand Admiral Karl Doenitz, who had been named Fuehrer either by Hitler himself, just before the latter committed suicide, or by Martin Bormann, Secretary of the Nazi Party. The surrender at Berlin also had been signed by Germans accredited by Doenitz. All of the Big Three governments had recognized the authority of the Grand Admiral to make these surrender arrangements from his temporary "capital" in Flensburg on the Danish frontier. But arguments broke out a few days later in London and Washington concerning whether Doenitz should be regarded as head of a government, and the problem was referred to the Supreme Commander. Eisenhower instructed me to proceed with Major General Lowell W. Rooks, one of his leading staff officers since African days, to Flensburg in Schleswig-Holstein, which now was in the British zone. Eisenhower believed Doenitz was trying to make trouble between SHAEF and the Russians, and he told us to investigate this situation.

Flying to Flensburg on May 17, we quickly went to work. The ancient port dating from the twelfth century had been badly battered, but a Hamburg-American luxury liner in the harbor had escaped serious damage and it served as comfortable billets for the numerous British staff officers assembled there who welcomed Rooks and me. We immediately met with Doenitz who, although he said his nomination to succeed Hitler had come as a complete surprise to him, had already set up all the paraphernalia of a going government, with honor guards around his headquarters, and a sizable civilian office staff including women typists and file clerks. The most prominent member of the "cabinet" which Doenitz had managed to get together was Dr. Albert Speer, Hitler's chief economist, who had performed wonders as the Nazi Minister of Munitions. Speer, on his own initiative, had disobeyed Hitler's last mad orders to blow up every utility within German control.

Doenitz received us ceremoniously and showed us two radiograms he had received purporting to come from Martin Bormann, Hitler's most trusted lieutenant in his last days. The first message stated that Hitler had changed his political testament, substituting Doenitz for Hermann Goering as his successor in case Hitler died. The second radiogram announced that Hitler had committed suicide and that Bormann had personally confirmed his death, so Doenitz now was the Leader. Doenitz impressed me at first as being much like conventional military officers I had met in other countries. He talked in almost the same phrases as the Frenchmen who swore allegiance to Pétain, and the Italian Badoglio who was loyal to his King. The German Admiral said he was merely trying to do his duty and to carry out orders from the authority which he considered legitimate.

But after talking in this vein for a little while, Doenitz declared solemnly that all Westerners, including the Germans, must work together now to prevent the Bolshevization of Europe. He related how he had organized a radio campaign which had induced an estimated million Germans to flee westward to escape the Russians. He boasted that he had arranged to bring out the ablest Germans, particularly the scientists, who could be most useful to the West. (A number of those scientists are American citizens now.)

This attitude of Doenitz was precisely what Eisenhower had asked us to watch for. It never occurred to the Admiral that Germany was to be deprived of a national government and that his suggestion of a provisional government, headed by himself under a Nazi mandate, was incompatible with Allied objectives. There could be no doubt that he was completely earnest in his expressed alarm about Bolshevization of Europe, but he seemed totally unaware that the entire continent hated and feared Germany more than Russia. We reported the circumstances to Eisenhower and to Washington, but investigators from the U. S. Strategic Bombing Survey group, including Paul H. Nitze and Henry C. Alexander, requested us not to disclose our recommendations for a day or two while they were obtaining information on the results of Allied bombing. Speer's files contained much useful data, and his women secretaries were well informed, eager to be helpful, and willing to work hours overtime to assemble the desired information.

While we were waiting for orders from Eisenhower, I learned to my great surprise that the notorious Heinrich Himmler, chief of the dread Gestapo, has been discovered near Flensburg by British Intelligence officers and arrested. Of all the Nazis, I would have supposed that Himmler, with his vast means and apparatus, would have been able to escape to another continent, perhaps by submarine. But there he was, at the end of the road, in Schleswig-Holstein. He was crudely disguised and carried false identity papers. Shortly after his arrest, he swallowed a cyanide capsule and died.

Word soon came from the Supreme Commander not to delay longer. Our report about the conversations with Doenitz confirmed Eisenhower's suspicions that these Germans were trying to create a rift between Anglo-Americans and Russians. Doenitz, in his memoirs published several years after the war, denied he ever had such intentions, but his remarks at Flensburg could be interpreted only as an offer to join us in a crusade against the Bolsheviks. Inasmuch as Rooks and I listened dead-pan to his proposal, the Admiral may have thought we were favorably disposed toward it. At any rate, Doenitz and his "cabinet" were stunned when we returned to inform them that the Supreme Commander not only did not recognize their "government," but had issued orders to arrest everybody connected with it. British military police made the arrests and, in the manner of soldiers from time immemorial, they simultaneously "liberated" some souvenirs for themselves. The German staff, including the helpful women secretaries and clerks, were ordered by the MPs to hand over everything detachable, especially money and wrist watches.

Probably I was the only witness to both the first and the last big failures of Adolph Hitler. The first was the "beer hall *putsch*" which I watched in Munich. Most people believed then that Hitler's career ended with that abortive attempt to seize power. A quarter of a century later, at Flensburg, I observed Hitler's final failure to perpetuate his Third Reich. After the arrest of Grand Admiral Doenitz and his associates, not even a remnant remained of any German government. The conquerors of the Nazis were in complete control and the administration of Germany was their responsibility.

EIGHTEEN

LAST SAD EVENING WITH ROOSEVELT (MARCH 1945)

Six weeks before the surrender of Germany, I was hurriedly summoned to Washington for urgent consulations. A last minute change had been made in selecting the administrator for the American occupation zone. An officer of the regular Army, Major General Lucius DuBignon Clay, was to become Eisenhower's Deputy Commander in Chief for Military Government, to perform the functions which had been intended for a civilian High Commissioner. It had been expected that Assistant Secretary of War John J. McCloy, an executive with wide business experience in Europe, would be appointed to this post. But now I was informed that it had been decided not to have a High Commissioner in Germany, and that I was slated to be the ranking civilian there, serving as political adviser to Clay as well as to Eisenhower.

Since I never had met Clay and recalled hearing of him only vaguely, I hastened to look up his official record. The Army's outline was not very enlightening: Clay was a West Pointer, class of 1918. He had not been sent overseas in World War I, being kept at home as instructor of engineering. Although promoted to captain late in 1918, his grade reverted to first lieutenant when peace came—and Clay remained a first lieutenant for seventeen years. That was not unusual in the period between World Wars, when military promotions came only if someone retired or died. But even while an obscure officer, Clay directed some great public projects, including a fifty-five million dollar dam on the Red River in Texas. He also served in the Philippines for a year as General MacArthur's Chief Engineer. By 1941 Clay had risen to full colonel. After the attack on Pearl Harbor, when men of Clay's experience were desperately needed in Washington, he was assigned there to help organize war production. His only overseas duty came during three weeks in 1944 when the flow of supplies to Eisenhower's advancing armies was threatened by delays in the French port of Cherbourg. Clay speedily removed that bottleneck, to Eisenhower's great relief, and then was sent back to Washington to make sure that the Armed Forces got enough ammunition.

Clay obviously was an excellent engineer and administrator, but there was nothing in his official record to suggest that he had the political qualities or experience demanded by the post in Germany. Since I would have to work very closely with him, I decided to call upon him at the Office of War Mobilization and Reconversion where he was Deputy Director. The General greeted me politely but with a somewhat puzzled air, as if wondering why I had come, and his politeness vanished when I congratulated him upon his German assignment. He replied sharply that I must be mistaken, that he knew nothing about such an appointment. According to my information, President Roosevelt had personally approved Clay's appointment to this key post, and I could not imagine why the General was giving me such a curt brush-off. After an awkward moment I apologized and left. Our brief meeting did not forecast a particularly pleasant future relationship.

It also was dismaying to learn the next day that the occupation directive for Eisenhower was not ready yet. This directive, which was to furnish a precise occupation program for military government, had been revised again and again. Now it was being revised once more, and I was told that it could hardly take final shape before the surrender. Meanwhile, nobody in SHAEF knew how many million Germans would be in the American zone, how long they would remain under American control, or how we were supposed to govern them. We did not even know what our zone would be, because De Gaulle's Government was still dissatisfied with the area assigned to France.

I had been told shortly after my arrival in Washington that the President wanted to talk with me, and I had been hoping he would provide the guidance which I sorely needed. I was conscious of the heavy responsibilities which my new assignment would impose, and was eager to ascertain what Roosevelt wanted done in Germany. In particular, I needed to know whether the President still regarded Germany as the testing ground for Soviet-American cooperation, as he had so earnestly impressed upon me in our conversation six months before. Washington was full of rumors that Roosevelt had come close to open quarrels with Stalin on several recent occasions, and it was important for me to find out whether these disagreements—if they really had occurred—affected the President's attitude toward postwar settlements. But no word came to me from the White House although the date for my return to Europe was almost at hand.

Then, suddenly, I received an invitation to dine with the President. I was lunching with friends at the Army and Navy Club when I was called to the telephone to talk with John Boettiger, Roosevelt's son-in-law. Boettiger said the President wanted me to come to dinner that evening. Only members of the family and one house guest, the Canadian Prime Minister Mackenzie King, would be present, and the Canadian visitor had to depart immediately after dinner. Boettiger said this would give the President an opportunity to talk with me alone about Germany. This was what I had been hoping for. Now I would be able to get the authoritative version of our occupation policy, on which the President would have the last word.

But when Roosevelt was wheeled into the second floor oval study of the White House that evening his appearance was a terrible shock; he was a mere shadow of the buoyant man who had talked so confidently to me the previous September. He was aware of how badly he looked and mentioned that he had lost thirty-six pounds. But he mixed martini cocktails in his usual jaunty manner, and neither Mrs. Roosevelt nor the Boettigers gave any indication of anxiety about the President's health. Two conversations I had had with Edward Stettinius flashed through my memory: Stettinius told me the previous summer that Roosevelt's health was a matter of grave concern to his friends. Some days he would seem utterly worn out; then he would bounce back incredibly. Stettinius said that a few of Roosevelt's most trusted supporters had made an agreement among themselves to call upon the President in a body, to beg him not to run for a fourth term because he was so near collapse. The next time I saw Stettinius was after the election, and I asked him how Roosevelt had received the group's suggestion. Rather shamefacedly Stettinius admitted that all of them had lost nerve and nobody had mentioned the President's health to him before the election. Now Roosevelt's physical decline was so obvious that I was startled when he exclaimed, "Well, it's almost over!" But he was referring to the war in Europe, not to his own life.

Conversation during the dinner was inconsequential, and the Canadian Prime Minister took his leave immediately after coffee was served. The President then invited me to his study for our serious discussion. But the man who sat across from me that night was unable to discuss serious matters. He talked for an hour, but aimlessly. Roosevelt scarcely mentioned the Russians; the Germans were on his mind. He reminisced about his visits to Germany during his student days, and told how arrogant some Germans had been in their uniforms. He said the important thing was to keep the Germans out of uniform because "the uniform does something bad to them, especially to the young men."

I tried several times to draw the President out on urgent matters—how the diverse interests of the occupying powers might be reconciled; how the natural resources of a partitioned Germany might be utilized; how he pictured the future of Europe. But Roosevelt was in no condition that night to offer balanced judgments upon the great questions of war and peace which had concerned him for so long. His conversation illumined for me why the Army during this period was making decisions which the civilian authority of our government normally would have made, such as the one relating to the capture of Berlin. General Marshall bore the brunt of this responsibility and deserves enormous credit for loyally protecting the President while remaining as anonymous as he could under the circumstances. The situation demonstrated a weakness which exists in our government structure despite our superb Constitution.

Shortly after my return to France I received word of the death of President Roosevelt on April 12 at Warm Springs, Georgia. His passing inspired sober reflections. I had been privileged to serve as the President's personal representative through four and a half years of the greatest war in history, and I was deeply grateful for the trust he had shown in me. Roosevelt had profoundly affected my personal life and my service to the State Department. The President never asked me to do anything involving party politics. He was well aware that although I started my career during the Democratic regime of Woodrow Wilson, I served thereafter under three Republican Presidents prior to Roosevelt's own administration. He understood, too, that I would continue to serve Democrats and Republicans impartially throughout the remainder of my career.

A few days after the President's death, I had my second encounter with General Clay when the two of us met at SHAEF in Reims. The General lost no time in explaining why he had been so abrupt when I congratulated him upon his assignment to Germany. In his pleasant Georgian drawl, Clay told me that I was the first to bring him the unwelcome news. All through the war he had endeavored to get a combat command to round out his military career, and Eisenhower had promised he would achieve that ambition. When I called, Clay was awaiting the coveted chance to lead a fighting division and he fervently hoped my information was a mistake. A few minutes after I left Clay's office, he received a telephone message from James F. Byrnes confirming that the President had appointed him to military government.

The substitution of the Army officer in place of a civilian High Commissioner in Germany was arranged almost singlehandedly by Byrnes. The influence of Byrnes upon Roosevelt was so great at that time that Byrnes was popularly known around Washington as the "Assistant President." This former senator from South Carolina had relinquished his lifetime appointment as an Associate Justice of the U. S. Supreme Court in order to undertake the responsibility of adjusting the American economy to its fantastic wartime burdens. During the final winter of the war, Byrnes had insisted upon "borrowing" Clay from the Army to become his deputy in the Office of War Mobilization and Reconversion. It was Clay's performance in that complex task which convinced Byrnes that his deputy should be the man to take charge of the American occupation of Germany. Byrnes believed that our military government should be administered by an Army officer, since it would have to depend so much upon garrison forces, and Byrnes succeeded in persuading everybody concerned that Clay was the officer for that job. Thus the civilian from South Carolina was largely responsible for putting the American occupation of Germany into the hands of a professional soldier—contrary to the advice of Eisenhower and most other military chiefs.

Clay told me that he had not talked with anybody in the State Department before leaving Washington; nobody had suggested that he do so. He had no idea how the occupation authority was to be divided between the War and State Departments; neither had I. Clay had been rushed off to Europe without any information about Eisenhower's directive which was still in process of revision, or about any of the international agreements concerning the occupation. As I tried to explain the current status of the intricate four-power negotiations, Clay's analytical mind perceived what difficulties lay ahead, and he expressed complete agreement with Eisenhower's opinion that the German occupation should become a civilian undertaking as soon as possible. He would have been horrified that day if he had realized that he was to serve four years in Germany as the man chiefly responsible for the administration of the American zone.

The first administrative problem which confronted Clay was to reshape a haphazard organization, called the American Group Control Council, which had been laboring for months under the impression that it was going to govern the American zone. The AGCC had been set up in England to prepare for the occupation, and most of its members were comfortably settled in headquarters at Kingston-on-Thames, which had been vacated by Eisenhower when the Supreme Commander moved to France. The council had a staff of a few civilians and several hundred Army officers, and it had embarked with earnest enthusiasm upon its preparations, under command of Brigadier General Cornelius W. Wickersham, a well-known New York lawyer in civilian life. To the surprise of everybody, it had been difficult for the AGCC to find German-speaking Americans who could be assigned to administrative posts in Germany. World War I had made unpopular in the United States everything German, including the language. This lack of American citizens who could speak German was a great handicap to our occupation authorities from the outset.

One of the first tasks undertaken by the AGCC was to compile a manual for the guidance of American occupation officials. This policy guide was patterned on a similar Army manual used in Germany after the First World War, and it not only tolerated but encouraged friendly relations between American soldiers and German civilians. Suddenly word arrived from Washington that the new manual had aroused indignation in the highest quarters and was to be scrapped almost entirely. Secretary Hull sent me a copy of a long Roosevelt memorandum on the subject. In the light of what happened later in Germany, one part of the memorandum is interesting. Roosevelt wrote that the AGCC manual "gives the impression that Germany is to be restored just as much as the Netherlands or Belgium, and the people of Germany brought back as quickly as possible to their prewar estate." The President emphasized that this decidedly was not American policy. Another manual, prepared by a rival section in the Army, was substituted for the AGCC compilation. The substitute forbade "fraternization" with the German people, banning personal relations of any kind between American occupants and Germans. Some of the planners in the AGCC were dismayed. One West Point officer asked me, "How the hell can soldiers be prevented from fraternizing with pretty girls?" As a matter of record, they never were!

Clay put the American Group Control Council to more practical use by promptly breaking up the top-heavy organization at Kingston-on-Thames and sending most of its officers and civilians into portions of Germany which already were occupied, thus giving the staff immediate first-hand experience in the field. But other administrative problems were not to be coped with so quickly. Eisenhower's directive for the occupation finally arrived, and Clay and I were permitted to study the top-secret document about ten days before the surrender. This directive, which later became notorious, was entitled JCS 1067, 6–7. The letters stood for Joint Chiefs of Staff and the tag numerals signified that this version combined the sixth and seventh drafts of this much revised plan. The reason there had been so many revisions and such long delays was because JCS 1067, in its definitive form, combined details from the original occupation programs of the State and War Departments together with incongruous additions inspired by the Morgenthau Plan.

To appraise JCS 1067, Clay consulted two men on his hastily assembled staff whose technical opinions he greatly respected. One of these experts was Brigadier General William H. Draper, Jr., who served as his economics adviser, and the other was Lewis W. Douglas, who had been appointed his financial adviser. Draper had been an investment banker in New York and a combat officer in the First World War, and he remained active later in the Army Reserve. When

World War II broke out, he went back to combat, becoming a regimental commander. His combined financial and military experience was unusual, fitting him to play the role in the occupation which he later performed. Douglas was a former congressman from Arizona and a highly successful businessman, president of a great insurance company, who served briefly as Roosevelt's first Director of the Budget. During the war, Douglas worked in the War Shipping Administration.

Both of Clay's advisers were shocked by the detailed prohibitions described in JCS 1067. Douglas exclaimed, "This thing was assembled by economic idiots! It makes no sense to forbid the most skilled workers in Europe from producing as much as they can for a continent which is desperately short of everything!" Clay agreed, and he asked Douglas to fly back to Washington at once to try to get the directive modified. But Douglas returned to France dejected. The only change he had been able to obtain was an ill-defined authority to exercise certain financial controls if adjudged necessary to prevent inflation. I shared quarters with Douglas during this period, and observed his gloom increase the more he studied JCS 1067. He came to the conclusion that the disputes in Washington had tied American occupation plans into fatal bowknots, and before long he quietly resigned. Two years passed before he resumed activity in European affairs as Ambassador in London.

As for Clay, he was destined to become the most influential American in Europe during several crucial postwar years. His sponsor, Byrnes, was Secretary of State from July 1945 to January 1947, and a Byrnes-Clay partnership not only changed the American conception of the German occupation, but affected the whole pattern of European events. The politican Byrnes showed extraordinary perception when he selected Clay, whose interest in European affairs was minimal in 1945, for a post which became so politically important. When Byrnes induced President Roosevelt to appoint Clay instead of a civilian High Commissioner, he told Roosevelt that "after dealing with officials of all the government departments, I found no man more capable than Clay, and no Army officer with as clear an understanding of the point of view of the civilian." My own years of association with Clay, which began so unpromisingly when I first met him in Washington, confirm this opinion. Nobody was more devoted to the Army than Clay, but he deliberately organized a predominantly civilian administration in Germany. Of all the Army officers I have worked with, none has matched Clay's respect for the civilian viewpoint, none has revealed more talent for true statesmanship.

NINETEEN

ISOLATED BERLIN

Not until June 5, 1945, did Eisenhower, Clay and I pay our first visit to conquered Berlin. Almost a month had passed since the surrender of Germany and the establishment of SHAEF at Frankfurt, but all of us had been nearly overwhelmed with multiple new activities. The Japanese war was reaching its peak, and redeployment to the Pacific had top priority. Four hundred thousand soldiers were being transported monthly from Eisenhower's command to the other side of the earth, together with incredible amounts of war matériel. The planning for this formidable operation in logistics was entrusted to Clay.

A huge secondary task was informally called Operation Rescue. It seemed to us that SHAEF was being asked to help save the entire population of Europe from starvation and disease. Hitler's fanatical resistance had exhausted reserves of food, medicines, and other essentials, and it devolved upon SHAEF to provide personnel and transport for what must have been the most gigantic life-saving enterprise of all time—the return of millions of "slave laborers" from German-occupied Europe to their own countries; the care of millions of starving displaced persons, including Jews, who were too weak to move or had no immediate place to go; massive deliveries of necessities to all liberated countries; provision of bare subsistence to about forty million Germans in the western zones.

But SHAEF's most difficult problem that spring was to get its own multi-million soldiers unscrambled and established in their designated zones. It was generally understood at the Yalta Conference that all Allied armies would push ahead as rapidly as possible, without regard to zones, but nobody had suspected how swiftly American armies could move. Now some of my British colleagues at SHAEF ruefully admitted to me that they had overestimated the Red Army and underestimated American military capabilities. Americans had managed to put seventy divisions into Europe before the war ended, four times the number of effective motorized divisions which the British produced. British planners had not believed this possible, and they had been equally mistaken about the Russian rate of advance. Most Britons had been pleased when Stalin agreed to accept a Russian occupation zone smaller than the territory which SHAEF expected the Red Army to overrun. What the British had not sufficiently taken into account was that most of the Red Army was not motorized, so that millions of its men moved on foot or depended upon horse-drawn and even camel-drawn vehicles.

Before the German surrender, American armies had penetrated the Russian zone on a four-hundred-mile front to a depth in some places of 120 miles. Churchill wanted our troops to stay there until the postwar bargaining began. The British Prime Minister informed Eisenhower he was convinced that Stalin intended to grab every place within reach of the Red Army, and he urged therefore that Anglo-American armies should seize and hold for bargaining purposes as much as possible of Germany and central Europe. As Supreme Commander, Eisenhower represented the British Government as well as his own, and he had to give due consideration to Churchill's arguments. But Eisenhower was determined to do nothing which might arouse Russian distrust, so he exercised the authority conferred upon him by the Combined Chiefs of Staff to politely disregard Churchill's pleas.

Western troops could have pushed much further than they did. For example, Eisenhower ordered General Patton to halt his motorized divisions almost within sight of Prague, the capital of Czechoslovakia, because the Russian commander who was approaching that city requested it. Patton also was ordered not to accept the proffered surrender of German armies which had been fighting on the eastern front, because the Russians wanted to take this surrender of their foes. As a result of these orders, disgruntled Americans were required to halt their spectacular advance and await the arrival of the Red Army. Czechoslovakia, unlike Germany, was not a conquered country but had its own government which was recognized by all the victors. It was a rather explosive situation, and Eisenhower dispatched Lieutenant General Harold R. Bull and me to Prague late in May to negotiate for the gradual withdrawal of American troops from this area.

Patton's advance headquarters at Pilsen were under the command of Major General Ernest N. Harmon, a colorful tank commander popularly known as "Hell on Wheels." Harmon wired Bull and me to stop off in Pilsen to attend a luncheon he was giving for the Soviet High Command in the area, and Field Marshal Bernard Montgomery's personal plane, which he had just turned in, was assigned to us for the trip. But the honor of being transported in this aged C-47 was not appreciated by us after its batteries caught fire, filling the plane with acrid smoke, and we had to come down hastily on an abandoned Luftwaffe fighter strip. The emergency landing resulted in our being late for the luncheon, and when we slipped into the dining hall at Pilsen's Grand Hotel we found Harmon in the midst of a vigorous speech.

There were about fifty Russian officers present, including a few generals and a number of Soviet WACs. In characteristic fashion Harmon was verbally attacking his Russian guests for their tendency to treat Americans like potential enemies instead of allies. Harmon had located an American lieutenant from Brooklyn whose parents had emigrated from Russia, and he was using this young man as his interpreter. The lad obviously was anxious to please his commander, but "Hell on Wheels" suspected the interpreter was toning down his purple remarks. Several times Harmon broke off to say to the lieutenant in a loud voice, "If you don't translate my exact words, so help me, I'll bust you!" Thus exhorted to use Russian equivalents for the General's salty phrases, the interpreter produced all the emphatic words he had ever heard in Brooklyn, including some profanity—and the effect upon the listening Russians, especially the WACs, was sensational. Continuous roars and shouts of laughter filled the hall, to the perplexity of Harmon who was very much in earnest.

The comic relief unintentionally provided by Harmon's interpreter helped to relax the tension of a local situation which was basically serious. While American soldiers were waiting at Pilsen for the arrival of the Red Army, delegations of non-Communist Czechs had visited American headquarters to urge our troops to enter Prague before the Russians could get there. The Czechs argued that Soviet military maneuvers were inspired by political motives, and that the liberation of Prague by the Red Army would fortify the Czech Communist Party. The American Army, they declared, by cooperating at that moment with the Russians, was inadvertently aiding the Communists.

Eisenhower's decision not to enter Prague was widely interpreted, as a matter of fact, as proof that the Soviet Government had been accorded a "sphere of influence" in Czechoslovakia. If Prague had been liberated by American forces, our action would have had considerable political effect in Europe; less than if we had taken Berlin, but important. When similar questions arose whether Anglo-American troops should proceed into the zone assigned to the Soviet Government, Eisenhower would remark at staff meetings, "Why should we endanger the life of a single American or Briton to capture areas we soon will be handing over to the Russians?"

13. First postwar American Ambassador to Japan; 1952. *Left to right:* Secretary of State Acheson, Rosemary Murphy, Robert Murphy. (ASSOCIATED PRESS PHOTO)

14. Visiting the Bonin Islands in the Pacific aboard the U.S.S. *Toledo;* 1952. *Left to right:* Admirals Overesch, Briscoe, and Radford; Robert Murphy; John Conroy of the U. S. Embassy in Tokyo. (U. S. NAVY)

15. Backstage ambassadorial visit with actor of famous Kabuki Theater; 1952. (SANGYO-KEIZAI)

16. Field Marshal Earl Alexander, British Defense Minister, visits Tokyo; 1952. At the right is General Mark W. Clark. (U. S. ARMY SIGNAL CORPS)

17. President and Mrs. Syngman Rhee visit the American Embassy in Tokyo; 1952. (UNITED PRESS INTERNATIONAL)

18. Generalissimo Chiang Kai-shek receives Ambassador Murphy in Taipei; 1953.

19. A briefing on the main line in Korea at a critical moment in 1953; in the foreground, left to right, are Robert Murphy, General Clark, General Van Fleet, and General White. (U. S. ARMY SIGNAL CORPS)

20. His Eminence Francis Cardinal Spellman of New York arrives in Tokyo; 1953.

21. A quiet moment at the American Embassy in Tokyo; 1953.

(THE MAINICHI)

22. Meeting with Marshal Joseph Broz Tito in Brioni in 1954. At extreme left is James W. Riddleberger, U. S. Ambassador to Belgrade. (TANJUG)

23. Meeting in London for talks on the Suez Canal crisis; 1956. *Left to right:* French Foreign Minister Pineau, British Foreign Secretary Selwyn Lloyd, Robert Murphy. (THE TIMES, LONDON)

24. King Hussein of Jordan is a guest at Blair House in Washington; 1959. At the left are Representative Walter Judd and Admiral Arleigh Burke.

25. The acting heads of the Department of State during Secretary Dulles' illness. *Left to right:* Under Secretary Douglas Dillon, Acting Secretary Christian A. Herter, Deputy Under Secretary Robert Murphy; February 1959.
(HANK WALKER, COURTESY OF LIFE MAGAZINE,© 1959 TIME INC.)

Eisenhower had emotional as well as strategic reasons for opposing Churchill's attempts to take advantage of Anglo-American momentum. The General had been deeply affected by the mass atrocities uncovered by our motorized divisions as they sped over Hitler's superhighways, catching Nazi extremists still at work. In mid-April, Patton's Third Army overran Ohrdruf and Buchenwald and other prison camps, and Eisenhower made flying inspection trips a few hours after the arrival of our troops. The Nazis had not been given time to destroy the evidence. Those prisons, unlike many death camps farther east, were not limited to Jews. Their victims came from almost every country in Europe. Gathered here were men and women who had organized resistance to Hitler. The prison tortures had been designed to crush the spirit of these resisters by every kind of degradation and agony. General Patton could not stomach the sights he saw at Buchenwald; he went off to a corner thoroughly sick. The inmates liberated by our forces were skeletons, having been fed barely enough to keep them alive. Many of the captives were professional soldiers who had become guerrillas when their armies could no longer fight in Europe, and they pulled up their wasted bodies into gallant salutes as Eisenhower, Patton, and their staffs passed them. It was enough to make strong men weep—and some American officers did so unabashedly. (One of the inmates was French Air Force General Maurice Challe, who sixteen years later was convicted of treason against the De Gaulle Government.) Confronted with the evidence of the prison camps he visited, Eisenhower's hatred for Nazism intensified his determination to have no conflict with Russia about Germany.

Eisenhower's attitude toward the Nazis was consistent with similar reactions which I observed during the years I worked with him. For instance, when in London in 1942 we first discussed the African expedition, I mentioned that it would be helpful to keep Generalissimo Franco of Spain quiescent during our landings. Eisenhower expressed distaste for even pretending to be friendly with a dictator who owed his position to Hitler and Mussolini. Another characteristic reaction occurred in Tunisia in 1943, when German forces surrendered en masse there. Eisenhower refused to meet the German commander, General von Arnim, saying, "I won't shake hands with a Nazi!" Years later, when Eisenhower was President of the United States, he became more resigned to the complexities of international politics; I accompanied him in December 1959 on a state visit to Spain when Franco acted as his host.

In 1945 Eisenhower's mind was fully made up on his policy toward Russia, and I cannot recall that any of his American staff disagreed with him. Roosevelt's faith in Soviet-American cooperation had been reaffirmed at Yalta by British as well as American military and political chiefs, and President Truman during his first months in office could hardly have reversed Roosevelt's policy even if he had so desired. Actually the new President did not want to alter the Roosevelt program then; he endeavored to do just what he believed Roosevelt would have done under the circumstances. Accordingly, when it suddenly became necessary to prop up Roosevelt's policy toward Russia, it was natural for Truman to seek help from one of Roosevelt's most intimate advisers, Harry Hopkins. Being seriously ill, Hopkins had resigned shortly before Roosevelt's death, but Truman induced him to leave his sickbed to go to Moscow. Few men of this century have exerted more influence upon American politics, domestic and foreign, than Hopkins. Through his unique relationship with Roosevelt, this social service worker became world famous; he negotiated as an equal with Stalin and Churchill. But none of his assignments for Roosevelt had more far-reaching results than the only assignment he performed for Truman, his mission to Moscow.

The immediate cause for Hopkins' mission was a threat to the United Nations which almost shattered that institution before it could be set in motion. The UN was an indispensable instrument in Roosevelt's Grand Design for the postwar world. It was the agency intended to assure Soviet-American cooperation. Roosevelt had persuaded Stalin at Yalta that the UN should be established before the war ended. Truman respected his predecessor's intentions, and he vigorously pushed the organization of the UN. The Charter Conference assembled at San Francisco on April 25, 1945, two weeks before the German surrender. To millions of war-weary people everywhere, the appeal of the UN was so great that two thousand accredited correspondents covered the opening session, which received more newspaper and radio attention than the war itself.

But soon after it started, the Charter Conference seemed hopelessly deadlocked. The Soviet Government demanded voting procedures which American delegates refused to accept. Furthermore, the behavior of the Russians in Poland and other eastern European countries was arousing much resentment among delegates in San Francisco. It looked as though Roosevelt's conception of the postwar world might evaporate even before World War II ended. It was in these circumstances that several people in Washington suggested to President Truman that Harry Hopkins had a better chance of reaching an understanding with Stalin than any other American. Truman acted upon the suggestion and prevailed upon Hopkins to fly to Moscow. His talks with Stalin lasted for eleven days in May and June.

At SHAEF, our first word from the Hopkins mission came on May 30. It was an enthusiastic message stating that Hopkins had persuaded the Soviet dictator to make satisfactory compromises concerning the administration of the UN and other disputed points. As a result Hopkins had been able to arrange for a meeting of Truman, Stalin and Churchill, to begin about July 15 in the vicinity of Berlin. Hopkins also sent word to Eisenhower that Stalin had appointed Marshal Georgi K. Zhukov, the conqueror of Berlin, as the Soviet member of the Allied Control Council, the supreme authority for the German occupation. We interpreted this to mean that now we could get a joint military government operating in Berlin without further delay. We were all in a hopeful, almost a holiday mood as we set out from Frankfurt for Berlin on the morning of June 5. Clay and I took along packed bags, expecting to spend several days in Berlin arranging for American headquarters and garrison there. Because of Hopkins' optimistic report on Stalin's attitude, we anticipated few difficulties.

The specific purpose of Eisenhower's first trip to Berlin was to sign the Declaration on the Assumption of Supreme Authority in Germany by the Allies, and to participate in the organizational meeting of the Allied Control Council for Germany. As was his custom, Eisenhower had insisted that an exact time schedule be prepared in advance and accepted by all concerned, including the Russians. The Supreme Commander always was annoyed if an agreed schedule was not carried out. We arrived in Berlin exactly on the dot, with plenty of time to pay a brief formal call upon Marshal Zhukov at Russian headquarters precisely at noon. The afternoon was left open for lunch and discussions with the Russians about how soon the Allied Control Council could get to work in Berlin. The schedule called for Eisenhower to take off from the airport at six o'clock on his return to Frankfurt.

We were welcomed at Templehof airport by Zhukov's deputy, General Vassily Sokolovsky, and an imposing Russian honor guard, and after a depressing drive through the prostrate center of Berlin with its wan population aimlessly shuffling about, we reached Zhukov's headquarters in a suburb. The odor of death was everywhere. The canals were choked with bodies and refuse. The subway had been flooded by some mad last-minute order of the Nazis, and thousands who had sought refuge in it had died. The Russian Commander in Chief greeted Eisenhower with great cordiality, making a fine impression. At the conclusion of the preliminary courtesies, the American party was taken to a very comfortable house and the British party, under Field Marshal Montgomery, to another house.

Eisenhower expected to wait only a few minutes before being escorted to a conference hall. But instead we were informed that lunch would be served in the house assigned to us, and that the British party would have lunch in their house. The schedule obviously was not being followed, and Eisenhower became increasingly restive when the meal ended and still no explanation of the delay came from the Russians. Finally Eisenhower asked me, "What's going on here? Do you think these people are giving us a runaround?" I replied that I could not see why they should, and I volunteered to ask Vinshinsky about it. Eisenhower remembered our association with Vishinsky in Africa and Italy where we had found him quite approachable.

Vishinsky received me at once and explained what had gone wrong. One of the three proclamations we had come to sign contained a clause pledging the Big Three to intern Japanese within their respective jurisdictions. But the Russians were not yet at war against Japan and therefore could not publicly agree to such cooperation. That proclamation had been discussed and scrutinized for months by specialists in Washington, London, and Moscow, and of course every expert who examined the document should have noticed this slip. But no one had. A minor Russian official discovered the clause while taking a last look at the documents in Berlin. "But this is an obvious error," I told Vishinsky. "I am sure that General Eisenhower will agree to eliminate the clause without reference to Washington or London." Vishinsky merely said, "We must await word from the Soviet Government." He seemed somewhat embarrassed, which may have indicated why this complication had not been explained to us sooner. Perhaps Vishinsky and Zhukov were influenced by what had happened to the unfortunate General Susloparov, who had innocently approved General Smith's surrender documents.

At any rate the Russians in Berlin were taking no chances and it was midafternoon before word came from Moscow. The three Commanders in Chief then were assembled, the proclamations duly signed, hundreds of photographs taken, and genial Marshal Zhukov, with Vishinsky close beside him, informally convened the first meeting of the Big Three military governors in Berlin. Eisenhower proposed that an immediate start be made toward establishing the Allied Control Council, explaining that he wanted to leave Clay and me in Berlin for that purpose.

After consultation with Vishinsky, Zhukov politely rejected this proposal. He said that each occupying power must withdraw its troops into its own zone before interntional controls could operate. This meant that the Russians were asking Americans to evacuate all portions of the Russian zone which we still held in Thuringia, Saxony, and Pomerania, without any quid pro quo. It became apparent even at that first short parley that it was Vishinsky, a civilian, and not Zhukov who was deciding matters with political implications, decisions of a type which Eisenhower could and did make on his own authority. Having watched Vishinsky's skillful maneuvers in Italy, I had not been surprised to hear he was setting up Communist regimes in eastern Europe, and now he clearly was pulling the strings in Berlin. It was evident that Zhukov was not empowered to accept Eisenhower's proposal for immediate entry into Berlin, and Eisenhower did not press the matter.

While the Commanders in Chief were conferring, a lavish assortment of food and drink was spread out on long tables in adjoining rooms by nice-looking Russian girls in uniform. It was evident that this was preliminary to a Russian-style banquet, and that Zhukov expected Eisenhower to delay his departure to participate in the celebration. Indications were that the feast would be a tremendous affair for which the Russians had made enormous preparations, even importing their best dancers, musicians, and entertainers. In the conditions then prevailing in Berlin, this was spectacular. But Eisenhower had not liked the whole procedure of the day and he insisted upon returning to Frankfurt with his entire staff at the scheduled hour. Zhukov, amazed and uncomprehending, could not believe at first that Eisenhower was determined to leave. "I shall arrest you and make you stay!" he exclaimed jovially. But Eisenhower remained only long enough to drink the first toasts, explaining that he had not been informed about the dinner and had made other arrangements. On the way back to the airport, he graciously invited Zhukov to visit Allied Headquarters. So, feeling rather deflated, we came back to Frankfurt only a few hours after we had left. Eisenhower had an uneasy feeling that he had been pushed around, despite Zhukov's flamboyant hospitality and personal amiability, and the immediate outlook was confused.

As we came to realize in time, the Russians obtained everything they wanted at that first Eisenhower-Zhukov meeting. Another month was to pass before we could negotiate permanent entry into Berlin, and we did not manage to get the Allied Control Council started until the Potsdam Conference was almost over. The proclamations which were released at the Eisenhower-Zhukov meeting served Russian purposes admirably. They became the basis of a joint occupation of Germany, and even today affect the relations between Germany and the Berlin signatories.

Proclamation Number One dissolved the last vestiges of any national German government, entrusting supreme authority in Germany to the Commanders in Chief of the victorious powers. Writing several years later, in 1950, General Clay declared: "This was a fateful decision which can be fairly judged in its effect only by time and history." Today, in the 1960s, time and history have not yet rendered a clear judgment.

Proclamation Number Two stipulated that unanimous agreement among the victorious powers must be reached in matters affecting

Germany as a whole; and that, in the absence of unanimous agreement, each Commander in Chief would be supreme in his own zone. In effect, this gave each occupying government an absolute veto, and resulted in the division of Germany indefinitely between the zones of the Eastern and Western conquerors.

Proclamation Number Three fixed the boundaries of the zones and confirmed the London agreement that the city of Berlin should be divided into sectors, each sector garrisoned by one occupying power. That document, together with the London protocols of September 12 and November 14, 1944, remains today the chief legal basis for keeping Western garrisons in Berlin.

Four days after our visit to Berlin, Harry Hopkins stopped in Frankfurt on his return from Moscow to Washington. He was bubbling with enthusiasm about his meetings with Stalin, and his confidence in Soviet-American cooperation was impressive. Hopkins changed our perspective at SHAEF. Germany had seemed to us the most difficult problem in Europe, but Hopkins made it clear that Germany was pretty far down on Washington's priority list. He explained that no disagreements about Germany had arisen in his talks with Stalin. The future of Poland caused more concern, he said. The most important result of the Hopkins mission to Moscow, I believe, was that he and all the Americans with him thought it was a spectacular success. With obvious sincerity Hopkins said to us in Frankfurt, "We can do business with Stalin! He will cooperate!"

Hopkins dwelt upon the concessions which Stalin had made, and his renewed faith in the Russians discredited Churchill's warnings about Soviet intentions. Hopkins made the alarm of the British Prime Minister seem exaggerated, even hysterical. Churchill during the war had been almost as laudatory as Roosevelt himself about Hopkins' judgment of men and events, and this fact gave added weight now to Hopkins' discount of Churchill's warnings. Churchill attempted to induce Hopkins to stop off in London before returning to Washington, but Truman vetoed this request. What Hopkins told us in Frankfurt was a preview of his report to Truman, who was still cautiously feeling his way, and it was only natural that the new President should want to hear Hopkins' report direct, without interpretations from Churchill.

Hopkins told us about the day he spent in Berlin on his way back from Moscow, and how the Russians in Berlin had been almost embarrassingly hospitable, even permitting him to carry off some books from Hitler's private library as souvenirs. He described how Vishinsky had answered political questions addressed to Zhukov, and Hopkins explained that no Russian military man, however high in rank, would have authority in political affairs. Hopkins said that Stalin frankly told him that Zhukov could decide only questions of military import. The

Soviet dictator seemed more determined than Americans to observe the principle of military subordination to civilian authority. Hopkins said Stalin always was thinking of how Napoleon had run away with the French Revolution.

Eisenhower listened thoughtfully to this part of Hopkins' remarks. All through the war, Marshall had insisted that American field commanders must have supreme over-all authority in their own war theaters, and Roosevelt had supported this policy even when decisions involved international affairs. Accustomed to so much authority for so long, Eisenhower seemed a little startled when Hopkins pointed out that all of the Commanders in Chief in the German occupation would have less power than they had had in wartime. Hopkins correctly predicted that the British Foreign Office, not the military chiefs, would hereafter largely determine British occupation policy. He added, with a sly smile, that several governmental departments in Washington would be sure to claim a loud voice in American occupation policy. Eisenhower glumly admitted that he already had abundant evidence of that. When Eisenhower explained that he was determined to pull back all American troops from the Russian zone as soon as possible, Hopkins heartily approved. However, Hopkins listened carefully to my explanation of why we did not have written specifications for corridors assuring access to Berlin. He agreed that we should by all means insist upon definite undertakings, and he promised to call this matter to the personal attention of both Truman and Marshall as soon as he returned to Washington.

A memorandum in the Hopkins papers shows that he kept this promise, and official documents show what happened then. On June 14, President Truman sent a message to Stalin requesting that in the program for mutual transfer of Russian and American forces in Germany and Austria, provision be included "of free access for U.S. forces by air, road and rail to Berlin from Frankfurt and Bremen." At the same time Churchill sent a similar request to Moscow. Stalin's replies to both men made no mention of access, and both Washington and London apparently assumed that unrestricted access could be taken for granted. On June 25 Marshall sent to Frankfurt the draft of a proposed directive for troop transfers, with the comment: "It will be noted that the proposed directive contains no action to obtain transit rights to Berlin and Vienna on a combined basis. . . . In accordance with the President's message to Stalin [June fourteenth], these should be arranged with Russian commanders concerned simultaneously with arrangements for other adjustments." In other words, Washington still regarded the access problem as merely a military detail.

On June 10 Zhukov flew to Frankfurt to repay Eisenhower's courtesy call, and gracious compliments were again exchanged. The next day Eisenhower departed for a month's leave. He made a grand tour of victory celebrations, receiving tumultuous welcomes first in London and Paris, then in Washington and other American cities. After addressing a joint session of Congress, Eisenhower began on June 25 a quiet fortnight's golf-playing vacation at White Sulphur Springs, West Virginia. He did not return to Germany until July 10, a week before the opening of the Potsdam Conference. In Eisenhower's absence during that month, Clay laid the foundations for American military government in Germany; he became its chief architect.

Eisenhower was still on vacation when Clay, as his deputy, was required to settle the final intricate details for the transfer to the Russains of hundreds of square miles of American-occupied German territory. To complete these arrangements, Clay flew back to Berlin on June 29 to see Zhukov again, more than three weeks after their first meeting. This was a conference between military commanders only, and all of us regarded it in that light, so I did not accompany Clay. The next morning, after his return from Frankfurt, Clay informed me orally of his negotiations with Zhukov. I must confess that no alarm bell rang in my mind when Clay mentioned that the question of access to Berlin had been arranged only on a temporary basis. The Americans and British asked for exclusive use of several railways and highways, but Zhukov eloquently described his own transport difficulties in moving millions of troops around. Americans had seen how inadequate Russian motorized transport was compared with SHAEF's, so Clay agreed to use only one railway and one highway to supply our garrison in Berlin, as a makeshift until the situation settled down. The British commander agreed to limit himself likewise.

Clay told me that since Zhukov was so reasonable about everything, it seemed best to assume, as the American and British Governments already had assumed, that all the occupying powers would have unrestricted access to Berlin as soon as the zonal areas were completed. It was agreed that modifications could be arranged later in the Allied Control Council, but it occurred to me that the veto power of each of the nations represented in the council would enable any single country to block agreements on any point, and I discussed this with Clay. The General understood that there was a veto power, but in the glow of that early honeymoon period this "technicality" seemed one of those things that would fall into place. At any rate, Clay said this was the best he could do. In my summary of Clay's oral report, which I sent to the State Department on June 30, I expressed satisfaction with Zhukov's acknowledgment that the movement to Berlin of men and supplies—whether American, British, or French—would not be subject to any kind of inspection or delay.

It is characteristic of Lucius Clay that he always has accepted full responsibility for the failure to obtain written assurances of access to Berlin while Americans still held control of a large part of the Russian occupation zone. The truth is that all of us overlooked what ultimately turned out to be the most dangerous factor in the Berlin situation—the two and a half million Germans then residing in the American, British and French sectors. Nobody foresaw that Zhukov, three years later, would refuse to supply food for Berlin's own population, and that the Western powers would become responsible for providing food, coal and raw materials for German civilians as well as for our own garrisons. When the Russian blockade was put into effect in 1948, it was aimed primarily at the Germans in the Western sectors, not at our garrisons. It was the Germans in Berlin who made us vulnerable to a Russian squeeze play—and who still make us vulnerable today. But I doubt that the Kremlin in 1945 even considered the possibility of a blockade. I believe the Russians thought it would be just a matter of time before the Western nations would lose interest and pull out of the Berlin area. It seemed such an artificial position.

From the outset of our occupation proceedings in Germany, Clay emphasized the civilian aspects of our administration. As a matter of personal conviction as well as American policy, he deliberately stressed my authority as our ranking civilian and treated me as a full partner. Clay and I were determined to coordinate all State and War Department activities, realizing that many potential sources of conflict existed. In organizing my own offices in Germany, I had no precedents to go by. Since the conquerors had abolished all German central administration, each occupying power devised means of its own to fill the vacuum. Members of my staff personally inspected local conditions throughout our zone, and we created what amounted to a miniature State Department type of organization to handle foreign affairs for the twenty million Germans in the American zone. My office also was responsible for American relations with the numerous countries which soon would be sending diplomatic missions to Berlin, accredited to the Allied Control Council.

Clay and I officially opened for business in Berlin on July 7, a few days before Eisenhower's return from vacation. The Russians had been generous in dividing the city with us. Our sector included a fair share of comparatively undamaged buildings in which to house our people; the Russians greeted us warmly whenever we met them; they put relatively few bureaucratic obstacles in our way, and during the honeymoon those obstacles usually were removed if we appealed to higher-ups. For several days American military government had only two telephones connecting Berlin with Frankfurt headquarters. One phone was in Clay's office, the other in mine, so everybody who needed to telephone paraded through our offices. As Clay wryly remarked, that was one way to keep in close touch with the operations of our staffs.

Two months after their surrender, Berliners still were moving about in a dazed condition. They had endured not only thousand-plane raids for years but also weeks of Russian close-range artillery fire. In addition to three million Germans in Berlin, thousands of displaced persons were roaming around the shattered city. None of us could be sure how these people might behave, whether their experiences had made them apathetic, revengeful, or crazy. Nearly all of them were existing on a fraction of the food considered essential for health. Hundreds of thousands were seeking shelter in cave-like ruins, or in tiny shacks which had been built in the suburbs for weekend vegetable gardeners. Many whose homes had not been destroyed were being expelled on short notice, with no place to go, in order to provide for the incoming conquerors. Even those of us who got the best available houses had to make major repairs before our quarters were livable. The house assigned to me on Spechtstrasse in Dahlem had been occupied for two months by Russian officers who, according to the old housekeeper, disposed of the wine cellar of more than two thousand bottles and amused themselves by shooting up the place every night. Ceilings, walls and family portraits were full of holes. The Russians especially enjoyed shooting at the crystal chandeliers. The housekeeper told me that when the officers arrived they found a badly wounded young German soldier on a divan and promptly shot him.

This was the setting which Stalin chose for his first meeting with Truman and his last meeting with Churchill. Berlin also had been Roosevelt's choice for the first postwar summit conference. When Roosevelt bade goodbye to Stalin at Yalta, he said, "We will meet again soon—in Berlin!" And, in a sense, Roosevelt was present at Potsdam. His Grand Design still strongly influenced all of us who had worked closely with our wartime President, as we made hurried preparations for the fateful conference of which Roosevelt had expected so much.

TWENTY

POTSDAM CONFERENCE: UP TRUMAN, DOWN CHURCHILL

When notice was sent to Eisenhower's headquarters at Frankfurt that Berlin would be the site of the first major postwar conference, the Russians were still holding exclusive control of that city. We assumed therefore that the Soviet Government would be host to all the delegates, as it had been at Yalta. However, Churchill had other ideas. The British Prime Minister pointed out that if the Anglo-Americans accepted Soviet hospitality in Berlin, this would imply that the Russians had special rights there, whereas the Yalta agreement specified equal rights for all the occupying powers. Churchill also contended that it was Stalin's turn now to come to London or some other Western city, inasmuch as Roosevelt and Churchill had journeyed to Stalin's country to attend the previous conference. When this matter was submitted to President Truman, he cast the deciding vote in favor of Berlin, because that city had been favored by Roosevelt for the first postwar conference.

But Truman agreed that Americans and Britons should go to Berlin as independent delegations, not as guests of the Russians. So Washington and London instructed their Military Governments to set up separate compounds in the ruined German metropolis at some site acceptable to the Russians. The location of this important conference could hardly have been more unfortunate. We had to make preparations in a city where our authority existed only on paper, a city one hundred miles distant from the American and British zones. We had to negotiate for accommodations in Berlin for our visiting delegates before we had made arrangements even to move our own Military Government there. This rush order complicated all our other Berlin negotiations and helped the Russians to bargain effectively—a situation of which they took full advantage.

The conference instructions addressed to Eisenhower arrived on June 11, the same day he was leaving Germany for a month's round of victory celebrations in England, France, and the United States. The

Supreme Commander assigned Major General Floyd L. Parks to direct preparations for the American delegation and asked me to supervise whatever political arrangements might be necessary. Those of us who had attended previous V.I.P. conferences were not surprised to learn the standards of comfort expected. The orders made clear that, even amid the rubble of Berlin, our delegates required adequate offices and living quarters and also ample space for entertaining. The Russians had set a pattern of lavish hospitality at Yalta, so our delegates must be prepared to reciprocate with their own equivalents of caviar and vodka, and they also must have their own cooks and valets, their own security agents and guards, and their own protected communication lines to Washington and London. Conscious of the magnitude of his assignment, General Parks felt we should get started immediately, but the Soviet Government controlled the situation. Eleven days elapsed before we could get permission even to send an exploratory group from Frankfurt to examine the Berlin site proposed by the Russians. Frantic cables were exchanged between Frankfurt, Washington, London, and Moscow without result. We were informed that Zhukov had gone home for victory celebrations at the same time Eisenhower did, that he would not return to Berlin until June 29, and that nothing could be done in the meantime.

Not until an appeal was addressed directly to Stalin was permission granted on June 22 for our advance American group to fly to Berlin. This delay demonstrated again how different our circumstances would have been if American or British troops had captured Berlin instead of the Red Army. We would not have needed to negotiate about entering the city; we would have been there. However, our advance party was cordially welcomed by Colonel General Kruglov, Stalin's personal Chief of Security, who had supervised arrangements for the Yalta Conference. Despite the numerous cablegrams to Moscow, Kruglov was still under the impression that the Russians would act as hosts again and would provide everything needed for all three delegations. Further cabled exchanges were required to straighten out this point. Kruglov also had assumed that our delegations would be about the same size as at previous conferences, but we broke the news to him that this time we were bringing four or five times as many people. Kruglov shrugged cheerfully and remarked that he would have to throw a few thousand more Germans out of their homes.

We were well pleased with the site and conference hall proposed by the Russians. They selected one of the most beautiful wooded sections of Greater Berlin, along the shores of winding Lake Griebnitz, twelve miles southwest of the capital's flattened center. The area included two towns—Potsdam, once the summer seat of the Hohenzollern Kaisers;

and Babelsberg, which had been popular with the Nazi motion picture colony. There were enough comparatively undamaged buildings in Babelsberg to lay out three adjoining large compounds. American quarters were about three miles from the conference hall in Potsdam, with the British and Russian quarters along the way. The building selected by the Russians for the formal meetings was the Potsdam summer palace of former Crown Prince Wilhelm, an imposing two-story brownstone structure, surrounded by splendid gardens extending to Lake Griebnitz. The palace, called the Cecilienhof, had been used by Germans and later by Russians as a hospital during the war. The original furnishings had disappeared, but our Russian escorts proudly pointed out good-looking furniture which they told us had been rushed from Moscow. The palace ballroom provided more than enough space for plenary sessions, and separate suites were made ready for each of the Big Three chiefs, plus additional consulting rooms for each delegation.

Because the Potsdam Conference was regarded as an extension of the Teheran and Yalta Conferences, and because the war against Japan was still raging, Germany's three conquerors agreed to abide by the same ground rules observed at previous meetings. These provided maximum seclusion for the conferees and maximum secrecy for their discussions. The Russians assigned thousands of green-capped frontier guards to ensure that all the conference enclosures were tightly protected against intruders of any kind. The American and British compounds were doubly protected by swarms of their own guards and security agents. For the sake of convenience, the Anglo-American negotiators agreed that Berlin would continue to operate on Moscow time, as it had done since its capture by the Red Army. I recalled how Paris under the Nazis had operated on Berlin time.

During our month of organizing the Potsdam Conference I learned that Andrei Vishinsky was directly in charge of arrangements. He was shrewd enough to utilize the preparations for the conference while simultaneously negotiating other German issues. When the Russians delayed our advance party for eleven days, they made it clear that they expected all American troops to withdraw from the Russian zone before the conference opened. President Truman's letter to Stalin dated June 14, 1945 linked the withdrawal of our troops from the Soviet zone to the question of our access to Berlin, but this was not made a condition in any negotiation. By thus interweaving various negotiations, the Russians won almost every controversial point. For instance, to enable President Truman to communicate privately with Washington, Americans had to install wireless relays and teleprinter circuits across the hundred miles of Soviet territory which separated Berlin from our zone. This project required weeks of around-the-clock labor, and the need to get started immediately put additional urgency upon General Clay to conclude his other Berlin negotiations. The result was that all American troops were evacuated from the Soviet zone with remarkable speed and efficiency, and Military Government offices were opened in Berlin a few days before the conference convened.

With separation of American and British forces thus completed, SHAEF ceased to exist on July 14, 1945. Eisenhower lost his title of Supreme Commander, Allied Expeditionary Force, and became responsible only for the American share of the German occupation. He returned from his month's leave just in time to participate, rather sadly, in the dissolution of SHAEF.

The following day President Truman flew into Berlin. The vast "Forbidden City" which had been fenced off for the conference possessed even its own airport at Gatow, and it was there that we met the presidential party, which arrived in three planes. As usual on such occasions, there was a large group at the airport and little opportunity to express more than perfunctory greetings. But Admiral Leahy caught sight of me and shouted as he was driving off in Truman's limousine, "Come and see me as soon as you can! I am staying with the President." That was a most welcome invitation, because I had lost my own direct contact with the White House. From the moment of Roosevelt's death, I no longer was anyone's "personal representative," but I knew that Leahy would bring my information up to date now. Nobody was better informed than the Admiral about what had happened in Washington since Truman became President. Leahy had acceded to Truman's request that he remain at the White House as personal Chief of Staff to the President. That position had been created for the Admiral by Roosevelt, who was an old personal friend, and Leahy performed the same duties for Truman until 1949, a solid link between the two administrations.

When the Admiral shouted his invitation at the airport, I took him at his word and called upon him at the "Little White House" shortly after his arrival there. The three-story, somewhat flamboyant mansion assigned to the President was old-fashioned, with minimum plumbing, but it was the most suitable which the American advance party had found in Babelsberg. The house was secluded, set back in large attractive gardens which fronted on the lake. The Russians told us that its last occupant, head of the Nazi motion picture industry, was now working in a "labor battalion" in Siberia. The President had invited Byrnes, the new Secretary of State, and Leahy to stay with him in his spacious billet, and they also had their offices there. Leahy was ready for me when I called, and led me to his private suite for a confidential talk.

The Admiral was a forthright naval officer, more affected by personal likes and dislikes than by partisan issues. He said to me at once, "This new President is all right. He couldn't be more different from Roosevelt, but he has the necessary qualities to make a good President and Commander in Chief." Leahy described how the President had depended upon him, Byrnes and Hopkins to fill the enormous gaps in Truman's information during his first weeks in office. Roosevelt never had confided in Truman, not even after the latter was elected Vice President, and it was only after Roosevelt's death that his successor learned from Leahy and other "insiders" about many wartime decisions. The Admiral was familiar with most of Roosevelt's secret or tacit understandings with foreign statesmen, some of which never were put on record.

Leahy told me that Truman was a quick learner and a tremendously hard worker. He described how meticulously the new President had prepared himself for Potsdam. As soon as the conference was scheduled, Truman asked the State Department and the Joint Chiefs of Staff to prepare condensed information on all subjects which might arise; and during the eight days crossing the Atlantic on a cruiser, the President had gone over these papers with his well-selected shipboard staff of experts. Leahy said, "He squeezed facts and opinions out of us all day long." He added that the President was more systematic than Roosevelt, and had considerably revived the morale of long-neglected government departments, notably the Department of State.

For the benefit of our Military Government staff, Leahy had thoughtfully made a summary of Truman's private opinions on matters affecting Germany. The Admiral said that the President desired to carry out the policies of his predecessor, and had intensively studied the secret reports of Roosevelt's commitments and understandings. For example, at both of the previous conferences at Tehran and Yalta, Roosevelt had accepted the principle that Germany should be partitioned, and the Yalta conferees had approved extensive annexations of German territory by both Russia and Poland. Roosevelt had informally suggested a split into five pieces. Another proposal favorably discussed was to separate Germany from its richest industrial regions in the Rhineland, perhaps placing the Ruhr's coal and iron mines and steel plants under international control. Leahy said that Truman also was rather attracted by another idea which Roosevelt and Churchill both favored—a southern confederation to include Austria and the German states of Bavaria, Baden, and Württemberg, with Vienna as the confederation capital. In fact, Leahy commented, the new President was favorably disposed, on the basis of Roosevelt's ideas, toward any proposals which might be made at Potsdam for partitioning Germany. Apparently the idealistic pronouncements of the Atlantic Charter had not bothered either President.

I explained to Leahy that these various schemes for breaking up Germany were worrying us in Military Government because one of our main problems was how to prevent the occupation from becoming an intolerable financial burden upon the American people. The situation, as we saw it, was that most European countries undoubtedly had legitimate claims for damages against the Nazis, and desperately needed immediate help, but that the war had been prolonged until nearly all of Europe was in ruins and the accumulated capital of generations used up. Since almost every nation was bankrupt except the United States, the American Government might be saddled now with the entire cost of the German occupation, as well as huge reparations for Nazi victims. The Admiral reassured me, "That danger is uppermost in the President's mind, too. I have heard him say that the American people foolishly made big loans to Germany after the First World War, and the money was used to pay reparations. When the loans were defaulted, Americans were left holding the bag. The President says he is determined not to let that happen again." I was relieved to hear this. Like Truman himself, I failed to foresee how insignificant those previous loans would seem, compared with the billions of dollars the United States would soon be pouring into Germany and the countries devastated by the Nazis.

On July 5, the day before the President's cruiser started for Europe, it was announced in Washington that Morgenthau had resigned, and I asked Leahy whether this sudden resignation of the Secretary of the Treasury had any significance for our occupation plans. "It was very significant," the Admiral replied. "Morgenthau wanted to come to Potsdam and threatened to resign if he was not made a member of our delegation. Truman promptly accepted his resignation. While the President was still a senator, he read in the newspapers about the Morgenthau Plan and he didn't like it. He also felt that the Treasury was exceeding its authority in presuming to make foreign policy. The President has told us emphatically that Treasury proposals for the treatment of Germany are out." However, that did not prove to be quite the case. In the long process of compiling Eisenhower's directive for administering the American zone in Germany, various compromises had been accepted by the numerous planners in Washington. The spirit—and sometimes the letter—of the Morgenthau Plan was reflected in many mandatory provisions of the top-secret directive JCS 1067, which haunted Military Government for several postwar years.

At the end of our conversation, Leahy took me to the President's study where I met Truman and Byrnes. The President was very interested to hear about conditions in Berlin, the attitude of the Russian High Command, and the conduct of the Russian forces. He was especially interested in the extent of looting and black marketeering, and the fact that many Russian soldiers were receiving months of back pay in the form of German occupation currency. This money would be worthless after the soldiers returned to the Soviet Union, so the men were converting the paper into goods of all kinds, especially watches. Thus, by printing occupation currency with engraving plates provided by the U. S. Treasury, the Soviet Government was relieved of the burden of paying its troops.

The Potsdam Conference opened formally on July 17, 1945, and continued through August 2. Although the two most famous men then alive—Stalin and Churchill—personally attended the plenary sessions, neither of these world celebrities attracted as much attention as the recent senator from Missouri, Harry S. Truman, who was completely unknown outside his own country. Only eight months had passed since Truman was elected Vice President of the United States; less than four months had gone by since the death of Roosevelt made Truman the Chief Executive of his country and Commander in Chief of all its Armed Forces. The tremendous authority of the presidency was further extended by its wartime emergency powers, and everyone at Potsdam was wondering what the newcomer would do. In one of Truman's first public statements after becoming President he had promised to fulfill all of Roosevelt's commitments, but this pledge could be interpreted variously. It had been Churchill's practice, when visiting wartime Washington, to seek out American senators who were active in foreign policy matters, but Truman had been so little concerned with foreign affairs that the British Prime Minister had never bothered to meet him. Now the former senator was in a position to help settle the grave disputes which had arisen between Churchill and Stalin.

Potsdam's portentous drama was played out before a very small audience. Only five members of each delegation were seated at the central roundtable in Cecilienhof's ballroom, and one of these was the interpreter. Behind the central table sat about twenty other members of each delegation, specialists who came and went as different topics were discussed. No journalists were admitted, to the chagrin of two hundred Western correspondents who had made their way to Berlin to report the proceedings. In accordance with security and secrecy policies, reporters were barred not only from the conference sessions but even from Potsdam and Babelsberg. Thus cut off from their carefully cultivated "informed sources," the correspondents had access to no information except formal communiqués and background talks with cautious "official spokesmen."

President Truman had chosen Leahy, Byrnes and Joseph E. Davies, a former American Ambassador to Moscow, as his three associates, with Foreign Service officer Charles E. Bohlen as interpreter. Bohlen was uniquely equipped for this assignment. He had been a member of our embassy in Moscow for years, had met Stalin several times, and was the only American who had been present at private conversations between Stalin and Roosevelt at both Tehran and Yalta. Harry Hopkins had so much confidence in Bohlen that he had arranged for him to be appointed State Department liaison officer at the White House during the last months of the Roosevelt administration. Bohlen had stayed on at the White House when Truman took over, another valuable link between administrations.

I was the only member of American Military Government attached to our delegation at Potsdam. Eisenhower and Clay were most concerned with the military conferences being held simultaneously in Berlin that fortnight. All the American and British Chiefs of Staff were on hand to confer with commanders of the Red Army about the war in the Pacific, and to decide about Anglo-American military cooperation around the globe. Eisenhower asked me to make daily reports to him and Clay concerning the discussions at Potsdam which affected Military Government.

Truman, being the only Chief of State present at the conference, was invited to preside at the plenary sessions, as Roosevelt had done at Yalta and Tehran. The new President presided with dignity and competence, but at first he was somewhat ill at ease in the presence of the fabulous Churchill and Stalin. He was under the great disadvantage of dealing with situations which were familiar to them but strange to him. But after a few sessions it seemed that Truman and Churchill were being drawn together as a result of Stalin's high-handed demands. The Russians had obtained at the Yalta Conference sweeping generalized benefits, and now they were insisting upon retaining those tentative concessions. One of the generalizations which had been accepted by Roosevelt and Churchill "as a basis for discussion" was a total of twenty billion dollars for German reparations, half of this to go to Russia. The Soviet delegates at Potsdam interpreted this to mean that Russia had been definitely promised ten billions, much of which could come only from the Anglo-American zones. To allow this interpretation would have meant inevitable American underwriting of reparation payments.

Of course disputes of this magnitude could be settled only at the highest level, but an Economic Subcommittee had the duty of preparing drafts on such questions for use at the plenary sessions. As in all international conferences, the "donkey work" was done in subcommittees, and because I was the only American member who would be staying on in Germany, I was assigned to the most controversial committee, the one dealing with reparations, permissible German production, living standards and other economic matters. It was an arduous, tedious business, and the Russians scored more points than we did because they never were in a hurry. Most of my Anglo-American colleagues and I were trying to perform four or five jobs simultaneously during the conference. My Berlin office had been open only a few days and needed constant attention. Eisenhower had several problems with political aspects which required my consideration. And there were numerous informal discussions to try to iron out disputed points which the Big Three could not find time to discuss in detail.

Stalin's favorite economist, Eugene Varga, inadvertently presented us with startling evidence of the type of bargaining which the Kremlin apparently expected concerning Germany. Varga, who arrived two days late for the conference, was assigned immediately to our Economic Subcommittee while we were clarifying what was meant in the Yalta agreements by the phrase "minimum needs of the German people." We concluded that the expression indicated barely enough to keep the Germans alive and working. To our astonishment, Varga then produced much lower estimates of the food needs of the Soviet zone than our own calculations. After a confused discussion we discovered that Varga had not included the German states of Thuringia and Saxony in his figuring. When asked to explain this omission, Varga said, "American troops occupy those sections of the Soviet zone." He was informed that American forces had been evacuated from this and all other Soviet areas before the conference convened, and that Russians were in full control of all the territory assigned them. Varga was incredulous; he seemed to suspect we were jesting. It became transparently clear that he had made his calculations upon the assumption that Americans would remain for some time in those districts of the Soviet zone which they had conquered. When Varga finally was convinced that Americans had relinquished portions of the Soviet zone without seeking any quid pro quo, he withdrew to revise his estimates. If a man so close to Stalin expected Americans to exploit their conquests, it seems probable that Stalin himself had similar expectations.

On July 21, as Truman presided over the fourth day of plenary sessions, we noticed a decided change in the President's manner. He seemed much more sure of himself, more inclined to participate vigorously in the discussions, to challenge some of Stalin's statements. It was apparent that something had happened, and the consensus among American delegates was that Stalin had overplayed his hand and that Churchill was winning Truman over to the Prime Minister's point of view. This seemed confirmed by a similar change in Churchill's manner. During earlier sessions, Churchill had disappointed his admirers by making a poor showing in some verbal exchanges with Stalin. Sometimes he got facts and figures wrong, sometimes he presented illogical or unconvincing arguments at wearying length. The President had been noticeably restless during some of the Prime Minister's more repetitious speeches. Stalin, however, although relentless in argument with Churchill, had been surprisingly patient in listening to him.

Everyone understood that Churchill was under tremendous strain when he arrived in Potsdam. It was not only that he was seventy years old and had led the British Empire through six exhausting years of total war. Now, to cap the triumph over Germany, Churchill had decided to challenge his political rivals at home, and a British general election had been conducted on July 5. Although this election had taken place ten days before Churchill came to Berlin, nobody knew the results yet and the suspense was becoming intolerable. This extraordinary delay occurred because the vote-counting was being deferred until July 25 so that soldier ballots from all points of the globe could be included. It had not been at all necessary for Churchill to burden himself with a domestic election campaign prior to the Potsdam Conference. By British rules, an election was due in 1945 but it could have been postponed until October. But leaders of the Conservative Party had persuaded Churchill to hold the election that summer. They told him he was at the height of his popularity and was sure to win, and public opinion polls confirmed this wishful thinking. The Conservatives feared that the Japanese war might drag on for another year and become increasingly unpopular with the British people. In spite of Germany's surrender, there certainly was no decrease in the suicidal resistance of the Japanese. So Churchill decided to hold the British general elections on July 5, and after attending nine plenary sessions at Potsdam he returned home confidently to learn the results of the vote-counting.

When Churchill returned to England on July 25 he carried with him a secret which was literally earth-shaking—the secret that an atomic bomb had been successfully exploded nine days before in a test in New Mexico. Scarcely a dozen men at Potsdam had heard about this new weapon, but the explosion had been hopefully awaited by Truman and Churchill. The bomb was still untried when the President left Washington, but the test was imminent, which was why Secretary Stimson flew into Berlin at about the same time the President did. Stimson's arrival had surprised me, since he was not listed as a member of the Potsdam delegation, but I had supposed he wanted to make himself available for consultation. As I learned later, the Secretary of War actually had a much more specific reason. He wanted to inform Truman personally about the final results of the atom bomb tests, whose development Stimson had directed for two years. The New Mexico explosion took place on July 16, on the eve of the conference opening, but Stimson received only a brief coded cablegram then. It was not until four days later that an Army courier arrived with vivid detailed accounts which showed how greatly the power of the bomb exceeded expectations. It was this exhilarating report which so changed the manner of Truman and Churchill. Like nearly everyone else in the world, I knew nothing about this until August 6, when atom bomb no. 1 was dropped on Hiroshima. By that time, the Potsdam Conference was over and Truman was at sea on his way home.

The full report on the test explosion was also read by Stimson personally to Churchill, who was entitled to be informed immediately because the bomb was a joint Anglo-American venture from its beginning. Churchill has related how he was more determined than ever, when he carried this secret to London, not to compromise basic issues with Stalin at Potsdam. He expected on his return to the conference also to have the increased prestige of political victory in Britain. The very worst he had reason to anticipate was the possibility of a narrow defeat in the elections, in which case he still could properly remain in office long enough to finish his Potsdam program, and he has recorded that this is what he intended to do. But Churchill's defeat was not narrow; it was overwhelming. It could be interpreted only as a repudiation of his postwar policies, and Churchill felt impelled to resign at once. The wartime Prime Minister, by permitting himself to become involved in politics at home that summer, forfeited his opportunity to force a showdown with Stalin. Had Churchill delayed the British elections until autumn, it would have made a tremendous difference to his career, and perhaps to the world.

Churchill's unexpected defeat suspended the Potsdam Conference in midair for two days while the surprised Labor Party victors formed a government. Then the new Prime Minister, Clement Attlee, and his Foreign Secretary, Ernest Bevin, returned to Berlin. Attlee had attended the plenary sessions from the beginning of the conference, having been invited by Churchill to serve as a full member of the British delegation while awaiting the delayed election results, but the head of the Labor Party had scarcely opened his mouth when Churchill was present. Not knowing Attlee, I assumed his silence indicated tactful respect, but when Attlee moved into Churchill's place during the final Potsdam sessions, he remained almost as silent as before. Attlee was an abnormally unassuming politician, and the last four plenary sessions were anticlimactic. It may have been my imagination, but it seemed to me that Stalin lost interest after the departure of his arch-rival. Stalin was visibly suspicious of Bevin, the trade unionist, and there was a touch of condescension in the Soviet dictator's unvarying politeness to Attlee, a contrast to his sharp interchanges with Churchill.

When the plenary sessions resumed after the British elections, many observers commented admiringly upon how smoothly the transition had been made, with little or no perceptible effect upon British foreign policy. But this outward appearance was misleading. The negotiators of the Labor Party were moderate socialists who viewed world problems differently than the Conservatives, and they were disinclined to press issues which Churchill considered vital. Furthermore, the new delegation was in a great hurry to return to England. The election platform of the Labor Party had promised "a new way of life" for the British people, and this prospect fascinated Attlee and his associates at least as much as international affairs. Thus they permitted the conference to adjourn with major issues unresolved or hastily compromised.

Years later when Churchill wrote his memoirs, he declared flatly: "Frustration was the fate of the final conference of the Big Three." That undoubtedly was true for Churchill, and to a lesser extent for the American delegates also. Among other matters which I found personally frustrating was that the American Government made no official transcript of the proceedings because overzealous security officers ruled against admitting stenographers to plenary sessions. The American daily minutes were written by two advisers who did not know shorthand and therefore could not record a verbatim report. Limited in scope as their notes were, even this incomplete record was given to nobody except the President and Secretary of State.

When I was informed that American stenographers were barred, I immediately obtained permission for members of my Berlin staff to take my place whenever subcommittee meetings prevented my own attendance at plenary sessions. But Truman's military attaché, Brigadier General Harry Vaughan, thwarted me. Vaughan was a Missouri politician who had played a prominent part in Truman's election campaigns for the Senate, and after the outbreak of war, Vaughan rejoined the Army as a reserve officer. Although Potsdam was Vaughan's first international conference, he somehow became a kind of stage manager at Cecilienhof. He was convinced that whenever we increased the number of American advisers at any session, the Russians did the same, and he expounded this highly doubtful theory to Secretary Byrnes when the latter's thoughts were centered on other matters. Byrnes replied absently, "All right, cut down our delegation." As a result of that casual decision, American Military Government never did get any American record of what occurred at Potsdam, whose top-secret Protocol shaped our administration in Germany. The

British Foreign Office came to our rescue; it made a complete transcript, with copies to spare.

President Truman's most conspicuous frustration at Potsdam has never been adequately recorded, so far as I know. Truman's favorite project at that time was the internationalization of inland waterways —rivers, canals, straits. During my first talk with Leahy at Babelsberg, he told me that the President attached singular importance to this subject and was sponsoring a proposal about it. The only inland waterway controversy of immediate interest to our Military Government was the Danube River. Most boats on the Danube sought refuge from the Red Army by moving to the river's upper waters which were controlled by Anglo-Americans. The crews refused to return to Soviet territory for fear that their boats would be seized. Revival of traffic on the Danube was desperately needed because other means of transport were badly damaged, so Eisenhower had recommended that regulations of Danubian traffic should be placed on the Potsdam agenda.

But Truman's goals were more ambitious. The President wanted the conferees to consider permanent internationalization of all inland waterways, even the Panama and Suez Canals. He introduced his proposal with a long statement at the plenary session on July 23, explaining that the immediate issues were the Danube and Rhine rivers, the Kiel Canal and the Bosporus. He declared that his study of history convinced him that all major wars of the previous two centuries had originated in the area from the Black Sea to the Baltic, and from the eastern frontier of France to the western frontier of Russia. He said he did not want to become engaged in another war over the Dardanelles or the Danube or the Rhine. It should be the business of this conference and of the coming Peace Conference, he said, to remove this source of conflict. The President mentioned how beneficial American rivers and canals had been in opening up the United States. He said he wanted the Russians, British, and everybody else to have free passage of goods and vessels along inland waterways to all the seas of the world, and he had prepared a paper on this subject which he now would circulate.

The earnestness of the President's speech was evident. Noting his manner, Churchill expressed cordial support in general terms. But Stalin replied merely that he would read the President's paper. At a second session that same day Truman raised the question again, declaring that he hoped the conference would treat the Danube, the Rhine and the Dardanelles as parts of the same question. Churchill again agreed generally, but Stalin said, "Our ideas differ widely. Perhaps we can pass over this point now." However, Truman circulated a second paper which he and his advisers had prepared. The next day the President brought up the subject again, reiterating his keen personal interest in it. Churchill again supported him but Soviet Foreign Minister Molotov interjected a sardonic reference to British control of the Suez Canal. Stalin cut short this interchange by saying, "We have many more urgent problems before us. This one can be put off." On July 25, Churchill's last day at the conference, Truman asked that his proposal be referred to the three foreign ministers for possible agreement, and that was how the matter stood when Churchill left for London.

Everybody could see that the President was intensely interested in this matter, more than many of us believed justified at that moment, and Byrnes did his best to get some action on it. At his suggestion the foreign ministers appointed a special committee to consider the question, the American member being Foreign Service officer James Riddleberger. He and the British representative prepared almost identical drafts for reference to the foreign ministers, but they could not induce the Soviet representative even to submit a statement. Moscow evidently was determined to avoid debate on this subject. However, on July 31, with Attlee and Bevin now heading the British delegation, the President again brought up his waterways proposal, making another earnest presentation. He declared that European waterways had been a hotbed for breeding wars throughout the history of the continent, and he believed that proper control would contribute greatly toward peace. Like Churchill before him, Attlee expressed general agreement, but Stalin repeated that the topic needed special study. At the President's request it was once again referred to the foreign ministers for reconsideration.

At the August 1 plenary session, the conference began to consider the final communiqué which soon would be made public. The President said he regretted that no agreement had been possible on control of waterways, but he believed nevertheless that the communiqué should mention that this subject had been discussed. Attlee agreed, but Stalin objected. He said the communiqué already mentioned more subjects than the public could easily digest, and no more should be added. Truman then turned to Stalin and made a frank personal plea. He said, "Marshal Stalin, I have accepted a number of compromises during this conference to conform with your views, and I make a personal request now that you yield on this point. My request is that the communiqué mention the fact that the waterways proposal has been referred to the Council of Foreign Ministers which we have established to prepare for peace settlements." The President pointed out that if the communiqué mentioned his proposal, that would give him an opportunity to explain it to the American Congress in a message which he planned to deliver after his return to Washington.

Stalin listened closely to the President's statement, which was addressed directly to him, and apparently the Soviet dictator understood most of the English words. Before the translation into Russian was finished, he broke in abruptly with the familiar Russian negative, "*Nyet!*" Then, very deliberately, he repeated in English, "No. I say no!" That was the only time I heard Stalin speak English at the conference. Truman could not mistake the rebuff. His face flushed and he turned to the American delegation and exclaimed, "I cannot understand that man!" I happened to be sitting directly behind Truman and Byrnes at the moment and overheard the President's further remarks to the Secretary of State. "Jimmy, do you realize that we have been here seventeen whole days?" he asked. "Why, in seventeen days you can decide anything!" It was evident that the new President would never enjoy playing the elaborate game of power politics which so delighted Roosevelt. The proceedings at Potsdam made Truman first uneasy, then impatient, and the final curious passage with Stalin infuriated him. He wrote later that he left Berlin resolved never again to participate personally in another similar meeting—and he never did.

After Churchill's departure, the American delegates were as impatient to return home as were the British. Truman was more concerned with the possible effect of the atom bomb on the war in the Pacific than with the squabbling aftermath of the war in Europe. Byrnes was equally anxious to get back to Washington. He had taken over the State Department only a few days before starting for Berlin, and had not even met many of his chief subordinates. The only delegates who showed no particular haste or desire for compromise were the Russians, whose government was not undergoing any change of administration. The imperturbable Stalin gave the impression of placid willingness to spend months of his rather valuable time on the major subjects under negotiation, in contrast to Truman who gave the impression of having much more important things to do in Washington. The Russians revealed at Berlin a more definite postwar policy than the United States or Great Britain, and Stalin and his group either obtained the settlements they sought, or managed to sweep ticklish questions under the rug. Roosevelt had hoped that this meeting of the Big Three would further advance his Grand Design for the postwar world. But it was Churchill who had suggested the code name for the Potsdam Conference: TERMINAL.

TWENTY-ONE

ARMY ENGINEER TAKES CHARGE IN GERMANY

Great events piled upon each other during the fortnight immediately following the Potsdam Conference. The first atom bomb was dropped on Hiroshima four days after the conference ended. Two days later, the Soviet Union declared war against Japan. Perhaps the atom bomb hastened the Soviet declaration, but Stalin had promised Roosevelt several months earlier that Russia would strike against Japan within three months of Germany's surrender. The three months ended on August 8, the precise day that the Russians attacked. A second bomb was dropped on Nagasaki the day after Moscow's declaration of war, and the Tokyo Government surrendered on August 14, 1945. As a result of this bewildering rush of events, the Red Army experienced only a week of desultory fighting before it became co-victor in the Pacific with Americans and Britons who had fought the Japanese for almost four years.

All of us working in Germany were caught by surprise when the Japanese halted resistance so suddenly and so completely. Eisenhower and Clay had flown to Moscow on August 10 for a state visit at the invitation of Stalin, and the arrival of the wartime Supreme Commander of the Western Allies inspired a jubilant demonstration the like of which never has been extended to any other American in Russia, before or since. The crowds in the Moscow streets were gay and friendly, Soviet Army officers heaped hospitality upon the famous guest, and Stalin personally showed Eisenhower every courtesy. While reviewing a spectacular parade in Red Square, Stalin amazed everyone by inviting Eisenhower to stand beside him on Lenin's Tomb, a public honor never previously accorded to any foreigner who was not a supporter of Communism. On the last night of the state visit, at an American Embassy party attended by Kremlin officials and Red Army chiefs, announcement was made of the surrender of Japan, and Americans and Russians joined in toasts to their shared victories in war and to their future cooperation in peace. Then Eisenhower and Clay flew back to their problems in Frankfurt and Berlin.

With the abrupt cessation of hostilities, intense unrest developed among American soldiers who still were in Europe. When the Nazis surrendered in May, more than three million American soldiers were on the continent. By August, through incredible feats of transportation, almost half of them had been sent either to the Pacific or to the United States. But a million and a half were still in Europe when Japan surrendered, and a deafening clamor arose to "bring the boys home." President Roosevelt had repeatedly declared during the war that it would not be necessary for American troops to remain abroad very long or in large numbers after military victory had been achieved over Germany and Japan. He believed that protection against future German aggression could be entrusted to the troops of Russia, Britain, and other European nations which had fought the Nazis. Roosevelt pictured the United Nations as a substitute for old-fashioned alliances, and the American Joint Chiefs of Staff unanimously approved Roosevelt's military ideas for postwar Europe. All plans made in Washington assumed that America's chief contributions to Europe would be twofold: first, massive temporary aid; second, vigorous and permanent participation in the United Nations. When President Truman took office, he also did not question this Roosevelt program for several months.

Nowadays the bombing of Hiroshima is recalled chiefly because it introduced the horrors of nuclear warfare, but in that summer of 1945 the atom bomb was widely hailed as a peacemaker. The immediate effect of the bomb was to terminate the Pacific War months sooner than had been generally expected, and hundreds of thousands of soldiers and their families felt that the new weapon may have saved the lives of these fighting men. Most American soldiers believed that they had done their duty and were entitled to prompt return to civilian life. But ships and planes were needed for many purposes besides ferrying Americans home, so the Army established a point system by which soldiers with long and superior records were released first.

This reluctance of most Americans to accept further service overseas created great administrative difficulties for our Military Government in Germany. Because a brief occupation was taken so much for granted, the only permanent staff originally available had to come from our regular Army and from career employees of federal departments and agencies. These are the only Americans obligated in peacetime to go wherever they are sent and to stay as long as ordered. But our Military Government needed as many specialists on German affairs as we could recruit. Eisenhower and Clay gradually assembled enough experts to provide them with the technical information they needed, and my own staff of one hundred and forty Americans was made up of the best I could obtain from inside and outside the Foreign Service. The men from the State Department were required to advise and support our Military Government and also to make preparations for eventual restoration of German independence.

Our chief trouble in the beginning was that Military Government was permitted to offer only one-year contracts, and we lost some of our best volunteers because they could not be guaranteed longer tenure. Many felt they could not afford such temporary work, that it behooved them to hurry back to the United States to get permanent civilian jobs before all the best ones were taken by ex-soldiers. Clay managed to retain a few key officials only by personally promising them two years' work in Germany, a guarantee which he had no authority to make. The maximum salary at the outset for Military Government employees was ten thousand dollars a year, and it happened that my salary as a Foreign Service Officer Class One was also about ten thousand dollars at that time. I had been offered the post of Minister to Portugal in 1944, which would have paid twenty thousand dollars annually, and in 1947 I could have become Ambassador to India at twenty-five thousand dollars, but I declined both offers because I was intensely interested in Germany.

From the very beginning of the German occupation, geography favored the Russians—as it still does today. Because Berlin was deep inside the Soviet zone, the Russian military governor, Zhukov, was able to establish his headquarters as soon as the capital city was captured, and also to establish the Russian political offices in Berlin. But the American, British and French military governors were not permitted to install their representatives in that city until two months later, and by that time all Western occupants had settled down in their own zones. Military governors could have moved to Berlin, but they were reluctant to set up their headquarters surrounded by the Soviet zone. Moreover, living conditions in Berlin also made it inadvisable to bring numerous soldiers into that area. So Eisenhower remained in Frankfurt.

However, the London agreement of 1944 specified that the headquarters of the four-power Military Government for Germany would be in Berlin. That international agreement also specified that each of the four military governors would have a civilian political adviser. The U.S.S.R. appointed Ambassador Arkady Aleksandrovich Sobolev; the United Kingdom, Sir William Strang; the French, Jacques St. Hardouin; and the United States appointed me. The result was that the political advisers established their offices in Berlin; the western military governors journeyed back and forth about three times a month to attend meetings of the Allied Control Council; and Eisenhower assigned his Deputy, General Clay, to remain in Berlin to direct the American political and economic share of the occupation. In this fashion, the military and political branches of the Western Military Governments developed in widely separated cities. Because the German population never created the trouble for the garrison troops which had been anticipated, military considerations soon became subordinate to political and economic issues, and Berlin grew more important than any of the scattered Army headquarters.

My four-year partnership with Lucius Clay did not really begin until the war in the Pacific ended. Until then, much of Clay's time was absorbed in arranging the transfer of combat troops to the Far East. But after the surrender of Japan, Clay and I installed ourselves in adjoining offices in Berlin in a rambling Nazi Air Force building which had survived years of air raids. Our rooms were severely plain and little was ever done to relieve their austerity. The official name of our Berlin headquarters was Office of Military Government, United States, a cumbersome designation which was promptly abbreviated to OMGUS.

Early in our association, Clay and I decided to rate our major problems in order of their importance by drawing up separate lists which we then could compare. I asked my ablest assistants to help with this project, and I believe Clay did the same. It is interesting now to recall that in the beginning nobody considered Soviet-American relations as our greatest obstacle. The consensus was that our no.1 problem was DOCUMENTS. The American occupation was controlled by two documents— Eisenhower's directive JCS 1067, which had been concocted in Washington; and the Potsdam Protocol, signed by Stalin, Truman and Attlee at Potsdam. The reason these documents presented overwhelming difficulties for Clay and me was because we were prohibited by JCS 1067 from doing some things which were absolutely essential; we were commanded by the Potsdam Protocol to perform the impossible; and because both of these directives were classified secret, we could not refer publicly to them.

The first essential for administering the American zone in Germany was to associate with Germans, but Americans were forbidden by JCS 1067 from having any personal relations with the people we had defeated. Eisenhower found it easy to obey this instruction meticulously. In fact, during his brief period as military governor, he usually managed to avoid even official contacts with Germans by delegating almost all negotiations to members of his staff. Eisenhower and President Truman, in their aloof and distrustful attitude toward Germans, typified the sentiments of millions of Americans. During Truman's eighteen days at Potsdam, while he was charting Germany's future, he did not ask to meet any anti-Nazi German statesmen, publicly or privately, and almost everyone in the President's entourage followed his example. The non-fraternization rule was also rigidly upheld by the War and Navy Departments (which combined into the Defense Department in 1947), even to the extent of insisting that separate toilets must be provided for Germans and Americans in Military Government office buildings—a sort of Jim Crow feature. But Clay's duties, as well as my own, necessitated associating with Germans even before we moved to Berlin. From the outset, our Army required extensive German assistance to maintain order in the cities and villages we had so swiftly overrun. The conquered people obeyed even our severest orders because they considered themselves fortunate to be under Western protection. SHAEF's Civil Affairs section, organized as a division of the General Staff (G-5), found German cooperation vastly more dependable than had been expected.

The second essential for administering our zone was to get things running again—utilities, railroads, factories. But JCS 1067 prohibited employment as executives or skilled workmen of any Germans who had been more than nominal members of the Nazi party. And we were promptly made aware that the great majority of executives and skilled workmen in Germany had undeniably been Nazis. American Intelligence agents, just after the surrender, were delighted to discover tons of Nazi files which listed in detail the activities of every member. The party files for Bavaria were captured almost intact. The German passion for classifying and preserving records persisted to the end. Those files did enable us to "denazify" the American zone with remarkable thoroughness, but there were times when this achievement did not seem an unmixed blessing.

As we got around to denazifying one enterprise after another, we had to dismiss thousands of efficient workers because their records placed them in categories which JCS 1067 marked for automatic exclusion from skilled employment. On the railways, for example, we tried for months to operate largely with untrained German personnel under the direction of the few skilled Americans available. It did not make us any happier when we learned that many of the workers whom we had been compelled to discharge found jobs immediately in the Russian, French and British zones. One day Clay went out on a limb and announced that thereafter we would employ minor ex-Nazis in skilled jobs. The American Government never did cancel this JCS 1067 prohibition; it merely refrained from repudiating Clay's action.

Washington urged Clay and me to try to induce the other three occupying powers to accept JCS 1067 as a basis for uniform treatment of Germans in all four zones, and we made a valiant attempt to do so. But the Russians, British and French replied, in effect: "No thank you. You are welcome to your JCS 1067." They all disliked the explicit prohibitions in the American directive and all had devised methods of their own for handling Germans. The Russians made it possible for minor ex-Nazis to redeem themselves by joining the thinly disguised German Communist Party. The French, after rounding up the leading Nazis in their zone, assumed that Germans are Germans and should be treated alike. The British, after a halfhearted attempt to keep in step with us, abandoned our regulations as impractical.

The third essential for administering our zone in Germany was to make it self-supporting, so that the occupation would not become an intolerable burden on the American taxpayer. But here again our attempts were thwarted by JCS 1067, with its traces of the Morgenthau Plan which threatened to delay Germany's economic recovery indefinitely. The occupation directive forbade Germans in the American zone from making more iron and steel than the minimum needed for domestic consumption. The Russians and the French also insisted that the total steel production for all Germany should be limited to a maximum of three million tons annually. (It is close to thirty million now.) Chemicals, automobiles, electric equipment, and machine tools were similarly restricted to absolute minimums. Germany had long depended on the manufacture and export of these and similar products to provide foreign currency for necessary imports, but now we were required to dismantle hundreds of German plants in our zone and to turn the machinery over to the Russians as war reparations. The admirable purpose in thus restricting German industrial production was to make any sort of German military revival impossible, but it also prevented economic recovery.

Our difficulties with the arbitrary restrictions of JCS 1067 were aggravated by the fact that OMGUS could not publicly explain that it was functioning under an explicit directive from Washington. The treatment of Germans was a very controversial subject at that time and every move by OMGUS was scrutinized by the oversized corps of foreign journalists assigned to Germany. Our rulings were brought to the attention of millions of interested persons in many countries, and some of our actions were severely criticized. But it was not until late in October 1945 that we were even permitted to admit that an American directive existed. As soon as the War Department made this fact public, Clay flew to Washington to try to get some of the JCS 1067 terms modified. Everyone he consulted, from President Truman down, conceded that drastic modifications were in order, but discussions about the proposed changes ran on and on and on because so many different agencies were involved. It was not until two years later, after Clay was promoted to succeed McNarney as military governor, that a revised JCS 1067 was officially approved and made public.

In the meantime, OMGUS not only was shackled by its inflexible directive from Washington, it also was burdened with international duties assigned to it by the Potsdam Protocol. This secret agreement specified that inasmuch as Germany had no government of its own, "supreme authority" would be entrusted to the commanders of the occupation forces, each military governor in his own zone, and "also jointly in matters affecting Germany as a whole." The "joint decisions" of these military governors were to be made at their meetings in Berlin as members of the Allied Control Council. So far as Washington was concerned, this was intended to be only a temporary expedient because American troops were not expected to stay long in Germany. But as matters turned out, "supreme authority" remained in the hands of the commanders for the next four years, and an impossible task was assigned to them—to "treat Germany as an economic unit."

This order, according to American interpretation, meant arrangements for nationwide operation of railroads, telegraph lines, postal service and the like. But as early as the Control Council meeting on September 22, 1945, the French representative, General Louis M. Koeltz, sharply rejected an American proposal for a central transport administration. Koeltz declared that railroads are a war potential and that an organization which centralized their operations would be as dangerous as a German General Staff. This French objection nipped in the bud the American effort to organize a unified German railroad system, because each of the military governors held veto power in the Control Council which could be used to nullify any proposal. The British or Russian commanders could not have summarily dismissed our railroad plan in this fashion because they, like Eisenhower, were working under the Potsdam agreement to "treat Germany as an economic unit." But the French military governor possessed what amounted to a double veto in the Control Council. He not only was endowed with the same veto power as the other commanders, but he also was free to veto the Potsdam Protocol itself, as the other three were not. Thus when Truman, Stalin and Attlee instructed the four military governors to "act jointly in matters affecting Germany as a whole," they were commanding the impossible because they had put the French Government in a position to prevent such united action.

This unique power of the French Government, which sometimes proved more effective than the combined strength of the Big Three, had emerged as a sort of by-product of a clash between De Gaulle and Truman. While the Allies were fighting Germans in Italy, De Gaulle attempted to make a few "corrections" in the French-Italian frontier by annexing some bits of Italian territory. In order to accomplish this, De Gaulle dispatched an order to the French forces in Italy which disregarded a battle order which had been issued by

Eisenhower. Like the British and American soldiers at that time, the American-equipped French troops were under the command of SHAEF, but when the French general assigned to Italy received contradictory orders there from Eisenhower and from De Gaulle, he understandably chose to obey De Gaulle. This insubordination so outraged Truman that when De Gaulle subsequently requested to be included in the Potsdam Conference, the President saw to it that his request was never even considered formally.

But instead of being crushed by this snub, De Gaulle utilized it to bring about a diplomatic triumph. Since France was not represented at Potsdam, its government did not sign the Protocol and therefore France was not bound by its provisions. The Four-Power occupation thus began with a disgruntled French Government in a position to block all plans for Germany. During the next three years, French officials freely exercised their unique veto. Several constructive Anglo-American proposals were hamstrung by the French, and the result was that the Soviet Union consolidated its own European schemes. It is ironic to reflect now that Stalin, who always deplored French participation in the occupation of Germany, became the chief beneficiary of early French policy there. Fortunately for our peace of mind, OMGUS could not foresee all the difficulties which France would make for us. But our staff encountered enough obstructions at the outset so that after listing our no. 1 problem as DOCUMENTS, we rated FRANCE as our no. 2 problem.

Concerning our numerous other problems, ranging from catastrophes to nuisances, opinions at OMGUS varied. All of us were aware that our relations with the Russians were often strained, but we did not regard that as an insurmountable obstacle. Our thinking was governed by Roosevelt's mandate to get along with the Russians because Germany, and especially Berlin, was to be the proof whether U.S. and U.S.S.R. postwar cooperation would be possible. Eisenhower had surmounted countless international misunderstandings when he was in command at SHAEF, and he was confident that with friendliness and tact we now could influence Soviet policy to our mutual advantage. Moscow's enthusiastic welcome of the General made a very favorable impression on him, and he felt that Americans and Russians should be able to get along in Germany. In particular, he was convinced that professional soldiers of all countries have much in common and that he and Zhukov would understand one another.

During one of Eisenhower's first visits to Berlin, the General told me that he was thinking of extending, through Zhukov, an informal invitation to Red Army personnel to visit the American zone whenever they desired, without any red tape. "That will give them a chance to get acquainted with our people and see how we run things," Eisenhower said. "Don't you think the Russians would like that?" I replied that in my associations with the Russians, they always seemed inclined to become suspicious when offered something for nothing. I suggested that Zhukov might be more receptive to a proposal for an exchange of visits between zones. "Now, none of your State Department quid pro quo's!" Eisenhower exclaimed impatiently. "What I have in mind is a straightforward unconditional friendly invitation." I said, "Well, try it out and see what happens."

A day or two later Eisenhower extended the invitation to Zhukov in my presence. There was an awkward pause, and then the Soviet Marshal inquired, "How many of your men would you expect us to admit to the Soviet zone?" Eisenhower replied, "I am not asking for any visiting privileges there. What you do about your own zone is your own business." Zhukov seemed genuinely embarrassed. Finally he said, "In that case I must refer the matter to my Government." While Zhukov's reply was being translated, Eisenhower continued to look straight at him, but out of the corner of his mouth he muttered to me, "Okay. You win." Nothing more was heard about that offer of hospitality.

A few weeks later Eisenhower attempted to make, through Zhukov, an even friendlier gesture to Red Army personnel in Germany. Eisenhower, like President Truman, was amazed by the Soviet Government's use of Allied occupation currency to pay the accumulated back pay of Red Army soldiers in Germany. This paper money was not negotiable in Russia so the troops had to spend it before going back home. As the Soviet forces under Zhukov numbered some three million troops then, this neat capitalistic device saved the Communist government hundreds of millions of rubles at the expense of Russian soldiers, many of whom had not been paid at all during the last three years of the war. Upon inquiry, Eisenhower learned that the Red Army had no real equivalent of the American Post Exchanges, so that few Russian soldiers possessed even such trifles as cheap fountain pens, and they were offering ridiculous prices for watches and other items which were available at our PX at wholesale cost. Our G.I.s could not be expected to ignore such an opportunity for quick profits, and Eisenhower said to me, "This profiteering is no way to win friends!" He went on to explain that the PX could lay in enough stock to provide limited supplies for the Soviet garrison in Berlin, and he asked, "Wouldn't it be a good idea to offer the Red Army limited shopping privileges at our PX?"

The General's suggestion reminded me of an incident which I related to him. I told him how a Soviet staff major appeared at our Berlin office one morning seeking penicillin for a senior Russian commander afflicted with syphilis. Penicillin was then the latest wonder drug and it was in very short supply. The major produced one hundred thousand occupation marks, which he said he had been authorized to pay for the necessary dosage. That paper money, which the Soviet Government had printed on its separate set of U. S. Treasury plates, was the equivalent of ten thousand dollars in the occupation currency then being used in Germany by Allied personnel. But when we politely declined payment and handed over the penicillin as a token of good will, the Soviet major was not at all pleased. Apparently his pride was hurt. Eisenhower listened to this tale and commented that he thought Zhukov would be more sensible. However, when Eisenhower made his PX offer to Zhukov, the Soviet Marshal curtly rejected the proposal. The Soviet Government had accepted many billions of dollars worth of Lend-Lease supplies from the United States, but Zhukov apparently considered Eisenhower's offer to be of a different sort.

At the beginning of our work at OMGUS, neither Clay nor I had any precedent to guide us in our assorted German, French, and Russian problems. We had to improvise as we went along. Clay's attitude was that of a highly trained Army engineer whose experience in war production had taught him what marvels can be performed by modern technology. Although the General expected to spend only a few months in Germany, until civilian agencies were ready to take over, he tackled the job of organizing the American zone with the same crisp efficiency that he had demonstrated the previous year at Cherbourg, when in three weeks he removed the bottlenecks which clogged that French port.

When I was notified in Washington that Clay had been appointed deputy military governor of our occupation zone, I was rather dismayed to learn that he knew virtually nothing about Germany. But I discovered in Berlin that Clay had much more valuable knowledge than that. In addition to his technical skills, Clay had political know-how. Information about Germany's history, its former financial and industrial ramifications, its prewar personalities and so forth, might merely have cluttered the mind of a deputy military governor. The war had so completely disarranged everything in Europe that many past events were irrelevant. But the ability to interpret ambiguous regulations, to avoid paper roadblocks, to persuade obstinate officials—these universally useful political talents were bred in Clay's bones and nurtured in his childhood. I gradually found out that Lucius Clay is a member of one of the most renowned political families of the South, a great-grandnephew of the statesman Henry Clay. The General's father had been a senator from Georgia and the son had lived from early boyhood in Washington's higher political atmosphere, even including service as a page boy in the United States Senate.

As an example of Clay's political sagacity, I recall an incident which occurred in January 1948 when he and I were summoned to Washington to testify before a congressional committee on appropriations. One evening we were invited to a dinner where Eisenhower also was a guest and he asked us to drive back with him to his headquarters at Fort Myer. Clay and I thought that the General wanted to talk more about Germany, but his mind was full of another subject. Eisenhower was nearing the end of his period as Army Chief of Staff, and he told us that he had mailed a letter that day in reply to a publisher who was urging him to become the Democratic candidate for the presidency. Eisenhower said he never had spent so much time on a letter, that he had drafted this one at least twenty-five times. Everybody expected that year that Governor Thomas E. Dewey of New York was sure to be elected, that the Democrats did not have a chance. When Eisenhower read his letter to us, with comments, it was clear that he was leaving sizable loopholes for a different response at a more favorable time. Eisenhower was not asking advice from Clay or me on domestic politics; he just wanted to unburden himself to sympathetic listeners who he knew could be trusted to keep their mouths shut. After we left Eisenhower that night, Clay shrewdly pointed out that Ike was a Republican, whether he realized it or not, and that if Dewey failed to be elected, Ike was the logical candidate next time. Four years later, Clay took the lead in pressing Eisenhower to run for President on the Republican ticket. Politics never tempted Lucius Clay to abandon his own Army career, but his familiarity with the inner workings of Washington was a prime asset in his German assignment, proving at least as useful as any acquaintance with prewar Germany might have been.

Although "supreme authority" in the American zone was wielded first by Eisenhower and then by McNarney, both of them delegated most political and economic matters to OMGUS, that is, to Clay. This division of military and civil duties functioned well so long as Eisenhower remained in Frankfurt, but it suffered severe strains after McNarney took over. McNarney's combat record was impressive and his handling of the American garrison was unexceptionable, but he lacked the flair for politics which distinguished both Eisenhower and Clay, and he seemed to take little interest in German political affairs. So, after about six months of friction with Frankfurt, Clay wrote a letter to McNarney in June 1946 stating that he intended to retire from the Army. McNarney's reply did not indicate much regret at the prospect, but by that time I was convinced that Clay was indispensable. I knew that Clay would resent any interference from me in this matter between Army officers, but I secretly sent word of the situation to Secretary of State Byrnes. Without revealing his knowledge of the personal equation involved, Byrnes tactfully reassured Clay, thus bridging that administrative rift for the time being.

My own status in the occupation hierarchy was more independent of the Army than Clay's. I never was subject to the Army chain of command, as I would have been in uniform. As representatives of the State Department in Germany, my staff and I were directed only by our own Department. My position was established by international treaty, as was also the position of the Russian, British, and French political advisers. But the other countries exercised a firmer control of their military, through civilian agencies such as their Foreign Offices, than did the Americans. During the first years of OMGUS, responsibility for the American occupation was shared by the State Department and the Defense Department. It was a dangerously cumbersome arrangement and would never have functioned at all if the representatives of State and Defense had not been able to establish the closest accord.

Fortunately Clay and I enjoyed mutal confidence from the outset. The General realized that my devotion to the State Department was comparable to his loyalty to the Army and we respected each other's views even when we did not accept them. We appreciated that our knowledge and experiences were complementary and we tolerated each other's defects and idiosyncrasies. Ours was the kind of give-and-take relationship which all intergovernmental associations ought to be, but frequently are not. Our harmonious partnership eliminated disputes between State and Defense which might have become a serious defect in the American occupation machinery. Clay and I rarely had disagreements, but when they did occur we tried to settle them ourselves without submission to Washington for prolonged discussions and negotiations, and they never came out in the open.

In his book *Decision in Germany*, published in 1950, Clay was kind enough to say that he could not recall a single major issue upon which he and I differed. But I can recall one which I, at least, considered an important issue. It was my contention, which Clay accepted, that the State Department, as the President's chief instrument for foreign affairs, must be in a position to think and act independently. It was therefore imperative, I maintained, that my staff and I should be able to communicate in our own code with the State Department. I pointed out that the British, French, and Soviet diplomatic officers in Germany reported privately to their respective Foreign Offices, and that the State Department's representatives must have the same privilege. But this business of our using a separate code distressed Clay at times, as it had the American officers in Eisenhower's commands in Africa and later in SHAEF. Even when I had access to military secrets in active theaters of war, I had insisted upon communicating in code with the State Department, but it had been a constant struggle to maintain that privilege. Clay never did become fully reconciled to independent reports from me, and especially from my staff, about matters for which he was responsible.

As soon as Clay and I were settled in Berlin, we made a practice of talking things over at least once a day when both of us were in the city. One morning, after I thought our procedure was well established, Clay walked into my office with a letter from an officer friend on General MacArthur's staff in Tokyo. According to the letter, MacArthur also had challenged the State Department's code privilege, and moreover had settled it in characteristic fashion. Since MacArthur's headquarters controlled all physical communications in Japan, it so happened that code messages from representatives of the State Department often "got lost" or were delayed. Clay told me that he was uncomfortable about the separate code messages to Washington dispatched from my office in Berlin, and thought the practice should be discontinued. I replied that in that case I would urgently recommend closing down the Department of State office completely, giving the military a free hand, and after a few hours I sent over to Clay's office a draft telegram recommending that action. Later, over a cup of coffee, we agreed to drop the matter. Our personal relations once again enabled us to arrive at an amicable solution on the spot.

Despite all the handicaps imposed upon OMGUS, Americans nevertheless managed in a short time to bring order out of chaos in our zone. This is all the more remarkable when it is recalled that not one of our top-ranking American officers could speak German. It is no mean feat to govern a country whose language you do not know. But the docility of the Germans and their eagerness to get back to work were a great help to us, and so was the comparatively dispassionate attitude of our people toward their recent enemies. Geography had saved the United States from such Nazi atrocities as the massacres in Russia, the aerial bombardments in Britain, and the imposition of forced labor upon French men and women. Americans had relatively few bitter memories and so could approach the reconstruction of our zone in a businesslike manner. However, victorious armies inevitably expect certain perquisites, and for some time our soldiers felt justified in "liberating" anything they could transport. The disorder and destruction of war seem to change most men's attitude regarding private ownership, so that the sanctity of personal property appears unimportant under the circumstances. But the Germans in our zone were partly protected by Clay's deep feeling about what had occurred in his own state of Georgia after the American Civil War. Clay discouraged looting and did everything in his power to control the activities of "carpetbaggers" intent upon making exorbitant profit out of Germany's defeat.

Even some high-ranking Americans developed peculiar twists in their attitude toward German possessions. I remember in particular one officer whom I invited to dinner soon after I was settled in Berlin. American troops in Germany were quartered in tents, Quonset huts, and other barrack constructions, but German residences had been commandeered for most of our officers and civilian staffs. I was lucky enough to have assigned to me a pleasant but unpretentious house with a small garden. Among the furnishings was an upholstered chair which my officer guest found agreeably comfortable. After lounging in it for an hour after dinner, he said to me, "The chairs in my house are too stiff. I need this chair to put next to my reading lamp." I thought he was merely making conversation, so I smiled amiably. But the next day his aide appeared at my residence, saying that his superior had instructed him to collect the upholstered chair. I sent the aide away empty-handed, with a verbal message for his chief which probably was toned down before delivery. To be sure, the requisitioned furniture in my official residence did not belong to me, but neither did it belong to my appreciative guest.

Another startling idea about how to dispose of German property was presented to me in the earliest occupation days. A very high-ranking American officer came to my office to inform me privately that the Army had just captured a huge cache of German gold bars. Nobody knew how large the treasure was because the bars had not yet been counted. "Do you see any objection to distributing some of this gold among the Americans chiefly responsible for defeating Germany?" my caller inquired. He explained that top British commanders in SHAEF expected to be rewarded with large cash bonuses, in accordance with ancient British custom. "The American Government has no such sensible tradition," my caller went on to say, "but can't some of us quietly arrange our own bonuses?" I tried to laugh off his proposal, but the officer was not joking. He dropped the idea only when I convinced him that Eisenhower would be furious if he learned that such a scheme had even been suggested. So far as I know, all the gold bars we captured were turned over to the proper Washington agencies.

A few OMGUS officers, when they found themselves holding powers of life and death over Germans, could not resist the temptation to play God. One day a senior American medical officer dropped into my Berlin office and said he wanted to show me something if I could spare an hour. We drove to an American internment camp in the suburbs, where the occupants were "little Nazis" awaiting classification. These were former party members who had held insignificant jobs in the party organization, including even charwomen in Nazi offices. It should be remembered that when U.S. forces moved into Germany, their directives prescribed thirty-three automatic arrest categories, mostly on account of membership, high or low, in a Nazi organization, of which there were that many. The commandant of the camp we were inspecting was a serious young American officer who showed us around conscientiously. I was startled to see that our prisoners were almost as weak and emaciated as those I had observed in Nazi prison camps. The youthful commandant calmly told us that he had deliberately kept the inmates on starvation diet, explaining, "These Nazis are getting a dose of their own medicine." He so obviously believed that he was behaving correctly that we did not discuss the matter with him. After we left, the medical director asked me, "Does that camp represent American policy in Germany?" I replied that of course it was contrary to our policy, and the situation would be quickly corrected. When I described the camp's conditions to Clay, he quietly transferred the grim young officer to a post for which he was better suited. On another occasion we were informed that a Nazi torture camp, equipped with devices to extort confessions, was still operating under American auspices. A zealous American Intelligence officer had found out how effectively Nazi devices persuaded Nazis to confess their own misdeeds, and he was chagrined when ordered to close down this establishment.

Sometimes American officers ventured to openly question the wisdom of directives from Washington. Most prominent of these outspoken officers was General George S. Patton, who was appointed military governor of Bavaria after the surrender. In two separate talks which we had together, Patton asked whether I thought he had fought his last battle. He inquired, with a gleam in his eye, whether there was any chance of going on to Moscow, which he said he could reach in thirty days, instead of waiting for the Russians to attack the United States when we were weak and reduced to two divisions. Patton expressed this opinion to me privately, but throughout his career this brilliant commander could not desist from also making controversial remarks publicly.

At one press conference in Bavaria, Patton asserted that Military Government would get better results if it employed more former members of the Nazi party in administrative jobs and as skilled workmen. One of the correspondents, detecting an opening for a sensational news story, asked a loaded question: "After all, General, didn't most ordinary Nazis join their party in about the same way that Americans become Republicans or Democrats?" The unsuspecting Patton replied, "Yes, that's about it." Within a few hours newspapers around the world were reporting: "American General Says Nazis Are Just Like

Republicans and Democrats!" The public was in no mood then to believe that any kind of Nazis could be as innocuous as Republicans and Democrats, and Eisenhower decided he could not again overlook Patton's verbal indiscretions, as he had done several times during the war. This decision was extremely difficult for Eisenhower because Patton was not only a celebrated combat officer but also a personal friend of long standing.

I happened to be in Bavaria when this incident occurred, and Patton invited me to luncheon at his headquarters near Munich in the large country home which formerly had belonged to Uxmann, the publisher of Hitler's *Mein Kampf.* I arrived a little early and talked with the General in his study while a Polish artist was painting his portrait. Afterwards we had lunch and then went to his office for a business conversation, where we were interrupted by Patton's efficient WAC secretary who announced an urgent telephone call from Frankfurt; General Smith, Eisenhower's Chief of Staff, was on the line. There was no love lost between Smith and Patton, and the latter suspected trouble. Pointing to the extension telephone, he said to me, "Listen to what the lying SOB will say." I did not know that the decision had been taken to relieve Patton of his command until I heard Smith performing his duty as tactfully as possible. Patton vigorously pantomimed for my benefit his scornful reactions to Smith's placatory remarks. Patton was transferred immediately to the Frankfurt area to work on an historical assignment, where he maintained a disciplined and for him unnatural public silence until his death a few weeks later in a traffic accident.

One constructive feature of JCS 1067 was its mandate to encourage anti-Nazi political activity among Germans in the American zone. Germany's unconditional surrender left Europe's largest country without any government of its own, federal, state, or local. Germany emerged from the war split up into six distinct pieces, the American, British, Russian and French zones, and two huge areas annexed by Russia and Poland. The American directive recommended that democratic government should be stimulated first in local communities, then expanded to wider areas. I was particularly hopeful about Bavaria, where I had lived for almost four years in the 1920s, and which was the only state which remained intact and entirely within our zone. By encouraging proper procedures in Bavaria, we might set a model for all Germany. So I traveled early and often to Munich, the capital city.

One old acquaintance there whom I thoroughly trusted was Anton Pfeiffer, who had been secretary of the anti-Nazi Bavarian People's Party before the war. From captured German records, we knew that Pfeiffer had been consistently anti-Nazi ever since. On one of my visits to Munich I invited Pfeiffer to dinner and he asked if he might bring along another local politician, Fritz Schaeffer, whom anti-Nazis in Bavaria had recently selected as their Deputy Minister-President. The three of us had an agreeable discussion and I was favorably impressed with Schaeffer. But early the next morning Pfeiffer telephoned in great agitation to tell me that a message had arrived from American headquarters in Frankfurt ordering the dismissal of Schaeffer on grounds that he was a pro-Nazi reactionary. I had difficulty persuading my old friend that I was not responsible for this action, that it was all news to me.

It was not until I returned to Berlin that I was able to find out that Schaeffer's dismissal had been ordered in Frankfurt without consulting Clay or the State Department. A subordinate Civil Affairs officer, who had been recruited from the history department of an American college, was convinced that Bavaria should be governed by the Social Democrats, notwithstanding that this socialist party had always been a small minority group in this predominantly Catholic state. Schaeffer, as a leader of the People's Party, opposed the Social Democrats, so the American professor considered him pro-Nazi and prevailed upon Major General Clarence L. Adcock, chief of G-5, to dismiss Schaeffer. The embarrassing mixup had the happy result, however, of fortifying the status of OMGUS thereafter. General Adcock was a friend of Clay's, a fellow Army engineer, and he shared Clay's views that G-5 should not attempt to compete with OMGUS or prescribe which of several anti-Nazi political parties should be supported by the Germans. As for the dismissed politician, Schaeffer, he became the first Finance Minister of the West German Government in 1949.

Eisenhower did not like Berlin and never stayed there longer than necessary. He was conscientious about studying the questions which arose and about making the considerable journey back and forth from Frankfurt to attend the sessions of the four-power Control Council, but his heart never was in the German occupation. His assignment as military governor was an anticlimax to his war years, and he regretted to see the separate zones become involved in wearisome jurisdictional disputes. Under the circumstances, Eisenhower was understandably happy to relinquish to his successors the administration of the American zone in Germany and to take up his new post in Washington as Army Chief of Staff.

About a year after Eisenhower's departure, Clay decided once more that he, too, wanted to get out of Germany. Clay and I were summoned home for consultation in November 1946, and Clay told me that he intended to apply for retirement from the Army when he reached Washington. But when we got there, Eisenhower informed

Clay privately that another post had been lined up for McNarney, and that Clay could expect soon to become military governor, the "supreme authority" for our zone in Germany. This prospect induced Clay to remain in Berlin for two and a half more years—those difficult and dangerous years which produced the Soviet blockade of Berlin, the spectacular defeat of the blockade by the Western airlift, and the swift advance of West Germany along the road to independence.

TWENTY-TWO

DECEPTIVE VICTORY OF THE BERLIN AIRLIFT (1949)

This chapter describes one of the strangest episodes in the foreign relations of the United States. It tells how the American people, for the first time in their history, formed a virtual alliance with the German people. The relationship prevailing today between Americans and Germans would have been unthinkable during the war against Nazi Germany. Yet the present German-American association probably would have been impossible without that war.

The evolution of the West German state, and of American relations to it, were a totally unforeseen result of the peacemaking after World War II. All through that war there was continuous discussion in Washington about the kind of peace which would come after the defeat of the Nazis. The peace planners of the Roosevelt administration, following the Presidents' lead, committed themselves to a reorganization of Europe under the auspices of Soviet Russia, Great Britain, and the United States. The planners assumed that the Big Three would eventually agree on an imposed peace for Germany. That was the prospect for Europe, foreshadowed by the Tehran and Yalta Conferences during the war.

There has been much speculation over what Roosevelt might have accomplished if he had lived to attend the third Big Three meeting, the Potsdam Conference in 1945. It is my personal feeling that Roosevelt's presence at Potsdam would have made little difference. By that time the enormous gap between Soviet and American ideas about Europe could no longer be ignored by any American President. It was at Potsdam that I suddenly realized that a peace treaty for Germany in the traditional sense might not be possible. This thought came to me at one plenary session after I listened to Stalin's extraordinarily frank revelations of his plans for eastern Europe. If the Big Three could not agree upon a German settlement, then Germany would become a permanent cause of conflict among the conquerors. It was an ominous idea.

However, the Potsdam Protocol made more concessions to our point of view than might have been expected. American slogan-makers wrote into the Protocol what they called the Four D's—Demilitarization, Denazification, Decentralization and Democratization. These mouth-filling words expressed lofty objectives, but lent themselves to a wide range of interpretations. But the most important portions of the agreement were not the propaganda features designed to attract public attention. The chief practical value of the Protocol was the agreement to treat Germany as an economic unit. I do not know why Stalin personally approved that provision, since the Russians never did apply it, but perhaps he anticipated the United States would soon lose interest in Germany, so the agreement would not be implemented. At any rate, the agreement did provide a basis for constructive action in the Western occupation zones.

The world's yearning for peace influenced American policy from the moment the war ended, and nobody worked more earnestly for this than Secretary of State Byrnes. Like many Americans before and since, Byrnes hoped that he could succeed with the Russians where routine diplomacy might fail. Byrnes' negotiating skill in domestic matters was a Washington legend. When President Truman made Byrnes his Secretary of State, the Department presented him with peace plans of considerable originality. One notable innovation was the decision to conclude treaties first with the lesser enemies, postponing the German treaty. This arrangement was based on the theory that peacemaking failures after the First World War resulted largely from the misguided attempt to settle everything simultaneously at the Versailles Conference in 1919. The victorious powers undertook there to resolve, in one all-inclusive assembly, every issue arising from the war, including creation of a League of Nations. The negotiators after World War II sought to avoid previous mistakes by dividing the peacemaking into many portions. The first stage, well started before the war ended, was to set up the United Nations as successor to the League of Nations. Then, at Potsdam, it was agreed to postpone consideration of a treaty for Germany until peace was concluded with Italy, Hungary, Bulgaria and Romania. At that time Germany had no central government of any kind, and some central government had to be organized before negotiations could begin.

To direct the peacemaking, the Big Three at Potsdam established a Council of Foreign Ministers with offices and staff at London. The members of this council represented the same five governments which were permanent members of the Security Council of the United Nations—Russia, Britain, the United States, France and China. A few weeks after Potsdam, when the excitement about the sudden ending of the Pacific War subsided, the council met in London to set the stage for Peace Conference Number One. Secretary Byrnes asked Clay and me to attend as consultants on German questions.

This meeting provided startling evidence of the disunity among Germany's conquerors. The business before the council was relatively simple: to fix a time and place for the preliminary conference, and to decide which governments should participate in it. But agreement even on this procedural question proved impossible. The Soviet Foreign Minister, V. M. Molotov, insisted upon debarring France, on legalistic grounds, from any share in negotiations with Bulgaria, Romania and Hungary. Molotov argued that the French Government dropped out of the war more than a year before those three countries became belligerents. The British Foreign Secretary, Ernest Bevin, persuasively urged that no mere technicality should debar the French from participation in the discussions, and Secretary Byrnes agreed. When Molotov would not yield, the council adjourned in confusion. Peacemaking thus came to an abrupt halt before it even got started, and the Russians seemed quite content with the impasse. Delayed peacemaking was an advantage to Moscow, enabling the Kremlin to consolidate its vast territorial acquisitions and spheres of influence in eastern Europe and Asia.

After this head-on collision in London in September 1945, peace negotiations marked time until Secretary Byrnes assumed the initiative and flew to Moscow in December. Stopping off briefly in Berlin en route to Russia, the Secretary told us how he had arranged this meeting. While Byrnes was thinking about how to break the diplomatic deadlock, Charles E. Bohlen, the State Department's Russian expert, suggested that if the Council of Foreign Ministers would meet in Moscow, Byrnes would have opportunity there to talk with Stalin, who had intervened personally to break previous deadlocks. Byrnes decided to cable directly to Molotov to ask if the Soviet Government would invite the council to meet there. This was not conventional diplomacy; embassies normally put out feelers first. But Byrnes was not a professional diplomat, and he was in a hurry. It had been agreed at Potsdam that the council would meet at least every three months, and the next council meeting was almost due. In order to sidetrack the controversial French issue, Byrnes proposed that the Moscow meeting be limited to the Big Three. Molotov promptly issued the invitations, and Byrnes and the British Foreign Secretary flew to Moscow, where they soon arranged to continue the peace talks.

However, that Moscow meeting got Byrnes into serious trouble with Truman, who happened to be on vacation in Florida when the resumption of peace negotiations was being improvised. When the results of these Big Three talks were announced, they won wide-spread public approval, but it soon became known that Byrnes' conduct of this affair had deeply disturbed the President. Truman thought that Byrnes had "appeased" Stalin by yielding on some of the Soviet demands which had been rejected at London, and also that the Secretary had made several decisions without consulting the President.

There can be no doubt that Truman and Byrnes held different views at that time concerning Roosevelt's Grand Design. FDR had personally confided to Byrnes the task of following through with the Russians, and the South Carolinian made a valiant attempt to reconcile irreconcilable objectives. But Truman, although he had publicly undertaken to honor all of FDR's commitments, never did feel responsible for the Grand Design. Roosevelt had not even tried to arouse Truman's enthusiasm for this concept when the latter was Vice President. And at Potsdam, Truman's distrust of the Russians became a very personal matter. Accordingly, soon after Byrnes returned from Moscow, Washington correspondents printed stories (evidently inspired) that the President no longer retained his original confidence in the judgment of his Secretary of State. But Byrnes stayed on the job despite this semi-public expression of little confidence. Byrnes was keenly aware that America's foreign affairs were more important than ever before, and that the State Department needed firm guidance.

Part of the Grand Design was to overcome Russian distrust of the Western powers. With this in mind during his visit to Moscow, Byrnes remarked to Stalin that Germany's principal conquerors could feel more secure if they signed a long-term pact to keep the Germans disarmed. The Secretary suggested a twenty-five-year treaty, and Stalin replied, "If you propose such a pact, I will support it." Following up this informal talk, Byrnes formally proposed a treaty at a meeting of the Council of Foreign Ministers in Paris in May 1946. When Molotov objected that twenty-five years was not long enough, Byrnes offhandedly said, "Then make if forty!"—a proposal which, if accepted, would have guaranteed German disarmament until 1986. But instead of supporting an agreement so advantageous from Moscow's viewpoint, Molotov torpedoed it by insisting upon crippling amendments.

While this demilitarization proposal was being discussed, I explained to a staff meeting in Berlin how the Russian amendments would undermine the pact. According to my notes on that talk, I concluded: "The United States, I think, should adhere to its present position and insist that the pact be kept simple and confined to its one basic purpose—to keep Germany incapable of waging war." The willingness of Americans at that time to disarm Germany was apparent in the attitude of my audience. No one present questioned my conclusion. A number of American staff officers were there, but not one of them pointed out that Germany should be considered a potential military ally of the United States. A demilitarized Germany would have created a vacuum in the center of Europe. It would have neutralized what has since become western Europe's most important country —the Federal Republic of Germany. It would have given Soviet Russia much stronger influence in Germany than it possesses today. Why did Stalin and his advisers, led by Molotov, miss this rare opportunity? The evidence seems to indicate that they were greedy. They sought not only to disarm Germany, but to render that country economically impotent.

The Russians were not alone in trying to retard German economic recovery. At that same meeting of the Council of Foreign Ministers in May 1946, the French Government proposed that Germany's richest industrial region, the Ruhr, should be detached and placed under international control. During the war and even at the Potsdam Conference, some Americans favored an internationalized Ruhr, but by 1946 this plan conflicted with the American program for making Germany self-supporting. Our economists at OMGUS had marshaled impressive statistics which proved that Germany could not possibly organize an industrial revival without the skilled workers and the coal and iron of the Ruhr.

Yet, discussing this matter with Byrnes and his staff in Paris, we agreed that Washington could not dismiss the French proposal summarily. Nazi atrocities had been so monstrous, prolonged and extensive, that fear of German recovery was deep throughout Europe. With feeling against Germany so bitter, we realized that amputation of the Rhur would have wide popular appeal and that we must proceed carefully in order to keep this area in the German economy. The American position was further embarrassed because two Presidents, Roosevelt and Truman, at the Yalta and Potsdam Conferences, had condoned absorption by Russia and Poland of vast German territories in eastern Europe. Under these circumstances, the United States now could scarcely reject outright France's proposal for equivalent amputations in the west.

After studying the problem from every angle, Byrnes' advisers came up with an adroit scheme. Byrnes agreed to fly to Stuttgart, Germany, in September to address a scheduled gathering of American military government administrators. In his speech, the Secretary of State raised doubts about the virtual annexations of territories which had taken place in eastern Germany. Byrnes reminded everybody that permanent Russian and Polish control of those areas had not yet been confirmed, because the Potsdam Protocol provided that Germany's boundaries would not be finally fixed until the peace treaty was signed. This Stuttgart meeting, over which I presided at Clay's request, attracted international attention. As we anticipated, the news reports emphasized the status of German territories in the east, and this diverted pressures for amputations in the west.

This gathering had particular significance because German officials were invited to Stuttgart to meet with Americans in a public place for the first time since the surrender. As an added gesture, Byrnes included in the first draft of his speech a pledge that the United States would keep armed forces in Germany as long as any other occupant did. However, Byrnes felt that this pledge of indefinite American military occupation might be going too far, and he deleted it. But Clay persuaded the Secretary to reinsert it, saying, "We can't expect the Germans to work all-out unless they have some assurance that their country will survive. The pledge of American troops serves that purpose."

From the very beginning, each of the occupying powers had different ideas about how Germany should be administered. The British decided very soon after Potsdam that Germany probably was permanently divided between East and West, and they proposed then that the United States and France cooperate with them in the three Western zones. But the French Government was adamant in opposing the Potsdam agreement to treat Germany as an economic unit. Several of my French friends told me privately that they were in favor of joint economic management of all occupation zones, and many Frenchmen working with us in Berlin were sympathetic. But they felt that any move to reunify Germany was abhorrent to French voters. So every time the British or Americans suggested fresh ideas for nationwide agencies in Germany to operate railways, power grids, and the like, the French Government would invoke its unique veto to block our plans. The Russians could sit back and let the French carry this ball for them.

Thus thwarted in our endeavors to administer Germany efficiently, Americans in military government began to consider a revised version of a recommendation which Eisenhower had made. The Supreme Commander had urged the retention of a SHAEF type of organization to handle the occupation problems. More than once while he was military governor of the American zone, the General ruefully remarked that jurisdictional conflicts might have been avoided if this had been done. Along similar lines, a plan now evolved for an economic merger of the American and British zones. Because of French intransigence, this seemed the most hopeful immediate prospect, but in order not to close the door on French and Russian cooperation, we again urged that all four occupying powers join in an economic merger.

This invitation was broadcast by Byrnes just one year after the Potsdam Conference, and the Secretary of State announced that only the

British Government had indicated willingness to accept this proposal. In Berlin, we were instructed to repeat the invitation at a meeting of the Allied Control Council, and this was done. But Paris and Moscow denounced our plan, and so it came about that the Potsdam provision for administering Germany as an economic unit was applicable in only two of the four occupation zones. The resulting American-British merger—called Bizonia—was officially approved on July 30, 1946.

I doubt whether anyone in Germany realized at that time the full significance of Bizonia. Our staff at OMGUS was pleased with the arrangement because we thought it would make the American share of the occupation more efficient and less costly, but none of us foresaw what a vital role Bizonia would have in Europe. Bizonia really laid the foundation for western Europe's most powerful state, West Germany, destined to make possible a vigorous non-Communist Europe. I think the Soviet Government also failed to grasp immediately the full importance of Bizonia, because it was not until several months later that the Russians began their determined effort to obstruct this new administration in Germany.

Throughout 1946 Allied peacemakers had to juggle several balls at once, with almost continuous meetings of one kind or another in European capitals. Whenever matters affecting Germany came up at London, Paris or New York sessions, Clay and I were summoned from Berlin as consultants to the Secretary of State, and we appeared so frequently at these various meetings that members of Byrnes' staff included us with themselves as "riders on the peace circuit."

The lesser peace treaties were debated in Paris from July 29 to October 15, 1946, and as things finally worked out, those sessions constituted the only formal European Peace Conference of World War II. All the nations which had fought on the winning side of the war were represented, and so were the four minor enemy countries. These Paris agreements were then referred for approval to the next meeting of the Council of Foreign Ministers, held in New York from November 4 to December 11. Byrnes presided at this council meeting, to which Clay and I were summoned, and Byrnes almost singlehandedly pushed through acceptance when another deadlock threatened. But of course the treaties were not effective until confirmed by the U. S. Senate and the other governments. The Senate debated at length, especially about the Italian treaty, which did not satisfy some Italian-American groups. American confirmation did not come until June 5, 1947, more than two years after the Nazi surrender. Even this belated settlement could not have been reached if the relatively simple claims against Italy, Hungary, Bulgaria and Romania had not been separated from the massive German issues.

On January 20, 1947, six weeks after Byrnes finished his work on the lesser peace treaties, he left his post as Secretary of State. Many months earlier President Truman had secretly asked the wartime Chief of Staff of the Army, General George Catlett Marshall, to become his Secretary of State as soon as Byrnes completed the minor peace treaties. All through 1946, the President and Byrnes lacked the mutual confidence which should prevail between the man in the White House and his chief foreign affairs adviser. For that reason, a change in the State Department was advisable, but it came at a very difficult moment for Marshall. For almost a decade, this five-star general had supervised the construction of America's war machine and had directed its battle campaigns around the world. The end of the war had not permitted him to relax, for he had to preside then over the hasty demobilization which he sadly described as "the disintegration of America's military power." Next, at President Truman's request, Marshall undertook to check the civil war between Generalissimo Chiang Kai-shek and the Chinese Communists. Marshall's assignment in the Far East resulted in many months of disappointments and frustrations. Nevertheless, Truman persuaded the conscientious soldier to take charge of the Department of State just as he was completing his China assignment. The General took on this formidable new job after having been completely out of touch with European affairs for many months.

The appointment of Marshall as Secretary of State startled Washington, because American tradition has not favored naming a professional soldier for the highest foreign policy post; several Washington commentators deplored what they called the "military takeover." General MacArthur already was exercising supreme authority in Japan and Korea; General Mark Clark was the chief American representative in Austria; General Clay was the key figure in Germany, about to become military governor; General Smith was Ambassador to Moscow; Admiral Alan G. Kirk was Ambassador to Belgium; and now General Marshall had become Secretary of State. Personally, I appreciated why President Truman felt justified in placing so many military men in important posts abroad. I knew how difficult it had been to get support from Congress for the State Department, how few qualified men our Foreign Service had, and how thin these good ones were spread. Still, there was no denying that when Marshall flew to Moscow a few days after assuming his post as Secretary of State, he was inadequately prepared to direct negotiations for a German peace treaty. The formal discussions opened on March 10, 1947, and the new Secretary had to begin his duties in an important and conspicuous position, heading the large American delegation at the Soviet capital.

This was not my first visit to Moscow. I had spent a fortnight there less than a year before as a guest of the American ambassador. Mrs.

Lucius Clay also was there then as a guest of Ambassador and Mrs. Bedell Smith, and she and I tried to see every phase of Soviet life. At that time the Russians banned tourists altogether and admitted very few official guests or journalists. The people in Moscow were living under postwar conditions not much better than conditions in Berlin, but the Russians had won the war and were in better spirit than the Germans. Everyone was extremely friendly to us wherever we went.

When I returned to Moscow to attend the discussions on the German peace treaty, there seemed to be very little material improvement in the city, at least on the surface. But on this trip I was not in Moscow for sight-seeing. The staffs of all the delegations to the conference were kept busy day and night—especially at night. It is an old Russian custom to work at night, and some of our subcommittee meetings did not break up until dawn. Although the American delegation was rather short on clerks and stenographers, we had plenty of V.I.P.'s. In fact, we had so many generals, ambassadors, and consultants that Ambassador Smith set up improvised desks in every cubbyhole of his official residence.

As the conference got under way, Marshall performed under severe handicaps. This probably was the only occasion when the General, celebrated for his retentive memory, ever was in such an embarrassing position. He had been rushed to Moscow before he had time to master the details of European peacemaking, and it must have been galling to his pride to lead debates in which it was evident to everybody that he was unfamiliar with relevant facts. However, it is unlikely that any Secretary of State could have accomplished more at the 1947 Moscow Conference, because by this time the cold war was being fought openly. Truman's misgivings about the Russians had hardened into certainties, as a result of Stalin's behavior, and the President was in no mood to concede anything. The Soviet Government, for its part, finally put its German cards on the table at the Moscow Conference, leaving no doubt that Russia's goals were a direct threat to Anglo-American objectives in Germany. The Russians frankly revealed their confidence that they could thwart Western plans for Germany's economic recovery, and thereby could jeopardize rehabilitation of non-Communist Europe.

The immediate focus of Soviet-Western conflict was Greece, where civil war was raging between Greek pro- and anti-Communists. Churchill, when he was Prime Minister, had secretly arranged with Stalin that Greece should be included in a British sphere of influence, but this agreement broke down when Moscow indirectly began to help the Greek Communists. The Labor Government in London, whose leaders had long urged reduction of imperial obligations, thereupon announced that Britain could no longer afford to underwrite Greek and Turkish anti-Communists.

This abdication inspired Truman's first major challenge to Communist expansion. On March 12, when the Moscow Conference was getting started, the President asked Congress to take over, in effect, British obligations in Greece and Turkey. After due deliberation, Congress agreed to supply limited aid for three months—and that was the beginning of the world-wide "mutual assistance" obligations which are carried today by the United States.

The Moscow Conference lasted for almost six weeks, as long as there was any chance of partial agreement, and the delegates patiently plowed through all the questions at issue. Detailed papers on more than thirty German problems had been prepared by Clay's staff and mine in Berlin. The State Department had prepared other detailed papers in Washington. John Foster Dulles, representing the Republican party in our delegation, was assigned conspicuous tasks, partly because of his ability but also because Washington wanted to convey the impression that American foreign policy was bipartisan. Specialists from Great Britain and France had likewise spared no efforts to cover every German problem thoroughly. But the three Western powers sometimes disagreed among themselves, and the Russians invariably came up with objections, amendments, and counterproposals. In a private talk with Marshall, Stalin cheerfully observed, "These are only the first skirmishes of reconnaissance forces on the German question."

But we could not view the outcome so placidly. The conference was such a complete failure that we departed from Moscow in mid-April with very sober thoughts indeed, aware that from now onward all our economic plans for Germany would encounter relentless Soviet opposition. We had not expected to reach full agreement on a German peace treaty at this initial meeting, but neither did we suspect that an all-inclusive German peace treaty would remain uncompleted up to the time that this is written sixteen years later. It was the Moscow Conference of 1947, I believe, which really rang down the Iron Curtain.

Soviet-American relations deteriorated rapidly after the abortive Moscow Conference, and the cold war developed with bewildering speed. Ever since Potsdam, President Truman had no faith in the usefulness of conferences, and Secretary Marshall felt the same way. In a radio report delivered shortly after his return to Washington from Moscow, Marshall said: "The patient is sinking while the doctors deliberate." It was this belief that Europe was in desperate need—and might swallow Communism as a remedy for its critical condition—

which resulted in the recovery program which became known as the Marshall Plan.

The Moscow Conference has been called the "birthplace of the Marshall Plan," but the program actually was not launched until June 5, 1947, when Marshall was awarded an honorary degree at Harvard University's commencement exercises. The Secretary of State made a speech on that occasion inviting all European governments, regardless of ideology, to join with the United States in restoring Europe's prosperity. Marshall announced Americans might be willing to provide the necessary financing for a joint effort if European governments were prepared to cooperate. Of course this tremendous concept was not tossed off as a casual suggestion. Ever since the war, hundreds of specialists in many countries had been investigating the plight of Europeans. The basic principles behind the Marshall Plan can be traced back to many men, including Henry L. Stimson, John J. McCloy and Lewis Douglas, among the Americans, and a number of farsighted Britons and Europeans.

The responses to Marshall's speech at Harvard were not quite as spontaneous as they were made to seem. Thanks to diplomatic preliminaries, the vast enterprise got under way so smoothly that representatives of sixteen countries met in Paris from July 12 to September 22 to consider the program. Foreign Minister Molotov flew to Paris to represent Russia, and he could have embarrassed Washington if he had expressed polite interest in the Plan. Congress might have balked if asked at that time to appropriate money for the benefit of Communist countries. But Molotov denounced the Plan as another form of imperialism, and dramatically rejected the American offer not only for Russia but for all the war-ravaged Soviet satellites. The western European nations accepted the program, thus dividing Europe more sharply than ever. I have always believed that the Russians committed a major policy blunder at that meeting in Paris. Stalin and Molotov would have shown great astuteness if they had agreed to participate to some extent in the Marshall Plan, thereby obtaining American help for the Soviet bloc, or at least deflating American enthusiasm for an aid program which included Russia.

A week after the Marshall Plan countries met at Paris, Truman asked Congress for a special appropriation of half a billion dollars to tide over those nations until the program could be approved. Congress appropriated a somewhat smaller amount for this emergency period, and by December 19 a comprehensive report was ready. The President announced that the task of rehabilitation could be completed in four years with an expenditure of seventeen billion dollars, and he asked Congress to authorize that amount. After debating for three months, Congress finally approved the recommendations of its own experts, with unimportant cuts, and Truman signed the measure on April 3, 1948.

During the congressional debates on the Marshall Plan, relatively little attention was paid to Germany. American and European experts proposed a secondary status for the American and British occupation zones, although Clay and I contended from the outset that Bizonia was better prepared than any part of western Europe to use Marshall Plan funds effectively. Germany's production had fallen much lower than that of neighboring countries, and it was capable of rising much faster. Clay and I believed that the very success of the Plan itself might depend on prompt increase in German productivity. We asked our economists in Berlin to devise measures to assure Bizonia an adequate place in the Marshall Plan, and our staffs assembled a formidable collection of statistics to bolster Bizonia's claims. One fact which spoke loudly for us was that American taxpayers were heavily subsidizing the German occupation, and were being asked to assume a still larger share of the deficit. We were able to show that Bizonia could quickly become self-supporting if it received adequate help, and might even become the most important contributor to Europe's recovery.

The official name of the Marshall Plan became the European Recovery Program, and Congress established a wholly American agency, the Economic Cooperation Administration, to dispense the funds. However, the two top Americans named by the President to administer the program were less interested in Germany than Clay and I were. One of these officials was W. Averell Harriman, who had become Truman's principal adviser on foreign policy. Harriman, an ardent supporter of President Roosevelt's New Deal, had executed many important assignments for FDR. Before Pearl Harbor, Harriman had been in charge of Lend-Lease missions to Britain and Russia. For three years he had served as wartime Ambassador at Moscow, and then he became Ambassador at London. After the war Harriman became Truman's Secretary of Commerce, from which post he organized European aid until the President appointed him representative in Paris of the Economic Cooperation Administration.

Paul G. Hoffman became administrator of the ECA with cabinet rank. Hoffman had been president of the Studebaker Corporation and was a Republican. His appointment was intended to win the support of big businessmen for the Marshall Plan, and to assure that the Plan would be administered without regard to party politics. Hoffman had been a supersalesman and he undertook now to "sell" the Marshall Plan both to Congress and to Europeans. He was impressed with the technological advances which had been made in the United States during the war, and his chief interest was that European industrialists should catch up with American "know-how." They did that very soon indeed.

A curious nonstop debate developed between the American administrations in Paris and in Berlin. The issue was how much Marshall Plan assistance should be given to the Western zones in Germany, and upon what terms. Harriman thought that Clay exaggerated the potential usefulness of Bizonia, and these two strong-minded men tangled in many a spirited argument. As a professional diplomat, I was supposed to suggest tactful compromises, but I felt as strongly on this subject as Clay. The curious aspect of this debate was that no Germans took part in it. It was agreed that the Western occupation zones should participate in the European Recovery Program only through their military governors. That arrangement proved a great deal more advantageous to the Germans than if they had represented their own country at that time. Germans could be certain of a hostile reception in any international gathering in 1947, and they were well content to have Americans plead their case.

Clay and I knew that we risked being labeled pro-Nazi in pressing for a larger German share of Marshall Plan funds—and we were. But Clay was not a man to be intimidated by unfair labels, and I was accustomed to criticism. In the end, Germany did receive substantial aid, although merely a fraction of what was allocated even to Italy. France got the largest share, with Britain second. The funds generally were dispensed as outright grants, but help for Germany came in the form of loans. As we had foreseen, Germany used very advantageously the aid which it received, and its Marshall Plan participation did much to revive the economy of Europe.

One great difficulty, however, was the inflated condition of German currency, a problem then still unsolved. At the time of the surrender, German finances had been utterly chaotic. The public debt was enormous and there was no central government to manipulate it. The Nazis had issued paper money so lavishly that their paper notes multiplied fourteen times during the war. The conquerors arranged to print special occupation currencies to meet their own expenses and pay their troops, but this temporary currency was of no help to the Germans; they were not supposed to use it.

Aware of this grave situation, Clay had persuaded Joseph M. Dodge, a prominent Detroit banker, to become his chief financial adviser in 1945, even before OMGUS was established in Berlin, and Dodge had directed many surveying and planning groups in Germany. Early in 1946 Dodge assembled a commission of eminent Americans to study German financial reorganization, and this commission accomplished wonders in getting cooperation from Russian, British and French consultants, assisted by German technicians. After ten weeks' study, these international experts recommended that new currency be issued, exchangeable for the old at one to ten; and that Germany's national debt be canceled, with reduced amounts apportioned among separate German states. The commission emphasized that these reforms should be introduced quickly, because inflation already was a dangerous threat.

Both Clay and I had strong personal feelings about inflation. I could never forget my experiences in Munich in the 1920s, when runaway inflation demoralized Germany's most useful citizens and launched the Nazi movement. Clay remembered his family's stories about what happened to them in Georgia after Confederate money became worthless. So Clay and I sent a continuous stream of reports to Washington urging prompt action on the Dodge commission's recommendations. We also brought up the subject at every conference we attended in every world capital. But innumerable departments and agencies in many countries were concerned with this matter, and delay was inevitable. Opposition was particularly strong in Paris and in Moscow.

During this waiting period, Americans and Britons in Berlin conceived the idea that we might be able to bypass France and Russia and introduce currency reforms in Bizonia alone. Jack Bennett, an able fiscal expert, devised a detailed program. But we realized that the Russians could make trouble if we issued new German banknotes without Soviet co-operation, especially in Berlin. The German metropolis had become an American showplace after Clay was appointed military governor and made his principal headquarters there. Time and again Clay and I reported to Washington that Western-backed currency would inspire more confidence than Soviet-backed currency, and that this would be particularly embarrassing to the Russians if two currencies circulated in Berlin.

As the years passed we were becoming increasingly conscious of our precarious position in Berlin, isolated deep within the Soviet zone, but our access arrangements served fairly well until 1948. The Western powers had exclusive use of one railway, on which they operated military trains; one main highway, reserved for convoys of personnel and supplies; and three air corridors. The famous German network of canals converged upon Berlin, and much heavy freight came by barge. When the first hints of a blockade appeared, we re-examined the precise status of all these transport arrangements. Our surveys reminded us that the only written agreement was the one made in September 1945 concerning air corridors. If the Russians chose to ignore verbal agreements, they could obstruct access to Berlin by land and water routes. We sent fresh warnings of this ominous situation to all the agencies concerned in Washington, London and Paris. We asked the American and British Governments for specific directives as to whether Bizonia should proceed with financial reforms and thus risk Soviet counteraction, and whether our troops should use force if necessary to resist a Russian blockade of Berlin. This urgent query was brought to the attention of our highest officials not merely once but several times.

It became evident that Washington policy-makers differed on this matter. A few Roosevelt disciples still clung to the wartime President's hope that the United States could work harmoniously with the Soviet Union. Some practical politicians felt that the currency reforms might be an unwarranted provocation to the Russians; that it would be better to "let the Nazis stew in their own juice" than to antagonize the Russians by assisting Germans. Many men in the Pentagon regarded Berlin as a purely military problem. According to their reasoning, Berlin was "indefensible" because Russian ground forces could overpower the city with ease.

German questions reached a climax when the Council of Foreign Ministers met in London on November 23, 1947 for what turned out to be its last session until 1949. The Ministers and their staffs had been meeting dutifully ever since September 1945, and now they attempted once more to reach some agreement on Germany. The council argued acrimoniously for four weary weeks. No important agreement was reached on any subject. Nothing specific was accomplished. Finally—a few days before Christmas—Secretary Marshall proposed that the council adjourn indefinitely, to Molotov's obvious surprise. Marshall's decisive move suspended the Potsdam agreement for bringing the Foreign Ministers together at least once every three months.

American and British officials in London were in no mood to enjoy a gay Christmas that week, and immediately after the New Year holidays seven of us met privately at the American Embassy to discuss "What next?" Our group consisted of Secretaries Marshall and Bevin; Generals Clay and Sir Brian H. Robertson, the military governors of the American and British zones; Lewis Douglas, the American Ambassador in London; Frank K. Roberts of the British Foreign Office, and me. Clay and I urged that German currency reforms be started without further delay, but Marshall and Bevin instructed us to make a final attempt to obtain acceptance of the new currency by the Allied Control Council in Berlin. If that failed, the Secretaries approved our plans to introduce the new banknotes in Bizonia. Clay then warned Marshall and Bevin once more that the Russians might make trouble for us in Berlin. Clay said he believed the use of force would not be necessary, but he stressed again how important it was to have emergency directives if need should arise. The Secretaries promised to give careful consideration to this matter, and Clay and I returned to Germany with this understanding.

Meanwhile, rumors began to circulate in Germany that new banknotes were being printed in Leipzig, in the Russian zone. This was not true, but the rumors gave Clay an idea which he put into effect when he and I had occasion to make a quick trip to Washington. We ascertained there that the Treasury Department was willing to print new paper money for Germany, and that the plan met with the approval of President Truman and Secretary Marshall. Tons of this money printed in Washington were transported to Germany in great secrecy, to prevent speculative profits, in a project called "Operation Bird Dog."

The record shows how reluctant our government was to issue this new money without Russian cooperation. Currency reform proposals were on the agenda of the Allied Control Council in Berlin for many months before the council finally disintegrated on March 20, 1948, when the Russians walked out. Only then was the decision taken to circulate the new currency in Bizonia on June 1. Just before that date, the French Government suddenly and belatedly agreed to extend the new money to the French zone. This caused a further delay to correlate three-power programs, but the new currency was put into circulation in all three zones on June 20, 1948—two years and one month after the Dodge commission declared that this reform was "urgent."

The Russians certainly gave us plenty of warning about the Berlin blockade. During the three months preceding the dissolution of the Allied Control Council, Moscow began cautiously to test the determination of the Western powers to stay in Berlin. Soviet inspectors sometimes would board military trains and insist upon their right to examine passengers. When the Western train commanders reported this, they were ordered to refuse inspection, and delays of several hours resulted. These occasional interruptions did not seriously inconvenience us, being little more than pinpricks, but they increased the prevailing uneasiness. I attended a private dinner given for a visiting British general where some American and British officers argued that the Western Military Governments should evacuate Berlin before we were forced out. The guest of honor agreed, saying, "We should pull out while we can still do so without too much loss of prestige. In military terms, our exposed salient in Berlin doesn't make sense." Several of us protested that our rights in Berlin were indisputable and that to surrender them as a military precaution would be politically disastrous, but we seemed to be in a minority that evening.

A few days later I discussed this with a remarkable German politician, Ernst Reuter, upon whom I depended a great deal for information and advice. Reuter was elected mayor of West Berlin in 1947 by the majority political party there, the Social Democrats, but the Russians utilized their veto power in the Allied Control Council to prevent him from taking office until the ACC itself was dissolved. The Russians had good reason for vetoing the selection of Reuter; he was a formidable foe of the Soviet system, which he knew well from the inside. Reuter had been a Communist at the time of the Russian Revolution, and in the early years he was a close associate of Lenin and held high positions in both the Russian and German Communist Parties. But he was too independent a spirit to tolerate the increasingly harsh Bolshevik creed, and early in the 1920s he renounced Communism, and for many years afterward fought in Germany against both Communism and Nazism. After Hitler came to power Reuter escaped to Turkey, where he lived throughout the war, operating an intelligence group to keep in close touch with developments in Russia and Germany. When he returned to Berlin after the surrender, nobody was better equipped to judge what was happening there.

When I told Reuter that some American and British officials believed we should withdraw from Berlin because it was "indefensible," he expressed the opinion that Moscow's blockade threats were a bluff. A few days previously the Russian military governor, Marshal Sokolovsky, had addressed a letter to General Clay informing him that the highway to Berlin would be closed for repairs until further notice. A wooden pole had been put across the road at Helmstedt, the point where the highway from West to East Germany met, and that wooden pole, guarded by only two Mongolian soldiers, represented at that time the Berlin blockade. Reuter suggested it would be a very simple matter to call Russia's bluff. The Western occupants need only send a small combat force to Helmstedt and notify the Russians that, as the highway was essential to our occupation of West Berlin, we were moving in and taking over maintenance of the road ourselves.

Reuter believed the Soviet Government would not risk a military operation of even a minor nature until Russia could recover from its war losses, which Reuter's information showed were much more serious than generally realized. Reuter repeated to me graphic stories he had heard from Russians about the appalling conditions in their country as the war ended. The German-Russian campaigns had been infinitely more brutal than those in the West. As Reuter put it: "It was a death struggle between two equally relentless governments who waged war as one vast merciless atrocity. They imposed sacrifices upon their own people far beyond anything Americans can imagine." I agreed that the Russians were bluffing now, and I took up Reuter's suggestion with Clay. Then I cabled to the State Department recommending the action proposed at Helmstedt, and Clay as I recall it cabled the same proposal to the Defense Department. But Washington did not accept our recommendations—and the Russians continued to test our will to maintain our position in Berlin.

On March 31, 1948, the Russians ordered that unless inspectors were permitted to examine passengers and luggage, Western military trains would be not merely delayed but would be turned back. An order also was issued that no freight trains could leave Berlin without a Soviet permit. To ascertain how far the Russians would go, Clay dispatched a train full of soldiers. The test train was shunted onto a siding for several days and had to return ignominiously. Clay informed the Joint Chiefs of Staff at Washington that his previous optimism about avoiding force was diminishing and he urged that decision be made at the highest level about whether to use force if the blockade was extended. But no decision was taken.

The next Soviet move was to stop all passenger trains departing from Berlin. About this time, Americans in Berlin seemed to be the only Westerners who were determined to stay there. French officials repeated the familiar remark that not a single Frenchman would vote to fight for Berlin. The British, believing that Berlin's geographical position makes the city indefensible, opposed an outright showdown—as they often do today. The British and French Governments began to reduce their garrisons and to evacuate women and children. Clay, on the contrary, thought that the departure of soldiers' dependents would arouse panic among the Germans, and he announced that any American who asked permission to send his family home should apply at the same time for his own transfer, which he could do without prejudice. Most Americans chose to stay.

In April the Russians expelled from the Soviet zone the American Signal Corps teams which had been stationed there since July 1945 to keep communications open. In May the Soviet Military Government imposed impossibly complex documentation for Western freight shipments to Berlin. In June civilian supply trains were held up on various pretexts. Freight and mail cars were detached from trains and got "lost." On June 18 the Russians stopped Western freight and passenger cars at western borders of the Soviet zone, explaining that these cars were "out of order."

On June 24, four days after the new German currency was put into circulation, the full extent of the Soviet threat became clear when all rail traffic between Berlin and the West was halted "due to technical difficulties." The same excuse was offered for stopping traffic on the autobahn and canals. This made the blockade complete. Two and a half million Germans in West Berlin were now dependent upon reserve stocks. They had enough food on hand to last thirty-six days, coal for forty-five days. The Germans had built up these reserves only with great difficulty because traffic facilities were inadequate. On June 24 electricity also was cut off by the Soviet-controlled power stations which served West Berlin. The power stations located in the Allied sectors had capacity enough to provide German homes and factories for only a few hours daily. The Soviet officials in Berlin showed justified confidence in their squeeze play. They had tested our will to insist upon access rights, and the three Western powers had not been able to conceal their doubts and hesitations.

After prolonged exchanges of cablegrams and teletype conversations between Berlin and Washington, Clay and I were summoned home to present our views in person. We discovered immediately that several extraneous factors were influencing the momentous decision. For one thing, Truman was up for election in November and all polls showed he was far behind Thomas Dewey. If the President were to approve action in Berlin which the voters considered reckless, his election chances would diminish still further. In spite of his personal predicament, Truman was more disposed than his military advisers to take chances. The Joint Chiefs of Staff were extremely conscious of how inadequate our Armed Forces were, due to headlong demobilization, and they considered our defense establishment much too weak to enter into any contest against the Red Army.

Marshall, who had been a soldier all his life, was naturally inclined to give more consideration to military factors than a civilian Secretary of State might have done. Marshall told me that the Joint Chiefs estimated they would need eighteen months to prepare for what might happen in Berlin if the Russians were challenged there. Truman reluctantly approved this opinion of the JCS, although he said that if the JCS would put a paper before him ordering what Clay and I proposed, he would sign it. Strangely enough nobody, either military or civilian, mentioned that the United States Government in 1948 possessed a growing stockpile of atomic bombs while Russia had none yet.

The final decision about Berlin was made on July 20 at a meeting presided over by President Truman in the Cabinet Room of the White House. From what I had heard from the Secretary of State and from friends at the Pentagon, it was a foregone conclusion that no decision would be taken affirming military action at Helmstedt, because of determined opposition by the Joint Chiefs of Staff. Whatever persuasive powers I possessed had been insufficient. The Grand Design people and the military prevailed. During that last meeting, Secretary Marshall gave me a fair chance by asking whether I wanted to add anything to my previous arguments, but in my discouragement I declined.

There always is the question what a career official should do when his government adopts a policy which he believes is a tragic mistake, a policy which he cannot in good conscience support. Discussing this subject in Berlin later with Henry Luce, the publisher, he told me with some asperity that one of the defects of public service in the

United States is that very few officials resign from their jobs as a matter of principle. In the early days of the Republic, he said, there were many resignations on issues, and that is a healthy situation. There is much truth in this view, but there is inconsistency in modern American practice because of the career principle, and ordinarily I have little sympathy with a Foreign Service officer who resigns because he disagrees with some policy. A professional diplomat understands when he accepts government service that he is obedient to official policy, no matter how repugnant a particular line may be to him personally. It is the function of a career diplomat to carry out his government's policy, a function which critics often do not understand. If an official is not willing to abide by this principle, it would be better for him not to enter the Foreign Service. In this respect, a career diplomat's position is comparable to that of a regular Army officer. Under the American system, officers and officials are free to make their opinions known to their superiors—up to the point where policy is definitely decided. After that everybody is expected to support policy to the best of his ability.

But the Berlin blockade is the one occasion in my long career where I feel I should have resigned in public protest against Washington's policy. My resignation almost certainly would not have affected events, but if I had resigned I would feel better today about my own part in that episode. I suffered anguish over this decision of our government not to challenge the Russians when they blockaded Berlin, and I still deeply regret that I was associated with an action which caused Soviet leaders to downgrade United States determination and capability, and led, I believe, to the subsequent Communist provocation in Korea.

When Clay and I flew to Washington, we had hoped for permission to try to break the blockade of ground access to Berlin. But the National Security Council did not share our confidence that the Russians were bluffing. With all ground routes thus ruled out, Berlin could receive its supplies only by air. During the intermittent traffic stoppages prior to the all-out blockade, we had discovered that airplanes could bring in a surprising amount of essentials. The National Security Council therefore decided that we should enforce only our written agreements for use of specific air corridors. Those agreements were down in black and white. That decision became the inspiration for the fabulous Airlift, whose achievements astonished even the Air Force. Our legal right to fly planes into Berlin was incontestable. None of us in Berlin thought much about it when Marshal Zhukov cheerfully signed the four-power pact in 1945 providing for separate air routes for the Western occupants. That agreement had been made almost casually because it was so obvious that safety is imperative in air traffic. I often have wondered whether we could not at that time have obtained the same kind of written agreement for our ground corridors.

In Washington, Air Force chiefs were flabbergasted by Clay's confidence that a city of two and a half million people could be supplied wholly by air. The Chief of Staff, General Hoyt S. Vandenberg, opposed the project because he correctly predicted that the Berlin Airlift would require almost every military transport plane, leaving us unequipped everywhere else in the world. But the Airlift was accepted as a challenge by the Air Force commander in Europe, General Curtis E. LeMay. Once the decision was made, the British Government threw itself wholeheartedly into the Airlift. But they had only a fraction of our air transport so Americans had to do most of the flying. The French decided to stay in Berlin as long as the others did, but they did not participate in the Airlift. Even the French garrison and community in Berlin were supplied almost entirely by American and British planes.

A few days after Clay and I returned to Berlin from Washington, Clay telephoned to LeMay in Frankfurt. Clay asked: "Have you any planes there that can carry coal?"

"Carry what?" asked LeMay.

"Coal," repeated Clay.

"We must have a bad phone connection," said LeMay. "It sounds as if you are asking if we have planes for carrying coal."

"Yes, that's what I said—coal."

Rallying quickly, LeMay said stoutly, "The Air Force can deliver anything!"

The German people, who had been somewhat apathetic ever since their defeat, came back to life during the Airlift. This was especially true of Berliners. For the first time since the war, all their organizing talents were brought into full play—and organizing genius was needed in this unprecedented attempt to feed and maintain two and a half million Germans in addition to the Western military and diplomatic communities. Nearly every country in Europe had set up its own diplomatic mission in Berlin, and most of the diplomats stayed on.

The Potsdam Protocol prohibited Germans from flying planes or serving as members of plane crews, but the Germans gave marvelous support on the ground. The American and British air forces operated separate sections of the Airlift, each using the corridor agreed to by the Russians in 1945, and during the early weeks the plane loadings were supervised by American and British pilots to make sure that the loads were balanced and secure. But before long this part of the Airlift was entrusted almost entirely to the

Germans. In Berlin and elsewhere the Germans worked ten and twelve hour days loading and unloading planes, and their super-efficient methods permitted many more round trips daily than had been estimated. Those Germans working on the ground at airports included celebrated aircraft engineers, flying executives, and much-decorated pilots. The Americans managed to fly even electric power station equipment into Berlin, considered impossible.

The community spirit of Berlin businessmen and housewives also revived, and they contrived ingenious schemes to keep going despite shortages of everything. Germans in the Western sectors organized to make the best of their tiny rations of heat, light, and the dehydrated foods which were being flown in. They dug out every hidden lump of coal and stick of wood. They rationed themselves more tightly than Military Government demanded. For several months that winter each household was permitted electricity for only two hours daily, and most of the cooking had to be done at that time. These two hours occurred in the middle of the night in some residential areas, but there were few complaints. The doubters wondered how long Berliners would put up with severe privations, lack of electricity, fuel, food, etc., in order to enable Western occupants to remain in their city. But most of us who were there were certain that Berliners would endure such hardships indefinitely, the alternative being Soviet control.

Under Mayor Reuter, the municipality made a master plan of its own. Resolution after resolution was passed by the city government in support of the Airlift, and by early September Reuter decided a big public demonstration would be desirable. Half a million Germans turned out to pledge their support, the biggest mass meeting since Hitler's biggest days. Luckily the blockade started in June, so Berlin enjoyed fine weather during the first few months, but before long the cruel winter of 1948–49 began to grip the city. The Russian authorities in East Berlin published tempting offers of food and coal for West Berliners, declaring that the Soviet Government did not want the German people to suffer because of the imperialistic aims of the Western powers, but only a few thousand Germans in the Western sectors made application for the proffered nourishment and warmth.

One incongruous aspect of the Airlift epoch was the help which black marketeers brought to Berlin. When the blockade went into effect, the three Western powers canceled the controls on consumer goods which previously had been enforced, and suddenly black marketeers discovered innumerable ways to move desired goods into the beleagured city, including many welcome items which Germans had not seen for a decade. Anybody who had money could buy almost anything. Thousands of Germans engaged in these merchandising operations, obtaining much of their stuff from ration-free Switzerland. Luxuries flowed in from the east, too—caviar and vodka, Russian cigarettes and champagne. All this was accomplished by simply demobilizing bureaucratic controls. The American community, which had expected an austere existence during the blockade, found itself deluged with luxuries at reasonable prices. As one of my aides remarked to me, "We are a capitalist oasis in a socialist desert!"

The end of my assignment to Germany came suddenly when I was recalled to Washington by the new Secretary of State, Dean Acheson, to serve there as Director of the Office of German and Austrian Affairs. It was a snowy night in February 1949 when my friends bade me farewell at Tempelhof, the airport in the American sector of Berlin. The Airlift was at its spectacular peak, with four-motor planes arriving every twenty minutes around the clock when weather permitted—and even when it didn't. Powerful searchlights turned night into day, and great snowshovels kept the airfield clear, with snow banked high around its edges. The terminal building had a solid glass front overlooking the landing field, and we watched in fascination as the roaring planes came down, unloaded, and took off again with minimum delay, while German citizens worked as team members with American soldiers. As my plane started down the runway, I looked out at my friends who were standing in the snow waving goodbye, and at the unloading crews who did not even glance at them. Those German-American teams never wasted a moment.

When I reached Washington, I learned that top-secret negotiations for ending the Berlin blockade had been going on for some time at the United Nations in New York between the Soviet delegate there, Jacob A. Malik, and Dr. Philip C. Jessup, who at this writing is a member of the International Court of Justice at The Hague. In 1949, when he was negotiating with Malik, Jessup was a professor of international law at Columbia University, on leave to serve with the American delegation to the United Nations. Stalin, in an interview with an American correspondent at Moscow, had hinted that he might be ready for some kind of settlement in Berlin, and Acheson had asked Jessup to sound out Malik on this point very privately.

When I talked with the Columbia professor, his attitude reminded me of Ambassador Winant's attitude in London five years earlier. Like Winant, Jessup felt that he had achieved an exceptionally cordial relationship with the Soviet diplomat, and he depended heavily upon Malik's good will to reach an agreement on Berlin. I did not succeed in convincing Jessup, any more than I had Winant, that Soviet negotiators cannot be influenced by personal friendships. At first Malik proposed outrageous conditions, making acceptance impossible. But after weeks of talk Malik receded from this extreme position, thus giving the impression of substantial Soviet concessions. The Jessup-Malik talks were kept so secret that I was not permitted to tell even Clay about them when I made a quick trip to Germany that spring. Clay was put in the embarrassing position of first hearing about the negotiations from his British colleague in Berlin.

May 12, 1949 marked the end of the Berlin blockade, and I went to Paris with Secretary Acheson to attend the first meeting of the Council of Foreign Ministers since December 1947. The Foreign Ministers agreed in principle upon a Berlin settlement, and then turned over the details to delegations of experts. Professor Jessup was left in charge of the American group. When the year-long blockade finally was lifted, the American press and public hailed the outcome as a great victory for the Western powers. The success of the Airlift provided a heady sense of triumph, but actually the Washington policy-makers had limited themselves to an experiment which merely proved that it was possible to keep alive a great modern city by the use of air transport alone. Few observers seemed to realize that our decision to depend exclusively upon the Airlift was a surrender of our hard-won rights in Berlin, a surrender which has plagued us ever since. The crucial point of the Berlin settlement was that the United States Government failed to ensure its legitimate claims for surface-level access to that city. During the entire period of the blockade the Russians denied the Western powers the use of ground and water routes to Berlin, and access was made no more secure by the terms of the settlement than before the blockade.

Could the Western powers have obtained better terms from Stalin in the Berlin settlement? In my view, the answer is "Yes!" Stalin was getting nowhere in this skirmish and had intimated that he was disposed to cut his losses. Stalin must have been both surprised and pleased when the American negotiators permitted Moscow to retain virtually all the controls which had made trouble for us in Berlin. Years later the chief British delegate at that conference in Paris, Sir Ivone A. Kirkpatrick, wrote: "The conference, which lasted a month, brought the Berlin blockade to an end. Privately the Russians admitted that they had gambled and lost, and the only thing to do was to liquidate the adventure. For the rest, no progress was made . . . There was disagreement over every aspect of future policy in Germany."

The settlement of the Berlin blockade which we agreed upon with Russia made our status in Germany even more precarious than before, because the Airlift tremendously increased our responsibility to the Germans in West Berlin. Those people—women and children as well as men—contributed remarkable support to the Airlift, accepting minimum food and heat through a severe winter, resisting Soviet temptations, unloading our planes hour after hour, day after day, month after month. The behavior of the Berliners transformed their relationship with Americans. During the blockade they became, for all practical purposes, our allies.

By coincidence, the Berlin blockade was lifted on the same day that two other prolonged negotiations in Germany were also concluded. The French Government completed arrangements to merge the economy of its occupation zone with the economy of the American and British zones in an organization to be named Trizonia. At the same time, the trizonal powers agreed upon an Occupation Statute for the eventual establishment of a Federal Republic of Germany. This new German nation soon became the most populous and important country in western Europe, but it was not until six years later, on May 5, 1955, that the United States, Britain and France removed their controls, thus enabling West Germany to become truly independent.

The French Government was very reluctant to grant administrative rights to West Germany. The first grudging French concession had been to extend the Bizonia currency reforms to the French zone, but Frenchmen opposed giving appreciable further authority to Germans, even authority to tax their own people. And this at a time when Washington was meeting heavy financial deficits in all the Western zones. The negotiations concerning the West German state and Trizonia were carried on through a tortuous series of parleys in which I participated for eighteen months, negotiations made more dramatic by the pressure of the Berlin blockade which naturally overshadowed our talks in urgency and public attention. The French were influenced somewhat by the blockade, but not much.

After completing his work on Trizonia and the plans for a revived German Republic, Clay flew home to retire from the Army. I had gone back to Berlin to participate in the final details of the negotiations, and returned to New York with Clay to ride in a ticker-tape parade. I was gratified, in that spring of 1949, that Americans had supported a remarkably constructive program in Germany. Our Military Government had stressed from the outset the constructive features of its directives. Because Great Britain and France were virtually bankrupt, only the United States possessed the capital and the initiative to stimulate German recovery in those first years of the occupation. It was good, too, that German-American relations during those formative years developed not entirely upon the negative basis of anti-Sovietism, but upon the positive concept that the economic recovery of Germany would help the economic recovery of Europe.

It had been decided in Washington that the successor to Clay in Germany should be a civilian High Commissioner, not another Army general, and it was a source of lively satisfaction to me to negotiate, on behalf of the Department of State, the appointment of John J. McCloy. I had had a great deal of contact with McCloy when he was the Assistant Secretary and right hand of Secretary of War Stimson. A brilliant lawyer, McCloy's practical approach and thorough understanding of American foreign policy were inspiring, whether in Washington or during his visits to the Mediterranean and Europe. McCloy became president of the World Bank after the war, but when he resigned from that post it was particularly fitting for him to become our first High Commissioner, especially in the light of McCloy's healthy effect on American policy in Germany when proponents of the pastoral theory were vocal and powerful in Washington.

Today, for better or worse, the German-American alliance has become the key to the American military position in Europe. It seems to me that Americans came out of their German experience as winners on the whole, and the Russians as losers. Even the isolation of Berlin has worked out more in our favor than the Kremlin's. The Russians inadvertently gave us an outpost one hundred miles inside the Iron Curtain, where the inadequacies of the Communist system show up more conspicuously than anywhere else, in full view of everybody in the world. Dangerous and explosive as the situation is in Berlin, due partly to Western hesitations in the past—and sometimes still in the present—I believe that the Berlin position is an invaluable asset, worth whatever it may cost to hold it for the West.

TWENTY-THREE

VISITS TO THE BELGIAN CONGO (1951 AND 1960)

It was a great relief to me, after years of concentrating upon the problems of Germany, to be accredited in September 1949 as American Ambassador to the King of the Belgians and to live once more among free people who controlled their own affairs. Following more than four years' occupation by the Nazis, Belgium had made a remarkable recovery, due largely to free enterprise, the prompt elimination of government restrictions, and sound financial practices which the Belgians adopted immediately after their liberation in 1944. Naturally, Marshall Plan money and over a billion dollars of American assistance to the Belgian military budget also gave great impetus to Belgian recovery. This dynamic nation of less than ten million inhabitants also devised practical means for cooperating after the war with other independent countries of Europe. The Belgians aspired, for one thing, to act as a catalyst between their two great neighbors, France and Germany, whose wars had repeatedly crushed them. By the time I arrived in the capital city, Brussels already was headquarters for the economic union called Benelux (Belgium, Netherlands, Luxemburg), which later expanded and embraced West Germany, France and Italy to become what is today the powerful Common Market.

Another reason why Belgium's prosperity revived quickly after the war was because Belgian industrialists planned in advance for the postwar reconstruction of their enterprises. Even before the end of hostilities, several Belgian corporations at their own expense sent technicians to the United States to investigate technological advances made during the war. These visitors were cordially welcomed by American corporations and little escaped their expert attention. So when Marshall Plan aid became available, Belgian industrialists already knew how to utilize efficiently their share of the funds. However, in the broad sweep of its conscientious generosity, Paul Hoffman's Economic Cooperation Administration dispatched productivity teams to teach the Belgians how to increase production. The Marshall Plan was at peak activity while I was in Belgium, and one corporation executive there consulted me about how to work with his American team. "Your men are very eager to be helpful," the puzzled industrialist told me, "and they explain that their services cost us nothing because the United States Government is paying all expenses of their group. But we really don't know what to do with them! Of course we listen politely, and we show them anything they want to see, but is there anything else we should do?"

Brussels also was a labor center of worldwide importance after the war because it was selected as headquarters for the International Confederation of Free Trade Unions, an anti-Communist association established to counteract the World Federation of Trade Unions, the outfit which had been set up by Moscow. A number of foreign labor organizations established officers of their own in Brussels, and meetings of the International Confederation attracted representatives from all non-Communist countries, including delegates from the AFL-CIO, headed by Irving J. Brown, who gave me loyal cooperation. One time while I was Ambassador, five directors of the confederation held a special meeting in Brussels. Eric Kocher, the labor attaché of our embassy, had no difficulty obtaining complete details of this session for our report to Washington, but to his astonishment he found that seventeen other Americans, including photographers, had arrived to cover this meeting of five individuals. The State Department agreed with my urgent suggestion that this kind of performance was if anything more harmful than our former practice of ignoring similar meetings.

Just before I departed from Washington, after briefings by the State Department and the excellent Belgian Ambassador, Baron Robert Silvercruys, President Truman asked me to call at the White House. Many European political irons were in the fire at that time, and I prepared myself so I could discuss whatever might be on the President's mind. However, I neglected to study the only subject which he wanted to talk to me about at that moment. One of Truman's diplomatic nominations had been the appointment of Mrs. Perle Mesta, the celebrated Washington hostess, to the newly created post of Minister to the Grand Duchy of Luxemburg, a tiny country so closely associated with Belgium that heretofore the American ambassador in Brussels had also been accredited to Luxemburg. The President explained to me that Mrs. Mesta was "a very wealthy woman" who had given much time and money to public affairs. As everybody in Washington believed, Truman had reason to be personally grateful to Mrs. Mesta because she made a generous contribution to the Democratic Party in 1948 when few people thought Truman had the slightest chance of being elected. As a reward to Mrs. Mesta, a separate legation was set up in the Grand Duchy and she became Madame Minister. The President told me that the lady did not pretend to be familiar with the subtleties of European politics, although she was well acquainted with many European diplomats who had attended her lavish parties. "I want you to do everything you can for Mrs. Mesta," the President instructed me.

That turned out to be a pleasant duty. The new Minister to Luxemburg frequently telephoned to me at Brussels, she was willing to take advice, and as a matter of fact I learned a great deal from her. No American envoy in any of the great capitals of the world attracted more public attention those years than Minister Mesta in her picturesque little legation which served admirably as a setting for the parties she delighted to give. During her term of office quite a few American V.I.P.s made it a point to include Luxemburg when they toured Europe, and Mrs. Mesta also extended hospitality to hundreds of our soldiers on leave from Germany.

Luxemburg officials regarded her appointment with mixed emotions, but Prime Minister Joseph Bech told me that Madame Mesta had helped to put Luxemburg on the map. "She and I are good friends," he said. "Of course, I don't talk with her any more about European politics." Mrs. Mesta herself jested about her unfamiliarity with European geography and economics. She enjoyed meeting people of consequence and mentioned to me that she would like to meet the Belgian Foreign Minister, Paul-Henri Spaak, whom she referred to as "very interesting." After dinner I asked Spaak if they had gotten along well. He replied blandly, "We had a thorough discussion about the weather and all such matters."

But Mrs. Mesta did not treat her job lightly. She was a quick learner and she knew what she wanted. One of the things she wanted was suitable quarters for the American Legation in Luxemburg. While I was working in Berlin, Washington confiscated the former German Legation in Luxemburg as part of American war reparations. The action was of doubtful wisdom because this picayune acquisition, like the seizure by our Government of the German embassy in Washington, supported in principle the more extensive seizures of the Russians and other powers. When I became Director of the Office of German and Austrian Affairs I vigorously opposed this feature of our reparations policy, but by then our Government was committed. The old-fashioned German Legation in Luxemburg required major renovations, and when that uncomfortable building became Mrs. Mesta's official residence, she consulted me about her problem. I told her that the State Department had a Director of the Office of Foreign Buildings, my friend Frederick Larkin, who was in Madrid at the moment. He was the man who decided priorities. "I'll telephone him at once!" exclaimed Mrs. Mesta, and she told me later what happened.

She informed the director about her difficulties and requested immediate attention. Larkin replied rather casually that Luxemburg was far down on the list and he could not possibly reach it for a couple of months. "Oh," said Mrs. Mesta, "I hoped you would come tomorrow!" When Larkin politely said that was out of the question, Mrs. Mesta said, "But I'm talking to President Truman on the telephone this afternoon, and I know he would want you to come right away!" Somehow the director arrived in two days, and eventually the Minister's residence in Luxemburg was all plushed up by Jansen of Paris. And Brussels also got a dividend because, under the spell of the Mesta experience, Larkin returned to Belgium and approved a new embassy building there.

When I arrived in Brussels, King Leopold III was still in exile in Switzerland where he had been residing with his second wife, Princess de Rethy, and his son Baudouin ever since released from Nazi custody in Austria. Leopold III did not go home immediately when freed from internment, because the Belgium Parliament opposed his return to the throne. A regency government had been set up in September 1944 with the King's brother, Prince Charles, as Regent. So it was to Prince Charles that I presented my letters of credence in the elaborate manner established by Belgian protocol. I was driven from my embassy residence in an ornate coach drawn by six horses, accompanied by a cavalry escort, to the royal palace where I was graciously received by the Regent. I liked Prince Charles, who could not have been more helpful and understanding, and he always was cooperative and friendly to the United States.

It was not until July 1950 that Leopold III finally decided to return to Brussels, a decision which brought out an extraordinary public display for and against the King. The Prince Regent was excluded from the palace; I had not appreciated the extent of personal hostility between the two brothers. I witnessed fighting in the streets, listened to violent speeches at mass meetings, and saw prominent patriots including Paul-Henri Spaak leading demonstrations. There was a rush of tension between the Walloons in the south and the Flemings in the north. The reputedly phlegmatic but actually emotional Belgian people trembled on the brink of civil war, and it was doubtful whether the monarchy would survive or be replaced by a republic.

The chief grievance against the King was that he had allowed himself to become a captive of the Nazis instead of escaping to lead the provisional Belgian Government which maintained headquarters in London during the war. But wiseacres in court circles told me that Leopold III might have returned to his throne, despite his questionable war record, if only he had not married again while in exile. His second wife was unacceptable to some Belgians, partly because of the deep affection which the nation felt for her predecessor, the lovely Swedish Princess Astrid who lost her life in an automobile accident in 1935; partly because the charming Princess de Rethy was a commoner. Fortunately, in this explosive situation, there existed a basis for compromise in the person of Baudouin, the son of Princess Astrid, who was devoted to his country, to his father, and to his stepmother. Dowager Queen Elisabeth supported the cause of her young grandson, and her views had considerable influence in the family councils. As the widow of Albert I, the heroic King of the Belgians during World War I, the Queen Mother was respected, and she also was held in personal esteem for her devotion to music and other cultural pursuits. Baudouin himself showed admirable character and courage, and suddenly the whole country united to uphold the Crown Prince and the monarchy. Leopold III abdicated; Baudouin became King on his twenty-first birthday, September 7, 1951; the former King and Princess de Rethy conducted themselves with dignity; and gradually calm was restored throughout the land.

Visits of interesting Americans are a pleasant feature of Embassy routine. Brussels enjoyed many. Among them, Mrs. Eleanor Roosevelt spent three energetic days as our guest, examining at first hand many aspects of the Belgian situation, and working late in the night on articles she was preparing. At a luncheon in her honor attended by a variety of Belgian officials there was a spirited conversation on the subject of the contrasts between American and Belgian life. Pierre Wigny, then Minister of Colonies, provided Mrs. Roosevelt a useful item for "My Day" with the jocular remark that he would not want to live in the United States. Mrs. Roosevelt, surprised, asked him why. The Minister, smilingly but with conviction it seemed to me, replied, "Because it is nothing but a matriarchy!"

I was impressed with the significance to the Belgians of their colony in the Congo, a region almost eighty times larger than Belgium itself. When Nazi troops invaded Belgium, the Congo remained beyond their reach and the mineral wealth of this African colony nourished the Belgian Government-in-Exile in London all through the war. The relationship between the United States and the famous Congo mining corporation, Union Minière du Haut-Katanga, controlled by the great banking complex, Société Générale, was very important. Union Minière aided the United States in creating the atom bomb several years before Soviet Russia produced this weapon.

During the war, the then chairman of Union Minière, Sir Edgar Sengier, learned authoritatively that the Germans were experimenting with atomic devices for which immense quantities of uranium were required—much more uranium in those early experiments than now. Katanga Province in the Belgian Congo was then the only known source of an ample and readily accessible supply of this metal. Although the United States Government had not yet undertaken its A-bomb experiments, Sir Edgar decided in 1940 that Washington soon would be in urgent need of uranium. In great secrecy, he arranged shipment in steel drums of a thousand tons of ore from the Congo to a New York warehouse. A year later, when American and British scientists were frantically seeking uranium for their A-bomb project, Sir Edgar amazed them by producing the ore in the warehouse—the first consignment of a steady flow of uranium. It was erroneously reported that Union Minière made excessive profits from this deal, and the corporation might easily have done so because governments in wartime are willing to pay any price for essential materials. But Sir Edgar supplied his uranium ore at very reasonable cost. He was as eager as anyone to defeat the Nazis.

In 1951 the United States found itself waging war again, this time in Korea. For years we had been able to import substantial amounts of uranium ore from Katanga at prices below what was paid elsewhere, but now Union Minière justifiably felt it was entitled to a price increase. This amounted to a number of million dollars annually, and I was summoned home to participate in the negotiation. The appropriate agencies in Washington thought we should approve the sum the Belgians were asking, and so did I. But as a matter of negotiation I felt that if we agreed at once to the entire increase, our friends might regret they had not asked for more. So I suggested that we offer half the amount requested. To my surprise, the Belgians promptly accepted the offer and both sides were quite happy. Critics often allege that American diplomats are poor negotiators, and Will Rogers used to say that the United States never lost a war nor won a conference, but in this instance one of my colleagues in Washington computed that the millions which my proposal saved for our government amounted to much more than I would earn for my lifetime services, and he told me I should consider myself a self-supporting diplomat.

Actually, I regarded myself as reasonably well paid ever since being appointed Ambassador to Belgium—$20,000 annually plus various perquisites. Although I had held the title of Ambassador for many years, I never before had received an Ambassador's salary. Several times during the arduous days in Berlin, I did feel that my work warranted more than the $13,500 salary of Career Minister which I received during my last years in Germany, but this idea never seemed to occur to anybody in the State Department. My own needs were adequately provided for in Berlin, but my wife and three daughters in Washington could have used more money. On my hurried trips home,

I would almost decide to broach this matter to someone in the Department, but everyone there was always engrossed in such momentous affairs and discussing such vast expenditures that my personal finances seemed too trivial to mention. Lucius Clay, while bearing full responsibility as military governor of the American occupation zone, also never received more than the regular pay of a soldier of his rank, comparable to mine as a diplomat. But when Clay and I left Germany and John J. McCloy was appointed High Commissioner to perform the political and diplomatic functions which we had shared, McCloy was allotted more remuneration than both of us had received together. And he earned it.

Probably my most interesting experience while Ambassador to Belgium was an extensive tour of the Congo, accompanied by my wife and daughter Mildred and several members of the embassy staff. I wanted to see that Belgian colony in equatorial Africa, one-third as large as the United States, where seventy-five thousand Europeans were living among some twelve million Congolese tribesmen. My years in French North Africa had shown me how dangerous conditions could be where native races so greatly outnumbered European settlers. Overtures were made to me in Morocco, Algeria, and Tunisia by different nationalist groups seeking independence from France, and my talks with these men made me aware of the difficulties confronting all colonial administrations. My little expedition to the Congo was encouraged by the Belgian Government, and an airplane and crew were provided by the United States Air Force. The Pentagon welcomed this opportunity to supplement its information about flying facilities in the heart of Africa.

The Belgians in the Congo were proud of their achievements in establishing a peaceful regime among tribes which had been feuding for centuries and whose ancient loyalties were still strong, and the European administrators were eager for us to inspect their operations. We were invited to go anywhere we desired, and we covered much territory in our plane. From the air we received an awesome impression of the vast extent of the colony's forests and grassy plains, the enormous sweep of the great Congo River, and the thousands of primitive villages. In this tropical region, men and women were hunted down like animals in the eighteenth and nineteenth centuries, usually by Arab traders, sometimes with the connivance of rival tribal chieftains, and were shipped under miserable conditions to be sold as slaves in the United States and elsewhere. The contrast now between the still primitive villages in the bush and the modern cities of Leopoldville, Stanleyville, and Elisabethville was startling—a jump from two thousand years ago to the age of motor, radio, and air conditioning. The Belgians were extending highways, electric power, and sanitation.

The Rockefeller Brothers were pioneering the first large American enterprise in the colony, a textile combine. In Katanga, the paternalistic policy of Union Minière had created marvels of modern housing, schools, and hospitals.

But the Congo, rich in mineral and other resources, required immense capital outlays to develop, so everything could not be accomplished at once. The Belgian program for its colony provided for a slow but steady rise in African standards of living. About half a million children were enrolled in the Belgian school system, more than in any other African colony, but schooling for the natives was limited for the time being to elementary education, plus vocational training for subordinate jobs in Belgian-controlled industries and plantations. Most of the teaching was done under the direction of missionaries. There were no medical, law, or engineering schools of university rank, but some missionary institutions sent a few Congolese to Belgium and France for higher education. Since French was the common language of the Congo, almost none of the French-speaking African students were sent to English or American schools. The colonial administration did not encourage sending students abroad because Belgians believed the time was not yet ripe for advanced education for Africans. One government official said to me, "With most of the population still illiterate, we think it best to lay solid foundations at lower scholastic levels before undertaking higher education." The administrators were convinced that their program was more suitable for Africans than the British and French colonial system which provided college courses for youths of superior intelligence, notwithstanding that very few executive positions were open to them. Several Belgians told me, "Our system, unlike the British and French, avoids creating a discontented group of men who cannot get work for which they think they are qualified."

The segregated social order in the Congo seemed to have unanimous support of the European residents, and general acceptance among Africans. Quite a few Europeans remarked to me that their relations with the Negroes were better than conditions in the United States. Intermarriage was not permitted, and there was great economic disparity between the races, but there were no segregated buses, and white and colored customers sat side by side in open-air cafés. Belgian newspapers occasionally published accounts of race clashes in America, and one sympathetic Belgian lady said to me, "You Americans really do not know how to cope with the color problem. You should investigate our methods in the Congo. We never have lynchings here because the Belgians have created a relationship of mutual understanding and trust." There was so little disorder in the Congo that more than one European woman assured me she would not hesitate to travel alone through any African community, even at night.

But I already had noted that in the Belgium homeland the Congo "system" was viewed with considerable misgivings. The election victory in 1945 of the British Labor Party, with its policy of hastening self-rule in the colonies, made a deep impression on Belgian industrial workers. French colonial difficulties also alarmed the Belgians, who dreaded lest they, too, get bogged down in guerrilla warfare to protect the vested interests of European colonizers and corporations. The administration of the Congo had become a major issue in Belgium, so explosive that no political party could ignore it. Everyone in Brussels told me that the Congo must avoid violence if the administration there hoped to retain the support of Belgian voters.

This aversion of the Belgians at home for maintaining ties with the Congo dated back to the very beginning, when King Leopold II assumed responsibility in the 1880s for nine thousand square miles in central Africa. The Belgian Parliament refused then to accept the Congo as a colony, so the King organized a private consortium to administer the region. Leopold II invested a great part of his personal fortune to develop mines and rubber and coffee plantations, and he recruited Europeans to train native laborers by offering the alien settlers permanent administrative jobs and grants of land. But Congo tribesmen, unaccustomed to hard, steady work, proved indolent and irresponsible, and some European supervisors inflicted severe punishments to compel them to work. The treatment of these forced laborers was so harsh in some instances that, even in the nineteenth century when harsh treatment of colonial populations was generally taken for granted, the labor situation in the Belgian Congo aroused protests all over the world. The King's consortium also ran into financial difficulties, and a year before the death of Leopold in 1908, the Belgian Government reluctantly became owner of his majority holdings, after which conditions of the Africans rapidly improved.

By 1940, when the Nazis invaded Belgium, its Congo administration was so firmly established that it continued to function smoothly throughout the war, and when I toured the colony in 1951 it was cited as a model for Africa. However, none of the Europeans I talked with then, including missionaries of several denominations and nationalities, believed that the tribesmen would be ready for self-government for at least another generation. Therefore I was incredulous when, during a visit of Princess de Rethy to Washington in 1959, a friend of mine in her entourage told me that Congolese independence might be granted at any moment. I knew, of course, that a political scuffle in Leopoldville in January had flared into a murderous riot in the capital city, but

I did not see how that two-day episode could produce sudden independence for the Congo.

Eight years had passed since my visit to Africa, so I asked what had happened there in the meantime. How many Congolese had been prepared for administrative posts? "Almost none," I was told. "Then it is not evident," I asked, "that at least five years will be required to prepare a bare minimum of qualified African administrators?" The Belgian official admitted that this was true, and added, "We hope that Congolese leaders will see the wisdom of an interim period; a few do understand this. But no matter what happens, Belgian voters will not risk getting involved in an Algeria-type war. The prevailing feeling in Belgium is that if the Congolese insist on premature independence, we must give it to them. None of our political parties can ignore this sentiment." Thus forewarned, I was not surprised when a few months later a "roundtable" conference in Brussels agreed that the Belgian Congo would become the independent Republic of the Congo on June 30, 1960.

By that time I had retired from the State Department, but President Eisenhower asked me to head the American delegation selected to attend the inaugural ceremonies, the other members being Clare H. Timberlake, our Ambassador to the new Republic; William S. Paley, board chairman of the Columbia Broadcasting System; C. Vaughan Ferguson, Jr., director of the State Department's Office of Middle and South African affairs; and Thomas A. Cassilly, the Department's desk officer for Congo affairs. By coincidence, the American group landed at the modern airport at Leopoldville the same time the official party from Brussels arrived, so I had opportunity to greet many old friends immediately, including Premier Gaston Eyskens and several of his principal ministers. The next day the King of the Belgians arrived, attended by leading members of the Royal Household, and it was a pleasure to participate in the enthusiastic reception accorded the young monarch at the airport.

Conversing informally with Belgian officials, I found that their mood was hopeful. Congolese politicians apparently had recognized that they would require Belgian technical assistance, and hundreds of experienced civil servants had expressed willingness to stay on under an African regime. Directors of Union Minière du Haut-Katanga told me they had made satisfactory arrangements to assure continuance of the corporation's multiple activities. As for the colonials—the businessmen, plantation owners, investors—I was informed that most of them intended to remain in Africa, too. This was the only life many of them had known, and this was a poor time to try to sell out. Moreover, they sincerely believed they had treated their native workmen so much better than some other European colonizers had done that relations would remain harmonious.

The Belgian Government did its best to make the Republic of the Congo's debut impressive. The formal inaugural ceremonies were held in the new Parliament hemicycle in a colorful yet dignified atmosphere. Several hundred Congolese, some in tribal raiment, some in European clothing, mingled with foreign ambassadors and other guests. King Baudouin in a graceful speech turned over his authority to the new independent state, and Congo President Kasavubu made a moderate and conciliatory acknowledgment.

Then the Prime Minister, Patrice Lumumba, who had not been scheduled to speak, rose unexpectedly to address the audience. I had arranged the previous day to meet this thirty-year-old politician because it was apparent that he, more than any other individual, would probably determine the course to be taken by the infant republic. He made a good impression on me during that first meeting. Speaking fluent French, he was vivacious and cordial and I thought intelligent. I knew that Lumumba's schooling was about equivalent to that of an American high school graduate, but self-made men with limited formal education are in the American tradition. Perhaps this dark-skinned young man would become the "Father of His Country." Facing his distinguished audience in the Parliament building, the stage was set for him to become his republic's foremost statesman.

But to the consternation of all foreigners present, Lumumba chose this solemn occasion to deliver an inflammatory and bitter recital of all the wrongs, real and imaginary, committed in the past by Europeans in the Congo, ignoring their constructive contributions. Contrary to my initial impression of Lumumba's intelligence, his speech was not only in poor taste but in poor judgment. The Prime Minister already had victory in his pocket, yet he was insulting the Belgians to their face while in the same breath pleading for their economic and financial cooperation. Full of zeal, hostile to the Belgians, caring little for amenities or accuracy, a new demagogue was making his appearance on the world scene. His method had enabled him to fight his way to the power he obviously craved, and the vociferous applause he received from several hundred Congolese demonstrated that he understood native politics.

Of course Lumumba's harangue destroyed the carefully planned atmosphere of friendly transition. At one point King Baudouin half-rose from his chair, as if about to withdraw in protest. But his counselors persuaded him to remain, although the veins in his forehead stood out as indication of the violence of his feelings. Lumumba's demagoguery left all of us subdued and thoughtful as we adjourned for the luncheon and reception which followed for about two thousand people. When

Lumumba rose to speak again, we steeled ourselves to expect the worst. But to the general bewilderment, the unpredictable Prime Minister launched into an extravagant eulogy of the Belgian role in the Congo, of the numerous good works they had introduced, and ended with the hope of future cooperation between the two countries. Congolese guests applauded this effusion almost as vigorously as they had hailed his earlier denunciation. I remarked to Ambassador Timberlake that I did not envy him the task of reporting to the State Department just what these two contradictory speeches signified. Belgian ministers later explained to me that the second speech was the outcome of a rather stern conversation they had with Lumumba in the brief interval before lunch. One of these Belgian officials told me, "Lumumba seemed genuinely astonished that his speech upset us. He said he has been making the same speech for years."

Before returning to Washington I had another private conversation with Lumumba. The rumor had spread after his inaugural tirade that he was a Communist and that the Soviet representative at the ceremony had helped to write his speech. I ascertained that Lumumba's knowledge of Communism was extremely vague, though his confusion made him as useful for the Soviet Government's purposes as an outright agent. Obviously under great strain and fatigue, Lumumba extended himself to say friendly things about the United States, to plead for understanding and assistance, and to make additional denunciations against the Belgians. I tried to describe the impartial and constructive attitude of the United States Government vis-à-vis the Congolese people, not concealing my esteem for our Belgian friends, and I hoped my efforts made a good impression. I was certain that Lumumba had but little notion of the huge problems of a practical nature which lay before him. He seemed to believe that the Belgian administrative structure would continue to function, that Belgian technicians would operate the power plants and transport, and that funds would be provided somehow. If the Belgians failed to provide, then somebody else would—perhaps the United Nations with American support, or the Soviet Union.

The day following my long talk with Lumumba, I crossed the Congo River from Leopoldville to Brazzaville, formerly the capital cities of the Belgian Congo and the French Congo. These European-style cities had been erected scarcely more than a stone's throw apart, facing each other on opposite sides of the river, but their administrations had been altogether different and this difference was revealed in the very appearance of the two capitals. The Belgian Government had been paternalistic, and the up-to-date docks, efficient transportation, and modern buildings of Leopoldville showed the conscientious care which had gone into its management. The French Government had been content to leave control of its colony largely to the devices of the dominant tribe in its region, and the people of France never invested much effort or much money in Brazzaville. Yet the French Congo had been granted independence several months before the creation of the Belgian republic, and the transition to native self-government had taken place very smoothly. There had been no rioting, no interruption of public services, no serious financial problems.

I wanted to find out how this transition had been accomplished, so the American Chargé d'Affaires in Brazzaville, Alan W. Lukens, arranged a luncheon for me where I could meet several Congolese officials of the new government, and also meet the High Commissioner and the Commander in Chief of the Congolese armed forces, Frenchmen who still retained their posts in the now independent African republic. In talking with these men, it became clear to me that the real rulers of the area were the Congolese chieftains, the tribal heads who always had commanded the loyalty of the natives, who still wielded authority in thousands of villages, and who would continue to hold deep power regardless of newfangled voting, politics in Leopoldville and Brazzaville, and participation in the Assembly of the United Nations.

The Belgian and the French administrators had maintained order while they controlled their respective portions of the Congo area, but tribal feuds reasserted themselves as soon as the colonies began to prepare for independence. The transition from colonial rule to self-government in the French and Belgian territories thus depended primarily on how the Africans themselves settled their own differences. The French were fortunate that a remarkable Congolese named Fulbert Youlou became the first President of their former colony. Youlou prudently retained ties with France, including the employment of essential French technicians, and he assisted in organizing the Union of Central African Republics which loosely combined his new state with two other former French colonies. Youlou understood how to keep control of his government during the perilous transition period, to the great advantage of his own people and also their French associates. Patrice Lumumba, who might have exercised similar influence across the Congo River, had a disorderly mind which was reflected in his actions.

I was unable to meet Youlou personally when I visited Brazzaville, because he happened to be out of the country then, but I had opportunity to talk with members of his government and also to discuss the situation with a number of well-informed people in the capital. I learned that the new President was a Roman Catholic priest who had been suspended by his bishop, but who continued to use the title "Abbé" and to wear a cassock. Church authorities, eager to do everything possible to prevent a crisis, remained silent on this matter. There are two tribes in the region formerly known as the French Middle Congo, and although Youlou's tribe is the smaller one, it is more warlike. The President, who carried a gun in his cassock and was followed by armed bodyguards, was deeply involved in the tribal rivalries. I was told that his followers organized aggressive elements (the description given me was "goon squads") who penetrated the larger tribe and massacred about two hundred rivals who might have opposed the Abbé's aspirations.

When I returned to Washington, the State Department did not ask me to make any recommendations concerning American policy toward the former Belgian colony, merely to relate what I had observed. But even while I was writing my report, conditions were changing so rapidly that my observations became out-of-date almost before they could be recorded. There never was any genuine sense of nationalism in the Belgian Congo, and the impressively large native government set up by the Republic was designed primarily to include enough ministers to satisfy all the tribal rivalries. Even when these officials professed devotion to the regime, their real interest was in their old resentments. With the disappearance of Belgian authority, there immediately occurred a complete breakdown of central government, of orderly employment, of responsible finance, of police discipline. Colonial complacency of half a century was abruptly dissipated by terrifying Congolese mass brutalities against the white population. The Belgians became panic-stricken and departed pell-mell on every outgoing plane and ship. Patrice Lumumba was murdered. Katanga Province seceded from the rest of the Republic.

When Youlou's government applied for admission to the United Nations, all went smoothly. The political technique in the French Congo was held to be "an internal matter." But when rich Katanga Province announced that it wanted to be an independent state all by itself, with no responsibility for its poor relations in other parts of the Congo, the United Nations decided that this was "an international matter," and it immediately dispatched money, troops, and administrators to weld together its newest member. That costly United Nations expedition to Leopoldville was financed largely by the United States which already had committed itself to the policy of encouraging the national aspirations of the people of Africa. It was felt in Washington that the former Belgian Congo could be a proper self-supporting state if it included Katanga Province, but that the infant Republic would become a bankrupt derelict, susceptible to Soviet domination, if deprived of Katanga. Moreover, there was strong suspicion that the secession of Katanga was not a spontaneous action on the part of its native inhabitants but a calculated move by Union Minière to protect its great investments from the disastrous chaos which was shattering the Leopoldville area. On United Nations Plaza in New York, the Soviet-inspired word "mercenaries" was applied promiscuously to nearly any Europeans who cooperated with the Katanga Government.

This was the period when the impact of the fledgling countries was new and startling. There was intense concern on the part of some American leaders to give immediate recognition to these newly emerging African nations. This interest consisted in part of genuine solicitude for their independence and welfare; plus a desire to align them on the side of the free world, or at least to keep them neutral; and perhaps also a notion at times that the Negro vote in the United States might somehow be affected. This last motive was of interest to the politician, of course, rather than to the career diplomat. When Katanga tried to secede, I was asked by my friend George C. McGhee, then chairman of the State Department's Policy Planning Council, to support the United Nations policy of forcing unification in the Congo. But I could not agree with this proposal because I did not believe that forced unification would necessarily serve the interests of the United States.

The American policy of supporting African nationalism is now firmly established in the State Department. But Americans often apply their own attitudes to societies which have developed under completely different conditions and which still are basically tribal. For example, preparations were made in August 1963 in Brazzaville to celebrate the third anniversary of the independence of the former French colony. Instead, an angry mob stormed the city prison while another mob surrounded the presidential palace. Youlou, garbed in the white cassock of his priesthood, descended the palace steps to address the chanting demonstrators, but his appeal failed. Youlou resigned from the presidency, and the Congolese Army took over provisionally under its French commander. Youlou's resignation left the country with no government and with little public confidence in any administrators who might try to succeed him.

The dream of a Belgian empire in central Africa has vanished, but the pioneer colonizers built a strong foundation there and Belgium now has opportunity to exercise its genius for economic development in the independent Congo. This new relationship may become even more profitable and provide less headaches than the old. Responsibility for a primitive people sometimes is a thankless undertaking. Now some of that responsibility has washed off on the American taxpayer who, almost completely ignorant of African conditions, has accepted heavy commitments and is being asked to contribute more and more millions of dollars to support the military and economic efforts of the United Nations in the vast stretches of the Congo.

TWENTY-FOUR

AMBASSADOR TO JAPAN; WAR IN KOREA (1952–53)

Suddenly in the spring of 1952 I was asked to become our first postwar Ambassador to Japan. I was given only five days' notice to wind up my affairs in Belgium before returning to Washington for intensive briefing about the Far East, which I had never even visited. In fact, I had never even set eyes on the Pacific Ocean. The task of cramming information into me, which was the responsibility of the long-suffering Asian specialists in the State Department, did not shrivel their sense of humor. It was not flattering to be told by them that the reason I had been selected was because I was an ignoramus about the Orient. The United States had just pushed through a peace treaty with Japan, overriding Soviet objections, and President Truman and Secretary of State Acheson wanted the American ambassador to arrive in Tokyo without delay. But ambassadors must be confirmed by the Senate, and developments in Asia had aroused such partisan controversies that many senators were wary of diplomats with Far Eastern experience. Secretary Acheson wryly remarked that the Senate probably would confirm me speedily because I never had occasion to express an opinion about Far Eastern issues. The Senate did confirm my appointment promptly on April 18, 1952, three days after the President signed the Japanese peace treaty.

My unsullied Far Eastern record was not the only reason I was chosen for the Tokyo post. Acheson intimated that my long association with military officers was another point in my favor, because in Japan I once again would be a diplomat among warriors. The war against Japan came to an end with the signing of the peace treaty, but the war against Communist forces in Korea was going full blast when I was assigned to Tokyo. For nearly seven years, while Japan was ruled by American Military Government, thousands of our troops were stationed in that country. Now Japan was beginning to govern itself once more but thousands of American soldiers were still stationed there because, under the terms of the Administrative Agreement,

Japan had become a vital element in the Korean conflict. Thus, while I was to be in charge of reestablishing normal diplomatic relations between the United States and Japan, I was confronted at the outset with a very abnormal military situation.

Before departing for Tokyo, I attended a session of the Senate Foreign Relations Committee, and I also had a valued talk with President Truman, who was friendly and practical as always. But I felt that I also should call upon General Douglas MacArthur, who had commanded the Occupation Forces in Japan. MacArthur, although aware that Truman was opposed to extending the Korean war, wanted to pursue the Red Chinese across the Yalu River to their air depots in Manchuria, and notwithstanding that MacArthur had been ordered to make important announcements only through Washington, he openly threatened Communist China with air and naval attacks. This policy conflict between the General and his Commander in Chief could be resolved in only one way: MacArthur was abruptly relieved of his Far Eastern duties by the President on April 11, 1951. But MacArthur's personality and his program for Japan had dominated that country ever since its surrender in 1945, and I hoped that conversation with the General would give me needed insight concerning the problems I was about to encounter. I had met MacArthur in Paris before the war, when he was Chief of Staff of the Army, and he readily received me now in his Waldorf Towers apartment in New York, which was crowded with precious souvenirs of his illustrious career.

After a few minutes of amenities, including a reference to his Milwaukee beginnings and mine, MacArthur began a distressing recital of his wartime experience. His review revolved around his sense of injustice against what he regarded as the prejudice of "the Marshall cabal." He condemned our government's decision to undertake the North African operation under the command of General Eisenhower—whom he included as a member of the "cabal"—and declared that the African strategy was an egregious blunder which defeated his own plans in the Pacific. MacArthur ignored the necessity for the operation; the part which Roosevelt, Churchill, and Stalin had in making the decision; the spectacular success of the expedition; and, incidentally, that I had been a proponent of the venture. It was all part of a Marshall-Eisenhower machination, he said, to deprive him, MacArthur, of the shipping and logistical support he needed in the Pacific. While I have grown accustomed to soldiers' reactions about campaigns in which they participate, I was not prepared for this astonishing outburst.

Finally there was opportunity to change the subject and I asked MacArthur a question about Japan which was of great importance to my mission. That question concerned the amazing clause of the Japanese constitution, ratified in May 1947, which prohibited Japanese rearmament "forever." The Korean war seemed to make it imperative that the Japanese should rearm immediately, but their politicians were determined to avoid this issue. Most of the war-weary world of 1947 praised Japan's pacificism, though some Americans complained then that it was utopian, that no nation has ever completely renounced military power as an instrument of national policy. Critics pointed out that even the Swiss maintain conscription to protect their famed neutrality, and that the disarmament clause left Japan incapable of self-defense and therefore invited aggression.

Two years later, after Chinese Communists seized control of the vast Chinese mainland, Washington officials also began to question the wisdom of a wholly demilitarized Japan, and when two hundred thousand Chinese Communist "volunteers" crossed the border of Manchuria on November 26, 1950, forcing the evacuation of ninety-one thousand Korean civilians, MacArthur urged the Japanese to prepare for self-defense. But the General never proposed any change in the wording of the Japanese constitution, so now in 1952 I ventured to ask his opinion of the anti-war clause. I had been informed that this Article Nine of the constitution had been devised by MacArthur's staff in Tokyo under the supervision of General Courtney Whitney, in consultation with the Japanese, but I wanted an authoritative explanation of the ironbound language of the clause, which was the heart of the rearmament problem. MacArthur vehemently denied that his military government staff had anything to do with Article Nine, saying that the arms prohibition was entirely a Japanese affair, the work mostly of Baron Kijuro Shidehara. Naturally, I accepted his explanation, but later in Tokyo some doubts arose in my mind. For in Japan I was told that at a luncheon there before the Korean war, given by MacArthur for a group of visiting American publishers, the General discussed American policy in Japan and declared that if ever a monument were to be erected to him, it would be not for his victories, not for his successful occupation of Japan, but for Article Nine of the Japanese Constitution!

Regardless of how one interprets this apparent contradiction between what MacArthur was reported to have said at the luncheon and what he told me during the Korean war, there can be no doubt that the Japanese people were generally pleased with the remarkable innovation of pacificism. Whether disarmament was imposed upon them by their foreign conquerors, or whether it was a device of their own politicians, the Japanese still cherish it. Even today the electorate refuses to approve constitutional amendments which would authorize enough armed forces to rank Japan as a "great power."

Another startling postwar innovation in Japan was that the Emperor ceased to be divine and became a modern constitutional monarch. During the war there had been prolonged discussion in Washington about the future status of the Emperor of Japan. Some of Roosevelt's advisers urged that the descendant of the Sun Goddess should be deposed, or even executed as a war criminal. But Joseph Clark Grew, who was the American Ambassador in Tokyo at the time of Pearl Harbor, recommended that when Japan surrendered, Emperor Hirohito should be required publicly to disclaim the myth of his divine origin, and thereafter should use his immense personal influence to persuade his subjects that he could serve best as a limited monarch, similar to the head of the British Empire.

It was to this new-style Emperor of Japan that I presented my letters of credence in the Imperial Palace at Tokyo. The Emperor was living in improvised quarters because part of the palace had been destroyed by fire during the wartime bombing. I admired his order that there should be no reconstruction of his quarters until new housing was provided for the people of Tokyo who had suffered so much. The beginning of my presentation ceremony was extremely formal. The Chief of the Imperial Household ushered me into the long Audience Chamber, where Hirohito was seated on a low dias at the far end of the room, attended by a small retinue of court officials. Upon my appearance, the Emperor arose and waited stiffly while my escort and I moved silently across the chamber's vast expanse. This court etiquette, based on ancient imperial custom, was observed until I bowed politely and presented my credentials.

Hirohito and I then sat down together informally, as would never have been permitted by palace protocol before the war, and had a lively discussion on several topics of current interest. Hirohito seemed relieved that he no longer was required to maintain the myth of divine origin. On this day, and later on other occasions when I presented prominent Americans who felt that a visit to Tokyo would not be official unless they were received by the Emperor, I found that he possessed a delightful sense of humor and innate modesty. These qualities were reflected also in the attitude of the Empress and their children. I like to think that Professor Shinzo Koizumi, the former president of Keio University who was mentor to the Crown Prince while I was in Japan, and Miss Elizabeth Vining, the American Quaker who was appointed as the English-speaking tutor of the Prince, contributed to this happy disposition of the imperial family.

A few days after making my official call on the Emperor, I found time to inspect my official residence in the compound of the American Embassy. I was accompanied by the head of the household staff, Funayama-san, an impressively dignified Japanese butler who had served Ambassador Grew before the war and had been re-engaged by General MacArthur. While walking through the long room designed for embassy receptions, I happened to notice an electric push button on the massive table at the far end of the room and asked the butler what was the purpose of this electric bell. He explained that soon after MacArthur's arrival in Tokyo, the General ordered that the Emperor should call upon him—an unprecedented reversal of protocol intended no doubt to demonstrate the reduced status of the Emperor and the authority of the American Supreme Commander. The butler went on to say that the General himself planned the procedure for the imperial visitor, and that MacArthur rehearsed the impending ceremony. As arranged, the Supreme Commander, attended by his military aides, was seated beside the great table when the Emperor of Japan entered. The General then rose and waited while the Emperor slowly walked the seventy-foot length of the room. MacArthur invited the Emperor to be seated, and when the audience was concluded the General pushed the electric bell which signaled that the palace entourage should be ushered in and the Emperor escorted to his limousine. Listening to this account of how the Emperor called upon the General, I was struck by the similarity of MacArthur's procedure to the ceremony I had just gone through at the palace. It was obvious that MacArthur had modeled his own "court etiquette" upon Japanese imperial custom, requiring Hirohito, while paying his respects to the Supreme Commander, to behave in much the same manner as I had been required to do when presented to the Emperor.

From the very beginning of the occupation of Japan, Americans dominated that country as we never had authority to do in Germany. MacArthur did not have to consider the divergent views of the British, nor did the French hold any two-edged veto over him. As for the Russians, they had not earned the right to participate in military government in Japan, and we excluded them as completely as Moscow excluded us from the occupation of Bulgaria and Romania. However, the Soviet Government was permitted to maintain a military mission with diplomatic privileges in Tokyo, under Lieutenant General K. N. Derevyanko, the Soviet representative to the Supreme Commander Allied Powers. Derevyanko also was the USSR member of the Allied Council for Japan, and this enabled the Russians to exploit opportunities in political, social, and labor fields. Using the apparatus of the revived Japanese Communist Party, the Russians distributed cheap paperback translations of Communist publications, thus insuring that the ideas of Marx, Hegel, Lenin and Stalin were read by book-hungry students and intellectuals. In meeting hundreds of youths throughout Japan, I discovered that they learned from these books about the industrial revolution in England a hundred years ago, and that they thought capitalism in the United States existed unchanged in the 1950s.

The Russian mission, under cover of its diplomatic immunity and the protection of an unwitting American military government, also promoted Communist infiltration of Japanese trade unions, especially the Teachers' Union. In their eagerness to encourage trade unions, which were completely alien to Japanese tradition, American representatives welcomed even extreme left-wing elements to expedite the initial organizing. This led to many violent manifestations, including spectacular scenes on May Day 1952, when thousands of snake-dancers wound their way through the streets of Tokyo. The demonstrators threw some American automobiles into the moat which surrounds the Imperial Palace, and they stoned the American Embassy car in which I was riding through the crowds. This incident brought a prompt visit to the chancery by the Japanese Foreign Minister, Katsuo Okazaki, which developed into a close personal relationship which has lasted to the present. At this writing, he is the Japanese Ambassador to the United Nations in New York.

Officials like Okazaki cooperated with Americans during the occupation. The Japanese, unlike the Germans, were permitted to retain their own central government and their revered Emperor. Although the Emperor had tremendous symbolic significance for the Japanese, the actual administration of the country had been manipulated for centuries by its elder statesmen, and American Military Government did not have to cope with bothersome details because it could rely upon experienced Japanese officials to carry out orders. While I was in Tokyo, the Prime Minister was seventy-four-year-old Shigeru Yoshida. His outlook was conservative and tradition was important to him, but he had had extensive diplomatic experience in Europe, including having been Ambassador in London, and he was familiar with European problems. From my point of view, we got along well together.

Like most professionals, Yoshida had not participated in politics during his years in diplomacy. He had opposed the war and had grimly "sat it out" in retirement until, a few weeks before the surrender, he risked his life by joining a small group of conspirators who tried to persuade the Emperor to sue for peace. Japanese militarists discovered the conspiracy and Yoshida was imprisoned in the closing weeks of the war while one of his colleagues, Mamoru Shigemitsu, served as Foreign Minister. Shigemitsu was a distinguished Japanese patriot. While Consul General at Shanghai in the 1920s, he lost a leg when struck by a bomb tossed by a Korean revolutionary, but this amputation did not interfere with his diplomatic career. Shigemitsu was Ambassador at Moscow and at London for several years, and it was Shigemitsu who headed the Japanese delegation which surrendered to General MacArthur aboard the battleship U.S.S. *Missouri.* Soon after that ceremony, Shigemitsu was arrested by American Military Government, tried and convicted as a major war criminal. Yoshida, having watched from the sidelines, became Foreign Minister right away and Prime Minister a year later. Not being a politician, Yoshida made little effort to win popularity with the Japanese electorate. But he played all his cards right and his efficient administration delighted MacArthur. Yoshida wisely decided that Japan was in no position to resist most things the Americans really wanted, but he was by no means a yes-man. He was friendly to the United States and he knew when to yield.

Before I left Washington there were two views in our government regarding the Bonin Islands, which had been part of the Japanese Empire. The State Department wanted to return the Bonins to Japan but the Defense Department wanted to retain control of the islands. Seven thousand fishermen, who had lived on those islands before the war, had been evacuated by the Japanese Navy during hostilities and now were clamoring to go back home. It had been my intention to attend to this matter without delay, but Admiral Arthur W. Radford, Commander in Chief, Pacific, came to Tokyo to dissuade me from relinquishing the Bonins. He told me the Japanese had used the islands as one of their most important submarine bases, and he insisted that Americans should hang on to the Bonins until it became clear what was going to happen in eastern Asia.

To demonstrate his point, Radford invited me to go by cruiser with him and a group of his admirals on an inspection tour of the former fishing area. We visited three of the islands and saw elaborate submarine installations. Radford contended that since it was the Japanese themselves who had expelled the inhabitants, Americans were under no moral obligation to let them return, especially since most of the displaced fishermen had found other jobs. My investigation convinced me that Radford's views were right, and American control of this valuable base is still intact. Our naval authorities, who have charge of the administration of the Bonins, permitted about one hundred and fifty Caucasian civilians to return to their former homes, and these men were allowed to bring their Japanese wives, who are the only Japanese in the islands. Concerning this Bonin controversy, as with other issues, Yoshida's Government made many vigorous representations to the American Embassy in Tokyo.

One day after Yoshida and I were well acquainted, he told me about some of his early experiences with Americans. His first encounter with our soldiers occurred when he and two other officials were driving in an old rattletrap automobile from Tokyo to Yokohama to call upon MacArthur. Suddenly they were hailed on the highway by two doughboys, disheveled, unshaven, real combat soldiers, who looked pretty tough under their helmets. Yoshida and his companions were not sure whether it might not be a holdup, but they stopped. The soldiers asked for a ride to Yokohama and perforce the Japanese agreed, still very uneasy. After they had crowded into the small car, the soldiers reached in their pockets and brought out, not weapons, but chewing gum and chocolate bars. Japanese confidence returned and all the men enjoyed an amiable trip to town. Yoshida said this was for him the keynote of the American occupation of Japan, and he never forgot the incident.

Another experience which Yoshida related had to do with his voyage in 1951 to San Francisco, where he went to sign the peace treaty. Yoshida's travel schedule included a stopover in Honolulu, and he resolved to avoid all mention of Pearl Harbor. But the aide of the commanding admiral, who called to escort Yoshida to lunch, remarked, "By the way, if you look over there, you can see Pearl Harbor." Yoshida said nothing. At the door of the admiral's residence, Yoshida was welcomed by the naval executive officer, who said, "From here we get an excellent view of Pearl Harbor." A little later the admiral himself mentioned Pearl Harbor, pointing from his lanai to the U.S.S. *Arizona,* whose mast could still be seen rising from the ocean where it had been sunk by the Japanese. At first Yoshida thought this was a deliberate attempt to embarrass him, but finally he realized that such conversation had become customary small talk with all of the admiral's guests. Yoshida told me that he lost his inhibition after that, and better appreciated American psychology.

For my part, I also had some difficulty making polite conversation in Japan, but it was not the kind of difficulty I anticipated. Before the war I sometimes had occasion to talk casually with Japanese whom I met abroad at receptions and dinner parties, and those social talks were seldom sparkling. Usually the Japanese guest would merely smile courteously in response to my remarks and say softly, "Ah, so!" Then it would be up to me to think up another topic to keep the conversation going. Consequently I went to Japan under the impression that the Japanese people tend to be "inscrutable," but in Tokyo I was quickly disabused of that idea. The most attractive feature of the democracy which the Americans brought seemed to be "free speech," and I was deluged with torrents of it. Delegation after delegation, desiring to make serious appeals or to expound propaganda, waited upon me at the embassy and whenever I traveled around the country. My difficulty was not to induce the Japanese to talk but to insert a word myself. Especially articulate were the politicians, trade union leaders, students and teachers. The latter were the most vocal critics of American policy, and I spent many interesting hours listening to them.

As in all foreign assignments, my duties were not limited to the citizens of the country to which I was accredited, but also included attentions to a variety of American visitors. Among the interesting visitors to Japan while I was Ambassador was Mrs. Margaret Sanger, President of the International Planned Parenthood Federation, who arrived with a committee to advocate birth control. Mrs. Sanger had come to Japan twice before, in 1922 and 1937, but in 1952 her work seemed to elicit no more favorable notice than on her previous trips. The population of Japan prior to the war was about seventy-two million, and it was claimed then that this great number was more then the small islands could support. Japanese militarists used this population density as one excuse for conquering Manchuria and invading China. Greater Tokyo now has the world's largest metropolitan population, over ten million, and the population of the islands is more than ninety-four million, so a neat problem does exist.

The Korean war came as a godsend to the Japanese because it enabled them to rebuild their shattered industries at maximum speed in order to provide supplies and services required by American and other United Nations troops. When the Republic of Korea was invaded on June 25, 1950 by sixty thousand North Korean soldiers spearheaded by a hundred Russian-built tanks, MacArthur dispatched to the front all available combat troops then stationed in Japan. The General was confident that the Japanese Government would furnish a secure and orderly base, and the Japanese with amazing speed did transform their islands into one huge supply depot, without which the Korean war could not have been fought.

American troops in Korea at the time of the invasion comprised only a very small constabulary force. Under an agreement with the Soviet Union, the United States Government was entitled to occupy Korea up to the thirty-eighth parallel, but there had been an economy wave in Washington and it was calculated that withdrawal of American forces from South Korea would save millions of dollars. Besides, due to rapid postwar demobilization, our military strength had dwindled to almost nothing, not only in the Far East but all over the world. In June 1950 the United States Army did not have manpower even to maintain air strips in Alaska, to say nothing of ability to provide more than a division or two in case of emergency in Europe. The Japanese were not asked or permitted to recruit soldiers to help us, but Japanese shipping and railroad experts worked in Korea with their own well-trained crews under American and United Nations commands.

This was top-secret, but the Allied forces would have had difficulty remaining in Korea without this assistance from thousands of Japanese specialists who were familiar with that country. As for the Koreans themselves, they could do very little to defend their country. Congress had been unwilling to appropriate any substantial sums to equip the South Korean Army, and it lacked even adequate rifles. On the other side, the Soviet Union and Communist China had seen to it that North Korea was relatively well supplied with military equipment.

When I arrived in Japan I enjoyed a brief reunion with General Matthew Ridgway, a friend from the North Africa and SHAEF days. This paratroop commander had checked the invasion of Chinese Communists in Korea with the help of a brilliant landing by U. S. Marines at Inchon on September 15, and had performed the complicated functions of Supreme Commander at Tokyo headquarters since the recall of MacArthur. But Ridgway was getting ready to depart for Europe, very thankful to be transferred because he did not like the prospects in Korea. Ridgway was about to become Supreme Allied Commander of NATO, succeeding Eisenhower, who had just resigned to seek the Presidency. Less than a month after my own arrival in Japan, Mark Clark flew in to succeed Ridgway, and I had a reunion with another General I had known well in Africa. Once again Clark and I found ourselves associated in military-political-diplomatic negotiations as prickly as those with Frenchmen in Algiers. Again I heard Clark protesting because he, "a plain soldier," had to spend his time on "politics." But Clark understood very well why his Tokyo post was more political than military. The command he was now assuming was called the United Nations Command, and it was more complicated than SHAEF had ever been.

This United Nations Command represented sixteen countries which had undertaken to help resist the Communist attack on Korea. When the invasion occurred, the U. N. Security Council demanded cessation of hostilities and withdrawal of the North Korean forces back to the thirty-eighth parallel, and two days later the Council asked United Nations members to help enforce its demand. Although the United States had very few of its soldiers in South Korea, they were being attacked in an area where they had a right and a duty to be, and President Truman immediately ordered General MacArthur to aid South Korea. The Congress of the United States was not called upon to declare war formally because Truman designated the expedition to Korea as an international "police action," in which the United States participated merely as a member of the UN. This "police action" erupted so unexpectedly that it did not permit the prolonged consideration which decisions of such importance usually receive in Washington. Although several members of the UN sent troops to Korea, and other governments contributed non-military support, the Korean war was primarily an American-Korean enterprise, and the staff at Tokyo headquarters was predominantly American. When the UN asked Truman to appoint a Supreme Commander of the international forces, MacArthur was the logical choice.

The UN Command was thus organized to fight the first major "United Nations War," the first major attempt by an international organization to establish peace by using force. This joint effort became possible only because the Soviet delegation had walked out of a United Nations Security Council meeting in New York six months earlier, announcing that it would not return until Red China was admitted as a member. The Russians were still absent when the Communists drove through the thirty-eighth parallel, and therefore were unable to use their veto when the Security Council branded the North Koreans as aggressors. If the Russians had stayed in the Security Council, they could have blocked this action by using their veto. They recognized their blunder and have never repeated that kind of walkout.

The situation in Korea was dominated by one overpowering individual—seventy-seven-year-old Syngman Rhee, President of the Republic of Korea, a singleminded nationalist who, following the Japanese annexation of his country in 1910, had devoted his life to re-establishing its independence. Rhee had every reason to support the American-UN campaigns in Korea, but the old man's hatred of the Japanese almost equaled his hatred of the Communist aggressors. Soon after I arrived in Tokyo, the State Department directed me to go to Korea to talk with Rhee. As Ambassador to Japan, my territory was limited officially to the home islands to which the former empire was now reduced, but the State Department had been trying for some time to coordinate Korean policy with that of the United States Government, and it hoped that I might be able to persuade Rhee to cooperate in establishing a more harmonious atmosphere.

But my visit to Seoul was not a success; Rhee wanted no harmony with the Japanese. He was bitterly opposed to the presence of any Japanese whatsoever in Korea, and on several occasions he had even instructed his police to arrest some of the Japanese transportation experts who were working under the UN Command. Rhee also was creating infinite difficulties by demanding special privileges for the six hundred thousand Koreans who were living in Japan, and by refusing to moderate or postpone Korean reparations claims against Japan. Rhee also ordered Japanese fishermen not to come within twenty-five miles of the Korean coasts. This limit had been set by MacArthur in 1945 for purely strategic reasons and was called the

MacArthur Line. Rhee renamed it the Rhee Line, applied it to fishing, and ordered small Korean gunboats (formerly American vessels) to capture what he called intruders. A few unarmed Japanese fishermen were killed and hundreds were imprisoned. Rhee flatly refused to release them, listening in stolid silence to the American Ambassador to Korea, John J. Muccio, who had served with me in Berlin, who urged that such disputes should be arbitrated. Rhee was not impressed with our argument that most of the United Nations fighting in Korea, notably the United States, also had massive grievances against Japan, but that we were subordinating them to the necessities of the Korean war.

One reason why Rhee was ill disposed to our point of view was because he felt that a grave wrong had been committed against him at the Cairo Conference in 1943 when President Roosevelt agreed with Chiang Kai-shek and Churchill that Korea should become independent "in due course." Rhee was angered by that indefinite phrase "in due course," and insisted then and always that Korea's independence must be recognized immediately after the defeat of Japan. When I talked with Rhee about this in the summer of 1952, no explanation of Roosevelt's attitude was available, but the story was made public a few years later. It then became known that Roosevelt discussed the Korean question during a private talk with Stalin at the Yalta Conference in 1945, and that the American interpreter, Charles E. Bohlen, made a confidential memorandum of that conversation for the White House files. According to this memorandum, Roosevelt told Stalin that what he had in mind for Korea was trusteeship for about twenty-five years. Roosevelt believed that since Japan had governed Korea for decades, it would require a generation for the Koreans to learn how to govern themselves again. Roosevelt said he would prefer a three-power trusteeship limited to Russia, the United States, and China, but he supposed the British would be offended if not included. Stalin replied that he thought the trusteeship could be much shorter, probably no more than five years, and that Britain certainly should be included.

This secret exchange of views was reported to President Truman after Roosevelt's death, but despite the fact that Stalin and Chiang Kai-shek still favored the plan which they had approved at Cairo, and it was known that Rhee opposed any form of trusteeship, Truman nevertheless gave his consent for Rhee to return to Korea. So Rhee, after thirty-five years in exile, returned in triumph, to become President in 1948 of part of his country, South Korea, where he lost no time in setting up a tough personal regime, committed to rule without any interim trusteeship period. The stubborn nationalist made many difficulties for the UN Command, but it is quite possible that without his fighting qualities, all of Korea might be occupied by Communists today. There never was a doubt about his anti-Communism, and when the North Koreans and Chinese "volunteers" staged their invasion of South Korea, Rhee stood up in a very grim situation.

After my failure to mollify Rhee in his own country, Mark Clark and I decided to try to bring the President of Korea and the Prime Minister of Japan together in Tokyo, because orderly relations between their countries were imperative to the conduct of the war. With great reluctance, Yoshida agreed that he would see Rhee if the Korean visited Japan. Clark then invited Rhee to come to Tokyo as his personal guest, and he put him up in the special guest house in the Supreme Commander's own compound. It was arranged that Rhee and Yoshida would meet at a luncheon which I would give in the American Embassy. But when the luncheon day arrived, Yoshida sent his regrets at the last moment and appointed Foreign Minister Okazaki to confer with Rhee. Yoshida told me later that his personal dislike of Rhee was so intense that he realized he could not conceal it even in a brief meeting, and would therefore only make matters worse if he appeared at the luncheon. So he had a diplomatic illness, which Rhee naturally resented. Most Korean leaders were less inflexible than Rhee toward the Japanese, and an administration without Rhee would have made matters easier for American negotiators and commanders, who continuously had to walk a tightrope while fighting their dangerous war in Korea.

Taiwan (Formosa) was another area which, like Korea, had once belonged to the Japanese Empire but which presented difficult problems of its own now. Taiwan had been part of China until 1895, when it was seized by Japan after the first Sino-Japanese war, and it was this island one hundred miles off the coast of Fukien Province which provided refuge for part of Generalissimo Chiang Kai-shek's army when Communist rebels gained control of the Chinese mainland in 1949. One million Chinese civilians also found refuge in Taiwan at that time. Chiang Kai-shek's government in the capital city of Taipei was accepted by the United States as the same Republic of China which we had officially recognized in 1928 when the Generalissimo first established his administration at Nanking. Some time after I arrived in Tokyo, there was opportunity to visit Taiwan where I engaged in conversations with Chiang Kai-shek and discussed with Karl L. Rankin, our well-informed Chargé D'Affaires in Taipei, how the situation there fitted in with war conditions in Japan and Korea. Americans had become well aware of the risks involved in Taiwan and its off-shore islands of Quemoy and Matsu.

I was agreeably surprised to learn that Chiang Kai-shek did not have Syngman Rhee's emotional attitude against the Japanese, although China had suffered as much as Korea had. Chiang had been a cadet at a military college in Japan, and he respected certain qualities in the character of the Japanese people. I had met the Generalissimo and his gallant wife when they attended the Cairo Conference in 1943, and now I was pleased to become better acquainted under more relaxed conditions. They were living in a spacious Japanese-style residence which had been built in the suburbs of Taipei by a Japanese industrialist, and I was invited to be the first occupant of their new guest house which Madame Chiang had designed for the Generalissimo's garden. Madame Chiang's wealthy Chinese Christian family, the Soongs of Shanghai, had educated her in the United States where she was graduated from Wellesley, and she acted as interpreter for her husband in more ways than one. He spoke no English and trusted her to make his ideas clear to Americans. Her translations, I was told, were seldom literal. It might be said that she interpreted the spirit rather than the letter of what he said.

My talks with Chiang and members of his government—Vice President Chen, Foreign Minister George Yeh, and the military chiefs—ranged over many of the strategic problems of the area, and of course touched on Japan and the conflict in Korea. The Generalissimo expressed eagerness to be helpful in the fighting and would have been glad to provide manpower. Throughout our talks there naturally was an overtone of desire by the Chinese to return to mainland China—the ultimate hope which buoyed them up—but Chiang and his associates spoke of this with restraint. They seemed to have no illusion that invasion of the mainland could be a short and easy expedition, but they were convinced that Communism in China was an experiment which would fail. Meanwhile Chiang was utilizing most of his military appropriation to train troops for attack. I realized that he could scarcely maintain the morale of his soldiers unless they had this incentive of anticipated return to the homeland. A son of the Generalissimo by his first marriage, Lieutenant General Chiang Ch'ing-kuo, was in charge of security and was confident of the morale of the troops—but they were not growing younger.

I felt that Americans should be understanding of Chiang's problem. Taiwan is a naval base essential to the security of the free world, and we do not have a surplus of assets in the Far East. An army of six hundred thousand men on Taiwan, well-trained and well-equipped, dedicated to overthrow the Communist regime on the mainland, is a great restraining factor against aggressive action by Chinese Communists. Furthermore, the very existence on Taiwan of a progressive government is an important element in free world strength in Asia. The Republic of China under President Chiang has demonstrated that it can make significant progress in solving the basic problems of less-developed Asian countries.

If the Chinese Nationalists should collapse, United States forces would have the unenviable burden of holding their position. Some of our European friends who do not always see eye to eye with the United States on China policy would be alarmed indeed if Taiwan were lost. Our critics are confident, of course, that the United States will not permit that to happen. Yet they have been complacent about the Red Chinese nibbling at the off-shore islands. After I returned to Washington, the British Ambassador there told me: "Quemoy and Matsu obviously are part of the mainland and belong to Red China." I asked him if the same reasoning applied to Hong Kong, and he replied rather heatedly that that was different because Hong Kong is a British Crown Colony!

There were other divergent views concerning our objectives in the Far East. President Truman showed great political courage in resisting the Communist attack, and our forces prevented the conquest of Korea despite intervention of troops from Red China. Some officials in Washington asserted that the Peiping regime would crack under the strain if the United States would fight this Korean war to a finish. But many Americans were reluctant to push the war to a definite victory, and our United Nations allies also acted as a brake on that idea. Our allies had a voice in the settlement, and they did not want the situation to develop into renewed civil war for the unification of China. Most Europeans did not want to fight even for the unification of Korea, being satisfied to accept the thirty-eighth parallel division which existed before the outbreak of hostilities.

In May 1951 General Omar N. Bradley, then Chairman of the Joint Chiefs of Staff, told the Senate Foreign Relations Committee: "Red China is not the powerful nation seeking to dominate the world. Frankly, in the opinion of the Joint Chiefs, this strategy [fighting for a united Korea] would involve us in the wrong war, at the wrong place, at the wrong time, and with the wrong enemy." The five-star General was considering the problem as a military situation: Korea's geographical position was almost as awkward for the American Army as Berlin's position was—and as both places still are. Bradley's recommendation of a compromise settlement made strong appeal because by this time there were nearly 142,000 American casualties and the fighting had become a miserable, inconclusive, frustrating ordeal. Moreover, the United States presidential election campaign was beginning to take shape, and the Korean war was extremely unpopular with the American public. So negotiations were opened on July 10, 1951 between the United Nations Command and the Chinese-Korean Communists. It was understood by everybody that we could not impose surrender terms, so we were compelled to negotiate a truce under the indignity of daily contumely and insults from our enemies.

When the armistice talks started, Americans believed that the actual fighting in Korea could be halted in a few days. In order not to complicate matters, it was agreed that the negotiators of the United Nations Command would all be military men. The theory was that political issues would be raised if civilian specialists were included, and the parleys might drag on indefinitely. However, the representatives from Peiping were aware that any settlement in Korea was bound to have far-reaching political effects because the conflict itself was essentially political. The Communists therefore assigned shrewd civilian negotiators to bargain with our professional soldiers; the Communists were intent from the outset upon scoring maximum political points.

By the time Mark Clark and I arrived in Tokyo in the spring of 1952, the Korean armistice discussions had spun out for almost a year. Clark and I, both newcomers to the Far East, worked closely together. I accompanied the General on his visits to Syngman Rhee, on trips to different UN military headquarters, and on inspections along the Korean battle lines. Clark showed me the enormous difficulties of waging war in mountainous Korea, at the end of a supply and communications line six thousand miles long, against an implacable enemy who always could take sanctuary across the Yalu River in neighboring Manchuria. Clark was convinced that the Joint Chiefs had badly misjudged this Korean situation when they started armistice parleys, and he believed we already had lost much ground by permitting the negotiations to drag on so long. What Clark personally favored was immediate resumption of a drive to unite Korea, for he was convinced that any settlement which left Korea divided would amount to a grave American defeat. He was confident that we could obtain a decisive victory without getting bogged down in guerrilla warfare on the Chinese mainland. I shared his conviction that we either should fight to win our objective, a united Korea, or we should liquidate on the best terms we could get. The monthly attrition of thousands of American casualties could not be justified by a stalemate position.

After making intensive on-the-spot studies, the new Supreme Commander recommended to the Joint Chiefs very much the same strategy which MacArthur had proposed a year earlier, even including the use of Chinese divisions from Taiwan. Chiang Kai-shek had offered Chinese troop support to the UN Command as soon as the Korean war broke out, and an American military mission to Taiwan reported that at least two of Chiang's divisions were combat-ready. Clark said to me, "These Chinese are eager to fight the Communists who beat them in 1949. They have been training for this chance, with American material support, and it is not fair to them or to our own soldiers to keep them on the sidelines while Americans fight Chinese." But this recommendation had been rejected by Washington when MacArthur proposed it, and it was rejected again when Clark revived it. The White House, the Pentagon, and the State Department all declared that Chiang's troops were not sufficient to swing the military balance, and that their appearance in Korea would mean reviving the Chinese civil war.

I agreed with Clark that although Russia and Red China were finding it very convenient to use North Korea as their cat's-paw, the Communists were anxious not to extend the war to the Chinese mainland, and I believed we were being bluffed out of a well-earned victory in Korea, as I felt we had been in Berlin. The United States had the military capacity to drive the Chinese "volunteers" back into Manchuria, but for various reasons we were hobbling ourselves. We had greatly superior air forces which could have been used to destroy the sanctuaries across the Yalu from which the Chinese were operating with impunity. We had naval strength, and the Chinese had practically none. We had nuclear weapons, and the Chinese had none at all. If the United States would use its power, our military estimates indicated that we could win without any Taiwan troops, and it seemed to me that if we accepted that prohibition, we might overcome the objections of our United Nations allies to resuming a drive for victory in Korea. However, neither Clark nor I were policy-makers; it was our function only to execute as best we could the policy decided upon in Washington. And, in the absence of a national determination to win, the United States established precedent by being willing to accept a stalemate.

During those dismal Korean hostilities, the Roman Catholic Archbishop of New York honored me by staying at our embassy residence in Tokyo while making Christmas visits to American troops. Korea was the fourth battleground where I was associated with Francis Cardinal Spellman in his travels as Military Vicar for the United States. He had stayed at my residence in Algiers; we had met again in Italy; and I had been touched by his horrified reaction, during actual combat in southern France, when he saw some of war's gruesome results. It was at our meeting in North Africa, just after the Cardinal had visited the Vatican, that I learned that His Eminence had played semi-pro baseball as a young man. In reply to an indiscreet question which I asked concerning rumored peace negotiations, Cardinal Spellman said: "That was a fast one which I let go through my legs." It was my great fortune, while accompanying the Cardinal, to be in close contact with him during most of the twenty hours of activity which he managed to squeeze into every twenty-four, and I could see how this warm-hearted churchman had become such a dynamic force for good.

The war in Korea was a very important issue as the presidential election approached its climax in the autumn of 1952. An ingenious speech-writer, Emmet John Hughes, induced Eisenhower to pledge that if he were elected, he would make a personal trip to Korea. The implication was that such a trip would produce a settlement. The response of the public to this promise was so enthusiastic that politicians of the Democratic party put pressure on the Truman administration to sign a cease-fire prior to the election, in order to get credit themselves for making peace. This unmistakable evidence of the war's unpopularity among American citizens encouraged the Peiping negotiators to hold out for wholly unacceptable terms. So the sporadic fighting and the armistice wrangling dragged on past the election date and into the new Eisenhower administration.

When Eisenhower became President, his inevitable choice for Secretary of State was John Foster Dulles. This celebrated international lawyer was for years the consultant on American foreign policy for the Republican party, and he had cooperated with both the Roosevelt and Truman administrations at many conferences and peace parleys. Dulles, under the supervision of Secretary of State Acheson, had been the chief architect of the Japanese peace treaty and the Administrative Agreement which governed the disposition of our armed forces in and about Japan. I arrived in Washington to attend with Dulles the session of the United States Senate which ratified that treaty. As a former senator himself, Dulles had carefully paved the way for its ratification. The expert handling by both sides of the intricate process of moving the United States and Japan from war to friendly peacetime association is one of the happier episodes of our history.

In hammering out the text of the treaty and the Administrative Agreement, Dulles had been assisted by Dean Rusk and many others, including John M. Allison, a veteran Foreign Service Officer who speaks and reads Japanese. As a reward to Allison for his expert services, the new Secretary of State offered him appointment as American Ambassador to Japan. An ambassadorial appointment usually lasts about three years, and when I went to Japan I expected to remain there that long. However, a change of Administration in Washington usually entails many shifts of American Ambassadors, and the Eisenhower Administration was no exception in this respect. Dulles recommended Allison for the post and Eisenhower approved. Dulles also cabled that he wanted me to "join his team" and offered me assignment in Washington as Assistant Secretary of State for United Nations Affairs. So we packed our personal effects; my wife and daughter, Mildred, flew home; I made the customary farewell calls; Japanese officials and my diplomatic colleagues gave me the customary farewell parties; and I went to bed one night expecting to fly back to Washington the next day. Instead, I received a cablegram asking me to stay on in Tokyo as General Clark's political adviser—

a familiar role!—during the final stages of the Korean armistice negotiations.

For the next four months, the Korean parleys claimed my full-time attention. This was the fourth truce negotiation in which I participated. Always in the past, with the French in North Africa, with the Italians and the Germans, we had victory as a base to stand on. This time we did not have a victory or anything resembling one. The UN Command started this last round of armistice talks knowing now what had to be done. For almost two years, ever since Washington indicated willingness to compromise, the Peiping regime had recklessly expended the lives of Chinese troops in the determination to kill and wound as many UN soldiers as possible, thereby increasing the eagerness of UN governments to negotiate a cease-fire. When Eisenhower flew to Korea soon after his election, thus fulfilling his campaign pledge, he said his advisers had reached much the same conclusion about Korea as the Truman administration had reached in the summer of 1951. No all-out attempt would be made to expel the Red Chinese from Korea. An armistice along the current battle lines would be acceptable. We were instructed to push hard for a settlement, and we did so, although this was a bitter pill to swallow.

The Red Chinese battled with remarkable tenacity. The political commissars attached to their units drove the men with savage disregard, and the fortitude with which the "volunteers" endured inadequate food, cotton clothing in zero weather, and total lack of medical care was incredible. They had been grossly underestimated. For example, on one occasion General James A. Van Fleet, Commander of United Nations Forces in Korea, asked authority to capture an advanced hill position in front of the main line. He estimated the operation might cost two hundred casualties, but about six thousand UN soldiers were killed or wounded and the hill position never was captured. The horde of badly equipped Chinese soldiers could have been forced to evacuate if the United States had been willing to utilize all our resources, including atomic weapons. It was this kind of indeterminate warfare which Clark and I felt must be stopped at the earliest possible moment. Such local operations were costing lives and also were giving the Red Chinese a distorted idea of American striking power. But the UN Command had little room for maneuver in its dealings with Peiping's representatives. When your adversary is aware of your anxiety to conclude negotiations, you are distinctly at a disadvantage, and that was the situation at Panmunjom, the remote Korean village where the negotiators were meeting.

At the beginning of the armistice talks in 1951, the first subject taken up was the exchange of prisoners-of-war, which the UN negotiators thought would be a simple matter to arrange. They proposed that the UN Command would give back the Chinese and Koreans we were holding, and the Communists would release our captive soldiers. But the Peiping regime anticipated that many Chinese who had surrendered, especially in large groups, would be unwilling to go back to China, fearing court-martial. So the Red Chinese negotiators insisted from the outset that all prisoners must be exchanged, regardless of what the men themselves desired. Wanting to effect a truce as quickly as possible, the UN Command did its utmost to persuade Chinese prisoners to return home. Assurances of immunity were circulated in all of our prison camps, and a poll was taken of the Chinese prisoners on April 10, 1952 in the hope that most of the men would express willingness to go back. But to the dismany of the UN Command, sixteen thousand of the twenty thousand Chinese prisoners voted against repatriation. When a poll of Korean prisoners was completed a few days later, it showed that about half of the Koreans voted to go home, which made the reflection upon the Peiping regime even more humiliating. The Red Chinese denounced what they called American "brainwashing," and by the time Clark and I undertook to wind up negotiations, this prisoner exchange problem still remained the only real barrier to an armistice, all other important issues having been virtually settled by then.

In addition to humanitarian sentiment, there were two other reasons why the UN Command could not forcibly exchange sixteen thousand Chinese prisoners who refused to be handed over to the tender mercies of the Communists. The United States Army had already had an experience of that sort when thousands of Russian prisoners, who had been captured by the Germans and then freed by American forces, fought desperately against repatriation when Red Army units came to get them. The Soviet soldiers who did not want to go home barricaded themselves in camp dormitories, in schools, and even in churches. Authorities in Washington feared that those painful scenes in Germany might be repeated in Korea if the UN Command tried to return Chinese prisoners without regard for their wishes. Moreover, the UN Command had dropped a million leaflets over enemy lines at the beginning of the war promising, in effect, political asylum to enemy soldiers who surrendered voluntarily. Hundreds of Chinese came into our lines waving those leaflets over their heads. So Washington laid down the policy that the UN Command should not return prisoners who resisted exchange. However, by the beginning of June 1953, the UN Command had about 100,000 Chinese and Korean prisoners who were willing to be repatriated, and we proposed to exchange this immense number for our men who had been captured by the Communists, about thirteen thousand. The armistice at long last seemed imminent.

But we were underestimating Syngman Rhee, who was as determined to prevent an armistice as Washington was determined to conclude one. Rhee foresaw dire consequences if the United States permitted Chinese Communists to dominate North Korea while the country remained divided at the thirty-eighth parallel. Rhee protested passionately that the United States, as well as all Asian anti-Communists, would suffer a disastrous defeat unless Korea recovered its territory up to the borders of Manchuria. He insisted that it is Communist tactics to penetrate countries by the armistice method, creating a divided nation as prelude to complete conquest later. Believing this, Rhee felt justified in taking extreme measures to disrupt our negotiations. And he very nearly succeeded. The UN Command, all through the war, entrusted control of most Korean captives to Rhee's administration. Only his officials had the language and knowledge of Korean customs necessary for this task. Now, during four days of 1953, June 18–21, Rhee dramatically ordered several camps thrown open, and the whereabouts of 27,160 Korean prisoners became a mystery. Those camps had held prisoners who were ready for repatriation to North Korea, where their families and homes were located. Rhee expected his defiance would upset the truce negotiations, and for a few days we thought he might have done so. But his flamboyant gesture had not involved any Chinese prisoners, so the Peking representatives finally agreed not to make the UN Command responsible for Koreans who had vanished from Rhee's camps.

Some American officers, including General Van Fleet, openly sympathized with Rhee's defiance because they shared his belief that the war should not end until the Communists were driven out and Korea was united. But most UN staff officers were sick and tired of this war, which they were waging with one hand tied behind them. For two long years Americans and Koreans and soldiers of other nationalities had been fighting and dying with victory virtually ruled out, while the Communists kept reminding us how costly this kind of fighting can be. On July 13–14, just two weeks before the armistice, the Chinese mounted their heaviest attack in two years, causing vast casualties on both sides.

The Communist negotiators were aggressive and insolent right down to the finish, but the American negotiators gritted their teeth and obeyed instructions. Under the circumstances, Mark Clark deserves great credit for restrained and intelligent handling of an assignment as distasteful to him as it was to me. I never admired the General more than when he carried out, in complete silence about his personal feelings, the directive of an old friend, another Supreme Commander who was now President of the United States. The armistice was signed on July 27, 1953. That ended my Far Eastern appointment and I flew back to Washington before the prisoner exchange began on August 5. The UN Command handed over 70,000 Koreans but only 5640 Chinese out of more than 20,000. The Communists released 12,760 prisoners, of whom about 3500 were American and nearly 1000 British. By the truce agreement, a political conference was to be held within ninety days to arrange permanent peace terms, and talks were held to discuss the agenda for that conference. But those preliminary discussions broke up on December 12 when the chief of the UN delegation, Arthur H. Dean, announced that no basis could be found for agreement. A decade later, the "temporary" settlement which we concluded is still the only settlement. Korea remains a country divided roughly at the thirty-eighth parallel, the same geographic division which prevailed before the attack by the Communists.

It is interesting to speculate what might have happened if, six months before that attack, the Russians had not stalked out of the United Nations meeting. Only by that fluke—the absence of the Soviet delegate at a crucial moment—did the Security Council of the UN approve the mobilization of armed force against the North Koreans. What would have happened if the Russians had been present to veto UN intervention and the United States had been left to face the Korean responsibility alone? It is not difficult to imagine the reaction which would have occurred throughout the Far East, especially in Japan, Taiwan and the Philippines, if we had simply walked away and allowed the small force of our military advisory mission in South Korea to be annihilated. Viscount Cherwell, addressing the House of Lords in London, asked rhetorically: "Does anyone believe that Americans would have abandoned to massacre millions of Koreans who had put their trust in the United States?" Yet it is unlikely that President Truman would have gone into Korea alone, because many of his advisers certainly would have considered such unilateral action unwise.

But if Truman had disregarded their advice, and the United States had gone into Korea without international allies, we would have played to win. The United Nations was a restraining influence. Some members of the UN, who recognized the Peiping Government, acted as go-betweens throughout the fighting period. For instance, when the Communists were intolerably delaying truce negotiations, word was passed to Peiping through Prime Minister Nehru of India that we intended to put an end to the fighting by using A-bombs. Whereupon other UN members told the Red Chinese, in effect: "We cannot let this go all-out! We will restrain the Americans." This was not in any way treacherous. It was simply a different kind of thinking which makes half-measures a constant objective of warfare and diplomacy.

General Clark certainly would have fought all-out if given authority, and President Truman was temperamentally disposed that way.

However, the way the Korean war actually ended, it became possible to claim only that the United States—and the United Nations—prevented Communist seizure of all Korea, and prevented an immediate threat to Japan. It also became possible for Peiping propagandists to claim a victory over Americans, and this they have done with immense effect ever since.

TWENTY-FIVE

DIFFICULTIES AT THE UNITED NATIONS

In addition to frequent trips to Korea, I had opportunity while serving as Ambassador to Japan to visit other points in Asia, including Taipei, Manila and Hong Kong. But I still was only feeling my way around that part of the world when I was unexpectedly recalled to Washington in 1953. I would have liked at least another year in the Orient, and for the first time in my career, I did not welcome my new appointment. But years of discipline and old loyalty to Eisenhower prevailed, and I flew back home anticipating with pleasure my first real vacation in eleven years.

Stopping first in Milwaukee to renew ties with family and old friends, I was in my hotel exactly twenty-five minutes when a telephone call came from Secretary of State Dulles in Washington. He expressed agreement in principle with the general theory of vacations and said he understood mine was long overdue. But, he remarked, that could be taken care of later. Right then he was faced with a difficult problem in the Korean debate which was coming up in the General Assembly of the United Nations in just ten days. There was an immense amount of work to be done in preparation for that meeting, and nobody else in the Department had my firsthand recent experience. So would I please proceed to Washington by the first available airplane? I remained in Milwaukee only that evening to attend a dinner given by one of my classmates at Marquette Academy, Dr. Arthur Raymond—and I never did collect that vacation. One of the former law partners of Dulles told me later that even during his busiest years in private practice in New York, Foster Dulles never missed his month's holiday in August, usually on Duck Island. But after Dulles became Secretary of State, he decided that vacations were overrated, both for himself and for those who worked with him. He once said to me that he thought occasional weekends did the trick nicely.

The main reason I was reluctant to accept direction of United Nations Affairs in the State Department was because I was not enthusiastic about the UN. My reservations concerning that organization dated back to the years between World Wars when I had a close-up view in Europe of the original League of Nations. Supporters of the League claimed that its failures occurred largely because the United States rejected Woodrow Wilson's idealism and refused to join the League. But I shared the opinion of many thoughtful Europeans and Americans that the very concept of the League was a delusion—it promised more than it could possibly perform in a world of sovereign nations, and thus misled millions of sincere people.

When the UN Charter was proclaimed, I was disappointed because the UN seemed little more than a repetition of the old League. It raised extravagant hopes without providing means to fulfill them. It was true that the United States which spurned the League at its beginning, and the Soviet Union which was not invited to join in 1919, were members of the UN now. But neither of these super-powers nor any other government delegated any important sovereign authority to the UN. It was deceptive to pretend that they had. Moreover, because basic conflicts exist between the objectives of the Soviet Union and the United States, the UN fell far short of the dream of the Roosevelt era. Nevertheless, having begun with the Grand Design of cooperation, many Americans still are unwilling to admit that there are basic conflicts. This refusal to recognize that the Soviet Union has no desire to cooperate with Western nations has led to many forms of self-reproach, suspicion, and dissension among Americans and their allies.

The persistent devotion of Americans to the principle of collective action may be partly explained by our desire to share with other nations some of today's staggering burdens which no one country can bear alone. But there are situations where the United States is too eager to merge its identify and destiny with the United Nations. Our associates at the UN, as well as our opponents, should know that on issues which involve our own security, we Americans are capable of going our own way. This requires, of course, not only national power but also determination by our people to use it. The use of fear as an element in foreign policy is abhorrent, but negotiation often is futile with an opponent who has no respect for weakness. Billions of dollars worth of equipment is worthless if Americans lack the will to use the weapons they possess. The United States seems reluctant at times to face up to a risk on our own national account, preferring to rely on a collectivity which includes weak, inexperienced and selfish nations, thus reducing the American position to the lowest common denominator in what one Frenchman has called "a tumultuous and scandalous forum of discord."

Personally, I never regarded the UN as a divine machine from which happy solutions to our problems would miraculously flow. Nor have I feared the consequences even if the UN should collapse utterly. The other day a friend exclaimed: "That would be the end of everything!" But it just wouldn't be the end of everything. I always have tried to take a practical view of the UN organization as an apparatus which is, or can be, useful to the United States in its diplomacy. This also was the policy of Secretary Dulles, who was active from the outset in the wartime planning of the UN and its establishment at San Francisco in 1945. Dulles respected the UN but he also regarded it at times as a receptacle where almost any thorny problem could be unloaded and stored away for a year or longer. Dulles occasionally liked to operate in that manner, so he found the UN particularly convenient. When somebody from Congress or another influential group would complain to Dulles, saying, "Why haven't you done something about this?" the Secretary of State could explain, "But the UN has the matter under advisement. They are handling this problem."

When I flew into Washington in response to the urgent summons from Secretary Dulles, I was surprised to see that I was to be in charge of about one hundred and forty men and women. The new office for UN Affairs had been in existence less than a decade, but already it had as many employees as the State Department's entire Washington staff in earlier days. Furthermore, my assistants were all busy, often frantically so, in an around-the-clock operation which went on every day of the year. It was the duty of the staff to keep in touch with everything affecting the relations of the United States with the UN, which comprised some sixty countries at that time. Of course, there has been rapid expansion of UN membership ever since, until now the flags of more than one hundred nations hang at UN headquarters in New York. The UN may be required at any moment to consider almost any military, political, economic, or social problem anywhere on earth, under the seas, or in outer space. So the UN office of the State Department is supposed to examine, at least superficially, all the incredible deluge of documents, resolutions, surveys, complaints, reports which pour in from the member-governments and all branches of the UN organizations—the Secretary-Generals' Office, the General Assembly, the Security Council, the Trusteeship Council, the Economic and Social Council, and numerous special agencies. Obviously a lot of people are needed merely to extract from this flood of paper essential information for the President and his chief foreign policy adviser, the Secretary of State.

It took no time at all for me to become aware that the morale of my staff was low, and I was not surprised. For three years a Senate subcommittee headed by Senator Joseph R. McCarthy had been investigating alleged penetration of the State Department by Communists and fellow travelers, and attention had been concentrated particularly upon people assigned to the office of UN Affairs. Those Senate hearings had aroused interest even in faraway Japan, because McCarthy was endeavoring to show that American officials sympathetic to Communism were partly responsible for Communist victories in China. Japanese newspapers published reports of the McCarthy inquisition and I was distressed, while Ambassador to Japan, to observe how newspaper readers there were getting the impression that the State Department was riddled with disloyal employees. But even that publicity in Japan did not prepare me for the attitude of Americans at home. Having lived abroad for years, I was startled when an old friend greeted me in Milwaukee with the question: "Bob, how can you bring yourself to work in that nest of Commies and homosexuals in the State Department?" I thought perhaps he was making a poor joke but found he was entirely in earnest. As this friend had never been near the State Department, I asked where he was getting his information and he told me he read about it in the Chicago *Tribune.*

Several government agencies were investigating my office when I took over direction of UN Affairs. A few doubtful staff members already had been dismissed, and I examined in detail the records of individuals who still were considered suspect. It seemed to me that all these men were loyal and competent, and I sympathized with their resentment at having been made victims of clumsy security measures which had opened the way for unjustifiable congressional and press attacks. I decided that one reason why this situation had developed was because a fundamental rule of the Foreign Service had been ignored in the new office. This rule was that Foreign Service officers should be rotated regularly. Sometimes a most capable officer, if left too long at the same post, may acquire a wrong attitude which can be rectified by transfer to a different environment. But ever since the establishment of UN Affairs, a number of officers had been left uninterruptedly in certain positions where their specialized knowledge was valuable. However, this was unfair to the men concerned, not only because it tied them to work which tended to become monotonous, but more importantly because it left them open to charges of being "internationalists"—a word which conveyed lack of patriotism to a good many Americans. There was a feeling that some members of the staff had become so imbued with UN ideas that they had lost their American viewpoint. Rightly or wrongly, the dog had acquired a doubtful name.

While the office of UN Affairs at the State Department in Washington was thus being half-smothered under a cloud of innuendo, the American delegation at UN headquarters in New York was flourishing.

Aware of Roosevelt's high hopes for the world organization, Truman decided in 1945 to enhance the status of the American Ambassador to the UN by informally ranking that official practically as a member of the President's cabinet, and he appointed to that post Warren R. Austin, a statesman of great dignity and charm who had been senator from Vermont for fourteen years. This selection by the Democratic President of a Republican Ambassador was indicative of the intention to lift United States policy at the UN indisputably above domestic politics.

Later, however, when the Ambassador to the UN was ranked formally as a member of the cabinet, the Presidents who followed Truman selected only members of their own party. Eisenhower named Henry Cabot Lodge, Jr., former Republican senator from Massachusetts, as his choice for Ambassador of the UN and Kennedy named Adlai Stevenson, the twice-defeated presidential candidate of the Democrats, as his appointee. Ambassador Austin was by nature a peacemaker; he disliked public controversy as much as he disliked personal publicity. In the UN debates, he rarely raised his voice or used a harsh word in response to strident Soviet propaganda against the United States, and his replies to Russian oratorical attacks were usually made only after careful preparation, thus enabling the Russians to gain the headlines unimpeded.

But Cabot Lodge was not the Austin type. When he became American Ambassador at the UN, he decided that every Russian attack should be countered sharply, and his method of immediately challenging Soviet misrepresentation had a salutary effect. His opponent at times was Andrei Vishinsky, my former traveling companion in Italy, who had become Soviet Foreign Minister and occasionally chief Russian delegate to the UN. When Lodge and Vishinsky exchanged verbal blows, both contestants seemed to enjoy the match, and so did American radio and television audiences. Knowing that he was cast by American viewers as the villain, Vishinsky played his role with relish. Taunting "capitalist" governments had been standard procedure with Bolshevik orators, and Vishinsky adapted this tactic to the UN forum with considerable effectiveness. All UN speakers know that whenever their views are broadcast, they are addressing an audience vastly greater than the delegates assembled at UN headquarters, and they plan their performances on the world stage as carefully as any actor. Offstage, Vishinsky's manner usually changed. No matter how bitter the official arguments had been, he would discuss the most controversial issue good-humoredly in the delegates' private lounge. In contrast to the public villain Vishinsky, the chief American delegate to the UN was well equipped to play a heroic role. Cabot Lodge, over six feet tall, youthful-looking and handsome, with a speaking voice well suited to television, became during his first few months at the UN one of the best-known personalities in American public life.

I quickly learned that I would have to practice a form of diplomacy in my new post which I had not anticipated. During the Korean debates, a resolution was proposed on which the vote promised to be closely divided. There were discussions at the office of UN Affairs in Washington about how the United States should vote, and after due consideration we decided that the American vote should be "Yes." We submitted our conclusion to Secretary Dulles and he approved it, so instructions were sent to the United States mission in New York to vote "Yes." But the next morning I was dismayed to read in the newspapers that Lodge had voted "No." As soon as I could talk to him by long distance telephone I said, "Apparently our instructions failed to reach you." Lodge repeated, "Instructions? I am not bound by instructions from the State Department. I am a member of the President's cabinet and accept instructions only from him." I knew that personal and official relations between Lodge and the President were exceptionally close. Lodge had been one of the original group which launched the "Eisenhower for President" movement, and he had directed Eisenhower's contest for the Republican nomination in 1952 against Senator Robert A. Taft. But no one had warned me that Lodge regarded himself as independent of the State Department and I protested, "But you also are head of an embassy, and our ambassadors accept instructions from the Secretary of State." After a moment's pause, Lodge replied, "I take note of the Department's opinions." I was flabbergasted. As an Ambassador myself, I had acted under instructions for many years. "This is a new situation to me," I said, "and I'll have to discuss it with the Secretary." Lodge replied coolly, "Yes, do that. He will set you straight." When I did report to Dulles, he listened carefully without comment until I finished, and then said, "This is one of those awkward situations which require special consideration. If it happens again, just tell me and I'll take care of it."

My personal relations with Lodge were always agreeable. Once I understood that the Secretary of State did not choose to challenge the virtual autonomy which Lodge claimed for his embassy at the UN, I realized it was not appropriate for me to do so. A word from President Eisenhower or a call from the Secretary of State personally were accepted by Lodge in good grace, but there were explosions from time to time if instructions, or even strong suggestions, were sent by the State Department to the American mission at UN headquarters. Lodge would tolerate no poaching on what he considered his own preserve. He was as anxious as anybody to promote a consistent American foreign policy, but he interpreted his functions as much broader than those of an ordinary ambassador. He believed that his position in New York entitled him to help formulate policy as well as execute it, and of course the State Department made every effort to have him participate in policy making.

The missions of most of the great powers at the UN operate like standard embassies, accepting instructions from their own Foreign Offices. Recently, however, problems have arisen due to the entry of many small, new countries. These are not always well organized and the home governments often fail to send instructions to their representatives in New York. The latter sometimes freewheel so it is difficult to determine whether they actually are representing the views of their governments.

The American mission's assertion of independence from the State Department continued through the eight years of the Eisenhower administration. The political influence and exceptional ability of Ambassador Lodge gradually transformed the American delegation at the UN until, as the years passed, our mission behaved less like an embassy than a second Foreign Office of the United States Government. The staff in New York grew at a tremendous rate—it numbered well over one hundred when I had dealings with it—and the range of its functions expanded accordingly. No other government maintains such an impressive bureaucracy to conduct its relations with the UN organization.

The public standing and cabinet rank of Lodge's successor, Adlai Stevenson, gave him great power in the Kennedy administration. But the existence of a two-headed Foreign Office is potentially dangerous because it can seriously hamper coordination of foreign policy. A conspicuous question of such coordination occurred in 1961, a few months after President Kennedy's inauguration. Cuban patriots living in exile crossed the small stretch of ocean which separated them from their homeland, and attempted an armed invasion of their country. The purpose of their daring expedition was to assist their countrymen in Cuba to revolt against Fidel Castro, who by that time was flaunting his affiliation with Soviet Russia.

But on the eve of the scheduled attack, the American Ambassador at the UN publicly announced in New York that there would be no United States military involvement in Cuba. Stevenson's statement apparently was made under instructions from the State Department, but also apparently in ignorance of military plans. Washington was persuaded to deny the use of the few American planes which with a great deal of luck might have enabled the weak Cuban invasion to succeed, and the absence of which guaranteed failure. There were various other factors in that Cuban affair, of course, and the confusion distracted public attention from the lack of coordination between American policy makers. President Kennedy accepted full responsibility, as he should, thereby choking off debate. The appointment of Harlan Cleveland as head of the UN office at the State Department suggests what probably is the most practical solution of the problem, a competent official in Washington who has the confidence of our Ambassador in New York.

The State Department and the United States mission to the UN are by no means always in conflict. More often than not, the two diplomatic groups see eye to eye on policies and usually on tactics, too. However, the State Department's point of view has special angles which sometimes are not appreciated by other departments. There was no conflict between the State Department and the Pentagon on some later phases of our Cuban policy, but those two branches of our government disagreed on policy during another Cuban episode which occurred before Castro seized power. At the time of this earlier episode, Castro was still an outlaw with secret headquarters in Sierra Maestra, and the question was whether the United States should use diplomacy or force to rescue thirty-one American Marines who had been kidnapped by his guerrillas. The unarmed Marines were returning to the Guantánamo Naval Base, after spending the evening at a movie in Guantánamo City, when their bus was stopped at a lonely spot and surrounded by guerrillas armed with machine guns. Our men were spirited to the mountains where they were hidden in separate small groups. We learned later that the idea had been developed by Raul Castro in the mistaken notion that this outrage would somehow persuade the United States to declare itself in favor of his brother's rebellion against Batista, who then ruled the island.

The kidnapping struck a sensitive nerve in the Pentagon which did not like the trend in Cuba anyway. The increasing boldness of the guerrillas seemed to be affecting American security in the Caribbean, and the Navy recommended an immediate intervention in Cuba of divisional size, with whatever naval support would be required to rescue the thirty-one Marines. Representatives of the State Department, however, had all kinds of reasons for opposing the Navy project, and there followed a series of meetings with representatives of the Pentagon, including a lengthy night session at the residence of Admiral Arleigh A. Burke, Chief of Naval Operations. Together with Roy R. Rubottom, Jr., Assistant Secretary of State for Inter-American Affairs, and members of his staff, I represented the State Department at that meeting.

While appreciating the Navy's justifiable indignation over the crude provocation, the State Department had distinct aversion to American military involvement in Cuba. We took the position that getting into the island would not be difficult but that getting out would be interminable. We reminded the military officers that the policy of the

United States Government is to keep out of the territory of our Latin-American neighbors. We recalled our obligations as members of the Organization of American States. We explained that we were bound by the Charter of the United Nations. Furthermore, we contended that if the objective was to recover the Marines alive, this could be accomplished by negotiation. If we intervened militarily, we might with luck find their corpses. Beyond the rescue of the Marines, it was the Navy's hope that American intervention would stabilize the situation in Cuba, although none of our military officers had confidence in Batista. The Pentagon was aware that the Cuban dictator had failed to subdue Castro's forces when they began activities as a mere handful of rebels, and our officers despised the incompetence and manifest corruption of Batista's associates. In the end, the Navy agreed to let the State Department try its hand at negotiation, and all the Marines were recovered alive by the American Consul at Santiago de Cuba, Park F. Wollam, who did a superb job as negotiator. But in retrospect it is intriguing to speculate what would have happened if the United States had intervened militarily.

The relationship of the United States Government with Batista's regime is sometimes cited as evidence that the State Department favors dictators. Batista in Cuba was a well-advertised dictator, and notwithstanding that his administration supported our policy in the UN and elsewhere, two or three American newspapers and congressmen goaded the State Department at every opportunity for allegedly favoring this dictator. But in my long years in the Department, I never detected affection or preference by any member of the staff for any dictator anywhere. Certainly our most determined opponents at the United Nations—the Soviet Union and its satellites—are all dictatorships. What critics of the State Department are inclined to ignore is that every Foreign Office, as a practical day-by-day matter, is obliged to deal with governments in power. Even if the relationship is distasteful to the State Department, it has no choice. For one thing, when an important topic is being debated in the UN, especially in the Security Council or General Assembly, it may be impossible to disregard the value of the vote of a particular country. The opposition leaders of that country, making agitated speeches back home, do not cast votes at UN headquarters.

The complexity and the diplomacy involved in "getting out the vote" at the UN can scarcely be imagined by anyone who has not toiled behind the scenes. The UN is not only an international forum—the greatest loudspeaker in the world—but it also is a center of information on the attitudes and policies of every nation represented there. Whenever an important resolution is under consideration, an enormous amount of preparatory work is done by the Department of State and by the American mission at the UN. Many foreign governments must be consulted, many must be supplied with facts, many must be advised on procedures.

By thus providing opportunity to other countries, whose self-interests coincide with ours, to harmonize their actions with our own, the United States Government has seldom been defeated in any significant political dispute in the U.N. This voting record has not been achieved without constant vigilance, as the Guatemala incident of 1954 illustrates. Guatemala was by no means the most troublesome of the many problems with which I was involved during my final years at the Department of State, but it is worth relating because it is typical of our times. In the latter part of 1953 I became aware of an unsatisfactory trend of events in the normally friendly Central American Republic whose President was Jacobo Arbenz, a left-wing army officer. After Arbenz took office in 1951, the Communist Party made rapid strides in Guatemala, proclaiming that it was working for social reform and against United States "imperialism." The Party membership was of standard pattern, comparatively small, perhaps three or four thousand, with a carefully selected group of competent leaders, many of whom made trips to Moscow. In May 1954, a Swedish cargo vessel, the M/V *Alfhem,* arrived at Puerto Barrios, Guatemala, with two thousand tons of arms listed in the manifest as "hardware and optical goods." The cargo actually consisted of fifteen thousand cases of rifles, machine guns and other military equipment, manufactured mostly in Czechoslovakia, and it was unloaded with great secrecy.

A group of Guatemalan anti-Communists were living in exile at that time in neighboring countries, and on June 18 about two hundred of these political exiles crossed the frontier to attack the followers of Arbenz, whom they believed had sold out to Soviet Russia. The invaders were led by Colonel Carlos Castillo Armas, and they were joined in Guatemala by some five hundred additional anti-Communists. The danger was whether Guatemalan soldiers would obey orders from President Arbenz to put down this revolt, but the Communists had not been able to infiltrate the regular Army and the soldiers refused to fight. Arbenz, after instituting a brief reign of terror, agreed to a cease-fire on June 29 and he and eight hundred of his followers took refuge in the Mexican Embassy.

Meanwhile, representatives of the Arbenz regime had lost no time in making formal protest against the neighboring countries of Honduras and Nicaragua, which were charged at the UN in New York with pursuing a policy of hostility and aggression. The Guatemala delegation made no direct accusation against the United States Government, though veiled hints were made against American individuals and business corporations. However, the Soviet Union blatantly charged the United States Government with having prepared armed intervention in Guatemala, and proposed in the Security Council that a UN Commission of Inquiry should investigate the matter.

From our point of view, the situation had been deliberately fomented by the Soviet Union as an agent of international Communism, and John C. Dreier, American Ambassador to the Organization of American States, made a brilliant exposé of this Communist penetration in an address to the OAS on June 28. The apparatus, he explained, was classical: A national front had been set up; the local government was permeated with Communists and their sympathizers; the labor movement was controlled; the acute need for social reform was exploited. Mass organizations were promoted—peace movements, women's clubs, youth "democratic" alliances, student groups, writers' and artists' clubs. Everything was done to appeal to young intellectuals who had adopted European cultural standards. When the forces of Castillo Armas captured the country, they found warehouses jammed with Communist propaganda material sent directly from Moscow. Arbenz, with the advice of the Russians, had been planning to arm the "agrarian workers" and the "people"—the customary last step before setting up a "proletarian revolutionary dictatorship."

In the hope of preventing establishment of a Soviet satellite in an area so vital to the security of Latin America and to the United States itself, the State Department naturally had watched this development with the closest attention, under the direction of Henry F. Holland, Assistant Secretary of State for Inter-American Affairs, and we had given whatever assistance we legitimately could to Castillo Armas and his fellow exiles. The United States delegation at the UN had no objection to an investigation of our government's activities with regard to Guatemala, but we contended that the inquiry should be conducted not by a commission of the UN but by the appropriate regional agency, the Organization of American States, as provided by the Charter of the UN. In view of the obvious attempt by Communist nations to engage in subversion in the heart of the American hemisphere, we believed it would be intolerable for a Commission of Inquiry to include representatives of those very nations.

The United States delegation had assumed it could count on the support of its friends when this question came to a vote, but to our dismay the British and French were inclined to favor the Soviet resolution. They believed the UN had authority to appoint a mixed lot of international delegates and saw no reason why it should not do so. The jurisdiction of the Organization of American States, they contended, was permissive but not mandatory. Britain and France were excluded from the OAS, of course, and it could be inferred that they wanted to participate in the investigation. Some nations always have been rather annoyed with United States power in Latin America, whatever form it assumes, just as they never have rejoiced over the Monroe Doctrine. We felt that the whole status of regional organization was at stake, but urgent representations to the UN Ambassadors of the United Kingdom and France were of no avail, and it became necessary for the President himself to appeal at the Prime Minister level. This was one of the few times the United States had ever sought the votes of its European allies in a matter affecting Central America, though we had been asked on sundry occasions to support them in matters concerning the Mediterranean and Middle Eastern areas. But the best we could obtain from our friends was their consent to abstain from voting. With this grudging assistance, the Soviet demand for a Commission of Inquiry was defeated, and the OAS made a report to the UN which was helpful to the United States point of view.

Castillo Armas was installed as President of Guatemala, through the process of a constitutional assembly and a plebiscite, and Jacobo Arbenz and his Communist associates fled to Mexico. Eventually some of them went to Cuba, including Arbenz and "Comrade" Che Guevara. The latter became head of the Cuban National Bank, a power in the Castro regime, and a frequent visitor to Moscow. Castro by that time already had made known that Communists who were forced to flee from the wrath of their own countrymen would be welcome in Cuba, and the island today is an assembly point for many Latin-American revolutionaries.

These restless men, living in exile so near to the United States, are a considerable threat to peace, as was demonstrated by the abortive invasion of Panama a few years ago. A handful of Panamanian exiles accompanied by a few Cubans, a group of about ninety in all, landed on a strip of jungle coast with the objective of overthrowing the government. The invaders were in possession of light military equipment and their advent caused near panic. The State Department in Washington was informed that some members of the Panamanian Government were packing their baggage for hurried departure, and an urgent request was received for machine guns and ammunition. In response to this request, an adequate supply was flown to Panama immediately. Then the Panamanians discovered that their security force was not qualified to handle the new equipment, so at another urgent request, a few American technicians were flown down to help them. Then Panama discovered a shortage of qualified personnel to direct its expedition against the guerrillas, and again help was promptly provided at Panamanian request. In the end the guerrillas were apprehended.

Soon after this episode, when perhaps one might have expected an atmosphere of appreciation to prevail, the President of Panama dispatched a lengthy communication to President Eisenhower listing demands for a series of adjustments relating to the Canal Zone, such as higher pay for Panamanian workers. President Eisenhower sent the President of Panama a friendly acknowledgment which was duly followed, in accordance with standard diplomatic procedure, by a note from the Secretary of State to the Panamanian Foreign Minister. This communication discussed the several items demanded by Panama and gave satisfactory assurance on some which already were under active study by our government. But this letter from Secretary Christian A. Herter was returned by Panama with an indication that only a personal message from Eisenhower himself would be acceptable. Even making due allowance for internal Panamanian politics, the contrast between the two incidents was not lost on those of us in Washington who were dealing with such matters.

Two months after my arrival in Washington, my friend and colleague, H. Freeman Matthews, was named Ambassador to the Netherlands, thus leaving a vacancy in the office which he held as Deputy Under Secretary for Political Affairs. That interesting post had been created largely to resolve differences of opinion which frequently arose within the Department itself. For example, the Assistant Secretary for Far Eastern Affairs might be inclined to favor President Sukarno in Indonesia, while the Office for European Affairs might recommend a contrary policy urged by Dutch officials at The Hague. I was appointed to take over concurrently the responsibilities of both the UN Affairs office and the work which Matthews had been doing, although Dulles was a bit doubtful, feeling that dealing with Lodge was a full-time job in itself. But Dulles agreed to let me try this arrangement, and a few months later the title and duties of Assistant Secretary for UN Affairs went to another experienced Foreign Service officer, another man in the middle, David Key, who had my warm sympathy.

In 1953 I had not wanted to be assigned to Washington at all, preferring a field post, but the job which I almost refused opened the way to six years of intense activity. From Deputy Under Secretary, I was promoted to Under Secretary for Political Affairs, the no. 3 spot in the Department of State and the highest post to which a career diplomat could reasonably aspire, since the two higher positions—Secretary of State and Under Secretary of State—are political appointments. As Under Secretary, I was the State Department's representative at the regular weekly meetings with the Joint Chiefs of Staff at the Pentagon, and I also came into top-level contact with other agencies of the government, the Federal Bureau of Investigation, the Central Intelligence Agency, the Washington diplomatic corps, and the White House. The work was grueling, but it concerned the entire sweep of American foreign policy and diplomacy and it provided my most satisfying years.

TWENTY-SIX

SUEZ CRISIS (1956)

One of the State Department's most difficult problems at the beginning of 1956 was the proposal to build the Aswan High Dam on the Nile River. This project was not only a formidable undertaking for Egypt but was also an important international undertaking, because the Middle East was in turmoil and Soviet Russia was fishing in the troubled waters. The focus of attention was Cairo, the capital of Egypt, where Gamal Abdel Nasser had led the 1952 revolt which resulted in the abdication of King Farouk. Economic conditions in Egypt at that time were impossible—the life expectancy of a peasant was perhaps thirty-five years and his average annual income about sixty dollars—and Americans sympathized with President Nasser's desire to raise the living standard of his country. The United States extended economic aid in various ways, but the most promising scheme appeared to be construction of an irrigation and power plant at Aswan. It was estimated that it would take sixteen years to complete this project, the largest of its kind in the world then, and that the total cost would be about two billion dollars, of which four hundred million would be needed in foreign currency. The State Department, in consultation with the British Government, worked out a plan with Eugene R. Black, president of the World Bank, to provide Egypt with the foreign money required, and a joint offer was announced on December 16, 1955. Shortly thereafter, Cairo publicly expressed its intention of accepting the proffered financial assistance.

Although the World Bank and the British Government were willing to contribute part of the funds for construction of the High Dam, most of the money would have to come from the United States—and the Aswan project was not popular in Congress. For one thing, American aid already given to Egypt had been provided in the face of many irritations. Another difficulty was the unresolved problem of dividing the waters of the Nile, a delicate question which remained a potential source of dispute. Furthermore, the publicity accorded the Aswan project had stimulated exorbitant requests from other Middle Eastern countries which did not favor strengthening Egypt unless they, too, received extravagant assistance. Nasser's ambition to establish an Arab empire from Casablanca to Baghdad had aroused uneasiness in the countries concerned, none of which yearned for Egyptian leadership. As for Israel, whose very existence was threatened by Arab hostility, that nation had special reason to fear Nasser's dominance, and Jewish organizations in the United States naturally opposed giving aid to Israel's enemies. Notwithstanding all these objections, the State Department believed that the Aswan plan was so humanely beneficial and so politically potent that it should receive our support.

While congressional committees were deliberating the pending Foreign Aid Bill, we were appalled to discover that Nasser had become involved in an extensive deal to purchase more than two hundred million dollars worth of airplanes, tanks, and other military equipment from the Soviet Union and Czechoslovakia, and had mortaged Egypt's stockpile of cotton in payment. Nasser had closed one deal with the Soviet Union in 1955, and now was arranging a second big arms deal. It was thought in Washington that the meager Egyptian economy simply could not support both the High Dam and Nasser's armament program. It already had been decided that one-third of Egypt's internal revenue should be diverted for ten years to the huge Aswan project, and an unproductive military drain would leave virtually nothing for necessities.

At this critical hour the Egyptian Ambassador returned from Cairo, where he had been on lengthy consultation with his government, and called upon Secretary Dulles. Even before departing from Egypt, Ambassador Ahmed Hussein announced that he was returning to Washington to sign the Aswan Dam agreement and that he foresaw no serious problems. The fact was, however, that there still remained large gaps in the agreement and that Nasser, despite our urging for six months, had chosen not to discuss these important details. The gaps were so formidable that extensive further negotiating would be required, but such talks inevitably would give the impression that we, rather than the Egyptians, were the hagglers. Hussein, carrying out his Cairo instructions, delivered on July 19 what was in effect an ultimatum demanding from the United States a commitment of hundreds of millions of dollars over a period of ten years or more. Such commitment would require congressional authorization, of course, and Congress had steadfastly refused to make long-term pledges. In fact, congressional leaders were disposed at that moment to disallow the use of American funds for the Aswan project even on a year-to-year basis.

So when the Egyptian Ambassador informed the Secretary of

State that if the United States would not guarantee to foot practically all of the Aswan bill, the Soviet Union would do so, Dulles told him in precise terms that the United States did not submit to blackmail and that our offer of aid was withdrawn. Dulles added politely that he hoped relations between the two countries would improve so that the matter could be re-examined at some future time. Hussein pleaded the Egyptian case skillfully, saying that reports exaggerated the quantity of arms which had been purchased from the Soviet bloc, and declaring that Nasser was anxious for an agreement with the United States, but Dulles reiterated that the American decision was firm. My own impressions of Hussein was that he was well disposed personally and felt that he failed in his mission. Certainly failure was not due to lack of effort on his part, but he was caught, as ambassadors often are, in a chancery of circumstances.

Those of us who worked with Dulles were never told explicitly why he acted so abruptly. We surmised that perhaps the main reason was because Nasser was scheduled to make a trip to Moscow early in August. If the United States would agree to the Aswan Dam financing, the Egyptian President could then concentrate in Moscow on concluding his second big arms deal with the Russians, thus getting the best of both worlds. Dulles guessed accurately that Nasser would not journey to Moscow at all if the Aswan Dam offer were rescinded, because that would compel the Egyptian to go hat-in-hand not only with regard to the High Dam project but on the arms deal as well.

But the effects of summarily withdrawing the Aswan offer had not been weighed carefully in advance. Although aware for several days of the Soviet arms deal, Dulles had summoned no staff meeting to discuss this new development. I was working with him at the time on related Middle Eastern problems, but he did not mention the Aswan matter to me. Even President Eisenhower was not consulted until the morning of Hussein's visit. There also was regrettable lack of adequate notice to the partners in the consortium, especially Britain which was chiefly affected. The British Ambassador in Washington, Sir Roger Makins, was notified of the American decision to cancel its offer to Egypt only an hour or so before Hussein called on Dulles. As Prime Minister Eden later said: "Her Majesty's Government were informed but were not consulted." Eugene Black, who had worked on the Aswan negotiations for more than a year on behalf of the World Bank, was particularly distressed by the sudden cancellation. Immediately after Hussein's visit, the Department of State issued a press release announcing its decision, but beyond that uninformative statement, Dulles never did explain his actions.

Five days passed without any visible reaction from Egypt. Then on July 24 Nasser made a speech at the opening of a new oil refinery near Cairo, and his address was marked by intemperate language to the effect that he would not permit the dollar to rule Egypt. Cairo newspapers chimed in with attacks against the United States. Two days later Nasser made his famous speech at Alexandria before an enormous crowd and recited his reasons for purchasing arms from the Soviet bloc. When the Western nations gave one rifle to seventy million Arabs, he declared, they gave two rifles to one million Zionists, so the Zionists could always be supreme. What was occurring in Palestine, Nasser said, was a process aimed at annihilating Arab nationalism. He accused the United States and the United Kingdom of perfidy, and charged the World Bank with generosity to Israel and a niggardly attitude toward the Arabs.

Nasser's theme was familiar up to this point, but then he went on to give his interpretation of the history of the Suez Canal, telling his audience that the Canal was dug by the sons of Egypt and that twenty thousand of them perished in the process. According to the Suez concession made in 1854 and 1856, Nasser said, Egypt was to have 44 percent ownership of the Canal Company, but Britain eventually cheated Egypt of its holdings. The income of the company in 1955 was one hundred million dollars, Nasser continued, and then he dramatically concluded his speech by announcing that he had signed a resolution nationalizing the Suez Canal. With income from Canal tolls, he declared, Egypt would not need American aid.

The first information the State Department received of Egypt's expropriation of the Suez Canal was what we read on the news ticker in our Washington office. Nasser's dramatic action came as a complete surprise to the American Government, as it did to others. Secretary Dulles had gone to South America to attend the inauguration of President Prado of Peru, and our well-informed Ambassador to the United Kingdom, Winthrop W. Aldrich, was on summer vacation in Maine. President Eisenhower and Prime Minister Eden got into transatlantic communication, and Eisenhower was invited to send an emissary to London to align a joint policy with Britain and France. Eden cabled: "My colleagues and I are convinced that we must be ready, in the last resort, to use force to bring Nasser to his senses. For our part we are prepared to do so. I have this morning instructed our Chiefs of Staff to prepare a military plan accordingly." Under the circumstances, it seemed to us in Washington no more than routine staff procedure that such a plan should be put in readiness. Eisenhower also was informed that Christian Pineau, the French Foreign Minister, was due to arrive in England on Sunday, July 29, "by previous arrangement."

Herbert Hoover, Jr., was Acting Secretary of State, and this was fortunate because he had extensive knowledge of the Middle East, the world's petroleum business, and related problems. Eisenhower asked Hoover and me to come to the White House to discuss the situation with him. Apart from Eden's brief message, we were uninformed regarding Anglo-French intentions, so our discussion actually was little more than a superficial review of recent events. The President was not greatly concerned, and there was no talk of recalling Dulles from Peru. The Middle East was regarded as of great importance to the United States, but American investments in the Canal Company were negligible. Eisenhower decided I should go to London "to see what it's all about," and he notified Eden that he was sending me as his representative. At the same time, he urged the British Prime Minister to extend the consultation to the largest possible number of maritime nations, since all of them were affected by the seizure of the Suez Canal. After my short talk with Eisenhower and Hoover, I departed on a few hours' notice, accompanied by Foreign Service officer William C. Burdett, a specialist in the Middle East area and a son of the consul whom I had succeeded at Seville way back in 1925. I went to London with no formal instructions whatever. "Just go over and hold the fort," the President told me.

I arrived in London late on Saturday night. The British Prime Minister was spending the weekend at his "cottage" in Wiltshire, but Foreign Secretary Selwyn Lloyd invited me on Sunday morning to meet with him and the French Foreign Minister, who had just flown in from Paris. I was not very well acquainted with Lloyd but I liked him and respected his ability. He confirmed that Her Majesty's Government had decided to be ready to use force if necessary, and I replied that of course the United States Government had made no such decision. The two Foreign Ministers did not appear to expect any affirmative assurances from me, but they seemed to assume that the United States would be involved in their plans. I asked a few questions, but mostly I just listened. The conversation was rather restrained and I did not learn anything very specific.

So I was pleased, upon telephoning to my old wartime associate Harold Macmillan, to be invited to dine informally with him that evening. Although Macmillan and I had worked together for twenty months in the Mediterranean, as British and American Political Advisers to General Eisenhower, I had enjoyed only sporadic visits with him since the end of the war. Macmillan now was Chancellor of the Exchequer, and I could see that he appreciated the dignity and traditions of his official residence at No. 11 Downing Street. Architecturally, the historic abode conveyed a certain Elizabethan atmosphere, especially the dining room, whose oak beams and pillars suggested the Tower of London. Yet I sensed that although Macmillan was well pleased with No. 11 Downing Street, he had aspirations to move some day to No. 10, the official residence of the Prime Minister. As things turned out in the Suez affair, Macmillan was to move next door sooner than any of us that evening suspected.

Only two other guests were invited to that dinner—Walworth Barbour, the able Chargé d'Affaires at the American Embassy, and the British officer I had known as General Alexander, Supreme Allied Commander in the Mediterranean Theater in 1944-45, now retired with rank of Field Marshal. Through many months of working closely with Macmillan and Alexander, I had developed great admiration for both of them. Both had successfully borne heavy reponsibilities and great honors, and both had successfully retained their sense of realism and sense of humor. Our conversation that night was easy and relaxed but it was not reminiscent of past associations. Our thoughts were on Suez, and as we sipped our admirable after-dinner brandy, Macmillan and Alexander discussed the situation frankly.

If Britain did not accept Egypt's challenge, Macmillan said, "Britain would become another Netherlands." I was left in no doubt that the British Government believed that Suez was a test which could be met only by the use of force, and I was not surprised at this reaction because it seemed not unjustified. I was told that the French saw eye to eye with the British on the necessity of making a stand, and that they were prepared to participate in a military operation. Although Alexander was retired, the distinguished soldier obviously was in close touch with the campaign plans and approved them. It was intimated that military moves might start in August and "would not take much"—perhaps a division or at the most two. And it would be all over in ten days, with the Suez Canal returned to international control. The British did not like the risk and expense involved—the government had set aside five million pounds for the venture—but "Nasser has to be chased out of Egypt." It was believed that the British people were unanimously behind the government in its determination to defeat Nasser. Macmillan and Alexander conveyed the impression of men who have made a great decision and are serene in the belief that they have decided wisely.

Although the little dinner party was private and unofficial, I realized after leaving No. 11 Downing Street that a full report must be sent to President Eisenhower, and instead of going to bed I went to the American Embassy to dispatch a cablegram. Personally, I thought that the straight-forward presentation I had just received of Anglo-French plans made good sense, and I shared British indignation over Nasser's high-handed action in seizing control of the Canal in defiance of international agreements. But I knew that United States policy opposed the type of eighteenth-century strategy which was in the minds of our friends, and the message which I prepared did not express my own opinions. It was a strictly factual amount of the evening's conversation. Since Secretary Dulles was absent and I was the President's emissary, I addressed my cablegram directly to Eisenhower. The dispatch was filed about 2 A.M. Monday in London, but it was Sunday evening in Washington when it arrived there, due to five hours' difference in time, and when I awoke in the morning, Eisenhower's reply was waiting for me. He made no comment on the contents of my report, but simply notified me that Dulles was returning from Peru and was being sent to London. There was no additional information. My only instructions still were to "see what it's all about" and "hold the fort."

The Secretary of State, it developed, was disinclined to proceed immediately to London. The Prime Minister informed the House of Commons on Monday that financial measures had been put into effect to freeze Egyptian sterling balances and thus to partially safeguard the assets of the Canal Company. It seemed in Washington that the British were taking a calmer view of the situation, and Dulles was content for me to carry on temporarily with talks with Lloyd and Pineau. They, however, were not happy about this as they felt that the United States was not taking the Suez affair sufficiently in earnest. Britain and France were understandably alarmed over the prospect of a vital artery, through which flowed much of their commerce, falling under the domination of the one-man government in Cairo. The importance of the Suez Canal had increased greatly since the war, due to expansion of oil fields in the Middle East and dependence of the industries of western Europe on this oil supply. In 1955, 14,666 ships had passed through the Canal, one-third of which were British, three-fourths serving NATO countries. Nevertheless, in my talks with Lloyd and Pineau on Monday, there was no hint that the United States would be expected to join any military moves.

On Tuesday I lunched with Sir Anthony Eden, Lord Salisbury, Selwyn Lloyd, Macmillan, and three Americans. No Frenchmen were present but there was nothing like the frank discussion of issues which I had heard on my first evening in London. The British seemed to feel that if a firm stand were taken at the outset, all maritime powers would support it, but there was no suggestion of imminent military activity. There was confident assumption, however, that the United States would go along with anything Britain and France did. As Eden expressed it, there was no thought of asking the United States for anything, "but we do hope you will take care of the Bear!" A neat way of saying that Britain and France would take care of the Egyptians, but in case of intervention by the Russian Bear, it was anticipated that the United States would step in. It seemed to me that Eden was laboring under the impression that a common identity of interest existed among the allies. That was not the American view, and I gave no encouragement to the idea.

Eden seemed at top form at this luncheon, but the Prime Minister had not adjusted his thoughts to the altered world status of Great Britain, and he never did. When the Conservative party returned to office in England in October 1951, and Eden became Foreign Minister again after a lapse of six years, he apparently expected to play the diplomatic starring role which he had performed for so long between the wars and during World War II. It seemed impossible for Eden to keep in mind how much Britain's power had diminished in relation to the United States and Russia. But Dulles never forgot this, and of course neither did the Russians. Macmillan understood from the time I knew him in Algiers, and he never spoke the way Eden did. Eden had suffered a serious operation, but he was taking care of himself and when I met him at the early conferences his health showed no ill effect. But perhaps his lowered physical stamina did affect his judgment when quick decisions became necessary later. He lost his nerve.

The French Foreign Minister was far more aggressive than the British Prime Minister. Nobody can be more ruthless in playing power politics or more intellectually insolent than French Socialists, once they believe their ox has been gored. Pineau did not conceal his contempt for what he called American naïveté. He acted as if he had received a blank check from the United States Government, but he did not take me into his confidence and I never was privy to French secret plans. The head office of the Suez Canal Company was in Paris, under terms of the Treaty of Constantinople of 1888, and Paris reacted vigorously from the moment Nasser seized control of the international waterway. Egyptian assets were frozen immediately and French canal pilots were ordered off duty. The French management confidently predicted that when their pilots left, operations would bog down and accidents multiply. They also declared that Egyptians lacked the technical training to enlarge the canal to accommodate the increasingly heavy traffic. American experts never were impressed with these scare arguments, and later events showed how mistaken were the French.

Pineau was annoyed with me from the start. There was a leak to the press at the end of the first day's meeting, and Pineau accused me of being responsible. It is notorious that most press leaks emanate from French delegations, and Pineau and I exchanged some sharp words on the subject. The Foreign Minister had another grievance. Nasser had used the cancellation of the Aswan deal as his excuse for expropriating the Suez Canal, and Pineau insisted that since the United States was responsible for the Aswan decision, it should not disinterest itself from the consequences. Our government, however, believed that the seizure and subsequent efficient administration of the Canal gave evidence of considerable forethought. This operation could not have been accomplished on a sudden whim and therefore should not be regarded as retaliatory. The Egyptians timed their seizure to exploit the optimum moment. Pineau was distraught by the notion that Europe would be cut off from oil, and he feared that Nasser was a tool of the Soviet Union and would bring the Middle East under Soviet domination. He emphasized the effect that Nasser's policy would have on Algeria and upon the entire French position in North Africa. Pineau felt that I was not taking the Suez crisis seriously enough. In fact, he said so in a speech in the French National Assembly some time later, when he asserted that Dulles was sent to London "to replace Robert Murphy, who did not attach to the situation the interest which was required."

Pineau was dead wrong about the degree of importance which all of us in the United States Government attached to the Suez incident. Americans fully appreciated the gravity of the situation and we made a very sober appraisal of the facts. As is often the case among allies, the material interest of the United States was not identical with that of either France or the United Kingdom. France and Britain had very substantial holdings in the Canal Company. American holdings were insignificant. France and Britain were directly dependent on the flow of Middle East oil. The United States was not nearly so dependent. But even though our commercial interests were not as vitally affected as those of our British and French friends, we certainly were fully aware of the importance of Western prestige in the Middle East.

As it became increasingly evident that there was serious and perhaps imminent prospect of Anglo-French military action, President Eisenhower decided that Dulles should depart immediately for London, although the Secretary told me when he arrived that he had not been anxious to come. Eisenhower had strong personal conviction that fundamental principles were involved—that the United States could not be a party to this type of military operation in view of its support of the rule of law and the United Nations Charter, and in view of what Eisenhower considered the injustice of insisting on these principles in the case of smaller countries if we were willing to wink at violations by greater powers. The fact that the issue affected our closest allies increased the embarrassment and difficulty. There were some in Washington who regarded Eden as "slippery," and Eisenhower was determined not to have the United States used as a cat's paw to protect British oil interests.

The policy of our government during the Suez affair strikingly demonstrated the close teamwork which existed between Eisenhower and Dulles. The President behaved like the chairman of the board, leaving it to his Secretary to handle details, and the latter acted as a buffer so far as the public was concerned. Dulles, operating under basic instructions to prevent military intervention, was acutely aware that a commitment to support hostilities could have a disastrous effect on Eisenhower's candidacy that year for re-election as President.

Dulles arrived in London on August 1 and the British Prime Minister gave a dinner in his honor the following evening. It was obvious that Eden and Dulles were uncomfortable with one another. Many Americans have found Eden uncongenial. Dulles disliked his attitude about Europe generally, and especially Eden's attitude at the 1954 conference on Indochina. Hoover "couldn't stand him." One State Department official asserted that he had never met a dumber man. Eden's memoirs give the impression that Dulles had a disastrous effect upon the Anglo-American alliance, with Suez as the outstanding example. Dulles died without writing his own memoirs, so his version of what occurred can be learned only eventually from his private papers and through accounts of other participants.

Until the arrival of Dulles, the tripartite conversations in London had been purely exploratory. But Dulles came accompanied by Herman Phleger, the shrewd legal adviser of the State Department, and the two lawyers had devised various delaying tactics designed to support Eisenhower's policy of avoiding military intervention. It was philosophically assumed that the danger of bellicose action would disappear if negotiations were prolonged, and that delays would reduce the heat and make possible some kind of nonviolent settlement in Egypt.

In his initial conversations with the British and French, Dulles stressed the need to "mobilize world opinion" as a preliminary to convening a large conference of the principal maritime users of the Canal, who should be organized in the hope of achieving a compromise. The American Secretary of State, who had been so abrupt with the Egyptian Ambassador a fortnight before, now counseled patience. He began to lean toward the opinion that the Suez question should be referred to an impartial tribunal such as the United Nations or the International Court. It became immediately apparent that our allies were opposed to entrusting this matter to the United Nations and favored direct action. Dulles pointed out the dangers of precipitate military action and urged that procedures be created which would bring about a peaceful and enduring solution. He said it was the view of the United States Government that no ultimatum should be presented which would require Nasser, under threat of force, to reverse his action nationalizing the Canal. It was Dulles' belief that Nasser would refuse and war would become inevitable.

Dulles and Phleger settled down to days of tedious parleys. Dulles' strength and weakness was in coming up with lawyers' devices to protect a case or a client. Ambassador Aldrich, who by this time had returned to London, became as impatient with the Secretary of State as Eden and the French representatives were. Aldrich told me that Dulles never could make up his mind even when he was in private law practice. The Secretary's approach now was the legal one of invoking the 1888 Convention of Constantinople, which guaranteed the international character of the Canal for all time. The Convention gave to all nations the same rights of transit through the Canal which the signatory countries enjoyed. Dulles took pains to explain the difference between the legal status of the Suez and Panama canals. Egypt retained sovereign rights in the Suez area, even though traffic was controlled by a privately owned company according to international agreement. The Panama Canal Zone, on the contrary, was "leased in perpetuity" to the United States and therefore was an American, not an international, waterway.

Secretary Dulles also reported that Eisenhower took the position that American ships in transit in the Suez Canal should be permitted to pay tolls to Egyptian officials. Britain and France, under their laws, were able to dictate to their commercial ship operators in a way that our government could not, and they had forbidden their vessels to acknowledge Egyptian authority even if the ships had to go around the Cape of Good Hope. Fortunately, the State Department had in Hoover an expert on the oil situation throughout the world. Under Hoover's experienced direction, the State Department and other agencies made valiant efforts to guarantee a provisional supply of oil to western Europe pending settlement of the Suez question. A plan to finance this immense and complicated undertaking was worked out with Secretary of the Treasury George M. Humphrey.

While the relationship between Eden and Dulles was correct during these preliminary conversations, there was evident strain which did not appear at the discussions which Dulles had with Macmillan or Lloyd. Macmillan asserted that the British public was determined not to let Nasser get away with aggressive violation of Egypt's treaty obligations, that Britain would be finished as a world power if that happened, and that the entire British position in the Middle East would be jeopardized. The great oil pipelines would be nationalized next, he said, and the Arab world would lose its respect for the British. If necessary, Britain would have to fight to defend its national security, even though this would be a hardship financially. "This is Munich all over again!" he exclaimed. France was with Britain on this issue, and Macmillan hoped for United States support.

It was finally agreed to invite twenty-four countries to send delegates to London for an international conference. Britain and France wanted the meeting to assemble immediately; Dulles thought there should be several weeks of preparation. A compromise date was fixed and it was announced that the conference would convene on August 16. The countries invited to participate were the eight signatories of the Constantinople convention—which included Russia but not the United States—plus the sixteen principal users of the Canal in terms of tonnage and trade. The three-power talks came to an end and our group flew back to Washington.

If John Foster Dulles ever was actually convinced of the possibility of organizing a Canal Users Association to operate the Suez Canal, I was not aware of it. Perhaps he considered the idea useful as a negotiating device. Probably he thought that a legal case could be made, sound enough to be upheld in any tribunal, which could demonstrate the good faith of the Association in keeping the Canal operating and in paying tolls to maintain it. A practical effect would be to divert tolls from Egyptian hands until a settlement and compensation for nationlization could be arranged. But Dulles did not spell this out and it seemed to me that he was skillfully working for time in the hope that public opinion in western Europe would harden against a military adventure. He recognized that it would be almost impossible to arouse Americans to join in defense of the Canal Company, especially considering the history of the original Suez concession and its long profitable enjoyment from 1888 to 1956.

It is true, as Eden reported, that Dulles once declared: "A way must be found to make Nasser disgorge what he is attempting to swallow!" But one never could be quite sure of the thoughts in the innermost recesses of the Dulles mind. He was entirely capable of suddenly ejaculating in the midst of a critical situation: "It's about time we started throwing bombs in the market place!" But that type of statement was a relief from the pressures and was to be taken with a warehouse full of salt. Perhaps Dulles wanted to show some sympathy, which I am certain he felt, for our Allies' indignation about Nasser.

Twenty-two nations accepted the invitation to attend the elaborate conference which convened in London on August 16. The objective, expressed in a declaration prepared mostly by the American delegation, was to establish an international board to govern operation of the Suez Canal. A new treaty to replace the one of 1888 was to be negotiated, and this treaty would recognize the sovereign rights of Egypt. Also, Egypt was to be a member of the governing board and was to receive fair compensation for use of the Canal. Prime Minister Eden's associates, determined to reach a quick conclusion, decided that this declaration should be put before Nasser at once, and a small committee was chosen to go to Cairo. Prime Minister Robert G. Menzies of Australia, who stoutly supported the British position, was named chairman of the committee, and he was accompanied by Deputy Under Secretary of State Loy W. Henderson, an expert on Middle Eastern affairs, who represented the United States, and by official representatives of Iran, Ethiopia, and Sweden.

When the committee arrived in Cairo, the Egyptian capital was full of rumors that British troops were mobilizing for attack, and contrary rumors that the British were bluffing. The Australian Prime Minister, in a detailed account published more than three years later, blamed the United States for the failure of his mission. He stated that he talked with Nasser first on September 5 and told him how public opinion in London and Paris opposed his Suez action, and added, in substance: "I am not making threats. Such things are not within either my authority or intention. But frankness as between two Heads of Government requires me to offer my personal opinion that you are not facing a bluff but a stark condition of fact which your country should not ignore." Menzies has recorded that Nasser thanked him, acknowledged his national responsibility and assured the Australian that he did not regard the British position as a bluff. But, according to Menzies, when he resumed talks with Nasser the following day, the attitude of the Egyptian President had stiffened. Menzies has written this explanation for Nasser's changed attitude: "He had, like the rest of us, read in the morning newspapers a statement of policy of the United States Government which said in headlines, 'There must be no use of force' and that if the proposals of the London conference were rejected, others must be considered. From that time on, Nasser felt he was through the period of danger."

It was my own opinion that the Menzies committee never had a chance of success. The Suez problem did not lend itself to negotiation because, in seizing the Canal, Nasser had burned his bridges and could not retreat. Nationalization had become an accomplished fact. The proposed new treaty did not seem to me a practical device because there was no adequate reason why it should be accepted by the Egyptians. Several of us in the State Department, including Hoover, Phleger and William M. Rountree, Assistant Secretary for the Near East and Africa, labored to produce a workable form of a Canal Users Association, but from Nasser's point of view this organization offered nothing of value. At that time Nasser believed he had support of the Soviet Union and, up to a point, he had. The Russians were backing Nasser in his nationalization of the Canal and had given him assurances of aid.

After the failure of the Menzies mission to Cairo, Secretary Dulles turned his attention once more to the United Nations on the theory that debate there would help formulate public opinion. Previously he had been reluctant to refer the question to the UN because the British and French did not want it to go there, and Dulles wanted to bring them into his own plans. The Secretary also felt, I believe, that maximum leverage could be brought upon Egypt better from outside the UN, through negotiations involving the principal users of the Canal.

At first we did not understand why the British and French were so opposed to recourse to the UN, but realized later that they knew their military schedule would be disarranged if they became entangled in drawn-out procedures in New York. But one British official said to me in August that a bow probably would have to be made to the UN sooner or later, and the courtesy gesture was made on October 13 when a resolution providing for free and open transit in the Canal was voted upon by the Security Council. As Dulles had foreseen, the action of the Council ended in a Soviet veto, thus leaving the Egyptians with a clearer international position regarding their seizure of the Canal.

With the Suez situation thus apparently at a standstill, Prime Minister Eden and Foreign Secretary Lloyd flew from London to Paris to discuss with French officials what might be attempted as their next move. Meanwhile, anxiety in Washington was relaxing. Dulles was confident that his delaying tactics were succeeding, that military plans were "withering on the vine," and that devices for safeguarding shipping through the Canal were developing. Eisenhower said in a television interview that progress in settling the Suez dispute was "most gratifying" and that "a very great crisis is behind us." Agitation in Europe seemed to be subsiding. British public indignation against Nasser was diminishing. Voices were heard in France urging moderation. In the United States there was not a vestige of a war party. But complacency in Washington was tinctured by an uneasy awareness that there had been a complete blackout of official information ever since the Anglo-French meeting in Paris. Dulles expressed the feeling of the State Department when he remarked at a staff conference: "It's very strange that we have heard nothing whatever from the British for ten days. We must try to find out what they and the French are up to."

A few more days passed quietly and then the State Department received a cablegram from the military attaché of the American Embassy at Tel Aviv conveying information which he had obtained confidentially regarding Israeli mobilization. That Israel might be preparing for action seemed plausible. The Egyptian Government had proclaimed war against Israel, and Nasser was invoking that technicality as justification for prohibiting Israeli ships from using the Suez Canal. There were numerous raids by Fedayeen, the commando unit trained to invade Israeli territory in small bands to commit sabotage and acts of violence. We in the State Department were painfully aware of the Egyptian military build-up in the spring and summer of 1956, and a Watch Dog Committee had been organized accordingly. We knew that substantial acquisitions of Soviet heavy equipment, including about fifty bombers, were stored on the edge of the Gaza Strip, the disputed truce-line between Egypt and Israel on the Mediterranean shore. In view of this aggressive Egyptian attitude, it did not appear surprising that the Israeli Government might have decided it would be safer to attack than wait to be attacked.

Yet, when I read the cablegram from our military attaché, I found it hard to believe that Israeli mobilization could be taking place in isolation. It seemed that France and Britain must have some intimation, however informally, of such activity. But we had no evidence that they did. Pineau had not so much as hinted of any French military arrangements with Israeli leaders. Eden did not suggest this even at official conferences with Ambassador Aldrich, and this deception of the American Ambassador may have been a factor in President Eisenhower's indignation later. Macmillan was very frank about all Anglo-French plans—except French encouragement to Israel. This never was revealed to any American, privately or otherwise.

Perhaps one reason why the British and French did not confide in us about this phase of their campaign strategy was because Dulles had insisted from the outset that the Suez crisis should be separated from the general Arab-Israeli situation. My own first contacts with that perpetual issue in the Middle East occurred when I was Assistant Secretary for United Nations Affairs. At that time Eisenhower and his associates had several ideas for solving a problem which was basically unsolvable. Arab-Israeli hostility was a chronic malady for which doctors could offer only relief, not cure. For example, Eric A. Johnston, acting as special representative of the President in the Middle East, worked for almost two years on an agreement for equitable distribution of the irrigation waters of Jordan, and devised a plan which was technically sound and fair to all concerned. But political factors made that solution, like many other solutions, unacceptable. Every American official who had dealings with Arab-Israeli matters could not escape unpleasant difficulties. The United States had replaced Europe as the center of world Jewry, and the large and influential Jewish community could bring heavy pressure to bear upon government officials, pressure which in the early days sometimes amounted to intimidation. Consequently Dulles was determined that negotiations with Nasser concerning Suez should not become entangled with Nasser's feud with Israel.

On the evening of October 29, 1956, the Sinai Campaign began. The invasion of the arid peninsula which separates Israel from the Gulf of Suez was a brilliant demonstration of Israeli military prowess.

Just before the attack commenced, the Department of State learned that the French were supplying the Israeli with fighter aircraft, and we made strong representations to Israel against precipitating military action. About British complicity we knew nothing. The Sinai invasion was a four-pronged venture which obviously had been in preparation for a long time. Using parachutists and moving with lightning rapidity, Israeli soldiers closed off the Gaza Strip, reached the Suez Canal at Ismailia in four days, and captured large quantities of equipment and supplies. Egyptian forces numbering about forty-five thousand were completely routed, with about one thousand killed and six thousand taken prisoner. Other Arab countries stood pat and did not come to Egypt's aid. Two years later, when I was in the Middle East on a different mission, I had an opportunity to get a vivid impression of the pattern of the military drive in this area. Flying low over the Negev to the growing port of Eilat on the Gulf of Aqaba, I was given a description of the Israeli attack and glimpsed some of the desert terrain in which the troops operated.

According to *Les Secrets de l'Expédition d'Egypte,* a book written by Merry and Serge Bromberg, two war correspondents who reported the campaign and later obtained military information to show that France was not responsible for the Suez fiasco, French air and naval forces immediately gave important assistance to Israeli troops, providing fighter cover to Israeli towns, destroying Egyptian fortifications, parachuting supplies of oil and food, and so on. But according to statements issued at the time, Britain and France had no prior notice of the Israeli attack and suddenly were confronted on October 30 with the problem whether to consult with others, such as the United States and the United Nations, or to act. They chose to act. The avowed Israeli objective was to forestall Egyptian aggression and open up Suez and the Gulf of Aqaba to Israeli shipping. The British and French Governments called upon the Israeli and Egyptians to cease fire and withdraw their troops from the Suez Canal. If they failed to comply, the British and French announced they would intervene to separate the combatants. In other words, the official reason for the British-French expedition was to safeguard the Canal and stop the Israeli-Egyptian fighting. Under the circumstances this explanation was less than convincing.

The big question was what the Russians would do. Their technicians got out of Egypt quickly and went to Khartoum, in neighboring Sudan. The Soviet Union declared that it might resort to force, threatened that the conflict could spread into general war, and hinted of nuclear bombs. Eisenhower was unperturbed. "Look at the map," he told a group of his advisers. "Geography makes effective Soviet intervention in Egypt difficult, if not impossible." But a high ranking official of the

State Department, who was not a career Foreign Service officer, could not conceal his alarm. "We must stop this before we are all burned to a crisp!" he exclaimed at a staff meeting after Russia had sent threatening notes to Britain and France. His reaction based on fear was not appreciated by his colleagues, and his remark remains in my memory as an example of the success sometimes achieved by Russian intimidation tactics. I am inclined to suspect that fear of the bomb motivated Sir Anthony Eden during this period more than he ever admitted, more perhaps than he himself realized.

The Anglo-French military operation was launched on October 31 strictly according to the staff plan which I had been told about in July. The scheme was to strike the Egyptian Air Force by bombings from Cyprus, Malta, Aden and from carriers. The British and French hoped to paralyze the Egyptians, black out Radio Cairo, chase Nasser from Egypt and, above all, prevent the Suez Canal from being blocked by vessels filled with concrete which the Egyptians had in readiness. For reasons of security, nothing was changed in this plan, which had been carefully prepared for use in August. The original program was not even dusted off before being put into effect. There was no time. Even the disposition of British naval and transport units was neglected, so that ships needed in the western Mediterranean were left undisturbed in the eastern end of the sea, while shipping which should have been in readiness in the eastern Mediterranean was toward the west, around Malta. Military officers, already bewildered by numerous delays and shifts of plans, became confused. I was reminded of the situation in North Africa in 1942 when General Eisenhower was similarly compelled to improvise plans hastily, on a vastly greater scale and at much greater risk.

Although the military operation thus got off to a poor start, there is no doubt it would have succeeded if it had been followed through. Successful bombings were made against Egyptian air bases, and Port Said was captured by Anglo-French parachutists. Since the Israeli forces had swept without difficulty through the Negev to the Suez Canal, capturing huge quantities of newly acquired Soviet equipment, it seemed to me that they alone could capture Cairo unaided. I mistakenly believed that the British and French would do so easily. Remembering British sentiment as I had observed it in July and August, I did not dream that our two major allies, so rich in military experience and tradition, would not be capable of overpowering the Egyptians. But to the amazement of many Americans, including myself, when the operation seemed about to achieve its goal, Prime Minister Eden decided to quit short of the objective.

What had happened was that while Anglo-French forces were accomplishing their tardy victories in Egypt, world opinion had become aroused; the British Labor Party had initiated attacks against Eden's Government; sterling reserves were evaporating. In addition to all this, messages from Moscow sounded more ominous than ever. Those communications from Marshal Bulganin did not impress me. I do not believe that if the British and French had persisted, and had succeeded in achieving their objective without long delay, there would have been direct Russian intervention. Because the British and French never intended to occupy Egypt but wanted merely to safeguard their Suez Canal treaty rights.

Eden's greatest miscalculation was that he was unable to enlist the support of Eisenhower. In fact the President made his displeasure very apparent. From his point of view the attack on Egypt in the final days of October was calamitous timing. Nationwide elections in the United States were to be held the first Tuesday in November, Eisenhower himself was running for re-election, and he was confronted with a situation in which three friendly nations, two of them allies, had decided to wage war without a word of consultation with him. That alone would be sufficient explanation for his attitude, but Eisenhower's wrath went further than that. The President already had made it very clear that he thoroughly disapproved of what he regarded as eighteenth-century tactics instead of recourse to diplomacy and United Nations procedures.

Eisenhower, Dulles and Lodge, working closely together, decided now upon a policy appropriate to the emergency. The United States took the initiative on October 30 by presenting to the Security Council a resolution opposing Israel's military action against Egypt. When that was promptly vetoed by the United Kingdom and France, Lodge introduced a resolution in the General Assembly condemning Israel, Britain, and France, demanding an immediate cease-fire, and proposing that UN forces should be put in charge of the combat areas temporarily. The resolution was adopted and the cease-fire went into effect at midnight of November 6.

The next day Eisenhower telephoned to Eden by the new transatlantic cable, which had just been put into service, to tell the British Prime Minister that he welcomed the end of hostilities. As a friendly gesture, very characteristic of Eisenhower, he added an invitation to Eden to call him from time to time by the new telephone system. While this would seem a natural and genial method of international intercourse, it is difficult for an overburdened Chief Executive to avoid impromptu commitments in such informal contact, and these can be embarrassing. The very next day, Eden telephoned back and asked in effect that he and French Prime Minister Mollet be invited to Washington. The President replied offhandedly, "Sure, come on over," and Eden wanted to fly over that very evening. Dulles was opposed to this visit, which would have been subject to all sorts of misinterpretations. There were many in the Soviet Union and elsewhere who believed the United States had connived secretly in the Anglo-French military venture and who were eager to tar the United States with the failure. An immediate visit to Washington by Eden and Mollet would have been regarded as confirmation of rumors of American complicity. It did not require any arguments from Dulles to persuade Eisenhower that Eden should be tactfully informed that it would be better to defer the visit. The President himself changed his mind within an hour, without consulting anyone, and Eden's visit never did take place. Under all the political and financial pressures, Eden's precarious health became worse, he announced his decision to retire, and it was not long before the Right Honorable Harold Macmillan became Prime Minister and First Lord of the Treasury and moved into No. 10 Downing Street, which remained his official residence until ill health compelled him in his turn to retire in 1963.

Many British newspapers blamed the American Secretary of State for the Suez fiasco, but their bitter comments did not bother Dulles. In fact, he seemed to enjoy their attitude. If they wanted to assign to him, rather than to Eisenhower, the dominant role in our Suez policy, that did not displease Dulles. And gradually, largely as reaction to this Suez criticism, Dulles' reputation grew in stature.

TWENTY-SEVEN

U. S. TROOPS IN LEBANON (1958)

Among disturbed places in 1957, one of the most conspicuous was Algeria, which for three years had been suffering the horrors of violent rebellion. When I was in North Africa during World War II, the French had golden opportunity to plan a progressive settlement of Algerian demands for independence, but French generals, admirals, and politicians at that time were declaring: "The only thing the Arab understands is force!" The French, who conquered Algiers in 1830 after the Dey slapped the face of the French Consul with a fly whisk, were understandably averse to relinquishing the country which they had been building up for more than a century. France deserves great credit for its achievements in Algeria, where a million Arabs and Berbers were living in miserable poverty when the country was annexed. The infant mortality rate was 90 percent when the French undertook to eradicate disease from Algeria, and it was the French who established law and order and who introduced modern roads, transport, communications, agriculture, and industry. The French also endeavored to raise educational standards, caught up in the complexities of Koranic rules and the Islamic social system. It was difficult for French settlers, after four generations in Algeria, to regard that country as anything but French. But the defeat of France by Germany stimulated Arab desire for independence, and there can be no doubt that the wartime presence of hundreds of thousands of American soldiers, with their easygoing contact with the native population, increased this restiveness of the *indigènes*.

The determination of the Arabs to govern themselves was not limited to Algeria but was widespread also throughout Tunisia and Morocco. Tunisia, which finally obtained its own independence in the summer of 1957, became headquarters for the Algerian rebels, and thousands of refugees and guerrilla fighters crossed the frontier to seek safety, rest, or medical care. These Algerians were a constant anxiety to the Tunisians, who believed that a French military group was looking for a pretext to turn the clock back and reoccupy Tunisia. Thus, when the French Air Force happened one day to bomb the village of Sidi Sakiet, President Bourguiba of Tunisia became frantic. He assumed that the bombing might be the signal for an invasion of his country, and he immediately broke off diplomatic relations with France; ordered a blockade of the naval and air bases at Bizerte and other French military installations; and entered formal protest at the United Nations.

The upshot was that France was censured by the United Nations, and the French Ambassador in Washington, Hervé Alphand, indicated it would be welcome if the United States and Great Britain would lend their good offices to arrange a settlement with Tunisia. In February 1958 Harold Beeley, in charge of Middle Eastern Affairs at the London Foreign Office, and I for the United States were designated as a Good Offices team, and we began hectic weeks of shuttling between conversations in Paris with Premier Felix Gaillard and Foreign Minister Pineau, and conversations in Tunis with President Bourguiba, Foreign Minister Sadok Mokkadem, and Defense Minister Bahi Ladgham. During the war years which I spent in Algiers, Ladgham, an Arab, was confined in a civilian French prison after conviction for activity with the Tunisian independence movement. No prison is attractive, but physical conditions in French military and civil prisons were shockingly medieval, due no doubt to unwillingness to spend money on them. Of course the Arabs themselves throughout history were no more humane to the unfortunate miscreants who fell into their hands. Ladgham told me that the five years he spent as a prisoner of the French were a nightmare, but in that prison in Algiers he managed to keep remarkably informed of American wartime plotting and of the operations of the underground groups with whom I was working at that time.

Valiant support was given to the Good Offices mission by the American Ambassador in Paris, Amory Houghton, and the British Ambassador, Sir Gladwyn Jebb, and also by their counterparts in Tunis, and a formula was laboriously devised which gave satisfaction to the Tunisians yet also enabled the French to retain much of their position in Tunisia. But De Gaulle's political party was in the opposition in France at that time, and Beeley and I were subject to caustic attacks in the De Gaulle press for interfering in a French "internal" matter. For example, there were some air bases in Tunisia which our formula left in French hands under neutral controllers. We knew those bases were virtually worthless, but the De Gaulle newspapers screamed every day that the destiny of France hung on them. Perhaps the most prominent writer for De Gaulle at that time was Senator Michel

Debré, who later became Prime Minister in the De Gaulle Government. Debré wrote several articles attacking the Good Offices mission and his thesis was, in effect, "Yankee Go Home!" Sidi Sakiet, he declared, was a French problem and France would settle it without American or British intervention.

Throughout the Tunisian negotiations we were constantly reminded by the French press and by our friends in government that our mandate did not include the war in Algeria. That, of course, was the very last thing in which we wanted to become involved, and we carefully avoided any implication of it in our talks. Yet French officials brought up the subject at almost every discussion, and the Tunisians also referred to it frequently. This was only natural because the Algerian conflict was weighing heavily on both countries. The Gaillard Government in Paris was politically vulnerable, and at the end of our negotiations a French friend said to me: "Your formula is all right and it will be adopted eventually, but two governments will fall before that." He was an accurate prophet. Gaillard fell on the Tunisian issue by a vote of 321 to 255, and was succeeded by Pierre Pflimlin who likewise failed, thus opening the way for De Gaulle.

It is interesting to reflect now that if the village of Sidi Sakiet had not been bombed, Gaillard might not have fallen, and if not, when would De Gaulle have come back to power? On my return to Washington, Dean Acheson greeted me cheerfully, saying: "You certainly fixed that one!" But it was not long before I had the satisfaction of seeing Prime Minister Debré conceding to the Tunisians far more than Beeley and I had proposed. The De Gaullists during the war years had insisted that Algeria must be French soil forever, and the 180 degree swing from that contention to the accord which was negotiated at Evian in 1962 by the astute Louis Joxe was an extraordinary feat of flexibility.

However, settlement of the Tunisian conflict in 1958 did not bring peace then to other Mediterranean countries, and machinations by Arabs throughout the Middle East created a perilous situation. This highly sensitive area was of political importance to the United States, and even more important to our European allies who depended on it as their major source of petroleum. Among other danger spots, the State Department was particularly concerned about the Republic of Lebanon. That small country had about a million and a half inhabitants, normally balanced delicately between Christians and Moslems, but now distorted by the presence of three hundred thousand Moslem refugees who had fled from Palestine. Many of these refugees were desperate men, bitter against the United States because it supported the State of Israel which had caused their exile. We learned that Arab nationalists, under the direction of President Nasser of Egypt, were spending money to influence the swollen Moslem population of Lebanon and were sending clandestine arms to rebellious elements there.

The prospect of the spread of Nasserism into Lebanon, one of the most pro-Western countries in the entire area, awoke lively reactions in Washington. Congress expressed considerable interest in helping our friends, especially when some Lebanese factions openly revolted against the duly constituted Government. By early June the situation had deteriorated badly, the country was in a state of civil war, and a vociferous radio and press campaign in Egypt was calling for the overthrow of the Republic of Lebanon. Charles Malik, who for ten years had been Lebanese Ambassador to the United States, was full of alarms and made excited appeals for large-scale financial aid. President Camille Chamoun, who was rumored to have sent his wife's jewels and his grandson out of the country, made urgent requests to the American Embassy in Beirut, the capital of Lebanon, for military equipment. He wanted tanks to be airlifted immediately. The Premier, Samy-es-Solh, informed our Ambassador that the Lebanese people would welcome assistance by American troops. President Eisenhower and Secretary Dulles expressed willingness to help Lebanon, if necessary, and the developing situation became a constant preoccupation of the State Department.

Suddenly the situation exploded—not in Lebanon as had seemed likely, but in another Middle Eastern country, Iraq, where King Faisal and his family were brutally murdered on July 14, 1958 by a group of their own Army officers who proclaimed a revolutionary regime in Iraq as "part of the Arab nation." President Chamoun, fearful that the independence of his country was also in gravest danger, urgently requested American intervention, and the U. S. Navy in cooperation with the American command in Europe was assigned the task of responding to his appeal.

Although I was keeping informed about these dramatic events, my own particular duty in Washington at that moment was tied up with an entirely different problem. Refusal by the State Department to issue passports to certain American citizens had been challenged in the federal courts; the Department was much concerned with pending legislation on this subject; and I was preparing arguments to present at a full-dress hearing of the Senate Foreign Relations Committee. The committee session was held on July 16 in the old Supreme Court Chamber in the Capitol, in order to accommodate the large number of interested citizens and reporters who wanted to attend, and I had just finished making the opening statement when I was notified that there was a telephone call from Secretary Dulles. He told me that President Eisenhower had decided to send me to Lebanon immediately, and that I should excuse myself from the committee hearing and return to the Department for hasty consultation prior to departure.

Dulles, who was waiting for me in his office, explained that I was to act in an advisory capacity to Admiral James L. Holloway, Jr., Commander in Chief of the United States forces which were landing in Lebanon at that very moment. This military action, undertaken at the expressed desire of the constitutional head of the Republic of Lebanon, was based on the traditional American policy of protecting our citizens and defending our national interests. In addition to our embassy personnel and other government employees, a good many Americans lived in Lebanon, most of them as teachers, missionaries, and businessmen. Beirut also was a popular seaside resort which attracted Americans residing throughout the Middle East and many tourists. Dulles told me that one of my functions would be to establish a smooth working relationship between the U. S. Military Command, the U. S. Embassy, and other American civilian authorities.

After this brief talk with Dulles, the two of us went to the White House where the President elaborated a little on his purpose in ordering U. S. Marines to land in Lebanon. He said that sentiment had developed in the Middle East, especially in Egypt, that Americans were capable only of words, that we were afraid of Soviet reaction if we attempted military action. Eisenhower believed that if the United States did nothing now, there would be heavy and irreparable losses in Lebanon and in the area generally. He wanted to demonstrate in a timely and practical way that the United States was capable of supporting its friends. It was our intention, he said, to act constructively in harmony with the Charter of the United Nations. One basis for American action was that Lebanon, of all the Arab states, had accepted the "Eisenhower Doctrine" and hence was in a position publicly and internationally to invoke it. My oral instructions from the President were conveniently vague, the substance being that I was to promote the best interests of the United States incident to the arrival of our forces in Lebanon.

It was obvious that this assignment as the President's personal representative was going to demand an altogether different type of diplomacy from what was required when I went as Eisenhower's emissary to investigate the Suez Canal incident. In both cases I was sent abroad on only a few hours' notice to find out what was happening in a crisis in the Middle East, and in both cases I was given no explicit instructions what to do when I arrived at my destination. My Suez assignment consumed nearly four months in London and Washington, with patient negotiation, written resolutions, infinite tact, and contrived delays. My Lebanon assignment called for four crowded weeks of on-the-spot decisions, frank explanations and immediate actions. How many spontaneous decisions I would have to make, and how many exotic cities I would have to visit, I was soon to discover.

Before going with Dulles to the White House, I telephoned my wife and asked her to pack a bag of tropical clothing for me, and three hours later she gave me the suitcase at the airport of the Materiel Air Transport Service, just outside Washington, where a military plane was waiting to take me to Westover Air Force Base in Massachusetts. At Westover I was delighted to find that one of the new tanker versions of the Boeing 707 jets, a KC-135, had been set up by the Air Force for a nonstop flight. We flew at forty thousand feet, making the fifty-five hundred miles in the record time of eleven hours exactly when the wheels touched down on the Beirut air strip.

I was greeted at the airport by Ambassador Robert M. McClintock, Admiral Holloway, and two harassed cabinet ministers of the Lebanese Government. McClintock had served with me years before in Brussels, when I was Ambassador and he was head of the political section of the American Embassy, and it was a joy to see him again and to obtain firsthand information. Considering that our military operations had been conducted on an emergency basis, the results were highly gratifying. Within twenty-four hours after President Chamoun's plea for help, thirty-six hundred Sixth Fleet Marines began landing on the beach near the Beirut airport and quickly secured the airport and downtown dock areas. Meanwhile, C-119 Flying Boxcars were ferrying more Marines of the 2nd Division from Camp Lejeune, North Carolina; C-124 Globemasters were being rushed from Donaldson Air Force Base, South Carolina, to pick up 24th Division Army paratroopers at Augsburg, West Germany; jet fighters were flying nonstop from Myrtle Beach, South Carolina; and a jet fighter and fighter-bomber strike force had departed from Langley Air Force Base, Virginia.

By the time I arrived in Beirut, almost seven thousand Marines had landed and were patrolling the vicinity with tanks, armored amphibians, and self-propelled atomic howitzers, although no nuclear weapons were unloaded. Under the experienced direction of genial Admiral Holloway, the landings had been made with éclat, with no unfortunate incidents and no casualties. By July 18 about seventy or seventy-five warships of the Sixth Fleet were near Beirut Harbor, providing quite a spectacle for the fashionable diners on the terrace of the Pigeon Rock restaurant. Marine columns were marching past the luxurious St. George Hotel, where girls were sunning themselves on yachts in the hotel's private basin while Navy jets from the carriers *Saratoga* and *Essex* were shrieking over the city. By July 25 the

American shore forces numbered at least 10,600 men—4000 Army, 6600 Marines—more than the entire Lebanese Army.

As our forces had come to Lebanon at the invitation of Chamoun, the first thing I did in Beirut was to pay my respects to the President at his official residence. There I found a tired and worried man, who for sixty-seven days had been a self-made prisoner. Apparently he had not so much as looked out of a window during that time, and this undoubtedly was wise as his chances of assassination were excellent. Under the Lebanese constitution the President of the Republic was limited to one term in office, but Chamoun was proposing to amend the constitution and seek a second term, and this political issue was one of the main reasons for the civil war.

Since Berlin in 1945, I had not been in a more trigger-happy place than Beirut was at that time. Wild fusillades, bombings, and arson were the order of the day and more especially the night. Almost across the street from the presidential palace was the Basta, a complex of ancient streets and buildings forming the type of district sometimes called the Casbah. The British Ambassador had asked for the protection of a Marine guard and this was assigned to him. But the first night the Americans were on duty, the British Embassy was peppered by shootings from the Basta which narrowly missed some of our Marines. President Chamoun told me that he had ordered and begged General Fuad Chehab, who was in command of the Lebanese Army, to clean out the Basta, but without success. My immediate reaction was that Chehab ought to be fired, a competent new commander appointed, and action taken to restore order and the authority of the Government. I found it was not quite that simple.

General Chehab, a highly intelligent person and a member of one of the leading Maronite Christian families, was a graduate of the French military academy at St. Cyr and L'Ecole Supérieure de Guerre. His Army consisted of about seven thousand soldiers plus technical command of the gendarmerie of about two thousand, and both forces were precariously balanced between Christians and Moslems. The General's principal preoccupation seemed to be to keep his military establishment intact. He opposed a major attack against the Lebanese rebels because he believed that if such an operation were attempted, the religious differences in his forces—particularly the pronounced sympathy of some of the Moslems for the rebel cause—would split them asunder. In effect, his Army would melt away. The United States Government had informed President Chamoun from the outset that Americans would not intervene unless the Lebanese themselves were willing to fight to defend their country, so now I was startled to learn that the President of the Republic seemed to think he had no authority to order the Commander in Chief of the Army to undertake military action. If so ordered, General Chehab undoubtedly would resign. Therefore the President had merely made suggestions to the General which over a period of months he successfully deflected. In turn, Chehab did not give orders to subordinate officers on his staff and in the line. He made recommendations to them. After some straight-from-the-shoulder conversation with the General and his staff, I became convinced that he honestly believed that if he attempted to clean up the Basta, his wobbly Army would fall apart.

Discussing this problem with Admiral Holloway, he and I agreed that Chehab's military establishment, flimsy as it was, nevertheless was the only element which was holding the Government together, paralyzed as it was. For all practical purposes the Lebanese Government was in control of only a small portion of the country, perhaps 30 per cent. Even the heart of the capital city was held by rebels. I had hoped that we could induce Chehab to take energetic action at least to rectify the disorderly situation in Beirut, but all that the General would offer was a mild process of gradually restricting rebel activity and containing it in certain districts. However, Chehab was willing to cooperate with the American forces, and although this was a slender reed on which to lean, Holloway and I felt it was sufficent for our immediate purposes.

As an illustration of Chehab's cooperation, Holloway told me about an incident which occured on the first day of the American landings. Lebanon has an unhappy history of foreign military invasions through the centuries—from the time of the Assyrians, through the conquests of Persians and Romans, to the Mamelukes and the modern Turks—and the Lebanese are deeply opposed to the presence of foreign troops on their soil. The Turks were the last military occupants, and their need for wood virtually eliminated the traditional cedars of Lebanon. Some Lebanese now were referring to the American forces as an occupation army, and a group of Lebanese staff officers decided to resist our intervention. When our Marines arrived at the Beirut airport there was but one road leading to town, and our troops proceeded down that road unaware that a dozen tanks had been lined up and orders issued to fire on our men. McClintock, learning of this at the last minute, made urgent contact with General Chehab and induced him to drive to the tank contingent with Admiral Holloway and the Ambassador in the embassy limousine flying Lebanese and American flags. Chehab gave orders on the spot to hold fire, and what might have been a tragic episode was narrowly averted.

Lebanon disputes were not limited to major political differences and division between Christians and Moslems. There also was factional strife within political parties and between religious sects. Lebanese tradition required that the President must be a Christian and the

Premier a Moslem, and this joint administration had been mutually satisfactory to Chamoun and Samy-es-Solh. Both of these officials had appealed to the American Embassy for assistance in putting down the insurrection and both were cooperating with McClintock and Holloway. However, the Premier was the target of rival Moslems who had set fire to his home and burned it down, with loss of most of Samy-es-Solh's possessions. Soon after I arrived in Beirut, the Premier invited several Americans including the Ambassador and me to lunch at his official residence, a colorful Arab-style structure. It was the daily routine of Samy-es-Solh to drive from this residence to his office in an automobile preceded by a police motorcycle escort. On the morning of our luncheon date the Premier had started out as usual, and had noticed a car parked beside the road with a flat tire. Actually about a hundred pounds of high explosives had been placed in this car, controlled by a concealed trip wire across the road. Seconds before the Premier's automobile passed over the wire, another car crossed into the lane and its five innocent passengers and the police escort were blown to bits. Samy-es-Solh escaped injury and he insisted on going through with the lunch, where with magnificent calm he carried on animated conversation.

About a month before the arrival of the American forces, an observation group had been dispatched to London by the United Nations. Lebanon had protested early in June that Egypt and Syria were interfering in its internal affairs, and the Security Council had authorized Secretary-General Hammarskjold to send UN representatives to Beirut to ensure that there was no illegal infiltration of persons and arms across the Lebanese frontier. The UN observers were headed by Galo Plaza, the dynamic former President of Ecuador, assisted by Rajeswar Dayal of India and Major General Odd Bull of Norway. David E. Blickenstaff, an American official of the UN, was executive officer of the group. This international party of investigators had reported they were unable to confirm the Lebanese charge that arms were being smuggled in, and they were inclined to minimize the extent of Egyptian and Syrian clandestine activities. But when I made contact with Gazo Plaza and his associates, I learned they had been able to work in the mountainous frontier area only during daylight hours, leaving the road network uninspected at night. And when our Marines tapped the telephone line between the capital of Syria and the Basta at Beirut, it was proved conclusively that the Basta rebels were receiving outside support. The American troop landings had been a surprise and a shock to the UN group, which regarded our military action with mixed emotions, as it seemed to interfere with their own efforts to settle the civil war.

Smuggling of small arms continued throughout the period of disturbance, and I was informed that it is the national custom in Lebanon for every family to be armed. Centuries of alien military occupation evidently had caused every Lebanese to desire some type of firearm, preferably a rifle or a pistol. Most of the men are good shots and they enjoy using their guns. At family celebrations there aways is a lot of playful shooting, and at one luncheon which I attended in the suburbs of Beirut, I noticed machine guns in the four corners of our host's rather large grounds.

Henry N. Taylor, representing the Scripps-Howard newspapers, decided to verify the firearms market in Beirut. I had known and liked this young correspondent in Washington and he told me about his little investigation. He hailed a taxi and asked the driver whether he knew where a machine gun could be purchased. Certainly, said the driver, and drove Henry to a small warehouse in the center of town. The affable proprietor had all kinds of machine guns for sale. Did Henry want a French, British, German, Czech or Russian brand? Maybe he could offer an American model, too. Henry said he wanted an Egyptian type. The proprietor pulled a used Egyptian machine gun from a burlap bag. Henry asked: "How do I know it will work?" The merchant of death suggested that they go up on the roof and try it out. A large sandbag installation was on the roof and several demonstration rounds were fired into it. The sound of shooting misled some rebels in the neighboring Basta and they started miscellaneous shooting of their own. After a little bargaining, Henry paid thirty-five dollars for the Egyptian machine gun and brought it back to his hotel in the taxi to prove to his fellow correspondents the ease with which firearms could be obtained in Beirut. Two years later Henry N. Taylor, only son of the American Ambassador to Switzerland, was killed in the Congo while reporting the Katanga fighting.

Popular sentiment in Beirut concerning United States intervention ranged from the beseeching invitation of President Chamoun to violent opposition by extreme Moslem groups. The Lebanese do not regard association of religion and politics as repugnant, and I found both Moslem and Christian leaders playing active roles in politics. In Lebanon one feels very close to the origins of Christianity. As a Roman Catholic, I had not been aware of the numerous Catholic rites which were functioning in that country. The many Christian sects have managed through the centuries to maintain relations with Islam, but often it is touch and go. American military intervention was generally well received by the Christian leaders, although some cautiously declined comment, fearful of eventual Moslem retribution.

Among those whom I called upon was the Maronite Patriarch, Paul Meouchi of Antioch, whom I visited at his mountain headquarters at Bkerke, an imposing establishment which includes his residence and a church. It was Sunday and I attended Mass which the Patriarch officiated in the Syrian rite. I then had a two-hour breakfast with the Patriarch, who reviewed the local situation and demonstrated a remarkable grasp of practical politics. Earlier in his life the Patriarch had lived for about fourteen years in the United States, whose Lebanese colony contributes handsomely to its families in the homeland. The Patriarch is well known in the United States and he wields substantial influence in Lebanese affairs.

I also paid my respects to Archbishop Saleeby of the Greek Orthodox Church, who told me that he had four thousand relatives in the United States, and Archbishop Nabaa of the Greek Catholic Church. Both were wise and helpful. Some Christians in Lebanon were relieved by the arrival of American forces and hopeful that they would end the civil and religious warfare which was threatening to destroy the integrity of the Republic. Others were disappointed because the Marines did not directly suppress rebel activity in several parts of the country. Inevitably there were some politicans who would have liked to exploit the American troops for selfish purposes of their own. Many accused President Chamoun of doing just that.

I continued to call upon Chamoun once or twice daily, in company with the American Ambassador, and I also had daily conversations with Holloway, with whom it was at all times a pleasure to work. The close cooperation between the diplomatic and military sides of the American house contributed greatly to the success of our Lebanese undertaking. We agreed that much of the conflict concerned personalities and rivalries of a domestic nature, with no relation to international issues. Communism was playing no direct or substantial part in the insurrection, although Communists no doubt hoped to profit from the disorders, as frequently happens when there is civil war. The outside influences came mostly from Egypt and Syria. From talks with Chamoun, McClintock, Holloway and others, my estimate of the situation was that arrangements should be made for an immediate election of a new President. Such election would be conducted by the single-chamber Parliament according to the constitution, and I urged Chamoun and the head of Parliament, whom I visited promptly, to hold an election without delay. I hoped this would bring about relaxation of the prevailing tensions and permit the withdrawal of American forces. The United Nations group would remain in Lebanon as observers. This, then, was the United States objective which was reported to and approved by the State Department.

But it seemed essential, before holding the election, that McClintock and I should talk with some influential rebel leaders in order to explain American policy to them and try to gain their cooperation. I made no contact with any of the rebels without fully informing

Chamoun in advance, and although these meetings with his opponents were not palatable to the President, he refrained from voicing objections. I believe those talks cleared away much misinformation about American intentions and contributed in the end to the peaceful settlement which followed our intervention.

I wanted first of all to meet Saeb Salaam, a former Premier who directed the group of Moslems which maintained headquarters in the Basta. I had been told that Saeb Salaam was inflamed against United States intervention and had taken the stand that there could be no presidential election in Lebanon until American troops departed. I tried to obtain an escort from General Chehab, but he continued to procrastinate about anything connected with the Basta, so I was very glad to meet in Beirut an old friend, Colonel William A. Eddy, then a consultant to the Arabian-American Oil Company. Eddy was our invaluable naval attaché in Tangier when I was preparing in 1942 for the American landings in North Africa. This retired Marine officer and former professor of English at Dartmouth, the son of missionaries and bilingual in Arabic, arranged a secret meeting outside Beirut with two of Saeb Salaam's associates. They seemed to think that American troops had come to Lebanon to perpetuate the administration of President Chamoun, and they recited a whole litany of complaints against him. They declared they preferred Nasser to Chamoun, and asserted that the Egyptians had no designs on Lebanon. They denied they were receiving aid from Syria, but their denials were not convincing.

After hours of conversation, Saeb Salaam's henchmen seemed reassured that the United States was seeking only to protect the independence of Lebanon, and they finally said that they were not unfriendly to Americans. This gave me an opportunity to refer to the safety of the American forces in Beirut. I explained that the first duty of a commanding officer is to take care of his men, and I pointed out that our Marines were being shot at every night, either intentionally or inadvertently, and that it was a miracle none had been killed. I added that since nobody had been killed in the entire landing operation, I interpreted this as evidence of the basic friendship between us, which we valued. The Moslem rebels quietly agreed. Then I went on to describe the equipment available to Admiral Holloway, potentially powerful enough to destroy all of Beirut in a matter of minutes. The Admiral, I assured them, was the friendliest of men, yet his first obligation was to his troops. Could not Saeb Salaam's associates end their indiscriminate shooting in the city, which might lead to very grave sanctions? My talk evidently had some effect, because the shootings died away the following day and except for occasional outbursts, life became quieter in Beirut. I always have been grateful to Bill Eddy for arranging that meeting because it seemed to mark a turn in events, and some days later I was able to meet Saeb Salaam himself and talk with him in the Basta.

My next contact with a rebel leader involved a strange journey into the Chouf Mountains where I called upon the Druze chieftain, Kamal Jumblatt, in his stronghold in the village of Sibline. Confidential arrangements for this visit were made through a member of Parliament who was vice president of the Socialist party. The tortuous path through the mountains would not have been a promenade under any circumstances, and the tough, bearded guards stationed along the way did not make it appear any more tranquil. But we were greeted cordially after our arduous climb. Jumblatt, formerly a close friend of President Chamoun, had been defeated in the last Parliament elections and he blamed Chamoun for interference in his campaign. He even said that American money had been used against him. Jumblatt's political ideas were fuzzy, but his family had been represented in Parliament for four generations and his defeat affected the prestige of his whole clan. It seemed to me that somewhere along the line a political error had been made in ousting him, and this was of a piece with various bits of other information I had picked up to the effect that Chamoun was trying to stay in office at the expense of his friends as well as his rivals. Conversation with Jumblatt indicated that he wanted a settlement, and he was pleased when I told him about the prospect of an early presidential election. He had thought the Marines had come to support Chamoun, and when he discovered this was not true, any opposition he might have had toward American intervention dissolved. Our meeting became most harmonious, not to say convivial, and McClintock and I returned over the mountains to Beirut convinced that progress was being made.

There was one more Moslem leader whom I felt I should meet, Rashid Karami, whose secret hideout was on the seacoast near Tripoli. With the help of General Chehab, whose authority over the Army continued to be the only stable influence, McClintock and I were able to cross the rebel lines and visit Karami. A leader in an irregular position, constantly in personal danger, is not apt to think in normal terms. His sources of information are often distorted. Karami did not regard Nasser as a threat to the independence of Lebanon, and he thought the United States was seeking to keep Chamoun in power. But Karami was not unfriendly to Americans, and when he later became Premier I enjoyed meeting him on a visit to Washington in that capacity.

Among Christian candidates to succeed President Chamoun, mention sometimes was made of a popular member of Parliament, Raymond Edde, and I was pleased when Edde invited me to be his guest one day on a visit to his constituency which included Byblos, the ancient Phoenician trading port. The curator of the museum at Byblos showed us among other fascinating relics the original Phoenician alphabet carved in subterranean rock. Funeral urns buried seven thousand years ago provided a healthy perspective for the current commotion. After a talk with local leaders and an excellent lunch up in the mountains, we visited two Arab villages where Edde was greeted by ceremonial revolver shots, much gaiety and coffee drinking. Edde knew his constituents and they obviously liked him.

Then we drove to the source of the Adonis River, the site of religious festivals through the ages, where pagan Roman ladies came to pray for fecundity and other blessings. The river gushes from a mountain opening beside a cave, from which to our surprise a guerrilla warrior emerged with rifle and cartridge belts slung from his shoulders. Our party had been preceded by two Army motorcycle escorts, and the guerrilla had not liked the looks of the men in uniform. Edde engaged the mountaineer in conversation but he was surly and suspicious. His companions on the other side of the river witnessed our gathering, thought that their friend was being apprehended, and started shooting. Up to that moment our excursion, which included the American Ambassador, had been appropriately dignified, but ceremony was forgotten as we scurried into our automobiles and drove hell-bent down the road. When Edde regained his breath and composure he explained that the guerrillas were not really shooting at us. They were perfect marksmen, he said, and if they had been in earnest, all of us would be dead. I felt that a member of Parliament in that area would need a robust constitution and Edde certainly had that.

However, Edde was not elected to succeed President Chamoun. Arrangements for assembling Parliament were difficult to organize because many members were hiding with the rebels, and Chamoun continued to keep his own intentions under a veil. It was not easy for him to withdraw as a candidate for a second term and he never said he would support any one else for the presidency. During my many conversations with him, he consistently disparaged the attitude of General Chehab and voiced suspicions of his loyalty and his capacity to command a vigorous opposition to the rebellion. But gradually, in spite of everything, prospects began to appear for an early meeting of Parliament, and shortly before the election Chamoun finally told me that he would not try to succeed himself. Then, to my agreeable surprise, he added that he had come to the conclusion that General Chehab, with all his defects, was the only possible choice. From that moment I knew the worst was over, and after congratulating the President on a statesmanlike decision, I said goodbye to him with a light heart. I regarded Chamoun as a good friend of the United States but I never really understood his motives. I felt that he was the victim of his own political excesses and that he had overreached himself in the brambles of Lebanese politics.

On July 31, General Fuad Chehab was elected President by the Lebanese Parliament by a vote of 48 to 8 on the second ballet. Raymond Edde received seven votes and there was one blank. Prior to the election, I heard many Lebanese speak of Chehab with contempt as spineless and weak, but remarkable unanimity developed after the balloting which augured well for national reconciliation. My own esteem for Chehab had grown through the difficult weeks in Beirut. He was devoted to his Army career and I am sure he did not seek the presidency. Although political ambition sprouts rapidly in some individuals, Chehab had a vast amount of common sense and he accepted the office only as a compromise essential to peace in Lebanon.

I had an understanding with the State Department that I would leave Lebanon on the eve of the election in order to minimize charges of American interference in the voting, and an itinerary was worked out for me to visit some other countries in the Middle East. But a few days after the election I had opportunity to stop over for a final brief visit in Beirut. I was told that notwithstanding gloomy predictions, there had been no rioting or other disorders. Chehab had deployed his soldiers to guard against any attempt to prevent the election, and all had gone well. The civil war was ended, and McClintock and Holloway agreed that they and I were entitled to what General Jumbo Wilson used to refer to as "a bit of a jolly."

The day after the first Marines landed in Beirut, jet planes showered a million leaflets all over Lebanon bearing the photograph of President Eisenhower and a message from him explaining that American troops had come at the request of the Lebanese Government to protect the freedom of that country, and that our forces would be withdrawn as soon as independence could be assured. But Chehab was in no hurry for our troops to leave. Occasional sniping was still occurring, and Chehab seemed eager for American advice. The United States had about fourteen thousand men in Lebanon on August 13, but on that day a Marine battalion returned to its ships in token withdrawal. An American aid program was being started, supplies were arriving, and the Lebanese could see that we were eager for our forces to depart. The conduct of our men had been exemplary. One soldier, an Army sergeant, had been killed by a sniper bullet but that was the only recorded fatality. On September 14, two more Marine battalions began shipping out, and the last Marines embarked on September 29, leaving seventy-five hundred G.I.'s on shore. Army paratroops began quitting Lebanon on October 4, and withdrawal of troops and tanks continued intermittently until the last American troops left on October 25. The 102-day operation, it was estimated later, cost the United States

$200,000,000. That financial reckoning reminded me of a call which I had received while in Beirut from Cevdet Dulger, the Turkish Ambassador there. He told me he was delighted with American military initiative, but said jocularly that the United States should have bought off the Lebanese—it would have been much cheaper than sending in the fleet.

At the time of the landings in Lebanon, it was decided to simplify that operation by restricting it to American forces, but the British simultaneously landed twenty-five hundred paratroops in the neighboring Hashemite Kingdom of Jordan, and Americans and British cooperated throughout the intervention. The British Navy provided support in the Mediterranean and made facilities in Cyprus available to us, while the United States gave logistic support by flying supplies into Jordan for the British contingent there. Americans, conscious of the historic association of the French with the Middle East, also maintained close consultation with our French allies. British Ambassador Middleton and French Ambassador Roche were highly experienced in this area and Americans could not have wished for better understanding than we received from both of them at Beirut. For instance, the French Government insisted on sending the cruiser *De Grasse* to Beirut waters in order to show the French flag. Much as we appreciated this evidence of solidarity, this was not the moment to stir up Moslem sympathizers for Algeria, and Ambassador Roche tactfully arranged with Admiral Jozan so that the *De Grasse* departed before the Damascus radio was aware of its presence.

The American intervention in Lebanon caused all kinds of wild rumors to circulate throughout the Middle East, and the State Department felt it would be advisable to give a firsthand account of the facts to some of the heads of governments in that region. Accordingly I was instructed to visit a number of countries before returning to Washington. One of my objectives was to convince leading officials that our intervention would exercise a stabilizing effect in the Middle East. There also were several specific questions which the State Department desired to have explored, and we hoped to find evidence that American prestige had risen appreciably in that part of the world.

The first three countries which I visited after finishing my assignment in Lebanon were Jordan, Israel and Iraq. Before leaving Beirut I had received word through the Egyptian Ambassador there that the United Arab Republic would also welcome me at Cairo to meet with President Nasser. The arrival of American Marines at Beirut had come as a surprise to Nasser. He seemed to be under the impression that the United States was not capable of independent action and would not provide military aid for a friendly nation. He thought Americans could be counted upon only to talk at the United Nations. Nasser happened to be in Yugoslavia at a meeting with Marshal Tito when the American forces landed, and he went immediately to Moscow, apparently expecting there would be strong retaliation by the Russians. When such measures failed to materialize, I believe that Nasser revised his exaggerated notions about how much he could depend on Russian protection and support. Our successful demonstration of American power, skillfully used without casualties, had a salutary effect upon Nasser, a professional soldier.

I was met at the Cairo airport by Raymond A. Hare, the American Ambassador, and an excitable group of Egyptian newspapermen, who asked all the embarrassing questions they could devise. Then Hare, an old Service friend especially qualified in Middle Eastern affairs, drove me to his embassy, where I was called upon by one of Nasser's associates to arrange the pattern for our conversation which was scheduled for eleven o'clock the following day. Later this official telephoned from Nasser's residence to confirm that our outline was entirely acceptable. But at seven o'clock the next morning, Nasser's associate telephoned that he had just had a stormy talk with the President and must see me immediately. He explained that although Nasser usually arose late, he had gotten up at six that morning to receive a report from New York about a speech which Henry Cabot Lodge, chief American delegate to the United Nations, had made before the Security Council. It seems that Lodge had brought up Lebanon's previous complaint concerning interference in its internal affairs by the United Arab Republic. Nasser was furious. If that was the American attitude, what use to talk with Murphy? Hare and I explained that the action in the UN was merely a technical procedure and that it was an unfortunate coincidence that it happened on the day I was to meet with Nasser. But Nasser canceled our appointment. A little later the American Ambassador was invited to call, without me, on Minister of State Ali Sabry, who told him the same thing. Hare replied that my visit to Cairo had been suggested by the Egyptians themselves and that I would depart the next morning whatever happened.

Hare and I waited until 6 P.M. and then, as there was no further word from Nasser, I telephoned to Assistant Secretary of State Rountree in Washington. Deliberately, I began our transatlantic conversation by saying that "a very amusing situation" had arisen—at which point the government-controlled telephone was cut off and we were unable to re-establish connections. I made a bet with Hare that we would hear from Nasser within an hour, but I lost because it took one hour and thirty minutes. Nasser asked us to come to his residence at nine o'clock that evening, where he received us informally in his living room accompanied by two of his principal Ministers. Our reception was cordial and the talk lasted until two the next morning, with Nasser doing most of the talking. I was impressed by the President's willingness to carry five hours of conversation by himself, ignoring any protective shielding which his Ministers could have provided. I remembered Calvin Coolidge's remark, "What I didn't say never hurt me," and I appreciated the risks assumed by Nasser in his loquacity.

Nasser was intensely interested in the American intervention in Lebanon. He appeared to accept my explanation that the intervention was designed simply to insure the independence of that country, and he seemed at least partly convinced that our military operation would be restricted to Lebanon. Nasser asserted that President Chamoun had been hostile to the Egyptian Government, but said he was pleased with the choice of General Chehab. He made voluble protestations of his desire to support the independence of Lebanon now that the hostile Chamoun propaganda machine would cease to function. Nasser added he would be delighted to maintain friendly relations with Chehab's administration and declared he did not want to dominate Lebanon.

Eventually I was able to change the subject and ask Nasser some questions about the Kingdom of Jordan, the first country I visited after leaving Beirut. King Hussein, with excellent reason, feared for the independence of his country and for his own life. When, accompanied by the American Chargé d'Affaires Thomas K. Wright, I talked with the twenty-four-year-old monarch in his palace at Amman, Hussein spoke vehemently of Nasser's hostility; of plots and conspiracies emanating from Cairo; of efforts to seduce Jordanian troops. Nasser laughed at rumors that he was about to invade Jordan or injure Hussein, saying that the last thing he desired was to add to his own present troubles and anxieties. He said Hussein was mistaken in suspecting him; the young man should be reassured. Nasser added that he could see no solution to Jordan's problems so long as it was determined to remain an independent state. The country simply did not possess the means to do so. However, Nasser said that he wished Hussein no harm and in fact admired his courage.

The fragility of King Hussein's position and his tremendous personal courage had also impressed me. When I talked with him in his study at the palace, he was seated below a large oil portrait of his grandfather who had been assassinated when Hussein was fourteen years old. The youth had been with his grandfather at the time and one of the assassin's bullets had cut a button from the boy's coat. Now his little kingdom was surrounded by revolutionaries in Iraq, rival Arabs in Syria, Jews in Israel, none of whom Hussein could trust. There were twenty-five hundred British soldiers camped outside the capital city; Jordan had only a slender supply line running through difficult terrain to the Gulf of Aqaba; half a million Palestinian refugees were superimposed on the country's own poverty-stricken population; there was practically no money in the till. King Hussein surely had a stacked deck against him, but he would not abdicate. I remarked to Nasser that Hussein told me he had complete confidence in the loyalty of his troops, whereupon Nasser laughed again, saying: "I overthrew the King of Egypt after plotting for five years, and nobody suspected anything. How can Hussein be sure what is going on in his Army? You know what happened last month to his cousin, King Faisal of Iraq!"

I knew indeed what had happened in Iraq because I had just visited Baghdad, the capital city, where King Faisal had been assassinated along with his Premier, the Crown Prince and other members of the royal family. During my call on Hussein, the young King expressed the hope that the Western powers would not grant official recognition to the murderers of his relatives, but I knew that the United States was going to recognize the new Iraq regime the following day. Soviet Russia had lost no time in recognizing the revolutionary government, and the United States had decided it must keep in close contact with the situation there.

The American Ambassador, Waldemar J. Gallman, had not been enthusiastic when informed that I was planning to visit Iraq so soon after the coup d'état, and even while I was flying to Baghdad, I appreciated my friend's misgivings. The Air Force had assigned a C-54 for my trip but we had hardly crossed the frontier when the Iraqi air center ordered our plane to turn around and leave the area. Our pilot sent messages that Baghdad had authorized the flight, but we received no clearance. We decided to maintain our course, however, and landed in a steamy heat of 113 degrees at the airport where we were greeted by the urbane Ambassador, members of his staff and representatives of the new Iraqi Government. While driving through the empty but heavily patrolled streets to the miniature White House which is our embassy in Baghdad, Gallman told me something of the horrors which the city had so recently experienced. Many innocent people had been swept to death by mobs whose violence surpassed all expectations and got out of control of the military officers who had instigated the revolt. Three American businessmen, who happened to be in the lobby of the modern Baghdad Hotel when the building was searched, were seized with other foreigners, loaded on military trucks and driven to the Defense Ministry. A traffic jam occurred, the mob caught up with the trucks, the unfortunate prisoners were dragged to the street and killed out of hand. The bodies of King Faisal and his family were torn to pieces and it was reported that the royal bones were sold in the bazaars as souvenirs.

The man who engineered this revolution, Brigadier General Abdul Karim Kassim, was now Premier, and Ambassador Gallman had arranged for us to pay him an official visit at the Defense Ministry, where he was working and sleeping in the same room which he had been occupying ever since the uprising. The ministry was swarming with nervous sentries, and Kassim had a tommy gun of his own within easy reach. Small of stature, alert and noncommittal, it was difficult at first to engage the new Premier in a discussion of our mutual problems, but we were aided by Foreign Minister Abdul Jablar al Jomard, a blonde blue-eyed native of Mosul. I learned that Jomard, who had not participated in the plot to destroy King Faisal, was surprised to hear on the radio that he had been designated Foreign Minister. Kassim told me that he had entertained thoughts of the revolution for a number of years. Its plan had been carefully worked out in secret with about one hundred of his fellow Army officers. When opportunity occurred in July, due to the shift of certain military units, Kassim and his conspirators were able to execute the plan swiftly and the surprise was total. The Premier justified the coup d'état with the explanation that only by such unconstitutional means was it possible for the impoverished people of Iraq to get rid of their corrupt royal regime. Kassim stressed the purely domestic character of the revolution, which he said had been organized for national rather than ideological reasons. He did not deplore the brutality of the accomplishment.

Changing the subject, I told Kassim that I had come to Baghdad to help my government better to understand the policies of his government, which the United States had been prompt to recognize. Coincident with the revolution in Iraq, my government had intervened militarily in neighboring Lebanon, and I had heard that Iraqi officials were suspicious of our motives. Was that true? Yes, Kassim said, he was suspicious because he believed that Americans did not intend to restrict their forces to Lebanon. He felt sure that our intervention was merely a prelude to an invasion of Iraq—which he proposed to resist. I replied that I had just flown over a good deal of Iraq and had observed that it was a vast expanse of arid country, most uninviting from a military point of view. I reminded Kassim that the President of the United States had to his credit a long and successful career as an Army officer. Kassim, I noted, was also a soldier, and I asked him to figure out one good reason why Eisenhower would want to send American troops to invade the Godforsaken stretches of Iraq. I said this with a smile, not wishing to make any reflection on his country, and after a moment Kassim smiled too. The argument seemed to make a favorable impression on him, and he expressed a desire for friendly relations with the United States and with other Western countries.

I mentioned that the Western nations were somewhat worried about the arrival in Baghdad of a large Russian mission who seemed to be working closely with the activated Iraqi Communist Party, and we discussed with great frankness the experiences of countries which had begun with acceptance of Soviet aid and ended up with a loss of independence. Kassim outlined in simple soldier language his ideas about social and economic reforms needed by his country and assured me that he had not risked revolution for the purpose of handing Iraq to the Soviet Union. He added that he and his associates also had not risked their lives in order to make Iraq subservient to Egypt. Kassim impressed me as a man walking a tightrope between Moscow and Cairo. He declared that his administration intended to support the policies of the United Arab Republic but that Iraq would honor its own international obligations. Kassim said that his country wanted to increase its oil shipments to the West by at least 50 percent, and that he had notified Nasser there was to be no disturbance of the pipelines in Iraq. There had been indication of infiltration by agents from Egypt, and Kassim spoke with quiet ferocity. I did not doubt that he was grimly determined to maintain Iraqi independence. But less than five years later, Kassim was assassinated by a group of his own former colleagues-in-arms led by Colonel Abdul Mohammed Aref, a fervent admirer of Nasser.

During Nasser's five-hour talk with me, he gave a long dissertation about the United Arab Republic, explaining the necessity of Arab unity for the security of a small weak country like Egypt. But Nasser did not elaborate on his views concerning Iraq, and our conversation moved on to Israel which I also had visited before flying to Cairo. Of all diplomatic problems, none is thornier than the Arab-Israeli difference and perhaps only time can provide a solution. Thus far no one has been skillful enough to develop a formula. The Department of State at least deserves credit for patiently trying through the years. Certainly our relations with Nasser were distorted by his oft-expressed view that, no matter what the issue, the United States would be found on the side of Israel. American policy in the Suez incident had shaken Nasser in his view but not entirely disabused him of it. When I introduced the subject of Israel, Nasser shrugged his shoulders with the intimation that nothing could be done about that situation. But he refrained from aggressive statements about his Jewish neighbors. Probably the lightning Israeli advance through the Sinai Peninsula had produced some realistic thinking in the Nasser hierarchy.

I had driven to Jerusalem over the excellent highway constructed with American aid, and in that Holy City I had seen how close to each other were the sacred places of the great religions, Christian, Jewish, Moslem. I noted how barbed wire barricades separated Israel from Jordan. On the Jordan side I was received graciously by the Governor, and at the Mandelbaum Gate there was a pleasant welcome by friends from the Israeli Foreign Office. I took advantage of the opportunity to visit the great Mosque of Omar, the Wailing Wall, the Holy Sepulchre and Gethsemane, and I spent an interesting moment with a group of Greek Orthodox prelates. Then I drove on to Tel Aviv, where a meeting had been arranged for me with Prime Minister David Ben Gurion. He was in fine form and we reviewed Middle East problems generally. He was enthusiastic about a plan he had evolved for an informal association of Israel with Turkey, Iran, Ethiopia and the Sudan. He declared that if Nasser invaded the Kingdom of Jordan by subversion or any other means, Israel would feel obliged to seize the left bank of the River Jordan regardless of international consequences. Ben Gurion hoped that Nasser had no illusions regarding either Israel's intentions or its capacity to carry them out. I thought ruefully of the fragile position of young King Hussein and of the failure of American efforts to make a start toward Arab-Israeli cooperation.

My long evening with Nasser provided opportunity for me to explain American policy in the Middle East and the desire of President Eisenhower and Secretary Dulles to work with other nations toward a solution of the basic problems. But Nasser contended that the United States had played fast and loose with Egypt. On the Aswan Dam project, he said, Dulles had been brutal. The Soviet Union, on the other hand, had taken a much broader view and Egyptians were grateful to the Russians for their understanding of Egypt's needs. I made some pointed references to the substantial aid the United States had provided for Egypt and to our attitude at the time of Suez. I also voiced hope that Nasser's attitude toward our British ally would improve in the general interest. But Nasser gave this a curt brush-off. It seemed to me that Nasser enjoyed indulging in national self-pity. He made emotional references to the three centuries of Turkish rule and the seventy-five years of British domination over downtrodden Egyptians.

I was surprised at Nasser's sensitivity to criticism in the American press. He had in his living room a stack of American newspapers and magazines and he picked up some of them with irritation. Apparently he had read every reference to himself and was cherishing every comment which he regarded as false or unjust. I told him that men in public life in the United States were accustomed to such treatment, and that one congressman had said to me that the only time a statesman should worry is when the press stops writing about him. Nasser laughed, but not heartily. Our meeting finally terminated in a cordial atmosphere. It was my impression that Nasser's respect for the United States had been enhanced by American intervention in Lebanon. There could be no doubt about the intensity of Nasser's patriotism and devotion to the Arab cause, and I respected him for his struggle with the crushing burden of trying to do something for Egypt's impoverished millions. But I left with a feeling of uneasiness about the pressures on Nasser which could lead to methods not conducive to peace.

From Cairo I flew to Addis Ababa, the capital of Ethiopia, because Emperor Haile Selassie had been pressing the State Department to send a ranking official with whom he could discuss urgent problems. My availability made this convenient now, and the Department instructed me to call on the Emperor before proceeding on my homeward journey. As customary, I was met at the airport by the American Ambassador, who as usual was an old Foreign Service colleague, and again I enjoyed the hospitality and the facilities provided by a competent embassy staff, all keenly interested in their mission. The Ambassador, Don C. Bliss, escorted me to the palace, where I was introduced to the Emperor who was seated with his pet terrier before a large fireplace glowing with crackling logs. It was chilly at that altitude of eight thousand feet, and I was conscious of the abrupt change from the sticky heat of sea level to this rarified atmosphere of Addis Ababa.

The three matters which Haile Selassie was most anxious to hear about were the American intervention in Lebanon, the destruction of the monarchy in Iraq, and Nasser's designs against Ethiopia. The Emperor approved our military action in Lebanon and asserted it undoubtedly would promote stability in the area. He was appalled by the assassination of the royal family in Iraq. And he manifested considerable disquiet over the increasing volume of propaganda on the Cairo radio directed toward the Moslem minority in Ethiopia, fearing that this might preface Egyptian interference in his kingdom. The Emperor told me that he had no illusions regarding Soviet ambitions, and that although the Russians were permitted to operate a hospital in Addis Ababa, the Ethiopians were on guard against Communist meddling in the affairs of their country. Haile Selassie, a sensitive, dignified and intelligent man, was acutely aware of his responsibilities and he wanted better American understanding of some of his anxieties. The United States already was cooperating with Ethiopia in a number of fields, and I tried to convey to the Emperor a sense of American participation in his problems.

Following instructions from the State Department, I enplaned next for Greece, with stopovers at the British Crown Colony of Aden and the island of Rhodes. At Aden I was informed concerning the continual tribal harassments on the Yemen frontier. At Rhodes I examined the Voice of America ship-based radio installation. Arriving in Athens, where the American Ambassador was my good friend James Riddleberger who had been on my staff in Berlin after the war, I learned that I had just missed British Prime Minister Harold Macmillan who had departed the previous evening after discussions with the Greek Government looking to a solution of the persistent Cyprus question. Riddleberger and I were invited to the country residence of Premier Constantine Karamanlis, where it would have been an interesting change for me if I could have listened to him and his Foreign Minister elucidate the Cyprus problem. But the two Greek statesmen were satiated with talk about Cyprus, so I was called upon to tell again about the American intervention in Lebanon, the precarious situation in Jordan, and Egypt's relations with the West. Greece had a very practical stake in Egypt, and the Premier did not despair of Nasser. He approved American intervention in Lebanon and I, for my part, admired his sturdy defense of democratic ideals and his opposition to relentless Communist pressures against the Greek Government.

Early the next morning, Sunday, I flew to London at the invitation of Foreign Secretary Selwyn Lloyd and spent the afternoon and evening at Chequers, the official country residence of the Prime Minister, in the stimulating company of our distinguished Ambassador, John Hay Whitney, and several members of the Foreign Office who met for an all-day discussion of the Middle East. During the war I grew to esteem the British colleagues who attended this meeting—Selwyn Lloyd, David Ormsby-Gore, Derek Hoyar-Millar, Patrick Dean, William Hayter, Evelyn Shuckburgh, Michael Hadow and Frank Account. Their trained and experienced minds are assets of great value in international negotiations.

The British platter was full of Middle East problems—Cyprus, Suez, Saudi Arabia, Bahrein, Qatar, Kuwait, the British military contingent in Jordan, the shocking assassination in Baghdad of King Faisal who so recently had visited London. What might happen in Iraq where Britain had a large stake? Would the United States stand firmly with its British friends along the Persian Gulf littoral? There were many grave probems, the area is of vital interest to Britain, and I respect British knowledge of it. I sometimes have wished that American concern for the Middle East had the same intensity, if for no other reason than that Britain is our major ally. It might seem entirely natural for Americans to share British urgency about the Persian Gulf—but we do not. Our geographic and material interests are different. Americans have not fulfilled British hopes of close association in some projects, because British interests and anxieties are not necessarily those of the United States.

After a restful night as the guest of Ambassador and Mrs. Whitney in London, I flew to Paris the next day for consultation with Ambassador Houghton and French Foreign Minister Couve de Murville. Once more there was another review of the problems of the Middle East.

In New York the following evening I found President Eisenhower and Secretary Dulles there for a United Nations meeting on the same subject. The President invited me to fly back to Washington with him the next day in his private plane, thus providing opportunity to relate to him in detail my observations and conclusions. By that time I had my Middle East recital quite well organized.

Throughout my tour, no matter how late each day ended, I always wrote for the State Department a long report of that day's happenings, and those field reports have provided most of the political information contained in this chapter. But I also saw and heard much which I never recorded for the State Department, and it is those experiences which I recall most vividly now. No field notes are required to remind me of the incongruity of Lebanese swimming, skin diving, and water-skiing against the gray backdrop of American warships anchored in Beirut Harbor . . . I can still smell the cool night breeze blowing off the desert, with that familiar odor reminiscent of the Sahara and Libya, while I talked with King Hussein in his palace at Amman . . . I still feel the serenity of the Mass which I attended on Sunday in the shadowy Roman Catholic church in Baghdad, while armed soldiers patrolled the hot streets outside . . . I remember my visits to the Holy Places in Jerusalem, which provided perspective of the past to contrast with ephemeral current troubles. And there was my visit to the kibbutz near Tel Aviv, which suggested hope for the future . . . I can still see the Aswan Dam project as I flew over it, dotted with Soviet engineers and technicians busily at work in the brilliant Egyptian sunshine . . . And there were those tame lions strolling around the palace garden in Addis Ababa to honor His Imperial Highness Haile Selassie, the Lion of Judah . . . On my night in Athens I witnessed field events between our team of American athletes and Greek track stars at the impressive Olympic Stadium, where the events were conducted in keeping with the finest Greek traditions . . . Then there was London and Paris and New York and Washington.

The next day I went back to work in my office at the Department of State. My twenty-nine-day Magic Carpet tour of the fabled East had come to its end.

TWENTY-EIGHT

AMERICAN RELATIONS WITH RUSSIA

Ever since I went to work for the Department of State in 1917, when the most important political event of the year was the Bolshevik revolution, the troubled relationship between the United States and the Soviet Union has overshadowed American foreign policy. During the final years of my diplomatic career, when I was Deputy Under Secretary and later Under Secretary for Political Affairs, the Russian policy of our government became my constant concern, notwithstanding that I lacked specialized training in that field. That is, I never was assigned duty as a Russian language student as were some other Foreign Service officers, notably Charles E. Bohlen who became President Roosevelt's interpreter at conferences with Stalin, and George F. Kennan whose analytical writings on Soviet policy won him worldwide distinction. Bohlen enjoyed three years on full-time active duty at L'Ecole Orientale des Langues Vivantes in Paris, studying Russian. Kennan was assigned to Berlin for two years in the same capacity. They and other Russian students spent their summers in places like Riga, the capital of Latvia, so that in addition to the language, those officers had opportunity to learn about Slavic history, issues, personalities and customs. Bohlen and Kennan later gave expert service in Washington and eventually each was appointed American Ambassador at Moscow.

Although I rather envied some of my colleagues their scholarly training, I had the benefit of a certain apprenticeship of my own in Russian affairs. My first involvement in Soviet diplomacy occurred in 1943 when Ambassador Bogomolov was attached to General Eisenhower's headquarters in Algiers. Bogomolov's status was roughly equivalent to Harold Macmillan's and mine as representatives of the British Foreign Office and the State Department, and the three of us saw each other frequently. Acquaintance with Bogomolov was followed by instructive association with another influential Russian when I was assigned to escort Stalin's emissary, Andrei Vishinsky, from Cairo to Algiers and thence on a tour of Italy. After the war my Russian contacts expanded through four years of work in Germany with an assortment of Soviet officials, including Marshals Zhukov and Sokolovsky and Ambassadors Sobolev and Semenov. Negotiating with Russian representatives about the Berlin blockade was a liberal education in itself, and that experience was extended when as American Ambassador to Japan, I encountered Communist techniques in the Far East.

Thus it was not as a novice that I took up my duties in Washington in 1953. At the beginning of my term there, Georgi N. Zaroubin was the Soviet Ambassador; later he was succeeded by Mikhail A. Menshikov. Both of these envoys were products of the Communist system, as were members of their embassy staffs, and sometimes I found myself actually sorry for the men and their families in the straitjacket existence required of them. Meeting these diplomats frequently on official business provided me with additional understanding of Soviet mentality and methods.

Most negotiations which I conducted on behalf of the Department of State involved exceptional matters, but there was one type of diplomatic exchange which occurred so many times that it became almost routine. Every once in a while a staff member of the Soviet Embassy would be detected in an attempt to acquire secret and strategic information in flagrant violation of American law. As part of the most intensive espionage network the world has ever seen, there was nothing novel about such spying, and the procedure for handling the situation was rather well established. The Ambassador would be asked to call and I would hand him a formal note, with appropriate deprecating gestures, reciting the facts and requiring the offending Russian to depart from the United States within a day or two as *persona non grata*. This would elicit a strong verbal denial of any wrongdoing, and the Ambassador would leave my office after suitable emotional expressions. Then the Ambassador would send me a formal communication denying everything in positive terms. And then the offending official would depart from the United States. No further reference to the incident would be made by either the Ambassador or me when he called again on other matters. There was a sort of tacit understanding that this was part of the game. But it would be just a question of time before a member of the staff of the American Embassy in Moscow would be arbitrarily accused of a similar offense, declared *persona non grata,* and asked to depart from the Soviet Union. It was the regular price we paid for success by our detection agencies.

Sometimes our government was compelled to pay a much higher

price for the privilege of maintaining diplomatic relations with the Soviet Union. One such instance occurred when a C-119 heavy transport plane, with seventeen American Air Force men on board, strayed about forty miles across the Soviet frontier while en route from Turkey through the Lake Van region. We never were able to determine why our plane flew off course into Soviet range. Flying conditions in that area are notoriously bad, due to weather, but in this case there was some indication that a false radio beam was transmitted and that the American pilot mistakenly followed it. Without warning, Soviet fighter planes attacked the unarmed transport and shot it down in flames. All seventeen airmen perished. The Soviet Government ignored requests from the State Department for permission for American representatives to visit the scene to verify what had happened and to recover the bodies. Weeks later six badly mutilated corpses were sent to the United States. The Soviet Government declared it had taken proper defensive measures to protect its air space, which the American plane had violated, and it warned that future offenders would be treated the same way.

By fortunate circumstances a radio operator in a nearby country made a tape recording at the time of the shooting, so we had a clearly audible record of the voices of the Soviet pilots and the orders emanating from their base. The conversations of the Soviet airmen included expressions in Russian such as "This time I got him!"—"Down they go!"—and similar excited comments. When the State Department received this tape recording, I invited Soviet Ambassador Menshikov, together with his air attaché, to come to my office. Representatives of our Air Force were also present. When all were seated, I explained the purpose of my invitation and the tape recorder was started. Menshikov jumped to his feet, protesting that he would not listen, that this was not his function, and furthermore that even if he did, he would not know what it was about because he was not a technician. I explained that was why his air attaché, a highly qualified technician, had been invited with him. He became vehement, almost incoherent. He objected that this was beyond his jurisdiction. I asked whether he did not have certain responsibilities as Soviet Ambassador to the United States, but he refused to stay. However, he and his air attaché did accept copies of the tape transcript which we had prepared for them. We also presented Menshikov with another souvenir which the American Embassy in Moscow had sent to the State Department—a copy of the official *Soviet Aviation Magazine*, which contained an illustrated account of the ceremony when the Russian fighter pilots were decorated for their valor in shooting down the unarmed American plane.

Continued efforts by our government brought no apology or any other satisfaction from the Soviet Government. Nevertheless the administration in Washington decided not to retaliate. We in the State Department could only speculate what effect this incident might have on the Russian mind—this knowledge that a brutal attack against unarmed Americans could be committed with impunity. Such a situation would traditionally have been sufficient cause for war. But the administration felt that risk of war was so perilous that it was advisable to limit action in the C-119 tragedy to protests and whatever publicity might be deemed useful.

The Soviet Union, in its aggressive ambition to expand its area of influence after World War II, occasionally made an error. One of these mistakes was Stalin's quarrel with his Communist colleague, Tito of Yugoslavia. Stalin was determined to control Party policies; Tito was equally stubborn in maintaining the independence of his country. Stalin, in his contemptuous plan to treat Yugoslavia like other Soviet satellites, ignored the fervent patriotism and the fighting qualities of the Yugoslavs. By the time Tito definitely broke with Stalin in 1948, the United States had learned some postwar lessons from the Berlin blockade and other Russian actions, and our government was making an effort to cultivate the sympathies of unaligned nations so that they would at least remain outside the Sino-Soviet bloc. Thus opportunity occurred for cooperation between the United States and Yugoslavia.

When I first visited that country during World War II, our government had no Yugoslav policy and I was instructed to call upon Tito only as a private visitor, unaccompanied by my staff. It was not until ten years later that I became involved again in Yugoslav affairs, and then rather by chance. One evening in 1954, while attending a Washington dinner party given by the Arthur Krocks, I happened to be seated next to Clare Boothe Luce, our Ambassador to Italy. Mrs. Luce had been summoned home for consultation about Yugoslavia's claims in Trieste against Italy, a dispute which had poisoned relations between the two countries for almost a decade and had received earnest attention from all the major European powers as well as the United States. While conversing with Mrs. Luce about this situation, I mentioned the amiable meetings I had had with Tito during the war. "You are just the man we need to bring Tito around!" she exclaimed. She told me she had an appointment with President Eisenhower the next morning and would suggest to him and to Secretary Dulles that I be sent to Yugoslavia. Ambassador Luce usually got what she wanted, and I received instructions that same day to confer with Tito.

When I was thus suddenly thrust into the Trieste negotiations as an additional mediator, confidential conversations already had been going on in London for seven months between Dr. Vladimir Velebit of Yugoslavia, Manlio Brosio of Italy, Geoffrey W. Harrison of the British Foreign Office and Llewellyn E. Thompson, the American Ambassador in Austria. This group of experienced diplomats had laboriously and skillfully settled many social, economic and ethnic questions, but a residue of marginal problems remained including one tiny bit of disputed land. The London discussions seemed to have reached an impasse on this matter, and under instructions from President Eisenhower I flew to Belgrade on September 14, accompanied by Robert G. Hooker, an able Foreign Service officer with special knowledge of Yugoslavia, to see what might be done about this situation.

After preliminary conversations with Yugoslav officials, Ambassador Riddleberger and I were invited to spend a day with Tito in his brand new "palace" on the island of Brioni off the Dalmatian Coast. I found my old wartime acquaintance in excellent form and good humor, and there was opportunity during lunch for the kind of informal banter which I knew he enjoyed. I told him that at the Chevy Chase golf course we had named Hole No. 8 "Trieste" because it encompassed about the same amount of territory which the Yugoslavs and Italians were arguing about. I also told him that a Texas friend had informed me that if Tito needed territory so badly as to squabble for months over a rock pile, my friend would buy him a whole county in Texas.

I had brought Tito a personal letter from President Eisenhower, and after lunch he excused himself and went to his study to read it carefully, leaving Riddleberger and me in the charge of his clever political adviser, Vilfan. Eisenhower's letter suggested some changes in the territorial division under consideration in London, and concluded: "I fully realize that your negotiators made concessions which represent great sacrifices on your part, and I want you to understand that in urging this further small concession, I am not blind to the great contribution you already have made." Tito rejoined our party after twenty minutes and said that he wanted a settement in Trieste as much as we did, but he asked for sympathetic understanding of his government's position because the problem was loaded with domestic political dynamite. I urged that the insignificant territorial concession be made, and promised I would also urge a compensating concession from our Italian friends whom I would visit in a few days. Tito did not quibble over details, and he himself suggested an alternative formula which he agreed I could present in Rome.

After two more days of discussions in Belgrade, I flew to Rome on September 18 where I was given a thorough briefing by Ambassador Luce regarding the fluid Italian political situation. There had been a government reshuffle that very day and Prime Minister Scelba had appointed a new Foreign Minister, Gaetano Martino, a professor from Sicily whom I did not know. He proved to be an ace. I found that all the Italian officials wanted a definite settlement of the tiresome and dangerous Trieste dispute, but the problem was loaded with dynamite in Italy just as in Yugoslavia. However, the Prime Minister said that public interest demanded a relaxation of tension and that he would take his political chances. The fact that I was able to offer an alternative formula of almost evenly balanced territorial concessions provided a face-saving device, and the staff of the Italian Foreign Office under the skillful guidance of Ambassador Zoppi seized on this eagerly. No one was happier about the satisfactory conclusion of the Trieste negotiations than Mrs. Luce, who had worked on this problem intelligently and unceasingly for months.

I flew to Paris on September 22 and touched base with Ambassador Douglas Dillon to inform him of the progress which had been made, and then proceeded the next day to London where the stage was being set for the end of the long drama. After appropriate instructions arrived from Belgrade and Rome, a boundary memorandum was initialed in London on October 5. The danger of conflict in the Trieste area, between the Italian forces and the Yugoslav divisions which had been mobilized against them, had been dissipated by diplomacy.

During my conversations in Belgrade I discovered that Vice President Svetozar Vukmanovic-Tempo, the economic boss of Yugoslavia, was greatly alarmed about his country's huge wheat deficit, the worst in its history. A deficit of 700,000 tons had been estimated, but now it was evident that the deficit would be at least 1,300,000 tons—this in a country which under capitalism had always been an exporter of cereals. The fact was that the collective farm system had failed miserably in Yugoslavia, there was an imperative need for wheat, and none seemed to be forthcoming from the Soviet Union. When Vukmanovic-Tempo brought up this matter, I told him that perhaps the United States could be helpful, but that I had come to Belgrade to ask for Yugoslav support on immediate settlement of the Trieste issue. Actually I was authorized to offer assistance if circumstances justified, and before departing for Rome I informed Deputy Foreign Minister Bebler in strictest confidence that the United States would be willing to deliver 400,000 tons of wheat to Yugoslavia. But it was incorrect for Sir Anthony Eden to suggest that I went to Belgrade and laid some wheat on the line, whereupon the Yugoslavs grasped the pen and signed the Trieste agreement. Tito sensibly wanted to bring the Trieste disturbance to an end, but I doubt that he would have surrendered on matters of principle for a shipment of wheat.

So far as I know, there never was any thought in Washington that we might persuade Tito to become our ally. Our objective was much more limited—to encourage a genuinely independent Yugoslavia not unfriendly to the United States. To achieve that purpose we were willing to provide extensive military and economic aid, so that Yugoslavia would not be at the mercy of Russia. I had nothing to do with the original concept of the military program which was negotiated in Belgrade by my friend General J. Lawton ("Lightning Joe") Collins while I was Ambassador in Brussels. I had no criticism of this aid policy which I believed sound, although I was critical later of extravagance in its application. It seemed to me that the United States could have obtained virtually the same political effect at a lower price, perhaps less than half what we actually spent. It is an American characteristic that when we once decide to pursue a policy, we are inclined to go all out and damn the cost. This was especially noticeable in France after the war, where we spent enormous sums with more generosity than discrimination. If we erred in Yugoslavia, it was on the liberal side. Sometimes it is not wise to shower lavish gifts on people accustomed to a meager economy, lest the recipients suspect that such generosity may have an ulterior motive. From the Yugoslav point of view, it was incomprehensible why we should press such substantial allocations upon them in the early days, and our extravagance made it difficult for us to deal with them later.

For instance, one day in 1953 I was authorized to inform the Yugoslav Ambassador in Washington that thirty-three million dollars had just been granted for the purchase of cereals and cotton under the aid program for his country. At that time the total amount which the United States had given to Yugoslavia exceeded a billion dollars in economic and military assistance, and I thought the Ambassador would express some appreciation. Instead, without a word of thanks, he said brusquely: "Yes, yes. I know all about that. But what about the additional twelve million dollars for wheat?" Apparently the Ambassador already had learned informally about the latest American grant, perhaps even before I heard of it myself. I let the thermometer drop about twenty degrees and then ushered him out of my office with some noncommittal remarks. Later a new Yugoslav Ambassador, Leo Mates, was assigned to handle the affairs of his country in Washington and at the United Nations. This former Partisan fighter was sympathetic and intelligent, and he became a dependable and effective diplomatic associate.

Nevertheless cooperation between Belgrade and Washington seemed to deteriorate. The United States Government had transferred hundreds of millions of dollars worth of equipment to the Yugoslav Army, and it was the duty of the American Military Assistance Mission in Belgrade to report on the use made of this equipment. But General Peter C. Hains, who was in charge of the military group, notified Washington that he could not get access to much of the information to which we were entitled by our agreement. As the complaints of our military establishment increased in crescendo, so did the voices of congressional critics, led by William F. Knowland, the Republican whip in the Senate, and Walter H. Judd in the House of Representatives. Knowland was an especially formidable opponent of the Yugoslav aid program, and I respected his reasons. Finally President Eisenhower and Secretary Dulles decided that I should go to Yugoslavia again to confer with President Tito and make a thorough review of our entire policy, military and economic.

I arrived in Belgrade on September 26, 1955 and remained there until October 3. This time I found Tito suffering from rheumatism in his knees, but notwithstanding his discomfort he manifested the greatest cordiality and good nature, and my visit provided useful opportunity for exchange of views. I explained in detail the difficulties which our Army representatives were encountering, and it was clear from Tito's reactions that he would undertake to improve matters. Some of the troubles of our mission occurred because Yugoslav officials and Army officers, as former guerrilla fighters and as Communists, had built-in prejudices against foreigners inquiring closely into their military establishment—especially capitalist foreigners. Traditional Slavic suspicions made this prejudice even more acute. Some of our other troubles were the result of experience which the Yugoslavs had had with the Russian military mission after the war. Minister of Defense Gosnyak told me frankly that the Yugoslavs were gun-shy. They had come close to domination by the Russians and they had no intention of incurring similar risk from Americans. They were inclined to see in every demand for verification, every attempt at inspection, a disposition on our part to dictate to and control them. Perhaps some of our people were too efficient and energetic. So the Yugoslavs had put obstacles in the way of our officers, refused facilities, and declined to accept additional American military personnel in the area.

General Hains had been succeeded by Major General John K. Waters, and out of the long talks which he and Ambassador Riddleberger and I had with Yugoslav officials, we were able to draw up a memorandum of understanding on October 1. General Waters was assured of direct communication with Minister Gosnyak, which previously had been denied to General Hains. The Yugoslavs gave assurances regarding our right to inspect matériel provided under the aid program. Facilities were promised for a staff of sixty American military men, and procedures were agreed upon for relations with their Yugoslav counterparts. There also was agreement on the delivery by us of specific military equipment.

These military negotiations in Belgrade were accompanied by some stubborn and rather stormy economic sessions with Vice President Vukmanovic-Tempo, who seemed determined by sheer aggressiveness to exact commitments of additional American aid to shore up the admittedly soggy Yugoslav economy. The name "Tempo" was a sobriquet of this Partisan hero, because "Tempo! Tempo!"—which means "Hurry! Hurry!" in Serbo-Croatian—had been his favorite expression during the war. So, according to Communist custom, "Tempo" had become his official name. Vice President Tempo did not request or attempt to negotiate; he demanded. I enjoyed the give and take, and the Yugoslavs did not seem to mind when we pounded the table just as hard as they did. We offered to supply three hundred thousand tons of wheat in the immediate future, but Tempo insisted upon five hundred thousand tons annually thereafter. Not receiving satisfaction from us, Tempo proposed going to Washington to continue the talks there, and this was agreed upon.

I presided at the opening session of our Washington meeting, which was attended by representatives of the State Department and the International Cooperation Administration. But I still could see no reason to yield on the question of allocating thirty million dollars for cereals, in addition to more than two hundred million dollars worth of other items, and my irritation with Tempo's bulldozing tactics must have been obvious. Harold Stassen, Director of the ICA, assumed charge of negotiations the next day while I attended as policy adviser representing the Secretary of State. Tempo continued to be offensively aggressive, and at one point in the discussion I slipped a note to Stassen saying: "Now it's your turn to get tough." But Stassen's scribbled reply was: "Let's get tough next year." The Yugoslavs received everything they demanded, about 260 million dollars' worth, for which we never got a bit of satisfaction or benefit.

Americans were disposed to be generous to Yugoslavia not only because that country was independent of Russia, but also because we hoped President Tito might have a liberalizing effect on other Communist countries. In my last talk with Tito, he told me that he wanted to improve relations with Hungary but his overtures were being balked by Matyas Rakosi, the Communist boss in Budapest, the capital of Hungary. Tito said that Rakosi, who had been a supporter of Stalin, was an evil influence, as unfriendly to Yugoslavia as he was to the United States, and Tito hinted that Rakosi must be removed from power. During the next few months I watched developments from Washington, and from that distance it appeared to me that Tito was achieving his objective. Beginning in February 1956 Communist politics in Budapest underwent one change after another. On July 18 Rakosi resigned. In October a delegation of Communists flew to Belgrade to discuss Yugoslav-Hungarian relations.

But Tito underestimated the passionate longing of the Hungarian people to regain their freedom. While negotiations were going on in

Yugoslavia to establish amicable relations with Hungary, ten thousand Hungarians assembled in Budapest to demand the withdrawal of Soviet troops and abolition of the secret police, and to plead for a new government with free elections. The Budapest demonstration began in orderly fashion, but later it burgeoned into a riot. Teletype reports from the American Legation informed the State Department that street fighting had broken out, that Stalin's great statue had been knocked down and trampled upon, and that Soviet troops were moving in from the countryside. It was clear that matters had gotten out of hand, and our fears of terrible reprisals were only too soon confirmed. The following day Soviet army units fired into an unarmed crowd in front of the Parliament building while Hungarian youths, as brave as they were reckless, attempted to block armored tanks. Soon the Hungarian revolt was spreading wildly into the provinces.

At three o'clock in the morning of Sunday, October 28, which happened to be my birthday, I was awakened at my home in Washington by a telephone call from Jacob D. Beam, head of the Eastern European Office in the State Department. Beam, an old friend who had served with me in Berlin, had been up all night with his staff, receiving teletype messages from our Legation in Budapest. The latest word was that Soviet armies were crossing the Carpathian frontier into Hungary. I dressed and hurried to the Department where we were able to exchange information with our Budapest staff and give last-minute instructions until all communication was cut off at seven o'clock.

I must admit that I did not expect that an anti-Soviet revolution would spread through Hungary like a forest fire, but I never doubted that if a revolt did break out, the U.S.S.R. would use every means no matter how brutal to suppress it. The United States Government had no advance information about this uprising, no plan of action. And neither did Tito in Belgrade nor the authorities in Budapest nor the rulers in Moscow. The State Department had welcomed the stimulation which Tito seemed to be giving to a liberalizing trend, but nobody anticipated anything like this Hungarian insurrection. The American Legation in Budapest was even without a Minister at the climax of the disorders. Christian M. Ravndal had done a superb job of reporting the political maneuvers which preceded the revolt, but he had been appointed in July as Ambassador to Ecuador. His successor, E. T. (Tom) Wailes, who had been Ambassador to the Union of South Africa, could not reach Budapest until November 2 and he never did present his credentials there. Although Wailes' experience and wisdom were invaluable during the last weeks of the crisis, many members of Congress were critical of the State Department and of American Intelligence services for having been caught so completely by surprise.

The movement into Hungary by large numbers of additional Russian troops was the most acute international situation since the invasion of Korea six years before, and far more dangerous because there was possibility of direct American contact in Europe with the Red Army itself.

While I was receiving in my office a stream of anxious visitors who were distressed because the State Department did not know what was going on behind the scenes in Hungary, other critics were accusing the State Department of having actively fomented the Hungarian uprising. It seemed to be a case of damned if we didn't, and damned if we did. Charges of our complicity in the rebellion were based chiefly on broadcasts from Radio Free Europe, a station maintained in Munich by an American organization. Radio Free Europe employs a number of Europeans to broadcast news and speeches in European languages, and it was only natural for the Hungarian announcers to give encouraging accounts of the rebellion in their native land. It is not unlikely that Hungarian challenges from the American broadcasting station did help to incite some patriotic insurgents, thus giving credence to the rumor that the United States was a party to the uprising, but actually we had nothing to do with it.

The impression that our government was sponsoring the Hungarian revolt was unfortunately enhanced by an appeal to Marshal Bulganin from President Eisenhower, who urged the Russian Premier to withdraw Soviet forces from Hungary and permit the people to exercise their rights in freedom. Eisenhower issued a statement declaring: "The United States considers the developments in Hungary as a renewed expression of the intense desire for freedom long held by the Hungarians." While I agreed with this sentiment, I regretted that the President expressed himself as he did just at that time, because the Russians were trying to blame Americans for the human slaughter which was occurring in Hungary. When the grim fighting finally ended on November 14, Eisenhower thought it advisable to issue another public statement explaining that he never had advocated open rebellion by an undefended population against forces over which they could not possibly prevail.

While the rebellion was blazing, everyone in the United States wanted to help the brave Hungarians, and the State Department was inundated with proposals ranging from outright military action to plans for welcoming thousands of refugees. Members of Congress and ambassadors from several embassies in Washington came to my office to urge "action," and some of our critics were bitter. I would analyze for each complainant the possibilities of "action" adequate to liberate Hungary, and would point out that palliatives could not possibly settle the issue but would only provoke the powerful Soviet armies to further massacre.

One suggestion frequently made was that the United States Air Force should at least fly in supplies to the patriots. But the geographic position of Hungary made this unfeasible. Our planes could not fly over Communist-controlled East Germany, Czechoslovakia or Yugoslavia, so we could approach Hungary only through Austria, and Austria declared in no uncertain terms that it would resist any form of overflights. Discussions with my visitors would conclude by my asking the complainant whether he would support a policy which would inevitably lead to a direct military attack by American forces against Russian forces. The sympathizer always would reply that he meant "action short of war." American policy of promoting liberation of captive nations always stopped short of war, and this was well known.

The Yugoslav Ambassador in Washington, Leo Mates, called on me several times. The Ambassador's forehead was wet with perspiration as he described the tense attitude of his government regarding the Soviet armies which were moving along the Yugoslav frontier. He was greatly alarmed by the clamor in the United States for counteraction against the Russians, and he begged that provocation be avoided. He believed that his country was trembling on the thin edge of war against the Soviet Union, and he urged that everything be done to confine the conflict to Hungary.

From Yugoslav sources I learned confidentially that before the Soviet Government decided on the grave step of military intervention, there were three days of violent discussion in the Kremlin. I was informed that strong influence was exerted by Peiping to induce Moscow to intervene in Hungary. Perhaps Peiping did support this brutal move, but even if the Chinese had opposed it, Moscow would have intervened anyway because its entire Eastern European security system was at stake. Once the decision was taken—and I was told that it was taken with the greatest reluctance—Marshal Zhukov was authorized to use every force needed for total suppression of the revolt. From the Russian point of view this was an absolute political and military necessity, and once the offensive was launched, they followed through. Putting ethics and the humanities aside, their judgment was sound. They understood the requirement to win.

The ruthless suppression of the Hungarian rebellion was somewhat dimmed by the Suez crisis, which could not have been timed more advantageously for the Russians. On October 24, units of the Red Army already stationed in Hungary went into action, and additional units invaded the country during the following days. On October 29, Anglo-

French-Israeli forces invaded Egypt. The Russians were determined in any case to crush the Hungarian insurrection, but the attack against Egypt provided them with an admirable distraction. For instance, when the President of Syria was urged at the United Nations to indicate some indignation about Russian conduct in Budapest, that estimable gentleman declared he did not care if there were fifty Budapests—what concerned him was what might happen to Syria as a result of the attack on Egypt. The concomitant of the military operations in Hungary and Egypt burdened the State Department with its most intense responsibilities since World War II, causing me and some of the other officers to work around the clock, while Secretary Dulles went to New York to take personal charge, with Ambassador Lodge, of the simultaneous proceedings in the United Nations.

Dulles succeeded—with cynical support from the Soviet Union!—in sponsoring measures in the UN which resulted in a cease-fire in Egypt. But measures adopted by the UN against Russia had no effect whatever on the situation in Hungary. The first step taken by Dulles was to have a resolution presented to the Security Council affirming the right of the Hungarian people to choose their own government, and calling upon the Soviet Union to desist forthwith from any form of intervention. Yugoslavia abstained from voting on this resolution and the Soviet representative—to the surprise of no one—vetoed it. The United States Government, under the direction of Dulles, then took the initiative in the General Assembly which passed a sturdy resolution by 53 to 9, with 13 abstentions, calling for immediate cessation of Soviet intervention in Hungary and providing for UN representatives to observe conditions in that country and to submit a report. But the Soviet Union would not permit Sir Leslie Munro of New Zealand to visit Budapest as an observer. We pushed as hard as we could in the UN forum, but we failed in our essential objective—release of the Hungarian people from bondage.

In the end, our government was reduced to the minimal policy of providing assistance to Hungarian refugees, and to impact on world opinion—whatever that may mean. On the assumption that the American people did not desire to go to war against the Soviet Union, and in Washington it was believed that they did not, there seemed no other policy to pursue. The American Legation in Budapest gave sanctuary to Cardinal Mindszenty; 21,500 refugees were offered asylum in the United States; and our government engaged in sundry welfare work for the Hungarian people. This was not a glorious position for the United States, and the words "roll back the aggressors" no longer appeared in speeches. General Ivan A. Serov, Soviet State Security Chief, arrived in Hungary and apparently was in charge of deportations which assumed massive proportions. Many patriotic men and women were executed.

Morally, the Soviet Union undoubtedly suffered in Western opinion. For one thing, the Soviet action doomed the "Spirit of Geneva" which had been exercising a divisive influence in the West and which was beginning to pay off for the Russians. But the U.S.S.R., as a practical matter, incurred little or no visible damage to its own world position. In fact the element of fear plays an important role in international affairs, and the effect of Hungary on some countries was evident in their subesquent willingness to yield to Soviet influence in the United Nations. In retrospect, world acceptance of the Russian aggression in Hungary is still incredible. For sheer perfidy and relentless suppression of a courageous people longing for their liberty, Hungary will always remain a classic symbol. Perhaps history will demonstrate that the free world could have intervened to give the Hungarians the liberty they sought, but none of us in the State Department had the skill or the imagination to devise a way.

Probably the most effective diplomatic device which the United States Government has been able to institute against the spread of Communism is our network of alliances. This international system got under way in 1949 when Secretary of State Acheson signed the NATO agreement. Creation of the North Atlantic Treaty Organization was closely related to the Marshall Plan and both were designed to safeguard the postwar world against Soviet expansion. After the establishment of NATO, Soviet expansion in Europe ceased. Today NATO has fifteen member nations, and it is one of a series of alliances, bilateral agreements, and other security arrangements in which forty-two nations are cooperating, including SEATO (Southeast Asia Treaty Organization), ANZUS (Australia, New Zealand, United States Treaty Organization) and CENTO (Central Treaty Organization).

For the staff of the State Department, the work required to develop those alliances was arduous. Innumerable details produced a heavy load of activities, and membership in an alliance, once achieved, created new responsibilities. During my last years in the Department, I devoted much of my time to problems which grew out of our alliances. Allies frequently felt privileged to make demands on a more prosperous fellow ally, especially demands for money or military know-how or equipment. Sometimes allies insisted on consultation before any policy whatever could be adopted. Even if a policy related to another area of the world, an ally by some stretch of imagination might contend that its own security was threatened. Allies also were likely to expect their partners to support them if they had difficulties in the United Nations or the Middle East or Africa or anywhere else. All of this necessitated consultation and consideration of every move on the international chess board, even when under pressure of fast-moving events, such as the situations in Algeria, Suez, Cyprus, Quemoy and Matsu, Indochina, Berlin, Cuba and the Iceland fisheries.

Algeria was one of the most persistent of our alliance problems and it often strained French-American relations. The difficulty was that France insisted Algeria was an internal problem and that France therefore was entitled to handle that situation without consulting its NATO allies. Accordingly the French would move troops and American-supplied military equipment to Algeria from Europe, thus weakening the line position on the continent. On many occasions the United States also was faced with awkward questions of voting on resolutions in the United Nations. If we voted in a manner offensive to the then French Government, there were emotional recriminations and aspersions cast on our loyalty as an ally.

Many of our allies do not comprehend what a radical departure from tradition it is for the United States to enter into military pacts with other nations. But every adult American has been taught that George Washington in his Farewell Address warned his countrymen against permanent alliances. In keeping with that prudent advice from our first President, the United States Senate rejected the covenant of the League of Nations. And the charter of the United Nations was approved only because it was intended to create an alliance which would banish war. Nothing less than the Soviet threat of world domination, accompanied by a series of provocative actions, could have persuaded the Senate to accept the NATO agreement, especially Article Five which provides that an attack against one is considered an attack against all.

Of course the United States could have remained aloof from our present intricate system of alliances if our government had chosen instead to rely on its own power, developing its conventional ground forces and also its nuclear weapons, and indicating a readiness to use both. We had the atom bomb when no country had defense against it. We had demonstrated in Hiroshima and Nagasaki the destructiveness of this bomb, and we could have aroused apprehension around the globe if we had based our position on our nuclear strength. But we had exploded atom bombs only during a war. It was repugnant to American principles to use them in peacetime even as a threat, to say nothing of seriously considering using them as a weapon. The U.S.S.R., on the contrary, did not hesitate in time of relative peace to fling about threats of rockets and bombs. Rightly or wrongly, our government has not done so, and the result has been that the aggressive Sino-Soviet moves in Berlin and Korea literally drove the United States into its policy of collective security. No network of military alliances is perfect, and ours certainly is not. But I believe it is more valuable than most Americans appreciate, and that credit is due to Dean Acheson for the Pact of Rio de Janeiro and the North Atlantic Alliance, and to Foster Dulles whose grim determination developed our security system in depth and effectiveness.

Another possible means of protecting the free world from Communist aggression might be for the United States to enter into an arms agreement with the Soviet Union. Such an agreement is commonly referred to as "disarmament," but that is a misnomer. The perennial hope—except among the starry-eyed—is not for disarmament but only for some reduction in armaments, a very different thing. Many conferences have been held since World War II with this objective in view. I was spared the ordeal of attending such conferences in Geneva, London and elsewhere abroad, but in the course of my duties I had to be present at dozens of meetings in Washington. Armaments often are regarded by the innocent as the cause of conflict between power groups, instead of the result, and there are those who believe that if the right disarmament formula could be invented, the world no longer would be in danger of nuclear holocaust.

One discussion held by Secretary Dulles was attended by the Chairman of the Atomic Energy Commission, the Secretary of Defense, the Joint Chiefs of Staff, and several officers of the Department of State. One of our officers, an ardent proponent of achieving agreement with the Soviet Union, pushed the tone of urgency a bit far until Dulles, who was fond of him, said: "Tell me, if you could specify precisely the disarmament agreement which you think that we should have with the Soviet Union, and if the Russians would accept your terms, do you believe the security of the United States could rely on that agreement?" The officer emphatically replied, "Yes, I do!" Dulles declared that was exactly the point on which they differed. In the light of all his postwar experience, the Secretary said, no Soviet pledge could be depended upon. This has been my experience also and it is one of the reasons why I do not support the notion that the United States must keep on discussing disarmament. Constant urging by us to induce the Russians to talk disarmament may please the neutral nations, but the Soviet Government regards such overeagerness as sign of weakness. The Russians interpret this as indication that we are fearful and will make greater concessions.

Disarmament is a hardy perennial in the United Nations, and the number of papers prepared and the number of meetings held on this subject have been legion. American representatives found that the Russians were willing to spin out talks for days and weeks and months. Then, when backed against a wall—usually on a concrete question involving inspection, verification and controls—the Soviet representatives would move adjournment and come up later with some procedural wrinkle, some new grouping or form of commission. Once the Russians proposed that a new disarmament commission should be created in the UN with the same number of members as the General Assembly, which at that time was eighty-one—an impossible monstrosity. All of these moves meant a lot of work for the staff of the State Department, and for me. It was obvious that the Russians were stalling for time through the years while they were building up their supply of nuclear weapons, rockets, submarines, military power of all sorts. I do not mean that the Soviet Union would not like reduction of armaments, in order to be relieved of the enormous costs, but it would have to be on its terms which simply are not reconcilable with ours. The Russians, I think, are cynical on this subject as, I fear, am I. The idea of having a permanent agency of qualified people in Washington to stay on top of this question is excellent, but our tactics should vary.

At present the United States is being exposed to Sino-Soviet threats which sound as insane as the mouthings of Hitler. Many Americans could not believe that Hitler really meant what he said, and did not become convinced until after we were attacked. The issues became clear then, but our military power was inadequate for many months to cope with the situation. During the fine idealism of the war years, Americans were led by Roosevelt's Grand Design and by other visions to make many concessions to the Russians. Those concessions were intended to create a climate in which sincere world cooperation would become possible. That this idealism should have affected many Americans in the first flush of victory is to our credit, but when such concessions were continued despite unwelcome realities, there was grave risk in blithely assuming that the United States was invulnerable.

A more sober view is taken nowadays. Americans appreciate the dangers of Communist expansion at weak points, of local wars of "liberation" in Southeast Asia, of plots to convert Cuba and Latin America into focal points of subversion, of arsenals of modern equipment designed to destroy the United States. Occasionally these threats are modified by not too adroit overtures of peaceful coexistence, that moldy Lenin doctrine which has misled many through the years. Even today there are those in places of influence who have convinced themselves that a cooperative understanding with Moscow and even with Peking can be arranged. There always seems to be a supply of individuals persuaded that they personally possess some peculiar charm or ability to negotiate such a deal. Some of these would-be peacemakers are eager to make almost any concession in the hope of avoiding an atomic holocaust which, naturally, they fear.

But it is one thing to engage in academic discussions, ignoring the lessons of Berlin and Korea, and another thing to negotiate directly with unyielding Muscovites, grasping for every advantage no matter how minute, supported by a military establishment of the first magnitude. Americans have learned, not without cost, that agressive tactics may be suspended at times by negotiation, but that basic Communist policy is never abandoned. Until that system deteriorates or collapses, the United States can deal with it only at arm's length from positions of strength. And strength does not consist solely of industrial and agricultural wealth and of vast quantities of military equipment. Our opponents must understand that there also is capacity and determination to use our resources whenever American security is threatened.

In Washington there were varying degrees of hope, which I shared through the years, that a schism would develop in Sino-Soviet relations. A power conflict between those two ruthless groups, ambitious for world hegemony, seemed inevitable. Some of the differences between China and the Soviet Union were ideological; others were pragmatic and historic. There was Russian discomfort over the drain on its economic resources from the insatiable requirements and lofty demands of the Chinese. We in the Department of State often tried to imagine the anxieties of the Soviet General Staff, or of the Red Chinese, concerning the security of those thousands of miles of Sino-Soviet frontier. Ethnic conflicts and Chinese contempt for Russian "barbarians" were also elements of conflict. We did not doubt that a schism would develop eventually, but in our frustration to accelerate it, we did not know whether the elapsed time would be measured in years or decades. There were many factors favoring a break, but the West, apart from the maintenance of its own power and its peripheral pinpricks, seemed to lack the ingenuity to promote a definite split.

In all our relations with the Soviet Union, the German question has played a continuous role. Khrushchev's tiresome threats that Moscow will conclude a separate peace treaty with the East German regime are still orchestrated, and no doubt such a treaty may be concluded if considered advantageous to the U.S.S.R. But Khrushchev knows that he cannot convey power to East Germany which the Soviet Union itself does not possess. Transferring Russian rights to the East Germans, whom the Russians do not trust, would not alter the Western legal or military status in Berlin so long as Americans are determined to fight to retain our position. This stalemate, which has produced a split country in the heart of Europe, involved me during my last years in the Department of State in constant negotiations, policy formulation and questions of German rearmament.

The Department also was concerned with various theoretical solutions for the German problem. One proposal which attracted a good deal of favorable attention in Europe was promoted by Prime Minister Eden of Great Britain and Paul van Zeeland of Belgium. According to this scheme, a reunited Germany—or at least an important strip of

Germany—would be constituted into some kind of neutral zone from which nuclear weapons and other offensive armament would be excluded by agreement among the great powers. This proposal was one of the subjects facing the Berlin Conference of 1954, where the United States was represented by Secretary Dulles. Just before that important meeting, George Kennan, who happened to be in London on personal business, was invited by the British Broadcasting Corporation to talk on the European situation. He advocated this neutral zone plan and many people mistakenly assumed he was speaking for the American Government. This caused quite a furor at the time and had to be disavowed by the State Department. The neutral zone idea arose from a certain reluctance, especially in England, to accept a revived Germany as a member of the Western military alliance.

Throughout this period I consistently helped to promote a policy favoring French-German rapprochement, which I always have regarded as essential to peace in Europe. The French themselves, in the immediate postwar years, did not favor this view—and they also were unenthusiastic then about Chancellor Adenauer, German economic restoration, and NATO partnership—but President de Gaulle eventually embraced this policy and he perhaps has pushed it farther than our British friends approve.

The Soviet Union, in its effort to establish domination in the German area, has deliberately agitated the situation there. Such agitation has taken the form, from time to time, of acute and alarming pressures on Berlin, and in those recurring crises the State Department naturally has worked in close consultation with the White House and the Defense Department. In addition to making our own political and military decisions, it also became necessary for our government to coordinate its plans with the plans of friendly nations. During such periods of strain concerning Berlin, I chaired numerous meetings with the British and the French in attempts to achieve agreement with them upon a program of action. Although this might seem like routine procedure, it always was an exhausting undertaking. Our allies were headed by their respective Ambassadors, assisted by special advisers from London and Paris, and after weeks of negotiations, we would arrive at an agreement "on the technical level." This meant that we had decided a host of details as to what would be done if the Soviet Union moved militarily—what forces would be employed, what equipment would be required, what emergency measures would be taken along the autobahn and at check points, and various other matters. But on the key question, what precisely would be done in case of a Soviet crunch on Berlin, the British would only say that this would be a problem for decision by the Cabinet in the light of circumstances prevailing at the time. In other words, they would not commit themselves in advance, thus leaving open the most vital question of all—would the British fight?

A few months before I retired from the Foreign Service, it occurred to some of my State Department colleagues and me that a substantial impact might be made on the thinking of the Soviet masses if President Eisenhower could tour the length and breadth of the Soviet Union, appearing at all kinds of public gatherings, giving interviews to the Communist press, making radio and television speeches. Such a tour by Eisenhower, we thought, would vary the monotonous Soviet diet of official distortion and misrepresentation regarding the United States. In addition to the President's personal charm, the name of Eisenhower had special significance for the Russian people, who associated it with American support of the Red Army and victory in World War II. Other than Roosevelt, no American name meant so much to so many Russians, and during Eisenhower's visit to Moscow in 1945, the people generously displayed their friendly sentiments.

So we conceived the plan that Nikita Khrushchev should be invited to visit the United States, with the understanding that the Russians would reciprocate by inviting Eisenhower to tour the Soviet Union. Khrushchev was to be authorized to travel all over our country and to express his views freely, and the same hospitality was to be offered to Eisenhower, to the extent of the more limited press, radio and television facilities available in Russia. I think I had as much to do with initiating Khrushchev's trip to the United States as anybody, and I prepared the recommendation to the White House urging it. It was a grievous disappointment to me when the scheme turned out badly, but it seemed a good idea at the time. I must say for Eisenhower that he agreed very reluctantly, but he did issue the invitation in writing, and Foy D. Kohler, later our Ambassador to the U.S.S.R., and I took the letter on a hot Sunday evening in New York to Frol Kozlov, a close associate of Khrushchev, who was returning to Moscow the next day. Kozlov delivered the invitation to Khrushchev and it was accepted promptly.

There followed weeks of sticky negotiations, which I conducted with the Soviet Ambassador in Washington. When Mikhail A. Menshikov arrived in the United States in 1957, newspapermen dubbed him "Smiling Mike" because he customarily looked cheerful in public. But in discussions I had with him at the State Department, the Soviet Ambassador usually neglected to put on his façade and I am sure he removed it when alone with his own staff. I remember the sweaty palm of his counselor when we shook hands. The counselor must have lived in terror of Smiling Mike, whom I found a cold-blooded ruthless somebody. My talks with Menshikov concerning Khrushchev's visit included decisions on itinerary, security, transportation, people to see, dinners, lunches, speeches and a thousand and one other details, about each of which Menshikov was arrogant and difficult.

For example, Eisenhower rather liked to use helicopters, and he suggested a sight-seeing flight over the Washington area, ending with a private visit to Camp David, the President's secluded mountain retreat. Menshikov said "No," that Mr. Khrushchev did not like helicopters and would not do it. I urged a second time, and again was rebuffed by Smiling Mike. Then I cabled the American Ambassador in Moscow, asking him to put the question, but got nowhere. Finally, after Khrushchev's arrival at the White House, Eisenhower had a helicopter waiting on the lawn and invited the Premier to ride with him. Khrushchev accepted with alacrity and, I was told, ordered the purchase of two helicopters of the same model. Menshikov later explained to me that he thought we were suggesting a flight for Khrushchev alone. Perhaps the Ambassador suspected we were plotting to assassinate the distinguished visitor.

Then there were questions about where to go, keeping in mind that all arrangements were to be reciprocal. There are many restricted areas in the Soviet Union where Americans are not admitted, and years ago our government staked out somewhat equivalent areas in the United States, such as Detroit and San Francisco, which Russians could visit only by special permission. We really did not care, but it was hoped that this inconvenience to visitors from the Soviet Union might cause the Russians to relax their restrictions on our citizens. They never did. Thus no American is allowed to go to Vladivostok, the seaport at the extreme eastern end of Siberia, near Japan. It was Eisenhower's intention at that time to visit Japan at the conclusion of his Russian tour. Khrushchev wanted to see San Francisco, which Mikoyan apparently had recommended to him. All Russian officials love San Francisco. So do I. We said "Certainly"—we would be delighted for Khrushchev to visit San Francisco, provided Eisenhower could go to Vladivostok. "But why does the President want to see Vladivostok?" demanded Menshikov. "There is nothing there but snow and ice!" We held our ground on that point for two weeks, until the White House indicated to hell with it and agreed to include San Francisco in the Premier's itinerary. A number of times during my exasperating talks with Unsmiling Mike, I wanted to call the whole thing off, but I clung to the hope that Eisenhower's tour might achieve some good inside the Soviet Union.

History will tell whether Khrushchev's visit to the United States was harmful, but I would not have recommended that the American President should play host to the Communist dictator if I had dreamt that Eisenhower, a few months later, would give Khruschev an excuse for canceling the reciprocal invitation to visit the Soviet Union. The unfortunate incident which ruined all our careful planning was that an American reconnaissance plane was shot down in the Soviet Union; its pilot, Francis Gary Powers, was arrested by the Russians as a spy; and President Eisenhower assumed personal responsibility for that U-2 flight.

I had handled State Department clearances for U-2 overflights for some time, and those flights were of really great value to us. They were conceived because of the tight Russian security and police system. The Soviet Union obtains a tremendous volume of information in the United States for the asking and through the courtesy of our press and other media, all eager to tell about things. In addition the Communists resort to other means, legal and illegal, to dig out defense and strategic data. But Russian security is so strict that Intelligence in that country is hard to come by. I have not the slightest doubt that our national safety justified our U-2 surveillance. As Secretary of State Christian Herter expressed it: "The Government of the United States would be derelict to its responsibility if it did not, in the absence of Soviet cooperation, take such measures as are possible unilaterally to lessen and to overcome the danger of surprise attack." The fact that Russian radar, anti-aircraft, and fighter planes could not for years down the U-2, even when flying at much lower altitudes than today, was in itself extremely valuable military information obtainable by us in no other way. While the Russians screamed about this, they recognized the justice of it. What infuriated them was their inability to touch the U-2 over such a long period of time.

The plane piloted by Powers was shot down on May Day, 1960, and for the next two weeks there was an almost daily exchange of diplomatic notes between Moscow and Washington. Meanwhile, Eisenhower, Khrushchev, De Gaulle and Macmillan were assembling in Paris for their long-heralded Summit Conference. But Khrushchev, on arrival there, declared he would not participate in the conference unless the United States would cease its flights over the Soviet Union, apologize for past "aggressions," and punish those responsible. When informed of Khrushchev's attitude, President Eisenhower accepted responsibility and said that the U-2 flights had been halted and would not be resumed. Eisenhower has made a vast number of difficult decisions during his years of service to the United States, and his percentage of errors is small indeed. The chief incidents which I recall were his imposition of press censorship in French North Africa, his order to General Patton not to enter Prague, his decision not to capture Berlin, and his authorization to sign the wrong armistice terms at Rheims. Eisenhower's impulsive *mea culpa,* his declaration in Paris that the U-2 flight was his fault, is the least comprehensible.

The immediate and most conspicuous result of the President's statement was that Khrushchev refused to attend the Summit Conference, and on May 17, 1960 that international meeting was called off. But, except for a certain humiliation, the cancellation represented only the loss of an exercise in futility. There was no profit in that exercise anyway. What was important was that Khrushchev also utilized the U-2 flight as an excuse to revoke the invitation to Eisenhower to visit the Soviet Union. The President's tour could have made a tremendously favorable impression on the Russian people. Communist leaders feared it. Khrushchev must have been incredulous when informed of Eisenhower's acceptance of blame for the U-2 flight. Up to that moment Khrushchev had merely made a bald assertion and the Soviet press had published a false news photo of the wreckage of some other airplane. The Russians might have hit upon a different subterfuge to avoid their promised hospitality, but the U-2 statement by Eisenhower provided an easy way out, and they grabbed it.

When the Summit Conference was canceled, ostensibly as a result of the U-2 incident, American newspapers and speech-makers demanded why had our government ordered a surveillance flight at such an inappropriate time, when the Russian, British, French and American heads of state were about to negotiate? I was no longer in government service then, having retired four months previously, but I inquired of my former colleagues in Washington and was told that weather was one important consideration. There were urgent reasons why the flight should be made, and it was calculated that weather conditions were likely to be unfavorable for some weeks because fog and heavy clouds make high altitude flights unsuitable for photography. Careful consideration was given to the scheduled Summit Conference, but nothing was expected from that event anyway—that is, there would have been no benefit from the talks even if they had taken place.

President Eisenhower went to Paris largely because of British pressure, and Prime Minister Macmillan wanted the meeting mostly for domestic political reasons. Macmillan did everything he could to save the Summit Conference. He had two private conversations with Khrushchev and urged the Soviet Premier not to wreck the four-power meeting. And if Eisenhower had not been so hasty in providing Khrushchev with a pretext for taking offense, it would have been practicable for the United States Government to use the formula which Macmillan informally suggested to me: "We do not discuss in public our Intelligence activities." Certainly the Russians never do, nor the British. A few years ago some British frogmen made passes at a Russian naval unit anchored in a British port, and one or two divers died in the process. There was great public outcry in Britain, but the government remained silent.

While American reconnaisance planes were making a determined effort to ascertain the growth of offensive military strength in the vast stretches of Russia, another more immediate danger was developing only ninety miles from the United States. In Cuba there was a gradual buildup of striking power which reached its climax in 1962. This danger did not happen overnight. It began in 1958 when Anastas Mikoyan, then Deputy Premier of Foreign and Domestic Commerce of the U.S.S.R., paid his first visit to Havana. On that occasion he stopped in Washington en route, and Secretary Dulles honored him with a dinner party at the F Street Club. The fourteen guests included Mikoyan's twenty-six-year-old son, some members of the Soviet Embassy staff and a few State Department people. Mikoyan's son, a bright, reserved young man, very respectful of his powerful father, told me that it was unbelievable that Dulles should be giving this party. His astonishment seemed to imply that he thought his father was our foe. The dinner was informal, with wide-ranging conversation including some discussion of Communism, which elicited the comment that Dulles knew more about Communism than Mikoyan had realized. In response to our questions, Mikoyan explained that he was going to Havana on a good will visit in the hope of setting up a trade mission.

In the State Department the next morning we speculated on Mikoyan's real motive and concluded that the trade mission would be a cover for clandestine and subversive operations throughout the hemisphere. It did not occur to any of us in 1958 that the Soviet Union would use Cuba as a major base for the installation of some of its most modern military equipment and powerful striking weapons. Our Kremlinologists believed that such overt provocation, which might entail direct confrontation with American forces, would not be in the pattern of Soviet policy. Yet that is what took place. Incredible as it may seem, considering that the United States spends billions of dollars annually to obtain Intelligence reports throughout the world, our government was ignorant in 1962 of what was transpiring in Cuba. That island had been an area where traditionally we had no difficulty obtaining military and other information, but with the establishment of the police state and the severance of diplomatic relations, the tradition had been destroyed.

Our government was alerted suddenly in October 1962, and reconnaissance airplanes were sent over sites in Cuba where lethal missiles were in the process of being installed and erected. Some of our military planes flew at the low level of two hundred feet and their photographs showed minute details. The Russian weapons in Cuba were capable of delivering warheads in megatons, and could destroy New York, Philadelphia, Pittsburgh, Cleveland, Fort Worth, Mexico City, the Panama Canal, Caracas and strategic installations in a range of two thousand miles. The missiles in Cuba would double the striking power of the U.S.S.R. against the United States. Our reconnaissance photographs illustrated more than ballistic details. They revealed the new technical competence of the Russians to mount in secrecy this huge and complex operation on the very threshold of the United States, and they revealed also the arrogance of the Russians in assuming they could do this with impunity.

It is too soon now to judge the Cuban episode, which still is developing. Some Americans are appalled by our complacent tolerance of Soviet military power in Cuba. Some of us worry about what has been called our "docile submission to a dangerous violation of the Monroe Doctrine." Some of us believe that we should not have intimated that United States forces might not invade the island. Some of us doubt the wisdom of having accepted, in effect, Anastas Mikoyan as mediator—the wily Mikoyan who inspired the Russian venture in the Caribbean in the first place. Most Americans are dismayed at the willingness of the United States Government to barter with and pay ransom to a hostile, sawdust dictator.

But perhaps history will be indulgent and will record that American policy during the Cuban episode was sagacious, since it avoided or postponed war between the Soviet Union and the United States. "Millions for defence, but not one cent for tribute!" has always been a popular cry in our country, but our government has not always acted upon that grandiose principle. This patriotic slogan, which is inscribed on the cenotaph erected in Charleston, South Carolina, in memory of Charls Cotesworth Pinckney, was Pinckney's impulsive reply, when he was Minister to Paris in 1797, to the proposition that the infant American nation should make a gift to France, thinly disguised as a loan. Pinckney's indignant refusal is recorded in history, but history also records that his mission to France accomplished nothing.

During the early years of our Republic, Congress appropriated millions of dollars for payments to the Barbary pirates, to protect American seamen from capture and confinement in the fetid North African jails which Arab leaders of those days regarded as suitable for dogs and infidels. Thomas Jefferson, however, was opposed to paying this tribute. It was his conviction that fighting the pirates would be less expensive and more honorable than bribing them, and would guarantee a better future. It is my view that, in the long run, Jefferson's policy is preferable to the recent easy procedure of our government in buying off Cubans and Russians. But I am not in possession of all the facts, of all the exchanges which have occurred, and I was not particeps to President Kennedy's innermost thoughts. He had my profound sympathy because the core of the Cuban problem, and the danger, still confront us.

TWENTY-NINE

THE DEPARTMENT OF STATE

It seemed incredible, as no doubt it seems to many, when my crowded years of government service brought with them the time to retire. I had never dreamt that I would remain in the Department of State until my sixty-fifth birthday, the automatic retirement age for career ambassadors. At about that time, the American Ambassador to the German Federal Republic, David K. E. Bruce, was resigning from his post and I was offered the appointment to succeed him. This was an honor which I appreciated, but I declined because I believe the automatic retirement provision is wise. Among other things, it offers incentive to the younger men. When I first went to work in Washington the Federal civil service had no pension plan, and every morning I would see employees hobbling on crutches to their offices or even being pushed along in wheelchairs. It was said in those days: "Few die and none resign!"

The President may extend an officer's time, and in my case a short extension was arranged because Eisenhower was planning a good will tour of eleven countries. He invited me to accompany him once more as his political adviser. The President's itinerary included the capitals of Italy, Turkey, Afghanistan, Pakistan, India, Iran, Greece, Tunisia, France, Spain and Morocco. While it may be difficult to measure in practical terms the value of brief visits in rapid succession with heads of government on three continents, this presidential tour promoted our national interest. The area embraced many vital concerns of the United States, and the President took full advantage of the opportunity for serious conversations, achieving solution of some problems and better understanding of many.

The success of this good will expedition was enhanced not only by Eisenhower's own delightful personality, but also by his amazing physical stamina. It required endurance to stand with Prime Minister Nehru of India in an open automobile for more than two hours while our caravan pushed slowly through a throng of two and a half million people. It was the marigold season and almost every spectator seemed eager to throw a flower into the Eisenhower automobile. The marigold is a rather heavy flower, but the President stood in marigolds up to his waist and the blossoms bounced off his bare head as our automobile crept in the murky evening through the crowds which pushed into our narrow road. Because of obvious risks, the strain on the President's bodyguards was acute. When we arrived at Rashtrapati Bhavam in New Delhi, James J. Rowley, now chief of the U. S. Secret Service, was dripping with perspiration. He recalled that he had been with us in a battle area in North Africa and claimed that was a comfortable, tranquil experience compared with the marigold barrage. Before the end of Eisenhower's tour, some members of his entourage succumbed to exhaustion and had to be flown home, but the President, recently recovered from two serious illnesses, never allowed his good nature and keen interest to flag.

Countries which flank the Soviet Union and Red China must regard security problems in the light of geography. Five countries which we visited were in that situation—Afghanistan, India, Iran, Pakistan, Turkey. Viewed from Kabul or Tehran, right under Communist guns, things look different than in New York or Lima. I was impressed by the contrasts in attitude, strength, weakness and policies which we encountered, and could only admire the sturdy courage of many top officials in those countries. Beset by acute economic and social problems, they faced their external threat philosophically.

In India I obtained a sharp picture of the magnitude of the daily problems of four hundred million people struggling with poverty, illiteracy and disease. I respected the determination of Nehru, his brilliant daughter, Mrs. Gandhi, and Nehru's associates in government, to raise India's living standard if only a millimeter at a time, but to raise it. I could sympathize with the government's unwillingness to take on the burden of military budgets when the minimum needs of the huge and growing population were so pressing. Yet I also found what I thought was a rather disdainful attitude toward the American power position and toward free world alliances, and I sought to understand the policy of nonalignment which Nehru had pursued so tenaciously through the years. I recalled attitudes, hardly friendly to my country and often supporting the Communists, which Krishna Menon had assumed, and I wondered how much India's former Ambassador to the United Nations may have influenced or even inspired India's nonalignment policy. Nehru knows England well after long residence there, but his knowledge of the United States is slight. I doubt that he comprehended American disarmament after World War II, or credited the sincere efforts of our government to promote world disarmament. He never fully grasped the implications of the Berlin blockade or the war in Korea. In his leadership of the neutralist block of unaligned countries, and in the pride of Panch Shila of Djakarta memory, Nehru probably never realized that he was merely trading on the western power position which he disdained.

When in 1962 Red China brushed aside the flimsy Indian frontier posts, and an alarmed Indian population saw in its nakedness that the Himalayas are not an adequate substitute for organized defense against aggression, it was sheer drama for Nehru to appeal to the West for arms. How long will that salutary lesson prevail? Having listened to leaders of the block of so-called unaligned nations—Nehru, Tito, Nasser, Sukarno and various Afro-Asians—I am curious as to their motivation. Is it a desire for peace, sincere antimilitarism, ambition to play an independent role, eagerness to obtain maximum benefits from the West and also from the Communist orbit, or is it an effort to deceive one side or the other or both? Perhaps all of these elements are involved at times.

Important discussions with heads of state were not the only benefits which Eisenhower derived from his good will tour. Probably every President has been dubious at times about the effectiveness of his representatives abroad. The American people are inclined to be indifferent to their Foreign Service, sometimes even contemptuous of its members whom they damn with the phrase "cookie pushers in striped pants," and few public servants are more widely misunderstood and misinterpreted than American diplomats. This tour gave Eisenhower opportunity to see at first hand eleven of our diplomatic missions in action. They performed well and they demonstrated that the American representation in foreign countries includes a modern, well-equipped, professional diplomatic service which need take second place to none.

A few years ago an Assistant Secretary of State was invited by the Encyclopædia Britannica to describe the Department of State. He explained that the top-ranking department of our government "is primarily the Foreign Office of the nation and, under the supervision of the President, it exclusively directs the foreign relations of the United States." This is a correct description of the theoretical structure —if it be added that such direction is performed through power delegated by the President—and the State Department might even be able to function like that if given a chance. But the career diplomat who wrote for the Encyclopædia must have been indulging in wishful thinking, because in my experience I never found that the Department possessed exclusive direction. On the contrary, the American antitrust philosophy has been carried into the field of foreign relations, where competition is rampant enough to satisfy every disciple of the Sherman Act.

Under our Constitution, the Secretary of State can exercise only such authority as the President may see fit to grant him. These two officials should enjoy warm sympathetic relationship, but from time to time they unfortunately do not. President Franklin Roosevelt had little respect for Cordell Hull's knowledge and judgment of foreign affairs, but he felt he could not replace Hull for domestic political reasons. So the President delegated only a limited number of matters to his Secretary of State. Three months after the Tehran Conference, I had occasion to return from the Mediterranean to report briefly to Secretary Hull, and I took the opportunity to mention that Foreign Service officers like myself would be strengthened in our operations if we could be informed of the secret conversations which Roosevelt had had with Stalin. "Oh, you think so, do you?" exclaimed Hull with a touch of humorous sarcasm. "Well, please know that the operations of the Secretary of State would also be strengthened if he knew what happened at Tehran!" On another occasion when I made a quick trip from North Africa to Washington, there was a crisis in our relations with the French concerning a delicate question of sending American naval units to Beirut. I arrived on a Monday morning and Admiral Leahy, then the President's personal chief of staff, told me cheerily that Roosevelt and he had decided on Sunday to send the naval vessels despite French opposition. I inquired whether the State Department had concurred. The Admiral briskly informed me that the Department had not been consulted. "We decided what to do in twenty-five minutes," he said. "If we referred this to the Secretary of State, it would take twenty-five days."

In addition to personal intervention by Roosevelt and other Presidents in the exercise of their constitutional right to direct foreign policy, there also is in the American tradition what amounts to competition from members of the President's entourage, sometimes referred to as the Palace Guard. Colonel Edward M. House established precedents after World War I when Woodrow Wilson, while he was ill, suspected that Robert Lansing was exceeding his authority, and there was serious disaffection between the President and his Secretary of State. Harry Hopkins expanded those precedents when he enjoyed close daily association with and the confidence of Roosevelt. Every President has his own work habits. Under Eisenhower the White House liaison officer for the Department of State was General Andrew J. Goodpaster, who had no personal ambition to influence foreign policy and was invaluable in putting the views of the Department before the President. At times he could do this more effectively than the Secretary of State because he was in constant touch with Eisenhower, knew when the President was overburdened or when he was relaxed and receptive. Goodpaster believed that the Department of State was best equipped to advise on foreign relations, but he presented every side of a question from all sources. Few men in my experience equaled Goodpaster in this respect. At times the Department has no dependable link of this sort with the White House.

In the field of competitive diplomacy, members of Congress also assume an important role. This is a blessing but not an unmixed one. The knowledge and wisdom possessed by many congressmen and congresswomen is impressive, and their activity in foreign affairs is important. Their criticism usually is constructive, and even in rare instances when members are hostile, the Foreign Service may gain by additional insight into problems. But when an individual congressman voluntarily takes on operational duties within the scope of the Department there may be difficulties. Quite apart from constitutional restrictions, the average congressman with his own heavy legislative responsibilities scarcely has time to conduct private diplomatic negotiations or engage in administrative activities or pursue intelligence investigations. Yet occasionally an individual tries to perform such tasks because interest in foreign relations has grown enormously since World War II. I recall being confronted by one member of Congress who demanded: "Why is it that a country boy like myself knew all about the Hungarian revolution before it happened, while you fellows in State and CIA were asleep?" Further conversation disclosed that he had had a talk with a Hungarian from his district who told him "all about it." The only thing Foreign Service officers can do with such individuals is to roll with the punch. It is better for congressmen to take possessive interest in foreign affairs than to take none at all.

The Secretary of State must be sensitive to congressional competition. A Vandenberg or a Connally, a Mansfield or a Fulbright, can make all the difference in the projection of policy in our relations with a foreign country. Such powerful political figures—the strong committee chairmen, the whips and the floor leaders—can and do call the turn on many matters. Senators Styles Bridges of New Hampshire and William Knowland of California exercised strong influence on the Department of State during the first term of Eisenhower. Bridges put in his assistant, Scott McLeod, as administrator of the Bureau of Security, Consular Affairs and Personnel, and Knowland had his assistant George F. Wilson, as assistant administrator of that bureau. Between them, McLeod and Wilson, each of whom seemed to entertain ready-made prejudices about the Foreign Service, had final say on many security and personnel matters and other things besides. Secretary Dulles' policy perforce was to get along with Congress at almost any cost.

At times a Secretary of State encounters more foreign policy disagreements from leaders of his own party than from his political opponents. An example was a congressional briefing session which Dulles held after his return from Berlin in 1954. The Secretary extended his customary invitation to thirty members of the Senate and the House, equally divided between Republican and Democrats, to inform them what had taken place at the Berlin Conference. The night before Dulles' return to the United States, Senator Knowland had made a speech in Philadelphia criticizing Dulles' conduct of affairs at Berlin, and at the briefing session the Senator quizzed the Secretary in the manner of a district attorney. At the close of the meeting, most of the Democrats congratulated Dulles while his fellow Republican stalked out.

Domestic politics demand much time and deft handling from a harassed Secretary of State who often is bereft of political strength in his own right, as is the case of Dean Rusk, the present Secretary. Unable to speak on the floor of Congress, like Foreign Ministers in countries where the parliamentary system prevails, the American Secretary can only present his views to individual congressmen or to congressional committees. Appearing before the Foreign Relations Committee of the Senate or the Foreign Affairs Committee of the House of Representatives is usually a rewarding experience. Individuals on those committees, and of course the Appropriations Subcommittees, are perhaps closer to the State Department than those of other committees, and they show lively concern in the work of the Department. I always learned something when I had the privilege of testifying before them, and I had high regard for their knowledge of foreign affairs. Views of committee members usually rise above partisan politics and personal considerations, and they are fully respected. Those committees provide our diplomats with information regarding the attitude of Congress not otherwise readily obtainable. Their hearings are something like the question period during debates on foreign policy in the British House of Commons.

In attempting to formulate foreign policy the Department of State encounters competition not only from the White House staff and congressmen, but from dozens of departments and agencies whose work nowadays requires association in one form or another with countries abroad. Their offices promote not only their own special objectives but some have positive notions about foreign policy generally. More than half a million American military personnel and their families are scattered over the globe, and it is inevitable that the Department of Defense and State occasionally disagree on correlation of foreign policy. This might happen on acute problems relating to such issues as Berlin and Korea, Quemoy and Matsu or Cuba. Ever since World War II thousands of American military men have been learning about foreign affairs, and some of them are persuaded they could do a better job in diplomacy than the career diplomat. And, no doubt, some of them could.

Besides competition which our Foreign Service officers meet from other government officials, they are challenged from time to time by individual citizens who believe they possess peculiar talents or means entitling them to take initiative in the diplomatic field. There is the Cyrus Eaton type, hostile to the Department of State because of disagreement on policy vis-à-vis the Soviet Union; or a Linus Pauling, impatient with nuclear policy. There is the well-intentioned executive who heads a private foundation or civic group which is promoting foreign policy ideas of its own. The appointment of American ambassadors from private life provides another element of competition to career diplomats. The State Department naturally views with a jaundiced eye the appointment of an unqualified political party hack, but it usually welcomes outside appointments of able men. Competition from capable non-professional ambassadors is often a source of strength, for such men bring wide knowledge and valuable fresh ideas developed in other fields.

The State Department cannot be expected to rejoice when foreign ambassadors stationed in Washington attempt to administer American foreign affairs. During my last years in the Department I attended functions in many embassies in our capital, and found it interesting to study the personalities in the diplomatic corps. At that time there were more than eighty diplomatic missions accredited to the President, and some of the foreign envoys had lived in Washington a long time. A few deliberately ignored the Department of State and tried to negotiate directly with members of Congress, and occasionally were welcomed. It seemed to give some legislators a heady sense of importance, and ambassadors on occasion achieved advantages they might not have obtained through regular channels. One ambassador told me he never bothered going to the Department of State. "I do all my business on the Hill," he said. He had been in Washington a number of years but was transferred shortly afterwards. In many countries the dean of the diplomatic corps is able to exercise a certain restraining influence, but protocol is liberal in Washington where the corps is loosely organized and authority of the dean exceedingly limited.

Perhaps it would be prudent to refrain from mentioning the State Department's most active rivalry of all—competition from American journalists. Some have a vast fund of knowledge gained from long experience in the foreign field; all are untrammeled by responsibility for application of policies. Foreign Service officers are inhibited from talking freely, partly by their disciplined training, partly for security reasons, but prompt dissemination of information is the duty of news reporters. Some Foreign Service officers are quite skillful in handling this delicate relationship with the press. If clumsily done, another source of hostility to the State Department may be created or stimulated, and for this reason an experienced newspaperman is often made an Assistant Secretary of State, such as Carl W. McCardle or Andrew H. Berding. George Marshall's wartime method was to take into his confidence a few selected correspondents, telling them a great deal about top-secret matters. He said they never violated his trust. But when the General became Secretary of State, he said he had to be more careful about foreign affairs than he had been about wartime strategy. "When a Washington correspondent makes an inquiry," Marshall explained, "I must first ask myself: Do I know the answer? Then I must think: Is there any reason why I should not answer? Third, I must consider: Why is he asking this question?"

That Marshall was not being unduly cautious was demonstrated to me a few years later. One morning our then Secretary of State informed his staff meeting that he was to have a quiet lunch that day with a well-known columnist in order to have a good talk with him. He realized that some of us would not approve, he said, but the columnist was capable and discreet. There was an awkward moment of silence, several shook heads, and we passed on to another subject. Less than forty-eight hours afterwards, the columnist broke a story which divulged what had been told him in strictest confidence. The Secretary bravely faced his staff meeting the next morning with such frank genial contrition that he retained our affectionate regard.

During the four years of World War II, Secretary of State Hull suspended recruiting for the Department of State and the Foreign Service in order to avoid charges that diplomats were draft dodgers. As a result of this policy, a manpower shortage developed and the Department was woefully unprepared to handle the staggering amount of work imposed on it at the end of the war. There was inadequate planning for the war's aftermath because nobody inside or outside the Department correctly anticipated the future. The failure of the State Department to make preparations for responsibilities in Germany, Japan and elsewhere caused unbelievable administrative confusion. The Armed Forces, which had absorbed the manpower, filled the vacuum—in some cases, with the utmost reluctance; in others, as for example General MacArthur, with the utmost determination.

Meanwhile, in Washington, the weakened Department of State suffered a postwar influx of manpower from unexpected sources, some of it dumped by President Truman and Secretary Byrnes from liquidated war agencies such as the Office of War Information, the Office of Strategic Services and others. The new employees arrived—certainly not at the request of the Foreign Service—without qualification examination or security screening, and they created an awkward situation. There had been practically no security precautions in the State Department prior to the war. Suddenly we had too much. Every report seemed to contain secrets; the most innocuous information was "classified"; a swollen staff of security agents hampered the work of everybody. At the same time greatly increased responsibilities were heaped upon the State Department. Foreign Service officers, no longer limited to orthodox consular and diplomatic activities, were allocated to propaganda, intelligence and military government, and became involved in many of the conflicts arising from Soviet expansion.

To cope with this changed situation, a commission headed by former President Herbert Hoover recommended in 1948 that the personnel of the State Department be integrated with the Foreign Service, and this was again urged in 1949 by the Rowe-Ramspeck-DeCourcy Advisory Committee on Personnel. But when I returned to Washington from Tokyo in 1953, no positive action had yet been taken to effect such consolidation. There still were sharp differences between the Foreign Service and the Department, poor coordination, and jurisdictional conflicts. Discussing this matter with Walter Kenneth Scott, Director of the Executive Secretariat of the Department, whom I had known as a lieutenant colonel in Algiers, we agreed that the Department had been dilatory. We believed that a consolidation should be organized which would provide greater opportunities to members of both the Department and the Foreign Service, and we made some recommendations to Secretary Dulles.

Dulles suggested that Henry M. Wriston, then President of Brown University, should head a committee to make specific proposals, and the "Secretary's Public Committee on Personnel" was selected. It consisted of eight members of whom I was one. The committee's proposals were approved for integration of the Foreign Service and Department personnel, for an improved plan of recruitment, and a vigorous in-training system. There were in 1954 some fifty-four hundred Department positions, and it was expected that fourteen hundred of these would be declared dual-service positions to be filled by Foreign Service officers. The proposals contemplated an enlarged corps of these officers, infusion of outside talent, and development of specialists in commerce, agriculture, public affairs and other fields. The program was rapidly executed, causing a certain amount of individual hardship in effecting transfers abroad from Washington. This organization now is an established element of foreign affairs, and I believe that the results on balance support the committee's hope that the new Service assures "a more faithful mirroring of American life."

Accompanying this new organization, there fortunately came recognition at long last that our Foreign Service officers, like our military officers, require technical training, and special educational opportunities are now available for American diplomats. I note this not without envy because I received a total of twenty minutes' "instruction" before proceeding in 1917 to my first post abroad. Reporting to Chief Clerk Miles Shand to take my oath of office, I was awed by the dignified white-haired gentleman in morning coat, seated at a huge rococo desk in the Victorian surroundings of the old State Department, and I was impressed by his gentle lecture on conduct. At the end of his twenty-minute talk the Chief Clerk picked up a glass paperweight and, holding it as a monocle, he concluded with mock formality: "And above all, young man, be circumspect with the ladies!" No doubt excellent advice for a young man—or, for that matter, any man —but scarcely in the nature of specialized training for the Foreign Service. Even after I passed State Department examinations which qualified me as an officer, my "instruction" was limited to thirty days before I was dispatched to foreign duty. Those thirty days and twenty minutes included all the educational assignments of my career. By contrast, General Bedell Smith, Eisenhower's Chief of Staff who later was appointed Under Secretary of State, enjoyed eleven years as student and instructor in a number of Army-financed courses. This imbalance between United States military and diplomatic education is now being corrected, and in particular great strides have been taken to establish State Department facilities for the study of foreign languages. A debt of gratitude is due to men like G. Howland Shaw who, sometimes using personal funds, promoted language study which produced the Bohlens and Kennans of the war period.

Not long ago President Kennedy asked Congress to implement the recommendation of a special committee, headed by former Secretary of State Christian Herter, that a "National Academy of Foreign Affairs" be set up near Washington to train selected men and women who should be cooperating in our nation's foreign relations. Perhaps the most valuable instruction which such an academy could provide would be to explain to the students American international objectives. I recall some of my colleagues in China who suffered great injustice during the McCarthy investigations because nobody had ever taken the trouble to indoctrinate them with American foreign policy in the light of Soviet expansion. Those Foreign Service officers were sent to China because they knew the language and the people, and they were given various assignments including details to Chinese Communist Army commands, where they often lived in squalor and hardship. They reported what they saw: some called it agrarian reform, some called it Communist penetration. A vast revolution was occurring in China. How could Americans in isolated places grasp all the implications? But if those "Old China Hands" had received the excellent courses at the National War College which were given to Dwight D. Eisenhower when he was a major, perhaps they would have avoided some errors committed because they had no policy direction.

The Department of State now has charge of about three hundred posts scattered all over the globe in addition to its thousands of employees stationed in Washington. Some of the problems of this far-flung organization were beyond the capacity of the Department's early postwar administration, and I have been interested in the substantial progress that has been achieved since then. Businessmen with whom I have discussed the Foreign Service are inclined to translate its problems into terms of their own tightly knit private corporations, with financial flexibility and power to hire and fire. By comparison it seems to me that representatives of the United States Government bear grave responsibilities and many handicaps.

Of course no government can or should compete with private enterprise in the larger financial rewards, and no one enters the Foreign Service under the impression that it will make him rich. Some diplomats have private means, most of them have not. They take up this career because there is pride and satisfaction in service to one's country which are not translatable in tangible terms, and because the work is significant and provides variety for those who can endure it. One man who told me that he envied Foreign Service officers was Ernest Hemingway who lived in Paris part of the time I was stationed there. Hemingway said he deplored the working habits of authors, with their absence of routine between intensive writing periods and their empty spells between productions, and he admired the methodical way the diplomatic service operated. But Hemingway chuckled when I asked if he would be willing to submit to the discipline of the diplomatic framework, especially as a subordinate to some ambassadors we knew.

One of the problems concerning our Foreign Service officers is how frequently they ought to be transferred from one post to another. It is the practice of the Department of State to move our career diplomats every three or four years, but this often occurs more frequently. In complicated situations, especially if an officer is unfamiliar with the language of the country to which he is assigned, our rotation system may move too swiftly. It may require several years for a diplomat to become sufficiently acquainted with the issues and personalities of his post to be able to represent American interests effectively. I have been told by friends in foreign capitals that they no longer bother trying to know American Embassy people because the latter are transferred so soon it is hardly worth the effort. Of course, such rotation avoids partisan attitudes and affiliations which may be politically embarrassing at times. During the first eight or ten years of an officer's career, it might be well for him to be assigned for relatively brief periods in each of the major world areas. With that background he then could specialize in one area, becoming truly an expert.

It is necessary for a Foreign Service officer to return often to the United States lest he ignore important trends in the country and in Washington. Prolonged absence can affect the judgment of a diplomat so that he may err in presenting his own country's posture to the government to which he is accredited. This sometimes also affects the military service. I recall a wartime comment made by a Deputy Chief of Staff while visiting the European Theater. "We've just got to get Eisenhower back home," he exclaimed earnestly. "The General has forgotten the facts of life!"

Sometimes it is not easy for a Foreign Service officer and his family to readjust themselves suddenly to "the facts of life" after they have become accustomed to embassy living abroad. One of my colleagues, summoned back to Washington after a tour of duty in Peiping, ruefully told me the legend of a Chinese philosopher who dreamt he was a butterfly. The sensation of fluttering among the flowers seemed so real that the philosopher said he did not know, upon awakening, whether he was a man who had dreamt he was a butterfly, or whether he was a butterfly dreaming now that he was a man. An American diplomat who is accredited to a foreign government is expected to associate with the leading government, business, cultural and labor representatives of that nation. From such a position of prominence, the Foreign Service officer may abruptly be transferred to an obscure job in the Department of State or some other Washington agency where he becomes a very small cog in a very big wheel. For some officers and their wives, this is a welcome relief; for others, it is a depressing shock. Probably such letdown is especially painful to a diplomat who, misinterpreting the honors he was accorded abroad as a representative of the United States Government, accepted those courtesies as personal tributes.

The Secretary of State himself is stationed only in Washington, of course, but some critics contend that in recent years this cabinet member has been spending an undue amount of time abroad, flying hither and thither to various conferences. Robert A. Lovett, formerly Secretary of Defense and Under Secretary of State, presented this opinion when he testified before the Senate Subcommittee on National Policy Machinery. Lovett pointed out that in a world which carries an open threat to our national security, the Secretary of State is the President's principal adviser on foreign policy, and that the Secretary's voice in council is of cardinal importance if delay and vacillation are to be avoided. This responsibility is enough to keep anyone fully occupied, Lovett declared, and he suggested that in view of the formidable burdens of his office, the Secretary of State remain in Washington instead of dashing all over the world to an increasing variety of meetings. Lovett proposed that a possible solution might be to regard the Secretary of State as the first ranking cabinet member, but to add a new cabinet officer who would devote full time to meetings and negotiations. He suggested that the new official could be given whatever title needed to do the job, perhaps Minister of Foreign Affairs. Dean Rusk, before he became Secretary of State, rather shared this opinion.

Lovett's idea had a comfortable ring. Certainly the work load of the Secretary of State is at a dangerous level, even without counting the necessary and wearisome social functions of his office. But I fear that the proposal to isolate our Secretary is not practicable. We are living in a jet age of worldwide travel, and the day has passed when the leader of our foreign relations could afford to remain at home. Apart from the fact that many ranking foreign officials dislike to deal with a no. 2 man, it is extremely valuable for our Secretary of State to attend international meetings in person. He learns many things and gains inspiration from associations in other countries. Frequently a difficult situation appears quite different when viewed from a European or a Latin American, a Middle Eastern or an Asiatic vantage point. It has been my observation that our Secretaries of State usually accomplish more substantive diplomatic work while on visits abroad than when in Washington with its countless distractions. Foster Dulles, for instance, was able to concentrate on problems and do more work on airplanes than at his desk. Moreover, modern communications are so good that the Secretary is always available to the President, who can get in touch with him instantly no matter where he may be.

What really disturbs American foreign relations is not the sporadic comings and goings of the Secretary of State, but the inevitable comings and goings of all the highest officers of the Department every time a new President is elected. The State Department is a mine of information, but its utility depends entirely on how it is used. By the time new men have learned how to take advantage of its complicated facilities, most of them are out of office. The Department always functions below par during change of administrations. Every American ambassador automatically tenders his resignation to an incoming President, and career diplomats in the field become confused and are inclined to be overcautious in their reports. Washington associates of the new President frequently are prejudiced against the career officers. President Truman expressed his own attitude when he declared: "Those fellows in the State Department, who stay there no matter what happens in elections, can't be trusted to carry out a President's policies."

Nothing is more demoralizing to members of the Foreign Service than to feel that they do not have the confidence of their superiors, and our career officers have passed through difficult periods in recent years. Like most human beings, a diplomat wants to be understood and at times even appreciated, but his work by its very nature does not lend itself to popularity. The Foreign Service, like any other organization—whether a government agency, a trade union or a corporation—looks to its own head office for leadership. When an American diplomat comes home from abroad with strange problems to discuss, he should be able to go to someone in Washington for understanding consultation. All too often, in the State Department, the career officer finds that he is a professional working under amateurs. At times, especially during change of administrations, there literally is no one to whom he can look for guidance, much less for protection.

Not all the troubles of our career officers come from without. There is at times a cloistered attitude in the Department of State, a detachment from daily American realities, an expectation that a vague someone will fight the battles of the Foreign Service. I believe it was Dean Acheson who recommended that career officers should take the offensive, and with that I agree. But what is needed most is continued leadership by strong, qualified persons in authority who provide stature, inspiration and a certain fighting spirit to the Foreign Service, persons who know the men and women of the State Department, who understand world conditions and problems, who are respected by Congress and by the public, and who are able to insist both on Service needs and Service discipline in the national interest.

Other countries, such as the British Government with its system of Permanent Under Secretaries, make provision for that type of leadership. In Britain the head of each department is a political appointee, but the no. 2 man is a career officer and it is he who provides continuity in policy between changing administrations, as between Labor and Conservatives. This post of Permanent Under Secretary is normally the highest position in the British diplomatic service to which a career officer can aspire, and it usually caps the career of a leading senior officer. The Foreign Office personnel depend on the Permanent Under Secretary to safeguard their work. The British have had this system for many years and it has served them well. They evolved it because they had worldwide commitments, and now that Americans are confronted with similar responsibilities, the United States Government no doubt will also place more reliance on our "men who stay no matter what happens in elections."

In 1959 the Department of State created a position somewhat analogous to that of a Permanent Under Secretary. In the American diplomatic hierarchy the ranking career officer was to be the no. 3 man. It was intended that this experienced diplomat should work closely with the Secretary of State and the President in the whole field of American foreign policy, and the title selected for his office was Under Secretary for Political Affairs. But this top career position lasted less than one year. It was abolished because of domestic politics and the title was given to a non-career official appointed by the President.

The quality of the men and women in our Foreign Service today is excellent. They have been drawn from every section of the United States, and most of them have enjoyed comprehensive educations and a variety of experiences. The seed planted by our first diplomat, Benjamin Franklin, is growing into the finest diplomatic instrument in the world. In linguistics, in technical knowledge, in contacts with peoples and problems of different parts of the world, in quality of reporting and negotiating, and in promotion of the national interest, our Foreign Service now rates with the best. The fact that the morale of the career officers has held up under acutely discouraging circumstances is a credit to the dedication of the staff, who are proud to be in the public service. A new generation, competent and resourceful, is overcoming prejudice and doubt. From its own vigorous ranks it will produce its leaders and it will receive the understanding and appreciation of the American public. What is past is prologue.

INDEX